The Identification of 1792 JOHN WRIGHT of Fauquier County Virginia

As Not the Son of 1729/30 JOHN WRIGHT of Stafford County Virginia

Robert N. Grant

HERITAGE BOOKS
2009

HERITAGE BOOKS
AN IMPRINT OF HERITAGE BOOKS, INC.

Books, CDs, and more—Worldwide

For our listing of thousands of titles see our website
at
www.HeritageBooks.com

Published 2009 by
HERITAGE BOOKS, INC.
Publishing Division
100 Railroad Ave. #104
Westminster, Maryland 21157

International Standard Book Numbers
Paperbound: 978-0-7884-4935-2
Clothbound: 978-0-7884-8214-4

ACKNOWLEDGEMENT

A number of people have assisted in the research which is the basis of this work. I would like to thank:

1. Jeffrey A. Wright, co-administrator of the Wright DNA Project, for permitting the inclusion of his excellent charts in this work and his continuing support, encouragement, and research on these Wright lines,

2. Lois Stuart Moore for her research on the descendants of Skelton Wright and for persuading her cousin David R. Wright, now deceased, to participate in the Wright DNA Project,

3. Tom Wright for his assistance in tracing his line of descent and for participating in the Wright DNA Project,

4. Mary Doris Wright for her research on the descendants of 1789 John Wright of Surry County, North Carolina, and for persuading her brother Thomas Carr Wright, now deceased, to participate in the Wright DNA Project,

5. Thad Tatum for sharing the many documents he has found in northern Virginia regarding these Wright families, for persuading his uncle James Logan Wright, now deceased, to participate in the Wright DNA Project, and for finding Greg Wright,

6. Greg Wright for his prompt and enthusiastic willingness to help document his family, for sharing photographs of his family tombstones, and for participating in the Wright DNA Project,

7. Diane Hayter for posting her family genealogy so that it could be found on the internet, permitting the inclusion of her family report in this work, and for persuading her uncle Peter Wright to participate in the Wright DNA Project,

8. Justin Glenn for sharing his vast collection of data on the Wright and Washington families, for permitting the inclusion of a portion of his work on those families in this work, and for his willingness to review and critique drafts of this work and the arguments and evidence relating to those lines, and

9. John A. Washington for reviewing and critiquing drafts of this work.

All of these people have contributed to the successful sorting out of these two Wright families and have helped in correcting a longstanding mis-identification by Charles Hoppin and others.

Thanks again to all of you for your contribution to this project.

Robert N. Grant
December 31, 2008

TABLE OF CONTENTS

The Identification Of 1792 John Wright Of Fauquier County, Virginia, As Not The Son Of 1729/30 John Wright Of Stafford County, Virginia

The Identification Of 1792 John Wright Of Fauquier County, Virginia, As Not The Son Of 1729/30 John Wright Of Stafford County, Virginia

I. Background And Recent DNA Results

1792 (year of death) John Wright of Fauquier County, Virginia, (place of death) has been extensively researched and discussed by Charles Arthur Hoppin in three publications:

1) "Some Descendants of Richard Wright, Gentleman, of London, England, and Northumberland, Va., 1655," published in Tyler's Quarterly Historical and Genealogical Magazine, Vol. I, pages 127-141 and 177-191, 1919, and reprinted in Genealogies of Virginia Families From Tyler's Quarterly Historical and Genealogical Magazine, published by Genealogical Publishing Company, Baltimore, Maryland, 1981;

2) "The Washington-Wright Connection and Some Descendants of Maj. Francis and Anne (Washington) Wright," published in Tyler's Quarterly Historical and Genealogical Magazine, Vol. IV, pages 315-356, 1923, and reprinted in Genealogies of Virginia Families From Tyler's Quarterly Historical and Genealogical Magazine, published by Genealogical Publishing Company, Baltimore, Maryland, 1981; and

3) The Washington Ancestry and Records of The McClain, Johnson, and Forty Other Colonial American Families, prepared for Edward Lee McClain, and printed by Yale University Press, 1932.

The last work incorporated the material from the prior two works.

1792 John Wright of Fauquier County has also been discussed by Ann Reed Ritchie in her work Major Francis Wright And Ann Washington With Allied Families, 1973.

1792 John Wright of Fauquier County has also been discussed by Myrtle Viola (Sears) Steiner and Velma (Wright) Ellis Wakefield in their work Wright-Washington and Allied Families "Descendants of Capt. Richard Wright - From the Eastern Shore of Virginia to the Pacific Coast of California 1630-1967", undated but apparently published in 1967.

Charles Hoppin in his works identified William Wright, the son of 1792 John

Wright of Fauquier County, Virginia, as 1805 William Wright of Fauquier County, Virginia. Ann Reed Ritchie and Myrtle Steiner and Velma Wakefield followed Hoppin in that identification. However, Ann Reed Ritchie referenced a "Bible record" which listed 1805 William Wright's birth in 1740. That reference led to a Family Record prepared by 1834 William Wright of Coshocton County, Ohio, which was attached as supporting documentation to the DAR Application #696077 of Eloise Wilma Ramsey Maynard, Shaker Heights, Cleveland, Ohio. That documentation made possible the determination that 1805 William Wright of Fauquier County, Virginia, was not the son of 1792 John Wright of Fauquier County, Virginia, and in my work The Identification Of 1809 William Wright Of Franklin County, Virginia, As The Son Of 1792 John Wright Of Fauquier County, Virginia I presented the evidence that identified William Wright, the son of 1792 John Wright of Fauquier County, as 1809 William Wright of Franklin County, Virginia. That work is available from Heritage Books, Inc., (heritagebooks.com).

Charles Hoppin in his works also identified 1792 John Wright of Fauquier County, Virginia, as the son of 1729/30 John Wright of Stafford County, Virginia, and the grandson of 1713 Francis Wright of Westmoreland County, Virginia, and the great grandson of 1663 Richard Wright of Northumberland County, Virginia. Ann Reed Ritchie and Myrtle Steiner and Velma Wakefield also followed Hoppin in this identification.

These works have in turn been relied on for numerous internet postings listing the same lineage.

However, in February 2008 and August 2008 significant DNA results were posted at the Wright DNA Project at http://www.wright-dna.org/ under the headings "1792 John" and "1540 John". The consequence of the posted results is that 1792 John Wright of Fauquier County, Virginia, was not the son of 1729/30 John Wright of Stafford County, Virginia, or the grandson of 1713 Francis Wright of Westmoreland County, Virginia, and his wife Anne (Washington) Wright. The explanation of this consequence is set forth below.

Y-DNA passes unchanged from father to son, except for periodic random mutations. If Y-DNA sequences of two males differ significantly, then they are not related in the male line. Y-DNA sequences are organized into haplogroups. Males whose Y-DNA comes from different haplogroups cannot be related within a time period covered by recorded history.

Six participants in the Wright DNA Project are documented as descendants of 1792 John Wright of Fauquier County, Virginia, through his son 1809 William Wright of Franklin County, Virginia. However, one of those participants does not match the other five and there was probably a "non-marital" event in his documented line which altered the Y-DNA. A seventh participant in the Wright DNA Project is a documented descendant of 1792 John Wright of Fauquier County, Virginia, through his son 1789 John Wright of Surry County, North Carolina. The Y-DNA of all seven participants, and most importantly the six who match with no or limited differences in Y-DNA, is posted under Haplogroup R1b1, the most common haplogroup found for Wright families, and more particularly under Haplogroup R1B1b2 and in the listings titled "1792 John". There is one perfect match of 37 of 37 markers for one of the descendants of 1809 William Wright (David R. Wright, Kit 38121) and the one descendant of 1789 John Wright (Thomas Carr Wright, Kit 94975), which confirms their common heritage and descent from 1792 John Wright. If the reader will click on "1792 John" at the Wright DNA Project site, you will be taken to a chart prepared by Jeff Wright showing the line of descent from 1792 John to all of the participants. A copy of that chart is attached as Exhibit A.

Two participants in the Wright DNA Project who are documented as descendants of 1713 Francis Wright of Westmoreland County, Virginia, have participated in the Wright DNA Project. The first participant is James Logan Wright, Jr., Kit 71409, whose line of descent goes through 1713 Francis Wright of Westmoreland County and his second son 1741 Richard Wright of Westmoreland County. The second participant is Werter Gregory Wright III, Kit 123670, who also descends from 1713 Francis Wright of Westmoreland County through his second son 1741 Richard Wright of Westmoreland County. Werter Gregory Wright III still resides on Wright family land located in Westmoreland County, Virginia.

The Y-DNA sequences of James Logan Wright and Werter Gregory Wright III match at 36 of 37 markers. However, both are from Haplogroup J2 and do not match the Y-DNA sequence of the descendants of 1792 John Wright of Fauquier County, Virginia. The descendants of 1713 Francis Wright of Westmoreland County and the descendants of 1792 John Wright of Fauquier County are from two different Wright lines.

Charles Hoppin identified 1713 Francis Wright of Westmoreland County, Virginia, as the son of 1663 Richard Wright of Northumberland County, Virginia. 1663 Richard Wright in turn has been listed on numerous internet postings as the son of 1655 Francis Wright of Yorkshire County, England. This relationship and the evidence supporting this identification are discussed more fully below. The consequence is that James Logan Wright, Kit 71409, and Werter Gregory Wright III, Kit 123670, descend from 1655 Francis Wright of Yorkshire County, England.

A third descendant of 1655 Francis Wright of Yorkshire, England, was located in the United Kingdom. Peter Wright, Kit 108246, descends from 1655 Francis Wright of Yorkshire County, England, through 1655 Francis Wright's son 1674 George Wright of Yorkshire, England, and is also from Haplogroup J2.

The Y-DNA sequence of Peter Wright, Kit 108246, most closely matches that of James Logan Wright, Kit 71409, and establishes that the Y-DNA of the family of 1655 Francis Wright of Yorkshire, England, also does not match that of the descendants of 1792 John Wright of Fauquier County, Virginia. They are two different Wright lines.

If the reader will click on "1540 John" at the Wright DNA Project site, you will be taken to a chart also prepared by Jeff Wright showing the lines of descent from 1655 Francis Wright of Yorkshire County, England, to James Logan Wright, Werter Gregory Wright III, and Peter Wright. A copy of that Chart is attached as Exhibit B.

The consequence of these two sets of Wright Y-DNA being from different haplogroups is that the two lines could not be related. The six participants who match in Haplogroup R1B1b2 and whose documentation shows them to be descendants of 1792 John Wright of Fauquier County, Virginia, are not related to the three participants who match in Haplogroup J2 and whose documentation shows them to be descendants of 1655 Francis Wright of Yorkshire, England, two through 1663 Richard Wright of Northumberland County, Virginia, and his son 1713 Francis Wright of Westmoreland County, Virginia, and one through 1663 Richard Wright's brother 1674 George Wright of Yorkshire County, England.

And the further consequence of these results that necessarily follows is that 1792 John Wight of Fauquier County, Virginia, could not have been the son of 1729/30 John Wright of Stafford County or the grandson of 1713 Francis Wright of Westmoreland County who married Anne Washington. The difference in Y-DNA sequences precludes that.

II. Potential Objections To Results

After the posting of these Y-DNA results, various interested researchers have engaged in further discussions of this evidence and some questions have been raised which deserve a response. Those questions included the following:

1. What are the weaknesses of Charles Hoppin's case as presented in The Washington Ancestry?

2. What is the documentation for each of the ancestral lines of the Wright DNA Project participants that shows their descent from 1792 John Wright of Fauquier County, Virginia, or 1713 Francis Wright of Westmoreland County, Virginia, or 1655 Francis Wright of Yorkshire County, England?

3. What is the evidence that identifies 1663 Richard Wright of Northumberland County, Virginia, as the son of 1655 Francis Wright of Yorkshire County, England:

4. What is the probability of a "non-marital event" occurring in the ancestral lines of the Y-DNA participants that could produce false results?

Each of these questions is discussed below.

III. The Weakness Of Hoppin's Evidence Identifying 1792 John Wright Of Fauquier County, Virginia, As The Son Of 1729/30 John Wright Of Stafford County, Virginia

The first question to be addressed is whether Charles Hoppin presented a compelling case for the identification of 1792 John Wright of Fauquier County, Virginia, as a son of 1729/30 John Wright of Stafford County, Virginia.

A review of Hoppin's The Washington Ancestry results in four bases for Hoppin's identification:

1) Physical presence of 1792 John Wright in Prince William County where 1729/30 John Wright owned land;

2) A deed which included a phrase that might be interpreted to indicate that 1729/30 John Wright had a second son in addition to his known son 1742 Francis Wright of Prince William County;

3) 1792 John Wright's election as a justice of Prince William County, the same position his father 1729/30 John Wright held in Stafford County, and

4) Similarity of occupations.

A. First Basis - Physical Presence

The first basis for Hoppin's identification of 1792 John Wright as the son of 1729/30 John Wright was his physical presence in Prince William County at the time 1729/30 John Wright owned property there.

Hoppin stated at page 384 that John Wright was appointed one of the original justices of Prince William County:

> "The following record of the action of the Governor and Council is taken from Virginia Council Orders, V, 1420-1447, 1448:
>
> 1731, April 27. The Governor, with the advice of the Council is pleas'd to nominate Justices of the peace for the new erected County of Prince William, viz: Thomas Harrison, Dennis McCarty, Willm Linton, Francis Awbry, Robert Jones, Burr Harrison, & Moses Quarles of the Quorum; and Leonard Barker, Wm Harrison, Valentine Barker, John Wright, John Allen, Willm Hackney, and Joseph Hudnal, Gent."

Hoppin then argued that 1792 John Wright and not 1729/30 John Wright was the subject of that appointment, because of the prior death of 1729/30 John Wright, which seems reasonable.

On March 23, 1740, at Prince William County, Virginia, D.B. E/170 1792 John Wright purchased 236 acres of land from Jeremiah Darnall and his wife Catharine Darnall:

> "This Indenture made this 23d day of March in the fourteenth year of the Reign of our Sovereign Lord George the Second . . . . in the year of our Lord one thousand seven hundred & forty Between Jeremiah Darnal of ye parish of Hamilton & County of Prince William planter & Catharine his wife of the one part and John Wright of the aforementioned parish & County Gent. of the other part Witnesseth that the said Jeremiah Darnal & Catharine his wife for and in consideration of the sum of sixty pounds Current money of Virginia to them in hand paid by the said John Wright . . . . Have given granted bargained sold aliened remised released enfeoffed & confirmed . . . . unto the said John Wright & to his heirs & Assigns for ever all that tract or parcel of land containing two hundred & thirty six acres situate lying & being ye parish of Hamilton & County of Prince William being part of a greater tract taken up by Waugh Darnall father to ye said Jeremiah and is bounded as followeth Vizt. Beginning at a Red Oak standing in Colonel Corbins line & extending thence along the said line South eighty eight degrees West four hundred & fourteen poles to a Hicory & Gum in ye said Corbins line & in the line of the land of John Ambrose thence along ye said line North nine degrees West ninety poles to a Stone Stake & Hicory in ye said line thence North eighty four degrees East three hundred & thirty six pole to two Red Oak Saplins on a hill thence South thirty two degrees East one hundred & forty two poles to the beginning. . . . . In Wittness whereof the said parties to these presents have interchangeably put their hands & affixed their Seals ye day month and year first above written.
>
> Signed Sealed & Delivered in the presence of
> John Frogg
> Jacob Holtzclaw
> George Crump
>
> Jeremiah Darnall
>
> . . . .
>
> At a Court held for Prince William County March 23d 1740. Jeremiah Darnall acknowledged this Release with the Receit endorsed to be his Acts & deeds and they were thereupon admitted to Record
>
> Test
> Catesby Cooke Cl Cur."

This is the first evidence of 1792 John Wright owning land in Prince William County.

The result of the above evidence establishes that 1792 John Wright of Fauquier County was resident in Prince William County by 1731 and first owned his own land there in 1740.

However, Hoppin also stated that at the time of appointment of 1792 John Wright to the position of justice, he was the only John Wright in that area:

> "[page 385] . . . . the father had died, and his *son was the only John Wright then alive* in all the wide domain now covered by the counties of Stafford, Prince William, King George, Fauquier, Fairfax, and Loudoun."

This last statement is more than can be shown by the records. As Hoppin pointed out, the Stafford County records have been substantially lost for that period. In addition, numerous Prince William County deed books are missing for that period. While no record of another John Wright has yet been located in those counties for this period, it is not possible to state with certainty that one did not exist.

In addition, Hoppin did not include Westmoreland County in his list of counties. There were three other John Wrights in Westmoreland County and Hoppin included separate sections on each. These three John Wrights are discussed more fully below.

Nevertheless, the physical presence of 1792 John Wright in Prince William County shortly after the death of 1729/30 John Wright would seem to be established. But without additional evidence, this alone would not be sufficient to identify 1792 John Wright as the son of 1729/30 John Wright.

B. Second Basis - Implication From Deed Of A Second Son

The second basis for Hoppin's identification of 1792 John Wright as the son of 1729/30 John Wright was the implication of a statement in a deed by 1742 Francis Wright.

On July 27, 1741, at Prince William County, Virginia, D.B. E/339 1742 Francis Wright sold to Henry Lee the remaining 667 acres of the land that Francis had inherited from his father 1729/30 John Wright, land which Henry Lee had previously sold to 1729/30 John Wright of Stafford County:

> "This Indenture made the twenty Seventh day of July in the fifteenth year of the reign of our Sovereign Lord George the Second . . . . Annog Domini One

thousand Seven hundred & forty one Between Francis Wright of Hamilton parish in Prince William County planter of the one part & Henry Lee of Cople parish in Westmorland County Gent of the other part Witnesseth that for & in Consideration of the Sum of Two hundred and Sixty pounds Current money of Virginia in hand paid to the said Francis Wright by the said Henry Lee . . . . he the said Francis Wright . . . . doth give grant enfeof & Confirm unto the said Henry Lee his heirs and Assignes for ever all that Messuage or Tenement of Land . . . . containing Six hundred Sixty Seven acres Scituate lying & being in the aforesaid parish of Hamilton & County of Prince William & is bounded or incuded between two Creeks now known & Called by the names of powels Creek & Nyapscoe Creek also binding on a parcel of Land the said Francis Wright sold to Mr. Benjamin Gresham the said Six hundred and Sixty Seven acres of Land being part of One thousand acres of Land Conveyed by the abovesaid Henry Lee to John Wright (father of the aforesaid Francis) in fee Simple as by Deed dated the twelfth day of June annog Domini One thousand Seven hundred & twenty five relation being thereunto ____ more fully & at Large appear & the said John Wright father of the said Francis Wright dying intestate the said Francis Wright as his eldest Son is heir at Law to the said Land . . . .

Signed Sealed & Delivered Francis Wright
in the presenceof us
John Frogg
R Blackburn
Wm Elliott.
. . . .
At a Court held for Prince William County the 27th day of July anno Domini 1741.

Francis Wright acknowledged this deed of feofment Livery of Seisin and receipts to be his acts and deeds & Ann the wife of the said Francis being first privatly Examined relinquished her right of dower to the Land by the said deed Conveyed and they are thereupon Admitted to Record.

Test.
Catesby Cooke Cl Cur"

Hoppin referenced the statement in the deed that Francis Wright "his [John Wright's] eldest Son is heir at Law to the said Land", and suggested that the statement indicated that there was a living younger son:

"[Page 387] Whereupon, on May 28, 1739, the eldest son sold one-third of that Leesylvania estate for cash and other land and on July 27, 1741, sold for cash the remaining two-thirds. In his deed of conveyance he referred to his father and himself, and indicated that his brother was then alive, viz.: . . . ."

One interpretation of the quoted phrase is that it implied that there was more than one son of 1729/30 John Wright, that is, that Francis Wright was the eldest of a set of sons. But if there were two sons and if the phrase was indicating that fact, then the proper term would have been "elder son", rather than "eldest son", since the latter implies three or more sons. However, this may be expecting too much grammatical correctness from writers of that period.

But there is a second interpretation that is equally plausible and that is that the scrivener of the deed was simply paraphrasing the standard rule of primogeniture that the eldest son of a decedent inherited the land and there was no implication, or necessity, of a younger brother in the statement of that standard rule.

The latter interpretation would seem the more probable, but in any event the meaning of the phrase is at best ambiguous.

There is no other document presented by Hoppin that directly supports his assertion that 1729/30 John Wright had a son John Wright or even a second son in addition to 1742 Francis Wright and no such document has as yet been located.

And there is circumstantial evidence discussed by Hoppin that indicates there was only one son of 1729/30 John.

Hoppin argued at page 399 that John Wright was offended by Francis Wright's sale to Benjamin Grayson in 1739 and to Henry Lee in 1741 of the land Francis Wright had inherited from his father:

> "That John[4] Wright, though powerless in the face of the law of primogeniture to prevent the sale of the fine estate on the western bank of the Potomac at Freestone Point and on the northern side of Powell's Run, did not approve the proceeding by his elder brother is evident from subsequent records. The rift in the personal associations between their families was decisive and as complete as John could make it without discredit to himself: . . . ."

There is no direct documentary evidence for this asserted taking of offense. And it is not clear why a younger son would be offended by a sale of land by an older brother that had been properly inherited under the law of primogeniture of that time.

Hoppin based the assertion of offense on a non-act by 1792 John Wright, that is, John Wright's permitting Thomas Stribling to be appointed guardian of 1742 Francis

Wright's children and permitting William Stribling to be overseer of 1742 Francis Wright's estate:

> "The rift in the personal associations between their families was decisive and as complete as John could make it without discredit to himself: . . . .This is shown in John's attitude toward the widow and children of his deceased brother Francis in permitting the appointment by the Court of his (Justice Wright's) fellow justice, Thomas Stribling, guardian of the children, while William Stribling was allowed to be overseer of the estate . . . . instead of his showing a more brotherly regard by taking charge of the children and estate himself, as under ordinary circumstances might be expected."

However, this non-action of 1792 John Wright is perhaps more properly evidence that 1792 John Wright was not related to 1742 Francis Wright. If 1792 John Wright had been related to 1742 Francis Wright, "under ordinary circumstances" (as Hoppin stated) he would, as the nearest male relative, have taken on the roles of guardian and overseer. Rather than evidence that 1792 John Wright was offended by his brother's sale of inherited land, this non-action by 1792 John Wright is evidence that he was simply not related to 1742 Francis Wright. As a non-relative, 1792 John Wright would have had no reason to become involved with Francis Wright's children or estate and that responsibility was properly left to others, who also happened to be closer neighbors.

The result is that the Francis Wright deed does not necessarily indicate that 1729/30 John Wright had more than one son and there is circumstantial evidence that 1742 Francis Wright was his only son.

C. <u>Third Basis - Selection As Justice Of Prince William County</u>

The third basis for Hoppin's identification of 1792 John Wright as the son of 1729/30 John Wright was the selection of 1792 John Wright as a justice of Prince William County.

As set forth above, Hoppin stated at page 384 that John Wright was appointed one of the original justices of Prince William County in 1731. Hoppin then argued that 1792 John Wright and not 1729/30 John Wright was the subject of that appointment because of the prior death of 1729/30 John Wright. This seems reasonable and it seems established that 1792 John Wright was the justice of Prince William County appointed in 1731.

However, Hoppin then went on to assert that the appointment was remarkable and that remarkable quality was evidence that 1792 John Wright was a son of 1729/30 John Wright. Hoppin gave three reasons why the appointment was remarkable: 1) 1792 John Wright's young age of 23 or 24 at the time of his appointment, 2) the influence of 1792 John Wright's great uncle and fellow justice Francis Awbrey, and 3) the honoring of 1792 John Wright's father 1729/30 John Wright, who had been a justice of Stafford County. These reasons are set forth in several places:

> "[page 382] This appointment of the young son would not have occurred had the father been alive; the father would have been honored instead. It was particularly an honor because the right to such an honor belonged to the men who had worked to have a new county made from the northern part of Stafford County; that the son was appointed to the position by the Governor of Virginia, to which the father would seem to be entitled by virtue of social rank, previous service, political activity, and ownership of the Leesylvania plantation on Powell's Run, is good evidence as to their relationship as father and son. Furthermore, it is obvious that the presence among the justices who, in 1731, constituted the quorum of Francis Awbrey, the probable uncle of John[3] Wright's wife, Dorothy Awbrey, had an influence in securing the preferment of the son, John[4] Wright, to membership in the body of justices. The choosing of the son was a tribute to the memory of the father; likewise the honors and emoluments due to the father were extended to the son after the custom in that region and time.
>
> [page 383] Hence his memory was honored by his colleagues' substituting the name of his son, John[4] Wright, in the nominations to the Governor and Council of Virginia for confirmation. The chief influences operating for the appointment of the son immediately after the death of his father may be stated as (1) the ambition of the son himself, (2) the presence of his mother's uncle, Francis Awbrey, as one of the seven older and chief members of the body of fourteen justices.
>
> [page 406] He succeeded his father as a justice upon his father's death by virtue of being his father's son. He was inducted into that preferment at a time when the influences and customs of the society into which he was born and in which he moved, made for such preferment of sons in order to maintain family prestige, to protect family property and prerogatives, and to continue political power and control in a few families. He succeeded to these honors at an age when he would not have been so preferred if he had not been son of John[3] Wright.
>
> (7) The recorded presence of the uncle of John[4] Wright's mother, Dorothy (Awbrey) Wright, namely, Francis Awbrey, as a first justice of the quorum of the first court of Prince William County in 1730-31, with John[4] Wright, suggests that

this elder justice had an influence in effecting the preferment of John[4] Wright, as a first justice of the first court.

. . . .

(9) . . . . the nomination in 1730 and the confirmation in 1731, for the honor of a first justiceship of the very young John[4] Wright not because of his personal merits and ability, without his having come to that nomination through the usual process of time and previous experience as a warden, a vestryman, and in other of the lesser town, parish, and county offices, is indirect proof that he was the son of the honored justice whose name he bore and who had then but recently died. Were there no other indications, evidences, proofs, either indirect or circumstantial, as to the relationship of these two John Wrights, the circumstances of this appointment to a justiceship conveys, alone, sufficient intelligence as to the truth."

Each of these reasons, when examined, turns out to be invalid and provides no support for the conclusion asserted.

1. Young Age At Time Of Appointment

The first reason offered by Hoppin for describing as remarkable the appointment of 1792 John Wright as a justice was Hoppin's assertion that 1792 John Wright was young at the time of his appointment. This assertion is not based on any documentation and is incorrect.

Hoppin stated that 1792 John Wright of Fauquier County was born in about 1707 as the son of 1729/30 John Wright of Stafford County and Dorothy (Awbrey) Wright:

"[page 394] John[4] Wright (John[3], Francis[2], Richard[1]), vestryman, captain, justice, and sheriff, was born in the "great house" on the Wright "manour plantation" on the Lower Machodoc peninsula in Westmoreland County as has been indicated, *circa* 1707, his parents, John[3] and Dorothy (Awbrey) Wright, having married about the year 1705, and his brother Francis[4] having been born as their eldest son, there being no evidence as to there being daughters by this marriage."

This statement of the date of birth is incorrect.

On October 2, 1790, in the case of Darnall v. Turberville, Prince William County, Virginia, Land Causes 1789-93/358, John Wright gave his deposition in connection with a survey of the lands in dispute between the parties:

". . . .

Fauquier Sct

The Deposition of Capt John Wright aged ninety years and upwards Deposed and sayeth that a red oak that he is now at that he the said Deponent has heard it called Colo. Corbins line for sixty years and upwards and he bought land of Jeremiah Darnall by this said line at Colo. Corbins and further saith not

John Wright

Fauquier Sct.

This day Capt. John Wright made oath in presence of Jeremiah Darnall Pltf and George Turberville Deft to the above given under my hand this 2d day of October 1790

Jo Blackwell

Fauquier Sct.

The Deposition of Capt. John Wright aged ninety years and upward Deposed and sayeth that the old field he now shows has been cleared about forty five years ago by Colo. Corbins Overseers and this Deponent further saith not

John Wright

Fauquier Sct.

This day Capt. John Wright made oath in presence of Jeremiah Darnall Pltf and George Tuberville Deft given under my hand this 2d day October 1790.

Jo Blackwell"

This deposition was also published in Prince William County Land Causes 1789-1793 by Sam and Ruth Sparacio.

As set forth above, on March 23, 1740, at Prince William County, Virginia, D.B. E/170 1792 John Wright of Fauquier County purchased 236 acres of land from Jeremiah and Catharine Darnall. The reference in the deposition to the land John Wright purchased of Jeremiah Darnall identifies the John Wright of these depositions as 1792 John Wright of Fauquier County. The result is that these depositions establish that 1792 John Wright of Fauquier County was born before October 2, 1700.

However, John A. Washington correctly noted that the reference to John Wright being "aged ninety years and upwards" was an introductory statement by Joseph Blackwell and not part of the deposition of John Wright. The age stated may have been an estimate of Joseph Blackwell rather than a statement by the deponent himself. In addition, John A. Washington and Dr. Luke F. Wright both stated that it is not unusual when persons become older to tend to exaggerate their age, feeling "a secret delight in surviving our contemporaries and even our juniors." Both points are well taken and in recognition of that, the date of birth must also be given as circa 1700.

Hoppin's listing of the date of birth in about 1707 was simply an extrapolation of an estimated date of birth based on the estimated marriage date of an incorrectly identified marriage. Hoppin also stated at pages 366 and 370 that 1729/30 John Wright of Stafford County's sons Francis and John were born between 1705 and 1708:

> "Of the marriages of Francis[2] Wright and his son John[3], which marriage occurred first can not be definitely determined. Doubtless the marriage of John[3] occurred first. That the two events were not more than two years apart is evident from the fact that Francis[4] Wright and John[4] Wright, the two sons of John[3] Wright, are shown by records to have been born between 1705 and 1708; . . . ."

It is unclear what records Charles Hoppin was relying on that showed the dates of birth of the sons Francis Wright and John Wright as between 1705 and 1708. A review of the remainder of <u>The Washington Ancestry</u> disclosed no such records to support those asserted dates of birth. The John Wright deposition in 1790 suggests that there were no such records and that Charles Hoppin made assertions that were not supported by the evidence.

This last conclusion is bolstered by a prior work of Charles Hoppin. <u>The Washington Ancestry</u> was published in 1932 and incorporated material from his two prior articles published in <u>Tyler's Quarterly</u>. In "Some Descendants of Richard Wright, Gentleman, of London, England, and Northumberland, Va., 1655," published in 1919 Charles Hoppin asserted that 1792 John Wright was born in about 1712:

> "John[4] Wright (John 3, Francis 2, Richard 1), "Gent.," "Churchwarden," "Captain," "Sheriff" and "Justice" of Prince William county, and later "Justice" of Fauquier county, was born in Cople parish, Westmoreland county, Virginia, about 1712, his father having married his mother Dorothy between 1707 and 1710."

This 1712 birth date is inconsistent with Hoppin's later conclusion in <u>The Washington Ancestry</u> that the birth date was in about 1707 and once again, no documentation was given for this birth date of 1712. Hoppin probably realized that if 1792 John Wright had been born in 1712, then he would have been only 18 or 19 years old when appointed in 1731 as a justice of Prince William County. Since that would be far too young for the appointment, Hoppin simply adjusted the marriage date and birth date back five years to more artfully fit his argument.

The result is that Hoppin was simply guessing as to the date of birth of 1792 John Wright.

And the further result is that 1792 John Wright was not 23 or 24 years old in 1731 and was not a young man receiving special preferment when selected as a justice for Prince William County, but a fully mature man who was 30 or 31 years of age.

2. <u>Influence Of His Great Uncle And Fellow Justice Francis Awbrey</u>

The second reason offered by Hoppin for describing as remarkable the appointment of 1792 John Wright as a justice was the influence of his great uncle Francis Awbrey, who was also a justice:

> "[page 406]
> (7) The recorded presence of the uncle of John[4] Wright's mother, Dorothy (Awbrey) Wright, namely, Francis Awbrey, as a first justice of the quorum of the first court of Prince William County in 1730-31, with John[4] Wright, suggests that this elder justice had an influence in effecting the preferment of John[4] Wright, as a first justice of the first Court."

This assertion is also incorrect, because Francis Awbrey was not the great uncle of 1792 John Wright.

The wife of 1729/30 John Wright of Stafford County was Dorothy (____) Wright. On September 22, 1714, at Westmoreland County, Virginia, D.&W.B. 5/332 John Wright gifted 300 acres of land to his brother Richard Wright, son of John Wright's father Francis Wright, and John Wright's wife Dorothy relinquished her right of dower in the land:

> "At a Court held for the sd. County the 29th day of Sept 1714 John Wright Gentl: personally acknowledged the above Instrument to be his proper act & deed to be & enure to the uses above in the same specified which Youell Watkins accepted in behalfe of Richard Wright and the sd. Watkins alsoe by a power from Dorothy wife of the said John (being duely proved) relinquished the right of dower & thirds of the said Dorothy at the comon law in and to the lands and prmisses above

menconed."

Hoppin went on to identify the wife of 1729/30 John Wright as Dorothy (Awbrey) Wright. He did this by a process of elimination and not by documented evidence:

> "[page 366] One event was the second marriage of Francis[2] to Martha Cox, and the other the marriage (about 1705) of John[3] to a Dorothy, probably Dorothy Awbrey.*
>
> *This marriage occurred about 1705. The exact date is not recorded as the records of marriage licenses, and bonds, and of the parish churches for Westmoreland are lost. Other records indicate the fact of the marriage. It has required exhaustive search and study to determine the identity of John[3] Wright's wife Dorothy, because of the prevalence in the Northern Neck of Virginia of women named Dorothy. Seventeen Dorothys of marriageable age, *circa* 1705, appear in the records. The surnames of these Dorothys were Ransone, Gouldman, Armstrong, Henry, Ripley, Dudley, Gatewood, Smith, Baughan, Durham, Strother, Maclanan, Abbott, and Awbrey. No one of these Dorothys, save the last, extant records show, could be the Dorothy who married John[3] Wright. The last one, Dorothy Awbrey, by a process of exclusion is decided to be the wife of John[3] Wright.
>
> Dorothy[3] Awbrey was a granddaughter of Henry[1] Awbrey (sometimes written Aubrey, Awbury, Aubery, and Awberry - Aubry and Aubrey being the spelling in Virginia of the name of another Aubry family that came direct from France). . . . Our particular interest is in the son, Richard[2] Awbrey, as he was the father of Dorothy[3] Awbrey who, it is believed, married about 1705 John[3] Wright. . . ."

However, a deed from Essex County establishes that this identification of Dorothy Awbrey as the wife of 1729/30 John Wright of Stafford County and the daughter of Richard Awbrey and granddaughter of Henry Awbrey was incorrect. Essex County, Virginia, Deed 19/28 dated February 11, 1729, provided as follows:

> "To all Christian people to whom this present Indenture shall come Know ye that John Billups & Dorithy my wife of the parish of St. Ann's in the County of Essex within the Colony of Virginia Daughter & heir Apparant of Richd. Aubery Decd Son of Henry Aubery Decd. do for diverse good Causes & Considerations me moving . . . . in wittness whereof we have hereunto set our hands & Seals this

Eleventh Day of February in the year of our Lord One thousand Seven hundred & Twenty eight Nine

Signed Sealed & Delivered) Jno. Billop
In the presence of us) her
Joseph Lovill Dorithy X Billips
Edward White
Mark Morgan

At a Court held for Essex County on the 17th Day of June 1729 John Billups and Dorithy his wife Acknowledged this their Indented release of Land to James Garnett Gentl. which on his Motion is Admitted to record

Test
W Beverley C Cur"

This record clearly identifies Dorothy Awbrey, the daughter of Richard Awbrey and granddaughter of Henry Awbrey, as the wife of John Billups in 1729.

In addition, Colonial Families of the Northern Neck of Virginia by Ralph and Catherine Beverly stated the following:

"8. Dorothy Awbrey, b. 1685 in Westmoreland Co. VA, dau. of Richard (4) Awbrey and Dorothy North, m. John Billings/Billups.

In a bond dated 11 March 1713/14, L500 Sterl, John Billups and Dorothy his wife admin. of est. of Henry Awbrey deceased. Signed Jno Billups, James Baughan, John Boughan. Rec. 11 Mar. 1713/14. {Fleet, citing Vol II Essex Co. Wills and Deeds 1711-1714}

In a lease and release dated 21 Feb 1715/16, John Billups and Dorothy his wife of Essex sell Thomas Smith of Middlesex Co., 200 a. in So. Farn. Par., being part of a tract granted Mr. Henry Awberry, adj the main run of Hoskins Creek, etc. Signed Jno Billups and Dorothy Billups. {Fleet, citing Essex Co. DW 1714-1716 14:460}"

These documents indicate that Dorothy Awbrey was married to John Billups by March 11, 1713/14, and was still married to him on February 21, 1715/16. Colonial Families also listed Essex County Deed 19/28 previously referred to.

Since 1729/30 John Wright of Stafford County was married to his wife Dorothy (____) Wright on September 29, 1714, and Dorothy (Awbrey) Wright was married to John Billups before March 11, 1713/14, and was still married to him on February 21,

1715/16, Dorothy (____) Wright, the wife of 1729/30 John Wright, could not have been Dorothy (Awbrey) Wright.

And if Dorothy Awbrey was not the wife of 1729/30 John Wright, then Francis Awbrey was not the great uncle of 1792 John Wright and would have had no reason to exert his influence for the appointment of 1792 John Wright as a justice.

3. Appointment To Honor The Father

The third and most important reason offered by Hoppin for describing as remarkable the appointment of 1792 John Wright as a justice was that the appointment honored 1792 John Wright's father 1729/30 John Wright, who had been a justice of Stafford County. This statement is based on a false premise and is also incorrect.

Hoppin asserted that it should be inferred that 1729/30 John Wright of Stafford County was a justice of Stafford County:

> "[page 382] The court order books in which were recorded the commissions of the justices, and the minutes of their sittings, are lost. That he did serve as a justice in Stafford* is to be inferred from the facts (1) that he was one of the very few men of his standing then living in the part of the county where he settled; (2) that within about a year after his death his young son, John, then aged not over twenty-four years, was proposed and soon after chosen a justice of the new county of Prince William created out of that same part of Stafford.
>
> . . . .
>
> *The original minutes of the Council of Virginia are lost for the period 1726-53. A copy or abstract of them was made yearly and sent to England. From these Virginia Council Journals, now at the Public Record Office in London, we extract two entries showing that new justices for Stafford County were appointed in 1727 and 1728, though the entries in the journals for these years omit to give the names of the men appointed, --among who, we are forced to believe from subsequent events, was John[3] Wright, Senior. Whether his wife's uncle, Francis Awbrey, was also a justice in 1727 or 1728 we do not know, but he is of record as one of the justices in 1731:
>
> *May 2, 1727.* "New Commissions of the Peace for the Countys of Stafford [etc] were this day Ordered in Council, and several persons appointed to be Justices in the room of those lately deceased."
>
> March 30, 1728 . . . "Commissions of the Peace. New Commissions of the Peace for the counties of Stafford, Northumberland, Isle of Wight, Gloucester, and Prince George being this day regulated and settled in Council were ordered

to be issue." [No names given.]"

Hoppin provided no documentation that 1729/30 John Wright was ever appointed as a justice of Stafford County. The only remaining records of the appointments cited by Hoppin do not list the names of the appointees. The appointment was merely inferred, in part from the appointment of 1792 John Wright as a justice in 1731. But in relying on the latter appointment to infer the earlier appointment, Hoppin assumed that 1792 John Wright was the son of 1729/30 John Wright. Hoppin then relied on the inferred appointment of 1729/30 John Wright as a justice to support the assertion that 1792 John Wright was a son of 1729/30 John Wright.

In other words, Hoppin assumed that 1792 John was a son of 1729/30 John to infer the appointment of 1729/30 John as a justice and then used the appointment of 1729/30 John to support the assertion that 1792 John was 1729/30 John's son. This is circular reasoning!

Unless independent evidence is found that 1729/30 John Wright was a justice of Stafford County, there is no documentation to support Hoppin's assertion that 1729/30 John Wright was a justice of Stafford County.

And if 1729/30 John Wright was not a justice of Stafford County, then the appointment of 1792 John Wright as a justice of Prince William County had nothing to do with honoring the supposed father or putting the son in the place the father would have received if the father had lived.

Notwithstanding the foregoing discussion, there is some support for Hoppin's argument. Hoppin stated that 1729/30 John Wright had been appointed as a justice of Westmoreland County in 1720, citing a Westmoreland County order to that effect:

"[page 378] [Westmoreland Orders, &c, 1705 to 1721, p. 399]:

At a Court held for the Said County the 22th Day of ffeb'ry 1720.

Present. Willoughby Allerton, Thomas Lee, Henry Ashton, Thomas Newton, Benja. Berryman, Augustin Washington, John ffitzhugh, George Turberville, Gentl. Justice &c Court Proclaimed.

Pursueant to a Comission of the peace under the hand of Alexr Spotswood his Majties Lieut Govr of Virga and a Dedims under the Same hand for Administring

> the oaths to the Justices in the sd Commission nominated (dated the 23d Day of December 1720) Henry Ashton & Thomas Lee two of the gentlemen nominated in the Dedimus Adminstred the oaths (by Act of Parliment Appointed to be taken instead of the oaths of Allegiance & Supremacy, the oaths appointed to be taken by Act of Parliament made the Sixth year of the reign of her late Majtie Queen Ann Entituled an Act for Security of her Majties person & Government & of the Succession of the Crown of Great Britain in the Protestant Line, As Also, the oaths appointed by a late Act of Assembly of this Colony to be taken by Justices of the Peace) to Willoughby Allerton, Benja Berryman, Daniel McCarty, Burditt Ashton, Augt Washington & George Turbervile Adminstred all the above oaths to the said Henry Ashton & Thomas Lee, As Also: to John Wright, Jno Elliott & Wm Lord. And each & Every of the above named Justices Subscribed the Test. According to the Direccons of the aforementioned Dedimus.
>
> . . . .
>
> 23d: ffebry 1720. Henry Ashton, Thomas Newton, Geo: Turbervile, Thomas Lee, Jno Wright, Wm Lord, Gentl: Justices &c. Court *Proclaimed.*
>
> . . . ."

This record makes clear that 1729/30 John Wright of Stafford County was a justice of Westmoreland County, even if there was no record of his being a justice of Stafford County.

Hoppin also stated that 1729/30 John Wright did not appear in the Westmoreland County records after August 23, 1723, after which he moved to his new lands in Stafford County in a part which later became Prince William County:

> "[page 379] The name of John Wright is not to be found in any of the records of Westmoreland County after May 31, 1723, save for a brief mention in the will of his half-brother, Richard Wright, and his final appearance three months later."

Hoppin then asserted that 1729/30 John Wright was active in the affairs of Stafford County:

> "[page 381] . . . . That he had an active interest in the political affairs of Stafford County, as he had had previously in Westmoreland, is scarcely open to doubt -- as, also, that he served as a justice of Stafford County as in Westmoreland. . . . . Since practically all of the records of Stafford County are lost for the years during which John[3] Wright resided there, namely from 1723 to 1730, as well as for years before and after that period, the details of his participation in the political and judicial affairs of Stafford County are missing. . . . ."

These assertions of political service in Stafford County may be correct, but they are undocumented and are merely speculations on Hoppin's part.

Hoppin's argument then has to be limited to an assertion that 1792 John Wright was appointed a justice of Prince William County in honor of 1729/30 John Wright's service as a justice in Westmoreland County eight years before, a much less compelling argument.

D. Fourth Basis - Similarity Of Occupations And Name

The fourth basis for Hoppin's identification of 1792 John Wright as the son of 1729/30 John Wright was the similarity of their occupations and given name.

Hoppin stated in point six of his summary of arguments that 1792 John Wright, 1729/30 John Wright, and 1713 Francis Wright were similar by having the same careers or occupations and given name:

> "[page 406] . . . .
> (6) John Wright was particularly the "son of his father." He was an Episcopalian, as were his father and grandfather. He was a vestryman, as were his father and grandfather. He was a captain in the militia, as were his father and grandfather. He was a lawyer, as were his father and grandfather. He was a justice, as were his father and grandfather. He bore his father's Christian name. . . . "

While this listing is partially correct, there are four points of similarity that are either irrelevant or incorrect.

That all were Episcopalians is not unique, since that was the established church of the Colony and all persons were required to be members.

That all were captains in the militia follows from all being justices at one time or another and does not add to the similarities.

That all were lawyers is not necessarily correct. They each may have acted in a lawyer like manner, especially in their role as justices, but Hoppin himself said that 1729/30 John Wright was probably not admitted to the bar:

> "[page 377] . . . . While he acted as an attorney in some special causes, he does not appear of record as having practiced law, thought the docket books bearing the names of attorneys in civil actions are now missing. . . ."

And that 1792 John bore his father's name would be just as true whether 1792 John was the son of John Wright (Westmoreland County Overseer), discussed more fully below, or was the son of 1729/30 John Wright and adds nothing to the argument.

The unique similarities among the three men then amount to the three men being vestrymen and justices, again a much less compelling argument.

E. Hoppin's Summary Of Arguments

Hoppin provided at page 406 a summary of his arguments for the identification of 1792 John Wright as the son of 1729/30 John Wright. Those arguments are set forth below, with a discussion following each point.

Point One:

> "Inasmuch, as has been previously observed, as John^{3} and Dorothy (Awbrey) Wright both died intestate, and as the county records of the distributions of their estates are lost, and as the baptismal records of their children are also lost from Yeocomico Church, we may summarize, at this moment in addition to what is said before, what it is that renders certain the parentage of John^{4} Wright.
>
> (1) John Wright, the father of John Wright, was the only living male Wright of the third generation who married. *This fact, alone, were there no other proof, is proof sufficient.*"

The fact of 1729/30 John Wright's marriage is not disputed, but the conclusion drawn from that fact is nonsense. The fact that 1729/30 John Wright married is no evidence that he was the father of 1792 John Wright. It is by itself not even evidence that 1729/30 John Wright had any children. The italicized (in the original) portion of Hoppin's statement is simply false.

Point Two:

> ". . . .
>
> (2) John^{3} Wright, the father of John^{4} Wright, was the only living male Wright of the third generation who did not die a minor and without issue, lawful or unlawful, of his body."

While this statement is probably true, it does nothing to establish the parentage of 1792 John Wright.

Point Three:

> ". . . .
>
> (3) John^{4} Wright could not have been a son of either of the only other two male Wrights of the second generation, namely, the brothers Mottrom^{3} Wright and Francis^{3} Wright, because Mottrom^{3} died in England not less than six years before John^{4} Wright was born in Virginia, and because Francis^{2} had but one son by his first wife, Anne Washington -- the son they named, in honor of her own

father (John Washington), John[3] Wright -- and Francis[2] had but one son by his second wife, Martha Cox -- the son he named in honor of his own father, Richard Wright. *The land and probate records of Westmoreland in this Wright chapter repeatedly prove these facts.*"

Again, this statement is correct and does exclude 1713 Francis Wright and 1700 Mottram Wright from being the father of 1792 John Wright. This method of excluding potential parents of 1792 John Wright is more significant in connection to Hoppin's next two points.

Points Four and Five:

". . . .

(4) John[4] Wright, son of John[3] Wright, was the only man named John Wright in the fourteen counties of northern Virginia and southern Maryland who could have been the second son of John[3] Wright. *This fact is proven by the records in this Wright chapter, by records copied but not in this chapter, and by records read but not of sufficient importance to be copied -- records which prevent the substitution of any other John Wright by either record or implication.*

(5) John[3] Wright, the second son of John[4] Wright, was the only Wright of any Christian name whatsoever alive in 1730, in the said fourteen counties, not already eliminated, by the quoted records alone, from the possibility of being substituted in the place of John[4] Wright as the second son of the said John[3] Wright. The latter's eldest and only other son was the Francis[4] Wright who died young in 1742 without male issue. *This is a statement of fact, not "a genealogist's opinion."*

. . . ."

These two points assume that there was a second son of 1729/30 John Wright. While the points are probably true in the sense that there was no other John Wright who could be substituted for 1792 John Wright as a second son of 1729/30 John Wright, that does not show that there was a second son of 1729/30 John Wright. And in addition, Hoppin changed the question from point three, which addressed whether there was another Wright who could be the parent of 1792 John Wright. That is a critical question and Hoppin avoided the question by not addressing it. The answer to that last question is more important than the answer to point three.

Hoppin had indirectly addressed the issue by discussing in his prior article "Some Descendants Of Richard Wright, Gentleman, Of London, England, And Northumberland, Virginia, 1655" published in Tyler's Quarterly in 1919, the three other

John Wrights who lived in Westmoreland County in the late 1600's and early to mid 1700's. The three John Wrights were (1) John Wright (Westmoreland County Planter), (2) 1714 John Wright of Westmoreland County and his son 1736 John Wright of Westmoreland County, and (3) John Wright (Westmoreland County Overseer).

John Wright (Westmoreland County Planter) died in about 1711 and left a widow Hannah and no heirs.

1714 John Wright of Westmoreland County left a son John Wright, who was 1736 John Wright of Westmoreland County, and a posthumous son Thomas Wright. This line of descent precludes 1792 John Wright from being the son of 1714 John Wright.

John Wright (Westmoreland County Overseer) was described by Hoppin through various Westmoreland County court orders, which indicated that this John the Overseer was born in about 1659, had a daughter Virlandoe and sons Aaron, William, and possibly Charles, and died sometime after 1734. No documentation has been found clearly identifying a John Wright as a son of John Wright (Westmoreland County Overseer). However, John the Overseer was old enough to have had a son John in about 1700 and the existence of three and possibly four other children is evidence that there may have been more children.

Hoppin did not address the question of whether 1792 John Wright might have been the son of John the Overseer. Hoppin simply disparaged this John Wright as having a discreditable background (reveling and drinking on Sunday during divine service and relieved of taxes in old age as an object of pity). One wonders whether Hoppin would have been paid by his patron and had his work published by Yale University Press if he had suggested a possible line of descent from such an ancestor rather than an association with the prestigious Washington family and, therefore, had an incentive to avoid discussing this possibility.

As set forth below, there are several pieces of circumstantial that connect the family of John Wright (Westmoreland County Overseer) to 1792 John Wright, so that it is possible that 1792 John Wright was a son of John Wright the Overseer.

The purpose of this discussion is to illustrate that Hoppin changed the focus of his questions between point number three and points number four and five and thereby avoided the issue of whether there was a possible alternative parent for 1792 John Wright, which there is.

Point Six (Part):

> " (6) John Wright was particularly the "son of his father." He was an Episcopalian, as were his father and grandfather. He was a vestryman, as were his father and grandfather. He was a captain in the militia, as were his father and grandfather. He was a lawyer, as were his father and grandfather. He was a justice, as were his father and grandfather. He bore his father's Christian name. Why, if he was not that father's son?. . . . "

This point has been discussed above in Section III.D and that discussion is not repeated here.

Point Six (Part):

> ". . . . He succeeded his father as a justice upon his father's death by virtue of being his father's son. He was inducted into that preferment at a time when the influences and customs of the society into which he was born and in which he moved, made for such preferment of sons in order to maintain family prestige, to protect family property and prerogatives, and to continue political power and control in a rew families. . . ."

This point has been discussed above in Section III.C.3 and that discussion is not repeated here.

Point Six (Part):

> ". . . .He succeeded to these honors at an age when he would not have been so preferred if he had not been son of John[3] Wright. . . ."

This point has been discussed above in Section III.C.1 and that discussion is not repeated here.

Point Seven:

> " (7) The recorded presence of the uncle of John[4] Wright's mother, Dorothy (Awbrey) Wright, namely, Francis Awbrey, as a first justice of the quorum of the first court of Prince William County in 1730-31, with John[4] Wright, suggests that this elder justice had an influence in effecting the preferment of John[4] Wright, as a first justice of the first Court."

This point has been discussed above in Section III.C.2 and that discussion is not repeated here.

Point Eight (Part):

> " (8) John[3] Wright lived from 1723 until his death upon the estate known as Leesylvania, situated along Neapsco Creek, near to the church of Hamilton Parish and near to the courthouse of Prince William County, both of which structures were built at the ferry of the Occaquan River. . . ."

This part of point eight may be correct, but does not address the issue of whether 1792 John Wright was a son of 1729/30 John Wright who was living at Leesylvania.

Point Eight (Part):

> "His widow, Dorothy, and their two sons lived there; she until her death (by 1739) and they until 1741. The elder of these two sons, Francis[4], lived there on the estate, Leesylvania, until he completed the sale of it on July 27, 1741. That his brother, John[4] Wright, was living there, as a vestryman at the church, as a lawyer, and as a justice of the quorum of the court of Prince William County as late as March 23, 1741 (new style), is proved by the evidence of the records of that court . . . ."

Hoppin's point is interrupted at this place to note a half-truth by Hoppin. While it may be true that the court records show 1792 John Wright active as vestryman and justice, those records do not show that 1792 John Wright was living on Francis Wright's land. There is no documentation to support that claim. 1792 John Wright may have been living on leased land or someone else's property, perhaps as an overseer, during this time.

Point Eight (Part):

> ". . . . and by the fact that he (John[4]) did not acquire from Jeremiah Darnall until March 23, 1741 (new style), the estate to which he then or soon afterward removed from the Neapsco. The date of this purchase was exactly twenty-two months after Francis[4] Wright sold the minor one-third of Leesylvania, and exactly four months and four days before Francis[4] Wright completed, on July 27, 1741, the sale of the major two-thirds of Leesylvania. These events are significant; they were interdependent. . . . ."

Hoppin's point is interrupted again at this place to note that his statement that the sale and purchase were interdependent is merely his interpretation of the events. There is nothing presented, other than his opinion, that the sale and purchase were interdependent. The precision with which Hoppin counts the time between the three transactions does not make them more interdependent or interdependent at all.

Point Eight (Part):

". . . . While the exact date of the removal of Justice John[4] Wright to the new home that he was obliged to acquire because of the sale of Leesylvania is not of record, ..."

Hoppin's point is interrupted once again at this place to note that there is nothing presented, other than his opinion, that the sale required 1792 John Wright to move from the area of the original courthouse.

Part Eight (Part):

". . . . it is clear that in removing so many miles away from the courthouse at Occaquan to the southwestward near the Licking Branch of Cedar Run, he did not suffer much inconvenience as a justice holding court, because he could have been, at the longest possible, settled in his own new home (the first that he had ever owned) but twenty-one months before the Council of Virginia, on December 15, 1742, ordered the removal of the court from the Occaquan to Philemon's Branch of Cedar Run, fifteen miles nearer to the new home of John[4] Wright near the Licking Branch of Cedar Run. . . ."

While this commentary may be correct, it is irrelevant to the issue of whether 1792 John Wright was a son of 1729/30 John Wright.

Point Eight (Part):

". . . . The upshot of these facts is (1) that John[3] Wright, father of John and Francis[4], lived and died on his estate along the Neapsco and near to the parish church of Hamilton and the county courthouse at Occaquan; . . . ."

While this commentary may be correct as to 1729/30 John Wright's residence at Occaquan, the statement that he was the father of John and Francis has not been shown. This is just an unsupported assertion by Hoppin.

Point Eight (Part):

". . . . (2) that John[4] Wright lived there until within four months and four days, at the longest, before Francis[4] Wright completed the sale of the same estate. . . . ."

Again, there is nothing in the "facts" that shows that 1792 John Wright was living "there", meaning on Francis Wright's land. It remains an unsupported assertion by Hoppin.

Point Eight (Part):

". . . . *This is circumstantial evidence that John[4] and Francis[4] were the only sons of John[3] and Dorothy (Awbrey) Wright, because the fact that John[4] did so remove at the time Francis[4] sold out the ground from under their feet and the roof from over their heads is good evidence of their relationship; otherwise, any act of Francis would have had no influence or bearing upon the movements and acts of John Wright, the justice, neither then nor at any other time. . . . ."*

Ironically, the last statement by Hoppin is more true than he perhaps appreciated. Since there is no independent evidence of a connection between 1742 Francis Wright's sale of his land and 1792 John Wright's purchase of his land and the asserted interdependence of those two actions is based solely on Hoppin's opinion, it is all too true that "any act of Francis . . . . had no influence or bearing upon the movements and acts of John Wright, the justice, neither then nor at any other time."

Point Eight (Part):

". . . . *The recorded facts of their lives and of the lives of their relations prove that the relationship between John[4] and Francis[4] could not have been other than that of brothers."*

Once again, there is nothing presented that supports this assertion, other than Hoppin's opinion, which in turn was partly based on a mistaken identification of the wife and in-laws of 1729/30 John Wright.

Point Nine (Part):

" (9) If one accepts, as we must, the record of the granting of letters of administration on the estate of John[3] Wright deceased dated in 1729 or 1730, as being proof of his death within that short period of time; and if one accepts, as we must, the record of the Council of Virginia dated April 27, 1731, in confirmation of the previous nomination, as a first justice of Prince William County, of John[4] Wright when he was aged no over twenty-four years, one at once becomes involved, inextricably, in a position from which neither retreat nor escape from the relationship of these men as father and son is possible - because of the nonexistence of any other two men who can be placed in the same positions; and, likewise, because of the nonexistence of any other one man who can be placed in the position of either John[3] Wright or John[4] Wright. Nor can either of the two John Wrights be removed from the positions they are found recorded in. Even were these facts not true, the nomination in 1730 and the confirmation in 1731, for the honor of a first justiceship of the very young John[4] Wright not because of his personal merits and ability, without his having come to that nomination through the usual process of time and previous experience as a warden, a vestryman, and in other of the lesser town, parish, and county offices, is indirect proof that he was the son of the honored justice

> whose name he bore and who had then but recently died. Were there no other indications, evidences, proofs, either indirect or circumstantial, as to the relationship of these two John Wrights, the circumstances of this appointment to a justiceship conveys, alone, sufficient intelligence as to the truth."

Hoppin has taken two facts which are established by documentation, the administration of the estate of 1729/30 John Wright of Stafford County in 1729 or 1730 and the appointment of 1792 John Wright as justice of Prince William County in 1731, and then attempted to connect them with a fact which is not established and actually is incorrect, the age of 1792 John Wright at the time of his appointment. Hoppin's incorrect assertion of the year of birth of 1792 John Wright has been discussed above in Section III.C.1 and is not repeated here.

F. Conclusion

The result of this review is that Charles Hoppin made a number of erroneous assertions that were unsupported by any documentary evidence, including the following:

1) Awbrey as the maiden name of 1729/30 John Wright's wife Dorothy,

2) 1708 to 1710 as the first listing of the time of marriage of 1729/30 John Wright and Dorothy ____,

3) 1705 as the second listing of the date of marriage of 1729/30 John Wright and Dorothy ____,

4) 1712 as the first listing of the year of birth of 1792 John Wright of Fauquier County,

5) 1707 as the second listing of the year of birth of 1792 John Wright of Fauquier County,

6) great uncle as the relationship of Francis Awbrey to 1792 John Wright,

7) the appointment of 1729/30 John Wright as a justice of Stafford County,

8) the residence of 1792 John Wright on the land of 1729/30 John Wright and later on the same land inherited by 1742 Francis Wright of Prince William County,

9) the story of resentment by 1792 John Wright against 1742 Francis Wright when 1742 Francis sold his land inherited from his father 1729/30 John Wright,

10) the claim of interconnection between the sale of 1742 Francis Wright's

land in 1739 and 1741 and the purchase of land by 1792 John Wright in 1740,

11) the story of a refusal by 1792 John Wright to act as guardian or overseer of the children and estate of 1742 Francis Wright, and

12) lawyer as the occupation of 1729/30 John Wright and 1792 John Wright.

The further result of this review is that the only evidence that supports Hoppin's assertion that 1792 John Wright of Fauquier County was a son of 1729/30 John Wright of Stafford County was the following:

1) the physical presence of 1792 John Wright in Prince William County in 1731,

2) an interpretation of the phrase "John Wright father of the said Francis Wright dying intestate the said Francis Wright as his eldest Son is heir at Law to the said Land" as implying there was more than one son of 1729/30 John Wright,

3) that 1729/30 John Wright was a justice in Westmoreland County in 1723 and 1792 John Wright was a justice of Prince William County in 1731, and

4) that they were both vestrymen.

In the absence of the Y-DNA evidence discussed below, this was possibly sufficient evidence to indicate that 1792 John Wright was possibly a son of 1729/30 John Wright, but it is hardly compelling. When the erroneous and undocumented assertions are removed from Hoppin's arguments, his case for 1792 John Wright of Fauquier County as the son of 1729/30 John Wright of Stafford County is no longer convincing.

IV. The Documentation For The Ancestral Lines Of The Wright DNA Project Participants

The second question that needs to be addressed is what the documentation is for the ancestral lines of the Wright DNA Project participants that shows their descent from 1792 John Wright of Fauquier County, Virginia, or 1713 Francis Wright of Westmoreland County, Virginia, or 1655 Francis Wright of Yorkshire County, England.

The ancestral lines of the following participants in the Wright DNA Project are attached as exhibits:

A) David R. Wright, Kit 38121, a descendant of 1792 John Wright of Fauquier County, Virginia, through his son 1809 William Wright of Franklin County, Virginia, and his grandson 1830 William Wright of Franklin County, Virginia, is attached as Exhibit C;

B) Thomas Wright, Kit 38118, a descendant of 1792 John Wright of Fauquier County, Virginia, through his son 1809 William Wright of Franklin County, Virginia, and his grandson 1823 James Wright of Franklin County, Virginia, is attached as Exhibit D;

C) Thomas Carr Wright, Kit 94975, a descendant of 1792 John Wright of Fauquier County, Virginia, through his son 1789 John Wright of Surry County, North Carolina, is attached as Exhibit E;

D) James Logan Wright, Jr., Kit 71409, a descendant of 1713 Francis Wright of Westmoreland County, Virginia, through his son 1741 Richard Wright of Westmoreland County, Virginia, is attached as Exhibit F;

E) Werter Gregory Wright III, Kit 123670, a descendant of 1713 Francis Wright of Westmoreland County, Virginia, through his son 1741 Richard Wright of Westmoreland County, Virginia, is attached as Exhibit G; and

F) Peter Wright, Kit 108246, a descendant of 1655 Francis Wright of Yorkshire County, England, through his son 1674 George Wright of Yorkshire County, England, is attached as Exhibits H, I, J, and K.

V. The Evidence That 1713 Francis Wright Of Westmoreland County Was A Descendant Of 1655 Francis Wright Of Yorkshire County, England

The third question to be addressed is the evidence that connects 1713 Francis Wright of Westmoreland County, Virginia, as a descendant of 1655 Francis Wright of Yorkshire, England.

James Logan Wright, Kit 71409, is a descendant of 1713 Francis Wright of Westmoreland County, Virginia, through his son 1741 Richard Wright of Westmoreland County, Virginia.

Werter Gregory Wright III, Kit 123670, is also a descendant of 1713 Francis Wright of Westmoreland County, Virginia, through his son 1741 Richard Wright of Westmoreland County, Virginia.

Peter Wright, Kit 108246, is a descendant of 1655 Francis Wright of Yorkshire County, England, through his son 1674 George Wright of Yorkshire County, England.

For James Logan Wright, Werter Gregory Wright III, and Peter Wright to be related, thereby confirming their common Y-DNA haplogroup, 1713 Francis Wright of Westmoreland County, Virginia, must be shown to have been a son of 1663 Richard Wright of Northumberland County, Virginia, and 1663 Richard Wright of Northumberland County must in turn be shown to have been a son of 1655 Francis Wright of Yorkshire County, England.

A. The Identification Of 1713 Francis Wright Of Westmoreland County As A Son Of 1663 Richard Wright Of Northumberland County

1713 Francis Wright of Westmoreland County was a son of 1663 Richard Wright of Northumberland County and Ann (Mottram) Wright.

The will of Richard Wright dated on August 16, 1663, and probated on December 10, 1663, at Northumberland County, Virginia, W.B. 1658-1666/114 listed Francis Wright as one of his children:

> "In the name of God Amen I Richard Wright of Chickacone . . . . doe make this my last will & testement in maner & forme following:
>
> . . . .
>
> Item I will & bequeath unto my loveing wife Anne Wright the one halfe of my land lying & being upon Machoatick & Patomack River, she takeing that halfe

that issues [or ioynes] upon my brother Spencer, & the land to have as long as she lives & after her death to goe to my sonne Francis . . . .

Item I give & bequeath unto my ____ land lying & being upon ____ halfe at present & the other ____ to him & his heirs for ever ____ francis all my money in Engl____ for the dischargeing the ____ education, Likewise I doe ____ Sonne francis Wright my ____ last will & Testament.
. . . ."

On February 25, 1685/6, at Westmoreland County, Virginia, D.B. 4/1 Francis Wright and his wife Ann (Washington) Wright sold to Michael Halbert 100 acres of land which had been granted to Ann (Washington) Wright's father John Washington and descended to her by reason of her father's death:

". . . . Francis Wright and Ann his wife send greeting . . . . Know Ye that I Francis Wright of the County of Westmoreld in Virga Gentl and I the said Ann daughter of Col John Washington of the County aforesaid decd now wife to the said Francis Wright . . . . for the sum of four thousand pounds of tobacco in cash to us in hand delivered . . . . do grant, bargain, sell, alien enfeoff and confirm unto Michael Halbert one hundred acres of land situate in Westmorld County in Virga. at the head of Madox granted to the said John Washington by patent and now by the death of the said Washington devolving and dissending to Ann his daughter (now wife to the said Wright by hereditary right together with all buildings fences, orchards, woods, rivers, waters, privileges members and appurtinances to the same belonging or in any wise appertaining. . . . . In witness whereof we the said Francis Wright and Ann Wright have hereto put our hands and seals this 25th day of February in the first year of the reign of our Sovereign Lord James the second Annoque Dom: 1685

Signed, Sealed and deli-) Francis Wright
vered in the presence of us) Ann Wright
Thomas Baker) John Wright
Thomas Marshall
Ann Read

March the 31st 1686. Acknowledged in Court by Francis Wright and then recorded

P. Tho: Marson D.C.C.P.

Westmorld: SS

At a Court held for the said County the 26th day of March 1707.

John Wright Gentl. son and heir apparent of Francis Wright Gent: party to this present conveyance by subscribing his name to the same and by himself in person acknowledged and voluntarily disclaimed any right, title or interest in and to the lands and premises in the said conveyance contained or to any part or parcel thereof for divers and especial considerations at this time him thereunto moving.

Test
Ja: Westcomb Cler Com Pred

Recordatz: primo die April 1707.

Pr. Eund'm Cler'um

Know all men by these presents that I Francis Wright of the County of Westmorld in Virga. do acknowledge and confess myself to be indebted to Michael Halbert his heirs, Exors Admrs in the full and just sum of ten thousand pounds of good tobacco in cash to be paid upon all demands after the date of these presents and to the performance hereof well and truly to be done I do bind myself my heirs and assigns firmly by these presents and in testimony to the truth hereof have hereto put my hand and seal this 25th day of Febry 1685.

Test
Ja: Westcomb Cler. Cler. Com Pred

The condition of this obligation is such that if the above bounded Francis Wright his heirs and assigns do from time to time and at all times hereafter save defend and keep harmless the Michael Halbert his heirs and assigns in the quiet and peacable possession of one hundred acres of land which he holds in right of Ann his wife and now by deed of feofment from the said Wright and Ann his wife granted sold aliened and confirmed to the Michael Halbert his heirs and assigns for a valuable consideration Recd. according to all the parts members and claims and things mentioned in the aforesaid deed of feofment bearing date with these presents And shall and will make such further assurances in law as by the said Michael Halbert and his learned counsel in the law shall be devised, or advised, then this obligation to be void and of none effect, otherwise to stand in full force and virtue.

Signed, Sealed & deli-) Francis Wright
vered in the presents of us) John Wright
Tho: Baker
Tho: Marshall

Westmorld: SS

At a Court held for the said County the 26th day of March 1707.

John Wright, Gentl, son and heir apparent of Francis Wright Gentl. party to the within Bond in open Court acknowledged himself a party to the said bond by subscribing his name thereto and the penalty therein specified to enure and be good and valued to all intents and purposes therein declared against him his heirs, Executors and Admrs to the benefit and advantage of the therein named Michael Halbert according to the true meaning and purport of the said bond.

Test
Ja: Westcomb Cler. Com Ped

Recordatz: primo die Aprilis 1707

Pr Eund'm Cler'um"

This record indicates that Francis Wright had married Ann Washington, daughter of John Washington, prior to February 25, 1685/6, and that they had a son John Wright who was an adult before March 26, 1707.

On August 30, 1711, at Westmoreland County, Virginia, D.&W.B. 7/230 Francis Wright quitclaimed to Francis Spencer 900 acres of land which had been formerly sold by Francis Wright's father Richard Wright to Nicholas Spencer and in which Francis Wright's mother Ann (Mottram) Wright had not properly joined:

"This Indenture made this 30th day of August in the yeare of Our Lord One thousand Seven hundred and Eleven Between Francis Wright of the parish of Cople in the County of Westmorld on the One part and Francis Spencer of the pish and County aforesaid on the Other part Witnesseth that Whereas Richard Wright father of the aforesaid Wright formerly (to Witt) the 18th day of August in the Yeare of Our Lord 1662 sold and Conveyed Over unto Nicholas Spencer esqr father of the aforesaid Francis Spencer a certaine tract of Land lying scituate on Nomony bay Containing Nine hundred acres of land more or less contained in Certaine bounds in the said Deed menconed which said Land was the Just right and inheritance of Ann the daughter of Coll John Mottrom and Wife of the said Richard and Mother of the said Francis Wright and forasmuch as the said Ann did not Joyne in the said sale nor was any party to the said deed nor did not pass her right in the said land as the law requires and that by meanes thereof the same is descended & come to the aforesaid Francis Wright as heir at Law to his mother therefore he the said Francis Wright as well for and in consideracon of the sum of Seven thousand pounds of good sound merchantable Tobacco in Cask to him in hand by the said Francis Spencer already paid . . . . doth . . . . give grant bargaine sell . . . . unto the said Francis

Spencer the same in his actual possession now being all that his the said Francis Wright his right and tittle of in and to the aforesaid tract of land Containing nine hundred acres be the same more or less being bounded as by the said parties to these prsents is now concluded Confirmed and agreed on (Vizt) Begining at a marked white Oake standing on the maine branch of King Copssco Pond at the head thereof by the road side that that leads from the house of the said Wright to the said Spencers running thence a streight Course to a marked red Oake standing by a swamp or branch that issueth out of Armsbys creek and near the now dwelling house of Samll Chamberlin and thence down the said swamp cove and creek to the head line of the whole dividend of land of the aforesaid Wright or Mattrom thence along the said head line and the water Courses of nominy Bay to the mouth of King Copssco Pond and up the said Pond according to the meanders thereof to the first menconed beginning White Oake . . . . In Testimony the aforesaid parties to these prsents hath interchangeably hereunto sett their hands and affixed their seales the day and year first above Written, Memorandm (the words the same in his actual possession now being on the eighteenth line was interlined before sealed & signed Frances Wright sealed and delivered in prsence of D McCarty Nath Pope - Westmld SC At a Court held for the said County the 29th day of August 1711 Francis Wright gentl: the above subscriber personally came into Court and acknowledged the above instrument to be his proper act and deed and the lands and prmisses therein menconed to be conveyed to Francis Spencer gentl: to be the Just right and inheritance of him the said Francis Spencer his heires and assignes forever.

Test.
Tho: Sorrell Depty Clu Comp'd

Recordate sixto die Septembris 1711

Pr Eundm Cluum"

This record confirms the identification of Francis Wright as the son of 1663 Richard Wright of Northumberland County and Ann (Mottram) Wright.

Married Well And Often by Robert K. Headley, Jr., also listed the Francis Wright as a son of Richard Wright and the marriage of Francis Wright and Anne Washington as before January 8, 1682/83:

> "Wright, Francis & Washington, Anne; bef. 8 Jan 1682/83; groom was a son of Rich. & Ann (Mottrom) Wright; bride was a dau. of Lt. Col. Jn. Washington; (RapC RB 1682-88:351; RC OB 4:333; WC DW 2:188a; DW 4:1; OB 1675-89:269; Wright 1:130; Wright 2:54)"

B. <u>The Identification Of 1663 Richard Wright Of Northumberland County As A Son Of 1655 Francis Wright Of Yorkshire County, England</u>

Although internet postings have often asserted that 1663 Richard Wright of Northumberland County, Virginia, was a son of 1655 Francis Wright of Yorkshire County, England, that has been done without documentation of the sources relied on for the identification. The following evidence I believe establishes that connection.

In her letter dated March 30, 2005, Jo Anne Mackby enclosed an excerpt from <u>The First Gentleman Of Virginia</u> by Louis B. Wright which stated that sometime before August 20, 1655, Richard Wright was accused of ravishing a young woman:

> ". . . . One Alice Atkinson accused Richard Wright, "aged 22 yeares or thereabouts," of ravishing her. In a deposition she testified that she told a certain Mrs. Salisbury of her misfortune and that Mrs. Salisbury replied "that Mr. Wright was a gentleman and it was a pity." In Record Book No. 2, under date of Aug. 20, 1655, there is the following entry (spelling modernized and abbreviations expanded): "Whereas it appeareth unto the Court that Alice Atkinson hath in a most infamous manner defamed Mr. Richard Wright in taxing him of ravishment and no proof thereof, the Court do therefore order that the said Alice Atkinson shall have twenty stripes upon her bare shoulders forthwith." Apparently Wright, probably a rowdy young blade just arrived in the colony, had been mixed up in a drinking brawl, and the evidence is vague as to precisely what happened. The clues are to be found in Beverley Fleet, *Virginia Colonial Abstracts. Vol. II. Northumberland County Records, 1652-1655* (Richmond, Va., 1937), pp. 62, 129-31."

This record indicates that Richard Wright was born in about 1633.

<u>York County, Virginia, Records 1659-1662</u> by Benjamin Weisiger stated that on October 31, 1661, at York County, Virginia, Record Book 1659-1662/136 the following bond was recorded:

> "I, Richard Wright of Northumberland County, Va., Merchant, am indebted to William Strange of London, Merchant, for £28 and bind my self to pay, 27 Sept. 1661
>
> Condition is that if Richard Wright repay £14 to Strange by 10th March next, bond is void.
>
> Wit: Tho Ballard, Ro. Pyland Richard Wright
> Recorded 20 Oct. 1661"

This record connects Richard Wright to at least one London merchant.

The will of Richard Wright was dated on August 16, 1663, probated on December 10, 1663, at Northumberland County, Virginia, W.B. 1658-1666/114. The copy remaining is very badly deteriorated and difficult to read. A copy of that will is shown on the following pages.

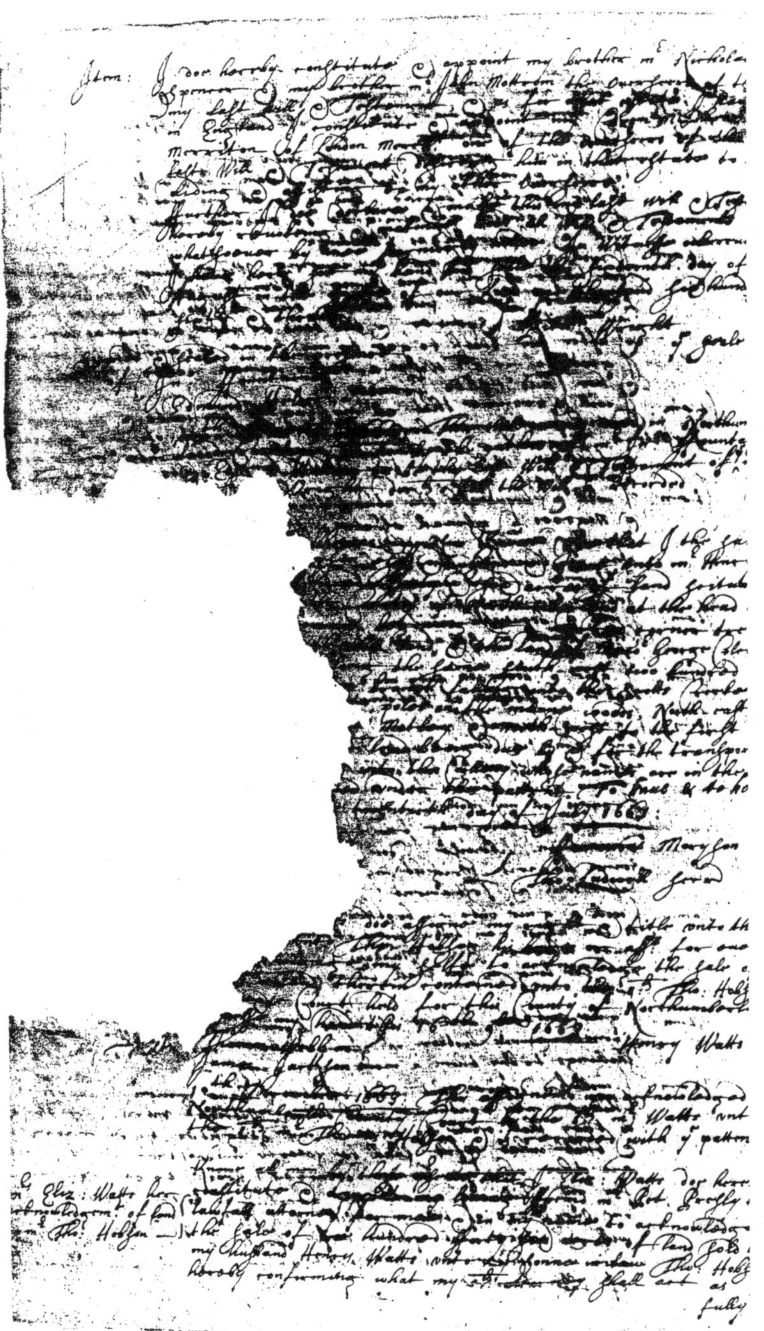

1956: Northumberland Co., VA
Record Bk 1658-1666:114-115

In the name of God Amen I Richard [illegible]

115

In his work <u>The Washington Ancestry</u> Charles Hoppin included a transcription of this will of Richard Wright. Unfortunately, Hoppin interpolated into his transcription words he thought should be in the document, but were not there. Most, but not all, of those interpolations were indicated by brackets. Hoppin's transcription read in part as follows:

> "Item: I doe hereby constitute & appoint my brother Mr Nicholas Spencer & my brother Mr John Mottrom the Overseers of this my Last Will & Testament, & as for what estate I have in England, I constitute & appoint my Cozen Mathew Merriton of London, Mercht. one of the Overseers of this my last Will & Testament, desireing him in that estate to be aiding & assisting to my other Overseers."

<u>Virginia Colonial Abstracts</u> by Beverley Fleet provided an abstract of that will which stated the will referenced a cousin Matthew Merriton:

> "Richd. Will. Entry mutilated. Dated 16 Aug 1663. Prob 10 Decr 1663. Wife Anne. Son Francis, the only name of child appearing, but refers to 'my children'. Est div in 3 parts so evidently another child. Overseers in Va brothers Nicholas Spencer and Jno Mottrom. Overseer in England "my Cozen Matthew Merriton of London merchant". Wit: Jno Fountaine, Edmund Helder. 15.114"

In 1993 I also requested Westmoreland County researcher Margaret Hill to transcribe the document and her transcription reads in pertinent part as follows:

> "Item I doe hereby constitute & appoint my brother Mr. Nicholas Spencer & my brother Mr. John Mottrom the Overseers of this my last will & Testament, & aas for what estate I have in England I constitute & appoint my Cozen Mr. ____ Merriton of London merch one of the Overseers of this my last Will & Testament, desiring him in that estate to be aiding & assisting to my other Overseers. . . . ."

Using these transcriptions and several xerox copies of the original document, I transcribed the will in pertinent part as follows:

> "Item: I doe hereby constitute & appoint my brother mr Nicholas Spencer & my brother Mr John Mottrom the Overseers of this my last will & Testament, & as for what estate I have in England I constitute & appoint my Cozen Mr [Thomas?] Merriton of London mercht one of the Overseers of this my last Will & Testament, desiring him in that estate to be aiding & assisting to my other Overseers."

The result of these readings is that 1663 Richard Wright had a cousin Mathew or Thomas Merriton who was a London merchant.

The marriage record of Francis Wright and Ann Meryton is listed in Paver's

Marriage Licenses for the year 1626 at http://www.genuki.org.uk/big/eng/YKS/Misc/Transcriptions/YKS/Pavers1626.html:

"Date	Surname	Christian name	Comment	Surname
1626	Wright	Francis	of Bolton-upon-Swale	Meryton

Christian name	Comment	Where to be married
Ann	of Kirk Leavington	either place.(8)

(8) Son of Francis Wright, of Bolton-on-Swale. She was daughter of George Meryton, D. D., Dean of York (See Dugdale's Visitation)."

History Of The Landed Gentry Of Great Britain & Ireland by Bernard Burke, published in 1875, (hereafter "Burke's Commoners") listed 1655 Francis Wright of Yorkshire, England, as married to Anne Merriton, daughter of George Merriton:

> "The Rev. Francis Wright, D.D. of Bolton-on-Swale, espoused Anne, daughter of the Very Rev. George Meryton, Dean of York, and by her, who died 29th March, 1670, had six sons and two daughters, namely,
> I. Francis, who died s. p.
> II. George, heir to his father,
> III. Thomas,
> IV. Richard,
> . . . .
> George Wright, esq. of Bolton-on-Swale, born in 1629, ... "

A copy of the relevant portion of Burke's Commoners is attached as Exhibit H. The date of marriage and the listing order of the births of the sons indicate that Richard Wright, the son of 1655 Francis Wright, would have been born in about 1633 or so, which is consistent with the 1633 birth of 1663 Richard Wright of Northumberland County.

Burke's Commoners information was probably drawn in part from The Visitation Of The County Of Yorke by William Dugdale, compiled in 1665 and 1666 and printed in 1859, (hereafter "Dugdale's Visitation") which listed Francis Wright as married to Anne Meryton and died in 1665 with a son Richard, among other children. A copy of that portion of Dugdale's Visitation is attached as Exhibit I.

Burke's Commoners also listed Grace Wright, the daughter of 1651 Francis

Wright of Yorkshire County, England, and Grace (Beckwith) Wright as married to Thomas Meryton, a son of George Meryton, Dean of York:

> "Francis Wright, of Bolton-on-Swale in the county of York, who died about the year 1651, leaving by Grace, his wife, daughter of ____ Beckwith, esq. of Aldborough, in the same shire, one son and three daughters, viz.
>
> . . . .
>
> Grace, m. to Thomas Meryton, esq. of Castle Levington, in the same county, son of George Meryton, D.D. Dean of Peterborough , and subsequently York."

Dugdale's Visitation listed George Meryton as married to Mary Rande and died in 1624 and with son John Meryton and son Thomas Meryton, who died in 1652, and who in turn had a son Thomas Meryton, among other children. A copy of that portion of Dugdale's Visitation is attached as Exhibit K. This record establishes a person who could be the cousin of 1663 Richard Wright named Thomas Meriton in the will of 1663 Richard Wright.

Finally, in her WorldConnect posting dated January 9, 2006, Renia Simmons stated that George Meryton was born in about 1581 in Yorkshire, married Mary Rande, and died in about 1624, and they had the following children, among others:

1) Thomas Meryton, born in about 1607 in Hadleigh, Suffolk, England,
2) Anne Meryton, born in about 1611 in Hadleigh, Suffolk, England, and
3) John Meryton, born in about 1615 in Hadleigh, Suffolk, England.

Ms. Simmonds also stated that Thomas Meryton married Grace Wright, daughter of Francis Wright and Grace (Beckwith) Wright, in about 1614 in Yorkshire, England, and that they had the following son, among others:

1) Thomas Meryton, born in 1638.

Ms. Simmonds also stated that Anne Meryton married Francis Wright in 1626 in Yorkshire, England, and that they had the following son, among others.

1) Richard Wright, born in 1633 in Yorkshire, England.

This information of Ms. Simmonds was probably drawn from Dugdale's Visitation.

However, Ms. Simmonds also stated that John Meryton married Elizabeth Smithson and that they had the following son:

1) Matthew Meryton.

Once again, John Meryton's son Matthew Meryton would have been a cousin of 1663 Richard Wright of Northumberland County.

So whether the will of 1663 Richard Wright of Northumberland County, Virginia, should be read as listing his cousin as Matthew Merriton or Thomas Merriton, there was a Meryton/Meriton of that name who would satisfy the description of cousin of 1663 Richard Wright and who connected him to 1655 Francis Wright of Yorkshire, England, and his wife Anne (Merriton) Wright.

The Dictionary Of National Biography, edited by Sidney Lee, 1909, also has a short biography of George Meriton or Meryton at Volume XIII, page 277, which mentions that the baptisms of his children were recorded in the registers of Hadleigh Parish.

The evidence connecting 1663 Richard Wright to Richard, the son of Francis Wright and Ann (Merriton) Wright, therefore, includes:

1) the marriage record of 1655 Francis Wright and his wife Ann in 1626,

2) the listing of Ann's maiden name as Meryton,

3) the listing of Ann (Meryton or Merriton) Wright as the daughter of George Meryton,

3) the date of birth of 1663 Richard Wright in 1633 consistent with the probable date of birth of Richard, the son of 1655 Francis Wright,

4) the reference in 1663 Richard's will to his cousin Thomas or Matthew Merriton in London, and

5) the listing of George Meryton as having grandsons Thomas and Mathew Meryton, the same name (or names) listed in 1663 Richard Wright's will,

The conclusion seems fair that this evidence indicates that 1663 Richard Wright of Northumberland County, Virginia, was the same person as the son of 1655 Francis Wright of Yorkshire, England, and Anne (Merriton) Wright.

VI. The Probability That A Non-Marital Event Tainted The Y-DNA Of Either The Descendants Of 1792 John Wright Of Fauquier County, Virginia, Or The Descendants Of 1655 Francis Wright Of Yorkshire County, England

The last question to be addressed is whether there is a significant probability that a "non-marital event" may have occurred in the ancestral line of either the descendants of 1792 John Wright of Fauquier County, Virginia, or the descendants of 1655 Francis Wright of Yorkshire County, England, that would produce a false result for the Y-DNA.

A. The Haplogroup And Y-DNA Sequence Of 1792 John Wright Of Fauquier County, Virginia

Since Y-DNA passes unchanged from father to son, except for random mutations, the haplogroup and Y-DNA of 1792 John Wright can be established from his male Wright descendants.

1. Line Of Descent Of 1809 William Wright Of Franklin County

The identification of 1809 William Wright of Franklin County as the son of 1792 John Wright of Fauquier County was set forth in my work titled The Identification Of 1809 William Wright Of Franklin County As The Son of 1792 John Wright Of Fauquier County, copies of which are available from Heritage Books, Inc., at heritagebooks.com. Through the efforts of John A. Washington and Justin Glenn, this identification was presented to the membership of the Washington Descendants Society and, after one year for consideration, was accepted by the Society as the correct line of descent.

In addition, my work Sorting Some Of The Wrights Of Southern Virginia, Part III: 1809 William Wright Of Franklin County sets forth the documentation for the line of descent of 1809 William Wright's sons 1823 James Wright of Franklin County and 1830 William Wright of Franklin County. Those lines lead to six participants in the Wright DNA Project, all of whom have the same haplogroup of R1b1c and five of whom have substantially similar Y-DNA sequences, one of which is identical to the sequence of Thomas Carr Wright discussed below. One of the six participants has a sufficiently large number of mutations in his Y-DNA sequence to indicate that there was probably a "non-marital event" in his line and that he is not descended from 1809 William Wright.

The line of descent of one of those descendants through the son 1830 William Wright of Franklin County is set forth in Exhibit C and the line of descent of one of those descendants through the son 1823 James Wright of Franklin County is set forth in Exhibit D.

If the documented lines of descent are correct and if there were no "non-marital events" in the line of descent from 1792 John Wright, then these Y-DNA results would alone establish the haplogroup of 1792 John Wright.

2. Line Of Descent Of Thomas Carr Wright

Thomas Carr Wright was a descendant of 1792 John Wright of Fauquier County through his son 1789 John Wright of Surry County, North Carolina.

As set forth at the Wright DNA Project site, the haplogroup for Thomas Carr Wright was R1b1c, the most common haplogroup for Wright descendants. The Y-DNA sequence for Thomas Carr Wright is set forth at the Wright DNA Project site and matched that of the modal sequence of a descendant of 1809 William Wright of Franklin County. The line of descent of Thomas Carr Wright is set forth in Exhibit E.

If the documented line of descent of Thomas Carr Wright is correct and if there were no "non-marital events" in that line of descent, then this evidence alone is sufficient to establish the haplogroup and Y-DNA sequence of 1792 John Wright of Fauquier County.

3. Improbability Of Non-Marital Event

The matching of the Y-DNA of six documented descendants of 1792 John Wright through two different sons seems to clearly establish the haplogroup and Y-DNA sequence of 1792 John Wright and his male descendants and male Wright ancestors.

However, a question that has to be addressed is whether it is possible that a "non-marital event" could undermine the conclusion regarding the haplogroup and Y-DNA sequence of 1792 John Wright and the answer is yes, that it could. However, with one participant from the line of 1789 John Wright and five participants from the line of 1809 William Wright who match Y-DNA, the "non-marital event" would have had to occur either (1) at the first generation of 1792 John Wright or (2) at the second generation of 1823 James Wright , 1830 William Wright, 1789 John Wright, or (3) among the male descendants of those last three men.

For the "non-marital event' to occur at the first generation, 1792 John Wright's wife Elizabeth (Bronaugh) (Darnall) Wright would have had to commit adultery twice with the same man within four years of her marriage to 1792 John Wright. While possible, this seems an improbable event. Ironically, if the "non-marital event" did occur at this generational level, then while 1792 John Wright might be a son of 1729/30 John Wright, none of his male descendants would be from his line.

For the "non-marital event" to occur in the second generation, there would have to have been multiple "non-marital events". Each of the wives of 1823 James Wright, 1830 William Wright, and 1789 John Wright would have had to have committed adultery with men with the same Y-DNA. If we assume a 30% probability that each of the wives would have committed adultery and if we use the same probability of the man being R1B1c that exists for Wrights, which is 60%, then the probability of all three wives having committed adultery with R1b1c men would be about .06% (.3 x .6 x .3 x .6 x .3 x .6). And the fact that the Y-DNA sequences match closely means the probability would be based on each man having not just R1b1c as a haplogroup, but the subset Y-DNA sequence of that haplogroup exhibited by the descendants. That probability would be even smaller than .06%.

And for "the non-marital event" to occur in the later generations, an even larger number of adulteries would have had to occur and all with men having similar Y-DNA. The probability of such an event has to be even smaller than .06%.

The same analysis would apply if the "non-marital event" were an undocumented adoption.

4. Conclusion

The result of the matching of these six participants, five from 1809 William Wright and one from 1789 John Wright, excludes with reasonable certainty the chance of a "non-marital event" altering the results and thus establishes with reasonable certainty the haplogroup and the Y-DNA sequence for all male descendants of 1792 John Wright and his male Wright ancestors. That haplogroup was R1b1c and that Y-DNA sequence is set forth at the Wright DNA Project site.

And as a consequence, if 1792 John Wright of Fauquier County was a son of 1729/30 John Wright of Stafford County and consequently a grandson of 1713 Francis Wright of Westmoreland County, great grandson of 1663 Richard Wright of Northumberland County, and great great grandson of 1655 Francis Wright of Yorkshire County, England, then the Y-DNA of those four persons and their male descendants has to match, subject to random mutations, that of the descendants of 1792 John Wright of Fauquier County.

B. The Haplogroup And Y-DNA Sequence Of Descendants Of 1655 Francis Wright Of Yorkshire County, England

As set forth above, 1713 Francis Wright of Westmoreland County was the father of 1729/30 John Wright of Stafford County. 1713 Francis Wright had a second son by his second marriage who was 1741 Richard Wright of Westmoreland County and 1741 Richard Wright had further male descendants. 1713 Francis Wright was also the son of 1663 Richard Wright of Northumberland County and the grandson of 1655 Francis Wright of Yorkshire, England, who had further male descendants.

Fortunately, two male Wright descendants of 1713 Francis Wright through his son 1741 Richard Wright have been located.

1. Line Of Descent Of James Logan Wright, Jr.

James Logan Wright, Jr., Wright DNA Project Kit #71409, is a male Wright descendant of 1713 Francis Wright of Westmoreland County. The line of descent for James Logan Wright, Jr., is set forth in Exhibit F. This line of descent is also set forth in the chart prepared by Jeffrey A. Wright set forth in Exhibit B.

The Y-DNA of James Logan Wright, Jr., is haplogroup J2, a relatively rare (4%) haplogroup for Wright descendants. His Y-DNA sequence is given at the Wright DNA Project site at http://www.wright-dna.org/dna/OtherResults.html.

If his line of descent is correctly stated and if no "non-marital event" occurred, then this Y-DNA result is sufficient alone to establish that 1792 John Wright of Fauquier County was not the son of 1729/30 John Wright of Stafford County. The difference in haplogroups is so great as to preclude a common ancestor within recorded history.

2. <u>Line Of Descent Of Werter Gregory Wright III</u>

Werter Gregory Wright III, Wright DNA Project Kit #123670, is a male Wright descendant of 1713 Francis Wright of Westmoreland County. The line of descent for Werter Gregory Wright III is set forth in Exhibit G. This line of descent is also set forth in the chart prepared by Jeffrey A. Wright set forth in Exhibit B.

The Y-DNA of Werter Gregory Wright III is again haplogroup J2, a relatively rare (4%) haplogroup for Wright descendants. His Y-DNA sequence is given at the Wright DNA Project site at http://www.wright-dna.org/dna/OtherResults.html and matches in 36 of 37 markers that of James Logan Wright, Jr.

If his line of descent is correctly stated and if no "non-marital event" occurred, then this Y-DNA result is again sufficient alone to establish that 1792 John Wright of Fauquier County was not the son of 1729/30 John Wright of Stafford County. The difference in haplogroups is so great as to preclude a common ancestor within recorded history.

3. <u>Line Of Descent Of Peter Wright</u>

Peter Wright, Wright DNA Project Kit 108246, is a male Wright descendant of 1655 Francis Wright of Yorkshire County, England, the grandfather of 1713 Francis Wright of Westmoreland County. The full line of descent for Peter Wright is set forth in Exhibits H, I, J, and K.

One researcher stated that Burke's <u>Commoners</u> was not considered reliable for lines of descent in the middle ages. While that may be true, the line of descent in this case begins in 1655, which is well beyond the middle ages and would seem a reliable source. And the material in Burke's Commoners is verified by the material from Dugdale's <u>Visitation</u>, a contemporaneous primary source.

The Y-DNA of Peter Wright is haplogroup J2. His Y-DNA sequence is set forth at the Wright DNA Project site at http://www.wright-dna.org/dna/OtherResults.html. and matches with five mutations that of James Logan Wright, Jr., and Werter Gregory Wright III.

If his line of descent is correctly stated and if no "non-marital event" occurred, then this Y-DNA result is also sufficient alone to establish that 1792 John Wright of

Fauquier County was not the son of 1729/30 John Wright of Stafford County. The difference in haplogroups is so great as to preclude a common ancestor within recorded history.

4. Improbability Of Non-Marital Events

As in the case of the descendants of 1792 John Wright of Fauquier County, it is possible that one or more non-marital events altered the transmission of the Y-DNA for the lines of James Logan Wright, Jr., Werter Gregory Wright III, and Peter Wright.

However, with three participants in three different lines in two countries, there would have to have been at least one wife who committed adultery in each line with a male who was of the same haplogroup of J2. If we assume a 50% chance of adultery in the nine generations for James Logan Wright, Jr., the ten generations of Werter Gregory Wright III, and the ten generations of Peter Wright, and if we take the percentage of all males with J2 haplogroup to be 4%, as it is for Wright participants in the Wright DNA Project, then the probability of the posited set of events would be about .000008% (.5 x .04 x .5 x .04 X .5 X .04). This probabiltiy is so low as to exclude a non-marital event for these three lines.

The same analysis would apply if the "non-marital event" were an undocumented adoption.

5. Conclusion

The result of this review is that the line of descent of each of James Logan Wright, Jr., Werter Gregory Wright III, and Peter Wright is well documented and the probability of a non-marital event in these lines is extremely small. The matching of their Y-DNA indicates that the lines of descent are probably correct.

As a consequence, the haplogroup of the Y-DNA of the line of Wrights from 1655 Francis Wright of Yorkshire County, England, including his grandson 1713 Francis Wright of Westmoreland County, is established as J2 and the Y-DNA sequence is set forth at the Wright DNA Project under 1540 John.

VII. Overall Conclusion

The result of this analysis is that (1) the case presented by Charles Hoppin for the identification of 1792 John Wright of Fauquier County as the son of 1729/30 John Wright of Stafford County is weak to the point of near non-existence, (2) the descendants of 1713 Francis Wright of Westmoreland County, Virginia, were also descendants of 1655 Francis Wright of Yorkshire County, England, (3) the Y-DNA results for the descendants of 1792 John Wright of Fauquier County and for the descendants of 1655 Francis Wright of Yorkshire County, England, with a high degree of probability, were all not tainted by a non-marital event, and (4) those Y-DNA results are so different that the two lines would not have a common ancestor within recorded history.

Since 1729/30 John Wright of Stafford County, Virginia, was a son of 1713 Francis Wright of Westmoreland County, Virginia, a grandson of 1663 Richard Wright of Northumberland County, Virginia, and a great grandson of 1655 Francis Wright of Yorkshire County, England, his Y-DNA would not match that of 1792 John Wright of Fauquier County and, therefore, 1729/30 John Wright of Stafford County could not be the father of 1792 John Wright of Fauquier County.

VIII. The Identification Of John Wright (Westmoreland County, Virginia, Overseer) As The Possible Father Of 1792 John Wright Of Fauquier County, Virginia

If, as set forth above, 1792 John Wright of Fauquier County, Virginia, was not the son of 1729/30 John Wright of Stafford County, Virginia, then the next logical question is who was the father of 1792 John Wright. There is circumstantial evidence that John Wright (Westmoreland County Overseer) was the father of 1792 John Wright of Fauquier County.

The first circumstantial evidence involves Virlandoe Wright, daughter of John Wright the Overseer, and her connection to 1792 John Wright.

In his work "Some Descendants of Richard Wright, Gentleman, of London, England, and Northumberland, Va., 1655," published in 1919, Charles Arthur Hoppin stated as follows with regard to John Wright (Overseer of Westmoreland County):

> "One June 30, 1709: "Ordered Virlandoe Wright, daughter of John Wright of Upper Machotique, mark of Cattle & Hoggs be Recorded. [Westmoreland Orders &c. 1705 to 1721, page 126.]"

"Greening - (And Variants) Early Records" by Sadie Greening Sparks stated that:

1) On October 25, 1725, at Northern Neck Grant A/190 Owen Greenin was granted 467 acres of land in King George County on the branches of Summerduck Run;

2) On February 4, 1730, at Northern Neck Grant C/96 Owen Grinan of King George County was granted 119 acres of land in King George County adjacent to his existing land; and

3) On September 1, 1731, at Northern Neck Grant D/28 Owen Grinan of Prince William County was granted 481 acres of land on the northern head branch of Broad Run.

On October 18, 1731, at Prince William County, D.B. B/64 Vellender Greenin appointed John Wright, Gentleman, as her attorney in fact to acknowledge her right of dower in 200 acres of land sold by her husband Owin Greenin:

> "Know all men by these Presents that I Vellender Greenin the Wife of Owin Greein of the Parish of Hanover in the County of Pr. Wm. Doe Constitute and appoint Jon. Wright Gent to acknowledge my right of Dowrey and thirds at the Common Law of in to Two hundred acres of Land Sold by my Said Husband

unto William McBee and his heirs for Ever relation thereto being had it doth and may fully and at Large Appear and for so Doing this shall be his Sufficient Warrent as witness my hand and Seal this Eighteen Day of Obr Anno Domini 1731

Signed Sealed and De- livered In the Presence of us Tested by Owin Greenin, Thos :T Dunigan	Vellender V Greenin her mark and Seal

At a Court Continued & held for Prince William County the Twenty first Day of october 1731

The Within Power of Atturney from Vellender Greenon to John Wright was Proved by the oaths of the Witnesses thereto admitted to Record

Test
Catesby Cooke Cl Cur."

The given female names of Virlandoe and Vellender are so unusual and so similar sounding that Vellender Greenin of Prince William D.B. B/64 was probably the same person as Virlandoe Wright of Westmoreland County Court Order 1705-1721/126. The only John Wright, Gentleman, in Prince William County in 1731 was 1792 John Wright of Fauquier County, who had been elected a justice of the county. A power of attorney was typically given to a trusted relative, which suggests that 1792 John Wright of Fauquier County was related to Vellender (Wright) Greenin. As set forth above, 1792 John Wright of Fauquier County was born before October 2, 1700, and Virlandoe/Vellender (Wright) Greenin was in 1709 old enough to record a mark and yet young enough not to be married and was married by 1731, indicating that John and Virlandoe/Vellender were of similar ages and, therefore, probably siblings.

Also, as set forth above, Vellender Greenin was described in Prince William County D.B. B/64 as of Prince William County and, as will be set forth below, Charles Wright was possibly a son of John Wright (Westmoreland County Overseer) and Charles Wright moved to Prince William County by 1741. This has the appearance of the migration of a family away from Westmoreland County to Prince William County in approximately the same time period.

The second piece of circumstantial evidence involves Charles Wright, a possible son of John Wright the Overseer, and the similarity of his residences to those of 1792 John Wright.

In his work "Some Descendants of Richard Wright, Gentleman, of London, England, and Northumberland, Va., 1655," published in 1919, Charles Arthur Hoppin stated as follows with regard to Charles Wright:

> "Charles Wright of Westmoreland, later of Prince William county, against whom nothing discreditable is found recorded, may have been an estimable son of John Wright the overseer, though recorded proof thereof is lacking; so one may accord to this Charles Wright the benefit of any doubt."

On September 28, 1741, at Prince William County, Virginia, D.B. E/468 Charles Wright purchased from Thomas and Judith Davies or Davice or Davis 250 acres of land on Occoquan River:

> "This Indenture made the twenty eighth day of September in the fifteenth year of the reign of our Sovereign Lord George the Second . . . . in the year of our Lord God one thousand Seven hundred and forty one Between Thomas Davice & Judith his wife of the County of Prince William in the parish of Hamilton of the one part & Charles Wright of the County of Westmorland in the parish of Washington of the other part Witnesseth that the said Thomas Davice and Judith his wife for and in Consideration of the Sum of fifteen pounds Currt. money of Virginia to him in hand paid by the said Charles Wright . . . . have given granted bargained & Sold . . . . unto the said Charles Wright and his heirs for ever the said Charles Wright being in actual possession of all and Singular the Premisses hereinafter mentioned and expressed by vertue of a lease thereof made for a whole year bearing date the day next before the day of the date hereof & of the Statute for transferring uses into possession it being part of a certain tract of Land lying upon the North side of Occoquon for two hundred & fifty acres be the ame more or less & is bounded as follows begining upon Reeves mill branch there the first course buts upon the said branch & runing on the said branch the meanders thereof to a maple at the mouth of a small branch thence binding with Reeves west eighty six degrees & a half West eight six pole then North thirty three degrees west twenty two pole thence North Seventeen degrees & 1/2 west ninety four pole to a white oak corner between Reeves & Stribling thence binding on Stribling South Seventy five degrees North one hundred pole to a hickory which was Corner to a tract of Land formerly taken up by John Florance thence along Florances Line South eighty degrees West two hundred and forty poles to a white oak corner to Bland & Davice thence binding on their Lines South twenty degrees East twenty poles to a White oak thence West Eighty degrees east sixty four pole to a red oak thence South Sixty one degrees East Seventy five pole to

two white oaks standing on a gulley on occoquon thence down Occoquon the meanders thereof to a hickory & white oak & a maple the beginning corner to this Tract thence to Reeves branch where it first began . . . .

Sealed & Delivered in presence of	Thomas Davies
Taylor Chapman	Judith X Davies
Benja Rush	
Peter Daniel	

Received of Charles Wright this __ day of ____)
1741 the Sum of fifteen pound Currt. money being)
the Consideration money within mentioned to be by) £15
the said Charles Wright paid to me)

Taylor Chapman	Thomas Davies
Ben: Rush	
Peter Daniel	

At a Court held for Prince William County the 28th day of September 1741.

Thomas Davies & Judith his wife (She being first privately examined) acknowledged this release from themselves with receit endorsed to Charles Wright to be their acts & Deeds and they were thereupon admitted to Record.

Test.
Catesby Cooke Cl.Cur"

This record indicates that Charles Wright had moved from Westmoreland County to Prince William County by 1741 on Occoquan Creek where the courthouse was originally located. This record also indicates that Charles Wright resided in the same parish of Washington in Westmoreland County in which John Wright (Westmoreland County Overseer) resided, suggesting a possible relationship.

On May 29, 1750, at Prince William County, Virginia, D.B. M/86 Charles Wright gifted to his son Joseph Wright 125 acres of his land on Occoquan River in exchange for his support:

"To all Christian People to whom these Presents shall come I Charles Wright of the County of Prince William and Parish of Detingen send greeting Know yee that I the said Charles Wright for & in Consideration of the Natural love & Paternall affection which I have & do bear unto my son Joseph Wright of the parish & County aforesd as also for & toward his personal support and better maintenance have given granted . . . . and confirm unto the said Joseph Wright and his heirs all that tract or Parcel of land with the appurtenances Cictuate lying & being in the Parish & County aforesaid upon ocquaquan Containing one hundred twenty five acres to be laid of in the most Convenient manner adjacent to the houseing and Plantation where the said Joseph Wright now lives. . . . . In Witness whereof I have hereunto set my hand and affixed my seale the xxixth day of May in the year of our Lord one thousand seven hundred & fifty

Sealed & Delivered in) Charles Wright
the presence of us)
Thomas Reno
Jno. Sturman

At a Court Contd. and held for the County of Prince William 29th May 1950
Charles Wright acknowledged this Deed & admitted to record

Test
p. Wagener Cl"

If Charles Wright was the son of John Wright the Overseer, then his move from Washington Parish, Westmoreland County, to Prince William County is further circumstantial evidence of a migration of the members of the family of John Wright the Overseer in the 1730's and 1740's, including possibly 1792 John Wright.

The third piece of circumstantial evidence involves the common given names. Parents often named one of their sons after the father, so it would be likely that John Wright (Westmoreland County Overseer) would have a son John. No other John Wright has been identified as a possible son of John Wright (Westmoreland County Overseer), which means that 1792 John Wright could fill that role.

The fourth piece of circumstantial evidence involves the Williams family. As set forth above, the wife of John Wright the Overseer was ____ (Williams) Wright. The wife of 1792 John Wright's son 1789 John Wright of Surry County, North Carolina, was Ann (Williams) Wright. The connection of John Wright the Overseer to the Williams family in Westmoreland County and the son of 1792 John Wright to the Williams family in Fauquier County indicate a connection between the two Wright families involved with the Williams families.

The fifth piece of evidence involves common connections of John Wright the Overseer and 1792 John Wright with the Corbin family. As set forth above, John

Wright the Overseer was described as the overseer for Gawin Corbin. As also set forth above, on March 23, 1740, at Prince William County Deed E/170, 1792 John Wright of Fauquier County purchased 236 acres of land from Jeremiah and Catharine Darnall, land which was described as adjacent to that of Colonel Corbin's:

> ". . . . bounded as followeth Vizt. Beginning at a Red Oak standing in Colonel Corbins line & extending thence along the said line South eighty eight degrees West four hundred & fourteen poles to a Hicory & Gum in ye said Corbins line . . . ."

The Encyclopedia Of Virginia Biography edited by Lyon Gardiner Tyler provides a biography of Gawin Corbin, Sr., at page 217 that indicates Gawin Corbin was a county lieutenant and, therefore, would have had the courtesy title of Colonel Corbin, and a second biography of his son Gawin Corbin, Jr., who lived in Westmoreland County:

> "Corbin, Gawin, of Middlesex county, son of Henry Corbin, of the colonial council, was naval officer of the Rappahannock in 1705. He was burgess for Middlesex county in 1698, 1699, 1700-1702, 1703-1705, 1718-1720 and for King and Queen county in 1715. He was county lieutenant. He married three times: (first) Catherine Wormeley; (second) Jane Lane, widow of Willis Wilson of Elizabeth City county, and daughter of John Lane of King and Queen, and (third) Martha Bassett. He died January 1, 1745, and was father of : 1. Richard Corbin, of "Laneville." 2. John Corbin, of "Portobago," Essex county. 3. Gawin Corbin, of "Pecatone."
>
> Corbin, Gawin, son of Gawin Corgin and Jane Lane, his wife, lived at "Pekatone," Westmoreland county, and at "Laneville," King and Queen county. He was burgess for King and Queen county in 1736-1740 and for Middlesex county in 1742-1747. He married Hannah Lee, daughter of Thomas lee of "Stratford," Westmoreland county, Virginia, and his will was proved in Westmoreland county January 29, 1760."

These records indicate a connection between John Wright (Westmoreland Overseer) and 1792 John Wright of Fauquier County through either Gawin Corbin, Sr., or his son Gawin Corbin, Jr..

For these reasons 1792 John Wright of Fauquier County was possibly the son of John Wright (Westmoreland County Overseer) and ____ (Williams) Wright, but further research will be required to confirm this identification.

Exhibit A

Chart Of Line Of Descent Of DNA Participants From 1792 John Wright

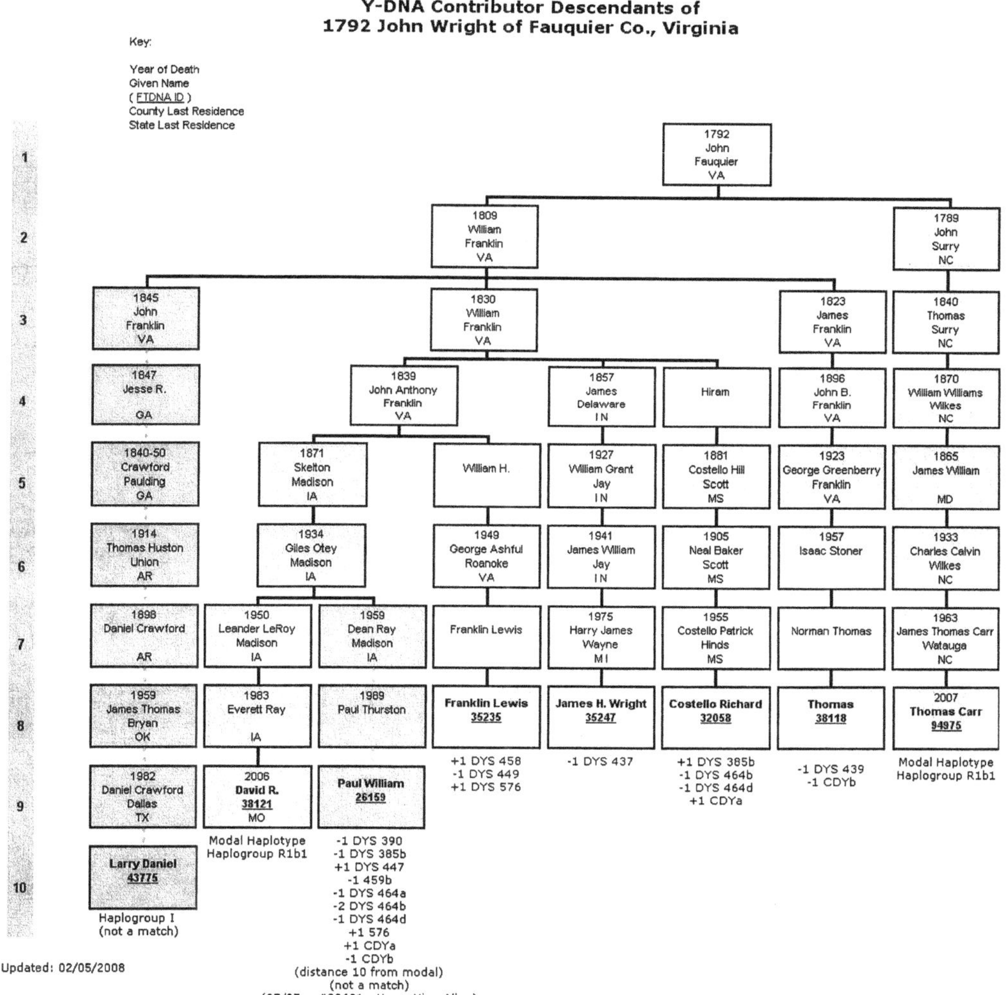

Jeffrey A. Wright

Exhibit B

Chart Of Line Of Descent For DNA Participants From 1655 Francis Wright

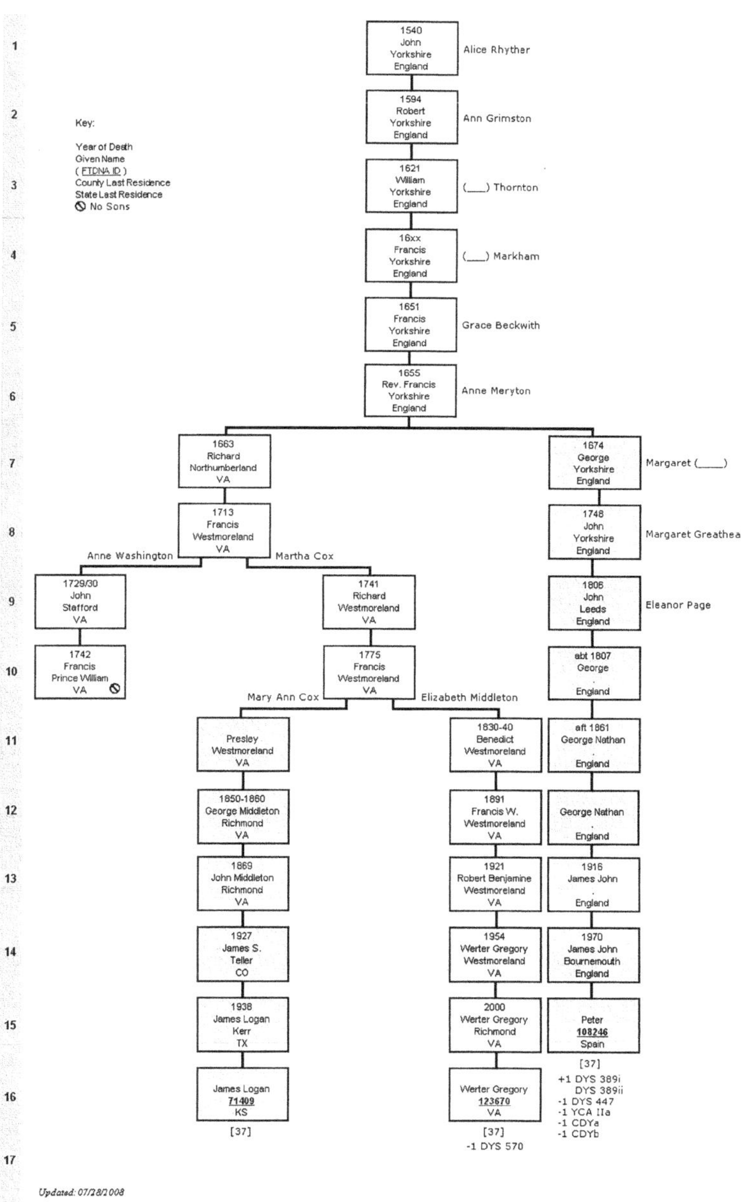

Jeffrey A. Wright

Exhibit C

Documentation For Line Of Descent Of David R. Wright

Kit 38121

Line Of Descent For David R. Wright, Kit 38121, From 1792 John Wright Of Fauquier County

This exhibit will trace the line of descent of David R. Wright, Kit 38121, from 1792 John Wright of Fauquier County.

First Generation:

1792 John Wright Of Fauquier County And Elizabeth (Bronaugh) (Darnall) Wright

The line of descent from 1792 John Wright of Fauquier County to 1809 William Wright of Franklin County has been given in my work The Identification Of 1809 William Wright Of Franklin County As The Son Of 1792 John Wright Of Fauquier County and the reader is referred to that work for the documentation relating to that connection.

Second Generation:

1809 William Wright Of Franklin County, Mary (Grant) Wright, And His Descendants

The will of Elizabeth (Bronaugh) (Darnall) Wright's first husband Waugh Darnall was probated on October 7, 1726, and the will of her father Jeremiah Bronaugh was dated on April 14, 1736, both listed her as Elizabeth Wright. This indicates that 1792 John Wright and Elizabeth (Bronaugh) (Darnall) Wright were married between October 7, 1726, and April 14, 1736. The marriage was probably after 1726 and thus perhaps in 1727, and if that were correct, then their first child would have been born probably in 1728. William Wright and Mary (Grant) Wright were married before September 4, 1751, when they executed King George County, Virginia, Deed 1743-52/442. Such a marriage date indicates that William Wright was probably born in before 1731.

The will of William Grant, Jr., undated and probated on May 4, 1733, at King George County, Virginia, W.B. A-1/98 listed Mary Grant as one of his daughters:

> "In the Name of God Amen. I William Grant, Junr. being sick and weak yet in perfect sense. First I return my soul to God that gave it and my body to the Earth, then my will and desire is that after my debts are paid that my well beloved wife Mary Grant should enjoy all my whole estate both real and personal

during her widdowhood & my desire after if my wife should marry again that my brother John Grant should take my two children and take care of them untill they come to the age of eighteen years and that my estate be equally divided between my two children Eliza & Mary. I appoint my beloved wife Mary Grant and my brother John Grant my sole Executors. Witness my hand and seal (*not dated*).

Test: Charles Dean		His	
John Briscoe	William	[/]	Grant
		Mark	

At a Court held for King George County the 4th. day of May 1733.

The last Will & Testament of William Grant was presented into Court by Mary Grant his Widdow & John Grant his Executors who made oath thereto and the same was proved by the oath of Charles Dean and admintted to record.

Copa. Test: T: Turner Cl: Cur:"

This record identifies Mary Grant as a daughter of William Grant, Jr., and Mary (_____) Grant and indicates that she was born after about May 1715.

The will of William Grant, Sr., dated January 24, 1726/7 and a nuncupative codicil dated January 4, 1733/4 and probated on February 1, 1733/4, at King George County, Virginia, W.B. A-1/101 made a gift to his son William Grant's children:

"In the Name of God Amen I William Grant of the Parish of Sittenburn in the County of King George being well in body & of perfect sense & memory thanks be to God for the same Do make & ordain this my last will & Testament in manner & form following Vizt Inprimis I give & bequeath all my Goods & Chattles upon my own plantation in the freshes which I bought of Cornelius Edmonds deced to my eldest son John Grant & his heirs forever & the same plantation & land I give between my two Sons John & Daniel the Survivor of them & their heirs forever Item I give & bequeath all the plantation & Land whereon I now dwell to my Son William Grant & his heirs forever And Whereas I gave formerly by deed of Gift given to my son John two Negroes named George & Sparry & an Indian Slave named Jo; To my Son William two Negroes named Mell & Sambo. To my Son Daniel two Negroes named Peg & Jenny & all their future increase & one Negro man named Tony which his brother John bought of Ansilem Bennet to him & his heirs forever Item I bequeath to my Son Daniel two feather beds & furniture and one flock bed & furniture three new pewter dishes & one small one four large basons six milk pans a quart Tankard a pint Do three porringers and dozen of plates and great large Iron pot & small ones & a brass shellet with my own horse bridle & Saddle holsters 2 pistols & all matterials belonging to a

Trooper Item I bequeath to my Son William & Daniel all my Stock of Chattels Hogs upon my own plantation Item I bequeath unto my Son Daniel a Servant Woman named Elizabeth _ndinant her with all my wearing apparell Item I bequeath to my son William Grant two feather beds 1 flock bed & their furniture all my horses mares & all matterials what is not willed to be divided amongst my three Sons John William & Daniel also if any debts come against me or my estate for my three Sons John William & Daniel to pay it in equall part of payment Item I give unto my wife Also one shilling sterling she being eloped from me & her basely abusing of me Item I make constitute & ordain my said three sons John William & Daniel Grant to be full & Sole Executors of this my last Will & Testament revoking all other wills by me heretofore made & confirming this & no other to be my last Will & Testament I appoint Collo Nicholas Smith Maj George Eskridge to be trustees of this my last Will & Testament As Witness my hand & Seal this 24th of Jany 1726/7

Sealed & Delivered
in the presence of
Francis Etteridge
Thos Stribling
his
John X Caddell
mark

his
William M Grant
mark

At a Court held for King George County the 1st day of Feby 1733

The last Will & Testament of William Grant deced was presented into Court by John Grant & Daniel Grant who made Oath thereto & the Same was proved by the Oath of Thomas Stribling one of the Witnesses thereto who also made Oath he saw Francis Etteridge another of the Witnesses evidence the Same which is admitted to record

Copa Teste
T. Turtner Cl Cur

Jany the 4th 1733/4

The last Will & Testament of William Grant my Will is that the labour of my two Negroes Jenny & Sarah shall be for the maintainance of my Son Willim Grants two Children

Item I give & bequeath to Catherine Taylor the bed that lyeth under my bed whereon I now lye with bed Clothes belonging to it

Item Three pound eight shillings due by Account from Anne Edmunds

Item Twenty shillings due by Account from John Brown

Item One Inspectors note of 720 lb of Tobacco

Item her resident on my dwelling plantation till Christmas next with Corn & meat to subsist on

Anthoney Carnabe

At a Court held for King George County the 1st day of Feb 1733

Anthony Carnaby presented the above Nuncupative Codicil into Court & made Oath that the deced William Grant desired him to take notice thereof & the Same was ordered to go with the Will & to be admitted to record

Copa Teste
T Turner Cl Cur"

On February 3, 1743, at King George County, Virginia, Fiduciary Account Book 3/18 John Grant filed his accounting for his guardianship of Mary Grant and her sister Elizabeth Grant:

"Dr.	The Estate of William Grant	£	S	_(?)
Settlement of the Estate of Wm Grant				
May 6	To 1 White Sheeting Jacket &c EG	2		0
1738	To 1 White Apron &c for Do	1		6
	To 1 Check Do for Do	1		6
	To 1 Brown Linnen Coat for Do	2		6
	To 1 Chaloes Coat for MG		2	
	To White Shift		2	
	To White Do EG	4		6
	To 2 Do for Do		6	
	To 2 Do for MG		5	
	To Caping for EG & MG		2	
	To 1 Coat for EG		3	
	To 1 Do for MG		2	
	To 1/2 m Pins			9
	To 1 Burmetar Hat for EG		4	
	To 1 pr Shoes for Do	3		6
	To 1 pr Ditto for MG	2		6
	To 1 yd. of Ribband for EG		2	
	To 2 Silk Girdles for Do			2
	To 2 pr. yarn Hose			3

		£	s	d
Decbr 30	To Boarding of Elizabeth & Mary Grant 1 Year	7		
	To 1 pr. of Linnen Britches & Shirt &c Sambo		5	
	To 1 Do of Do for James		5	
	To 1 Shift & Coat for Sarah		6	
	To 1 Do of Do		6	
	To 3 Narrow Hoes @ 2/2	6		6
	To 2 Broad Do 2/6		5	
	To 1 Shift for the Negro Child &c	1		6
	To 4 pr. of Shoes @ 5/ To 4 pr. of Stockings @ 2/6	1	10	
	To 2 Cotton Jackets & Britches for Sambo James		15	
	To 2 Coats & Jackets for Sarah & Abigail		17	
	To 2 Cotton frocks for the Negro Children		3	
March 26	To 1 pr of Shoes for EG	3		6
1739	To 1 Country Cloth Gown &c for EG		10	
	To 1 fine Shift &c for EG	4		6
	To 6 yds. fine Chints for a Gown &c E		18	
	To 1 fine Shift &c for Do	4		6
	To 1 pr. Worstead Hose for Do	2		6
	To 1 Muslin Workt Handkerchief for Do		3	
	To 1 pr of Kid Gloves for Do		2	
	To 2 fine Shifts for MG		6	
	To 1 Brown Linnen Coat for Do		2	
	To 1 Bible for EG		6	
	To 1 fine Linen Apron for EG	1		10
	To 1 Laced Hat for Do	16		6
	To 1 Chaloes Coat for Do		3	
	To 1 felt Hat for MG	1		3
	To 1 fine Shift for EG	5		6
	To Linnen for Caps & Handkerchiefs & Apron	4		6
	To 1 Shirt & Britches for James &c		6	
To 1 Shirt & Britches for Sambo &c			6	
	To 1 Shift & Coat for Abigal &c		8	
	To 1 Shift for the Negro Child &c	1		8
	To Schooling EG 1 year & Paper		15	
	To 1 Quilted Coat for Do		10	
	To 1 Cloth Gown &c for Do	10		6
	To the making 6 pr of Shoes	7		6
	To the making 1 pr of stick downs			6
	To 1 pr. of Yarn Stockings	1		6
	To 4 Brown Linnen Shirts for the Negroes		15	
	To 1 Cotten Coat & Jacket &c for Sarah	7		6
	To Do of Do for Abigail	7		6
	To 1 Kersey Jacket & Britches &c for Sambo		12	
	To 1 Cotton Jacket & Britches &c for James	7		6
	To 4 pr. Plaid Hose		5	

	To 2 Cotton Frocks for the Negros &c		5	
	To 1 Stear for the Overseer	1	5	
1739	To finding the Overseer Beding		10	
	To 1 Scarlet Cloak for EG	1	2	6
	To 1 Check Apron for Do		1	3
	To Shalloon Coat for MG &c		4	6
	To 1 Coat & Jacket &c for Do		2	6
	To 1 pr. of Shoes for James		5	
	To 2½ yds. of Yellow Canvas @ 2/6	6		3
	To 1 frying pan for the Negros		4	
1740	To Boarding of Eliza Jellary Grant	7		
	To 1 Pen knife for EG			6
	To finding the Overseer Bedd		10	
	To 6 yd. Seersucker for Gown &c		18	
	To Hilling Hoe	2		6
	To 1 fine Linen Shift &c for EG		8	
	To 6 yds. Coarser Do for Do		9	
	To 1½ yds. fine Do for Do	3		9
	To 1 yard of Muslin		3	
	To 1 yard of fine Linen	2		7
	To 1 Check Linnen Coat &c	2		6
	To 1 Apron of Do	1		3
	To 1½ yds. of fine Linnen	2		3
	To 1 pr. Worstead Hose		3	
	To 1 m of Pins	1		3
	To 2 pr. Kid Gloves for EG		3	
	To 2 fine Shifts &c MG	6		9
	To 2 Aprons for Do	1		6
	To 1 Check Linnen Gown & Coat for Do		8	
	To 1 Brown Do for Do	2		3
	To 1 felt Hat for Do	1		2
	To 1 Sack Bag		3	
	To Small Book			9
	To 36 yards of Brown Linnen	1	16	
	To 4½ yards of Cloth for EG &c @ 1/8	7		10
	To 1¾ yds of White Linnen for Do	2		2
	To Schooling of & Paper EG		11	
1741	To Boarding of Eliza. and Mary Grant	7		
	To 1 Necklace for EG			9
	To 1 fine Side Saddle & Bridle Whip EG	4	2	6
	To a pr. of Womens Shoes		3	
	To 1 pr. of Worstead Hose	3		9
	To 6½ yds. Wide Check Linnen	9		9
	To 6 yds. Chince &c for EG	1	4	
	To 1 Ounce of Nuns Thread			7

	To 1 pr. of Tape				9
	To 1 pr. of Bobin				5
	To 1 m of Pins				9
	To 5 yd of Shalloon			6	3
	To 5 yd of Worstead Stuff			6	3
	To 6½ yards of Sheeting Linnen 4/3			7	10
	To 1 yard of Muslin			4	6
	To 1 yard of Do			2	6
	To 4 yds. of fine Irish Linen @ 2/3			9	
	To 3 yds. of Edgen		2		3
	To 8 yds. of Irish Linen @ 12d			8	
	To 35 yds. of Brown Do. @ 9d		1	6	3
	To 2 Broad Hoes 1 Narro. Do			7	6
	To 1 yd. fine Irish Linen			4	4
	To 1 __ of Brown Thread @			2	6
	To ½ __ of Whited Brown			2	6
	To 1 pr. of Womens Shoes			3	6
	To 1 Worstead Hose			3	6
	To 1 pr. of Womens Shoes			3	6
1738	By 1 Crop of Tobacco	44 78			
1739	By 1 Do of Do	49 60			
1740	By 1 Do of Do	31 70			
1741	By 1 Do of Do	43 88			
		169 96			
	Deduct for Goods	120 77 @ 15/	90	11	8
		49 19 @ 14/	34	8	7
	By 2 Steers			3	
	By 1 Old Cow & Yearling			2	
	By Cash			3	2
	By 1 Cow Sold Ross			1	15
	By 1 Cow Sold Thos. Wood			2	
	By 1 Steer Sold Stephen Bowen			2	
	By Ballance due as by the Settlement in 1738		26	18	3
			162	16	8

February the 3d 1743

In Pursuance to an Order of King George County Court we the Subscribers have Setled the Acct. of Wm. Grants Orphans & find a Ballance in the Hands of John Grant Exr. of Forty Eight pounds One Shilling & Seven pence Currt. Money Given under Our Hands this day & year Above Written

Saml. Skinker
John Champe

At a Court held for King George County The 3d day of February 1743

This Settlement of the Estate of William Grants Orphans in Presented into Court by John Grant the Exor. & admitted to record.

Copa Test
Harry Turner Cl"

On August 26, 1751, at Prince William County D.B. M/169 1792 John Wright of Fauquier County gifted 185 acres of land to his son William Wright:

"To all to whom these presents shall come send greeting Know ye that for divers good causes and considerations but more especially for and in consideration of the natural love and affection which I have and Do bear unto my dear beloved son William Wright Do give grant and confirm and by these prsents do give grant and confirm unto the sd. William Wright all that messuage tract or parcel of Land which he now lives on containing one hundred and Eighty five Acres Situate lying and being in the parish of hamilton and county of Prince William and Collony of Virginia and Bounded as followeth Beginning at two red oaks being the dividing corner between Jonas Williams and Scimon Morgan and runs with the dividing line S: 7-1/2 degrees W: 185 poles to a box oak on a branch thence N. 83 d: W: 208 poles to a Chesnut on a hill in the old Line of the deeds thence with the line of the deeds to the beginning it being part of a greater Dividant taken up by Waugh Darnal Decd. by patent Dated the 17th day of feberuary 1725 To have and to hold the sd. tract or parcel of Land to him the aforesd. William Wright and his heirs for Ever together with all houses Edifices Gardens Building orchards woods and underwood timber and timbers trees ways water and water courses priviledges and Commodities wth. ye. appurtenances unto the same belonging which said land I do hereby do grant and Confirm unto the said William Wright and to his heirs for Ever in Witness whereof I hereunto set my hand & fixed my seal this 26th day of August AD 1751

Test: John Crump — John Wright
Weeden Smith

At a Court held for the County of Prince William 26 august 1751 John Wright Gent acknowleged this Deed which is admitted to record

Test
Z Wagener Cl

Deed deld. Mr Wm Wright & wife ye 20th May 1762."

This record indicates that William Wright was old enough to be living on his own land in

Hamilton Parish, Prince William County, in 1751 and, therefore, is evidence that he was born probably before 1733.

On September 4, 1751, at King George County, Virginia, D.B. 1743-1752/442 William Wright and Mary his wife sold to Jane Payne by lease and release one moiety of 180 acres of land inherited by Mary (Grant) Wright from her father William Grant:

> "This Indenture made the fourth day of September In the Twenty Fifth Year of the Reign of our Sovereign Lord George the Second by the Grade of God of Great Britain France & Ireland King Defender of the Faith &c. And in the year of our Lord God one Thousand Seven hundred and Fifty one Between William Wright of the Parish of Hammilton in the County of Prince Wm of the one part and Jane Payne of the Parish of Hanover in the County of King George of the other part Witnesseth that the said William Wright for and in Consideration of the Sum of Five Shillings Current Money of Virginia to him in hand paid by the said Jane Payne at or before the ensealing & delivery of these presents the Receipt whereof he the said Wm. Wright doth hereby acknowledge Hath Granted Bargained & Sold and by these presents Do Grant Bargain & Sell unto the said Jane Payne her heirs Executors Admrs. and Assigns, one certain Tract Piece or Parcel of Land and Premises, lying and being in the Parish of Hanover in the County of King George aforesaid Containing by Estimation Ninety Acres be the same more or less, it being one Moiety of one hundred & Eighty Acres of Land Given and Devised by the last Will and Testament of William Grant the Elder deced. to his son William Grant the Younger (who was the Father of the said Mary Wright party to these Presents) And by his Last Will did Devise the same together with his Personal Estate to be equally divided between his two Daughter's vizt. the aforesaid Mary & Elizabeth Grant, And all houses, Out houses Edifices, Buildings, Gardens, Orchards, Fences Woods, Underwoods, Ways, Waters, Watercourses, Profits, Comodities Heriditaments & Appurtenances whatsoever to the said Land & Premises belonging or in any wise Appertaining & the Reversion and Reversions Remainder & Remainders, Rents Issues & Profits thereof, And all and Singular the same Premises and every part and Parcel thereof with their and every of their Appurtenances, To have and to hold the said Piece or Parcel of Land and all and Singular the Premises herein before mentioned or Intended to be hereby Bargained & Sold with the Rights members & appurtenances unto the sd. Jane Payne her heirs Executors Admrs. and Assigns from the day next before the day of the date of these presents & unto the full end and term of one whole year from thence next ensuing & fully to be Compleat & ended Yielding and Paying therefore unto him the said Wm. Wright his heirs or Assigns, the Rent of one Ear of Indian Corn upon the Feast of St. Michael next coming if the same shall be Lawfully Demanded to the Intent & Purpose & that by virtue of these presents and of the Statute for Transfering Uses into Possession, the said Jane Payne be in the Actual Possession of the said Premises and be thereby the better enabled to

Accept and take a Grant & Release of the Reversion & Inheritance to her and her heirs forever by Indenture Intended to be made between the said William Wright & Mary his wife on the one part and the said Jane Payne on the other part and to bear date the day next after the date of these Presents In Witness whereof the sd. William Wright to this present Indenture hath set his hand & Seale the day Month & Year first above written

Sealed and Delivered) William Wright
In the presence of)
Wm. Bruce
John Grant
David Bronaugh

At a Court held for King George County on Thursday Sept. the 5" 1751. Then came William Wright personally into Court and Acknowledged this his Lease to Jane Payne which was admitted to Record

Copa. Test.
Harry Turner C.C."

This record identifies the wife of William Wright of Hamilton Parish, Prince William County, as Mary (Grant) Wright and identifies her as the daughter of William Grant, Jr., and granddaughter of William Grant, Sr. If William Wright and Mary (Grant) Wright were at least 18 years of age when they married, then their dates of birth would be probably before 1733.

On September 24, 1759, at Fauquier County, Virginia, D.B. 1/65 William Wright and Timothy Stamps were both witnesses to a deed from James Scott to Thomas Stamps.

The Washington Ancestry by Charles Arthur Hoppin stated that on September 27, 1759, at Fauquier County, Virginia, Court Minute Book 1/25 William Wright's military service was of record when "John Wright Present . . . John Cole, Elias Edmonds, William Wright, Armistead Churchill etc. Captains, took the usual oaths to his Majesty's person and Government and subscribed the Test."

In 1759 Captain William Wright incurred an account debt for 6£ 16s for 18 barrels of Indian corn, a copy of which account was filed in the case of Chadwell v. Wright, Fauquier County, Virginia, Chancery Court Loose Papers, Ended Causes 1763, Box 7:

"1759 Capt. William Wright	Dr £ S d
To 18 Barrells of Indian Corn @ 10/	9 0 0
Cr By Cash paid	2 4 0
	£6 16 0

. . . ."

On February 8, 1760, William Wright executed a promissory note payable to John Chadwell for the account due of 6£ 16s, a copy of which note was filed in the case of Chadwell v. Wright, Fauquier County, Virginia, Chancery Court Loose Papers, Ended Causes 1763, Box 7:

"Sr

I will pay you six pound fifteen Shillings Current money on account of John Chadwell

witness my hand this 8th Day of Fber or 1760(?)

To Color. John Champ William Wright

Mr William Wrights note of hand for £6" 15" 0 Curt money"

On February 28, 1761, at Fauquier County, Virginia, Chancery Court Loose Papers, Box 3/1761-003, William Wright executed a surety bond for 51£ 6S 2p to secure Peter Hon:

"Know all Men by these Presents, That I William Wright Junr of Fauquier County am held and firmly bound unto Peter Hon Esqr merchant in Whitehaven in the just and full Sum of Fifty One pounds six shillings & two pence Currt. money To be paid unto the said Peter Hon Esqr his certain Attorney, his Heirs, Executors, Administrators, or Assigns: To which Payment well and truly to be made, I bind myself, my Heirs, Executors, and Administrators, firmly by these Presents. Sealed with my Seal, and dated this Twenty Eigth Day of February Anno Dom. One Thousand Seven Hundred and Sixty One

The Condition of the above Obligation is such, That if the above bound William Wright do and shall well and truly pay, or cause to be paid, unto the said Peter Hon Esqr his certain Attorney, Executors, Administrators, or Asigns, the just Sum of Twenty five pounds Thirteen Shillings & one penny (like Currt. money) on demand Then the above Obligation to be void; or else to remain in full Force and Virtue.

Sealed and Delivered) William Wright

in the Presnce)
William Carr"

On about November 27, 1761, in Triplett v. Wright, Fauquier County, Virginia, Chancery Court Loose Papers, Ended Causes 1763-9-112, William Wright executed his surety bond for the payment of 18£ 5s 9p due to Francis Triplett:

"Know all Men by these Presents that I William Wright of Fauquier County and Colony of Virginia am Held and firmly Bound unto Francis Triplett of the County and Colony aforesaid in the full and Just Sum of Thirty Six Pounds Eleven Shillings and Seven Pence Current Money of Virginia to be paid unto the said Francis Triplett his Certain Attorneys Executors Administrators or Assigns to the which Payment well & Truly to be made and done I Bind my Self my Heirs Executors and Administrators firmly by These Presents sealed with my Seal and dated this twenty Seven day of November Anno domini one Thousand Seven Sixty one

The Condition of the above obligation is Such that The Above Bound William Wright do and shall well and Truly pay __ Cause to be paid unto the Said Francis Triplett his Certain Attorney Executors Administrators, or Assigns the Just and full Sum of Eighteen pounds five Shillings & Ninepence Halfpenny Current Money of Virginia at or upon the thirtyeth day of November Next Ensuing the Date hereof with Legall Intrest for the same then The Above Obligation to be Void Else to Remain in full force and Virtue in Law

Sealed and Delivered William Wright
in Presence of
Wm. McPherson
Wm. Edmonds

Wm Wrights Bond
to
Francis Triplett
1761
writ Issd. D. not I: in: of Virga"

On November 27, 1761, in Triplett v. Wright, Fauquier County, Virginia, Chancery Court Loose Papers, Ended Causes 1763-9-112, a summons was issued against William Wright to answer the complaint of Francis Triplett for the payment of 36£ 11s 6p due on William Wright's surety bond:

"George the third by the Grace of God of Great Britain France & Ireland King Defender of the Faith &c To the Sherif of Fauquier County greeting we

Command you that you take William Wright if he be found within your Bailiwick & him safely keep so that you have his Body before our Justices of our said County Court at the Courthouse of the said County on the fourth Thursday in this Month to answer Francis Triplett of a plea of Debt for Thirty six pounds Eleven shillings & seven pence Current Money of Virginia Damage forty shillings

And have then there this Writ Witness Humphrey Brooke Clerk of our said Court at the Courthouse the first day of December in the third Year of our Reign 1762

H Brooke

Triplett)
v) Caps
Wright

1763
March Atta

Not found Copy Left

pr. Orig Young S.S"

On about February 27, 1762, in How v. Wright, Fauquier County, Virginia, Chancery Court Loose Papers, Box 3/1761-003, Peter How filed a complaint for payment of 51£ 6s 2p due from William Wright on his bond dated February 28, 1761:

"Fauquier Sct. Peter How Esqr. complains of William Wright Jur. in Custody &c of a plea that he render to him Fifty one pounds six Shillings and two pence Current Money which to him he owes and unjustly detains &c. For that whereas the said Deft the 28th Day of February 1761 at the County aforesaid by his certain writing obligatory sealed with the Seal of the said Deft. and to the Court here shewn the Date whereof is the same Day and Year did acknowledge himself to be held and firmly bound to the said Pl. in the Sum of Fifty one pounds six Shillings and two pence to be paid to the said Pl. whenever he should be thereto required Nevertheless the said Def. altho often required the said Sum of Fifty one pounds six Shillings and two pence to the said Pl hath not paid but the same to him to pay hath and Still doth refuse to the Damage of the Pl. Forty Shillings and thereupon he brings this Suit &c.

W Ellzey for plt."

On February 27, 1762, in How v. Wright, Fauquier County, Virginia, Chancery Court Loose Papers, Box 3/1761-003, a summons was issued against William Wright,

Jr., to answer the complaint of Peter How for payment of 51£ 6s 2p:

> "George the third by the Grace of God of Great Britain France and Ireland King Defender of the Faith &c. To the Sherif of Fauquier County Greeting we command you that you take William Wright Jr if he be found within your Bailiwick and him safely keep so that you have his Body before our Justices of our said County Court at the Courthouse of the said County on the fourth Thursday in next Month to answer Peter How Esquire of a plea of Debt for Fifty one pound Six Shillings & two pence Damage Forty Shillings
>
> And have then there this writ Witness Humphrey Brooke Clerk of our said Court at the Courthouse the 27th Day of February in the second year of our Reign 1762.
>
> H Brooke"

The use of the term "Jr." in the summons was to distinguish this William Wright from 1789 William Wright of Fredericksburg, who was older than this William Wright and, therefore, identifies the William Wright of this suit as 1809 William Wright of Franklin County, the son of 1792 John Wright of Fauquier County. The resolution of the case of How v. Wright has not as yet been found.

On June 25, 1762, in Mercer v. Wright, Fauquier County, Virginia, Chancery Court Loose Papers, Ended Causes Box 8, Folder 7, William Wright executed a promissory note payable to James Mercer for 4£ 2s 6p:

> "I William Wright of Fauquier County do promise to pay Mr. James Mercer his Heirs or Assigns the Sum of four Pounds two Shillings & Six Pence on or before the first Day of June next ensuing for value reced To which payment well & truly to be made I do bind myself my Heirs &c. in the Penall Sum of eight Pounds Witness my hand & Seal this 25 day of June 1762
>
> William Wright"

On about August 26, 1762, at Fauquier County, Virginia, D.B. 1/369 William Wright and Mary Wright conveyed to Thomas Edwards by lease and release 125 acres of the land gifted to William by his father John Wright:

> "This Indenture made this _ day of ____ in the Year of our Lord One thousand seven Hundred and Sixty two Between William Wright and Mary his Wife of the Parish of Hamilton and County of Fauquier in the Colony of Virginia of the one part and Thomas Edwards of the Parish County and Colony aforesaid of the other part Witnesseth that the said William Wright and Mary his Wife for and in

Consideration of the Sum of five Shillings Sterling Money to them in hand paid by the said Thomas Edwards at and before the Ensealing and Delivery of these presents Have Granted Bargained and Sold and by these Presents do Grant Bargain and sell unto the said Thomas Edwards his Heirs Exors Administrators and Assigns a Certain Tract or Parcel of Land Containing one Hundred and Twenty five Acres it being the said Land whereon the said Wright now lives Adjoining to the Lands of Simon Morgan and Jonas Williams on the South side the Pignut Ridge and bounded as followeth (Vizt) Beginning at two Red oaks being the dividing Corner between the said Simon Morgan and Jonas Williams and Runs thence with the said Dividing Line S. 7-1/2° W. 130 poles to a Red oak a spanish Oak and Elm on a Branch thence North 83 degrees West 208 poles to a white oak Grub by two Red oak saplins on a hill in the old Line of the Deed thence with the line of the said Deed to the Beginning it being part of a Greater Dividend taken up by Waugh Darnall Decd by Patent Dated the 7th day of February 1725. Together with all Houses Outhouses Edifices buildings Woods Underwoods Orchards Ways Waters and Water Courses Priviledges Commodities and Appurtenances whatsoever to the said Land and Premisses belonging or in any wise Appurtaining and the Reversion or Reversions Remainder and Remainders of the same and of every part or parcel thereof together with all the Rents and Profits of the Premisses and every part thereof To have and to hold the said Seat and Parcel of Land and Premisses with all the Appurtenances unto the said Thomas Edwards his Heirs Exors Administrators and Assigns from the day before the Date of these presents for and during the Term of one whole Year thence next ensuing and fully compleated and Ended Yielding and Paying therefore the Yearly Rent of one pepper Corn at the feast of Saint Michael the Archangel if the same be Lawfully Demanded to the End Intent and purpose that by Virtue of these presents and of the Statute for Transfering Uses into Possession the said Thomas Edwards may be in the Actual Possession of the Premisses and may be enabled to accept a Grant and Releas of the Reversion and Inheritance of the same to him and his Heirs forever In Witness whereof the said William Wright and Mary his Wife hath hereunto set their hands and Seals the Day and Date first above written

Sign'd Sealed & delivered)
in Presence of)
Isaac Judd
James Bashan
Thomas Coleman

William Wright
her
Mary X Wright
mark

At a Court held for Fauquier County the 26th Day of August 1762.

This Indenture was acknowledged by William Wright and Mary his Wife (she being first privily examined as the Law directs, to be their Act and Deed and Ordered to be recorded

Teste
H Brooke

On about August 26, 1762, at Fauquier County, Virginia, D.B. 1/379 William Wright and Mary Wright released to Thomas Edwards 125 acres of the land gifted to William by his father John Wright:

> "This Indenture made this __ day of ____ in the Year of our Lord one Thousand seven Hundred and Sixty two Between William Wright and Mary his Wife of Hamilton Parish and County of Fauquier in the Colony of Virginia of the one part and Thomas Edwards of the Parish County and Colony aforesaid of the other part Witnesseth that the said William Wright and Mary his Wife for and in Consideration of the Sum of Sixty five Pounds Current Money of Virginia to them in hand paid by the said Thomas Edwards at and before the Ensealing and Delivery of these presents the receipt whereof the said William Wright and Mary his Wife doth hereby acknowledge and themselves therewith fully satisfied and paid Have Given Granted Bargained Sold Aliened Remised Released Enfeoffed and Confirmed and by thesse presents do Give Grant Bargain Sell Alien Remise Release Enfeoff and Confirm unto the said Thomas Edwards and to his Heirs and Assigns a Certain Tract or Parcel of land Containing one Hundred and Twenty five Acres it being the said Land whereon the said Wright now lives adjoining to the Lands of Simon Morgan and Jonas Williams on the South Side the Pignut Ridge and bounded as followeth Vizt. Beginning at two Red oaks being the dividing Corner of the said Simon Morgan and the said Jonas Williams and Running thence with the said dividing Line South 7-1/2° West 130 poles to a Red oak a spanish Oak and Elm on a Branch thence North 83° West 208 poles to a white Oak Grub by two Red oak Saplins on a hill in the Old Line of the Deed thence with the Line of the said Deed to the Beginning it being part of a Greater Dividend taken up by Waugh Darnall Decd by patent dated the 7th day of February 1725. Together with all Houses Outhouses Edifices Buildings Gardens Orchards Woods Underwoods Ways Waters Watercourses Priviledges, Commodities and Appurtenances whatsoever to the said Land and premisses belonging or in any wise Appurtaining all which said Premisses now are in the Actual possession of him the said Thomas Edwards by Virtue of one Indenture of Bargain and Sale to him thereof made for the term of one whole Year bearing Date the day next before the day of the Date of these presents and made Between the said William Wright and Mary his Wife of the one part and the said Thomas Edwards of the other part and by Virtue of the Statute for transferring Uses into Possession and all the Estate Right Title Interest Use Property Reversion Claim or demand whatsoever of them the said William Wright and Mary and to the Premisses and every part and parcel thereof Together with all and Singular Deeds Wills Evidences Writings Records Emplifications of Records Escripts and Minuments whatsoever touching or concerning the said Premisses or any part thereof To have and to hold the said Seat or Parcel of Land and

Premisses and every part and parcel thereof with their and every of their Appurtenances to the said Thomas Edwards his Heirs and Assigns the only proper Use and Behoof of him the said Thomas Edwards his Heirs and Assigns forever to be holden of the Chief Lord of the Fee by the Quit rents accustomed and the said William Wright and Mary his Wife their Heirs Exors Administrators the said mentioned Granted Premisses with the Appurtenances unto the said Thomas Edwards his Heirs and Assigns shall and will Warrant and forever Defend by these presents and the said William Wright and Mary his Wife for themselves their Heirs Exors and Administrators do Covenant and agree to and with the said Thomas Edwards his Heirs and Assigns by these presents that it shall and may be Lawful for him the said Thomas Edwards his Heirs Tenants and Assigns from time to time and at all times hereafter according to the purpose intent and true meaning of these presents for him Quietly to enter into and upon to have hold Occupy Possess and Enjoy to his and their Proper Use and Behoof of the aforementioned Tract or Parcel of Land and all and Singular other the Premisses herein before mentioned Meant or Intended to be hereby Granted Bargained and Sold without any Lawful or Equitable Lett Suit Trouble Demand Expulsion Eviction Interruption Claim or Demand of them the said William and Mary his Wife their Heirs and Assigns or any other person Claiming or to Claim by from or under them or any other Person whatsoever and that the said William Wright and Mary his Wife their Heirs &c shall and will at any time hereafter upon the Request and at the Cost and Charge in the Law of the said Thomas Edwards his Heirs and Assigns do make Levy acknowledge Execute suffer or cause to be done made Levied acknowledged Executed and suffered all and every such further Lawful and Reasonable Assurance and Act in the Law for further and better Absolute Assuring and Conveying the said Seat or Percill of Land and all and Singular other the Premisses herein before mentioned meant or Intended to be hereby Granted Bargained and Sold and every part thereof with the Appurtenances unto the said Thomas Edwards his Heirs and Assigns to the only proper use and behoof of him the said Thomas Edwards his Heirs and Assigns forever according to the Purport intent and true meaning of these presents as by the said Thomas Edwards his Heirs or Assigns his or their Council Learned in the Law shall be reasonably advised Devised or required In Witness whereof the said William Wright and Mary his Wife have sett their Hands and Seals the day and Year first above written

Sign'd Sealed and deli-) William Wright
in Presence of) her
Isaac Judd) Mary X Wright
James Basham mark
Thomas Coleman

At a Court held for Fauquier County the 26th Day of August 1762

This Indenture was acknowledged by William Wright and Mary his Wife, she being first privily examined as the Law directs and Ordered to be Recorded

Teste
H Brooke CC"

On October 13, 1762, at Fauquier County, Virginia, D.B. 1/433 William Wright and Mary Wright and David Williams and Betty Williams conveyed to John Waddle by lease and release 60 acres of the land gifted to William Wright by his father John Wright:

> "This Indenture made the 13th day of October in the Year of our Lord one thousand Seven Hundred & Sixty two and in the Second Year of the Reign of our Sovereign Lord George the the third by the Grace of God of Great Britain France and Ireland King Defender of the Faith &c Between William Wright and Mary his Wife and David Williams and Betty his Wife of the Parish of Hamilton and County of Fauquier of the one part and John Waddle of the same parish and County of the other part Witnesseth that the said William Wright and David Williams for and in Consideration of the Sum of Thirty five pounds Current Money of Virginia Hath Given Granted, Bargained and Sold unto the said John Waddle his Heirs and Assigns Sixty Acres of Land lying and being in the above said parish and County and Bounded as followeth Vizt Beginning at two Spanish Oaks thence So. 5° Wt. 46 poles to a Box oak in a branch thence No. 84° Wt. 220 poles to a Chesnut Oak on the Side of the Pignut Ridge thence No. 31° Et. 46 poles to a white oak Grub thence Et. 187 poles to the beginning in Simon Morgans line being part of a Tract taken up by Waugh Darnall Decd Containing Sixty Acres together with all Houses, Outhouses, Orchards, Woods, Underwoods Waters, Watercourses and Appurtenances whatsoever thereunto belonging to the said Land or in any wise Appurtaining To have and to hold unto the said John Waddle his Heirs and Assigns from the Day of the Date of these presents until the full end and Term of one whole Year thence next coming shall be fully Compleated and Ended. Yielding & paying the Fee Rent of one Ear of Indian Corn upon the feast Day of the Nativity of our Lord Christ only if the same be Demanded to the Intent that by Virtue of these presents and of the Statute for Transferring Uses into Possession the said Waddle may be in Actual possession of the said Sixty Acres of Land and Premisses and be thereby enabled to accept a Grant of the Reversion and Inheritance thereof In Witness the Parties to these

present Indentures have Interchangeably set their Hands and Seals the Day and Year above written.

Sealed and Delivered) William Wright
In Presence of) her
Simon Morgan Mary X Wright
Thomas Carter mark
William Norriss David Williams
Charles Morgan
Thomas Grubbs

At a Court Continued and held for Fauquier County the 25th Day of March 1763

This Indenture was proved by the Oaths of Simon Morgan, William Norriss and Charles Moran jun Witnesses thereto to be the Act and Deed of the said William Wright & Mary his Wife & David Williams & Ordered to be recorded

Teste
H Brooke CC"

On October 14, 1762, at Fauquier County, Virginia, D.B. 4/435 William Wright and Mary Wright and David Williams and Betty Williams released to John Waddle 60 acres of the land gifted to William Wright by his father John Wright:

"This Indenture made the fourteenth Day of October in the Year of our Lord One thousand Seven Hundred & Sixty two and in the Second Year of the Reign of our Sovereign Lord George the third by the Grace of God of Great Britain France and Ireland King Defender of the Faith &c. Between William Wright and Mary his Wife and David Williams and Betty his Wife of the parish of Hamilton and County of Fauquier of the one part and John Waddle of the same Parish and County of the other part Witnesseth that the said William Wright and David Williams for and in Consideration of the Sum of Thirty five pounds Current Money of Virginia to them in hand paid the Receipt whereof they do hereby acknowledge themselves to be fully Satisfyed and paid Hath Given Granted, Bargained, Sold Alienated, Released, Enfeoffed & Confirm'd and by these presents Doth fully and Absolutey Give, Grant, Bargain, Sell, Alien, Release Enfeoff and Confirm unto the said John Waddle Sixty Acres of Land now in the Actual Possession of the said John Waddle by Virtue of an Indenture of Bargain and Sale made to him for one whole Year bearing Date the Day next before the Date of these presents and of the Statute for Transferring Uses into possession which said Sixty Acres of Land is Situate in the above said Parish of Hamilton and County of Fauquier bounded as followeth vizt. Beginning at two Spanish Oaks thence So 5° Wt. 46 poles to a Box Oak in a Branch thence No. 84° West 220 poles to a Chesnut Oak on the side of the Pignut Ridge thence No. 31° Et.

46 poles to a white oak Grub thence Et. 187 poles to the Beginning in Simon Morgans line being part of a Tract taken up by Waugh Darnall Decd Containing Sixty Acres Together with all Houses Outhouses, Orchards, Woods, Underwoods, Waters, Water Courses, and Appurtenances whatsoever thereunto belonging To have and to hold unto the said John Waddle his Heirs and Assigns forever to the only proper Use and Behoof of the said John Waddle his Heirs and Assigns forever And the said William Wright and Mary his Wife and David Williams and Betty his Wife do by these presents Covenant and promise for themselves and their Heirs to warrant the hereby Granted Land and Premisses unto the said John Waddle his Heirs and Assigns from the Claim or Claims of any person or persons whatsoever subject only to the Quitrents which shall become due hereafter and the said William Wright and Mary his Wife and David Williams and Betty his Wife do for themselves and their Heirs promise and Grant to and with the said John Waddle his Heirs and Assigns that the hereby Granted Land and premisses now are and so from henceforth shall be and continue clearly acquitted and exonerated of and from all manner of former Gifts, Grants, Dowers, Jointures and Incumbrances whatsoever and that the said John Waddle his Heirs and Assigns shall for ever hereafter peaceably Occupy and Enjoy the hereby Granted Land and premisses without the lawfull Lett, Trouble or Interruption of any person or persons whatsoever and the said William Wright and Mary his Wife and David Williams and Betty his Wife do for themselves and their Heirs further Covenant and Promise with the said John Waddle his Heirs and Assigns that the said William Wright and David Williams their Heirs &c. shall and will at all times and from time to time at the request Cost and Charge of the said John Waddle his Heirs and Assigns make do and execute every Deed, Conveyance and other things that can be reasonably Desired by the said Waddle his Heirs or Assigns for the more sure Conveying an absolute Fee Simple Estate in the here _ Granted Land and premisses unto the said John Waddle _ Heirs and Assigns forever In Witness whereof the _ parties have Interchangeably set their Hands and seals the Day and Year above written

Sealed & Deliver'd)
in Presence of)
Simon Morgan
Thomas Carter
Charles Morgan
William Norriss
Thomas Grubbs

William Wright
her
Mary X Wright
mark
David Williams

At a Court Continued and held for Fauquier County 25th Day of March 1763

This Indenture was proved by the Oaths of Simon Morgan, William Norriss and Charles Morgan Jun Witnesses thereto to be the Act and Deed of the said Willi__ Wright and Mary his Wife and David Williams and ordered to be recorded

Teste
H Brooke CC"

On March 25, 1763, in Triplett v. Wright, Fauquier County, Virginia, Chancery Court Loose Papers, Ended Causes 1763-9-112, an attachment was issued against William Wright for payment of the debt due to Francis Triplett and the sheriff attached one candle mold:

"George the third by the Grace of God of Great Britain France & Ireland King Defender of the Faith &c To the Sherif of Fauquier County Greeting we command you that you Attach as much of the Estate of the within Named William Wright as will be of value Sufficient to Satisfy the within mentioned Debt & Costs & the same in your hands to Secure or otherwise provide that it may be forthcoming & liable for further proceedings therein to be had before the Justices of our said County Court at the Courthouse of the said County on the fourth Thursday in next Month & further to do & receive what our said Justices shall then & there in this behalf Consider And have then there this Writ Witness Humphrey Brooke Clerk of our said Court at the Courthouse the 25 day of March in the third Year of our Reign 1763

H Brooke

Triplett)
v) Atta
Wright)

By Virtue of the within I Attached one Candle Mold

p. Orig Young S.S

Fauquier Sc. March Court 1763

Francis Triplett Pl.)
ag.) In debt
William Wright Def)

The Deft not appearing On the Motion of the Pl. by his Attorney It is Ordered that an Attachment issue against the said Defts Estate for thirty six pounds eleven shillings seven pence Current Money & Costs returnable to the next Court

H. Brooke"

On about March 28, 1763, in Chadwell v. Wright, Fauquier County, Virginia, Chancery Court Loose Papers, Ended Causes 1763, Box 7, John Chadwell filed suit for payment of the promissory note due to him:

"Fauquier Sc

John Chadwell Complains of William Wright in custody &c of ____ a &c for that whereas they the said Plaintif and Defendt Upon the __ day of ____ in the year of our Lord one thousand seven hundred & sixty at the County aforesaid accounted together of and concerning Several Sums of money before that time due from the said Defendt to him the said Plaintif and then in arrear and unpaid & upon which said settlement and amount stated the said Defendt was then & therefor in arrear & indebted to the said Plaintiff in the sum of Six pounds fifteen shillings current money in consideration whereof he the said Defendant then & there undertook & to the said Plaintiff faithfully promised & assumed that he the said Defendant the six pounds fifteen shillings current money afsd unto him the said Plft would well & truly content and Pay when ever after the said Defendant should be thereunto Required Nevertheless the said Defendt his promise and assumpsit aforesaid inform aforesaid made not in the Least reguarding but contravening & fraudulently intending the said Plft in this Behalf craftily & subtilly to Deceive and Defraud the money aforesaid or any part thereof unto him the said Plft as yet hath not paid tho' thereto of times Required but the same to pay hitherto hath & still doth refuse to the Damage of him the said Plft Eight pounds and therefore he brings Suit &c

Bullitt the Plft
J. Doe
R Roe
Pledges &c

. . . ."

On March 28, 1763, in Chadwell v. Wright, Fauquier County, Virginia, Chancery Court Loose Papers, Ended Causes 1763, Box 7, a summons was issued against William Wright to answer John Chadwell in his suit for payment of the promissory note due to him and the summons was returned with the notation that William Wright was not found:

"George the third by the Grace of God of Great Britain France & Ireland King Defender of the Faith &c To the Sherif of Fauquier County Greeting we

Command you that you take William Wright if he be found within your Bailiwick & him safely keep so that you have his Body before our Justices of our said County Court at the Courthouse of the said County on the fourth Thursday in Next Month to answer John Chadwell of a plea of Trespass upon the Case Damage Eight pounds

And have then there this Writ Witness Humphrey Brooke Clerk of our said Court at the Courthouse the 28th day of March in the third Year of our Reign 1763

H Brooke

Chadwell)
vs.) Cap
Wright

May A Caps
Not found Copy Left

P. Origl. Young SS"

On May 28, 1763, in Chadwell v. Wright, Fauquier County, Virginia, Chancery Court Loose Papers, Ended Causes 1763, Box 7, a second summons was issued against William Wright to answer John Chadwell in his suit for payment of the promissory note due to him and the summons was returned with the notation that the summons had been executed on William Wright and his body was in gaol:

"George the third by the Grace of God of Great Britain France & Ireland King Defender of the Faith &c To the sherif of Fauquier County Greeting we command you as we have before commanded you that you take William Wright if he be found within your Bailiwick & him safely keep so that you have his Body before our Justices of our said County Court at the Courthouse of the said County on the forth Thursday in next Month to answer To John Chadwell of a plea of Trespass upon the Case Damage Eight pounds

And have then there this Writ Witness Humphrey Brooke Clerk of our said Court at the Courthouse the 28th day of May in the third Year of our Reign 1763

H Brooke

Chadwell)
vs.) Alias caps
Wright)

1763
May P.C.
June C.O in Court
Aug. Non Ap.
Executed and Body in gaol

p. W Grant Shef."

On June 13, 1763, John Chadwell assigned the account due to him from Captain William Wright to Richard Bryan, a copy of which assignment was filed in the case of Chadwell v. Wright, Fauquier County, Virginia, Chancery Court Loose Papers, Ended Causes 1763, Box 7, and with that assignment were the notes of counsel regarding his arguments in the case:

	Dr £	S	d
"1759 Capt. William Wright			
To 18 Barrells of Indian Corn @ 10/	9	0	0
Cr By Cash paid	2	4	0
	£6	16	0

I do hereby Assign and make Over the Above Acct. to Richd. Bryan as witness my hand this 13th day of June 1763

Test
James Armstrong

John Chadwell

King George County Ss

John Chadwell this day made Oath that the within acct. is just & that he never recd any satisfaction for the same Given under my hand this 13th June 1763

Wm Rowley

Dr a__ an order upon Coll Champ(?) who was indebted to Wright

---

The merchant endorsed a note which he took & no Protest

---

for to bring a suit upon an order & no protest sure he knows little of the Custom of Merchants & gives his note

---

a merchant agt a Planter he ought to Loose his Debt

---

but our Case"

Sometime in approximately 1763 and probably after May 28 a jury in Chadwell v. Wright, Fauquier County, Virginia, Chancery Court Loose Papers, Ended Causes 1763, Box 7, found for the plaintiff:

> ". . . .
> Chadwell)
> vs) Ded.
> Wright)
>
> we of the jury find for the plaintif six pounds fifteen shillings Dam
>
> William Delaney
> Foreman"

On about August 1, 1763, in Mercer v. Wright, Fauquier County, Virginia, Chancery Court Loose Papers, Ended Causes Box 8, Folder 7, James Mercer filed a complaint against William Wright for payment of the promissory note of 4£ 2s 6p due to him:

> "Fauquier to wit M. James Mercer complains of William Wright in Custody &c of a plea that he render unto him eight pounds which to him he owes and from him unjustly detains for that whereas the said Defen the 25th day of June 1761 at the County aforesaid made his certain penal Bill in writing sealed with his Seal dated the same day and Year and now here to the Court Shown whereby he promissed to pay to the Pl. or to his Assigns the Sum of four pounds two Shillings & Six pence on or before the first day of June next ensuing for Value received and for the same payment well and truly to be made the said Deft. bound himself his Heirs Exors Administrators in the penal Sum of Eight pounds and the said Plt. in fact saith that the said Deft did not pay the said Sum of four pounds two Shillings & Six pence as he ought to have done whereby Action Accrued to the pl. to demand and have of the said Def the Said eight pounds Nevertheless the said Def tho often required hath not paid the last mentioned Sum of Money to the pl. but the same to pay hath altogether refused and still doth refuse to the Damage of the said pl. and thereupon he brings suit &c
>
> W. Ellrey for pl.) J. Doe
> pledges &c.) R Roe"

On August 1, 1763, in Mercer v. Wright, Fauquier County, Virginia, Chancery

Court Loose Papers, Ended Causes Box 8, Folder 7, a summons was issued against William Wright to answer the complaint of James Mercer for payment of the promissory note of 4£ 2s 6p:

> "George the third by the Grace of God of Great Britain France & Ireland King Defender of the Faith &c To the Sherif of Fauquier County Greeting we command you that you take William Wright if he be found within your Bailiwick & him safely keep so that you have his Body before our Justices of our said County Court at the Courthouse of the said County on the Fourth Thursday in this Month to answer James Mercer of a plea of Debt for eight pounds Damage Forty Shillings
>
> And have then there this Writ Witness Humphrey Brooke Clerk of our said Court at the Courthouse the First day of August in the third Year of our Reign 1763
>
> H Brooke"

Genealogy Of John J. Wright Of Virginia, Indiana and Kansas by John Calvin Wright stated that on August 29, 1763, William Wright executed a promissory note for six pounds one shilling and by January 28, 1764, was not to be found in Fauquier County.

On June 1, 1785, John Wright named William Wright as a son in his will probated on February 27, 1792, at Fauquier County, Virginia, W.B. 2/219, and referred to William as having been given land by John Wright which William Wright had sold:

> "In The Name Of God Amen I John Wright of the Parish of Hamilton & County of Fauquier in the Common Welth of Virginia, being in a weakly state of bodily helth and calling to mind the uncertainty of this life, being at this time of sound and dispos'd mind and memory blessed be God for the same, do make this my last will and testament in manner and form following that is to say, and first as to what worldly goods it hath pleased God to bless me with, I give and desire and bequeath to my son James Wright all of that my land lying on the east side of the run, being part of the tract of land whereon I now live, in the County of Fauquier to him his Heirs & assigns forever. I also give to my son James Wright one negroe named tom and one negro named Moses to him his Heirs or assigns for ever,
>
> Item I give to my grand daughter Betsey Wright daughter to my son James Wright one negro named Jinny to her, her Heirs and assigns forever.
>
> Item I give likewise to my two daughters Mary Wright & Rosamond Wright the plantation whereon I now live and all the land I hold lying on the west side of the

said run above mentioned to them & their Heirs lawfully begotten of their bodys forever to be divided between the two as they can agree, and in case they die without such Heir. It is my Will and desire that the said land shall go to my son James Wright to him his Heirs & assigns for ever.

Item I give to my two daughters Mary Wright & Rosamond Wright the negroes as followeth, Vz. Dinah, Jude Ledie, Robin, Lucy, Will & Milley to them their Heirs and assigns forever, and all Future increes of the aforesaid negroes to the aforesaid Mary and Rosamond Wright their heirs and assigns forever to be divided by the two as they can agree.

I likewise give to my aforesaid two Daughters Mary Wright & Rosamond Wright all my house hold Furniture such as beds &c and all my stock such as horses cattle, sheep & Hogues to them their Heirs and assigns for ever.

Item I give to my son William Wright and my son John Wright twenty shillings each current money of Virginia the reason why I have left my two sons William and John Wright no more is that I gave them both land which they sold.

Item it is my will and desire that in case my daughter Elizabeth Parlow should ever apply that then my executors pay her fifteen pounds out of my estate, current money of Virginia. It is my will & desire that all my estate heretofore mentioned shall be kept to gether for the use of my wife Elizabeth Wright during her life, and after her Dec.e to be divided as before mentioned. And lastly I make and ordain constitute & appoint my son James Wright my execu.r and my two daughters Mary & Rosamond Wright my Executx. of this my last will and testament hereby revoking all former and other wills by me heretofore made declaring this to be my last.

In witness whereof I have hereunto set my hand and seal this first day of June in the year of our lord one thousand Seven hundred and eighty five.

Signed Sealed published and declared by the said testator as his last will & testament in our presence and his request subscribed our names as Witness hereto

George Maddox John Wright
John Nelson
his
Francis X Latham
mark
Wm Kernes.

At a Court held for Fauquier County the 27th day of February 1792. This will was proved by the oaths of George Maddux and William Kerns witnesses thereto and ordered to be recorded.

And on the motion of James Wright the executor therein named who made oath and together with Thomas Keith his security entered into and acknowledged bond in the penalty of one thousand pounds conditioned as the law directs Certificate is granted him for obtaining a probate thereof in due form.

Teste:
H. Brooke, C.C."

Sometime before January 28, 1764, William Wright and Mary (Grant) Wright moved from Fauquier County to Bedford County in a part that later became Franklin County on its formation in 1785. The further documentation regarding 1809 William Wright and Mary (Grant) Wright in Bedford and Franklin Counties follows.

On May 24, 1768, at Bedford County, Virginia, D.B. 3/276 William Wright acted as a witness to a deed from John Greer and Thomas Elliott to John Hall for 131 acres of land on the north side of Stanton River. This is the first record of William Wright found in the Bedford/Franklin County area and the location of the land in the deed in southern Bedford County indicates that the William Wright in this document was 1809 William Wright of Franklin County. As will be set forth below, 1809 William Wright's land was on Maggottee Creek in a part of Bedford County that became Franklin County.

On May 22, 1770, at Bedford County, Virginia, D.B. 3/443 William Wright acted as a witness to a deed from Justice Beech to Richard Brown for 93 acres of land on both sides of Maggotte Creek.

On November 14, 1772, at Bedford County, Virginia, W.B. 1/495 William Wright was named as executor of the will of John Miller and Mary Wright acted as a witness to the will:

"In the Name of God Amen I John Miller of Bedford County am sick and Weak but of Perfect Sense and Memory, thanks be to God for it, and it is ordered that all men should dye I do make Constitute ordain and appoint this my last Will & Testament, in Manner and form following Viz - Item I give and bequeath my Land and plantation on Maggottee Creek unto the Male Heir of my Daughter Jean Miller lawfully begotten of her Body To him at the Age of Twenty One Years and his Heirs for ever, I likewise desire my Stock of Cattle may be sold for the use of Such Heir - Item I give and bequeath unto my Wife Ann Miller One Shilling Sterling she being Elopd from me and her Basely abusing me.

Item, I give & bequeath to my Daughter Elisabeth one Shilling Sterling.

Item I give to my Daughter Jean Miller One Shilling Sterling - I likewise make constitute ordain & appoint William Wright my whole & Sole Executor and Trustee of this my last Will and Testament, as Witness my hand this 14th day of November 1772

	his		his	
Patrick	O Johnson	John	X	Miller
	Mark		Mark	
	her			
Eva	X Johnson			
	Mark			
	her			
Mary	X Wright			
	Mark			

At a Court held for Bedford County at the Court House the 26th day of July 1785 - This Last Will & Testament of John Miller Deceased was proved by the Depositions of Patrick Johnson & Eve Johnson Witnesses thereto Subscribed - & Ordered to be recorded

Teste
Ja Steptoe Cl. B.C.

The Commonwealth of Virginia To Isaac Rentfro and Thomas Arthur Gentlemen of the County of Bedford Greeting: Know Ye that we trusting to Your Fidelity & provident Circumspection in Diligently examining Patrick Johnson & Eve his Wife Witnesses to the Will of John Miller deceased, Command you or any two or more of You, that at such certain Days and places as You shall appoint You Assemble Yourselves and the Witnesses aforesaid before You or any two or more of You You call and Cause to come, & diligently examine on the holy Evangelists of Almighty God and their Examinations into our County Court of Bedford distinctly & plainly without delay You shall send and certify inclosed under Your Seals returning also to us this Writ: Witness James Steptoe Clerk of our said Court at the Court House the 23d day of May 1785 in the Ninth Year of the Commonwealth.

Ja Steptoe.

Pursuant to an Order of Bedford Court bairing Date the 23d of May 1785 We Isaac Rentfro & Thos Arthur have met at the Dweling House of Patrick Johnson on the first day of June 85 have causeed the sd. Pattrick Johnson & Eve his wife to Apear before us & they being first Sworn on the holy Evangelist of Almightty God deposeth & Sayeth that they saw John Miller that is now deseas'd Sign Seal and Acknowledg a Sartain Will by him made bearing Date the 14th November 1772. Viz Signd with a Cross & his name Rote by William Wright to which will the said Pattrick Johnson & Eve his Wife subscribed their Names as Witnesses Given under our Hands this 1st day of June 1785

Isaac Rentfro
T Arthur

At a Court held for Bedford County at the Court House the 26th day of July 1785 - This Commission for the Examination of Patrick Johnson & Eve Johnson Witnesses to the last Will & Testament of John Miller deceased together with their Depositions were produced in Court & Ordered to be Recorded.

Teste
J Steptoe Cl.B.C"

On about April 28, 1774, at Bedford County, Virginia, County Court Loose Papers Timothy Stamps filed a complaint for debt against "William Wright Black Smith" based on a judgment previously obtained in Fauquier County:

"To the Worshipful the Court of Bedford County, Timothy Stamps humbly showeth, That William Wright Black Smith stands indebted to him in £1.7.0 122 w. Tobo. 15/ by former Judgment of Faquier Court and refuseth Payment: Wherefore your Petitioner prays Judgment against him for the same, with Costs.

And shall pray, &c."

This record both identifies William Wright's occupation as blacksmith and his prior residence in Fauquier County.

On April 28, 1774, at Bedford County, Virginia, County Court Loose Papers Timothy Stamps obtained a summons against William Wright Blacksmith to answer his complaint for debt:

"George the Third, by the Grace of God of Great Britain, France, and Ireland, King, Defender of the Faith, &c. to the Sheriff of Bedford County, greeting: We command you that you summon William Wright (BlackSmith to appear before our Justices of our said County Court, at the Courthouse of the said County, on the 4 Monday in next month then and there to answer the Petition of Timothy Stamps exhibited against him and have then there this Writ. Witness James Steptoe Clerk of our said Court, at the Courthouse, the 28th Day of April in the XIVth Year of our reign.

Robert Alexander D.C."

On August 30, 1778, at Bedford County, Virginia, County Court Loose Papers Timothy Stamps obtained another summons against William Wright Blacksmith to answer his complaint for debt:

> "The Commonwealth of Virginia to the Sheriff of Bedford County, greeting: We command you, that you summon William Wright (Black Smith) to appear before our Justices of our said County Court, at the Courthouse of the said County, on the 4th Monday in next month then and there to answer the Petition of Timothy Stamps exhibited against him and have then there this Writ. Witness James Steptoe Clerk of our said Court, at the Courthouse, the XXX Day of Augt in the Third Year of the Commonwealth.
>
> Ja. Steptoe"

On November 9, 1779, William Wright joined others in petitioning the Virginia Legislature for the formation of a new county. Franklin County, Virginia, A History by Marshall Wingfield stated that:

> "As early as 1779, the inhabitants of Bedford County living on the south side of the Staunton River began to petition the Virginia Legislature for a new county. In a petition dated May 24, 1779, it is set forth that a new county on the south side of the river should be formed because of the difficulty of crossing the water courses in order to reach the court house; and, further, because "many of the inhabitants of Bedford live fifty miles from the county seat" . . . .
>
> On November 9, 1779, Thomas Arthur, Thomas Doggett, William Wright, William Walton, John Underwood, William Slone and ninety-four others, living in Bedford on the south side of Staunton River, and having to go from thirty to fifty miles to reach the court house, petitioned the Legislature to add their section of the county to a part of Henry and form a new county."

On September 1, 1780, at Patent Deed D/80 William Wright patented 280 acres of land in Bedford County:

> "Thomas Jefferson Esquire Governor of the Commonwealth of Virginia, to all to whom these presents shall come Greeting: Know ye that in consideration of the ancient Composition of Thirty Shillings sterling paid by William Wright into the Treasury of this Commonwealth there is granted by the said Commonwealth unto the Said William Wright a certain Tract or parcel of Land containing Two hundred and Eighty Acres by survey date March the tenth one Thousand seven hundred and seventy five it being part of an Order of Council Granted Walton for ten Thousand acres lying and being in the County of Bedford adjoining Griffiths and bounded as followeth to wit Beginning at Rays Corner white Oak by a branch thence along his Lines North seventy degrees East thirty eight poles to a

Locust off South twenty degrees East one hundred and Sixty four poles to pointers in Murpheys Line thence along his Line South Sixty eight degrees west ninty six poles to his corner white Oak thence off North Eighty five degrees West one hundred and ninty four poles to a red Oak North Seventeen degrees East Two hundred and thirty six poles to a white Oak on Griffith's Mountain South Seventy degrees East one hundred and fourteen Poles to a white Oak in Rays Line and thence along his line South fifteen degrees East Thirty two poles to the Beginning with its Appurtenances: to have and to hold the said tract or parcel of Land with its Appurtenances, to the said William Wright and his heirs forever. In Witness whereof the said Thomas Jefferson Governor of the Commonwealth of Virginia, hath hereunto set his hand, and Caused the Seal of the Said Commonwealth to be affixed at Richmond on the first day of September in the year of our Lord One thousand seven hundred and Eighty and of the Commonwealth the fifth

Thomas Jefferson"

The purchaser of this land was probably 1809 William Wright of Franklin County, but may possibly have been 1830 William Wright of Franklin County, the son of 1809 William Wright of Franklin County. As will be set forth below, the legal descriptions confirm that this same land was sold in 1782 by Bedford County Deed 7/179. The land was described in Deed 7/179 as on Black Water, a creek in a part of Bedford County that later became Franklin County and that was near to Maggotty Creek where 1809 William Wright had most of his land. The witnesses on Bedford County Deed 7/179 included George and James Wright, sons of 1809 William Wright. This evidence indicates that 1809 William Wright was the probable purchaser. However, Mary Wright, the wife of 1809 William Wright, did not join in the execution of Deed 7/179, leaving open the possibility that 1809 William Wright's son 1830 William Wright was the purchaser of Patent Deed D/80 and the seller of Bedford County Deed 7/179.

On September 1, 1780, by Patent Deed D/94 William Wright patented 63 acres of land in Bedford County on Maggotty Creek:

"Thomas Jefferson, Esquire Governor of the Commonwealth of Virginia, to all to whom these presents shall come Greeting. Know ye that in consideration of the ancient Composition of Ten Shillings Sterling paid by William Wright into the Treasury of this Commonwealth there is granted by the said Commonwealth unto the said William Wright a certain tract or parcel of Land containing Sixty three acres by survey bearing date March the Sixteenth one thousand Seven hundred and seventy two, lying and being in the County of Bedford on Maggotty

Creek and bounded as followeth to wit, Beginning at Charles Vincents Corner Hornbeam on the said Creek and thence along his Lines South Sixty one degrees West thirty two poles to a white Oak South forty six degrees west thirty two poles to a hickory South fifty degrees East Seventy eight Poles to a red Oak South sixty Seven degrees west forty two poles to a red Oak South twenty nine degrees west thirty poles to a white Oak thence new lines South thirty four degrees East forty six poles to a white Oak South Seventy three degrees East Sixteen poles to a Gum North Seventy six degrees East One hundred poles to a small white Oak north fifty one degrees west twelve poles to Millers corner Chesnut thence along his Lines north twenty eight degrees west fifty four poles to a red Oak north forty five degrees west twenty poles to a white oak north thirteen degrees west forty four poles to the said creek and thence up as it meanders to the first Station with its appurtenances; to have and to hold the said tract or parcel of Land with its Appurtenances to the Said William Wright and his heirs forever, In witness whereof, the Said Thomas Jefferson Governor of the Commonwealth of Virginia, hath hereunto set his hand, and Caused the Seal of the Said Commonwealth to be affixed at Richmond on the first day of September in the year of Our Lord One thousand seven hundred and Eighty and of the Commonwealth the fifth.

Thomas Jefferson"

On February 21, 1782, William Wright and Mary his wife sold three parcels of land: Bedford County, Virginia, Deed 7/124 for 200 acres to Charles Vinson, Deed 7/124 for 100 acres to Abraham Abshire, and Deed 7/125 for 100 acres to Jacob Boon:

"This Indenture made the 2lst day of February 1782 Between William Wright and Mary his wife of the one Part and Charles Vinson of the other Part Witnesseth that the said William Wright for and in Consideration of the sum of Twenty Pounds Current money of Virginia to him in hand Paid the Receipt whereof he doth hereby acknowledge hath Bargained and sold and by these presents doth Bargain sell alien feoff Deliver and Confirm unto the said Charles Vinson his Heirs and assigns forever one Certain Tract or Parcel of Land Containing Two Hundred Acres more or less and Bounded on William Wright Abraham Abshire and Richard Brown on a Branch of Maggotty Creek in Bedford County Together with the Reversion and Reversions Remainder and Remainders and every part and Parcell thereof To have and to hold the above Granted Land and Premises unto the said Charles Vinson his Heirs and assigns forever and the said William Wright for himself his Heirs Doth Covenant and agree to and with the said Charles Vinson his Heirs and assigns that he the said William Wright and his Heirs the above Granted Land and Premises in an undefesible fee simple Estate unto the said Charles Vinson his Heirs and assigns forever against the Claim and Demand of all other Person or Persons whatsoever shall and will by these presents warrant and forever defend In witness whereof the said William Wright have hereunto set his hand and affixed his seal the day and Year above written.

Witness	)	William Wright
Thos. Arthur	)	Mary Wright
Isaac Rentfro	)	
his	)	
Laughlin + McGrady	)	
mark	)	
Daniel French	)	
John Talbot	)	

At a Court held for Bedford County March 25th 1782 This Indenture was Proved by the Oaths of Thomas Arthur and John Talbot witnesses thereto and at a Court held for said County the 22d day of April 1782 the same was further Proved by the Oaths of Isaac Rentfro another witness thereto and ordered to be Recorded

Teste
J. Steptoe Cl. Cur.

This Indenture made the 2lst day of February 1782 Between William Wright and Mary his wife of the one Part and Abraham Abshire of the other Part Witnesseth that the said William Wright for and in Consideration of the sum of Ten pounds Current Money of Virginia to him in hand paid the Receipt whereof he doth hereby acknowledge hath Bargained and Sold and by these presents Doth Bargain Sell Alien feof Deliver and Confirm unto the said Abraham Abshire his Heirs and assigns forever one Certain Tract or Parcel of Land Containing one Hundred acres more or less and Bounded on William Wrights Jacob Boons and Charles Vinsons Lines on a Branch of Maggotty Creek in Bedford County Together with the Reversion and Reversions Remainder and Remainders and every Part and Parcel thereof To have and to hold the above Granted Land and Premises unto the said Abraham Abshire his Heirs and Assigns forever and the said William Wright for himself his Heirs Doth Covenant and agree to and with the said Abraham Abshire his Heirs and assigns that he the said William Wright and his Heirs the above Granted Land and Premises in an undefesable fesimple Estate unto the said Abraham Abshire his Heirs and assigns forever against the Claim or Demand of all other Person or Persons whatsoever shall and will by these presents Warrant and forever Defend In witness whereof the said William Wright have hereunto set his hand and afixt his seal the day and year above written

Witnesses	)	William Wright
Thos. Arthur	)	Mary Wright
Isaac Rentfro	)	
his	)	
Laughlin + McGrady	)	
mark	)	
Daniel French	)	
John Talbot	)	

At a Court held for Bradford County March 25th 1782 This Indenture was proved by the oaths of Thomas Arthur & John Talbot witnesses thereto and at a Court held for the said County April 22, 1782. The same was further Proved by the oath of Isaac Rentfro another witness thereto and ordered to be Recorded.

Teste
Ja Steptoe Cl. Cur.

This Indenture made the 2lst day of February 1782 Between William Wright and Mary his wife of the one Part and Jacob Boon of the other Part Witnesseth that the said William Wright for and in Consideration of the sum of Ten Pounds Current Money of Virginia to him in hand Paid the Receipt whereof he doth hereby acknowledge hath Bargained and sold and by these presents Doth Bargain sell alien feof Deliver and Confirm unto the said Jacob Boon his Heirs and assigns forever one Certain Tract or Parcel of Land Containing one Hundred acres more or less and Bounded on William Wrights Line and Abraham Abshires Line on a Branch of Maggottee Creek in Bedford County Together with the Reversion and Reversions Remainder and Remainders and every part and Parcell thereof To have and to hold the above Granted Land and Premises unto the said Jacob Boon his Heirs and assigns forever and the sd William Wright for himself his Heirs Doth Covenant and agree to and with the said Jacob Boon his Heirs and assigns that he the said William Wright and his Heirs the above Granted Land and Premises in an undefesable fee simple Estate unto the said Jacob Boon his Heirs and assigns forever against the Claim and Demand of all other Person or Persons whatsoever shall and will by these presents Warrant and forever Defend In witness whereof the Said William Wright hath hereunto set his hand and afixt his seal the day and Year above Written.

Witness) William Wright
Thos. Arthur) Mary Wright
Isaac Rentfro)
his)
Laughlin + McGrady)
mark)
Daniel French)
John Talbot)

At a Court held for Bedford County March 25th 1782 This Indenture was Proved by the Oaths of Thomas Arthur and John Talbot Witnesses thereto and at a Court held for the said County the 22d day of April 1782 the same was further Proved by the oath of Isaac Rentfro another witness thereto and ordered to be recorded.

Teste
Ja Steptoe Cl. Cur."

The listing of Mary Wright as a grantor of these deeds identifies them as from 1809 William Wright. However, no document has yet been found prior to this date which shows the acquisition of these 500 acres of land. The probable explanation is that this represented land claimed by William Wright to which title had not as yet been perfected. As will be set forth below, William Wright, Sr., obtained a survey for 733 acres of land in 1784 and perfected that title by Patent Deed W/476 in 1786. This was probably the land of which the 500 acres constituted a part. The absence of clear legal descriptions in these three deeds supports such a conclusion.

The 1782 Personal Property Tax List for Bedford County, Virginia, listed William Wright with the following household:

Name	Free Males above 21 yrs	Slaves	Horses	Cattle	White Ty above 16 yrs	Blk Tithes above 16 yrs
William Wright	1		3	10	2	

The 1782 Land Tax List for Bedford County, Virginia, listed William Wright with the following property:

Name	___	Acres	Value Pounds, Shillings
William Wright	9/5	158	75.

Both William Wright, Sr., and William Wright, Jr., owned land in Bedford County and, therefore, either of them could have been the subject of this listing. However, the 174 or 172 acres of land first acquired by William Wright, Jr., was not listed in the Bedford County or Franklin County Land Tax Lists until 1788 and, therefore, this listing in 1782 was probably for William Wright, Sr.

On April 22, 1782, at Bedford County, Virginia, County Court Booklet II, Public Service Claims, Record Group 48, Virginia State Archives, William Wright was granted a certificate by Christopher Irvine, Commissioner of the Provision Law, on a Revolutionary War claim for having provided "3 diets, 2 pecks corn".

On December 5, 1782, at Bedford County, Virginia, D.B. 7/179 William Wright of Bedford County sold 280 acres of land to Christian Brewer:

> "This Indenture made the 5th day of December 1782 Between William Wright of Bedford County of the one part and Christian Brewer of the sd County of the other Part Witnesseth that the said William Wright for and in Consideration of the Sum of one Hundred Pounds to him in hand paid the Receipt whereof he Doth hereby acknowledge hath given granted Bargained and Sold and by these presents do Bargain sell deliver and Confirm unto the said Christian Brower his Heirs and assigns forever one Certain Tract or parcell of Land Lying and being in the County of Bedford on the Branches of Black Water Containing Two Hundred and Eighty acres and Bounded as followeth To wit Beginning at Rays Corner White Oak by a Branch thence along his Lines North Seventy degrees East Thirty Eight Poles to a Locust of South Twenty degrees East one Hundred and Sixty four Poles to Pointers in Murphys Line thence along his Line South Sixty Eight degrees west ninety six poles to his Corner white oak thence off North Eighty five degrees west one hundred and ninety four Poles to a Red oak North Seventeen degrees East Two Hundred and thirty Six Poles to a white oak on Griffiths Mountain South Seventy degrees East one Hundred and fourteen Poles to white oak in Rays Line and thence along his Line South fifteen Degrees East Thirty Two Poles to the Beginning Together with the Reversion & Reversions Remainder and Remainders and every Part and Parcel thereof To have and to hold the above Granted Land and Premises with the Priviledges and appurtenances profits and advantages thereunto Belonging or in any ways appertaining unto the said Christian Brower his Heirs and assigns forever and the said William Wright Doth for himself his Heirs Covenant grant and agree to

and with the said Christian Brower his Heirs and assigns that he the said William Wright & his Heirs the above Granted Land & premises with the appurtenances unto the sd. Christian Brower his Heirs and assigns shall and will by these presents warrant and forever defend In Witness whereof the said William Wright hath hereunto set his hand and affixed his seal the day year above written

Witnesseth William Wright
John Johnson
James Wright
George Wright

At a Court held for Bedford County 24th February 1783 This Indenture was acknowledged by William Wright party thereto and ordered to be Recorded.

Teste
Jas Steptoe C.C."

The legal description confirms that this was the same land as that patented by William Wright in Patent Deed D/80 and for the reasons set forth above in connection with that patent deed, the seller of Deed 7/179 was probably 1809 William Wright of Franklin County, but may possibly have been 1830 William Wright of Franklin County, the son of 1809 William Wright.

The 1783 Personal Property Tax List for Bedford County, Virginia, listed William Wright with the following household:

Name	No White & Blk Tithes	Tax on Covering Horses	Whites Over 21	Blacks Over 16	Blacks under 16	Total Blacks
William Wright	1		1		1	1

No Horses	No Nett Cattle	No Wheels R Carriages	Ordinary License
2	8		

On April 11, 1783, at Bedford County, Virginia, S.B. 2/467 William Wright obtained a survey for 72 acres of land:

"April 11 1783

> Surveyd for Wm. Wright 72 Acres of Land, Situate in Bedford County Lying on the Waters of Magotty Cr & bounded as follows to wit. Beg. at Abraham Abshers Co. wh.o Thence along his lines - N 40 W 60 po' to a Mehogany Stump & Poplar Thence off W - 40 poles to a Maple in a Br. N 4 W 40 pos to a wh.o in Boons & Langdons Lines Thence off new lines S 85 W 90 poles to a Chest. Thence S 9 W 44 poles to a wh.o Thence W - 8 poles to 4 wh.os on the top of a Small Mountain Thence S 9 W 44 poles to a Black Oak Thence S 56 E 32 pos. to a B-Oak Thence N 75 E 60 poles to a Black Oak Thence S 65 E 20 poles to a B-O Thence N 69 E 60 poles to a wh.o Thence S 47 E 54 poles to Johnson Co. Spanish Oak Thence along his Lines N 9 W 38 poles to the first station"

Since both William Wright, Sr., and William Wright, Jr., were acquiring land in Bedford County at this time, this survey could have been for either one and further research will be required to confirm the association of this survey with William Wright, Sr.

In July 1783 at Bedford County, Virginia, Court Order Book 7/57 William Wright, Sr., was ordered to view a road from Maggotty Creek to a new road leading to the court house:

> "Ordered that William Wright Sr. Richard Brown John Langdon & James Stone or any three of them be appointed to view a Road from Maggotty Creek into a New Road Leading from the Court House to James Slones Mill & make Report"

The reference to "Sr." and the location of Maggotty Creek identify this William Wright as 1809 William Wright of Franklin County.

The 1784 Personal Property Tax List for Bedford County, Virginia, listed William Wright with the following household:

Names	Total Tithes	Tax on Covg. Horses	Whites over 21 Years	Blacks over 16 Years	Blacks under 16
William Wright, Sr.	1		1		

Total Blacks	No Horses	No Nett Cattle	No Weals Ridg Carriages	Ordinary Licenses
	1	8		

The 1784 Land Tax List for Bedford County, Virginia, listed William Wright with the following property:

Name	[Quantity of Acres]	[Average price pr Acre]	[Amount Valuation]	Tax at 1½ pr Cent]
William Wright	158	15.4	204.15.4	3.1.5

On April 12, 1784, at Bedford County, Virginia, S.B. 2/479 William Wright obtained a survey for 733 acres of land:

> "April 12 1784 Surveyd. for Wm Wright 733 Acres of Land Situate in Bedford County Bounded as follows to wit, Beg - at Jacob Andersons Co. Spanish Oak in the point of a Hill, Thence along Andersons old Line S 84 E 163 poles to a R o, N 45 E 133 poles to a Spanish o, & Chesnut S 25 E 136 poles to a R o, E- 22 poles to a Chesnut N 37 E 74 poles to Andersons Lower Co. R o, Thence off along Meads Lines N 85 E 52 poles N 47 E 34 pos to Absher Co. Chesnut on the Creek, Thence down the Cr. N 76 E 44 poles to a Post Oak S 30 E 139 poles to a Post Oak S 76 E 74 poles to a R o, in a Br, Thence off new Lines S 35 W 336 poles to a wh.o N 56 W 73 poles to a wh.o S 50 W 29 poles to a Chesnut N 60 W 166 poles to a wh.o N 10 W 42 poles to Dilmans Co, wh.o Thence along Dilmons old line N 41 W Crossing Green Street Br. 116 poles to a wh.o N 83 W 82 poles to Browns & Dilmons Co, wh.o N 4 E 132 poles to the first Station"

As will be set forth below, the 1785 and later Land Tax Lists for Franklin County, Virginia, listed this land as owned by William Wright, Sr., thus identifying him as the person who obtained this survey.

The 1785 Land Tax List for Bedford County, Virginia, listed William Wright with the following property:

Landholder	Quantity of Acres	Average price pr Acre	Amount Valuation	Tax at 1 pr
William Wright	193	25.8	34.12.0(?)	3.10
Do	63	2.6	7.17.6	2.__

This record reflects the patent of 63 acres of land by Patent Deed D/94. As will be set forth below, William Wright, Sr., purchased 194 acres of land in 1787 by Franklin County Deed 1/324 and this record indicates that he was in possession of and taxed on the land even before the purchase was completed. The 1789 Land Tax List for Franklin County, Virginia, listed the land as taxed to William Wright, Sr., confirming the identification of this 1786 Land Tax listing as for 1809 William Wright.

On June 23, 1785, at Bedford County, Virginia, D.B. 7/519 William Wright of Bedford County sold six acres of land to John Langdon:

"This Indenture made this 23d day of June 1785 Between William Wright of Bedford County of the one Part and John Langdon of the said county of the other part witnesseth, that the said William Wright for and in Consideration of the sum of five Pounds current money of Virginia to him in hand paid the Receipt hereof he doth hereby acknowledge hath given granted bargained and sold and by these presents doth grant Bargain Sell Deliver and Confirm unto the said John Langdon his Heirs and assigns for ever one certain Tract or Parcell of Land lying and being in the County of Bedford containing six acres be the same more or less and bounded as followeth, to wit, Beginning at three horn Beames on Maggottee Creek in the said Langdons Line, thence on his line South fifty Degrees west Thirty two Poles to a white oak, South forty six west thirty two Poles to a Hickory South fifty East twenty eight Poles to a Red oak, thence off North twenty Nine East sixty two Poles to the first station together with the Reversion & Reversions Remainder & Remainders and every part and Parcell thereof to have and to hold the above granted land and Premises with the Priviledges & apurtinances thereunto belonging or any ways appertaining unto the said John Langdon his Heirs and assigns forever, and the said William Wright doth for himself his Heirs Covenant grant and agree to and with the said John Langdon his Heirs and assigns that he the said William Wright and his Heirs the above granted Land and Premises with the appurtinances unto the said John Langdon his Heirs & assigns shall and will by these presents warrant & forever Defend In witness whereof the said William Wright hath hereunto set his hand and seal the day and year above written.

Teste) William Wright
Thomas Arthur)
Isaac Rentfro)

At a Court held for Bedford County the 27th day of June 1785 This Indenture was acknowledged by William Wright Party thereto and Ordered to be Recorded.

Teste
Ja Steptoe C.B.C."

The sale to Langdon of only 6 acres of land suggests that it was adjacent to his property. The legal description of Bedford County S.B. 2/467 referred to Langdon's line, indicating that this 6 acres was probably part of that survey. It is not yet possible to determine whether 1809 William Wright or 1830 William Wright was the seller of this land.

In July 1785 at Bedford County, Virginia, Court Order Book 8/165 a report on the viewing of a new road to Maggotty Creek was filed:

> "A Report of a Road from the Widow Martins on Stanton River to Slones Mill on Maggotty Creek retd. to witt, We the Viewers being first sworn have viewed the way from the Widow Martins to Slones Mill & find it Passable crossing Gills Creek between Jno Charter's & Anthony Pate's & Establishd. Accg to Report. - Charles Simmons Appd. Surv. of Sd Road from Stanton River to Jos: Simmons Road - William Charter from Simmons Rd. to Gills Creek - & Wm Wright Jr. from Gills Creek to Maggotty - & all the Hands within two Miles on each Side of sd. Road to Attend the said Surveyors to Open the same"

This may have been the report on the road ordered in 1783.

In October 1785 at Bedford County, Virginia, Court Order Book 8/206 hands were alloted to work under William Wright on the road from Gills Creek to Maggotty Creek:

> "The Hands as p List filed are Ordered to Work under William Wright Survr. Rd. from Gills Creek to Maggotty Creek"

Since William Wright, Jr., was the surveyor of this road, it was probably him and not his father 1809 William Wright who was supervising this road work.

On April 4, 1786, by Patent Deed W/476 William Wright patented 733 acres in Bedford County:

> "Patrick Henry Esquire Governor of the Commonwealth of Virginia, To all to whom these Presents shall come Greeting; Know ye, that in Consideration of the ancient Composition of three pounds fifteen Shillings sterling paid by William Wright unto the Treasury of this Commonwealth there is Granted by the said Commonwealth unto William Wright a Certain Tract or Parcel of land containing seven hundred and Thirty three acres by Survey bearing date the twelfth day of April one Thousand Seven hundred & Eighty four lying and being in the County of Bedford on Magotty Creek and Bounded as followeth, to wit, Beginning at Jacob Andersons Corner Spanish oak on the Point of a hill thence along Andersons old lines South Eighty four degrees East one hundred and three poles to a red oak North forty five degrees East one hundred & thirty three poles to a Spanish oak and Chesnut South twenty five degrees East one hundred & thirty six poles to a red oak East twenty two poles to a Chesnut North thirty Seven degrees East Seventy four poles to Andersons lower red oak corner thence off along Meads line North Eighty five degrees East fifty two poles North forty Seven degrees East thirty four poles to Abshers chesnut corner on the Creek thence down the Creek North Seventy Six degrees East forty four poles to a Post oak South thirty degrees East one hundred and thirty Nine poles to a post

oak South Seventy Six degrees East Seventy four poles to a red oak in a branch thence off new lines South thirty five degrees West three hundred and thirty six poles to a white oak North fifty six degrees West Seventy three poles to a white oak South fifty degrees West twenty nine poles to a Chesnut North Sixty degrees West one hundred and Sixty Six poles to a white oak North ten degrees West forty two poles to Dilmons white oak Corner thence along Dilmans old lines North forty one degrees West Crossing Green Street Branch one hundred and Sixteen poles to a white oak, North Eighty three degrees West Eighty two poles to Brown and Dilmans white oak corner North four degrees East one hundred and thirty two poles to the Beginning with its Appurtenances to have & to hold the said Tract or parcel of Land with its appurtenances to the said William Wright and his Heirs for Ever. In Witness whereof the said Patrick Henry Esquire Governor of the Commonwealth of Virginia hath hereunto set his Hand & Caused the Lesser Seal of the said Commonwealth to be affixed at Richmond on the fourth day of April in the year of our Lord one thousand Seven hundred & eight six and of the Commonwealth the tenth.

P. Henry."

This is the same land as that surveyed in Bedford County, Virginia, S.B. 2/479.

The 1786 Personal Property Tax List for Franklin County, Virginia, listed William Wright, Sr., with the following household:

By Whom Taken	To Whom Belonging	Total Tithes	Whites Over 21	Whites Under 21
Arthur	William Wright Sr.	1	1	0

Slaves Over 16	Slaves Under 16	Horses	Cattle	Studd Horses
0	0	2	6	

The 1786 Land Tax List for Franklin County, Virginia, listed William Wright Sr with the following property:

Persons Names	Acres	Average Price	Amount	Tax
William Wright Sr	733	2.	73.06.00	1.1.11-1/2

This record reflects the patent of 733 acres of land by Patent Deed W/476 and confirms that William Wright, Sr., or 1809 William Wright, was the purchaser of Patent Deed

W/476.

The 1786 Land Tax List for Franklin County, Virginia, also listed William Wright with the following property:

Persons Names	Acres	Average Price	Amount	Tax
William Wright	193	25.8	234.12	3.10.4
Ditto	63	2.6	7.17.6	0.02.42

The 1787 Personal Property Tax List for Franklin County, Virginia, listed William Wright, Sr. with the following household:

	Whites Over 21	Whites Under 21	Blacks Over 16	Blacks Under 16	Horses	Cattle
William Wright Sr.	1	0	0	0	1	8

The 1787 Land Tax List for Franklin County, Virginia, listed William Wright Sr. with the following property:

Persons Names	Acres	Average Price	Amount	Tax
William Wright Sr	733	0.2.0	73.6.0	1.1.11-1/2

The 1787 Land Tax List for Franklin County, Virginia, also listed William Wright with 103 acres of land, but since there was one listing for William Wright, Sr., and William Wright, Jr., also owned land in Franklin County at this time, this second listing was probably for William Wright, Jr.

On September 19, 1787, at Franklin County, Virginia, D.B. 1/324 William Wright purchased a further 194 acres of land in Franklin County:

> "This Indenture made this l9th Day of September 1787 Between Samuel Gambell and Jane Gambell both of Franklin County of the one Part and William Wright of the said County of the Other Part Witnesseth that the said Samuel and Jean Gambell for and in Consideration of the sum of Twenty five Pounds Current money of Virginia to them in hand paid the Rect whereof they doth hereby acknowledge hath given Granted Bargain & Sold Deliver and Confirm unto the said William Wright his Heirs and Assigns forever one Certain Tract or Parcell of Land lying and being in the County of Franklin on Both sides of Magottee Creek formerly belonging to John Miller decd. Containing one hundred and ninety four

acres be the same more or less and Bounded as followeth viz Beginning at Talbots Corner white oak Sapling thence north Seventy five Degrees west fifty four Poles to a red oak thence north Thirty four Degrees west 20 Poles to a red oak, Thence South Eighty two Degrees West crossing a Branch ninety Two Poles to Pointers thence North Sixty degrees West ninety Poles to a white oak thence South Eighty Degrees West forty poles to Pointers in the Patton line thence on the Patton line South Ten Degrees East one hundred and thirty Poles Crossing a Branch to a corner in the said line thence South Sixty five Degrees, East two hundred Poles to Talbots Corner red oak in the sd. line Thence on his line north Twenty Degrees, East One hundred and forty Poles to the Beginning being Part off the Land bought by John Miller off Richard Randolph had and will at large appear. Together with Reversion & Reversions Remainder and Remainders and every Part and Parcel thereof. To have and to hold the above granted land and Premises with the appurtenances Profits and advantages thereunto Belonging as in any way appertaining unto the said William Wright his heirs and assigns forever and the said Samuell Gambell and Jane Gambell doth for themselves their heirs doth Covenant, Grant and bargain with the said William Wright his heirs and assigns that they the said Samuell Gambell and Jane Gambell and their Heirs the above Granted Land and Premises with the appurtenances unto the said William Wright his heirs and assigns shall and will by these Presents Warrant and for Ever Defend In Witness whereof the sd. Samuell & Jane Gambell hath hereto set their hands and affixt their seals the day and day above written.

Teste	)		his	
John Gibson	)	Samuell	X	Gambell
William Wright	)		mark	
David Margin	)		his	
James Bay	)	Jean	X	Gambell
George Wright	)		mark	

At a Court held for Franklin County on Monday the 3d day of Decr 1787.

The within Indenture was Proved by three of the Witnesses thereto to be the act & Deed of the Within named Samuel Gambell & the same was ordered to be recorded. By the Court.

Test
Stephen Smith ClC."

On February 2, 1788, at Franklin County, Virginia D.B. 1/351 William Wright sold 200 acres of land to Christopher Rebble. The deed recited a date of February 2, 1780, but was recorded on February 4, 1788, and since Franklin County was not formed in

1780, I believe the date of the deed was either miswritten or miscopied by the clerk and the correct date was February 2, 1788:

> "This Indenture, made this Second day of Feby, one Thousand Seven hundred & Eighty Between William Wright of Franklin County of the one part & Christopher Rebble of the said County of the other Part Witnesseth that the said William Wright for & in consideration of the sum of one hundred & thirty Pounds Current money of Virginia to him in hand paid the receipt whereof is hereby acknowledged hath granted Bargained & sold alined Enfeoffed & Confirmed & by these presents doth grant bargin Sell alien Enfeoff & confirm unto the sd. Christopher Rebble his Heirs & assigns forever one Certain Tract or Parcel of Land containing by Estimation two hundred acres be the same more or less lying & being in the County of Franklin the Branches of Gills Creek & bounded as followeth (to wit) Beginning at a white oak and Branch north thirty one Degrees East forty four poles to Early Hiccory Greel(?) thence his lines, north Eighteen degrees West one hundred & sixty Two poles to a Black oak, thence new lines South eighty Seven Degrees west thirty two poles to a Chesnut oak & red oak South thirty Seven Degrees West thirty six poles to a Gum & Hiccory. South eight Degrees, East seventy four Poles to Jones(?) line on his line South four(?) degrees West Twenty Eight poles to a double red oak South forty four Degrees, West seventy four poles to Pointers thence along McGradys lines South forty five Degrees east Sixty two poles to a white oak, South Seventy three degrees West forty four Poles to a Chesnut, South fifty five Degrees west sixteen Poles to a Chesnut, South thirteen Degrees west Sixty Poles to a white oak leaving McGradys line South fifty three Degrees East ninety four Poles to a Black Jack North forty nine Degrees East Seventy eight Poles to a Chesnut oak north seven Degrees East thirty four Poles to a white oak North Seventy Degrees, East Ten Poles to a Poplar in the fork of a Branch, thence up the north fork as it Meanders sixty one Poles to the Begining together with the Reversion & Reversions Remainder & Remainders of the Land & Premises above Mentioned with all & singular the appurtenances thereunto belonging or in any wise appertaining To have & to hold the said Tract or Parcel of Land with their & every of their appurtenances unto the said Christopher Rebble his Heirs & assigns forever & the said William Wright for himself & his Heirs doth covenant & forever agree to & with the said Christopher Rebble that he the said William Wright the above Mentioned Land & Premises with appurtenances unto the sd. Christopher Rebble his heirs & assigns forever against the Claim & Demand of each & every Person or Persons whatsoever shall & will Warrant & forever Defend In Witness whereof the said William Wright hath hereunto set his hand & seal the Day date above written.
>
> William Wright
>
> At a Court held for Franklin County on Monday the 4th Day of Feby 1788

The Within Indenture was acknowledged by the within named William Wright to be his Act & Deed & the same was ordered to be recorded, By the Court

Teste
Ste Smith Cl. C."

The 1788 Personal Property Tax List for Franklin County, Virginia, listed William Wright Senr with the following household on June 17:

		Whites Over 16	Blacks Over 16	Blacks Over 12	Horses
June 17	William Wright Senr	1	0	0	1

The 1788 Land Tax List for Franklin County, Virginia, listed William Wright Sr. with the following property:

Persons Names	Acres of Land	Price p Acre	Amount	Taxes
William Wright Sr	733	0.2.0	73.6.0	1.1.5/0

This record identifies the purchaser of 733 acres of land in Patent Deed W/476 as William Wright, Sr.

The 1789 Personal Property Tax List for Franklin County, Virginia, listed William Wright with the following household on July 6:

		16/ Whites	16 B	12Do	Horses
July 6	William Wright	1	0	0	1

The 1789 Land Tax List for Franklin County, Virginia, listed William Wright Sr with the following property:

Persons Names	Qty. Acres	Average Price	Amount	Taxes
William Wright Sr	735	0.2.0	73.10.0	0.14.8
Ditto	194	0.5.0	48.10.0	0.9.8

This record reflects the purchase of 194 acres by Franklin County Deed 1/324 and confirms that William Wright, Sr., or 1809 William Wright, was the purchaser of Franklin County Deed 1/324 and, in conjunction with the 1785 Land Tax List, of Patent Deed

D/94.

On June 10, 1789, at Franklin County, Virginia, D.B. 2/86 William Wright sold 200 acres to Joseph Stith:

> "This Indenture made this l0th day of June 1789 Between William Wright of Franklin County of the one Part and Joseph Stith of Bedford County of the other part, Witnesseth, that the said William Wright for the Consideration of Forty Pounds Current Money of Virginia to him in hand paid the Receipt hereof he doth hereby acknowledge hath Given, Granted, Bargained and Sold and by these Presents do Give, Grant, Bargain and sell unto the said Joseph Stith his heirs & assigns one Certain Tract or parcel of Land Containing Two hundred acres on the south Branches of Maggottie Creek and Bounded as followeth Begining at a Locust Rays Line Wrights Corner thence along the the said Line South Twenty east one hundred and sixty Poles to Pointers in Murpheys Line Thence on his Line North 62 East Thirty Eight Poles to Murpheys Corner Sorrel South 69 East Seventy Six Poles to a white oak South 15 East 52 Poles to a Corner Chesnut thence on his Line North 84 East 62 Poles to Pointers of New Lines North 58 West four hundred and Twenty Poles to the Begining, Together with the Reversion and Reversions, Remainder, and Remainders and Every Part and Parcel thereof to have and to hold the above Granted land and Premises with the Privileges thereunto Belonging or any ways appertaining unto the said Joseph Stith his heirs and assigns for ever and the said William Wright doth for him self his heirs Covenant Grant and agree to and with the said Joseph Stith his heirs and assigns that he the said William Wright and his heirs the above Granted Land and Premises with the appurtenances unto the said Joseph Stith his heirs & assigns shall and will By these presents warrant and forever Defend in witness hereof he the said William Wright hath hereunto set his hand and seal the Day and Year above written.
>
> In the Presence of Us) William Wright
> John Hall)
> Isaiah Willis)
> Thomas Hall)
>
> At a Court held for Franklin County on Monday the first Day of February 1790 This Indenture was Proved by the witnesses thereto Subscribed to be the Act & Deed of the within William Wright and the same was ordered to be Recorded.
>
> Teste
> Ste. Smith C.C."

The legal description does not produce a closed plat and there is apparently an error in the metes and bounds or a missing line. As will be set forth below, the legal description in this deed is virtually the same as that in Franklin County Deed 3/526 by which William Wright acquired 200 acres of land. For some reason, the sale of the land occurred before the purchase; the recording of the deed of purchase did not occur until almost eight years after the deed was executed.

The 1790 Personal Property Tax List for Franklin County, Virginia, listed William Wright, Sr., with the following household on March 27:

		Whites	Blacks Over 16	Blacks Under 16
March 27	William Wright Sn	1	0	0

Horses	Studs	£ S D
0	1	0 1 0

The 1790 Land Tax List for Franklin County, Virginia, listed William Wright Sr with the following property:

Persons Names	Acres	Average Price	Amount
William Wright Sr	705	0.2.0	73.10.0
Ditto	194	0.5.0	48.10.0

It is unclear why the amount of acreage listed decreased from 735 acres in 1789 to 705 acres in 1790 and this may have simply been a transcription error rather than reflecting an actual transfer of land. The adjustment of the amount of land taxed in 1791 suggests that this was the case.

On September 3, 1790, at Franklin County, Virginia, Suit Papers, Virginia State Library, William Wright executed a promissory note to Henry Buford for £6, 12s:

> "I promise to pay Henry Buford on or before the Tenth day of November next the Just and full sum of six pounds Twelve Shillings current money of Virginia to bear Interest from the date hereof It being for Value Received witness my Hand this third day septemr 1790
>
> £6.17 William Wright
> Test
> Jubal Early"

An execution on the debt set forth below identified the William Wright of this document as William Wright, Sr., or 1809 William Wright.

On October 6, 1790, at Franklin County, Virginia, D.B. 3/526 Martin Key of Albemarle County sold 200 acres of land to William Wright:

> "This Indenture made 6th day of October 1790 Between Martin Key of Albemarle County of the one part and William of Franklin County of the other part Witnesseth Witnesseth that the said Martin Key for and in consideration of twenty pounds to him in hand paid the Receipt hereof he doth hereby Acknowledge hath given granted Bargained and Sold and by these presents do give grant Bargain & sell unto the said William Wright his heirs and assigns forever one Certain tract or parcel of Land Containing 200 Hundred acres on the head Branches on Maggotty Creek and Bounded as followeth to wit, Beginning at a Locust Rays line Wrights said Line south twenty East one hundred and sixty poles to pointers in Murpheys line thence along his Line No 68 E thirty eight poles to Murpheys corner Sorrell So 69 E twenty six poles to a white oak South 15 E 52 poles to a corner Chesnut thence on his Line No 85 E 63 poles to Pointers of new Line N 58 W four hundred and 20 poles to the Begining - Together with the Reversion and Reversions Remainder and Remainders and Every part and parcel thereof to have and to hold the said Granted Land, and premises with the Priviledges thereunto belonging or any ways appertaining unto the said William Wright his his heirs & assigns forever and the said Martin Key doth for himself his heirs Covenant grant and agree to and with the said William Wright his heirs and assigns that he the said Martin Key and his heirs the above granted Land and premises with the appurtenances unto the said William Wright his Heirs and Assigns shall be and by these presents Warrant and for Ever Defend in witness whereof the Said Martin Key hath hearunto set my hand and Seal this Day and Year Above Written
>
> Witness Martin Key
> John Bowman
> Tobias Miller
> Abraham Miller
>
> And at January Court 1798 the Same was further proved by the affirmation of one other witness thereto subscribed and the same was ordered to be Recorded by the Court
>
> Test
> James Callaway Cl."

As with Franklin County Deed 2/86, the legal description does not produce a closed plat and there must be an error in the metes and bounds. As the deed recites, it was not recorded until 1798. The land did not show up on the Land Tax List for Franklin County, Virginia, until 1798 and then was listed with the other land of William Wright, Sr., thus identifying him as the purchaser of this land.

The 1791 Personal Property Tax List for Franklin County, Virginia, listed William Wright Sn with the following household on August 2:

		Whites	Blacks Over 16	Blacks Under 16
August 2	William Wright Sn	1	0	0

Horses	Stud Horses	£ S D
2	0	0 1 0

The 1791 Land Tax List for Franklin County, Virginia, listed William Wright with the following property:

Persons Names	Acres	Average Price	Total Amount	Tax
William Wright	534-1/4	0.2.0	53.9.0	
Ditto	144	0.5.0	36.0.0	

This record reflects the sale of 201 acres of the 735 acre parcel of land by Franklin County Deed 2/238 set forth below and 50 acres of the 194 acre parcel of land by Franklin County Deed 2/173 set forth below.

On February 7, 1791, at Franklin County, Virginia, D.B. 2/173 William Wright, Senr., sold 150 acres of land to James Wright:

> "This Indenture made this 7 Day of February 1791 Between William Wright Senr. of Franklin County of the one Part and James Wright of the Said County of the other Part witnesseth that the Said William Wright for the consideration of Thirty five Pounds Current money of Virginia to him in hand paid the Rect. hereof he doth hereby acknowledge hath Given Granted Bargained and Sold and by these Presents do Give Grant Bargain Sell Deliver & Confirm unto the said James Wright his heirs or assigns one Certain Tract or Parcell of Land Containing one hundred & fifty acres be the same more or less and Bounded as followeth to wit Begining at Talbotts Corner white oak Saplin on the Crooked Run thence north seventy five Degrees west fifty four Poles to a Red oak thence north Thirty four

Degrees west 20 Poles to a Red oak thence South 82 Degrees West Crossing a Branch seventy Poles to a white oak in the said Line thence new Line by agreement to a Corner white oak on the Bank of Maggottee Creek thence up the Said Creek as it Meanders Crossing the same to the mouth of warfords Branch, thence up the said Branch as it Meanders to a Corner white oak on Charles Vinsons Path thence along the said Path to a Corner red oak in Charles Vinsons Line, thence on his Line to the aforesaid Maggottee Creek thence Down the said Creek as it meanders to Tallbotts & Millers Dividing Line thence on the Said Dividing Line to the Begining Together with the Reversion and Reversions Remainder & Remainders and every Part and Parcell thereof to have and to hold the Above Granted Land and Premises with the Appurtenances Profits and advantages thereunto belonging or any ways appertaining to the said James Wright his heirs and assigns for Ever and the Said William Wright doth for himself his heirs, covenant Grant and agree to and with the said James Wright his heirs and Assigns that he the said William Wright and his heirs the above Granted Land and Premises with the appurtenances unto the said James Wright his heirs and assigns shall and will By these Presents warrant and for Ever Defend in Witness whereof the said William Wright hath hereunto set his hand and seal the Day & Year above written

William Wright

At a Court held for Franklin County on Monday the VII day of February 1791 This Indenture was acknowledged by the within named William Wright to be his Act & Deed and the same was ordered to be Recorded

Teste
Ste Smith ClC"

Although the deed recites that 150 acres of land was being sold, the 1791 Land Tax List for Franklin County listed only 50 acres as transferred from William Wright, Sr. In addition, that same Land Tax List showed James Wright for the first time with 50 acres of land. The result is that the deed probably misstated the amount of land as 150 acres when only 50 acres were transferred. And a comparison of the legal description of Franklin County Deed 1/324 to the legal description of Franklin County Deed 2/173 indicates that Deed 2/173 involved the northeast portion of Deed 1/324.

On April 2, 1791, at Franklin County, Virginia, D.B. 2/238 William Wright and Mary Wright, his wife, sold 201-3/4 acres of land to John Hook. The deed recites that the land was part of the land patented in Patent Deed W/476:

"This Indenture Made this 2d Day of April one Thousand Seven hundred and ninety one between William Wright and Mary Wright his wife of Franklin County of the one part and John Hook of said County of the other part Witnesseth that the said William Wright and Mary Wright his wife for and in Consideration of the sum of Fifteen pounds nine Shillings and three pence Current Money of Virginia in hand paid to them by the Said John Hook the Receipt whereof they do hereby acknowledge have and by these presents do Grant Bargain & Sell unto the said John Hook his heirs and assigns for ever one Certain Tract or parcel of Land Laying and Being in the County of Franklin on the South Side of Magotty Creek being part of a Patent of Seven hundred and odd acres Patented to William Wright about the Year one Thousand Seven hundred and eighty five on the South Side of Randolphs old order and patent of nine hundred and forty acres the same Known by Hooks line Containing Two hundred and one and three fourths acres and Bounded as follows viz Beginning at a corner Chesnut oak of the patent thence along the patent Line west one hundred and Seventy four poles to a Post Oak, thence off new Lines South thirty one Degrees East one hundred and fourteen poles to a Red oak South Eighty degrees East one hundred and Thirty two poles to a white oak North forty one Degrees East Four(?) hundred poles to pointers, North Thirty six Degrees west sixty four poles to two Dogwoods and Laurel on Hooks Line thence along Hooks Line South Eighty five Degrees west Sixty eight poles to a Red oak on the patent Line thence on the said Line South forty four Degrees west Eighty three poles to the Begining. Together with all the priviledges and appurtenances thereunto Belonging or in any wais appertaining To have and to hold the aforesaid Land and premises unto the said John Hook his heirs and assigns for ever, the said William Wright and his wife do by these Presents warrant and Defend the Said Land free from and against the Claim or Demand of all and every person or persons Claiming the Same, In witness whereof the said William Wright and Mary Wright his wife have hereunto set their hands and Seals the Day & Year above written.

Signed Sealed &	)	William Wright
Delivered	)	her
In presence of	)	Mary X Wright
George Wright	)	mark
George Spangler	)	
Edward Lewis	)	
Edward Lewis	)	
William Wright	)	
Chileman Smith	)	

Memo. That on the Day and Year within written Livery and Seizen of the with Land Premises mentioned was held by the Said William Wright and Mary Wright his wife and by them Given to the within named John Hook according to the True form and Effect of the within written Deed

Signed Sealed & Delivered in presence of

George Wright) William Wright
George Spangler) her
Edward Lewis) Mary X Wright
Edward Lewis) mark
William Wright)
Chileman Smith)

At a Court held for Franklin County on Monday the VI Day June 1791. This Indenture together with the Memorandum of Livery & Seizen herein Endorsed was proved by the oath of Three of the witnesses hereto Subscribed to be the acts and Deed of the within named William Wright and the same was ordered to be Recorded

Teste
Jas Callaway Jr ClC"

The legal description does not close, but if the line of uncertain length were changed to connect the two lines that follow the patent line, then the only location that would fit the legal descriptions would be the westernmost portion of Patent Deed W/476.
This record confirms William Wright, Sr., as the purchaser of Patent Deed W/476 and is apparently the 201 acres that was reflected in the 1791 Land Tax List as having been transferred from William Wright, Sr.

On December 6, 1791, at Franklin County, Virginia, Suit Papers, Virginia State Library, a summons was issued against William Wright, Sr., to answer the complaint of Henry Buford for payment of his debt of £6, 12s:

"The Common Wealth of Virginia to the sheriff of Franklin County Greeting: You are hereby Commanded to take William Wright Senr if he be found in your Bailiwick & him safely keep so that you have his Body before the Justices of our Court of our said County at the Court house on the first Monday in March next to answer Henry Buford of a Plea of Debt for Six pound Twelve Shillings Damage 40/- And have then there this Writ. Witness James Calloway Clerk of our said County Court at the Court house the VI day of Decmr 1791 in the XVI year of the Common Wealth.

Dcr 27.90 CN James Callaway ClC.

By Cash in part of the within ____
Wm Wright Sr to Buford £6.12 payable 10th November 90"

On February 6, 1792, at Franklin County, Virginia, D.B. 2/397 William Wright, Sr. and William Wright, Jr., sold thirty acres of land to Isaac Glass:

> "This Indenture made 6th Day of February 1792 Between William Wright and William Wright Senr. of the one part and Isaac Glass of the other part witnesseth that the said William Wright Junr. and William Wright Senr. for in Consideration of the sum of thirty pounds Current Money of Virginia to them in hand paid the rect. hereof they do hereby acknowledge hath Given Granted Bargaind and sold unto the said Isaac Glass one Certain Tract or Parcel of Land Containing Thirty acres be the same more or Less and bounded as Followeth to wit Begining at a Red oak in Overhols line then north East one Hundred poles to a post oak thence north 35 west 36 poles to Watts Corner white oak thence south 30 degrees West Sixteen Poles to waggon Road thence along the waggon Road north 25 west 50 poles to Maggotty Creek thence South 23 degrees West 120 poles to the begining together with revesion and Revesions remainder and Remainders and Every part and Parcell thereof to Have and to hold the above Granted Land and premises with the appurtenances above Granted Profits and advantages thereunto belonging or in any ways appertaining unto the said Isaac Glass heirs and assigns forever and they the said William Wright Junr. and William Wright Senr. and theirs Heirs and assigns the above Granted Land and Premises unto the said Isaac Glass and his heirs and assigns the forever against the Claim or demands of all person or persons whatosever Shall and will by these presents warrant and forever defend In witness whereof the said Senr. and William Wright Junr. hath hereunto set his hands & seals the day & year above &c
>
> Test Ambrouse Rains) William Wright
> Abraham Ashire) William Wright
>
> At a Court Held for Franklin County on Monday the ___ Day of August 1792 this Indenture was acknowledged by the within William Wright Junr. & William Wright Senr. to be their respective act and Deed and the same was ordered to be Recorded
>
> Test
> James Callaway Clk."

Both 1809 William Wright and 1830 William Wright joined in this deed to convey title, because this was apparently the 23 acres informally transferred by 1809 William Wright at the same time as the sale in Franklin County Deed 2/238 in 1791 and taxed to 1830 William Wright in 1791 and 1792. The 1793 Franklin County Land Tax List shows a reduction of 23 acres of land taxed to 1830 William Wright.

The 1792 Personal Property Tax List for Franklin County, Virginia, listed William Wright, Sr., with the following household on March 17:

Date Of Receiving Individuals	Persons Names Chargeable With The Taxes	Whites	Blacks Over 16	Blacks Over 12
March 17	William Wright Sn	1	0	0

Horses	Stud Horses	Amount of Taxes £ S D
2	0	0 1 0

The 1792 Land Tax List for Franklin County, Virginia, listed William Wright Sn with the following property:

Persons Names Owning Land	Quantity of Land	Rate of Land p Acre	Total Amount of Vallue of Land	Amount of Taxes @ 7/6
William Wright Sn	534	0.2.0	53.9.0	0.4.0
Ditto	144	0.5.0	36.0.0	0.2.9

On October 1, 1792, at Franklin County, Virginia, D.B. 2/417 William Wright sold 162 acres of land to Counrod Harter:

> "This Indenture made this 1st day of October 1792 between William Wright of the one part and Counrod Harter of the other part Witnesseth that the said William Wright for & in consideration of the sum of Thirty pounds Current money of Virginia to him in hand paid the rect. hereof he doth hereby acknowledge hath given granted Bargaind and Sold & by these presents do give grant Bargain Sell Deliver & Confirm unto the said Conrod Harter one certain Tract or parcel of Land Containing one Hundred & Sixty two acres be the same more or less, & Bounded as followeth Begining at Hooks Corner White oak thence north 44 East 60 poles to a red oak in Hooks line, thence of new lines South 67 East 102 poles to an ash in a Swamp Cald the Long branch thence down the same as it Meanders 66 poles to a white in Wrights line, thence along Wrights old line South 51 West 132 poles to a white oak thence north 31 West 70 poles to a white Oak, thence South 45 West 26 poles to Chesnut thence north 82 West 82 poles to a post oak thence north 72 poles to a chesnut, thence north 20 Degrees East 72 poles to a Chesnut thence north 45 East 62 poles to the begining Together with the Revision & Revisions Remainder & Remainders &

every part & parcel thereof to have & to hold the above granted land & premises with the appurtenances profits & advantages thereunto belonging or in any way appurtaining unto the said Conrod Harter his heirs and assigns for ever the above granted Land & premises with the appurtenances Profits and advantages thereunto belonging or any ways appurtaining & he the said William Wright his Heirs to & with the said Conrod Harter and his Heirs that he the said William Wright the above granted Land & Premises shall & will by these presents Warrant & forever Defend Witness my hand & Seal the day & Year above Written

William Wright

At a Court Held for Franklin County in October 1792 This Indenture was acknowledged by the within named William Wright to be his act & Deed & the same was Ordered to be recorded.

Test
James Callaway Cl"

On October 1, 1792, at Franklin County, Virginia, D.B. 2/424 William Wright and Robert Mead sold 72 acres of land to Mary Closser:

"This Indenture made this 1st day of October 1792 by and between Robert Mead & William Wright of the one part and Mary Closser of the other Part Witnesseth that the said Robert Mead & William Wright for the Consideration of Seven pounds Current money of Virginia to them in Hand Paid the Rect. hereof they Doth Hereby acknowledge Hath Given Granted Bargained and Sold unto the above said Mary Closer one Certain Tract or Parcell of Land Containing 72 acres be the same more Or less and Bounded as follows to wit Beginnig at Browers white oak Corner in floroes(?) Line thence north 70 Degrees West 180 poles to abshires Red Oak thence on His Line north 68 East 24 Poles to Vensons Corner Dogwood Thence on His Line north 30 Degrees East 100 poles to a red oak thence South 40 Degrees East on Browers Line 154 poles to flord (?) Sorrell Corner thence on His Line to the Begining Together with the Roversion and Reversions Remainder and Remainders and Every Part and Parcell thereof to Have and to Hold the above Granted Land and Premises with its appurtenances profits and advantages thereunto Belonging or any ways appertaining unto the said Mary Closser Her Heirs & assigns forever and to the said Robert Mead & William Wright doth for themselves their Heirs Covenant Grant and agree to and With the said Mary Closser and Her Heirs that we the above Granted Land and Premises shall and will by these Presents Warrant & for Ever Defend Witness our Hands and Seals the day & Year above Written

Robert Mead
William Wright

At a Court Held for Franklin County in October 1792 this Indenture was acknowledged by the within named Robert Mead and William Wright to be their Respective act & Deed and the same was Ordered to be Recorded by the Court

Test
James Callaway Clk"

On October 1, 1792, at Franklin County, Virginia, D.B. 2/427 William Wright also sold 300 acres of land to Michael Peters:

"This Indenture made this 1st Day of October 1792 Between William Wright of the one Part and Michael Peters of the other part witnesseth that the said William Wright for and in the Consideration of the sum of Fifty pounds Current money of Virginia to Him in Hand paid the rect. hereof He doth Hereby acknowledge Hath Given Granted Bargained and Sold and by these presents do Give Granted Bargain sell Deliver and Confirm unto the above said Michael Peters one Certain Tract or Parcell of Land Containing three Hundred acres be the Same more or Less and Bounded as Followeth Begining at Pointers in Murphys now Hooks Line Thence North 45 East 70 Poles to a Chesnut Oak in Sinks Line thence north 40 Degrees East 54 poles to a Large Chesnut oak thence north 45 East 59 poles to a Chesnut oak thence north Eight Degrees East 86 poles to a post oak thence N 20 East 70 to a chesnut thence N 45 East 62 poles to Hooks Corner white oak thence on His Line North 82 West 125 Poles to a red oak thence north 30 West 128(?) poles to a post a post oak in the order Line thence on the same West 63 poles to Browns Line South 8 Degrees West 53 poles to Browns Corner Red oak thence new Line South 63 East 8 poles to Peters Corner white oak thence South 60(?) Degrees E 20 poles to florons(?) Corner Sorrell Tree on a Branch thence up the Branch as it meanders South 30 West 20 poles to a Maggotty in Floroas Line South 60 poles to a white oak thence South 72 West 80 poles to Pointers South 11 West 100 poles to a Chesnut South 74 West 50 poles to a Locust thence south 58 East 120 (420?) poles to the Begining Together with the Reversion Reversions Remainder and remainders and Every part and Parcell thereof to Have and to Hold the above Granted Land and Premises with its appurtenances Profits & advantages thereunto Belonging or in any way appertaining unto the said Michael Peters His Heirs Heirs and assigns for Ever that the said William Wright His Heirs & assigns to and with the said Michal Peters His Heirs that he the said William Wright the above Granted Land and Premises shall and Will by these Presents Warrant and for ever Defend Witness my Hand and seal the day & Year above written

William Wright

At a Court Held for Franklin County in October 1792 this Indenture was acknowledged by the within named William Wright to be His act & Deed and the same was Ordered to be recorded by the Court

Test
James Callaway Clk"

An overlay of Patent Deed D/80, Franklin County Deed 2/86, Franklin County Deed 2/417, and Franklin County Deed 2/427 shows that the legal descriptions of the four deeds fit together.

On January 7, 1793, at Franklin County, Virginia, D.B. 2/473 William Wright sold 75 acres of land to Abraham Abshire:

> "This Indenture made this 7th day of January 1793 By and Between William Wright of Franklin Cty of the one part and Abraham Abshire of said County of the other Part Witnesseth that the said William Wright for & in Consideration of the sum of five pounds Current Money of Virginia to Him in Hand Paid the Receipt Hereof he doth Hereby acknowledge hath Given Granted Bargained and sold unto the said Abraham Abshire One Certain tract or parcell of land Containing Seventy five acres be the same more or less and Lying on the South side of Maggotty Creek and Bounded As followeth, to wit, Begining at a Red oak on a Ridge over his(?) Line thence South 45 D East 50 poles to Kislers Line Corner Spanish oak Thence south Eighty Degrees East 52 poles to a spanish oak thence S 75 E 60 poles to a Large white oak thence East 58 poles to Newer Wood Thence North 60 East 66 poles to a Dogwood thence north 70 Degrees West 111 poles to a Dogwood in Abshears Line thence on His old Line South 52 Degrees West 26 poles to a white oak North 40 Degrees West 33 poles to a white oak on a Ridge thence South 40 degrees West 30 poles to the Begining togethe with the Revesion and Revesions Remainder and Remainders and Every part and parcell thereof to Have and and to Hold the above Granted Land and premises with the appurtenances profits and advantages therto Belonging or in any ways appertaining unto the Abraham Abshear His Heirs and assigns and assigns For Ever and He the said William Wright doth for Himself his Heirs Covenant and agree to and with the said Abraham Abshire His Heirs and assigns that He the said William Wright the the above Granted Land and Premises with the appurtenances thereunto unto the said Abraham Abshear His Heirs assigns shall and will by these presents warrant and forever Defend in Witness hereof the said William Wright Hath Hereunto Set His hand and Year above Written
>
> William Wright
>
> At a Court Held for Franklin County in January 1793 this Indenture Was

acknowledged By the within named William Wright to be his act & Deed and the same Was ordered to be Recorded

Test
James Callaway Clk"

The 1793 Personal Property Tax List for Franklin County, Virginia, listed William Wright, Sr., with the following household on July 24:

	Persons Names	Whites	B a 16	B u 16	Hors	Studs
July 24	William Wright Sn	1	-	-	2	-

The 1793 Land Tax List for Franklin County, Virginia, listed William Wright Sn with the following property:

Persons Names Owning Land	Acre	Avarig	Total Amount	Taxes
William Wright Sn	144	0.5.0	36.0.0	0.1.9½

This record reflects the sale of 162 acres of land by Franklin County Deed 2/417, 72 acres of land by Franklin County Deed 2/424, and 300 acres of land by Franklin County Deed 2/427, for a total of 534 acres, and confirms 1809 William Wright as the grantor of those deeds.

On October 5, 1793, at Franklin County, Virginia, D.B. 3/53 William Wright, Sr., sold 20 acres of land to Luke Abshire:

> "This Indenture made this 5th day of October 1793 Between William Wright Senr. of Franklin County of the one part and Luke Abshire of the Said County of the other part Witnesseth that the Said William Wright for and in consideration of 6 pounds to him in hand paid the receipt whereof he doth hereby acknowledge hath given granted bargained and sold and by these presents doth grant bargain sell deliver and Confirm unto the said Luke Abshire his Heirs and Assigns for ever a Certain tract or parcel of Land lying and being in the County of Franklin on the South Side of Magottee Creek Containing 20 acres be the same more or less lines made by Agreement begining at Hooks pointers thence new line Markd. by Agreement to the head of a Small branch cornering on a white oak thence clean(?) said branch as the water runs to said Luke Abshires old line thence along his old line to said John Hooks line to the begining together with the reversion and reversions remainder & remainders and every part and parcel thereof to have and to hold the above granted Land and premises with its appurtenances previledges profits & advantages thereunto belonging or any

ways appertaining unto the said Luke Abshire his Heirs and assigns for ever and the said William Wright doth for himself his Heirs Covenant grant & Agree to and with the said Luke Abshire his Heirs and Assigns that he the said William Wright and his Heirs the above granted Land and Premises with appurtenances unto the Said Luke Abshire his Heirs and Assigns Shall and will by these presents warrant and for Ever defend in witness whereof the said William Wright hath hereunto set his hand and affixt his Seal the day and year above written.

Witness William Wright

Franklin October Court 1793 This Indenture was acknowledged by the within named William Wright to be his Act & Deed and the same was ordered to be recorded by the Court

Test
James Callaway Clk"

On November 20, 1793 (written 1783 in the deed), at Franklin County, Virginia, D.B. 3/78, recorded in December 1793, William Wright sold 150 acres of land to Peter Fisher:

"This Indenture made this 20th day of November 1783 Between William Wright of the one part and Peter Fisher of the other part Witnesseth that the said William Wright for and in Consideration of thirty pounds current money of Virginia to him in hand paid the Rect. hereby he doth hereby acknowledge hath given given granted bargained & sold unto Peter Fisher one Certain tract or parcel of Land containing one hundred & fifty acres be the same more or less on the south branches of Maggottee Creek & bounded by Delanys lines Peters & Zenks lines together with the Reversion & reversions remainder & remainders and every part & parcell thereof to have and to hold the above granted Land and premises with the priviledges and appurtenances thereunto belonging or any ways appertaining unto the said Peter Fisher his Heirs and Assigns for ever and the said William Wright doth for himself and his Heirs Covenant grant and agree to and with the said Peter Fisher his Heirs and Assigns that he the said William Wright & his Heirs the above granted premises with the appurtenances unto the said Peter Fisher his Heirs and assigns shall and will by these presents warrant and for ever defend in Witness whereof the said William Wright hath hereunto set his hand & Seal the day and year above written

Witness) William Wright
Abraham Abshire)
John Brown)
John Nofsinger)
Isaac Miller)

Franklin Decr. Court 1793. This Indenture was Acknowledged by the within named William Wright to be his act & deed & the same was ordered to be recorded by the Court

Test
James Callaway Clk"

On December 2, 1793, at Franklin County, Virginia, D.B. 3/52 William Wright, Sr., sold 100 acres of land to George Wright:

> "This Indenture made this 2nd day of December 1793 Between William Wright Senr. of Franklin County of the one part and Geo. Wright of the said County of the other part Witnesseth that the said William Wright for and in Consideration of £75 Current money of Virginia to him in hand paid the receipt whereof he doth hereby acknowledge hath given granted bargained and Sold and by these presents doth grant bargain Sell deliver and Confirm unto the said Geo Wright his Heirs and Assigns for Ever a Certain tract or parcel of Land lying and being in the County of Franklin on both sides of Magottee Creek being part of the land formally belonging to John Miller deseasd. Containing one hundred acres more or less lines by agreement begining at the white oak corner on the old Order line above the big Rocks then along that line to the creek then down the Creek as it meanders to the waggon ford then along the waggon Road to the within mentioned order line then along said line to Hooks line then along his line to Charles Vinson line at Said Vinsons Cart Road then along the Cart Road to James Wrights line then along his line to Millers Old line on the top of the hill by the Waggon Road then along Millers old line to the begining together with reversion & Reversions Remainder and remainders and every part and parcel thereof to have and to hold the above granted Land and premises with appurtenances previledges profits & advantages thereunto belonging or any wise appertaining unto the said George Wright his Heirs and Assigns for ever and the said William Wright doth for himself and his Heirs Covenant grant and Agree to and with the said Geo Wright his Heirs and Assigns that he the said William Wright and his Heirs the above granted Land and premises with the appertunances unto the said George Wright his Heirs and Assigns shall and will by these presents Warrant and for ever defend in Witness whereof the Said William Wright Senr. hath hereunto set his hand and Affixt his Seal the day and year above Written
>
> William Wright

Franklin December Court 1793

This Indenture was acknowledged by the within named William Wright to be his act & Deed and the same was Ordered to be recorded by the Court

Test
James Callaway"

On April 7, 1794, at Franklin County, Virginia, D.B. 3/142 William Wright and Mary, his wife, sold 200 acres of land to George Baker, Sr.:

"This Indenture made this VII Day of April one Thousand Seven Hundred and Ninety four Between William Wright and Mary his Wife of the County of franklin of the one part and George Baker Senr. of the said County of the other part Witnesseth that the said William Wright and Mary his Wife for and in Consideration of the Sum of one Hundred pounds Current Money of Virginia to him in hand paid at and Before the Ensealing and Delivering of these presents the receipt whereof he the said William Wright and Mary his wife Doath hearby Acknowledge hath Given Granted Sold and Confirmed and by these presents doth Give Grant Bargin Sell alien Enfoeff and Confirm unto the said George Baker Siner his heirs and assigns forever one Certain Tract or parcel of Land Containing two Hundred acres be the same more or less lying and being in the County of Franklin on the south Branches of Maggotty Creek and by Abshers Hooks and Longs line and hartors(?) Withal and Singular the rights and appertenance thereunto Belonging or in any Wise appertaining to the Same to have and to Hold, the Said Land and Premises unto the Said George Baker Sener. his heirs and assigns forever and the said William Wright and Mary his Wife doth for themselves their Heirs Executors &c Covenant and agree with the said George Baker Sr. his heirs Exors. &c that it shall and may be Lawful for the said George Baker Senr. his heirs Executors &c from time to time and all times forever Hereafter peaceably and Quietly to possess and Enjoy the said Land and premises and the right and title of him the said William Wright and Mary his wife without Trouble Suit or Molestation from them the said William Wright and Mary his Wife their Heirs Exors. Admrs. or assigns or any Person or Person lawfully claiming in by, from or under the said William Wright and Mary his Wife or any person Whatsoever and the said William Wright and Mary his Wife shall warrant and forever Defend the said Land and premises as before Expressd; unto the said George Baker Senr. his heirs & assigns forever and shall warrant and forever Defend by these presents In witness whereof William Write and Mary his wife hath hereunto set their hands and seals this day and year above Written Signed Sealed and Delivered in presence of

William Wright

At a Court Held for Franklin County in April 1794 this Indenture was acknowledged by the within Named William Wright to be his respective act and Deed and the same was ordered to be Recorded by the Court

Test
James Callaway Clk"

The 1794 Personal Property Tax List for Franklin County, Virginia, listed William Wright, Sr., with the following household on May 8:

	Persons Names	White Tithes	Blacks Over 16	Blacks 16 to 12	Horses
May 8	William Wright Sn	1	-	-	3

Stud Horses	£ S D
-	- 1 -

The 1794 Land Tax List for Franklin County, Virginia, listed William Wright Sr with the following property:

Persons Names	Acres	Amount of One Acre	Total Amount of Valuation	Tax
William Wright Sr	44	0.5.0	11.0.0	0.0.6½

This record reflects the sale of 100 acres of land by Franklin County Deed 3/52.

On October 6, 1794, at Franklin County, Virginia, D.B. 3/164 William Wright sold 50 acres of land to Charles Vinson:

"This Indenture made this 6th day of October 1794 Between William Wright of the one part and Charles Vinson of the other part Witnesseth that the said William Wright for and in Consideration of the sum of five Pounds Current Money of Virginia to him in hand paid the rect. whereof he doth hereby Acknowledge hath Given Granted Bargained and Sold and by These presents do Bargain Sell Deliver and Confirm unto Charles Vinson one Certain Tract or parcell of Land Containing fifty acres be the same more or less and Bounded by Charles Vinsons Samuel Hustons John Hirshaw lines Together with the Reversions and Reversions remainder and remainders and Every part and parcel thereof to have and to hold the above Granted Land and premises with the appertenances profits and advantages thereunto belonging or in any wise appertaining unto the

Said Charles Vinson and his heirs forever and that the said William Wright and his heirs do Covenant Grant and agree to and with the said Charles Vinson that the the Said William Wright the above Granted Land and premises Shall and will by these presents warrant and forever Defend

In Witness hereof the said William Wright hath hereunto set his hand and seal the day and year above Written

William Wright

At a Court Held for Franklin County in October 1794 this Indenture was acknowledged by the Within named William Wright and the same was ordered to be Recorded

Test
James Callaway ClC(?)"

This was probably an untaxed parcel of land owned by 1809 William Wright. The Land Tax Lists do not show the land being removed from either 1809 William Wright's taxable land or from 1830 William Wright's taxable land in 1795, but in 1796 fifty acres are taxed to a William Wright who is listed next to 1809 William Wright and then in 1797 the land is not listed. The source of this fifty acres has not as yet been traced.

The 1795 Personal Property Tax List for Franklin County, Virginia, listed William Wright S with the following household on March 28:

	Persons Names	Whites	Blacks	Blacks	Horses	Tax
March 28	William Wright S	1	-	-	2	- - 8

The 1795 Land Tax List for Franklin County, Virginia, listed

Persons Owning Land	Quant of Land	Amount of One Acre	Total Amount of Valluation	Tax
William Wright	44	0.5.0	11.0.0	0.0.6½

In March 1795 at Franklin County, Virginia, Survey Book _/72 a survey for 510 acres of land was recorded for William Wright:

"Franklin County V. March 1795. Surveyed for William Wright 510 Acres by Value of the following Land Office Treasury Warrants to wit, 300 Acres by Warrant Granted Charles McKinney the 4th November 1783 No ___ containing

1825 Acres also 100 Acres by Warrant granted Richard Smythe 9th April 1792 No 470 containing 200 Acres, and 110 Acres by Warrant granted Thomas S. Price the 13th September 1782 No 14227 Containing ___ Acres Begining at John Hooks corner Corner Chesnut Oak Thence new line No 73 W 89 po. to a Chesnut tree, So 70 W 28 po crossing Crooked run to a small Hickory, No 60 W 43 po Crossing a branch to a Chesnut Tree, No 27 W 32 po to a small RO No 10 W 34 po to five Chesnut trees, No 2 W 43 po to Three Chesnut trees So 88 W 114 po to a RO on the side of the mountain No 64 W 56 po to a RO So 74 W 48 po to a RO So 60 W 34 po to a RO So 34 W 66 po to a Chesnut tree, So 8 W 18 po to a RO So 20 E 44 po to a Chesnut & WO in Johnsons line And with it So 82 E 32 po to a Double Chesnut tree, So 71 E 70 po to a WO So 20 E 66 po to a Gum; No 23 E 26 po to a WO So 44 E 64 po to a Hickory So 28 E 32 po to a maple on a branch, and down the same as it meanders 20 po to a RO So 5 W 72 po to a RO in Boon's line and with it No 44 E 96 po to a WO So 85 E 128 po to a black Gum in Wrights line, North 20 po to Hooks corner WO Thence No 28 E 34 po to the Begining.

Will Greer Assistant to
Ste Smith Sur"

On May 4, 1795, at Franklin County, Virginia, D.B. 3/263 William and Mary Wright sold 300 acres of land to Ezekel Curtis:

"This Indenture made this 4th day of May 1795 Between William Wright and Mary Wright his wife of the one part and Ezekel Curtis of the other part Witnesseth that the said William Wright and Mary his Wife as for and in the Consideration of the sum of Thirty pounds Seven Shillings and four pence to them in hand paid the Receipt whereof they do Hereby acknowledge hath given granted Bargained, and sold unto Ezekel Curtis one Certain tract or parcell of land Containing three hundred acres be the Same more or less on the north branches of maggotty Creek and Bounded by Hooks Lindsays(?) Turners Harriss's and Talbotts lins Together with the Reversion and Reversions Remainder & Remainders and Every part and parcell thereunto belonging or any ways appertaining unto the said Ezekel Curtis his heirs & assigns forever and the said William Wright and Mary his Wife doth for themselves their Heirs Covenant grant & agree to and with the said Ezekel Curtis his heirs and assigns that they the said William and Mary Wright & their Heirs the above granted premises unto the said Ezekiel Curtis his heirs & Assigns shall and will by these presents warrant and forever Defend In Witness Whereof the said William & Mary Wright hath hereunto set their Hands Seals the day & year above Written

William Wright
Mary Wright

At a Court Held for Franklin in June 1795 this Indenture was Acknowledged by the party to the same Subscribed to be their Respective Act and Deed and the same was Ordered to be Recorded by the Court

Test
James Callaway Clk"

On August 30, 1795, at Franklin County, Virginia, D.B. 3/282 William Wright, Sr., of Franklin County sold 80 acres of land to David Overholt:

"This Indenture made this 3d day of August 1795 By and between William Wright Senr. of Franklin County of the one part and David Overholts of the said County of the other part Witnesseth that the said William Wright Senr for and in consideration of ten pound Current money of Virginia to him in hand paid the Receipt hereof he doth hereby acknowledge hath given granted Bargained and Sold and by these presents doth grant Bargain Sell Deliver and Confirm unto the said David Overholts his heirs and assigns forever a Certain tract or parcel of Land lying and being in the County of Franklin, on the Head Branches of Maggotty Creek Containing 80 acres be the same more or less and bounded as followeth Begining at a Red oak in Langdons line then South 85 Degrees W 100 poles to a white oak in Luke Keslars line thence on his line S 16 Do West 100 poles to a white oak in the said Line then west 8 poles to four white oak Saplins on a Ridge then South 9 West 44 poles to a black South 56 East 43 poles to a black oak North 75 East 85 poles to a Red oak South 65 East 28 to a black oak North 69 East 40 poles to a Chesnut oak then Division Line North 25 West 136 poles to the Begining together with the Reversion Reversions Remainder and Remainders and Every part and parcel thereof to have and to hold the above granted Land and premises with appurtenances Advantages and profits thereunto Belonging or any Wise appertaining unto the said David Overholts his heirs and assigns forever and the said William Wright Senr. doth for himself and his heirs Covenant grant and agree to and with the said David Overholts his heirs the above granted Land and premises with the appurtenances unto the said David Overholts his heirs and assigns shall and will by these presents warrant and forever Defend in Witness whereof the said William Wright Senr. hath hereunto set his hand and affixed his Seal the year above Written

William Wright

At a Court Held for Franklin County in September 1795 this Indenture was acknowledged by the within named William Wright to be his respective act & Deed and the Same was ordered to be Recorded by the Court

Test
James Callaway Clk"

An overlay of Franklin County Deed 3/282 and Franklin County Survey Book

2/467 shows that Deed 3/282 was the westernmost portion of S.B. 2/467. The angles are the same, but the distances of several lines were extended.

The 1796 Personal Property Tax List for Franklin County, Virginia listed William Wright with the following household on April 30:

	Persons Names	White Tithes	Blacks 0. 16	Blacks u 16	Horses
April 30	William Wright	1	-	-	1

Studs	£ S D
-	- - 4

The 1796 Land Tax List for Franklin County, Virginia, listed William Wright with the following property:

Persons Names Owning Land	Numr of Acres	Amount of One Acre	Total Amount of Valluation	Taxes
William Wright	44	0.5.0	11.0.0	0.0.6-3/4

On February 8, 1797, at Franklin County, Virginia, D.B. 3/407 William Wright of Franklin County sold 200 acres of land to William Linsey:

> "This Indenture made this 8th day February 1797 By and between William Wright of Franklin Cty of the one part and William Linsey of the said County of the other part Witnesseth that the said William Wright for and in Consideration of the sum of twenty pounds current money of Virginia to him in hand paid the Receipt hereof he doth acknowledge hath given granted Bargained and Sold unto the said William Linsey one Certain tract or parcell of Land Containing two hundred acres be the Same more or Less and bounded as followeth to wit, Begining at Hooks Corner Chesnut oak, thence new line N 73 W 30 pole to a Chesnut tree S 70 W. 28 poles Crossing Crooked Run to a Small Hickory N 60 W 48 poles Crossing a branch to a Chesnut tree N 27 W 32 poles to a small Red oak N 40 W. 34 poles to five chesnut trees thence South along the mountain Joining Turner's line fifty poles, thence down to Hooks Corner White oak, thence to the Begining Together with the Reversion & Reversions Remainder and Remainders and Every Part and parcel thereof to have and to hold the above granted land and premises With the appurtenances profits and advantages thereunto belonging or in any ways appertaining unto the said William Linsey his

heirs & assigns forever and the said William Wright doth for himself, his heirs Covenant Grant and agree to and with the said William Linsey his heirs and assigns that he the said William Wright and his heirs, the above granted Premises with the appertenances unto the said William Linsey his heirs and assigns forever shall and will by these presents warrant and forever defend, In Witness hereof the said William Wright hath hereunto set his hand and seal the day and year above Written

Witness) William Wright
Geo. Wright)
Elijah Wray)
James Wright)

At a Court held for Franklin in April 1797 the within Indenture was acknowledged by the within named William Wright to be his Respective act and Deed and the Same was ordered to be Recorded by the Court

Test
James Callaway Clk"

As will be set forth below, the land was the northwest portion of Patent Deed 37/514 acquired on November 30, 1797.

On February 24, 1797, at Franklin County, Virginia, D.B. 3/495 William Wright of Franklin County sold 200 acres of land to John Turner:

"This Indenture made this 24th day of February 1797 By and between William Wright of Franklin County of the one part and John Turner of the said Cty of the other Part Witnesseth that the said William Wright for and in consideration o the Sum of Seventy pounds Current money of Virginia to him in hand paid the Receipt hereof he doth hereby Acknowledge hath given granted, Bargained, and sold and by these presents do give grant bargain & sell one Certain tract or parcel of land containing two hundred acres be the same more or less and Bounded __ as followeth Begining at Johnsons Corner white oak, thence along the Same to a Small Chesnut tree in the said Lines, thence up the mountain to Wrights & Linseys corner Red oak thence on Linseys Line to white oak, thence to five Chesnut trees corner of Linsey and Curtiss thence on Curtiss Line to his & Curtisses Line to his and harriss Corner formed Chesnut tree thence along the side of the Mountain on Harriss Line to a Red oak, thence down the Ridge to a Double Chesnut thence to the Begining

Together, with the Reversion and Reversions Remainder and Remainders and Every part and parcell thereof to have and to hold the above granted Land and Premises with the appurtenances Profits & Advantages thereunto Belonging or any Ways appertaining unto the said John Turner his heirs and assigns forever and that he the said William Wright his heirs and assigns doth Covenant Grant and agree to and with the said John Turner his heirs and assigns that he the said William Wright & his heirs the above granted Land and Premises with the appurtenances unto the said John Turner his heirs and assigns shall and Will by these Presents warrant and forever defend In Witness whereof the said William Wright hath hereunto set his hand and Seal the day and year above Written.

Witness	)	William Wright
Margaret Wright	)	
William Linsey	)	
James Wright	)	

Franklin July court 1797 The within Indenture was proved by the oath of one of the witnesses thereto Subscribed to be the act & deed of the within named William Wright and the same was Certified and At September Court 1797 the Same was acknowledged by this Within named William Wright and ordered to be Recorded by the Court

Test
James Callaway Clk"

This was probably the land of 1809 William Wright, since it refers to boundaries on his own line.

The 1797 Personal Property Tax List for Franklin County, Virginia, listed William Wright, Sr., with the following household on March 17:

	Persons Names	White Persons	Blacks 0 16	Blacks U 16
March 17	William Wright Senr	1	-	-

Horses	Studs
1	

The 1797 Land Tax List for Franklin County, Virginia, listed William Wright with the following property:

Persons Names Owning Land	Number of Acres	Amount of One Acre	Total Amount of Valuation	Taxes
William Wright	44	0.5.0	11.0.0	0.0.6-3/4

On November 30, 1797, by Patent Deed 37/514 William Wright, Sr., patented 510 acres of land in Franklin County:

> "James Wood Esquire Governor of the Commonwealth of Virginia to all to whom these Presents shall come Greeting Know ye that by Virtue of three Land office Treasury Warrants Numbers twenty thousand three hundred and six, four hundred and seventy, and fourteen thousand two hundred and twenty seven There is Granted by the said Commonwealth unto William Wright senior a certain tract or parcel of Land Containing five hundred and ten Acres by survey bearing date the fifth day of March one thousand seven hundred and ninety five Lying and being in the County of Franklin and is bounded as followeth to Wit Beginning at John Hooks corner chesnut oak, thence new line North seventy three degrees West (eighty nine poles to a Chesnut, South seventy degrees West) twenty eight poles crossing Crooked Run to a small Hickory North sixty degrees East forty three poles crossing a branch to a chesnut tree. North twenty seven degrees West thirty two poles to a small red oak North forty degrees West thirty four poles to five chesnut trees North two degrees West forty three poles to three chesnut trees south eighty eight degrees West one hundred and fourteen poles to a red Oak on the side of a Mountain North sixty four degrees West fifty six poles to a Red oak South seventy four degrees West forty eight poles to a red Oak, south sixty degrees West thirty four poles to a red oak, south thirty four degrees West sixty six poles to a chesnut tree, south eight degrees West eighteen poles to a red oak, south twenty degrees East forty four poles to a chesnut and white oak in Johnsons line and with it, south eighty two degrees East thirty two poles to a double Chesnut tree south seventy one degrees East seventy poles to a white oak, south twenty degrees East sixty six poles to a gum North twenty three degrees East twenty six poles to a white oak south forty four degrees East sixty four poles to a Hickory south twenty eight degrees East thirty two poles to a Maple on a branch thence down the same as it meanders twenty poles to a red oak south five degrees West seventy two poles to a red oak in Boons line and with it, North forty four degrees East ninety six poles to a white oak south eighty five degrees East one hundred and twenty eight poles to a gum in Wrights line North twenty poles to Hooks corner white oak, and thence North twenty eight degrees East one hundred and thirty four poles to the beginning, with its appurtenances To have and to hold the said tract or parcel of Land with its appurtenances to the said William Wright senior and his Heirs forever In Witness whereof the said James Wood Esquire Governor of the Commonwealth of Virginia hath hereunto set his Hand and caused the lesser seal of the said Commonwealth to be Affixed at Richmond on the Thirtieth day of November In the Year of our Lord one thousand seven hundred and ninety seven and of the Commonwealth the Twenty second
>
> James Wood"

This was the same land as that surveyed in Franklin County S.B. _72.

The 1798 Personal Property Tax List for Franklin County, Virginia, listed William Wright Senr with the following household on March 10:

	Persons Names	White Tythes	Blacks Over	Blacks Under 16
March 10	William Wright Senr	1	-	-

Horses	Stud Horses	License	D C
1	-	-	- 9

The 1798 Land Tax List for Franklin County, Virginia, listed William Wright with the following property:

Persons Names Owning Land	Number of Acres	Amount of One Acre	Total Amount of Valluation	D C 38 Cts
William Wright	44	0.5.0	11.0.0	0.14
Ditto from Martin Key	200	0.1.6	12.10.0	0.16

This record reflects the purchase of 200 acres of land by Franklin County Deed 3/526 in 1790 that was not recorded until 1798.

On August 4, 1798, at Franklin County, Virginia, D.B. 3/607 William Wright sold 120 acres of Land to Abraham Overholt:

> "This Indenture made this 4th day of August 1798 By and between William Wright of Franklin County of the one part and Abraham Overholt of the said County of the other part Witnesseth that the said William Wright for the Consideration of ten pounds Current money of Virginia to him in hand the Rect. hereof he doth hereby acknowledge hath Given Granted Bargained and sold and by these presents doth grant Bargain sell deliver and Confirm unto the said Abraham Overholt his heirs and assigns forever one Certain tract or parcel of Land Containing one hundred and twenty acres be the same more or less and bounded as followeth Begining at a Large Chesnut tree in harveys Line thence along Harveys Lines to Turners line along Turners Line to Patrick Johnsons Lines along his Lines to a Gum on John Johnsons Lines along his Lines to the Begining. Together with the reversion and Reversions Remainder and Remainders and Every part and parcel thereof to have and to hold the above granted Land and premises with the Previledges and appertenances Profits and

advantages Thereunto belonging or in anyways appertaining unto the said Abraham Overholt his heirs and assigns forever and the said William Wright doth for himself his heirs Covenant Grant and agree to and with the said Abraham Overholt his heirs and assigns that he the said William Wright his heirs and assigns the above granted Premises with the Appertenances unto the said Abraham Overholt his heirs and assigns shall and will by these presents warrant and forever Defend, In Witnesseth whereof the said William Wright hath hereunto set his hand and seal the day and year above Written

Test) William Wright
Henry Brower)
Abraham Overholt)
Jacob Coloro)

At a Court held for Franklin County in September 1798 the Within Indenture was acknowledged by the within named William Wright to be his act and deed and the same was ordered to be Recorded by the Court

Test
James Callaway CC"

The 1799 Personal Property Tax List for Franklin County, Virginia, listed William Wright with the following household on May 6:

	Persons Names	White Tithes	Blacks Over 16	Blacks Under 16
May 6	William Wright Sr	1	-	-

Horses	Studs	Licenses	D C
1	-	-	- 12

The 1799 Land Tax List for Franklin County, Virginia, listed Wm Wright Senr with the following property:

Persons Names Owning Land	Number of Acres	Value of One Acre	Total Amount of Valuation	D C @ 48 Cts
Wm Wright Senr	44	0.5.0	11.0.0	0.12
Do	200	0.1.6	12.10.0	0.20

The 1800 Personal Property Tax List for Franklin County, Virginia, listed William Wright, Sr., with the following household on June 14:

		White Tithes	Blacks Over 16	Blacks Under 16
June 14	William Wright Sr.	1	-	-

Horses	Stud Horses	Rates p person	License	Dollars Cents
-	-	-	-	- -

The 1800 Land Tax List for Franklin County, Virginia, listed William Wright Sr with the following property:

Persons Names Owning Land	Number of Acres	Amount of One Acre	Total Amount of Valuation	D C
William Wright Sr	44	0.5.0	11.0.0	0.18
Same	200	0.1.6	15.10.00	0.20
Same	510	0.1.3	31.17.6	0.51

This record reflects the patent of 510 acres of land by Patent Deed 37/514.

The 1801 Personal Property Tax List for Franklin County, Virginia, listed William Wright Sr. with the following household on May 2:

		White Tithes	Blacks Over 16	Blacks Over 12 + 16
May 2	William Wright Sr.	-	-	-

Horses &c &c	Stud Horses	Rates pr Season	Roding(?) Chairs	Dollars Cents
1	-	-	-	- 12

The 1801 Land Tax List for Franklin County, Virginia, listed William Wright Sr with the following property:

Persons Names Owning Land	No. of Acres	Amount of One Acre	Total Amount of Valuation	D C
William Wright Sr	44	0.5.0	11.0.0	0.18
Same	200	0.1.6	12.10.0	0.20
Same	510	0.1.3	32.17.6	0.51

On July 1, 1801, at Franklin County, Virginia, D.B. 4/168, William Wright sold 330 acres of land to Ezekiel Curtis:

> "This Indenture made this 1st Day of July 1801 by and between William Wright of Franklin Cty. of the one part, and Ezekiel Curtis of the said County of the other part; Witness that the said William Wright for and in the consideration of fifty pounds current money of Virginia to him in hand paid the Rect. hereof he doth hereby acknowledge, hath given, granted, bargained & sold unto the said Curtis one certain tract, or parcel of Land containing three hundred and thirty acres, be the same more or less, and known by the name of the Flat Rock place, and bounded as followeth, Begining at Hook's corner white oak, thence new Line to Talbot's Line on the Top of the mountaine; thence along his Line crossing the Flatt Rock to Harriss Line; thence along his line to Linsey's thence Line along Linsey's Line to Hook's Line; thence along Hooks Line to the Begining together with the Revertion and Revertions, Remainder and Remainders, and every part, and parcel thereof. To have and to hold the above granted Land and Premises, with the previleges, and appurtenances thereunto belonging or any ways appertaining unto the said Ezekiel Curtis his Heirs & assigns for ever, and the said William Wright doth for himself, his Heirs covenant, grant, and agree, to and with the said Ezekiel Curtiss, his Heirs & assigns that he the said William Wright, and his Heirs, the above granted Land with the appurtenances, unto the said Ezekiel Curtiss, his Heirs & assigns shall and will by these presents, warrant and for ever defend. In Witness hereof the said William Wright hath hereunto set his hand and Seal The day and year above written.
>
> Witness William Wright
> James Wright
> Adam Wray
> Isaac Wray

At a Court held for Franklin County at the Courthouse in September 1801

This Indenture of bargain and sale between William Wright of the one part, and Ezekiel Curtis of the other part, was proved by the oath of James Wright, Adam Wray, and Isaac Wray, the subscribing witnesses & ordered to be Recorded.

Teste,
Ja Callaway C. C"

This was probably a sale by 1809 William Wright, since as will be set forth below, the 1802 Land Tax List showed the disposition of all but 44 acres of his land.

The 1802 Personal Property Tax List for Franklin County, Virginia, listed William Wright Sr with the following household on August 18:

	Persons Names	White Tithes	Blacks Over 16	Blacks Over 12 & Under 16
August 18	William Wright Sr	1	-	-

Horses &c &c &c	Stud Horses	Rates p Season	Store License	Dollars Cents
1	-	-	-	- 12

The 1802 Land Tax List for Franklin County, Virginia, listed William Wright Sr with the following property:

Persons Names Owning Land	No. of Acres	Amount of One Acre	Total Amount of Valuation	D C
William Wright Sr	44	0.0.5	0.11.0	0.18

This record reflects the sale of 200 acres and 510 acres of land by the various Franklin County Deeds listed above.

The 1803 Personal Property Tax List for Franklin County, Virginia, did not list a William Wright, Sr., but did list a Captain William Wright who was probably his son 1830 William Wright of Franklin County.

The 1803 Land Tax List for Franklin County, Virginia, listed William Wright Sr

with the following property:

Persons Names Owning Land	No. of Acres	Amount of One Acre	Total Amount of Valuation	D C
William Wright Snr	44	0.5.0	11.0.0	0.10

On September 4, 1803, at Franklin County, Virginia, D.B. 4/482 William Wright sold 220 acres of land to John Fishburn:

> "This Indenter made this 4th day of September 1803 by and between Wm. Wright of Franklin County of the one part, and John Fishburn of the said county of the other part, Witnesseth, that the said William Wright for and in consideration of Sixty pound to him in hand paid, receipt hereof he doth hereby acknowledge, hath given, granted, bargained, and sold, deliver, and confirm unto John Fishburn his hears and assigns forever, a certain tract or parcel of Land containing 220 acres be the same more or less, lying and being in the Count of Franklin on the head Branches of Ellits and Gills' Creeks and bounded as followeth, to wit, Begining at a small Hickory on his own Line, thence along Early's Line South 72 W. 52 poles to a Gum corner of Rays thence with his Line S. 28 E. 28 poles to white oak S. 10 E. 46 poals to white oak of Wright's S. 66 E. 38 poles to a Chesnut oak, S 78° E. 44 poals to a double Popler, S 70 E 26 poals to a small Spanish oak, S. 44 E 60 poals to a white oak, N. 58 E. 34 poals to a Chesnut, N. 25 E. 40 poals to a Dogwood and Chesnut, N. 39 E. 26 poals to a dead red oak, in Harkman Doarn's line, along his line N. 20 W. 34 poals to a white oak N. 22 E. 42 to a white oak, thence N. Seventeen degrees E. 30 poals to Popler in Harkman Doarn's line, thence lines by agreement along the loral ridge to the Hickory corner, togeather with reversion and reversions remainder and remainders and every part and parcill thereof: To have and to hold the above granted Land and Premises, with the appertanances, Previledges, Profits, and advantages thereunto belonging or any wise appertaining, unto John Fishburn his heirs, and assigns forever, and the said William Wright doth for himself covenant, grant, and agree to and with the said John Fishburn his Heirs, the above granted Land and Premises with the appertanances unto the said John Fishburn his Heirs shall and by these Presents warrant and forever defend. In Witness whereof the said Wm. Wright haith hereunto set his hand and fixed his seal, the day and year above written.
>
> Wm. Wright
>
> At a Court held for Franklin County at the Courthouse the fifth day of September 1803
>
> This Indenture of bargain and Sale between William Wright of the one part and

John Fishburn of the other part, was acknowledged by the said William Wright & ordered to be recorded.

Teste,
James Callaway C L.C"

The 1804 Land Tax List for Franklin County, Virginia, listed William Wright Snr with the following property:

Persons Names Owning Land	No. of Acres	Amount of One Acre	Total Amount of Valuation	Tax D C
William Wright Snr	44	0.84	36.68	0.18

The 1806 Land Tax List for Franklin County, Virginia, listed William Wright Sr with the following property:

Persons Names That Own Land	No. of Acres Land	Amt of One Acre D C	Total Amount of Valuation D C	Tax D C
William Wright Sr	44	0.84	36.68	0.18

The 1807 Land Tax List for Franklin County, Virginia, listed William Wright S. with the following property:

Persons Names That Own Land	No. of Acres	Amt of One Acre	Total Amount of Valuation	Tax
William Wright S.	44	0.84	36.68	0.18

The will of 1809 William Wright was dated on October 10, 1808, probated on January 2, 1809, at Franklin County, Virginia, W.B. 1/368, and provided as follows:

> "In the name of God Amen October the 10th Day 1808 I William Wright of Franklin County am well in helth and of perfect Sences and Memory thanks Be to God for his Mercies and Caling to mind the mortallity of man and that all men once must Die I Doe make constitute ordain and appoint this my last Will and testament in manner and Form followeth - Item I give and Bequeath unto my Grand Son Enoch Wright all my land and plantation where I now live and all my stock and firneture To him and his heirs for Ever and the sd. Enoch shall find the sd. William with all things that is Needs full During His life I Likewise appoint my

two sons James Wright and George Wright and Enoch Wright my whole and Sole Executors and trustees of this my Last Will and Testament Witness my hand and Seal the day and year above written

Witness   William Wright
Isaac Abshire
Philemon Smith
Abraham Abshire

At a Court held for Franklin County January 2d 1809

This last Will and Testament of William Wright deceased was proved by the oath of Isaac Abshire Philemon Smith & Abraham Abshire the witnesses hereto, and ordered to be recorded.

And at a Court held for Franklin County September 3d 1810, on the motion of George Wright one of the executors herein named, who took the oath prescribed by Law and together with James Wray his security entered into and acknowledged his bond in the penalty of fifty Dollars, conditioned according to Law, Certificate is granted him for obtaining a Probat in due form, liberty being reserved to the other Executors in the said Will named to join in the Probat when they shall think fit.

Teste,
Jas Callaway CFC"

Although the language is somewhat ambiguous, the will identifies two sons, James and George Wright, and one grandson, Enoch Wright. The reference to "sd. William Wright" is unclear and may be to a son, but is probably to himself.

The Inventory and Appraisement of the estate of William Wright was dated September 11, 1810, and filed on June 1, 1812, at Franklin County, Virginia, W.B. 1/443 and listed a value of $17.96 1/2:

"An Inventory and appraisment of the Personal Estate of William Wright decd.

To 1 Bed and furnurture	$10.00
To one Table	1.17
To a persel of old cloath	0.14
To one Bed sted and Cord and mattress	0.25
To one Small Chest of Dawers	1.00
To 1 Bason 1 Dish 2 plates 5 Spoons	1.17
To 1 Tea Kettle	0.75
To 1 Crock & Shegar Box	0.17

To fire dogs & rasor	0.25
To 1 Turnip Knife	0.12½
To 1 Butter Furcan	0.12½
To 1 Chest	0.42
To 1 Pott	1.17
To Small Table	0.25
To old Dresser	0.12½
To 2 old Pickling tub & Bred Tray	0.25
To Churn	$0.50
To do Chear	0.10

Agreeable to an order of Court to us directed we have meat at the late Dweling house of William Wright Decd. this 14th Day of Septemr 1810 and praisd the above property to the sums anext to there Ginven under our hands

Geo Wright
executor

Jacob Boon
Abram Abshire
Moses Greer

At a Court held for Franklin County June 1st 1812

This Inventory and appraisement of the Estate of William Wright Deceased, was returned and ordered to be recorded

Teste,
James Callaway C.F.C"

The 1810 Land Tax List for Franklin County, Virginia, listed William Wright Decd with the following property:

Persons Names That Own Land	Amount of Land	Amot of One Acre	Amount Of Vallueation	Tax
William Wright Decd	44	0.84	36.68	0.18

This record clearly identifies the William Wright who was taxed on 144 acres of land and 44 acres of land from 1791 to 1810 as 1809 William Wright of Franklin County.

However, a review of the land transactions for 1809 William Wright of Franklin County indicates that he was executing deeds for the sale of far more land than he was acquiring by patent deeds or grant deeds:

Date	Book/Page	Acres Acquired	Acres Sold	Net Acreage
Sep 1, 1780	Pat D/80	280		280
Sep 1, 1780	Pat D/94	63		342
Feb 21, 1782	Bdfd 7/124A		200	143
Feb 21, 1782	Bdfd 7/124B		100	43
Feb 21, 1782	Bdfd 7/125		100	-57
Dec 5, 1782	Bdfd 7/179		280	-337
Jun 23, 1785	Bdfd 7/519		6	-343
Apr 4, 1786	Pat W/476	733		390
Sep 19, 1787	Fr 1/324	194		584
Feb 2, 1788	Fr 1/351		200	384
Jun 10, 1789	Fr 2/86		200	184
Oct 6, 1790	Fr 3/526	200		384
Feb 7, 1791	Fr 2/173		150	184
Apr 2, 1791	Fr 2/238		201	33
Feb 6, 1792	Fr 2/397		30	3
Oct 1, 1792	Fr 2/417		162	-159
Oct 1, 1792	Fr 2/424		72	-231
Oct 1, 1792	Fr 2/427		300	-531
Jan 7, 1793	Fr 2/473		75	-606
Oct 5, 1793	Fr 3/53		20	-626
Nov 20, 1793	Fr 3/78		150	-776
Dec 2, 1793	Fr 3/52		100	-876
Apr 7, 1794	Fr 3/142		200	-1076
Oct 6, 1794	Fr 3/164		50	-1126
May 4, 1795	Fr 3/263		300	-1426
Aug 30, 1795	Fr 3/282		80	-1506
Feb 8, 1797	Fr 3/407		200	-1706
Feb 24, 1797	Fr 3/495		200	-1906
Nov 30, 1797	Pat 37/514	510		-1396
Aug 4, 1798	Fr 3/607		120	-1516
Jul 1, 1801	Fr 4/168		330	-1846
Sep 4, 1803	Fr 4/482		220	-2066

The total of over 2000 acres of land sold in excess of recorded acquisitions is difficult to explain. The timing of the acquisition and sale of lands were sometimes out of order, indicating that 1809 William Wright did not wait to formalize title to land that he was selling to others. In addition, he may have recorded deeds for the sale of the same land twice, once when legal title had not yet been formalized and then again later when legal descriptions of the property had been obtained and to confirm the title in the purchaser. The lack of legal descriptions in many of the deeds makes them difficult to trace. And there may have been recorded sales which thereafter were considered by the parties to be void because of the failure of the buyer to pay the purchase price; 1809 William Wright would then sell the same land without recording a document to clarify that title had returned to his name. These types of transactions all appear to relate to the two large Patent Deeds W/476 for 733 acres and 37/514 for 510 acres. For Patent Deeds D/80 and D/94 and Franklin County Deeds 1/324 and 3/526, the later sale of those lands can be traced. And finally, there seem to have been some informal transfers of land among 1809 William Wright and his sons that did not result in recorded documentation of the change of title.

Notwithstanding these explanations, there still seems to be a large amount of land unaccounted for. Although all patent deeds and grant deeds naming William Wright as acquirer have been traced, including those for both 1809 William Wright and his son 1830 William Wright, there may have been additional acquisitions that were not recorded, where the formality of title transfer was not followed, and yet no title dispute arose because the purchasers were in possession of the land. The Land Tax Lists reflect the confusion regarding the amount of land actually owned by 1809 William Wright and generally reflect the four patent deeds and two grant deeds by which he acquired land and their later sales, but not the numerous additional sales listed above.

The impression left is that 1809 William Wright, the blacksmith, was not knowledgeable in the legal formalities required for the acquisition and passage of title to land or the proper methods of establishing the metes and bounds of land, even though his father 1792 John Wright had been a justice of Fauquier County. 1809 William Wright functioned in an informal and unusual style with regard to his land transactions, but with the purpose of assuring his purchasers of their right to ownership of the land sold, even though leaving the chain of title and records confused for future genealogists.

<u>Enoch Wright and wife Susan Abshire</u> by Katherine M. Roehl stated as follows with regard to 1809 William Wright of Franklin County:

"Early Wrights
In England
And In New England

It seems that the name Wright was originally the old Saxon name Wryta, which referred to occupation; a Wryta was a skilled craftsman, and especially was he a builder of timber houses, an artisan in wood.

There were several Wright families in England, especially in Essex and in Norfolk -- early records in East Anglia include Wright families.

Where there is no documentary proof, it is the opinion of more than one genealogist, including a London researcher, that our Wrights in Virginia trace back to the Wrights of Massachusetts descended from Deacon Samuel Wright of Springfield, who was of the lineage of the Kelvedon Wrights of Essex, England.

A brief look at the Wrights of Kelvedon Hall in Essex tells us that they trace back to Sir John Wright who was born in 1488, died 1551, Lord of Kelvedon Hall in Essex, near Brentwood and about 16 miles northeast of London. Kelvedon Hall is still a beautiful manor, and was visited and photographed by the writer in 1965.

Several of the Kelvedon Wrights came to this country, one as early as 1621.

Samuel Wright of London (born at Wrightsbridge near Kelvedon Hall in 1600) was a direct descendant of Sir John Wright of Kelvedon Hall, and who had died there at Kelvedon in 1551. Samuel Wright of London had a wife Margaret and nine children, at least some of the children born in England. In 1630 Samuel Wright, wife Margaret, and family, came to New England, apparently with the Winthrop Fleet. They became residents of Springfield, Massachusetts, where he is recorded as Deacon Samuel Wright. Samuel and Margaret left numerous descendants.

A study of the descendants of Deacon Samuel and Margaret Wright brings to light a great-great-grandson by name of William Wright, born April 3, 1738 at Northfield, Massachusetts. This William Wright is recorded as having married Mary _____ (surname not known) and having sons James and George Wright. They seem to disappear from Massachusetts records with no clue as to where they went.

Are they the same William and Mary Wright, with sons James and George, recorded in Bedford County, Virginia just a few years later -- our proven ancestral line? William Wright of Bedford County, Virginia is our proven ancestor and he certainly had wife Mary and sons James and George Wright.

There is no documentary proof that our proven Wright family in Virginia was indeed the very same William and Mary, James and George, that had resided in Northfield, Massachusetts, but it is probable and thus is noted here as a probability, but not documented as factual.

There arises the question of transportation between the colonies. There was some coastal shipping between Massachusetts and Virginia at that time. And it is recorded that most of the early settlers of Franklin County, Virginia came there from Tidewater Virginia, moving westward along the James River.

There could have been more than one Wright Family in such a migration. By the mid-1700's Massachusetts was a well settled state and men with families were seeking new lands for themselves and their families.

Thus our proven Wrights in Bedford County, Virginia may or may not have been the Wright family from Northfield, Massachusetts. Proof has not been forthcoming.

It may be of interest to add that the lineage of Wilbur and Orville Wright, of fame in aviation history, traces back to the Deacon Samuel Wright line through Daniel Wright who served in the American Revolution, and whose wife was Sarah Freeman. Their lineage has been thus recorded."

As set forth above, 1809 William Wright of Franklin County was the son of 1792 John Wright of Fauquier County and was not related to the Wrights of Northfield, Massachusetts.

In Genealogy Of John J. Wright Of Virginia, Indiana and Kansas John Calvin Wright stated that the children of 1809 William Wright and his wife Mary were the following:

1) John Wright, born in 1747 or 1748 at Fauquier County, Virginia,

2) William Wright, born in 1751 or 1752 at Fauquier County, Virginia,

3) Wingfield Wright, born in 1753 or 1754 at Fauquier County, Virginia,

4) James Wright, born in 1756 or 1757 at Fauquier County, Virginia,

5) Elizabeth Wright, born in 1760 at Fauquier County, Virginia,

6) George Wright, born in 1763 at Fauquier County or Franklin County, Virginia,

7) Mary "Polly" Wright, born in 1765 at Fauquier County or Franklin County, Virginia, and

8) Rachel Wright, born in 1767 at Fauquier County or Franklin County, Virginia.

The will of 1809 William Wright identified James and George Wright as his children, but John Calvin Wright gave no supporting documentation for the identification of the other persons named as children of 1809 William Wright.

The John Wright identified as a child was 1845 John Wright of Franklin County. John Calvin Wright identified him as a child of 1809 William based on first Fauquier County Deed 1/168 in which a William and Mary Wright were listed as having a son John and second 1845 John's pension application which stated that he was born in Fauquier County. However, Fauquier County Deed 1/168 probably involved the 1789 William Wright of Fredericksburg who married Mary Brent rather than 1809 William Wright and his wife Mary (Grant) Wright. Nevertheless, as set forth in Sorting Some Of The Wrights Of Southern Virginia, Part III: 1809 William Wright Of Franklin County, 1845 John Wright of Franklin County was probably a son of 1809 William Wright of Franklin County.

The identification of Wingfield Wright as a son of 1809 William Wright is based merely on John Calvin Wright's belief stated as follows:

> "Little is known of the parents of Enoch Wright to whom William[5] left his land and property and whom he named as his grandson. The Franklin County personal tax records show a Wingfield Wright for the years 1790 to 1792 inclusive. In each of the years his taxes were paid on the same day as were those of William[5] of whom the author believes he was a son and that he died about 1792-3 leaving a daughter Margaret and a son Enoch[7] who was raised by he grandfather William[5]."

Nevertheless, as will be set forth below, Wingfield Wright was possibly a son of 1809 William Wright of Franklin County based on the circumstantial evidence of his probable age, his marriage to a sister of the wife of 1845 John Wright of Franklin County, and his presence in Bedford and Franklin Counties at the same time as that of the family of 1809 William Wright of Franklin County.

The identification of Elizabeth Wright as a daughter of 1809 William Wright was mistaken. John Calvin Wright apparently saw the marriage bond and assumed that she was the daughter of 1809 William. However, the marriage consent identifies her as a daughter of John Wright, not William Wright:

"to the Clerk of franklin Coart I John Right do wish for you to Issue licens of marrage between my daughter Elizabeth Right and William Gearhart freely giving my Consent &c

Test
Jos. Willis

James Callaway

Know all men by these Presents that We William Gearhart & Joseph Willis are held and firmly bound unto John Page Esqr of the Com Wealth of Virginia in the Sum of one hundred and fifty dollars current money; to the payment whereof well and truly to be made to the said Governor and his Successors, we bind ourselves and each of us, our and each of our Heirs, Executors & Administrators jointly and severally firmly by these Presents Sealed with our Seals, and dated this 16th day of April 1804

The Condition of the above Obligation is such that Whereas there is a marriage shortly intended to be had & solemnized between the above bound William Geerhart and Elizabeth Wright

Now If there shall be no lawful cause to obstruct the said Marriage then the above Obligation to be void, else to remain in full force & virtue

Signed sealed and deli-)
vered in presence of)
C. Tate"

William Gearhart
Jos Willis

The identification of Mary "Polly" Wright as a daughter of 1809 William Wright was also mistaken. Again, John Calvin Wright apparently saw the marriage bond and assumed that she was the daughter of 1809 William. However, the marriage consent identifies her as a daughter of John and Mary Wright, not William Wright:

"We frely give our Consent to James higly Juner our Dafter polly to Be marred as Witness our hands this 22d of December

Saml Akers
Tho Highley Jr

John Wright and
mary wright

Know all men by these presents that We James Highly Junr & Samuel Akers are held & firmly Bound unto John Tyler Esqr Governor Chief Magistrate of Virginia for the time being or to his Successors in the sum of 150 Dollars to which payment well & truly to be made we bind ourselves our Heirs &c firmly by these presents sealed with our Seals & dated the 23d day of December 1810

The Condition of the above obligation is such that whereas there is a Marriage shortly Intended to be had and solemnized between the above bound James Highly Jr. Polly Wright now if there shall be no lawful Cause to obstruct the same then the above obligation to be Void else to remain in full force power & Virtue

Test
Ja Callaway

his
James X Highly Jr
mark
Samuel Akers"

Finally, the identification of Rachel Wright as a daughter of 1809 William Wright was also mistaken. Again, John Calvin Wright apparently saw the marriage bond and assumed that she was the daughter of 1809 William. However, the marriage consent identifies her as a daughter of Johne Wright, not William Wright:

"Sir please to let the Adam Running have Licence to be Married to my Daughter Rachel Wright & thus Oblige

To the Clerk of Franklin County

Yr Mo Obt.
Johne Wright

Know all men by these presents that we Adam Running & Daniel Hoff are held & firmly bound unto Edward Randolph Esqr Governor or Chief Magistrate of the State of Virginia in the Sum of Fifty Pounds to wch payment well & Truly to be made we Bind unto the said Edward Randolph or his Successors we bind ourselves & each of us our & each of Our Heirs Extors Admrs or assigns Jointly & Severally firmly by these presents Sealed with our Seals & Dated this 20th Day of Septemr 1788

The Condition of the above Obligation is such that whereas there is a Marriage shortly intended to be had & Solemnized Between the above Bound Adam Running & Rachel Wright Now if there shall be no Lawful Cause to Obstruct said Marriage then the above Obligation to be Void or else to Remain in full force power & Virtue

Witness
Samuel Read

Adam Running
Danal Hoff

. . . .
Adam Running & Rachal Right Septr. 23d 88

The above persons Legally Joined Together in the holy Estate of Matrimony, on the Day & Date Anext to these Names by Mr. ____

Randolph Hall"

From the evidence set forth above and additional evidence set forth below, the children of 1809 William Wright of Franklin County and Mary (Grant) Wright were the following:

1) probably John Wright, born about 1747 or 1749 at Fauquier County, Virginia,

2) possibly Wingfield Wright, born before 1761,

3) James Wright, born before summer of 1761,

4) William Wright, born before summer of 1761,

5) George Wright, born in late 1762 or early 1763, and

6) ____ Wright, a son.

Third Generation:

<u>1830 William Wright Of Franklin County, Virginia, His Wife Catherine (Doran) Wright, And His Descendants</u>

1830 William Wright of Franklin County was a son of 1809 William Wright of Franklin County and Mary (Grant) Wright. (1809 William[1])

On September 1, 1780, by Patent Deed E/550 William Wright patented 174 acres of land in Bedford County on Maggoty Creek:

"Thomas Jefferson Esquire; Governor of the Commonwealth of Virginia to all to whom these presents shall come greeting: Know ye that in Consideration of the Ancient Composition of Twenty Shillings Sterling paid by William Wright into the Treasury of this Commonwealth there is granted by the said Commonwealth unto the said William Wright a certain Tract or parcel of Land containing One hundred and Seventy four acres by survey bearing date the sixteenth day of March One Thousand Seven hundred and Seventy four lying and being in the

County of Bedford on the south side of Maggoty Creek and bounded as followeth, to wit, Beginning at Pointers in Randolphs line off south fifty five degrees west fifty six Poles to a Hickory South Seventy poles to a Chesnut tree South thirty degrees West Twenty four poles to a Dogwood North seventy degrees West One hundred and twelve Poles to a Dogwood South fifty degrees West Twenty six poles to a white oak North forty degrees West Sixty six poles to a Mahogany tree on a Branch thence up the Branch as it Meanders fifty poles to a Maple off North one hundred and two poles to Johnsons Corner pointers thence on his lines North Seventy degrees East seventy poles to a Chesnut oak East seventy poles to Randolphs old Corner Red oak thence along his line South forty five degrees East one hundred and four poles to his Corner and East Thirty six Poles to the first Station with its Appurtenances; to have and to hold the said Tract or parcel of Land with its Appurtenances to the said William Wright and his Heirs forever In witness whereof the said Thomas Jefferson Governor of the Commonwealth of Virginia, hath hereunto set his hand and Caused the seal of the Said Commonwealth to be affixed at Richmond on the first day of September in the year of our Lord One Thousand Seven hundred and eighty and of the Commonwealth the fifth.

Thomas Jefferson"

As will be set forth below, the 1788 and 1789 Land Tax Lists for Franklin County, Virginia, listed 172 acres of land for William Wright, Jr. The similarity in the amount of land makes clear that the patentee of Patent Deed E/550 was William Wright, Jr.

The 1782 Personal Property Tax List for Bedford County, Virginia, listed William Wright Jr. with the following household:

Named Wright	Free Males above 21 yrs	Slaves	Horses	Cattle	White Ty above 16 yrs	Blk Tithes above 16 yrs
William Wright Junior	1		3	4	1	

This record indicates that William Wright was born before the summer of 1761.

On March 15, 1785, at Bedford County, Virginia, S.B. 2/495 William Wright, Jr., obtained a survey for 372 acres of land:

"Mar 15, 1785 -

Surveyd. for William Wright Jnr. 372 Acres of Land Situate in Bedford County, Bounded as follows to wit. Beg. at a wh.o in Limses Order line on the waters of

Gills Creek. Thence of new Lines N 41 W 160 poles to a white Oak N 76 W 72 poles to a R.o N 44 W 34 poles to a wh.o N 31 E 44 poles to a Hicory Grub in Earleys line, along his line N 18 W 162 poles to 2 R.o Thence new lines S 87 W 38 poles to a Chesnut Oak and a Red Oak S 37 W 36 poles to a Gum and Hicory S 8 E 24 poles to Slones line along his lines S 4 W 28 poles to a double Red Oak S 44 W 74 poles to Pointers, along McGradys lines S 45 E 62 poles to a wh.o S 73 W 44 poles to a Chest. S 55 W 16 poles to a Chesnut S 13 W 60 poles to a white Oak Leaving McGradys lines S 53 E 92 poles to a Black Jack N 49 E 28 poles to a Chesnut Oak N 7 E 34 poles to a wh.o S 12 E 28 poles to a wh.o S 66 E 28 poles to a wh.o S 27 E 20 poles to a wh.o S 74 E 18 poles to a wh.o S 51 E 58 poles to a wh.o in Hartman Dorons line along his hill N 80 E 172 poles to the first Station"

On March 17, 1785, at Bedford County, Virginia, S.B. 2/498 William Wright, Jr., obtained a survey for 233 acres of land:

"March 17th 1785 -

Surveyed for William Wright Jnr 233 acres of Land by virtue of a Land Office T. Warrant Granted to Thomas Arthur 30th Aug 1782 for 2550 Acres and Assd. to the sd. Wright &c: Situate in Bedford County Lying on the waters of Elliott Creek and Gills Creek Bounded as follows to Wit. Beginning at Laughlin McGrady Co. wh.o thence along his line S 88 W 78 pos. to a white Oak N 55 W 106 poles to a wh.o W 46 poles to a Red Oak S 2 E 20 poles to a Red Oak and Spanish Oak S 43 W 40 poles to a Gum S 16 E 64 poles to a Hicory S 16 W 74 poles to a wh.o S 66 E 38 poles to a Chesnut Oak S 78 E 44 poles to a double Poplar S 70 E 26 poles to a small Spanish Oak S 44 E 60 poles to a wh.o N 58 E 34 poles to a Chesnut N 25 E 40 poles to a Dogwood & Chesnut N 39 E 26 poles to a dead Red Oak in Heartman Dorons Line, along his hill N 20 W 34 poles to a white Oak N 22 E 42 poles to a wh.o Thence N 17 E 56 poles to the Beginning."

In July 1785 at Bedford County, Virginia, Court Order Book 8/165 a report on the viewing of a new road to Maggotty Creek was filed:

"A Report of a Road from the Widow Martins on Stanton River to Slones Mill on Maggotty Creek retd. to witt, We the Viewers being first sworn have viewed the way from the Widow Martins to Slones Mill & find it Passable crossing Gills Creek between Jno Charter's & Anthony Pate's & Establishd. Accg to Report. - Charles Simmons Appd. Surv. of Sd Road from Stanton River to Jos: Simmons Road - William Charter from Simmons Rd. to Gills Creek - & Wm Wright Jr. from Gills Creek to Maggotty - & all the Hands within two Miles on each Side of sd. Road to Attend the said Surveyors to Open the same"

This record indicates that William Wright, Jr., was residing on Maggotty Creek in July

1785.

The 1786 Personal Property Tax List for Franklin County, Virginia, listed William Wright, Jr., with the following household:

By Whom Taken	To Whom Belonging	Total Tithes	Whites Over 21	Whites Under 21
Arthur	William Wright, Jr.	2	1	0

Slaves Over 16	Slaves Under 16	Horses	Cattle	Studd Horses
1	2	2	2	

The 1787 Personal Property Tax List for Franklin County, Virginia, listed William Wright, Jr. with the following household on July 3:

		Whites Over 21	Whites Under 21
July 3	William Wright, Jr.	1	0

Blacks Over 16	Blacks Under 16	Horses	Cattle
1	2	2	11

The 1787 Land Tax List for Franklin County, Virginia, listed William Wright with the following property:

Persons Names	Acres	Average Price	Amount	Tax
William Wright	103	1.5.-	128.5.0	1.17.5¼

The 1787 Land Tax List for Franklin County, Virginia, also listed William Wright, Sr., with 733 acres of land, but since William Wright, Jr., also owned land in Franklin County at this time, this second listing for 103 acres of land was probably for William Wright, Jr.

On August 4, 1787, by Patent Deed 10/450 William Wright, Jr., patented 372 acres of land in a part of Bedford County which became Franklin County:

"Beverley Randolph Esquire Lieutenant Governor of the Commonwealth of Virginia to all to whom these presents shall come greeting Know ye that in Consideration of the ancient Composition of two pounds sterling paid by William Wright junr. into the Treasury of this Commonwealth there is granted by the said Commonwealth unto the said William Wright junr. a certain tract or parcel of Land Containing three hundred and seventy two acres by survey bearing date the fifteenth day of March one thousand seven hundred and eighty five lying and being in the County of Bedford and Bedford and Bounded as followeth To wit Beginning at a white oak in Sims's order line on the waters of Gills Creek thence off new lines North forty one degrees, West one hundred and sixty poles to a white oak North seventy six degrees, West seventy two poles to a red oak North forty four degrees West thirty four poles to a white oak, North thirty one degrees, East forty four poles to a hickory Grub in Earleys line thence along his line north eighteen degrees, West one hundred and sixty two poles to two red oaks, thence New lines South eighty seven degrees West thirty two poles to a chesnut oak and Red oak South thirty seven degrees West thirty six poles to a Gum, & hickory South eight degrees East twenty four poles to Stones lines thence along his lines South four degrees West twenty eight poles to a double Red oak, South forty four degrees West seventy four poles to pointers thence along McGradys lines South forty five degrees East sixty two poles to a white oak, South seventy three degrees West forty four poles to a Chesnut, South fifty five degrees, West sixteen poles to a Chesnut South thirteen degrees West Sixty poles to a white oak leaving McGradys line South fifty three degrees West ninety two poles to a black Jack, North forty nine degrees East twenty eight poles, to a Chesnut oak, North seven degrees East thirty four poles to a white oak, South twelve degrees East twenty eight poles to a white oak, South sixty six degrees East twenty eight poles to a white oak South twenty seven degrees, East twenty poles to a white oak South Seventy four degrees East eighteen poles to a white oak South fifty one Degrees East fifty eight poles to a white oak in Heartmon Dorams line along his line North eighty degrees East one hundred & seventy two poles to the Beginning With its appurtenances to the said William Wright junr. & his heirs forever In witness whereof the said Beverley Randolph Esquire Lieutenant Governor of the Commonwealth of Virginia hath hereunto set his hand and caused the lesser Seal of the said Commonwealth to be affixed at Richmond on the fourth day of August in the year of our Lord, one Thousand seven hundred & eighty seven & of the Commonwealth the twelfth.

B. Randolph"

The legal description confirms that this is the same land as that in Bedford County Survey Book 2/495.

On March 20, 1788, at Franklin County, Virginia, D.B. 2/263 William Wright, Jr., purchased 230 acres in Franklin County from Laughlin McGrady:

"This Indenture Made this 20th day of March 1788 between Laughlin MCgrady of Franklin County of the one part, and William Wright Junr. of the said County of the other part, Witnesseth that the said Laughlin McGrady for and in Consideration of the sum of 100 pounds Current Money of Virginia to him in hand paid, the Receipt Whereof he doth hereby acknowledge hath given Granted, Bargained and Sold & by these presents doth grant Bargain Sell Deliver and Confirm into the said William Wright his Heirs & Assigns for ever one Certain Track or parcell of Land lying & being in the County of Franklin On the Head Branches of Gills Creek Containing 230 Acres be the same More or less, and Bounded as followeth to wit, Begining at a Corner White Oak, thence off new lines N. fifty three Degrees W. forty poles to a Hickory, thence South Eighty Nine Degrees West fourteen poles to a Black gum, thence North Sixty Seven Degrees West Thirty-Two poles to a Chesnut, thence South Seventy Degrees West forty six poles to a White Oak thence North 81 Degrees East Thirty Two poles to a Sourwood, thence Thirty Two Degrees East Ten poles to a Chesnut, thence North Eighty One Degrees East thirty two poles to a sourwood, and Chesnut Oake, thence South forty six Degrees East Sixty four poles to a sourwood, and poplar, in a branch thence North thirty one Degrees East forty poles to a poplar on a branch One Hundred and Six poles to pointers East Seventy Two poles to a White Oak South Seventy Six Degrees East One Hundred & Six poles to a White Oak, N. Eighty Eight Degrees Seventy Eight poles to a White Oak North twenty Six Degrees West One Hundred poles to a white oak N. One thirteen Degrees West One Hundred and thirty Eight poles to a red oak North Sixteen Degrees East Sixteen pole to a Chesnut, South Seventy three Degrees East 44 poles to a White Oak N Forty Eight Degrees West 68 poles to a red Oak, in Kellys line, thence on Kellys line South fifty five Degrees West fourteen poles to his corner poplar, of South Twenty five Degrees West Twenty four poles Chesnut South Eighty five Degrees West fifty four poles to a Chesnut, South forty Eight Degrees West forty poles to a red oak, South fourteen Degrees East twenty two poles to a White Oak, South fourty four Degrees West thirty four poles to a Gum, South Seventy four Degrees West thirty four poles to a Red Oak, Together to have & to hold the above granted land & premises with the apurtinances thereunto belonging, or any ways appertaining unto the said William Wright his heirs & assigns for ever & the said Laughlin McGrady doth for himself his Heirs Covenant Grant and agree to and with the said William Wright and his assigns that he the said Laughlin McGrady and his Heirs the above Granted Premises with the appurtenances to the same William Wright and his assigns shall and will for ever defend in Witness Whereof the said Laughlin McGrady hath hereunto set his hand and affixed his seal the day & year above written.

Witness	)	his
Peter Abshire	)	Laughlin X McGrady
her	)	mark
Catharine McGrady	)	
mark	)	
Jacob McGrady	)	

At a Court held for Franklin County in November 1788. This Indenture was proved by the Oath of two of the Witnesses hereto subscribed to be the act & Deed of the within named Laughlin McGrady & the same was ordered to be Certified And at a Court held for the said County on the 5th day of September 1791

This Indenture was further proved by the oath of one other Witness hereto subscribed & Ordered to be recorded

Teste
James Callaway ClC"

The legal description crosses over on itself and there is obviously some error in the metes and bounds.

The 1788 Personal Property Tax List for Franklin County, Virginia, listed William Wright, Jr., with the following household on April 1:

		Whites Over 16	Blacks Over 16	Blacks Over 12	Horses
April 1	William Wright Jnr	1	0	0	1

The 1788 Land Tax List for Franklin County, Virginia, listed William Wright Jo with the following property:

Persons Names	Acres of Land	Price p Acre	Amount	Taxes
William Wright Jo	172	0.2.0	17.4.0	0.5.1-3/4

This record confirms that the purchaser of 174 acres of land by Patent Deed E/550 was William Wright, Jr.

The 1789 Personal Property Tax List for Franklin County, Virginia, listed William

Wright, Jr., with the following household on August 7:

		16/ Whites	16 B	12Do	Horses
August 7	William Wright, Jr.	1	0	0	2

The 1789 Land Tax List for Franklin County, Virginia, listed William Wright Jr with the following property:

Persons Names	Qty. Acres	Average Price	Amount	Taxes
William Wright Jr	172	0.2.0	17.4.0	0.3.5-1/2

The 1790 Personal Property Tax List for Franklin County, Virginia, listed William Wright, Jr., with the following household on March 12:

		Whites	Blacks Over 16	Blacks Under 16
March 12	William Wright Junr	1	0	0

Horses	Studs	L S D
0	1	0 1 0

The 1790 Land Tax List for Franklin County, Virginia, listed William Wright with the following property:

Persons Names	Acres	Average Price	Amount
William Wright	173	0.2.0	17.6.0

On October 4, 1790, at Franklin County, Virginia, D.B. 2/219 William Wright, Jr., purchased 150 acres of land from John Langdon:

> "This Indenture Made this 4th Day of October 1790 By and Between John Langdon of the County of Franklin of the one part and William Wright Junr. of the Said County of the other part, witnesseth that the Said John Langdon for and in Consideration of the Sum of one hundred pounds to him in hand paid the Reciept whereof he doth hereby Acknowledge hath Given Granted Bargained and Sold and by these presents do Bargain and Sell Deliver and Confirm unto

the Said William Wright his heirs and assigns one hundred and fifty acres of Land be the Same more or Less Lying and being in the County of Franklin on both sides of Maggotty Creek and Bounded as followeth Begining at a Chesnut Oak in William Wright Senr Line South 66D° West 76 to a Black Oak South 78 poles to a White Oak on a Ridge South 24 D° West 84 poles to a Gum then New Lines North 44 D West 40 poles to a Chesnut North 86 D West 34 poles to a Red Oak North 43 Degrees West 66 poles to a Dogwood North 39 D East 42 poles to Chesnut oak North 50 D East 48 poles to Gum North 24 D. East 6 poles to a White Oak in Jacob Boons line thence along his Line North 65 East 26 poles to a pine North 84 D East 16 poles to a Hickory Stump North 77 D East Crossing Maggottee Creek 70 poles to a Red Oak in the said Line thence with New Lines to a Locust Stake on the Waggon Road thence along the Waggon Road as it Meanders Crossing the Creek to the Begining to have and to hold the above Granted Land and premises with the Appurtenances privilidges profits and advantages unto the Said William Wright and his heirs and assigns for ever the said John Langdon doth for him Self his heirs and assigns Covenant Grant and aGree to and with the Said William Wright that he the said John Langdon his heirs and assigns shall warrant and forever Defend in Witness hereof the Said John Langdon hereunto Set his hand & Seal the day and Year above written

Teste John Landon LS
George Wright
James Wright
John Harris
Robert Goring
Thomas Lewis

At a Court held for Franklin County on Monday the 2nd Day of May 1791 This Indenture was proved by the oath of 3 of the witnesses hereto Subscribed to be the act & Deed of the within named John Langdon the Same was ordered to be recorded

Teste
__ Smith Clc"

On April 2, 1791, at Franklin County, Virginia, D.B. 2/238 William Wright acted as a witness to the sale of 201-3/4 acres by his father and mother William and Mary (Grant) Wright.

The 1791 Personal Property Tax List for Franklin County, Virginia, listed William Wright, Jr., with the following household on April 9:

		Whites	Blacks Over 16	Blacks Under 16
April 9	William Wright Jn	1	0	0

Horses	Stud Horses	L S D
2	0	0 1 0

The 1791 Land Tax List for Franklin County, Virginia, listed William Wright Jr with the following property:

Persons Names	Acres	Average Price	Total Amount	Tax
William Wright Jr	23	0.2.0	2.0.0	
Do	172	0.2.0	17.4.0	

On April 19, 1791, at Franklin County, Virginia, D.B. 2/223 William Wright, Jr., sold 150 acres of land to Jacob Boon:

> "This Indenture Made the 19th of April in the Year of our Lord One thousand seven hundred and ninety one, Between William Wright Jr. of the County of Franklin of the one part and Jacob Boon of the Same place of the other part Witnesseth that the said William Wright for and in Consideration of the Sum of one hundred pounds to him in hand paid doth Give Grant Bargain & Sell to the said Jacob Boon & his heirs one parcel of Land Lying and Being in the County aforesaid on Magotty adjoining the Land of the Said Jacob Boon and William Wright Senior Containing one hundred and fifty acres more or Less and Bounded as follows to wit Begining at a Red oak thence South 38 Poles to a Stake on the Waggon Road and with the Same S 78 E 64 poles to the ford of the Creek near the still house, thence S 3 E 146 Poles to a Red Oak Corner to William Wright Senr. thence S 52 E 20 Poles to a Large white oak S 88 W 84 poles to a Gum, N 44 W 40 poles to a Chesnut No. 26 W.34 poles to a Red oak N. 43 W. 66 poles to a Dogwood N. 39 E. 42 Poles to a chesnut oak, N. 50 E.48 poles to a Gum N. 24 E. 6 poles to a white oak on the said Boons Line thence with the same North 65 E. 26 poles to a pine, N 84 E. 16 poles to a Hickory Stump N 77 E. 90 poles Crossing the Creek to the Begining together with all its Appurtenances to have and to hold the Said parcel of Land with its Appurtenances to the said Jacob Boon and his heirs, to the Sole use & Behoof of the said Jacob Boon and his heirs and the said William Wright Jr. for him self and his heirs doth Covenant with the said Jacob Boon and his heirs, that the said William Wright Jr. and his heirs the said parcel of Land with the appurtenances

to the said Jacob Boon and his heirs against all persons whatsoever will for ever Warrant and Defend In Witness whereof the said William Wright Jr. hath hereunto Subscribed his name and affixed his Seal the Day and Year above written

Sealed and delivered in presence of

William Wright LS

At a Court held for Franklin County on Monday the 2nd Day of May 1791. This Indenture was acknoeldged by the within named William Wright to be his act & Deed & the same was ordered to be recorded.

Teste
Ste. Smith CIC"

On February 6, 1792, at Franklin County, Virginia, D.B. 2/323 William Wright purchased 200 acres from John Early and Jubal Early:

"This Indenture made this Sixth day of February One thousand Seven hundred & ninety two between John Early & Jubal Early of Franklin County of the one part and William Wright of the said County of the other part, Witnesseth that the said John & Jubal for and Consideration of the sum of Eighty pounds to them in hand paid the receipt whereof is hereby acknowledged hath Granted bargained & sold, & by these presents do Grant, bargain, & Sell unto the said William Wright one certain tract or parcel of Land containing Two hundred acres be the same more or less lying & being in Franklin County on the head branches of Gills Creek & bounded as followeth. To Wit: Begining at McGradys old line thence north Fifty two & 1/2 Degrees West, Seventy Six poles to a White Oak in said line South fifty five Degrees West twenty Six poles to a Chesnut north Eighty six West fifty four poles to a Chesnut South forty five Degrees West thirty nine Poles to a Red oak, South Seventeen Degrees East Twenty one poles to a White Oak, South forty two Degrees West thirty three poles to a Gum South Seventy four Degrees West thirty four poles to a Red Oak in Jacob McGradys Line, thence with his line north fifty six Degrees West forty Eight poles to a Hickory, thence new lines the same course seventy Eight poles to Earlys line and along their line South Eighty three Degrees East thirty two poles to a White Oak north ten Degrees West forth six poles to a poplar, north sixty Eight East forty six to a poplar, north Eighty five Degrees East Thirty six poles to a black Oak, north Sixteen Degrees East Twenty two Poles to a Rock & Chesnut South Eighty one Degrees East fifty four poles to a Hickory, north nineteen Degrees West Thirty two poles to a Chesnut Oak, thence new lines North thirty four Degrees East Sixty two poles to a Chesnut Oak in Kellys Line with his line South Degrees East Sixty four po to Red Oak South Ten East Seventy four poles to a Chesnut Oak, South Sixty two Degrees East forty four poles to a poplar stump north fifty three Degrees East

Sixteen poles to pointers, South forty six Degrees East Sixty six Poles to White Oak, South Eighty seven & 42, Degrees West Sixty Eight poles to a Chesnut, South forty Eight Degrees West fourteen poles to a Red Oak South three Degrees West to the Begining To have and to hold the said granted land and premises with appurtainances to the same belonging or in any wise appurtaining with the Reversion & Reversions Remainder and Remainders and every part and parcel thereof unto the said William Wright his heirs & assigns for ever, & the said John Early & Jubal Early do Covenant and agree to & with the said William Wright his Heirs & assigns that they the said John & Jubal for them their Heirs & assigns the above Granted Land and premises unto the said William Wright his heirs & assigns shall & warrant & forever Defend from them the said John & Jubal their Heirs & assigns & from all other persons whatever in Witness whereof they the said John & Jubal hath hereunto set their hands & seals the day & date above written.

John Early
Jubal Early

Franklin February Court 1792 This Indenture was acknowledg by the within named John & Jubal Early to be their respective act & Deed & the same was Ordered to be Recorded

Teste
James Callaway Cl."

The 1792 Personal Property Tax List for Franklin County, Virginia, listed William Wright, Jr., with the following household on May 17:

Date Of Receiving Individuals	Persons Names Chargeable With The Taxes	Whites	Blacks Over 16	Blacks Over 12
May 17	William Wright Jur	1	0	0

Horses	Stud Horses	Amount of Taxes L S D
2	0	0 1 0

The 1792 Land Tax List for Franklin County, Virginia, listed William Wright Jur with the following property:

Total

Persons Names Owning Land	Quantity of Land	Rate of Land p Acre	Amount of Vallue of Land	Amount of Taxes @ 7/6
William Wright Jur	23	0.2.0	2.6.0	0.0.2
Ditto pr Earleys	200	0.1.3	12.10.0	0.0.11½
Ditto	172	0.2.0	17.4.0	0.1.3½
Ditto per Megrayday	230	0.5.0	57.10.0	0.4.4½

This record reflects the purchase of 200 acres of land by Franklin County Deed 2/323 and 230 acres of land by Franklin County Deed 2/263.

On October 17, 1792, by Patent Deed 27/201 William Wright, Jr., patented 233 acres of land:

> "Henry Lee Esquire, Governor of the Commonwealth of Virginia, To all to whom these presents shall come, Greeting; know ye, that by Virtue and in Consideration of a Land Office Treasury Warrant Number fourteen thousand and thirty three, issued the thirtieth day of August, one thousand seven hundred and eighty two, there is granted by the said Commonwealth unto William Wright Junior a certain Tract or parcel of Land, containing two hundred and thirty three Acres by survey bearing date the seventeenth day of March, one thousand seven hundred and eighty five, lying and being in the County of Bedford on the Waters of Eliots Creek and Gills Creek and bounded as follows to wit, Beginning at Laughlin McGradys corner white oak along his lines South eighty eight degrees West seventy eight poles to a white oak, North fifty five degrees West one hundred and six poles to a white oak West forty six poles to a red oak South two degrees East twenty poles to a red and spanish oaks, South forty three degrees West forty poles to a gum, South sixteen degrees East sixty four poles to a Hickory, South sixteen degrees West seventy four Poles to a white oak South sixty six degrees East thirty eight poles to a Chesnut oak, South seventy eight degrees East forty four poles to a double poplar, South seventy degrees East twenty six poles to a small spanish oak South forty four degrees East sixty poles to a white oak North fifty eight degrees East thirty four poles to a Chesnut, North twenty five degrees East forty poles to a dogwood, and Chesnut, North thirty nine degrees East twenty six poles to a dead red oak in Heartman Dorams line along his lines North twenty degrees West thirty four poles to a white oak North twenty two degrees East forty two poles to a white oak thence North Seventeen degrees East fifty six poles to the Beginning With its Appurtenances; To have and to hold the said Tract or parcel of Land, with its Appurtenances, to the said William Wright Junior and his Heirs forever
>
> In Witness whereof the said Henry Lee Esquire, Governor of the Commonwealth of Virginia hath hereunto set his hand, and Caused the lesser Seal of the said Commonwealth to be affixed at Richmond, on the seventeenth day of October in

the year of our Lord, one thousand seven hundred and ninety two, and of the Commonwealth the Seventeenth

Henry Lee"

This was that same land as that surveyed in Bedford County, Virginia, S.B. 2/498.

Franklin County, Virginia, A History by Marshall Wingfield stated that:

"An Act for establishing several towns was passed on November 10, 1792, reading as follows: "That forty acres of land in the county of Franklin, the property of Moses Grier, shall be, and they are hereby vested in John Early, Jacob Boon, John Northsinger, Daniel Barnhart, Samuel Thompson, William Wright, jun., William Turnbull, and Swinfield Hill, gentlemen, trustees, to be by them, or a majority of them, laid off into lots of half an acre each, with convenient streets, and established a town by the name of Wisenburgh.

. . . .

These two places existed as villages for a short time, then ceased to be. . . ."

The 1793 Personal Property Tax List for Franklin County, Virginia, listed William Wright, Jr., with the following household on June 3:

	Persons Names	Whites	B a 16	B u 16	Hors	Studs
June 3	William Wright Jun	2	-	1	2	-

The 1793 Land Tax List for Franklin County, Virginia, listed William Wright Jun. with the following property:

Persons Names Owning Land	Acre	Avarig	Total Amount	Taxes
William Wright Jur	200	0.1.3	12.10.0	0.0.7-1/2
Ditto	172	0.2.0	17.4.0	0.0.10-1/2
Ditto	230	0.5.0	57.10.0	0.2.3-1/2

In September 1793 at Franklin County, Virginia, Court Order Book 3/16 William Wright, Jr., was recommended to be a Captain of the Militia, 2nd battalion, in place of John Early who was promoted.

In October 1793 at Franklin County, Virginia, Court Order Book 3/21 William Wright, Jr., qualified as Captain of the Second Battalion.

The 1794 Personal Property Tax List for Franklin County, Virginia, listed William

Wright, Jr., with the following household on August 9:

	Persons Names	White Tithes	Blacks Over 16	Blacks 16 to 12	Horses
August 9	William Wright Jur	2	-	1	2

Stud Horses	L S D
-	- 2 4

The 1794 Land Tax List for Franklin County, Virginia, listed William Wright Jur with the following property:

Persons Names	Acres	Amount of One Acre	Total Amount of Valluation	Tax
William Wright Jur	200	0.1.3	12.10.0	0.0.7½
Ditto	172	0.2.0	17.4.0	0.0.10½
Ditto	230	0.5.0	57.10.0	0.2.10½

The 1795 Personal Property Tax List for Franklin County, Virginia, listed William Wright, Jr., with the following household on May 16:

	Persons Names	Whites	Blacks	Blacks	Horses	Tax
May 16	William Wright Jr.	2	1	-	3	- 2 8

The 1795 Land Tax List for Franklin County, Virginia, listed William Wright Jun with the following property:

Persons Owning Land	Quant of Land	Amount of One Acre	Total Amount of Valuation	Tax
William Wright Jun	200	0.1.3	12.10.0	0.0.7½
Ditto	172	0.2.0	17.4.0	0.0.10½
Ditto	230	0.5.0	57.10.0	0.2.10½

The 1796 Personal Property Tax List for Franklin County, Virginia, listed William Wright, Jr., with the following household on May 2:

	Persons Names	White Tithes	Blacks 0. 16	Blacks u 16	Horses
May 2	William Wright Junr	2	1	-	2

Studs	L S D
-	- 2 4

The 1796 Land Tax List for Franklin County, Virginia, listed William Wright Ju with the following property:

Persons Names Owning Land	Numr of Acres	Amount of One Acre	Total Amount of Valluation	Taxes
William Wright Ju	200	0.1.3	34.1.3	0.0.7½
Ditto	172	0.2.0	17.4.0	0.0.10½
Ditto	230	0.5.0	57.10.0	0.2.10½

On October 2, 1797, at Franklin County, Virginia, D.B. 3/462 William Wright sold 170 acres of land to John Doran:

> "This Indenture made this 2d day October one Thousand Seven hundred and ninety seven between William Wright of the County of Franklin of the one part & John Doran of the same County of the other part Witnesseth, that the said William Wright for and in consideration of the sum of fifty pounds Current money of Virginia to him in hand paid at & before the Ensealing & delivery of these presents the receipt whereof he the said Wm. Wright doth hereby acknowledge doth give grant bargain Sell, alien Enfoeff, and Confirm unto the said John Doran his heirs & assigns forever one Certain tract of parcel of land, Containing one hundred and Seventy, acres be the same more or less lying and being in the County of Franklin being on the Branches of Gills Creek and bounded as followeth (to wit) Begining at a white oak in Simses(?) order line thence of new lines north fourty one degrees west one hundred & sixty poles to a white oak north Seventy six degrees west Seventy two poles to a Red oak north fourty four degrees west thirty four poles to a white oak on a branch thence down the Branch to a poplar corner agreed on thence west to a white oak in the aforesaid line, South Seventy four degrees East twenty poles to a white oak, South Seventy four degrees East Eighteen poles to a white oak South fifty one degrees East fifty Eight poles to a white oak in Harthmon Dorens(?) line along his Line north Eighty degrees East one hundred and Seventy two poles to the Begining with all and singular the Rights & appertenances thereunto, belonging or in any wise appertaining to the same, To have and to hold the said Land and premises

unto the said John Doran his heirs and assigns forever and the said William Wright doth for himself his heirs Executors &c Covenant and agree with the said John Doren his heirs Executors &c that it shall and may be lawful for the said John Doran his heirs Executors &c from time to time and at all times forever hereafter, peaceably and Quietly to possess and Enjoy the said Premises and the Right & title of him the said William Wright without trouble Suit or Molestation from him the said William Wright his heirs Exors Admrs or assigns or any other person or persons lawfully claiming in by from or under the said William Wright or any Person whatsoever and the said William Wright shall warrant and forever defend the said Land Premises before Express unto the said John Doran his heirs and assigns for ever and shall forever warrant and Defend by these presents In witness whereof the said William Wright hath hereunto set his hand and seal the day and year first above written.

William Wright

Franklin October Court 1794 the within Indenture was acknowledged by the within named William Wright to be his Respective act & deed and the same was ordered to be Recorded by the Court

Test
James Callaway CC"

The 1797 Personal Property Tax List for Franklin County, Virginia, listed William Wright, Jr., with the following household on April 1:

	Persons Names	White Persons	Blacks 0 16	Blacks U 16	Horses	Studs
April 1	William Wright Jr.	2	1	-	4	

The 1797 Land Tax List for Franklin County, Virginia, listed William Wright Junr with the following property:

Persons Names Owning Land	Number of Acres	Amount of One Acre	Total Amount of Valluation	Taxes
William Wright Junr	200	0.1.8	12.10.0	0.0.7½
Ditto	172	0.2.0	17.4.0	0.0.10½
Ditto	230	0.5.0	57.10.0	0.2.10½

The 1798 Personal Property Tax List for Franklin County, Virginia, listed William Wright, Jr., with the following household on April 7:

	Persons Names	White Tythes	Blacks Over	Blacks Under 16
April 7	William Wright Jnr	2	1	-

Horses	Stud Horses	License	D C
3	-	-	- 62

The 1798 Land Tax List for Franklin County, Virginia, listed William Wright Jur with the following property:

Persons Names Owning Land	Number of Acres	Amount of One Acre	Total Amount of Valluation	D C 38 Cts
William Wright Jur	200	0.1.8	12.10.0	0.16
Ditto	230	0.5.0	57.10.0	0.74

This record reflects the sale of 170 acres of land by Franklin County Deed 3/462 and confirms 1830 William Wright as the grantor of that deed.

The 1799 Personal Property Tax List for Franklin County, Virginia, listed William Wright, Jr., with the following household on March 19:

	Persons Names	White Tithes	Blacks Over 16	Blacks Under 16
March 19	Wm Wright Jr.	2	1	-

Horses	Studs	Licenses	D C
3	-	-	- 80

The 1799 Land Tax List for Franklin County, Virginia, listed Wm Wright Junr with the following property:

Persons Names Owning Land	Number of Acres	Value of One Acre	Total Amount of Valuation	D C @ 48 Cts
Wm Wright Junr	200	0.1.8	12.10.0	0.20

The 1800 Personal Property Tax List for Franklin County, Virginia, listed William Wright, Jr., with the following household:

		White Tithes	Blacks Over 16	Blacks Under 16
Apr 5	William Wright Jr.	1	1	-

Horses	Stud Horses	Rates p person	License	Dollars Cents
3	-	-	-	- 80

The 1800 Land Tax List for Franklin County, Virginia, listed William Wright Jrs with the following property:

Persons Names Owning Land	Number of Acres	Amount of One Acre	Total Amount of Valuation	D C
William Wright Jrs	200	0.1.8	12.10.0	0.20

On December 24, 1800, at Franklin County, Virginia, Survey Book _/105 a survey of 15-1/2 acres was recorded for William Wright:

"Franklin County the 24th of December 1800

Surveyed for William Wright 15-1/2 acres on the branches of Gills Creek by Virtue of a Land office Treasury Exchange warrant Granted of Stephen Smith Assee of Hugh French the 11 day of June 1801 No 110 Conts 94 Acres Begining at a Small Hickry on his Own Line thence With Earleys line S 72 West 52 po to a Gum Corner of Rays thence With his line So 28 East 28 po to a White Oak S 10 East 46 po to a White Oak on Wrights thence With his Line No 16 East 92 po to the Begining

William Greer asst to
Ste. Smith SFC"

The 1801 Personal Property Tax List for Franklin County, Virginia, listed Capt. William Wright with the following property:

		White Tithes	Blacks Over 16	Blacks Over 12 + 16
May 2	Capt. William Wright	1	1	-

Horses &c &c	Stud Horses	Rates pr Season	Roding(?) Chairs	Dollars Cents
1	-	-	-	- 56

The 1801 Land Tax List for Franklin County, Virginia, listed William Wright Jr with the following property:

Persons Names Owning Land	No. of Acres	Amount of One Acre	Total Amount of Valuation	D C
William Wright Jr	200	0.1.8	12.10.0	0.20

The 1802 Personal Property Tax List for Franklin County, Virginia listed one William Wright with the following household on April 10:

	Persons Names	White Tithes	Blacks Over 16	Blacks Over 12 & Under 16
April 10	William Wright	2	1	-

Horses &c &c &c	Stud Horses	Rates p Season	Store License	Dollars Cents
3	-	-	-	- 80

The 1802 Land Tax List for Franklin County, Virginia, listed William Wright Jr with the following property:

Persons Names Owning Land	No. of Acres	Amount of One Acre	Total Amount of Valuation	D C
William Wright Jr	200	0.1.8	12.10.0	0.20

On November 3, 1802, at Patent Deed 51/200 William Wright patented 15-1/2 acres of land:

> "James Monroe Esquire Governor of the Commonwealth of Virginia to all to whom these presents shall come greeting Know Ye that by vitue of an exchanged Treasury Warrant Number Eleven hundred and eight issued the eleventh of June Eighteen hundred and one There is granted by the said Commonwealth unto William Wright a Certain tract or parcel of land containing Fifteen and a half acres by Survey bearing date twenty fourth day of August Eighteen hundred and one, lying and being in the County of Franklin and bounded as followeth to Wit: Beginning at a small hickory in his own line, thence with Earleys line South Seventy two degrees West fifty two poles to a gum Corner of Rays thence with his line South twenty eight degrees East twenty eight poles to a white oak South ten degrees East forty six poles to a white oak of Wrights thence with his line North Sixteen degrees East ninety two poles to the beginning. With its appurtenances to have and to hold the said tract or parcel of land with its appurtenances to the said William Wright and his heirs forever. In Witness whereof the said James Monroe Esquire Governor of the Commonwealth of Virginia hath hereunto set his hand and caused the lesser Seal of the said Commonwealth to be affixed at Richmond on the third day of November in the Year of our Lord One thousand eight hundred and two and of the Commonwealth the twenty seventh.
>
> James Monroe"

This is the same land as that surveyed in Franklin County S.B. _/105.

The 1803 Personal Property Tax List for Franklin County, Virginia listed Captain William Wright with the following household on April 15:

	Persons Names	White Tithes	Blacks Over 16	Blacks Under 16 & Over 12
April 15	Capt. William Wright	3	2	-

Horses, Mares & Colts	Stud Horses	Rate per Season	Merchant License	Dollar Cents
4	-	-	-	1 36

The 1803 Land Tax List for Franklin County, Virginia, listed William Wright Junr with the following property:

Persons Names Owning Land	No. of Acres	Amount of One Acre	Total Amount of Valuation	D C
William Wright Junr	200	0.1.8	12.10.0	0.20
Same	235	0.2.0	23.10.0	0.38
Same	250	0.1.6	18.15.0	0.30

The 1804 Personal Property Tax List for Franklin County, Virginia, listed Captn William Wright with the following household on May 7:

Date of Recving lists	Persons Names Owning Property	White Tithes	Blacks Ov 16	Blacks 12 & 16
May 7	Captn William Wright	3	2	-

Horses	Stud Horses	Rate per Season	Merchant License	Taxes
5	-	-	-	1 48

The 1804 Land Tax List for Franklin County, Virginia, listed William Wright Jr with the following property:

Persons Names Owning Land	No. of Acres	Amount of One Acre	Total Amount of Valuation	Tax D C
William Wright Jr	200	0.29	41.68	0.20
Same	250	0.25	62.50	0.30
Same Paternal	15½	.25	3.87	0.02

This record reflects the patent of 15-1/2 acres of land by Patent Deed 51/200.

The 1805 Personal Property Tax List for Franklin County, Virginia, listed William Wright with the following household on August 8:

	Persons Names	White Tithes	Blacks Over 16	B under 16 & O. 12
Augt 8	William Wright	3	2	-

Horses	Studs	Rate per Season	Merchant License	Taxes
2	-	-	-	1 12

The 1805 Land Tax List for Franklin County, Virginia, listed William Wright Jur with the following property:

Persons Names That Own Land	No. of Acres	Amount of One Acre D C	Total Amount of Valuation D C	Tax D C
William Wright Jur	200	0.29	42.00	0.20
Same	250	0.25	62.50	0.30
Same	15½	0.25	3.87	0.20

The 1806 Personal Property Tax List for Franklin County, Virginia, listed William Wright with the following household on May 5:

date of B under Receiving Lists	Persons Names Owning Property	White tithes	B: Over 16	16 & over 12
May 5	William Wright	1	2	-

Horses	Studs	Rate per Season	Merchant License	Tax
2	-	-	-	1 12

The 1806 Land Tax List for Franklin County, Virginia, listed William Wright Cap with the following property:

Persons Names That Own Land	No. of Acres Land	Amt of One Acre D C	Total Amount of Valuation D C	Tax D C
William Wright Cap	200	0.29	42.00	0.20
Same	250	0.25	62.50	0.30
Same	15½	0.25	3.87	0.02

The 1807 Personal Property Tax List for Franklin County, Virginia, listed William Wright Sr. with the following household on April 6:

Date of Receiving Lists	Persons Names that Own Property	White Tithes	Blacks over 16	blacks under 16
Apr 6	William Wright Sr	2	2	

Horses	Studs	Rate of Season	Merchant License	Tax
4				1.36

The 1807 Land Tax List for Franklin County, Virginia, listed William Wright Jr with the following property:

Persons Names That Own Land	No. of Acres	Amt of One Acre	Total Amount of Valuation	Tax
William Wright Jr	200	0.29	42.00	0.20
Same	250	0.25	62.50	0.30
Same	15½	0.25	3.87	0.02

On September 7, 1807, at Franklin County, Virginia, D.B. 5/376 William Wright purchased 291 acres of land from Duvall Crowel:

> "This Indenture this 7th day of Sepr. one thousand eight hundred & seven between Duvall Crowel of Franklin County of the one part and William Wright of the said County of the other part Witnesseth that the said Duvall Crowel and Julian his wife for and in consideration of the sum of two hundred and ten pounds to them in hand paid the Recet whereof is hereby acknowledged hath granted bargain'd & sold and by these presence do grant bargin & sell unto the said William Wright one certain tract or parcel of Land containing 291 acres lying and being in the County of Franklin on the head Branches of Gills Creek and bounded as followeth Viz. Begining at a chesnut oak on the top of a mountain thence with the patent line North 19 Degrees West 20 poles to a dogwood North 67 degrees West 90 poles to a poplar South 46 degrees West 16 poles to a Linn North 44 degrees West 34 poles to a chesnut North 45 degrees West 10 poles to a popler North 92 poles to a pine North 70 degrees East 20 poles to a hickory South 77 degrees East 22 poles to a dogwood South 85 degrees East 38 poles to a Gum North 7 degrees West 24 poles to a hickory East 90 poles to Moraviana Road on a Ridge thence down the highest part of said Ridge as it

meanders 231 to Jubal Early's corner Black oak thence with William Wright's line South 87 degrees West 37 poles to a chesnut oak South 37 degrees West 36 poles to a Gum and hickory S 8 degrees East 76 poles to Slones line thence with the same to Early's & Wrights dividing line thence along the dividing to the Begining to have and to hold the above granted Land premises with appurtainances to the same belonging with the Reverser and Reversers Remainder & Remainders and each and every part and parcel thereof unto the said William Wright his heirs and assigns forever and the said Duvall Crowel & Julian his wife do covenant grant and Agree to and with the said William Wright his heirs and assigns that they the said Duvall Crowel and Julian his wife for them their heirs &c the above granted Land & premises unto the said William Wright his heirs and assigns shall and will warrent and forever Defend from them the said Duvall Crowel and Julian his wife their heirs and assigns and from all other persons whatever. In Witness whereof they the said Duvall and Julian have hereunto set their hands & Seals the day and year first above Written

Signed and delivered) Duvall Crowell
in presents of) Julian Crowl
Teste
John Dodd)
William Curtain)
John Campbell)

At a Court held for Franklin County September 7th 1807

This Indenture of bargain and sale between Duvall Crowel and Julian his wife of the one part and William Wright of the other part was acknowledged by the said Duvall Crowel and Julian his wife - the said Julian being first privily examined according to Law voluntarily relinquished her right of dower in and to the Land and premisses conveyed by the said Indenture which is ordered to be recorded

Teste,
James Callaway C.F.C."

On June 28, 1808, at Franklin County, Virginia, W.B. 4/100 William Wright, Jr., acted as a witness to the will of Francis Halley.

The will of 1809 William Wright dated October 10, 1808, and probated on January 2, 1809, at Franklin County, Virginia, W.B. 1/368 has an ambiguous clause that requires his grandson Enoch Wright to provide for a William Wright:

". . . .Item I give and bequeath unto my grand son Enoch Wright all my Land and plantation where I now live and all my stock and firneture To him and his heirs for ever and the sd. Enoch shall find the sd. William with all things that is need full during his life. . . ."

A possible implication would be that the grandson was to provide for the William Wright who was a son of 1809 William. The more probable reading is that the grandson was to provide for his grandfather William Wright and the gift of land in the will was made on that understanding.

On January 11, 1809, at Franklin County, Virginia, D.B. 5/680 William Wright, Sr., and James Wright sold 200 acres of land to John Vinson:

> "This Indenture made this 11" day of January 1809 by and between William Wright Senr. & James Wright both of Franklin County of the one part & John Vinson of the said County of the other part Witnesseth that the sd. William Wright Senr. & James Wright for and in consideration of 100 dollars current money of Virginia to him in hand paid the receipt hereof he doth hereby acknowledge hath given granted bargained & sold, and by these presents doth give grant bargain sell deliver & confirm unto the said John Vinson his heirs & assigns forever, a certain Tract or parcel of Land Containing 200 acres more or less lying & being in the county of Franklin on the south side of Maggottee Creek and bounded as followeth to wit: Begining at a post oak on the top of the ridge near the cart road, thence along Millers old line to a black oak corner in Millers & Browns dividing thence along said line to Maggottee Creek, thence up the Creek as it meanders to a corner Walnut Vinson & Wrights dividing line thence along the same to the Begining Together with the reversion & reversions, remainder and every part & part & parcel thereof To have & to hold the above granted land & premises with appurtenances previledges profits & advantages thereunto belonging or any wise appertaining unto the said John Vinson his heirs & assigns forever, and the said William Wright Senr. & James Wright doth for themselves & their heirs covenant grant & agree to & with the said John Vinson and his heirs & assigns that they the said William Wright Senr. & James Wright and their heirs the above granted Land and premises with appertenances unto the said John Vinson his heirs & assigns shall and will by these presents warrant & forever defend In Witness whereof the sd. William Wright Senr & James Wright hath hereunto set their hands & affixt their seals the day & year above written.
>
> William Wright
> James Wright"

1830 William Wright was described in this deed as "Senr." because of the death of his father 1809 William Wright prior to January 2, 1809.

The 1809 Personal Property Tax List for Franklin County, Virginia, listed William Wright with the following household:

date of Rec Lists	Persons Names that own Property	Whites	B over 16	Blacks over 12
	William Wright	2	2	-

Horses				Tax
5	-	-	-	1 48

The 1809 Land Tax List for Franklin County, Virginia, listed William Wright Jr with the following property:

Persons Names That Own Land	Amount of Acres	Amt of One Acre	Total Amount Of Valuation	Tax
William Wright Jr	200	0.29	42.00	0.20
Same	250	0.25	62.50	0.30
Same	15½	0.25	3.87	0.02
Same	291	.38	109.16	0.53

This record reflects the purchase of 291 acres of land by Franklin County Deed 5/376.

The 1810 Personal Property Tax List for Franklin County, Virginia, listed William Wright with the following household:

	Persons Names that own Property	Whites	Black over 16	B over 12 & under 16
	William Wright	2	2	-

Horses				Tax
5	-	-	-	1 48

The 1810 Land Tax List for Franklin County, Virginia, listed William Wright S with the following property:

Persons Names That Own Land	Amount of Land	Amot of One Acre	Amount Of Vallueation	Tax
William Wright S	200	0.29	42.00	0.20
Same	250	0.25	62.50	0.30
Same	15½	0.25	3.87	0.02
Same	291	0.38	109.16	0.53

This record reflects the redesignation of 1830 William Wright as "S" for "Senior" from "Jr." following the death of his father 1809 William Wright.

The 1810 Census for Franklin County, Virginia, listed two William Wrights, one of whom was 1854 William Wright of Campbell County and the other of whom was 1830 William Wright with the following household:

Name of Head of Family	Free White Males	Age	Free White Female	Age	All Other Free Persons	Slaves
William Wright	1	45+	1	45+		4
	1	26-45	1	26-45		
	2	16-26	2	16-26		
			1	10-16		

This record indicates that 1830 William Wright was born before 1765.

The 1811 Personal Property Tax List for Franklin County, Virginia, listed William Wright with the following household on April 1:

Date of Receivg Lists	Persons Names that Own Property	White tithes	Blacks over 16 years	Blacks over 12 & under 16 years
Aprl 1	William Wright	3	2	1

Horses	___	___	___	Tax D C
5	-	-	-	1 92

The 1811 Land Tax List for Franklin County, Virginia, listed William Wright Snr

with the following property:

Persons Names That Own Land	No. of Acres	Amount of One Acre	Total Amount Of Valuation	Tax
William Wright Snr	200	0.29	42.00	0.20
Same	250	0.25	62.50	0.30
Same	15½	0.25	3.87	0.02
Same	291	0.38	109.16	0.53

The 1812 Personal Property Tax List for Franklin County, Virginia, listed William Wright with the following household:

____	Persons Names that own property	White tithes	Blacks over 16 years	Blacks under 16 & over 12
	William Wright	3	2	1

Horses	___	___	____	Tax
4	-	-	-	1 80

The 1812 Land Tax List for Franklin County, Virginia, listed William Wright with the following property:

Persons Names That Own Land	No. of Acres	A Description and Situation of Each Tract of Land	Amount of One Acre	Total Amount Of Valuation	Tax
William Wright	200	on gills Creek	0.29	42.00	0.20
Ditto	250		0.25	62.50	0.30
Ditto	15½		0.25	3.87	0.02
Ditto	291		0.38	109.16	0.53

The 1813 Personal Property Tax List for Franklin County, Virginia, listed William Wright with the following household:

____	Persons Names that own property	White tithes	Blacks over 16	Blacks over 12 & under 16
	William Wright	3	2	1

Horses	___	___	___	Tax
5	-	-	-	2 57

The 1813 Land Tax List for Franklin County, Virginia, listed William Wright with the following property:

Persons Names That Own Land	No. of Acres	Description & Situation of Each Tract	Amount of One Acre	Total Amount Of Valluation	Tax
William Wright	200	on G Creek	0.29	42.00	0.27
Same	265½		0.25	66.37	0.43
Same	291		0.38	109.16	0.71

The 1814 Personal Property Tax List for Franklin County, Virginia, listed William Wright with the following household:

___	Persons names that own property	White tithes	Blacks over 16	Blacks 12 & under 16
	William Wright	3	2	1

Horses	Griss Merchant Mills	Rent	Saw Mills	Rent	Forges	Valu-ation
6	-	-	-	-	-	-

Cariages	Valu-ation	Stud Horses	Rate per Season	___	Valu-ation	___
-	-	-	-	-	-	-

Valu-ation	Free negroes & Mulatoes	Merchant License	_____	_____
-	-	-	-	3 63

The 1814 Land Tax List for Franklin County, Virginia, listed William Wright with the following property:

Name Of Owner	Residence	Estate	Number of Town Lots	Name of the Town
Willian Wright	in Franklin	fee Simple		
Same	" "	" "		
Same	" "	" "		

Yearly Rent of Lots	Amount of Tax on Lots	No of Acres of Lots	Description of Land
		200	Gills Creek
		250	Joining
		291	Joining

Distance & Baring from the Court House	Rate of Land [er Acre	Total Valua-tion of Land	Amount of Tax on Land	Total Amount of Tax on Land and Lots	Explanation of Alterations During the Preceding Year
15N	.29	42.00	.36	.36	
15N	.25	65.52	.53	.53	
15N	.38	109.16	.93	.93	

The land of 1830 William Wright of Franklin County was described in the patent deeds and grant deeds as partly on the south side of Maggotty Creek and as on the head branches of Gills Creek. The Land Tax List placed these lands approximately 15 miles north of the courthouse at Rocky Mount.

The 1815 Personal Property Tax List for Franklin County, Virginia, listed William Wright with the following household:

Dates of Receiving lists from individuals	Persons Names Charged with the Tax	No of white males above 16 years old
	William Wright	3

Slaves over 9 and und 12 years old	over 12 years old	above 16 years old	Horses Mules mares & Colts	Stud Horses No	Rate of Covering mares	no of head of Cattle
	5	4	6			16

Carrages 2 wheel riding Carrages	Pheatons & Stage Waggons	Publick Stages	all other 4 Wheel Carrag	Mills	Tole bridges & Ferrys

Tax Yeards	Free Male negros above 16 & under 45 years old	Watches Silver	Single Case Gold	Double Case Gold	Livery Stables	Houses in the Cuntry

Ice House for private use	from Which Ice is Sold	Clocks Works of Wood W out Case	Works of Wood With Case	Works of Metal	of Vallu between 50 & 100	over $100

Coal Pitts	Printers	Furniture Bureau & Bed Steds of Mahogany	Picturs & Glasses	Bureau & Book Cases	Total Pitchers and Decanters	Amount of Tax D C
						5.74

The 1815 Land Tax List for Franklin County, Virginia, listed William Wright with the following property:

Names Of Owner	Residence	Estate	No of Acres of Land	Description of Land
William Wright	Franklin	Fee Simp	200	Gills Creek
Same	Same	Same	250	Joining
Same	Same	Same	291	Joining

Distance an Baring from the Court House	Rate of Land Per Acre	Total Vallua-tion of Land	Amount of Tax on Land	Explanation of Conveyances During the Preceding Year
15N	.29	42.00	.36	
15N	.25	62.52	.53	
15N	.38	109.16	.93	

The 1816 Personal Property Tax List for Franklin County, Virginia, listed William Wright with the following household:

Dates of Receiving lists from individuals	Persons Names Chargeable the Tax	No of white males above 16 years old
_ 4	William Wright	3

no of Slaves above 12 years old	No of Horses	Stud Horses No $ Cts	2 wheeled riding Carriages & harness belonging thereto Not Exceeding in Value $100	Exceeding in Vallue $100
5	6	-	-	-

Phaetons Slay Waggons & harness belonging thereto		Coaches & Harness belonging thereto			
Not Exceeding in Vallue $200	Exceeding in Vallue $200	Not Exceeding in Vallue $300	Exceeding in Vallue $300	Total Amount of Taxes $ Cts	
-	-	-	-	4.58	

The 1816 Land Tax List for Franklin County, Virginia, listed William Wright with the following property:

Names Of Owner	Residence	Estate	No of Acres	Description of Land
William Wright	Franklin	in fee	200	Gills Creek
Ditto	"	in fee	250	Joining
Ditto	"	in fee	291	Joining

Distance an Bearing from the Court House	Rate of Land Per Acre	Total Valuation of Land	Amount of Tax on Land	Explanation of Conveyances During the Preceding Year
15N	.29	42.00	.32	
15N	.25	62.52	.47	
15N	.38	109.16	.82	

On July 16, 1816, at Franklin County, Virginia, D.B. 7/441 William Wright purchased all of the interest of Rachel Sanforde in the estate of Harkman Doran:

> "This Indenture made this 16th day of July 1816, between James Slone attorney in fact for Rachel Sanforde of the one part, and William Wright of the other part, Witnesseth that the said James Slone attorney in fact for Rachel Sanforde for and in consideration of the sum of one hundred and thirty five Dollars to him in hand paid, the Receipt whereof is hereby acknowledged, hath given, granted, bargained and Sold and by these Presents, doth give, grant, bargain and Sell, unto the said William Wright his heirs and assigns for ever all the Interest right and title which the said Rachel Sanforde has or may have in the estate of Harkman Doran decd late of the County of Franklin whether the same be real or personal which shall or may be coming to the said Rachel Sanforde as a Daughter and one of the Legatees of the said Harkman Doran Decd and all right which the said Rachel Sanforde had to a part of Land lying in Franklin County on which said Harkman Doran in his life time resided lying on the waters of Gills Creek adjoining the Lands of William Wright, Peter Abshire and others and is hereby transfered from James Sloan as attorney in fact as aforesaid to the said

William Wright and his heirs and assigns for ever the meaning and intention of this Indenture is to place the said William Wright precisely in the situation of the said Rachel Sanforde so that at the distribution of the estate of the said Harkman Doran Decd both of Land Negroes, Horses, cattle, hogs, sheep, household and kitchen furniture and Plantation utencils, that portion of which would have been assigned to the said Rachel Sanforde becomes the property of the said William Wright and his heirs and assigns for ever, and the said William Wright is hereby authorised to take such steps as may be necessary to effect a division of the said estate both real and personal either in Law or equity so that the same be at his own proper costs and charges and when a division shall take place to hold and enjoy whatever shall be collected for him by virtue of this deed free from the claim or claims of her the said Rachel Sanforde her heirs or assigns, executors and administrators. In Witness whereof the said James Slone attorney in fact for Rachel Sanforde have hereto set his hand and Seal the day and year first within Written.

his
James X Slone
mark
attorney in fact for
Rachel Sanforde

At the Clerks office of Franklin County July 16th, 1816.

This Indenture of Bargain and Sale between James Slone attorney in fact for Rachel Sanforde of the one part, and William Wright of the other part, was acknowledged by the said James Slone & admitted to be recorded.

Teste
Caleb Tate, C.F.C."

The 1817 Personal Property Tax List for Franklin County, Virginia, listed William Wright with the following household on April 12:

Date of Receiving lists from individs	Persons Names Chargeable With the Tax	No of white males above 16
Apl 12	William Wright	2

No of Slaves above 12 years old	No of head of Horses	Stud Horses No of	Stud Horses Rate per Season	2 wheel riding Carriages & harness Not Exceeding in Vallue $100	2 wheel riding Carriages & harness Exceeding in Vallue $100
5	5	-		-	-

Phaetons Slays Wagons & harness Not Exceeding in Vakkye $200	Phaetons Slays Wagons & harness Exceeding in Vallue $200	Coaches & Harness Not Exceeding in Vallue $300	Coaches & Harness Exceeding in Vallue $300	Total Amount of Tax	Proof
-	-	-	-	4.40	

The 1817 Land Tax List for Franklin County, Virginia, listed William Wright with the following property:

Names Of Owner	Residence	Estate	No of Acres	Description of Land
William Wright	Franklin	in fee	200	Gills Creek
Ditto	"	in fee	250	Joining
Ditto	"	in fee	291	Joining

Distance & Baring from the Court House	Rate of Land Per Acre	Total Value of Land	Amount of Tax on Land	
15N	.29	42.00	.32	
15N	.25	62.52	.47	
15N	.38	109.16	.82	

The 1818 Personal Property Tax List for Franklin County, Virginia, listed William Wright with the following household on April 6:

Date of Receiving Lists	Persons Names Chargeable With the Tax	No of white males above 16
April 6	William Wright	2

No Slaves over 16 yrs old	No Slaves over 12 & under 16 yrs old	Studs No of	Studs Rate per Season	2 wheel riding Carages Not exceeding in Vallu $100	2 wheel riding Carages Exceeding in Value $100
5	-	5	-	-	-

Phaetons & Stage Waggons not Exceeding in Vallue $200	Phaetons & Stage Waggons Exceeding in Vallu $200	Total Amount of Tax	Proof
-	-	4.40	

The 1818 Land Tax List for Franklin County, Virginia, listed William Wright with the following property:

Names Of Owners	Residence	Estate	No of Acres	Description of Land
William Wright	Franklin	in fee	200	Gills Creek
Ditto	"	in fee	250	Joining
Ditto	"	in fee	291	Joining

Distance & bearing from the Court House	Rate of Land Per Acre	Total Value of Land	Amount of Tax on Land	
15N	.29	42.00	.32	
15N	.25	62.52	.47	
15N	.38	109.16	.82	

The 1819 Personal Property Tax List for Franklin County, Virginia, listed William Wright with the following household on April 30:

date of Receiving Lists from Individs	Persons Names Chargeable With the Tax	White Males 16 years of age	No of Slaves above 16 years of age
Ap 30	William Wright	2	5

No of Slaves above 12 & under 16 years of age	No of Horses	Stude Horses: No of Studes	Stude Horses: Rate per Season	2 wheel Riding Carrages: Not exceeding in Vallue $100	2 wheel Riding Carrages: Exceeding in Vallue $100
1	4	-	-	-	-

Pheatons & Stage Wagons: Not Exceeding in Vallue $200	Pheatons & Stage Wagons: Exceeding in Vallue $200	Clocks: Not Exceeding in Vallue $300	Clocks: Exceeding in Vallue $300	Total Amount of Tax	Proof
-	-	-	-	4.92	

The 1819 Land Tax List for Franklin County, Virginia, listed William Wright with the following property:

Names Of Owners	Residence	Estate	No of Acres	Description of Land
William Wright	Franklin	in fee	200	Gills Creek
Ditto	"	"	250	Joining
Ditto	"	"	291	Joining

Distance & Bearing from the Court House	Rate of Land Per Acre	Total Value of Land	Amount of Tax on Land	
15N	.29	42.00		
15N	.25	62.52		
15N	.38	109.16		

On February 1, 1819, at Franklin County, Virginia, D.B. 8/120 William Wright appointed James Wright as his attorney in fact to acquire title to 200 acres of land purchased from Absalom Watkins located in Franklin County, Kentucky:

> "Know all men by these presents that I William Wright of Franklin County State of Virginia have made, ordained constituted and appointed, and by these Presents do make, ordain Constitute and Appoint, James Wright of the said County & State my true and lawful attorney for me and in my name, but to my use, to get a right and title in fee simple to a certain tract or parcel of Land purchased by me of a Absalom Watkins of Franklin County State of Kentuckey,

two hundred acres, lying and being in Lincoln County State of Kentuckey, being a part of Tract of granted to John Early of Franklin County State of Virginia, the terms set forth in the title Bond; and after getting a legal Title to the said Land to Sell and dispose of the said Land, on any terms he think proper, to make a legal title to the said Land; and further to do & execute all and every other lawful act and acts needful for the recovering or conveying the title to the said Lands as fully and effectually to all intents and purposes as if I were personally present, hereby ratifying & confirming whatever my said attorney shall lawfully do or cause to be done in or about the Premisses. In Witness whereof I have hereunto set my hand - Seal, this 1st February eighteen hundred and nineteen.

Witness
N. H. Claiborne
George Nafe
Mark R. Taylor

William Wright

Virginia, to wit

At a Court held for Franklin County, February 1st, 1819 This Letter of attorney from William Wright to James Wright was proved by the oath of George Nafe and Mark R Taylor, two of the Witnesses hereto, and ordered to be recorded

Teste,
Caleb Tate C.F.C"

The 1820 Personal Property Tax List for Franklin County, Virginia, listed William Wright with the following household:

Date of Receiving Lists from Individs	Persons Names Chargeable With the Tax	White Males 16 years of age	No of Slaves above 16 years of age
	William Wright	2	8

No of Slaves above 12 & under 16 years of age	No of Horses	Stude Horses: No of Studes	Stude Horses: Rate per Season	2 wheel Riding Carrages: Not exceeding in Vallue $100	2 wheel Riding Carrages: Exceeding in Vallue $100
7	5	-	-	-	-

Pheatons & Stage Wagons		Clocks			
Not Exceeding in Vallue $200	Exceeding in Vallue $200	Not Exceeding in Vallue $300	Exceeding in Vallue $300	Total Amount of Tax	Proof
-	-	-	-	6.50	

The 1820 Land Tax List for Franklin County, Virginia, listed William Wright with the following property:

Names Of Owner	Residence	Estate	Number of Acres of Land	Description of the Land
William Wright	Franklin	in fee	200	Gills Creek
Do	"	"	250	joining
Do	"	"	291	do

Distance and bearing from the Court House	Vallue of Land Per Acre	Sum added to the on account of the Below	Total Vallue	Amount of Tax upon Land	Remarks
15 Miles N	3.38	200.00	676.00	.85	
15 " "	3.38		845.00	1.06	
15 " "	3.38		983.58	1.23	

On about June 5, 1820, at Franklin County, Virginia, D.B. 9/73 William Wright purchased 130 acres of land from Joab Early, Henry Early, and Lamech Early:

> "This Indenture made and entered into this _ day ____ eighteen hundred & twenty between Joab Early, Henry Early, & Lamech Early of Franklin County and State of Virginia of the one part, and Wm Wright of the said County and State of one other part, Witnesseth that the said Joab, Henry & Lamech Hearly for and in consideration of the sum of three thousand weight of Tobacco to them in hand paid by the said Wm Wright the receipt whereof is hereby acknowledged, hath bargained, sold and by these presents doth bargain sell and confirm unto sd Wright a certain tract or parcel of Land lying and being in the aforesaid County on the waters of Maggotty Creek containing one hundred and thirty Acres more or less and bounded as followeth Begining at a Hickory on the Laurel Ridge S 60 West 58 poles to a Red Oak, S 88 West 164 Poles to a Black Gum N 17 East 62 poles to a White Oak N 54 West 40 poles to a Chesnut tree N 20 East 30 poles to a Chesnut tree N 32 West 42 poles to a Black Walnut N 32 East 16 poles to a poplar & Locust N 87 E 50 po. to a White Oak on the Ridge thence on the top of the same as it meanders to the Begining, together with all the appurtenances

priviledges, and every part and parcel thereto belonging or in any wise appertaining to have and to hold the above granted Land & premisses unto the said Wm Wright his heirs and assigns forever and said Joab Early, Henry Early & Lamech Early doth for themselves their Heirs and assigns covenant and agree to and with said Wright and his heirs & assigns that they the said Joab Early, Henry Early & Lamech Early & their heirs & assigns the above granted Land & premisses in an undefeasable fee simple estate unto the sd Wright his heirs and assigns from the claim or demands of all and every person or persons whatsoever shall and will by these presents warrant and forever defend. In witness whereof we have hereunto set our hands & Seals this day & date above written

Jb. Early
Henry Early
Lamech Early

At a Court held for Franklin County June 5th 1820

This Indenture of Bargain and sale between Joab Early Henry Early and Lamech Early of the one part and William Wright of the other part was acknowledged by the said Joab, Henry, and Lamech Early and the same was ordered to be Recorded

Teste,
Caleb Tate, C.F.C."

The 1820 Census for Franklin County, Virginia, listed two William Wrights, one of whom was again 1854 William Wright of Campbell County and the other of whom was 1830 William Wright with the following household:

Names of Heads of Families	Free White Males	Age	Free White Females	Age
William Wright	1	45+	1	45+
	1	16-26	2	26-45
			2	16-26

Foreigners	Number in Agriculture	Number in Commerce	Number in Manufacture
	10		

Male	Age	Slaves Female	Age	Free Colored Males	Age	Free Colored Females	Age	All Other Persons

The 1821 Personal Property Tax List for Franklin County, Virginia, listed William Wright Sr with the following household on April 7:

date of Receiving Lists from Individs	Persons Names Chargeable With Tax	Slaves above 12 years of age	Horses Mares Colts & Mules
April 7	William Wright Sr	9	6

Stude Horses		two wheeled riding and Harness		Phaetons & Stage Wagons & Harness	
No.	Dollars Cts	Not exceeding in Dollar $100	above the Vallue of $100	Not Exceeding in Vallue $200	above the Vallue of $200
-	-	-	-	-	-

Riding Carrages& Harness			
Not Exceeding in Vallue $300	above the Vallue $300	Amount of Tax	
-	-	5._	

The 1821 Land Tax List for Franklin County, Virginia, listed William Wright with the following property:

Names Of Owner	Residence	Estate	Numr of Acres of Land	Description of the Land
William Wright	Franklin	in fee	200	Gills Creek
Ditto	"	"	250	Joining
Ditto	"	"	130	Sorrel Ridge
Ditto	"	"	291	Joining

Distance and bearing from the Court House	Vallue of Land per acre Including Bildings	Sum added to the Land on act of Bildings	Total Vallue of the Land & Bilding	Amount of Tax at the Rate of	Explana- tion _ during the Pre- ceding Year
15 Miles N	3.38	200.00	676.00	.61	
15 " "	3.38		845.00	.77	
15 " "	1.00		130.00	.12	Deed from
15 " "	3.38		983.58	.89	Joab Early

This record reflects the purchase of 130 acres of land by Franklin County Deed 9/73.

On April 16, 1821, at Franklin County, Virginia, D.B. 9/294 William Wright purchased 139 acres of land from Joab Early, Henry Early, and Lamech Early:

> "This Indenture made this 16th day Apl 1821 between Joab Early, Henry Early and Lamech Early of the one part, and William Wright Sr of one other part of Franklin County Witnesseth, that said Joab Henry and Lamech Early for and in consideration of the sum of four hundred and fifty Dollars to them in hand paid the receipt whereof is hereby acknowledged hath given granted bargained and sold and by these presents doth grant bargain sell and confirm unto the said William Wright Sr his heirs and assigns forever one certain tract or parcel of Land lying and being in the County aforesaid on the waters of Gills Creek and containing 139 Acres be the same more or less and bounded as followeth, Begining at a Hickory N 85 W 20 po. to a Gum S 70 W 38 po to a Chesnut, S 58 po to a white Oak, thence down the branch East 38 po. to a Spanish Oak, S 35 E 10 po to a Chesnut, N 83 E 50 po to a Chesnut, S 45 E 70 po to a Poplar & some S 26 East 22 po. to a White Oak N 38 E 4 po. to a Gum, S 16 E 24 po. to a Locust, S 12 W 48 po to a Gum S 75 W 20 po to a Hickory on the Lorrel Ridge thence on the same up as it meanders to a White Oak in the Old line of John and Jubal Early's thence with that line N 87 E 30 po to two Gums and hickory N 72 E 48 po to a White Oak, N 12 W. 28 po. to a Poplar S 83 E 80 po to a White Oak thence to the Begining, together with all and singular the appurtenances unto him the said William Wright Sr his heirs and assigns forever and the said Joab, Henry and Lamech Early, doth hereby warrant and forever defend a good and lawfull right and title in fee simple to the above mentioned land and premisses unto him the said Wm Wright his heirs and assigns forever. In witness whereof we the said Joab Henry and Lamech Early hath hereunto set our hands and seals this day and date above written
>
> Teste) Jb. Early
> Lewis Turnbull) Henry Early
> Patrick Hix) Lamech Early
> Moses Green Jr)

At a Court held for Franklin County May 7th 1821

This Indenture of Bargain and sale between Joab Early, Henry Early and Lamech Early of the one part, and William Wright Senr of the other part was acknowledged by the said Joab, Henry and Lamech Early and ordered to be recorded

Teste
Caleb Tate CFC"

The 1822 Personal Property Tax List for Franklin County, Virginia, listed William Wright with the following household on March 4:

date of Receiving Lists from Individs	Persons Names Chargeable With Tax	Slaves above 12 years of age	Horses Mares Colts and Mules
March 4	William Wright	8	8

Stude Horses		two wheeled riding Carriage & Harndss		Phaetons & Stage wagons & harness	
No.	Dollars Cts	Not exceeding in Dollar $100	above the Value of $100	Not Exceeding in Value $200	above the Value of $200
-	-	-	-	-	-

Riding Carrage & Harness			
Not exceeding in Value $300	above the Value of $300	Amount of Tax	
-	-	5.32	

The 1822 Land Tax List for Franklin County, Virginia, listed William Wright with the following property:

Names Of Owners	Residence	Estate	Number of Acres of Land	Description of the Land
William Wright	Franklin	in fee	200	Gills Creek
Ditto	"	"	250	Joining
Ditto	"	"	130	"
Ditto	"	"	291	"
Ditto	"	"	100	"
Ditto	"	"	139	"

Distance & bearing from the Court House	Value of Land per acre Including the Bildings	Sum added to the Land on act of the Bildings	Total Vallue of the Land & Bilding	Amt of Tax	Explanation of alterations during the Preceding Year
15 Miles N	3.38	200.00	676.00	.61	
15 " "	3.38	"	845.00	.77	
15 " "	1.00	"	130.00	.12	
15 " "	3.38	"	938.58	.89	
15 " "	1.00	"	100.00	.09	fm J. Early
15 " "	1.00	"	139.00	.13	fm J.H. & L. Early

This record reflects the purchase of 139 acres of land by Franklin County Deed 9/294.

The 1823 Personal Property Tax List for Franklin County, Virginia, listed William Wright Sr with the following household on March 20:

date of Receiving Lists from Individs	Persons Names Chargeable With Tax	Slaves above 12 years of Age	Horses Mares Colts & Mules
March 20	William Wright Sr	9	9

Stude Horses			two wheeled riding Carriage & Harness		Phaetons & Stage waggons & Harness	
No.	D	C	Not exceeding in Vallue $100	Exceeding in Vallue Vallue $100	Not exceeding in Vallue $200	exceeding in Vallue $200
-	-		-	-	-	-

Riding Carrage & Harness			
Not exceeding in Vallue $300	above the Vallue of $300	Amount of Tax	
-	-	5.31	

The 1823 Land Tax List for Franklin County, Virginia, listed William Wright with the following property:

Owners Names	Residence	Estate whether held for life or in fee	No. of Acres of Land	Description of Land
William Wright	Franklin	in fee	200	Gills Creek
Ditto	"	"	250	"
Ditto	"	"	130	"
Ditto	"	"	291	"
Ditto	"	"	100	"
Ditto	"	"	139	"

Distance & bearing from the Court House	Value of Land per acre Including Buildings	Sum added to the Land on act of Buildings	Total Vallue of the Land & Buildings	Amount of tax on the value of	Explanation of alterations during the preceding Year
15 Miles N	3.38	200.00	676.00	.55	
15 " "	3.38		845.00	.68	
15 " "	1.00		130.00	.11	
15 " "	3.38		983.58	.79	
15 " "	1.00		100.00	.08	
15 " "	1.00		139.00	.12	

The 1824 Personal Property Tax List for Franklin County, Virginia, listed William Wright S with the following household on April 5:

date of Receiving Lists from Individuals	Persons names Chargeable With Tax	Slaves above 12 years of Age	Horses Mares Colts & Mules
Ap 5	William Wright S	10	10

No. of Studs	Dollars	2 Wheel Riding Carrages	4 wheel Riding and Harness	Amount of Tax
-	-	-	-	5.90

The 1824 Land Tax List for Franklin County, Virginia, listed William Wright with the following property:

Names Of Owners	Residence	Estate Whether held for life or in fee	No of Acres of Land	Description of the Land
William Wright	Franklin	in fee	200	Gills Creek
Ditto	"	"	250	"
Ditto	"	"	130	"
Ditto	"	"	291	"
Ditto	"	"	100	"
Ditto	"	"	139	"

Distance and bear-ing from the Court House	Vallue of Land per acre Including Building	Sum added to the Land on account of Building	Total Value of Land & Buildings	Amount of tax at the Rate of pr	Explanation of alterations during the Pre-ceding Year
15 North	3.38	200.00	676.00	.55	
15 "	3.38	"	845.00	.68	
15 "	1.00	"	130.00	.11	
15 "	3.38	"	983.58	.79	
15 "	1.00	"	100.00	.08	
15 "	1.00	"	139.00	.12	

The 1825 Personal Property Tax List for Franklin County, Virginia, listed William Wright Sr with the following household on February 12:

Date of Receiving Lists from Individuals	Persons names Chargeable With the Tax	Blacks over 12	Horses mares Colts & Mules
Feb 12	William Wright Sr	10	6

Amount of Tax	Carriages & Stallions	Remarks
5.42		

The 1825 Land Tax List for Franklin County, Virginia, listed William Wright with the following property:

Names Of Owners	Residence	Estate Whether held for life or in fee	Number of Acres of Land	Description of the Land
William Wright	Franklin	in fee	200	Gills Creek
Ditto	"	"	250	"
Ditto	"	"	130	"
Ditto	"	"	291	"
Ditto	"	"	100	"
Ditto	"	"	139	"

Distance and bear-ing from the Court House	Vallue of Land per acre Including Building	Sum added to the Land on account of Building	Total Vallue of Land & Buildings	Amount of tax at the Rate of pr	Explanation of alterations during the Pre-ceding Year
15 Miles N	3.38	200.00	676.00	.55	
15 "	3.38	"	845.00	.68	
15 "	1.00	"	130.00	.11	
15 "	3.38	"	983.58	.79	
15 "	1.00	"	100.00	.08	
15 "	1.00	"	139.00	.12	

The 1826 Personal Property Tax List for Franklin County, Virginia, listed William Wright with the following household on March 6:

Date of recg lists from Individuals	Names of persons Chargeable With the Tax	Slaves over 12	Horses &c
March 6	William Wright	12	5

Stallions Carriages &c	Amt of Tax	Proof
-	6.26	

The 1826 Land Tax List for Franklin County, Virginia, listed William Wright Sr with the following property:

Names Of Owners	Residence	Estate Whether held for life or in fee	Number of Acres of Land	Description of the Land
William Wright Sr	Franklin	in fee	200	Gills Creek
Ditto	"	"	250	"
Ditto	"	"	130	"
Ditto	"	"	291	"
Ditto	"	"	100	"
Ditto	"	"	139	"

Distance and bear-ing from the Court House	Vallue of Land per acre Including Building	Sum added to the Land on account of Building	Total Value of Land & Buildings	Amount of Tax	

The 1827 Personal Property Tax List for Franklin County, Virginia, listed William Wright with the following household on April 2:

Date of Receiving List from Individuals	Persons Names Chargeable With the Tax	Slaves over 12 years of age	Horses Mares Colts & Mules
Apl 2	William Wright	11	5

Stud Horses Carriages	The Amount of Tax	
-	5.77	

The 1827 Land Tax List for Franklin County, Virginia, listed William Wright Sr

with the following property:

Names Of Owners	Residence	Estate Whether held for life or in fee	Number of Acres of Land	Description of the Land
William Wright Sr	Franklin	in fee	200	Gills Creek
Ditto			250	
Ditto			130	
Ditto			291	
Ditto			100	
Ditto			139	

Distance and bear-ing from the Court House	Vallue of Land per acre Including Building	Sum added to the Land on account of Building	Total Vallue of Land & Buildings	Amount of Tax	
15N	3.38	200.00	676.00	.55	
	3.38		845.00	.68	
	1.00		130.00	.11	
	3.38		984.08	.79	
	1.00		100.00	.08	
	1.00		139.00	.12	

On June 2, 1827, at Franklin County, Virginia, D.B. 12/113 William Wright and Caty his wife sold to Patrick Hix their interest in a lot acquired from the Hartman Doran estate:

> "This Indenture made the 2d day of June in the year 1827 between William Wright and Caty his wife of Franklin County and State of Virginia of the one part and Patrick Hix of the County and State aforesaid of the other part Witnesseth that the said William Wright and Caty his wife in consideration of one hundred and twenty five dollars of lawful money of this Commonwealth to them in hand paid by the said Patrick Hix at or before the ensealing and delivery of these presents the receipt whereof is hereby acknowledged have bargained and sold and by these presents do and each of them doth bargain and sell the said Patrick Hix his heirs and assigns all there right and title and interest in the Land belonging to the estate of Hartman Doran desd. Towit Lot No 1st laying at lower end, To have and to hold said Land with the Tenements hereditaments and all and singular other the premises herein before mentioned or intended to be bargained and sold and every part and parcel thereof with every of there rights,

members, and appurtenances unto the said Patrick Hix, his heirs and assigns forever and the said William Wright and Caty his wife for themselves and there heirs the Said Land with all and Singular the premises and appurtenances before mentioned unto the said Patrick Hix his heirs and assigns free from the claim or claims of them the said William Wright and Caty his wife or either of them, their or either of their Heirs and of all and every person or persons whatsoever, shall will and do warrant and forever defend by these presents. In witness whereof the said William Wright and Caty his wife have hereunto set their hands and seals the day and year above written

William Wright
her
Caty X Wright
mark

Franklin County Towit, We Joab Early and John Wade justices of the peace in the County aforesaid, do hereby certify that Caty Wright the wife of William Wright parties to a certain Deed bearing dated on the 2d day of June, ahd hereunto annexed personally appeared before us in our County aforesaid and being examined by us privily and apart from her husband and having the Deed aforesaid fully explained to her she the said Caty Wright acknowledged the same to be her act and Deed and declared that she had willingly signed sealed and delivered the same and that she wished not to retract it. Given under our hands and seals this 2d June 1827

Jb. Early JP
John H. Wade"

The 1828 Personal Property Tax List for Franklin County, Virginia, listed William Wright S with the following household on February 4:

Date of Receiving list from individuals	Persons Names Chargeable With the Tax	Slaves over 12 years of age	Horses Mares Colts & Mules	Amount of Tax
Feb 4	William Wright S	8	5	4.36

The 1828 Land Tax List for Franklin County, Virginia, listed William Wright Senr with the following property:

Names Of Owners	Residence	Estate Whether held for life or in fee	Number of Acres of Land	Description of the Land
William Wright Senr	Franklin	in fee	200	Gills Creek
Ditto			250	
Ditto			130	
Ditto			291	
Ditto			100	
Ditto			139	

Distance and bear-ing from the Court House	Vallue of Land per acre Including Building	Sum added to the Land on account of Building	Total Vallue of Land & Buildings	Amount of Tax on Land	Explanation of alterations During the preceding Year
15N	3.38	200.00	676.00	.55	
	3.38		845.00	.68	
	1.00		130.00	.11	
	3.38		984.00	.79	
	1.00		100.00	.08	
	1.00		139.00	.12	

The 1829 Personal Property Tax List for Franklin County, Virginia, listed Wm. Wright Sr with the following household on February 25:

Date of Re-ceiving list	Persons Names Charable With Tax	______	Negroes over 12	Horses &c &c &c
Feby 25	Wm. Wright Sr	8	-	6

_____	Amount of Tax	_____
-	3.80	

The 1829 Land Tax List for Franklin County, Virginia, listed William Wright Sr with the following property:

Names Of Owners	Residence	Estate whether Fee for life &c	Number of Acres	Situation of Land
William Wright Sr	Franklin	Fee	200	Gills C
"	"	"	250	"
"	"	"	130	"
"	"	"	291	"
"	"	"	100	"
"	"	"	139	"

Distance and bear-ing from the Court House	Value of Land Pr Acre including Build-ings &c	Sum added to the Value of the Land on account of Improve-ments &c	Total Value of Land & Im-provements	Amount of Tax on Land	Explanation of alterations During the pre-ceding Year
15 N	3.38	200.00	676.00	.55	
"	3.38	"	845.00	.68	
"	1.00	"	130.00	.11	
"	3.38	"	984.08	.79	
"	1.00	"	100.00	.08	
"	1.00	"	139.00	.12	

The 1830 Personal Property Tax List for Franklin County, Virginia, listed Wm. Wright Estate with the following household on February 24:

Date	Persons Names Chargeable With Tax	Negroes over 12 years		
Feby 24	Wm. Wright Estate	8	-	-

Horses &c &c &c		Dollars Cents	Proff
6		3.28	

The 1830 Land Tax List for Franklin County, Virginia, listed William Wright Sen with the following property:

Names Of Owners	Residence	Estate whether in Fee or for life	Number of Acres	Situation of Land
William Wright Sen	Franklin	Fee	200	Gills C
"	"	"	250	"
"	"	"	130	"
"	"	"	291	"
"	"	"	100	"
"	"	"	139	"

Distance from C House	Bearing from C House	Value of Land Per Acre, including Buildings	Sum added to Value of Land for Improvements	Total Value of Land & Improvements
15	N	3.38	200.00	676.00
"	"	3.38	"	845.00
"	"	1.00	"	130.00
"	"	3.38	"	984.08
"	"	1.00	"	100.00
"	"	1.00	"	139.00

Amount of Tax on Land	Explanation of Alterations during the preceding Year
.55	
.68	
.11	
.79	
.08	
.12	

The will of William Wright was dated February 12, 1825, probated on February 1, 1830, at Franklin County, Virginia, W.B. 3/251, and provided as follows:

"I William Wright of Franklin County and State of Virginia do hereby make my Last Will and Testament in manner and form following that is to say 1st I Desire that my Just Debts and funeral expences be paid by my executors herein after named 2nd after the payment of my Debts and funeral Ecpences I give to my Wife Catharine Wright as much of the land on the Tract where I now live as she thinks proper to make use of during her natural life time and three negroes (to wit) Henry Fellice and Hannah During her life allso all the Stock of Horses Cattle Sheep and Hogs for her to Dispose of as She thinks proper at her death but it is to be understood that the Land that my wife is to make us of is goto my Son William Wright, at the Death of my said Wife, 3d I give to my Daughter Nancy Wright a tract or parcel of land Known by the of Crowls place Begining on the top of the Mountain at a chesnut oak corner thats mentioned in Crowls old deed thence down the ridge to a White oak that stands the road between Duvalt and Henry Crowls old place marked and Branded with W thence a North East Cours to the Middle fork of Gills creek thence down the creak as it meanders to Earleys line also eight negroes, to wit, Ama, Sarah, Harriet, Agee, Mary, Ceejor, Joshua & Lea and there increse to her and her Heirs and Assigns forever, 4th I give to my Daughter Rhoda Wright a tract or parcil of Land parte Known by the name Henry Crowls place Begining at the above named Chesnut oak corner thence down the main ridge to Earley Corner white Oak and Locus Stake Branded with W. W. on the road near the negroe field also one and a half part of the negroes that is coming to me out of the Estate of Hartmon Doran Decd and one negro fellow named Joe to her and to her heirs and assigns forever. 5th I give unto my Daughter Miram Wright one and a half shear of the part that is coming to me out the negros of the Estate of Hartmon Doran Decd also four hundred & Dollars to be paid to her by Daughter Nancy Wright & Rhoda Wright and Son William Wright Equally of the parts give to them. I give unto my Daugher Milley Shorewatter one part of the Land and Negroes coming to me out the Estate of Hartmon Doran Decd and Negro named Frank, I give unto my Son William Wright one certain tract or parcel of Land known by the name of the old place to Begining at a Chesnut oak Corner on the top of the Bue Ridge thence with a straight line to a Hickry Corner on the Sorrel ridge and three Negroes Mary James & Marean to him and to his heirs and assigns forever. My Son George Wright has received his part therefore I leave him nothing. My Son James Wright has received one thousand Dollars therefore he is to have now more of my Estate. I give unto my Son John Wright and my Daughter Polly Smith and Hiram Wright the Balance of my Land not heretofore Disposed of to be Equally Divided between them as they may think proper. And Lastly I do constitute and and appoint my Son William Wright Executor of this my last Will and Testament hereby Revoking all other or former Wills or Testaments by me heretofore made in Witness Whereof I have hereunto set my hand and affixed my seal this 12 day of February in the year of our Lord 1825

Signed and Sealed and published & Declared in presence of us   William Wright
Mosses Greer Jr
William Wright (Son of James)

At a Court for Franklin county held at the Courthouse the first day of February 1830. This last Will and Testament of William Wright deceased was produced in court and proved by the Oathe of Moses Greer Junior and William Wright (son of James) the subscribing Witnesses and ordered to be recorded, and on the motion of William Wright the Executor herein named, who took the Oath prescribed by Law and together with John Wright, Joseph Showatter, and James Wright, his securities executed bond in the penalty of five thousand dollars conditioned according to Law, certificate is granted him for obtaining a Probat in due form

Teste
Caleb Tate CfC"

From that will the following family of 1830 William Wright can be identified:

Wife: Catharine Wright

Children: William Wright
Nancy Wright
Rhoda Wright
Miram Wright
Milley (Wright) Shorewatter
George Wright
James Wright
John Wright
Polly (Wright) Smith
Hiram Wright

Grandson: William Wright, son of James Wright

The 1830 Census for Franklin County, Virginia, listed Nancy Wright as the head of a household with a female aged 70 to 80. Since Nancy Wright had been bequeathed real property by her father, this household was probably that of Nancy, the daughter of 1830 William, and the female aged 70 to 80 was probably Catherine (Doran) Wright, indicating a date of birth between 1750 and 1760.

The 1831 Land Tax List for Franklin County, Virginia, listed Catherine Wright and 1830 William Wright's children with the following property:

Names Of Owners	Residence	Estate whether in Fee or for life	Number of Acres	Situation of Land
Catherine Wright	Franklin	Life	200	Gills C.
"	"	"	250	"
Rhoda Wright	Franklin	Fee	145½	Gills C
Nancy Wright	Franklin	Fee	145½	Gills C.
Jno Wright & Hiram & Polly Smith	Franklin	Fee	130	Gills C.
"	"	"	100	"
"	"	"	139	"
William Wright	Franklin	Fee	200	
	Already charged to Catherine Wright			
"	"	"	250	
	Already charged to Catherine Wright			

Distance from Ct House	Bearing from Ct House	Value of Land Per Acre, including Buildings	Sum added to Value of Land for Improvement	Total Value of Land & Improvements
15	N	3.38	200.00	676.00
"	"	3.38	"	845.00
15	N	3.38	200.00	491.79
15	N	3.38	200.00	491.79
15	N	1.00	200.00	130.00
"	"	1.00	"	100.00
"	"	1.00	"	139.00

Amount of Tax	Explanation of alterations during the preceding year
.55	From Wm Wright decd. by will
.68	Same
.40	Same) 291 acre tract
.40	Same) 291 acre tract
.11	Same
.08	Same
.12	Same
	Same
	Same

<u>Genealogy Of John J. Wright Of Virginia, Indiana and Kansas</u> by John Calvin Wright stated that William Wright was a son of 1809 William Wright of Franklin County and Mary (Williams) Wright, was born about 1751 or 1752 at Fauquier County, Virginia, married Catharine Doran, died in 1830 at Franklin County, Virginia, and was buried at Franklin County, that Catharine (Doran) Wright was a daughter of Hartman Doran, was born about 1752 or 1753, and died between 1830 and 1832 at Franklin County, Virginia, and that 1830 William Wright and Catharine (Doran) Wright had the following children:

1) William Wright, born about 1773 at Franklin County, Virginia,
2) Mary "Polly" Wright, born about 1777 or 1778 at Franklin County, Virginia,
3) John Wright, born about 1780 at Franklin County, Virginia,
4) George Finney Wright, born about 1784 or 1785 at Franklin County, Virginia,
5) Hiram Wright, born about 1788 or 1789 at Franklin County, Virginia,
6) Mildred "Milly" Wright, born about 1791 or 1792 at Franklin County, Virginia,
7) James Wright, born about 1792 or 1793 at Franklin County, Virginia,
8) Rhoda Wright, born about 1793 or 1794 at Franklin County, Virginia,
9) Nancy Wright, born about 1800 at Franklin County, Virginia,

10) Miriam Wright, born about 1802 at Franklin County, Virginia,

However, John Calvin Wright incorrectly listed 1839 John A. Wright of Franklin County as a son of 1845 John Wright of Franklin County. As will be set forth below, 1839 John A. Wright was a son of 1830 William Wright.

Fourth Generation:

1839 John A. Wright Of Franklin County, His Wife Elizabeth (Abshire) Wright, And His Descendants

1839 John A. Wright of Franklin County was a son of 1830 William Wright and Catharine (Doran) Wright. (1809 William[1], 1830 William[2])

In his letter dated June 14, 1979, Mr. William Pullen enclosed a copy of the Family Bible of John A. Wright, now owned by the Virginia Historical Society. Mr. Pullen had referred to that Bible in his pamphlet Virginians and Hoosiers: Abshires, Hustons, and Wrights, Bedford, Franklin, Virginia and Union, Hamilton Counties, Indiana, 1977. That Family Bible provided as follows:

Page 1:

"John Wright December 26, 1810

James Mitchell was born October the 18th Day in year of Ninety-Four"

Page 2:

"John A. Wright

John Wright and Elizebeth his Wife was married 11th of february 1800 and there first born Child polley was born 29th of march 1801

Nancey Wright was born october 17th day 1803

Skelton Wright was born 27th of December 1805

Right W. Wright ws born january 30 1808

Matthew Wright was born 11th of aprile 181[0?]

John burrel Wright [____] (?) was born 18th day of March 1812

Ome Wright was born 3 day of May 1814

Asa Wright was born 26 day of March 1816

Rody Wright was born 1 day of february = 1818

William H. Wright son of John & Betsey was Born the 11th of December 1819

―――

february 13 Day James Wright Washington was Born in the year of 1823

Lewis Wright was born 7th day of July 1826

I(?)oty Wright was born March 4th 1829

Teste: Gabriel Swanson

Page 3:

"Right Wright [unreadable]

Joh[_]n[ ]abshire

Meredith Pate october the 30 1839

Oatey Wright and Caroline Pearson was married November the 29, 1855"

Page 4:

"ould mises polly James Died on 18 Day of January 1838

kitty Wright formerly kitty simmons Died the 7 Day of July 1839 Sunday

[remaining sentence unreadable]"

Page 5:

"Oatey Wright was born the [__]th 1828
Caroline Frances Wright was born February the 20 1836
Mary Elizabeth Wright was born September the 16 1856
Sally Ann Wright was born April 8 1858
John Otey Wright was born January the 4 1860
George Robert Wright was born September the 8 1862"

Page 6:

"Hiram Wright Children
Mehala Wright was born the 27th may 1810
Catherine Wright was born the 10th April 1812
July Wright was Born the 8th July 1813
Costalow H. Wright was Born 15 Day April 1815
Calvin Wright was Born the 24 march 1817

Washington Nunlys and Rody his wife first born child Elizabeth Mary was born 28 July 1836

William H was 6 Day Novem 1838"

The entry on the first page regarding John Wright was apparently the date of purchase, especially since the entries through Matthew Wright on the second page all seem to have been written at the same time. The entry on the first page regarding James Mitchell was not identifiable to Mr. Pullen. As will be set forth more fully below, the entries on the second page seem to be a clear identification of the children of John A. and Elizabeth Wright.

Mr. William Pullen tentatively identified this John A. Wright as the son of 1815 Joseph Wright of Bedford County, based on the fact that 1815 Joseph Wright had a son John Wright and both had children with similar names. Each had children named Right Wright and Matthew Wright, as well as a daughter Nancy. However, that identification is incorrect. As will be set forth below, the Franklin County Land Tax Lists and Personal Property Tax Lists clearly identify this John A. Wright as the son of 1830 William Wright of Franklin County.

There is other evidence as well that argues against the identification of 1839 John A. Wright of Franklin County as a son of 1815 Joseph Wright of Bedford County and in favor of his identification as a son of 1830 William Wright of Franklin County. That evidence is the following:

First, John Wright, the son of 1815 Joseph Wright, was identified in Bedford County, Virginia, Deeds 7/559 and 7/560 dated November 5, 1816, as then residing in Montgomery County. There is no indication that 1839 John A. Wright of Franklin County ever resided in Montgomery County and it would seem unusual for him to have lived in Franklin County, Virginia, for most of his life, to have moved to Montgomery County just before or at the time of sale of 1815 Joseph Wright's land, and then move back again to Franklin County.

Second, the John A. Wright Family Bible had entries which associate him with the family of 1830 William Wright of Franklin County, who had a son John. Those entries include the following:

Page 4:

. . . .

kitty Wright formerly kitty simmons Died the 7 Day of July 1839 Sunday
. . . ."

Keziah (Simmons) Wright was the wife of George Wright, a son of 1830 William Wright of Franklin County and a grandson of 1809 William Wright of Franklin County.

Page 6:

"Hiram Wright Children
Mehala Wright was born the 27th may 1810
Catherine Wright was born the 10th April 1812
July Wright was Born the 8th July 1813
Costalow H. Wright was Born 15 Day April 1815
Calvin Wright was Born the 24 march 1817
. . . ."

Hiram Wright was a son of 1830 William Wright of Franklin County and the listing above is of his children. It would seem to be highly unusual for 1839 John A. Wright of Franklin County to list the children of someone unrelated to him in his Family Bible, which would be the case if 1839 John A. Wright were the son of 1815 Joseph Wright. On the other hand, it would not be unusual for 1839 John A. Wright to record the births of his brother's children, which would be the case if he were the son of 1830 William Wright. This evidence I think strongly argues the 1839 John A. Wright was a son of 1830 William Wright of Franklin County.

Third, a number of members of the family of 1839 John A. Wright moved to Indiana, as did some other descendants of 1830 William Wright, but no such proximity in Indiana has yet been found for the descendants of 1815 Joseph Wright.

With regard to the family of 1839 John A. Wright, there are the following Indiana connections. Nancy Wright, the daughter of 1839 John A. Wright, married Pendleton Wright, the son of 1843 George Wright of Franklin County and the grandson of 1809 William Wright of Franklin County. As indicated, Pendleton Wright died in 1864 in Hamilton County, Indiana. Right W. Wright, a son of 1839 John A. Wright, died in 1877 in Hamilton County, Indiana. Matthew W. Wright, a son of 1839 John A. Wright died on February 20, 1865, at Hamilton County, Indiana. John Burrell Wright, a son of 1839 John A. Wright, resided in 1850 in Hamilton County, Indiana. Finally, Lewis Wright, a son of 1839 John A. Wright, resided on January 18, 1860, at Tippecanoe County, Indiana.

With regard to the descendants of 1809 William Wright of Franklin County, there are the following Indiana connections. Enoch Wright, a grandson of 1809 William Wright, resided on September 2, 1831, and until about 1851 in Elkhart County, Indiana. Oliver S. Wright, a possible but as yet unproved grandson of 1809 William Wright, resided in 1833 through 1848 at Kosciusko County, Indiana.

The marriage bond of John Wright and Elizabeth Abshire was dated on February 8, 1800, at Franklin County, Virginia, with Lodowick Abshire as surety:

> "Know all men by these presents that we John Wright & Lodowick Abshire are held & firmly bound unto James ____ Esq Governor of the State of Virginia in the Sum of ____ Dollars to which paymt Well and truly to be made we bind ourselves our heirs &c firmly by these presents Sealed with Our Seals & dated this 8th day of February 1800. The Condition of the above obligation is Such that whereas there is a marriage shortly Intended to be had & solemnized between the above bound John Wright & Elizabeth Abshire Now if there shall be no lawfull Cause to obstruct the same then the above Obligation to be Void else to remain in full force power & Virtue
>
> John Wright
>
> his
> Lodowick X Abshire
> mark"

In his booklet Virginians and Hoosiers, William E. Pullen identified this Elizabeth Abshire as the daughter of Lodowick or Luke Abshire (Apshear, Abshear) and Christina (McGrady or possibly McGown) Abshire, based on his will probated on April 5, 1821, at

Franklin County, Virginia, W.B. 2/603 and court orders in 1822 in Franklin County, Virginia, Court Order Book 24/84, 24/89, 24/91, and 24/101.

The 1801 Personal Property Tax List for Franklin County, Virginia, listed William Wright John son with the following household on May 2:

		White Tithes	Blacks Over 16	Blacks Over 12 + 16
May 2	William Wright John son	1	-	-

Horses &c &c	Stud Horses	Rates pr Season	Roding(?) Chairs	Dollars Cents
-	-	-	-	- -

Although the entry suggests that William Wright was the taxpayer, the 1802 List indicates that John Wright was the taxpayer. However, as set forth above in connection with 1859 William Wright of Muhlenberg County, Kentucky, this may have been a listing for William Wright, the son of 1845 John Wright of Franklin County.

The 1802 Personal Property Tax List for Franklin County, Virginia, listed John Wright W Son with the following household on August 18:

	Persons Names	White Tithes	Blacks Over 16	Blacks Over 12 & Under 16
August 18	John Wright W Son	1	-	-

Horses &c &c &c	Stud Horses	Rates p Season	Store License	Dollars Cents
1	-	-	-	- 12

The 1803 Personal Property Tax List for Franklin County, Virginia, listed John Wright Wm Son with the following household on August 6:

	Persons Names	White Tithes	Blacks Over 16	Blacks Under 16 & Over 12
August 6	John Wright Wm Son	1	-	-

Horses, Mares & Colts	Stud Horses	Rate per Season	Merchant License	Dollar Cents
1	-	-	-	- 12

On September 22, 1803, at Franklin County, Virginia, D.B. 7/225 John Wright purchased 120 acres of land from William and Sarah Brown:

> "This Indenture made this 22d day of September 1803 Between William Brewer of the County of Franklin of the one part and Sarrah his wife of the other part Witnesseth That for and in consideration of the Sum of fifty five pounds seven Shillings and seven pence half penny current money of Virginia to him in hand paid the receipt whereof is hereby acknowledged hath granted Bargaind and Sold and by these present do grant bargain Sell and Confirm unto the said John Wright his heirs &c one certain Tract or parcel of Land lying and being in the County aforesaid Containing one hundred and Twenty Acres be the same more or less and Bounded as followeth to wit Bordering on both sides of Maggotty Creek, Beginning at a sorrel and White Oak in Wrays and Browns line Thence lines of agreement a Straigh Line to a Branch on a corner White oak in Browns old line thence along that line to Browns old corner Persimmon Tree and White Oak Bush, Thence through the plantation of said Brown Samuel Huston being a dividing between said Huston and said Brown to a Chesnut Tree near the Creek in the mouth of Samuel Hustons Land Thence a straight Line north to Brown & Wrights corner White Oak near the crooked Run thence around the said Browns old Lines on the Eastward and lower end of his Land from thence to the first Begining To have and to hold the said Bargained Land and Premises to the said John Wright his heirs &c the said William Brown and Sarah his wife do warrant and for ever defend unto the said John Wright his heirs &c a good and Lawful right and Title in fee simple against him the said William Brown and Sarah his wife and against the Claim or demand of all persons or person whatsoever In

Witness whereof the said William Brown and Sarah his wife have hereunto Set their hands and Seals the day and date above written.

Signed Sealed & delivered   William Brown
in presence of
Samuel Huston
Thomas Wright
Edward Abshire
Joab Dodd
Guy Smith

At a Court held for Franklin County February 6th 1804

This Indenture of Bargain and Sale Between William Brown of the one part, and John Wright of the other part, was proved by the oath of Samuel Huston and Thomas Wright two of the witnesses hereto. And at a Court held for said County January 2d 1815. The said Indenture was further proved by the oath of Edward Abshire another witness hereto, and ordered to be recorded.

Teste,
Caleb Tate, C.F.C"

The 1804 Personal Property Tax List for Franklin County, Virginia, listed John Wright W son with the following household on August 11:

Date of Recving lists	Persons Names Owning Property	White Tithes	Blacks Ov 16	Blacks 12 & 16
Aug 11	John Wright W son	1	-	-

Horses	Stud Horses	Rate per Season	Merchant License	Taxes
1	-	-	-	- 12

The 1804 Land Tax List for Franklin County, Virginia, listed John Wright Jur per William Brown with the following property:

Persons Names Owning Land	No. of Acres	Amount of One Acre	Total Amount of Valuation	Tax D C
John Wright Jur per William Brown	120	1.00	120.00	0.62

This record reflects the purchase of 120 acres of land by Franklin County Deed 7/225.

The 1805 Personal Property Tax List for Franklin County, Virginia, listed John Wright WS with the following household on May 4:

	Persons Names	White Tithes	Blacks Over 16	B under 16 & O. 12
May 4	John Wright WS	1	-	-

Horses	Studs	Rate per Season	Merchant License	Taxes
2	-	-	-	- 24

The 1806 Personal Property Tax List for Franklin County, Virginia, listed John Wright Jur with the following household on May 24:

date of B under Receiving Lists	Persons Names Owning Property	White tithes	B: Over 16	16 & over 12
May 24	John Wright Jur	1	-	-

Horses	Studs	Rate per Season	Merchant License	Tax
2	-	-	-	- 24

The 1806 Land Tax List for Franklin County, Virginia, listed John Wright Jur with the following property:

Persons Names That Own Land	No. of Acres Land	Amt of One Acre D C	Total Amount of Valuation D C	Tax D C
John Wright Jur	120	1.00	120.00	0.60

The 1807 Personal Property Tax List for Franklin County, Virginia, listed John Wright Wm son with the following household on May 4:

Date of Receiving Lists	Persons Names that Own Property	White Tithes	Blacks over 16	blacks under 16
May 4	John Wright Wm son	1		

Horses	Studs	Rate of Season	Merchant License	Tax
2				.24

The 1807 Land Tax List for Franklin County, Virginia, listed John Wright Jur with the following property:

Persons Names That Own Land	No. of Acres	Amt of One Acre	Total Amount of Valuation	Tax
John Wright Jur	120	1.00	120.00	0.60

On February 14, 1807, at Franklin County, Virginia, D.B. 5/332 John Wright purchased 50 acres of land from James Wright:

> "This Indenture made this 14th day of Feby 1807 by and between James Wright of Franklin County of the one part and John Wright of the said County of the other part Witnesseth, that the said James Wright for and in consideration of 120 pounds to him in hand paid the Receipt hereof he doth hereby acknowledge hath given granted Bargained and Sold and by these Presents doth give grant Bargain Sell deliver and confirm unto John Wright his heirs and assigns forever, a certain tract or parcell of land containing 50 acres more or less lying in Franklin County on both sides of Maggottee Creek and bounded as follows begining at a white oak corner in Millers old line thence along said line N 75 degrees West 54 poles to a Red oak thence N 34 West 70 poles to a Red oak then South 82 De West 80 poles to a corner white oak in the sd line made by agreement thence

agreement line near a South course to the Creek, thence up the Creek as it meanders to the mouth of a small branch, thence up the same as it meanders to the fork and up the left hand fork to Vinsons old path, and thence along the path to the top of the Ridge to the old cart Road thence along the same as it meanders to the point of the Ridge thence along the agreement line between Wright and Vinson to the Creek, thence down the Creek as it meanders to Bowns old line, thence Along the same line North 20 De East 100 poles to the Begining, together with Reversion and Reversions Remainder and Remainders and every part and parcell thereof to have and to hold the above granted land and premises within appertenances priviledges profit and and advantages thereunto belonging or any wise appertaining unto the said John Wright his heirs and assigns for ever and the said James Wright doth for himself and his heirs covenant grant and agree to and with the said John Wright and his heirs the above granted land and premises with appertenances shall and will by these Presents warrant and forever defend in Witness whereof the said James Wright hath hereunto set his hand and affixt his seal the day and year above written.

Witness — James Wright

Geo. Wright)
Hiram Wright) — Peggy her X mark Wright
William Brown)

At a Court held for Franklin County April 6th 1807.

This Indenture of bargain and Sale between James Wright of the one part and John Wright of the other part was acknowledged by the said James Wright & ordered to be recorded

Teste,
James Callaway CFC"

The 1809 Personal Property Tax List for Franklin County, Virginia, listed John Wright WS with the following household:

date of Rec Lists	Persons Names that own Property	Whites	B over 16	Blacks over 12
	John Wright W S	1	-	-

Horses				Tax
4	-	-	-	- 48

The 1809 Land Tax List for Franklin County, Virginia, listed John Wright Jur with the following property:

Persons Names That Own Land	Amount of Acres	Amt of One Acre	Total Amount Of Valuation	Tax
John Wright Jur	120	1.00	120.00	0.60
Same	50	.84	42.00	0.20

This record reflects the purchase of 50 acres of land by Franklin County Deed 5/332.

The 1810 Personal Property Tax List for Franklin County, Virginia, listed John Wright WS with the following household:

____	Persons Names that own Property	Whites	Black over 16	B over 12 & under 16
	John Wright WS	1	-	-

Horses	___	___	____	Tax
5	-	-	-	- 60

The 1810 Land Tax List for Franklin County, Virginia, listed John Wright Jur with the following property:

Persons Names That Own Land	Amount of Land	Amot of One Acre	Amount Of Vallueation	Tax
John Wright Jur	120	1.00	120.00	0.60
Same	50	.84	42.00	0.20

The 1810 Census for Franklin County, Virginia, listed three John Wrights, one of whom was listed as John Wright, Sr., and was 1845 John Wright of Franklin County, the second of whom was listed as John Wright, Jr., and was 1848/50 John Wright of Muhlenberg County, Kentucky, a son of 1845 John Wright of Franklin County, and the third of whom had the following household:

Name of Head of Family	Free White Males	Age	Free White Female	Age	All Other Free Persons	Slaves
John Wright	1	26-45	1	16-26		
	2	16-26	1	10-16		
	3	0-10	1	0-10		

This record indicates that 1839 John A. Wright and Elizabeth (Abshire) Wright were born between 1765 and 1784 and is consistent with the Family Bible of John A. Wright listed above:

Female aged 10-16	Mary "Polly" (Wright) Abshire, born on March 29, 1801, at Virginia,
Female aged 0-10	Nancy (Wright) Wright, born on October 17, 1803,
Male aged 16-26	Probably a brother of of 1839 John A. Wright working on his farm,
Male aged 16-26	Probably a brother of of 1839 John A. Wright working on his farm,
Male aged 0-10	Skelton Wright, born on December 27, 1805, at Virginia,
Male aged 0-10	Right W. Wright, born on January 30, 1808,
Male aged 0-10	Matthew W. Wright, born on April 11, 1810, at Franklin County, Virginia.

The 1811 Land Tax List for Franklin County, Virginia, listed John Wright Jur with the following property:

Persons Names That Own Land	No. of Acres	Amount of One Acre	Total Amount Of Valluation	Tax
John Wright Jur	120	1.00	120.00	0.60
Same	50	.84	42.00	0.20

The 1812 Personal Property Tax List for Franklin County, Virginia, listed John Wright Jr with the following household:

	Persons Names that own property	White tithes	Blacks over 16 years	Blacks under 16 & over 12
	John Wright Jr	1	-	-

Horses				Tax
2	-	-	-	- 24

The 1812 Land Tax List for Franklin County, Virginia, listed John Wright Jur with the following property:

Persons Names That Own Land	No. of Acres	A Description and Situation of Each Tract of Land	Amount of One Acre	Total Amount Of Valuation	Tax
John Wright Jur	120	on maggotty Creek	1.00	120.00	0.60
Ditto	50		.84	42.00	0.20

The 1813 Personal Property Tax List for Franklin County, Virginia, listed John Wright J with the following household:

	Persons Names that own property	White tithes	Blacks over 16	Blacks over 12 & under 16
	John Wright J	1	-	-

Horses				Tax
4	-	-	-	- 64

The 1813 Land Tax List for Franklin County, Virginia, listed John Wright J with the following household:

Persons Names That Own Land	No. of Acres	Description & Situation of Each Tract	Amount of One Acre	Total Amount Of Valuation	Tax
John Wright J	120	Magoty	1.00	120.00	0.80
Same	50		0.84	42.00	0.27

The 1814 Personal Property Tax List for Franklin County, Virginia, listed John

Wright Jur with the following household:

___	Persons names that own property	White tithes	Blacks over 16	Blacks 12 & under 16
	John Wright Jur	1	-	-

Horses	Griss Merchant Mills	Rent	Saw Mills	Rent	Forges	Valuation
2	-	-	-	-	-	-

Cariages	Valuation	Stud Horses	Rate per Season	___	Valuation	___
-	-	-	-	-	-	-

Valuation	Free negroes & Mulatoes	Merchant License	______	_______
-	-	-	-	- 42

The 1814 Land Tax List for Franklin County, Virginia, listed John Wright Jur(?) with the following property:

Name Of Owner	Residence	Estate	Number of Town Lots	Name of the Town
John Wright Jur(?)	in Franklin	fee Simple		
Same	" "	" "		

Yearly Rent of Lots	Amount of Tax on Lots	No of Acres of Lots	Description of Land
		120	Magoty
		50	Joining

Distance & Baring from the Court House	Rate of Land per Acre	Total Valua-tion of Land	Amount of Tax on Land	Total Amount of Tax on Land and Lots	Explanation of Alterations During the Preceding Year
12N	1.00	120.00	1.02	1.02	
12N	.84	42.00	.35	.35	

The 1815 Personal Property Tax List for Franklin County, Virginia, listed John Wright J with the following household:

Dates of Receiving lists from individuals	Persons Names Charged with the Tax	No of white males above 16 years old
	John Wright J	1

Slaves				Stud Horses		
over 9 and und 12 years old	over 12 years old	above 16 years old	Horses Mules mares & Colts	No	Rate of Covering mares	no of head of Cattle
			3			15

Carrages					
2 wheel riding Carrages	Pheatons & Stage Waggons	Publick Stages	all other 4 Wheel Carrag	Mills	Tole bridges & Ferrys

		Watches				
Tax Yeards	Free Male negros above 16 & under 45 years old	Silver	Single Case Gold	Double Case Gold	Livery Stables	Houses in the Cuntry

Ice House		Clocks				
for private use	from Which Ice is Sold	Works of Wood W out Case	Works of Wood With Case	Works of Metal	of Vallu between 50 & 100	over $100

Coal Pitts	Printers	Furniture: Bureau & Bed Steds of Mahogany	Picturs & Glasses	Bureau & Book Cases	Total Pitchers and Decanters	Amount of Tax D C
						1._

The 1815 Land Tax List for Franklin County, Virginia, listed John Wright Jur with the following property:

Names Of Owner	Residence	Estate	No of Acres of Land	Description of Land
John Wright Jur	Franklin	Fee Simp	120	Maggoty

Distance an Baring from the Court House	Rate of Land Per Acre	Total Vallua-tion of Land	Amount of Tax on Land	Explanation of Conveyances During the Preceding Year
12N	1.00	120.00	1.02	

This record reflects a disposition of the 50 acre tract of land, but no recorded document has been found regarding this transfer.

The 1816 Personal Property Tax List for Franklin County, Virginia, listed John Wright Jur with the following household on March 4:

Dates of Receiving lists from individuals	Persons Names Chargeable the Tax	No of white males above 16 years old
March 4	John Wright Jur	1

no of Slaves above 12 years old	No of Horses	Stud Horses No $ Cts	2 wheeled riding Carriages & harness belonging thereto: Not Exceeding in Vallue $100	Exceeding in Vallue $100
-	4	-	-	-

Phaetons Slay Waggons & harness belonging thereto		Coaches & Harness belonging thereto			
Not Exceeding in Vallue $200	Exceeding in Vallue $200	Not Exceeding in Vallue $300	Exceeding in Vallue $300	Total Amount of Taxes $ Cts	
-	-	-	-	.72	Gigg 0.50

The 1816 Land Tax List for Franklin County, Virginia, listed John Wright Jur with the following property:

Names Of Owner	Residence	Estate	No of Acres	Description of Land
John Wright Jur	Franklin	in fee	120	Magoty

Distance an Bearing from the Court House	Rate of Land Per Acre	Total Vallua-tion of Land	Amount of Tax on Land	Explanation of Conveyances During the Preceding Year
12N	1.00	120.00	.90	

The 1817 Personal Property Tax List for Franklin County, Virginia, listed John Wright Junr with the following household on March 3:

Date of Receiving lists from individs	Persons Names Chargeable With the Tax	No of white males above 16
March 3	John Wright Junr	1

No of Slaves above 12 years old	No of head of Horses	Stud Horses		2 wheel riding Carriages & harness	
		No of	Rate per Season	Not Exceeding in Vallue $100	Exceeding in Vallue $100
1	2	-		-	-

Phaetons Slays Wagons & harness Not Exceeding in Vallue $200	Exceeding in Vallue $200	Coaches & Harness Not Exceeding in Vallue $300	Exceeding in Vallue $300	Total Amount of Tax	Proof
-	-	-	-	1.06	

The 1817 Land Tax List for Franklin County, Virginia, listed John Wright Junr with the following property:

Names Of Owner	Residence	Estate	No of Acres	Description of Land
John Wright Junr	Franklin	in fee	120	Magoty Creek

Distance & Baring from the Court House	Rate of Land Per Acre	Total Value of Land	Amount of Tax on Land	
12N	1.00	120.00	.90	

The 1818 Personal Property Tax List for Franklin County, Virginia, listed John Wright with the following household on April 22:

Date of Receiving Lists	Persons Names Chargeable With the Tax	No of white males above 16
April 22	John Wright	1

No Slaves over 16 yrs old	No Slaves over 12 & under 16 yrs old	Studs No of	Studs Rate per Season	2 wheel riding Carages Not exceeding in Vallu $100	2 wheel riding Carages Exceeding in Value $100
1	-	4	-	-	-

Phaetons & Stage Waggons			
not Exceeding in Vallue $200	Exceeding in Vallu $200	Total Amount of Tax	Proof
-	-	1.42	

The 1818 Land Tax List for Franklin County, Virginia, listed John Wright jr with the following property:

Names Of Owners	Residence	Estate	No of Acres	Description of Land
John Wright jr	Franklin	in fee	120	Maggoty

Distance & bearing from the Court House	Rate of Land Per Acre	Total Value of Land	Amount of Tax on Land	
12N	1.00	120.00	.90	

The 1819 Personal Property Tax List for Franklin County, Virginia, listed John Wright Jur. with the following household:

date of Receiving Lists from Individs	Persons Names Chargeable With the Tax	White Males 16 years of age	No of Slaves above 16 years of age
__ 1	John Wright Jur.	1	1

No of Slaves above 12 & under 16 years of age	No of Horses	Stude Horses		2 wheel Riding Carrages	
		No of Studes	Rate per Season	Not exceeding in Vallue $100	Exceeding in Vallue $100
-	3	-	-	-	-

Pheatons & Stage Wagons		Clocks			
Not Exceeding in Vallue $200	Exceeding in Vallue $200	Not Exceeding in Vallue $300	Exceeding in Vallue $300	Total Amount of Tax	Proof
-	-	-	-	1.24	

The 1819 Land Tax List for Franklin County, Virginia, listed John Wright Jr with the following property:

Names Of Owners	Residence	Estate	No of Acres	Description of Land
John Wright Jr	Franklin	in fee	120	Magoty

Distance & Bearing from the Court House	Rate of Land Per Acre	Total Value of Land	Amount of Tax on Land	
12N	1.00	120.00		

The 1820 Personal Property Tax List for Franklin County, Virginia, listed John Wright Jur with the following household:

Date of Receiving Lists from Individs	Persons Names Chargeable With the Tax	White Males 16 years of age	No of Slaves above 16 years of age
	John Wright Jur	1	1

No of Slaves above 12 & under 16 years of age	No of Horses	Stude Horses		2 wheel Riding Carrages	
		No of Studes	Rate per Season	Not exceeding in Vallue $100	Exceeding in Vallue $100
1	5	-	-	-	-

Pheatons & Stage Wagons		Clocks			
Not Exceeding in Vallue $200	Exceeding in Vallue $200	Not Exceeding in Vallue $300	Exceeding in Vallue $300	Total Amount of Tax	Proof
-	-	-	-	1.60	

The 1820 Land Tax List for Franklin County, Virginia, listed John Wright Jun with the following property:

Names Of Owner	Residence	Estate	Number of Acres of Land	Description of the Land
John Wright Jun	Franklin	in fee	120	Magoty

Distance and bearing from the Court House	Vallue of Land Per Acre	Sum added to the on account of the Below	Total Vallue	Amount pf Tax upon Land	Remarks
12 Miles N	10.00	300.00	1200.00	1.50	

The 1820 Census for Franklin County, Virginia, listed three John Wrights, one of whom was John Wright, the son of 1854 William Wright of Campbell County, the second of whom was 1845 John Wright of Franklin County, and the third of whom was 1839 John A. Wright with the following household:

Names of Heads of Families	Free White Males	Age	Free White Females	Age
John Wright	1	45+	1	26-45
	1	26-45	2	16-26
	2	10-16	2	0-10
	4	0-10		

Foreigners	Number in Agriculture	Number in Commerce	Number in Manufacture
	3		

Male	Age	Slaves Female	Age	Free Colored Males	Age	Free Colored Females	Age
		1	26-45				
		1	0-14				

All Other Persons

The 1821 Personal Property Tax List for Franklin County, Virginia, listed John Wright Jr with the following household on April 6:

date of Receiving Lists from Individs	Persons Names Chargeable With Tax	Slaves above 12 years of age	Horses Mares Colts & Mules
April 6	John Wright Jr	1	5

Stude Horses		two wheeled riding and Harness		Phaetons & Stage Wagons & Harness	
No.	Dollars Cts	Not exceeding in Dollar $100	above the Vallue of $100	Not Exceeding in Vallue $200	above the Vallue of $200
-	-	-	-	-	-

Riding Carrages & Harness			
Not Exceeding in Vallue $300	above the Vallue $300	Amount of Tax	
-	-	1._	

The 1821 Land Tax List for Franklin County, Virginia, listed John Wright Jur with the following property:

Names Of Owner	Residence	Estate	Numr of Acres of Land	Description of the Land
John Wright Jun	Franklin	in fee	120	Magoty Creek

Distance and bearing from the Court House	Vallue of Land per acre Including Bildings	Sum added to the Land on act of Bildings	Total Vallue of the Land & Bilding	Amount of Tax at the Rate of	Explanation _ during the Preceding Year
12 Miles N	10.00	300.00	1200.00	1.08	

The 1822 Personal Property Tax List for Franklin County, Virginia, listed John Wright Jun with the following household on February 23:

date of Receiving Lists from Individs	Persons Names Chargeable With Tax	Slaves above 12 years of age	Horses Mares Colts and Mules
Febru 23	John Wright Jun	1	4

Stude Horses		two wheeled riding Carriage & Harndss		Phaetons & Stage wagons & harness	
No.	Dollars Cts	Not exceeding in Dollar $100	above the Value of $100	Not Exceeding in Value $200	above the Value of $200
-	-	-	-	-	-

Riding Carrage & Harness			
Not exceeding in Value $300	above the Value of $300	Amount of Tax	
-	-	1.07	

The 1822 Land Tax List for Franklin County, Virginia, listed John Wright Jur with the following property:

Names Of Owners	Residence	Estate	Number of Acres of Land	Description of the Land
John Wright Jur	Franklin	in fee	120	Magoty

Distance & bearing from the Court House	Value of Land per acre Including the Bildings	Sum added to the Land on act of the Bildings	Total Vallue of the Land & Bilding	Amt of Tax	Explanation of alterations during the Preceding Year
12 Miles N	10.00	300.00	1200.00	1.08	

On March 1, 1822, at Franklin County, Virginia, D.B. 9/504 John Wright purchased 300 acres of land from James Saunders:

> "This Indenture made this first day of March in the Year of Christ Eighteen hundred and twenty two, Between James Saunders of the Town of Lynchburg, County of Campbell, and State of Virginia, of the one part, and John Wright of the County of Franklin and State aforesaid of the other part, Witnesseth that the said James Saunders, for and in consideration of nine hundred Dollars of lawful money of this CommonWealth, to him in hand paid by the said John Wright, the receipt whereof is hereby acknowledged hath, bargained and Sold, and by these presents doth bargain and sell unto the said John Wright his heirs and assigns, a certain Tract or parcel of Land, lying and being in the County of Franklin and State of Virginia, upon the waters of Crooked Creek, a branch of Maggotty, containing Three hundred Acres more or less, and bounded as follows, to wit, Begining at a chesnut Tree, thence North 57 Degrees West 78 poles to a chesnutt, North 88 Degrees West 92 poles to a red oak, North 21 Degrees West 68 poles to a White Oak, South 88 Degrees, West 74 poles to a chesnutt Oak, South 54 Degrees West 114 poles to a White Oak, South 58 Degrees, East 136 poles to a red oak, South 88 Degrees, East 196 poles to a post oak North 43 Degrees, East 62 poles a chesnut, and thence North 33 Degrees East 20 poles, to the first station; together with all and singular the appurtunances thereunto belonging or in any wise appertaining To have and to hold the said Tract or parcel of Land, with the tenements and herereditaments, together with all and singular the appurtenances and premises herein conveyed. And the said James Saunders for himself, and his heirs doth covenant and agree to and with the said John Wright and heirs to Warrant and defend the right and title of the said Land against the claim or claims of him the said James Saunders his heirs or assigns and all other persons whatsoever. In Witness whereof the parties have hereunto set their hands and affixed their Seals the day and date first within Written.
>
> Signed, Sealed & delivered) James Saunders
> In the presence of Test)
> Thomas Hale
> James S Mcallister
> Skelton Wright

At the Clerks Office of Franklin County the 3rd day of December 1822.

This Indenture of bargain and Sale, between James Saunders of the one part and John Wright of the other part, was exhibited into the Office and acknowledged by the said James Saunders, and admited to Record.

Teste
Caleb Pate C.F.C."

The 1823 Personal Property Tax List for Franklin County, Virginia, listed John Wright Jur with the following household on March 3:

date of Receiving Lists from Individs	Persons names Chargeable With Tax	Slaves above 12 years of Age	Horses Mares Colts & Mules
March 3	John Wright Jur	1	4

Stude Horses			two wheeled riding Carriage & Harness		Phaetons & Stage waggons & Harness	
No.	D	C	Not exceeding in Vallue $100	Exceeding in Vallue $100	Not exceeding in Vallue $200	exceeding in Vallue $200
-	-		-	-	-	-

Riding Carrage & Harness			
Not exceeding in Vallue $300	above the Vallue of $300	Amount of Tax	
-	-	.95	

The 1823 Land Tax List for Franklin County, Virginia, listed John Wright Jur with the following property:

Owners Names	Residence	Estate whether held for life or in fee	No. of Acres of Land	Description of Land
John Wright Jur	Franklin	in fee	120	Maggotty
Ditto	"	"	300	Mountain

Distance & bearing from the Court House	Value of Land per acre Including Buildings	Sum added to the Land on act of Buildings	Total Vallue of the Land & Buildings	Amount of tax on the value of	Explanation of alterations during the preceding Year
12 Miles N	10.00	300.00	1200.00	1.08	
13 " "	2.50		750.00	.60	fm Jas Saunders pr Deed

This record reflects the purchase of 300 acres of land by Franklin County Deed 9/504.

Before March 4, 1823, at Franklin County, Virginia, Chancery Court, Virginia State Library Reel 295/665, John Wright and Elizabeth (Abshire) Wright with other heirs of Luke Abshire filed a complaint for sale of the decedent's land:

> "To the worshipful Court of Franklin County in chancery Sitting, Humbly complaining sheweth unto your worships your orator's and Oratrix's Peter Abshire, Polly Abshire, Nancey Smith late Nancey Abshire, John Furguson and Susana his wife late Susanna Abshire, Jacob Abshire, Abram Abshire, John Wright and Elizabeth his wife late Elizabeth Abshire, Isaac Abshire, and John Showalter and Catharine his wife late Catharine Abshire children and distributees of Luke Abshire deceased and Sarah Abshire, Luke Abshire, Daniel Wray and Fanny his wife late Fanny Abshire Abram Abshire and Nancey Abshire children and distributees of Edward Abshire deceased who was the son of the aforesaid Luke Abshire deceased and Edward Abshire Abram Abshire William Abshire and children and distributees of John Abshire deceased who was ____ the son of the aforesaid Luke Abshire deceased.
>
> That Luke Abshire the father of your first mentioned complainants and the grand father of your last mentioned complainants departed this life some time in the year of ____ intestate seised of a considerable real estate to wit one tract of land containing 140 acres and one other tract of land containing 20 acres and also possessed of a considerable personal estate. That at the ____ term of your worshipful Court letters of administration were granted by the said court to George Wright senior and William Abshire and that the said G Wright and Abshire then and there took upon themselves the Administration and possessed themselves of the personal estate of the said intestate to the amount of ____ dollars. That your complainants are informed that all the debts of the said estate have been paid and that the administrators are willing that the same should be distributed among the children and representatives of the said Luke Abshire deceased but as a part of the distributees are infants under the age of twenty one years your complainants are informed that the same could legally be done unless by the decree of your worshipful court or some other Court of competent jurisdiction.

And your complainants further shew to your Worships that the aforementioned tracts of land of which the said Luke Abshire died seized are of small value and will not amount to $300.00 to each share and that it will be greatly to the interest of the parties to sell the same and divide the proceeds thereof among the parties according to their respective rights and claims. To the end therefore that the said George Wright Senior and William Abshire Administrators as aforesaid and George Wright senior and ________ his wife late Abshire and William Abshire children and distributees of Luke Abshire deceased Chritic ____ Abshire widow and relict of Luke Abshire deceased and Polly Abshire and Anselem Abshire children and distributees of Edward Abshire deceased who was the son of the aforesaid Luke, which said Polly and Ansolem are infants under the age of twenty one years and children and distributees of John Abshire deceased who was also the son of the aforesaid Luke which said ____ are infants under the age of twenty one years, be made defendants to this bill and compelled to answer the allegations thereof fully and unequivocally, that the said land be sold under the decree of this court and the proceeds thereof be divided among the complainants and others according to their respective rights and claims And that a division of the said personal estate be decreed in like manner and to grant such other and further relief as in equity to your worships may seem meet and finally may it please your worships to grant the commonwealths writ of subpoena commanding &c and your complainants as in duty bound will ever pray &c

Woods A plaintiff

To the worshipful Court of Franklin County in Chancery sitting:

The answer of George Wright senr and William Abshire administrators of Luke Abshire deceased and George Wright and ____ his wife late ____ Abshire and William Abshire children and distributees of Luke Abshire deceased to the bill of complaint exhibited against them in your worshipful court by Peter Abshire and other children and distributees of Luke Abshire deceased and Sarah Abshire and other children and distributees of Edward Abshire deceased and ____ and others the children and distributees of John Abshire decd The said respondants saving and reserving to themselves all benefit of exception to the many errors and imperfections in their said bill contained, for answer thereto or to so much thereof as it is material for them to answer, answereth and sayeth; that true it is that the said Luke Abshire departed this life some time in the year of ____ intestate siesed and possessed of a considerable real and personal estate, and that the sd George Wright and William Abshire took upon themselves the administration, and possessed themselves of the personal estate of the said intestate to the amount of ____ dollars. That it is also true that the debts due from the said estate are very small and inconsiderable, and that as administrators of ____ as children and distributees of the said Luke Abshire decd have they any objection to a division and distribution of the same, provided the distributees that have been advanced by the sd Luke Abshire decd in his life time will bring the same into hotch pot and also provided the sd distributees will enter into bond with sufficient security conditioned for the indemnity of your respondants ____ respondents farther answer that it is also true that the real estate of which the said Luke Abshire died siesed is not of great value, that it will not amount to $300.00 to each share and that it will be to the interest of the parties to sell the same and distribute the proceeds thereof according to their respective rights and claims and having answered the allegations of the sd bill your respondants pray to be dismissed &c and as in duty bound will ever pray &c

To the worshipful court of Franklin COunty in chancery sitting:

The answer of Polly Abshire and Ansolem Abshire children and distributees of Edward Abshire deceased which Polly and Ansolem are infants under the age of twenty one years by George Wright their guardian specially appointed to defend this suit and ____ children and distributees of John Abshire deceased which ____ are infants under the age of twenty one years by George Wright their guardian specially appointed to defend this suit to the bill of Complaint exhibited against them in your worshipful court by Peter Abshire and other children and distributees of Luke Abshire decd These respondants saving and reserving to themselves all benefit of exception from the many errors and imperfections in said bill for answer thereto or to so much thereof as it is material for them to answer answereth and sayeth that it is true that Luke Abshire intestate in the ptffs bill depart this life some time in the year of ____ intestate seised and possessed of a considerable real and personal estate, and that they have been informed that letters of administration were granted by the county court of Franklin to George Wright and William Abshire who as they also have been informed took possession of the personal estate that they are entirely ignorant of the value of either the real or personal estate. And these defendants being infants of tender years submit themselves to the judgement of this worshipful court and humbly hope that what right or title they or either of them have to the said real or personal estate of their grand father or father may be protected and saved to them respectfully and having answered pray to be dismissed &c and as in duty bound will ever pray &c"

The 1824 Personal Property Tax List for Franklin County, Virginia, listed John Wright with the following household on March 1:

date of Receiving Lists from Individuals	Persons names Chargeable With Tax	Slaves above 12 years of Age	Horses Mares Colts & Mules
Mar 1	John Wright	-	6

No. of Studs	Dollars	2 Wheel Riding Carrages	4 wheel Riding and Harness	Amount of Tax
-	-	-	-	1.19

The 1824 Land Tax List for Franklin County, Virginia, listed John Wright Jr. with the following property:

Names Of Owners	Residence	Estate Whe-ther held for life or in fee	No of Acres of Land	Description of the Land
John Wright Jr.	Franklin	in fee	120	Magoty
Ditto	"	"	300	Mount

Distance and bear-ing from the Court House	Vallue of Land per acre Including Building	Sum added to the Land on account of Building	Total Value of Land & Buildings	Amount of tax at the Rate of pr	Explanation of alterations during the Preceding Year
12 north	10.00	300.00	1200.00	.96	
15 "	2.50	"	750.00	.60	

On August 2, 1824, at Franklin County, Virginia, D.B. 11/67 John Wright purchased 93 acres of land from George Wright and Kessiah and Hiram Wright and Elizabeth Wright:

> "This Indenture made this second day of August Eighteen hundred and Twenty four, between George Wright and Kessiah his wife and Hiram Wright and Elizabeth his wife of the County of Franklin of the one part and John Wright of sd. County of the other part witnesseth that the said George Wright and Kessiah his wife and Hiram Wright and Elizabeth his wife for in consideration for the sum of one hundred and twenty pounds, current money of Virginia to them in hand paid the rect. whereof they the sd. George Wright Kessiah his wife and Hiram Wright and Elizabeth his wife doth acknowledge hath given granted bargin and sold and Delivered and by these Presents doth give grant bargain sell and deliver and confirm unto the sd. John Wright his heirs and assigns forever one ceytain tract or parcel of land lying in Franklin County on both sides of Maggotty creek containing Ninety three acres be the same more or less, being part of a grater tract and divided by agreement as followeth, To wit, Begining at Millers white oak Corner sapplin on the North side of the Crooked run, thence along his

line across Maggotty creek thence South fifty five West fifty five poles to a white oak in his line oft South twenty East 80 poles to a white oak North Eighty three East 60 poles to Wrays loin thence along the loin north forty East fifty four poles to his corner white oak and sorrel thence loins of agreement between sd Huston and Brown to the Begining together with all and singler appertanances thereunto belonging or in any wise appertaining to have and to hold the sd. tract or parcel of Land with tenements and hereditaments together with all and Singler the appertenances and premisses herein conveyed and the sd. George Wright and Kessiah his wife and Hiram Wright and Elizabeth his wife for themselfs & there heirs doth covenant and agree to and with the sd. John Wright and his heirs to warrant and defend the right and title of the said Land against the claim or claims of them the said George Wright and Kessiah his wife and Hiram Wright and Elizabeth his wife there heirs or assigns and all other persons whatsoever. In Witness whereof the partys have hereunto set their hands and affixed there seals the day and date first Written

Signed seald. and Deliverd) Hiram Wright
in the preasance of) George Wright
Teste) Elizabeth Wright

Franklin County SC

We Moses Greer Jr & Patrick Hix Justices of the peace in the County aforesaid in the state of Virginia do hereby certify that Elizabeth Wright the wife of Hiram Wright parties to a certain Deed bareing date on the 2nd day of Augt. 1824 and hereunto annexed personally appeared before us in our County aforesaid and being examined privily and apart from her said husband having the Deed aforesaid fully explained to her she the said Elizabeth Wright declared that she had Willingly signed sealed and Delivered the same and that she wish not to retract it. Given under our hands & seals this 27" day of October 1824

Moses Greer Jr
Patrick Hix

At a Court held for Franklin County at the Courthouse on the 1st day of November 1824

This Indenture of bargain and sale between George Wright and Hiram Wright and Elizabeth his wife, of the one part, and John Wright of the other part was acknowledged by the said George Wright and Hiram Wright and together with the certificate hereon endorsed of the relinquishment of dower of the said Elizabeth Wright ordered to be recorded

Teste
Caleb Tate cfc"

The 1825 Personal Property Tax List for Franklin County, Virginia, listed John Wright Jr with the following household on February 28:

Date of Receiving Lists from Individuals	Persons names Chargeable With the Tax	Blacks over 12	Horses mares Colts & Mules
Feb 28	John Wright Jr	1	3

Amount of Tax	Carriages & Stallions	Remarks
.83		

The 1825 Land Tax List for Franklin County, Virginia, listed John Wright Jr. with the following property:

Names Of Owners	Residence	Estate Whether held for life or in fee	Number of Acres of Land	Description of the Land
John Wright Jr.	Franklin	in fee	120	Magodee
Ditto	"	"	300	Mountain
Ditto	"	"	93	Magodee

Distance and bear-ing from the Court House	Vallue of Land per acre Including Building	Sum added to the Land on account of Building	Total Vallue of Land & Buildings	Amount of tax at the Rate of pr	Explanation of alterations during the Preceding Year
12 Miles N	10.00	300.00	1200.00	.96	
15 "	2.50	"	750.00	.60	
12 "	4.50		418.50	.34	pr H & G Wright

This record reflects the purchase of 93 acres of land by Franklin County Deed 11/67.

On July 3, 1825, at Franklin County, Virginia, D.B. 11/620 John Wright, Jr., and Elizabeth his wife sold 120 acres of land to Pleasant Farmer:

"This Indenture made this 3rd day of July 1825 between John Wright Junr & Elizabeth his wife of the one part & Plesant Farmer of the other part Witnesseth that for and in consideration of four hundred and fifty dollars to them in hand paid the receipt whereof is hereby acknowledged have granted bargained and sold and by these Presents doth grant bargain and sell unto Plesant Farmer his heirs and assigns One certain tract or parcel of Land in Franklin County on Crooked branch of Magotty Creek Containing 120 acres be the same more or less & bounded as followeth to Wit Begining at pointers in the old line thence with it South 88 West 31 poles to a chesnut oak South 54 West 140 poles to a white Oak South 58 East 140 poles to a red Oak South 88 East 57 poles to pointers off dividing lines North 24 West 98 poles to a white oak North 51 West 18 poles to a white oak on a ridge thence along the same as it meanders to the Begining Together with all and singular the appurtenances thereunto belonging or in any wise appurtaining To have and to hold the said bargained Land and premises unto him the said Plesant Farmer his heirs and assigns free from the claim of the said John Wrignt Junr and Elizabeth there heirs and assigns or any other person or persons whatsoever shall and will by these Presents Warrant and forever defend In Witness whareof the said John Wright Junr and Elizabeth his wife have hereunto set their hands and seals the day and year first above written

John Wright
Elizabeth Wright

Franklin County Sc.

We John H. Wade and Moses Greer Junr justices of the peace in the County aforesaid in the State of Virginia do hereby certify that Elizabeth Wright the wife of John Wright parties to a certain Deed bearing date on the 3rd day of July 1825 and hereunto annexed personally appeared before us in our County aforesaid and being examined by us privily and apart from her husband and having the deed aforesaid fully explained to her she the said Elizabeth Wright acknowledged the same to be her act and Deed and declared that she had willingly signed sealed and delivered the same and that she wished not to retract it Given under our hands and seals this 31st day of May 1827

John H Wade
Moses Greer Jr

At a Court held for Franklin County the 4th day of June 1827

This Indenture of bargain and sale between John Wright and Elizabeth his wife of the one part and Pleasant Farmer of the other part was acknowledged by the said John Wright and together with the certificate hereon endorsed ordered to be recorded.

Teste
Caleb Tate C.F.C."

The 1826 Personal Property Tax List for Franklin County, Virginia, listed John Wright with the following household on March 27:

Date of recg lists from Individuals	Names of persons Chargeable With the Tax	Slaves over 12	Horses &c
March 27	John Wright	2	4

Stallions Carriages &c	Amt of Tax	Proof
-	1.42	

The 1826 Land Tax List for Franklin County, Virginia, listed John Wright Jr with the following property:

Names Of Owners	Residence	Estate Whether held for life or in fee	Number of Acres of Land	Description of the Land
John Wright Jr	Franklin	in fee	120	Magoty
Ditto	"	"	300	Mountain
Ditto	"	"	93	

Distance and bear-ing from the Court House	Vallue of Land per acre Including Building	Sum added to the Land on account of Building	Total Value of Land & Buildings	Amount of Tax	

The 1827 Personal Property Tax List for Franklin County, Virginia, listed John Wright Jr with the following household on March 5:

Date of Receiving List from Individuals	Persons Names Chargeable With the Tax	Slaves over 12 years of age	Horses Mares Colts & Mules
March 5	John Wright Jr	2	4

Stud Horses Carriages	The Amount of Tax	
-	1.42	

The 1827 Land Tax List for Franklin County, Virginia, listed John Wright Jun with the following property:

Names Of Owners	Residence	Estate Whether held for life or in fee	Number of Acres of Land	Descrip-tion of the Land
John Wright Jun			120	Magoty
Ditto			300	Mountain
Ditto			93	Magoty

Distance and bearing from the Court House	Vallue of Land per acre Includ-ing Building	Sum added to the Land on account of Building	Total Vallue of Land & Buildings	Amount of Tax	
12N	10.00	300.00	1200.00	.96	
15	2.50		750.00	.60	
12	4.50		418.50	.34	

On May 31, 1827, at Franklin County, Virginia, D.B. 11/619 John Wright, Jr., and Elizabeth his wife sold 145 acres of land to Nelson Abshire:

> "This Indenture made this 31st day of May 1827 between John Wright Junr and Elizabeth his wife of the one part and Nelson Absheir of the other part Witnesseth that the said John Wright and Elizabeth his wife for and in consideration of the sum of three hundred and ninety dollars to them in hand paid the receipt whereof is hereby acknowledged have granted bargained and sold and by these Presents doth grant bargain and sell unto him the said Nelson Abshier one certain tract or parcel of Land in Franklin County on the waters of magoty Creek and contains 145 acres more or less and is bounded as followeth To wit Begining at a chesnut tree thence North 88 West 92 poles to a red Oak North 21 West 68 poles to a white oak South 88 West 30 poles to pointers on a ridge thence down the same as it meanders to a white oak South 51 East 18 poles to a white Oak South 24 East 98 poles to pointers South 88 East 138 poles to a post oak North 43 East 62 poles to a chesnut tree North 33 East 20 poles to a chesnut tree North 57 West 78 poles to the Begining To have and to hold the said bargained Land with the appurtenances thereunto belonging or in any wise

appertaining to the only use and behoff of the said Nelson Abshier his heirs and assigns forever free from the claim of them the said John Wright and Elizabeth his wife their heirs and assigns and from every other person or persons whomsoever shall and will by these presents Warrant and forever defend In Witness whereof the said John Wright and Elizabeth his wife have hereunto set their hands and seals the day and year first above written

John Wright
Elizabeth Wright

Franklin County Sc

We John H. Wade & Moses Greer Justices of the peace in the County aforesaid in the State of Virginia do hereby certify that Elizabeth Wright the wife of John Wright parties to a certain Deed bearing date on the 31st day of May 1827 and hereunto annexed personally appeared before us in our County aforesaid and being examined by us privily and apart from her said husband and having the deed aforesaid fully explained to her she the said Elizabeth Wright acknowledged the same to be her act and deed and declared that she had willingly signed sealed and delivered the same and that she wished not to retract it. Given under our hands and seals this 31st day of May 1827

John H. Wade
Moses Greer Jr.

At a Court held for Franklin County the 4th day of June 1827

This Indenture of bargain and sale between John Wright and Elizabeth his wife of the one part and Nelson Abshire of the other part was acknowledged by the said John Wright and together with the certificate hereon endorsed Ordered to be recorded

Teste
Caleb Tate cfc"

The 1828 Personal Property Tax List for Franklin County, Virginia, listed John Wright Ju with the following household on February 17:

Date of Receiv-ing list from Individuals	Persons Names Chargeable With the Tax	Slaves over 12 years of age	Horses Mares Colts & Mules	Amount of Tax	
Feb 17	John Wright Ju	2	4	1.42	

The 1828 Land Tax List for Franklin County, Virginia, listed John Wright Junr with the following property:

Names Of Owners	Residence	Estate Whether held for life or in fee	Number of Acres of Land	Description of the Land
John Wright Junr			120	Magoty Creek
Ditto			93	

Distance and bear-ing from the Court House	Vallue of Land per acre Including Building	Sum added to the Land on account of Building	Total Vallue of Land & Build-ings	Amount of Tax on Land	Explanation of alterations During the preceding Year
12 N	10.00	300.00	1200.00	.96	
12	4.50		418.00	.34	

This record reflects the sale of 265 or 300 acres of land, 120 acres by Franklin County Deed 11/620 and 145 acres by Franklin County Deed 11/619.

The 1829 Personal Property Tax List for Franklin County, Virginia, listed Jno Wright Jr with the following household on February 6:

Date of Receiving list	Persons Names Charable With Tax		Negroes over 12	Horses &c &c &c		Amount of Tax	
Feby 6	Jno Wright Jr	2	-	2	-	1.20	

The 1829 Land Tax List for Franklin County, Virginia, listed John Wright Jr with the following property:

Names Of Owners	Residence	Estate whether Fee for life &c	Number of Acres	Situation of Land
John Wright Jr	Franklin	Fee	120	Magotty C
"	"	"	93	"

Distance and bearing from the Court House	Value of Land Pr Acre including Buildings &c	Sum added to the Value of the Land on account of Improvements &c	Total Value of Land & Improvements	Amount of Tax on Land	Explanation of alterations During the preceding Year
12 N	10.00	300.00	1200.00	.96	
"	4.50	"	418.50	.34	

The 1830 Personal Property Tax List for Franklin County, Virginia, listed Jno Wright Jr with the following household on February 24:

Date	Persons Names Chargeable With Tax	Negroes over 12 years		
Feby 24	Jno Wright Jr	2	-	-

Horses &c &c &c		Dollars Cents	Proff
5		1.10	

The 1830 Land Tax List for Franklin County, Virginia, listed John Wright Jr with the following property:

Names Of Owners	Residence	Estate whether in Fee or for life	Number of Acres	Situation of Land
John Wright Jr	Franklin	Fee	120	Maggotty C
"	"	"	93	"

Distance from C House	Bearing from C House	Value of Land Per Acre, including Buildings	Sum added to Value of Land for Improvements	Total Value of Land & Improvements
12	N	10.00	300.00	1200.00
"	"	4.50	"	418.50

Amount of Tax on Land	Explanation of Alterations during the preceding Year
.96	
.34	

The will of 1830 William Wright dated February 12, 1825, and probated on February 1, 1830, at Franklin County, Virginia, W.B. 3/251 listed John Wright as one of his children:

> ". . . . I give unto my Son John Wright and my Daughter Polly Smith and Hiram Wright the Balance of my Land not heretofore Disposed of to be Equally Divided between them as they may think proper. . . ."

The 1830 Census for Franklin County, Virginia, listed John Wright with the following household:

Names Heads of Families	Free White Males	Age	Free White Females	Age
John Wright	1	50-60	1	40-50
	2	20-30	1	10-15
	2	15-20	1	0-5
	1	10-15		
	1	5-10		
	3	0-5		

Slaves Male	Age	Slaves Female	Age	Free Colored Males	Age	Free Colored Females	Age
1	24-36	1	36-55				
1	0-10	1	10-24				
		1	0-10				

	White Persons included in the foregoing				
Total	Deaf & Dumb Under 14	Deaf & Dumb 14 to 25	Deaf & Dumb 25+	Blind	Aliens - Foreigners & Naturalized
18					

Slaves and Colored Persons, included in the foregoing			
Deaf & Dumb under 14	Deaf & Dumb 14 to 25	Deaf & Dumb 25+	Blind

This record indicates that John A. Wright was born between 1770 and 1780 and that Elizabeth (Abshire) Wright was born between 1780 and 1790.

The 1831 Personal Property Tax List for Franklin County, Virginia, listed John Wright Jr with the following household:

Month Date	Names of Persons chargeable With Tax	Negroes over 12 years		
	John Wright Jr	3	-	-

Horses Mules &c &c		Amount of	
4		.99	

The 1831 Land Tax List for Franklin County, Virginia, listed John Wright Jr with the following property:

Names Of Owners	Residence	Estate whether in Fee or for life	Number of Acres	Situation of Land
John Wright Jr	Franklin	Fee	120	Magotty C
"	"	"	93	"

Distance from Ct House	Bearing from Ct House	Value of Land Per Acre, including Buildings	Sum added to Value of Land for Improvement	Total Value of Land & Improvements
12	N	10.00	300.00	1200.00
"	"	4.50	"	418.50

Amount of Tax	Explanation of alterations during the preceding year
.96	
.34	

The 1831 Land Tax List for Franklin County, Virginia, also listed Jno Wright & Hiram & Polly Smith with the following property:

Names Of Owners	Residence	Estate whether in Fee or for life	Number of Acres	Situation of Land
Jno Wright & Hiram & Polly Smith	Franklin	Fee	130	Gills C.
"	"	"	100	"
"	"	"	139	"

Distance from Ct House	Bearing from Ct House	Value of Land Per Acre, including Buildings	Sum added to Value of Land for Improvement	Total Value of Land & Improvements
15	N	1.00	200.00	130.00
"	"	1.00	"	100.00
"	"	1.00	"	139.00

Amount of Tax	Explanation of alterations during the preceding year
.11	Same
.08	Same
.12	Same

This record reflects the bequest of land in the will of 1830 William Wright to his children.

The 1832 Personal Property Tax List for Franklin County, Virginia, listed John Wright Jr with the following household on February 6:

Date	Names of Persons Owning Property	White Tyths	Blacks Over 12 Years	Blacks Over 16 Years
Feby 6	John Wright Jr (Maggotty)	3	3	2

Horses Mules		Amount of Tax	
5		1.05	

The 1832 Land Tax List for Franklin County, Virginia, listed John Wright Jr with the following property:

Names Of Owners	Residence	Estate whether in fee or for life	Number of Acres	Situation of land
John Wright Jr	Franklin	Fee	120	Maggotty Creek
"	"	"	93	"

Distance from Court House	Bearing from Court House	Value of Land Per acre, Including buildings	Sum added to Land in Improvement	Total Value of Land and Improvements
12	NW	10.00	300.00	1200.00
"	"	4.50	"	418.50

Amount of Tax	Explanation of alterations during the Preceding year
.96	
.34	

The 1832 Land Tax List for Franklin County, Virginia, also listed John Wright, Hiram, & P. Smith with the following property:

Names Of Owners	Residence	Estate whether in Fee or for life	Number of Acres	Situation of land
John Wright, Hiram, & P. Smith	Franklin	Fee	130	Gills Creek
"	"	"	100	"
"	"	"	139	"

Distance from Court House	Bearing from Court House	Value of Land Per acre, Including buildings	Sum added to Land in Improvement	Total Value of Land and Improvements
15	N	1.00	200.00	130.00
"	"	1.00	"	100.00
"	"	1.00	"	139.00

Amount of Tax	Explanation of alterations during the Preceding year
.11	
.08	
.12	

The 1833 Personal Property Tax List for Franklin County, Virginia, listed John Wright Jr (Maggotty with the following household on March 4:

Date of List	Owners Names	White Tythes	Blacks over 12 Years	Blacks over 16 Years
Mch 4	John Wright Jr (Maggotty	2	3	2

Horses &c &c		Amt. of tax $	
5		1.05	

The 1833 Land Tax List for Franklin County, Virginia, listed John Wright Jr with the following property:

Names Of Owners	Residence	Estate whether in fee or for life	No of Acres	Situation of land
John Wright Jr	Franklin	Fee	120	Magotty Cr
"	"	"	93	"

Distance from Ct House	Bearing from Ct House	Value of land Per acre, Including buildings	Sum added to Land for Improvement	Total Value of Land and Improvements
12	NW	10.00	300.00	1200.00
"	"	4.50	"	418.50

Amount of Tax	Explanation of alterations during the Preceding year
.96	
.34	

The 1833 Land Tax List for Franklin County, Virginia, also listed J. H. Wright & P. Smith with the following property:

Names Of Owners	Residence	Estate whether in fee or for life	No of Acres	Situation of land
J. H. Wright & P. Smith	Franklin	Fee	130	Gills Creek
"	"	"	100	"
"	"	"	139	"

Distance from Ct House	Bearing from Ct House	Value of land Per acre, Including buildings	Sum added to Land for Improvement	Total Value of Land and Improvements
15	N	1.00	200.00	130.00
"	"	1.00	"	100.00
"	"	1.00	"	139.00

Amount of Tax	Explanation of alterations during the Preceding year
.11	
.08	
.12	

The 1834 Personal Property Tax List for Franklin County, Virginia, listed John Wright Jr Maggotty with the following household on April 5:

Date of List	Names of Persons	White Tythes	Blacks over 12 Years	Blacks over 16 Years
Apl 5	John Wright Jr Maggotty	3	3	2

Horses Mules &c	___	Amount of Tax	____
6		1.11	

The 1834 Land Tax List for Franklin County, Virginia, listed John Wright Jr with the following property:

Names of Owners of Land	Residence	Estate whether in fee or life	Number of Acres	Situation of land
John Wright Jr	Franklin	Fee	120	Maggotty Cr
"	"	"	93	"
"	"	"	137	Gills creek

Distance from C House	Bearing from Court House	Value of Land Per Acre	Sum added for Improvements	Total Value of Land & Improvements
12	NW	10.00	300.00	1200.00
"	"	4.50	"	418.50
15	N	1.00	"	137.00

Amount of Tax of Land	
.96	
.34	
.12	By division

This record reflects an allocation of the 139 or 137 acre parcel of land of 1830 William Wright to his son John Wright in accordance with William Wright's will and clearly identifies the John Wright who owned 120 acres of land on Maggotty Creek from 1803 on as the son of 1830 William Wright of Franklin County.

The 1835 Personal Property Tax List for Franklin County, Virginia, listed John Wright Jr Maggotty with the following household on May 5:

Date of List	Names of Persons	White Tyths	Blacks over 12 Years	Blacks over 16 Years
May 5	John Wright Jr Maggotty	2	3	2

Horses Mules &c	Amt of Tax
5	1.05

The 1835 Land Tax List for Franklin County, Virginia, listed John Wright Jr with the following property:

Names of Owners of Land	Residence	Estate whether in fee or life	Number of Acres	Situation of land
John Wright Jr	Franklin	Fee	120	Maggotty Cr
"	"	"	93	"
"	"	"	137	Gills creek

Distance from C House	Bearing from Ct House	Value of Land Per Acre	Sum added for Improvements	Total Value of Land & Improvements
12	NW	10.00	300.00	1200.00
"	"	4.50	"	418.50
15	N	1.00	"	137.00

Amount of Tax of Land	Explanations of Alterations during the Preceding Year
.96	
.34	
.12	

The 1836 Personal Property Tax List for Franklin County, Virginia, listed John Wright Jr Maggoty with the following household:

Date of List	Names of Owners	White Tyths	Blacks over 12 Years	Blacks over 16 Years
	John Wright Jr Maggoty	2	4	2

Horses Mules &c	___	Amt of Tax	____
4		1.24	

The 1836 Land Tax List for Franklin County, Virginia, listed John Wright Jr Wm son with the following property:

Names of Owner	Residence of Owners	Estate whether in fee or Life	Number of Acres	Situation
John Wright Jr Wm son	Franklin	Fee	120	Maggotty Cr
"	"	"	93	"
"	"	"	137	Gills creek

Distance from Ct House	Bearing from Ct House	Value of Land Per Acre	Value of Improvements	Value of Land Including Improvements
12	NW	10.00	300.00	1200.00
"	"	4.50	"	418.50
15	"	1.00	"	137.00

Amount of Tax	Explanations of Alterations during the Preceding Year
.96	
.34	
.11	

This record also identifies the John Wright, Jr., who owned 120 acres of land on Maggotty Creek as the son of William Wright.

The 1837 Personal Property Tax List for Franklin County, Virginia, listed John Wright Jr Maggoty with the following household:

Date of List	Names of Owners	White Tythes	Blacks over 12 Years	Blacks over 16 Years
	John Wright Jr Maggoty	2	5	2

Horses &c	Amt of Tax	
5	1.55	

The 1837 Land Tax List for Franklin County, Virginia, listed John Wright Jr Wm son with the following property:

Names of Owner	Residence of Owners	Estate whether in fee or Life	Number of Acres	Situation of Land
John Wright Jr Wm son	Franklin	Fee	120	Maggotty Cr
"	"	"	93	"
"	"	"	137	Gills creek

Distance from Ct House	Bearing from Ct House	Value of Land Per Acre	Value of Improvements	Value of Land Including Improvements
12	NW	10.00	300.00	1200.00
"	"	4.50	"	418.50
15	"	1.00	"	137.00

Amount of Tax	Explanations of Alterations during the Preceding Year
.96	
.34	
.11	

On May 11, 1837, at Franklin County, Virginia, D.B. 15/416 John Wright and Elizabeth Wright sold 124 acres of land to William Wright:

> "This Indenture made this 11th day of May 1837 Between John Wright and Elizebeth his wife of the one part and William Wright of the other part Witnesseth that the said John Wright and Elizebeth his wife for and in consideration of the sum of four hundred Dollars to them in hand paid the receipt wareof is hereby acknowledged hath given granted bargained and Sold unto the said William Wright one certain tract or parcel of Land in Franklin County on the head waters of Gills Creek - Containing 124 acres and bounded as followeth to wit Beginning at a Gum thence North 5 West 340 poles to a Chesnut tree East 6 poles to a Hickory South 40 East 50 poles to a Chesnut oak South 16 East 270 poles to a Hickory South 60 West 72 poles to pointers South 88 west 24 poles to the Beginning. Together with all and Singular the appurtinances thereto Belonging or in any wise appertaining to have and to hold the said bargained Land and primisses unto the said William Wright his heirs and assigns forever and they the said John Wright and Elizebeth his wife doth warrant and forever defend a Good

and Lawful Right and title in fee Simple the said bargained Land and primisses unto him the said William Wright his heirs and assigns forever free from the claim of them the said John Wright and Elizebeth his wife there heirs and from all other persons whomsoever In wit whareof the said John Wright and Elizebeth hath hereunto put their hands and Seals the day and year above written.

John Wright
Elizebeth Wright

Franklin County SC

We John H Wade & J Early Justices of the peace on the County aforesaid in the State of Virginia do hereby certify that John Wright a party to a certain deed baring date on the 11th day May 1837 and hereto annexed personally appeared before us on our County aforesaid and acknowledged the deed aforesaid to be his act and deed and desired us to certify the same the Clerk of the County court of Franklin in order that the same may be recorded. Given under our hands this 19th Jany. 1838.

John H Wade JP.
J Early JP.

Franklin Cty. SC

We John H Wade & J Early Justices of the peace in the county aforesaid in the the State of Va do hereby certify that Elizabeth Wright wife of John Wright parties to a certain deed baring date on the 11th May 1837 and hereunto annexed personally appeared before us in our County aforesaid and being by examined privily & apart from her husband and having the deed aforesaid fully explained to her she the said Elizabeth acknowledged the same to be her act and deed and declared that she had willingly signed sealed and delivered the same and that wished not to retract it Given under our hands and seals this 19 July 1838.

John H Wade JP.
J Early JP.

In Franklin County Clerks office 5" February 1838

This Indenture of bargain and sale between John Wright and Elizabeth his wife of the one part and William Wright of the other part was exhibited into the said office and together with the certificates herein endorsed admitted to record

Teste
Caleb Tate C.F.C."

The 1838 Personal Property Tax List for Franklin County, Virginia, listed John Wright Ser Magoty with the following household:

Date of Receiving List	Names of Owners	White Tithes	Blacks over 12 years of age	Blacks over 16 Years
	John Wright Ser Magoty	2	6	4

Horses &c	Amount of Tax	
3	2.04	

The 1838 Land Tax List for Franklin County, Virginia, listed John Wright (Magoty) with the following property:

Names of Owners	Residence of Owners	Estate	No of Acres	Situation of Land
John Wright (Magoty)	Franklin	Fee	120	Magoty
"	"	"	93	"
"	"	"	137	Gills creek

Distance	and Bearing from the Court House	Value of Land Per Acre	Value of Improvements	Value of Land Including Improvements
12	NW	10.00	300.00	1200.00
"	"	4.50	"	418.50
15	"	1.00	"	137.00

Amount of Tax	Explanations of Alterations during the Preceding Year
1.20	
.42	
.14	

The 1839 Personal Property Tax List for Franklin County, Virginia, listed John Wright Magoty with the following household:

	Names of Owners	White Tythes	Slaves over 12 years of Age	Slaves over 16 years
	John Wright Magoty	2	6	8

Horses &c	Amount of Tax	
4	2.12	

The 1839 Land Tax List for Franklin County, Virginia, listed John Wright (Magoty with the following property:

Names of Owner	Residence of Owners	Estate whether in fee or Life	Numbers of Acres	Situation of Land
John Wright (Magoty	Franklin	Fee	120	Magoty
"	"	"	93	"

Distance from Court House	Bearing from Court House	Value of Land Per Acre	Value of Improvements	Value of Land Including Improvements
12	NW	10.00	300.00	1200.00
"	"	4.50	"	418.50

Amount of Tax	Explanations of Alterations during the Preceding Year
1.20	
.42	
.11	

This record reflects the sale of 124 or 137 acres of land by Franklin County Deed 15/416.

The 1840 Personal Property Tax List for Franklin County, Virginia, listed Widow Wright with the following household:

1840	Names of Owners	Slaves over 12 years of Age	Horses &c		Amount of Taxes
	Widow Wright	2	1		.68

The 1840 Land Tax List for Franklin County, Virginia, listed John Wright Decd with the following property:

Names of Owner	Residence of Owners	Estate whether in fee or Life	Numbers of Acres	Residence of Land
John Wright Decd	Franklin	in fee	120	Magoty
"	"	"	93	"

Distance from Court House	Bearing from the Court House	Vallue of Land Per Acre	Vallue of Improvements	Vallue of Land Including Improvements
12	North	12.00	400.00	1440.00
"	"	4.50	"	418.50

Amount of Tax	Expla of Alterations during the Preceding Year
1.44	
.42	

This record reflects the death of John Wright in 1839 and confirms the identity of the John Wright who owned 120 acres on Maggotty Creek from 1803 on as 1839 John A. Wright of Franklin County.

In February 1840 at Franklin County, Virginia, Court Order Book 6/304 in the case of Wright v. Wright in Chancery, on the motion of Elizabeth Wright, it was ordered that Moses Greer, Stephen Kessler, and John Flora lay off and assign to Elizabeth her dower in the land and slaves of her late husband John Wright, deceased, and that they also examine the remaining part of said decedent's land and note the value of the remaining slaves and after such assessment to report the proceeds in order that a further decree in the premises could be issued and on the motion of the plaintiff John H. Wade was appointed guardian ad litem for the infant plaintiffs William Wright, Lewis Wright, and Otey Wright.

On April 15, 1840, at Franklin County, Virginia, W.B. 15/119 the estate of John Wright was divided and allotted.

[Map not included]

"The above is a plat of Land of John Wright Dec containing 339 acres and is bounded as followeth to wit begining on Magety creek at A thence south & W 60 poles to Pointers at B S & W 60 poles to RO at C So 6338 [6 E 38?] poles to a WO at D So 43 W 31 poles to pointers at E N 76 W 90 poles to a Sorrel at F S 40 W 10° poles to a WO at G No 77 W 36 poles to a Sorrel at H So 75 W 25 to a WO I. So & 2 W 40 po to a WO at J No 21 W 88 po to a WO at K No. 55 E 132 poles to RO at L N 23 East 170 poles Crossing the to a WO at M So 75 E 62 poles to a red oak at N. S 48 E 100 to a dogwood at 0 So 14 E 22 to the begining all of which Land we the undersigned Commissioners value at $9500 out of which tract we have said of and assigned to Elizabeth Wright the widow of the said John Wright. dec 129 acres of Land at the price of $833 which may be known in the above plott By begining at A and runing So 8 W 60 poles to pointers at B So W 60 po to a RO E So 6398 poles to a WO at D So 43 W 31 poles to pointers at E N 76 W 90 po to a sorrel at F So 40 W 102 poles to a WO at G N 77 W 36 poles to a sorrel at H off dividing lines Lines No 55 W 80 poles to a Branch at R thence down the branch as it meanders in the wagan road at Q thence with the road west 20 po to the Creek at P thence down the creek as it meanders to the Beginning at A. We found the following slaves of the said John Wright Dec

To wit Martin which we value	at	$400.00
Sarah & child Jack	at	650.00
Mary & child Lovey	at	450.00
Joshua	at	600.00
one old woman	at	100.00
		2200.00

Out of the above slaves we have alotted Elizabeth Wright the widow of the said John Wright Dec the following slaves to wit

The Negroe boy Joshua	at	$600.00
and the old Amen		

All of which your undersigned commissioners appointed by the county court of

Franklin for the purpose beg leave to submit in order for a final Deecree. Given under our hands this 15th of April 1840

Moses Greer)
John Flora) Commissioners
Stephen Kosler)

At the court held for Franklin county the 8th day of June 1841. This report of assignment of dower to Elizabeth Wright of the estate of John Wright dec was confirmed and admitted to record.

Teste
M. G. Carper C.F.C."

The 1840 Census for Franklin County, Virginia, listed Elizabeth Wright with the following household:

Names of Heads of Families	Free White Persons Males	Age	Free White Persons Females	Age
Elizabeth Wright	1	30-40	1	50-60
	1	20-30		
	2	15-20		
	1	10-15		

Free Colored Persons Male	Age	Free Colored Persons Female	Age	Slaves Males	Age	Slaves Females	Age
				1	36-55	1	36-55
				1	10-24	2	10-24
				1	0-10		

	Number of Persons in each Family Employed in					
Total	Mining	Agri-culture	Commerce	Manu-facture and trades	Navi-gation of the ocean	Navigation of canals lakes and rivers
12		10				

Learned professions and engineers	Pensioners for Revoultionary or Military Services included in the foregoing		Deaf and Dumb, Blind and Insane White Persons included in the Foregoing		
			Deaf and Dumb		Blind
	Names	Ages	No.	Ages	

Deaf and Dumb, Blind and Insane White Persons Included in the Foregoing [Continued]		Deaf and Dumb, Blind and Insane Colored Persons Included in the Foregoing			
Insane and Idiots		Deaf, Dumb, and Blind		Insane and Idiots	
Insane and idiots at public charge	Insane and idiots at private charge	Deaf & Dumb	Blind	Insane and idiots at private charge	Insane and idiots at public charge

Schools, &c.						
Universities or College	Number of Students	Academies & Grammar Schools	No. of Scholars	Primary and Common Schools	No. of Scholars	No. of Scholars at public charge

No. of white persons over 90 years of age in each family who cannot read or write

The 1841 Personal Property Tax List for Franklin County, Virginia, listed Widow Wright with the following household on May 17:

Date of Receiving Lists from Individuals	Persons Names Chargeable With Tax	No of White Males	Slaves above 12 years old
May 17	Widow Wright	1	3

Slaves above 16 years old	Horses Mares Mules & Colts	Carriages whether four wheel or two Wheel riding Carriages phea stage wagons with the Vallue thereof	
3	1		1.32½

The 1841 Land Tax List for Franklin County, Virginia, listed John Wright Decd with the following property:

Names of Owners	Residence of Owners	Estate whether for Life or in fee	No of Acres of Land	Residence of Lands
John Wright Decd	Franklin	in fee	210	Magoty

Distance from the Court House	Bearing from the Court House	Vallue of Land Per Acre	Vallue of Improvements	Vallue of Land Including Improvements
12	North	7.00	200.00	1470.00

Amount of Tax	Expla of Alterations during the Preceding Year
1.84	Resant Survey

The 1841 Land Tax List for Franklin County, Virginia, also listed Elizabeth Wright (Widow) with the following property:

Names of Owners	Residence of Owners	Estate whether for Life or in fee	No of Acres of Land	Residence of Lands
Elizabeth Wright (Widow)	Franklin	Life	129	Magoty

Distance from the Court House	Bearing from the Court House	Vallue of Land Per Acre	Vallue of Improvements	Vallue of Land Including Improvements
12	North	7.00	200.00	903.00

Amount of Tax	Expla of Alterations during the Preceding Year

1.12 fm John Wright

On February 18, 1841, at Franklin County, Virginia, D.B. 16/460 John Nunley and Naoma his wife and William Wright and Nancy his wife sold their interest in certain land and slaves in the estate of John Wright:

> "This Indenture made this 18" day of February 1841 Between John Nunley and Naoma his wife and William Wright and Nancy his wife heirs and Legatees of John Wright Deceased of the one part and William Ward of the other part all of the County of Franklin and State of Virginia. Witnesseth that for and in consideration of two hundred fifty five Dollars paid unto the said John Nunley and Naoma his wife and three hundred Dollars paid unto William Wright and Nancy his wife the receipt whereof is hereby acknowledged hath granted bargained and sold and by these presents doth give, grant bargain and sell unto him the said William Ward all the Interest they now have or may hereafter accrue to them from the Estate of John Wright Decd both real and personal which consists of 331 acres of Land more or less on boath sides of Magoty Creek in Franklin County and bounded by the lines of Usalin Pate, Peter Hales heirs, Daniel Peters and Samuel Flora, also nine Negroes to wit, One Negroe man named Martin, one old Negroe Woman named Sinthy, one Negroe Boy named Joshua, one Negroe Woman named Sarah and two children named Jack and Martin, one Negroe Woman named Mary and her two Children named Lusey and Jim, also all money and bonds in the hands of the administrators or may come into their hands from the Estate of John Wright Decd we have by these presents sold unto the said William Waid his heirs and assigns forever and they the said John Nunley and Naoma his wife William Wright and Nancy his wife doth warrant and forever defend a good and lawfull right and title in fee Simple the said bargained Land and premis unto him the said William Waid his heirs Executors Administrators and assigns forever. also to the above mentioned Slaves to wit: Martain 1 Negroe Boy named Joshua, an Old Negroe Woman named Sintha, one Negroe Woman named Sarah and here two Children named Zack and Martin and one Negroe named Mary and her two Children named Lucy and and also all the money on hand that is now in the hands of or may come into the hands of the Administrators of John Wright Decd with the futer increase of the female Slaves, they the said John Nunley and Naoma his wife and William Wright and Nancy his wife doth forever defend a good and Lawful right and title to the said Land and premises the within named Slaves Martin, Joshua, Sinthia, Sarah Zack, Martin Mary Lucy with the furter increase of the Slaves which is 1/3 to each Legatee against the claim and demand of the said John Nunley and Naoma his wife and William Wright and Nancy his wife there heirs Executors Administrators & from all other persons whomsoever shall and will by these

presents warrant and forever defend. In witness whereof we have hereunto set our hands and seals the day and year above written.

his
John X Nunley
mark
Naoma Nunley
his
William Wright
mark
Nancy Wright

Franklin County SC

We Samuel Helm & Moses Greer Justices of the Peace in the County aforesaid in the State of Virginia do hereby certify that John Nunley and William Wright parties to a certain deed bearing date on the 18" February 1841 and hereto annexed personally appeared before us in our County aforesaid and acknowledged the same to be ther acts and deed and desired us to certify the said acknowledgments to the clerk of the County Court of Franklin in order that the same may be recorded. Given under our hands and seals this 19" February 1841

Saml Helm
Moses Greer

Franklin County SC

We Samuel Helm & Moses Greer Justices of the Peace in the County aforesaid in the State of Virginia do hereby certify that Naoma the Wife of John Nunley and Nancy Wright the wife of William Wright parties to a certain deed bearing dates on the 18" February 1841 and hereunto anned personally appeared before me in our County aforesaid and being examined by us privily and apart from ther Husbands and having the deed aforesaid fully explained them the said Naoma Nunley and Nancy Wright acknowledged the same to be there act and deed and declared that they had willingly signed sealed and delivered the same and that they wished not retract it. Given under our hands and seals this 19" February 1841.

Saml Helm
Moses Greer

In Franklin County Clerk's Office February 20" 1841

This Indenture of bargain and sale between John Nunley and Naoma his wife and William Wright and Nancy his wife of the one part and William Ward of the other part was exhibited unto the said Office and together with the certificates hereon endorsed admitted to record.

Teste
Mose G. Carper C.F.C."

The 1842 Personal Property Tax List for Franklin County, Virginia, listed Widow Wright with the following household:

Date of Receiving Lists from Individuals	Persons Names Chargeable With Tax	No of White Males Above 16	Slaves above 12 years old
	Widow Wright	1	2

Slaves above 16 years old	Horses Mares Mules & Colts	Carriages whether 4 wheel or two wheel riding Carriages Carryall and all others with Vallue thereof	Amount of Tax
2	2		1.50

The 1842 Land Tax List for Franklin County, Virginia, listed John Wright Decd with the following property:

Names of Owners	Residence of Owners	Estate Whether for life	No of	Residence of Lands
John Wright Decd	Franklin	in fee	210	Maggotty

Distance from the Court House	Bearing from the Court House	Value of Land Per Acre	Value of Improvement	Value of Land Including Improvements
12	North	7.00	200.00	1470.00

Amount of Tax	Explanations of Alterations during the Preceding Year
1.84	

The 1842 Land Tax List for Franklin County, Virginia, also listed Elizabeth Wright with the following property:

Names of Owners	Residence of Owners	Estate Whether for life	No of	Residence of Lands
Elizabeth Wright	Franklin	life	129	Maggotty

Distance from the Court House	Bearing from the Court House	Value of Land Per Acre	Value of Improvement	Value of Land Including Improvements
12	North	7.00	200.00	903.00

Amount of Tax	Explanations of Alterations during the Preceding Year
1.13	from John Wright 1840

The 1843 Personal Property Tax List for Franklin County, Virginia, listed Widow Wright with the following household:

	Names of Persons Taxable	White males over 16 years of age	Slaves over 12 years of age	Slaves over 16 years of age
	Widow Wright	1	2	2

Horses Colts	Carriages Carryalls and Livery wagons	Pianos(?)	Gold watches	Silver Lever watches	Common silver watches
2					

Wooden clocks	Metal Clocks	Amount of tax
		1.20

The 1843 Land Tax List for Franklin County, Virginia, listed John Wright Decd with the following property:

Name of Owners	Residence	Estate whether held in fee or Life	No of Acres	Description of the Land as to water Courses Mountains & Contiguous Tracts
John Wright Decd	Franklin	in fee	210	Magoty

Distance and bearing from the Court House	Vallue of Land Per Acre	Sum added on account of Buildings	Total Vallue of of Land & Buildings	Amount of Tax on ____ Tract at
12 North	7.00	200.00	1470.00	2.21

Explanations of Alterations during the Preceding Year for Whom Transferred

The 1843 Land Tax List for Franklin County, Virginia, also listed Elizabeth Wright with the following property:

Name of Owners	Residence	Estate whether held in fee or Life	No of Acres	Description of the Land as to water Courses Mountains & Contiguous Tracts
Elizabeth Wright	Franklin	Life	129	Magoty

Distance and bearing from the Court House	Vallue of Land Per Acre	Sum added on account of Buildings	Total Vallue of Land & Buildings	Amount of Tax on ____ Tract at ____
12 North	7.00	200.00	903.00	1.36

Explanations of Alterations during
<u>the Preceding Year for Whom Transferred</u>

On March 3, 1843, at Franklin County, Virginia, D.B. 18/120 William Wright conveyed his interest in the estate of his father John Wright to Washington Nunley:

> "This Indenture made the 3rd day of March 1843 between William Wright of Franklin County & State of Virginia of the one part, & Washington Nunley of said County & State of the other part Witnesseth that the said William Wright for & in consideration of a tract or parcel of Land supposed to contain about 50 acres be the same more or less has, granted bargained & sold & by these presents does grant bargain & sell unto the said Washington Nunley his heirs & assigns, all his interest of every sort & description in & to the estate of his deceased father John Wright. To have & to hold the said interest herein before mentioned or intended to be bargained & sold to the said Washington Nunley his heirs & assigns forever. In Witness of which the said William Wright has hereunto set his hand & affixed his seal the day & year first above written
>
> Test
>
> his
> William X Wright
> mark
>
> In the Clerk Office of Franklin County Court the 8th day of March 1843.
>
> This Indenture of bargain and sale between William Wright of the one part, and Washington Nunley of the other part was acknowledged in the said Office by the said Wright and admitted to record.
>
> Teste
> Moses G. Carper C. F. C."

The 1844 Land Tax List for Franklin County, Virginia, listed John Wright (Decd) with the following property:

Name of Owners	Residence	Estate whether held in fee or Life	No of Acres	Description of the Land as to water Courses Mountains & Contiguous Tracts
John Wright (Decd)	Franklin	In fee	210	Magoty

Distance and bearing from the Court House	Vallue of Land Per Acre	Sum added on account of Buildings	Total Vallue of Land & of Buildings	Amount of Tax on ____ Tract at ____
12 North	7.00	200.00	1470.00	1.84

Explanations of Alterations during the Preceding Year for Whom Transferred

The 1844 Land Tax List for Franklin County, Virginia, also listed Elizabeth Wright with the following property:

Name of Owners	Residence	Estate whether held in fee or Life	No of Acres	Description of the Land as to water Courses Mountains & Contiguous Tracts
Elizabeth Wright	Franklin	Life	129	Magoty

Distance and bearing from the Court House	Vallue of Land Per Acre	Sum added on account of Buildings	Total Vallue of Land & Buildings	Amount of Tax on ____ Tract at
12 North	7.00	200.00	903.00	1.13

Explanations of Alterations during the Preceding Year for Whom Transferred

The 1845 Personal Property Tax List for Franklin County, Virginia, listed Elizabeth Wright with the following household:

____	Persons Chargeable with tax	White males above 16 years of age	Slaves above 16 years of age	Slaves above 12 years of age
	Elizabeth Wright		1	1

Horses, mules, &c.	4 wheel pleasure carriages and harness and value	Stages, and value including harness	Carryalls and harness, and value	2 Wheel pleasure carriages and harness and value
1				

Gold watches	Patent lever or lepine silver watches	Other watches	Metallic clocks	Other clocks	Pianos, and value

Plate over the value of $50	Attorneys paying specific tax, and am't of tax	Physicians and surgeons paying specific tax, and amount of tax	Dentists paying specific tax and amount of tax	Am't of int, or profits on moneys loaned out, or on bonds acquired by purchase, including interest, pre__ or dividends on state or corporat'n bonds

Am't of monied yearly income over $400, received as salaries or fees of office	Bridges - am't of yearly rent or value over $100	Ferries - am't of yearly rent or value over $100	Newspaper printing presses and amount of tax	Total am't of tax. Dollars Cents

The 1845 Land Tax List for Franklin County, Virginia, listed John Wright with the following property:

Name of Owners	Residence	Estate whether held in fee simple, for life &c	No of Acres	Description of the land as to watercourses mountains and contiguous Tracts
John Wright	Decd	In fee	210	Magoty

Distance and bearing from the court house	Value of land per acre including buildings	Sum added to the land on account of Buildings	Total Value of the Land and Buildings	Am't of Tax on the whole tract, at the legal rate
12 N	7.00	200.00	1470.00	1.47

Explanations of alterations during the preceding year, especially from whom transferred

The 1845 Land Tax List for Franklin County, Virginia, also listed Elizabeth Wright with the following property:

Name of Owners	Residence	Estate whether held in fee simple, for life &c	No of Acres	Description of the land as to water courses mountains and contiguous Tracts
Elizabeth Wright	Franklin	Life	129	Magoty

Distance and bearing from the court house	Value of land per acre including buildings	Sum added to the land on account of Buildings	Total Value of the Land and Buildings	Am't of Tax on the whole tract, at the legal rate
12 N	7.00	200.00	903.00	.91

Explanations of alterations during the preceding year, especially from whom transferred

The 1846 Personal Property Tax List for Franklin County, Virginia, listed Elizabeth Wright with the following household:

____	Persons Chargeable With Tax	White males above 16 years of age	Slaves above 16 years of age	Slaves above 12 years of age
	Elizabeth Wright	1	1	1

Horses, mules, &c.	4 wheel pleasure carriages and harness and value	Stages, and value including harness	Carryalls and harness, and value	2 Wheel pleasure carriages and harness, and value
1				

Gold watches	Patent lever or lepine silver watches	Other watches	Metallic clocks	Other clocks	Pianos, and value

Plate over the value of $50	Attorneys paying speci- fic tax, and am't of tax	Physicians and surgeons paying spe- cific tax, and amount of tax	Dentists paying specific tax and amount of tax	Am't of int, or profits on moneys loaned out, or on bonds acquired by pur- chase, including interest, profits or dividends on state or corporat'n bonds

Am't of monied yearly income over $400, received as sala- ries or fees of office	Bridges - am't of yearly rent or value over $100	Ferries - am't of yearly rent or value over $100	Newspaper printing presses and amount of tax	Total am't of tax. Dollars Cents
				.42

The 1846 Land Tax List for Franklin County, Virginia, listed John Wright with the following property:

Name of Owner	Residence	Estate whe- ther held in fee simple, for life &c	No of Acres	Description of the land as to watercourses mountains and contiguous Tracts
John Wright	Decd	In fee	210	Magoty

Distance and bearing from the court house	Value of land per acre including buildings	Sum added to the land on account of buildings	Total Value of the Land and buildings	Am't of Tax on the whole tract, at the legal rate
12 N	7.00	200.00	1470.00	1.47

Explanations of alterations during the preceding year, especially from whom transferred

The 1846 Land Tax List for Franklin County, Virginia, also listed Elizabeth Wright with the following property:

Name of Owner	Residence	Estate whether held in fee simple, for life &c	No of Acres	Description of the land as to watercourses mountains and contiguous Tracts
Elizabeth Wright	Franklin	Life	129	Magoty

Distance and bearing from the court house	Value of land per acre including buildings	Sum added to the land on account of buildings	Total Value of the Land and buildings	Am't of Tax on the whole tract, at the legal rate
12 N	7.00	200.00	903.00	.91

Explanations of alterations during the preceding year, especially from whom transferred

The 1847 Personal Property Tax List for Franklin County, Virginia, listed Elizabeth Wright with the following household:

	Persons Chargeable With Tax	White males above 16 years of age	Slaves above 16 years of age	Slaves above 12 years of age
	Elizabeth Wright	1		

Horses, mules, &c.	4 wheel pleasure carriages& harness and value	Stages, and value including harness	Carryalls and harness, and value	2 Wheel pleasure carriages & value
1				

Gold watches	Patent L watches	Other watches	Metallic clocks	Other clocks	Pianos & value

Plate over the value of $50	Attorneys paying specific tax and amount of tax	Physicians &c paying specific tax	Dentists paying specific Tax & amount of tax	Am't of Interest and profits

Am't of monied yearly incomd over $400	Bridge value -	Ferry - value	Newspaper	Dollars Cents
				.10

The 1847 Land Tax List for Franklin County, Virginia, listed John Wright with the following property:

Name of Owner	Residence	Estate whether held in fee simple, for Life &c	No of Acres	Description of the land as to watercourses mountains and contiguous Tracts
John Wright	Decd	In fee	210	Magoty

Distance and bearing from the court house	Value of land per acre including buildings	Sum added to the land on account of buildings	Total Value of the Land and buildings	Am't of Tax on the whole tract, at the legal rate
12 N	7.00	200.00	1470.00	1.47

Explanations of alterations during the preceding year, especially from whom transferred

The 1847 Land Tax List for Franklin County, Virginia, also listed Elizabeth Wright with the following property:

Name of Owner	Residence	Estate whether held in fee simple, for Life &c	No of Acres	Description of the land as to watercourses mountains and contiguous Tracts
Elizabeth Wright	Franklin	Life	129	Magoty

Distance and bearing from the court house	Value of land per acre including buildings	Sum added to the land on account of buildings	Total Value of the Land and buildings	Am't of Tax on the whole tract, at the legal rate
12 N	7.00	200.00	903.00	.91

Explanations of alterations during the preceding year, especially from whom transferred

Franklin County, Virginia, Chancery Court Order Book A/__ dated May 13, 1847, and Court Order Book A/__ dated October 11, 1849, and Court Order Book A/444 dated June 5, 1850, listed the distributee children of John Wright as follows:

1) Asa Wright,
2) Otey Wright,
3) William Wright,
4) Naoma (Wright) Nunley,
5) Rhoda (Wright) Nunley,
6) Nancy (Wright) Wright,
7) Right Wright,
8) Matthew Wright,
9) John Wright,
10) James Wright,
11) Lewis Wright, and
12) Polly (Wright) Abshire.

Although Mr. Pullen was uncertain about the identification of the last three entries in the Bible, the Court order appears to confirm them as children of John A. Wright. The full text of Court Order Book A/__ dated May 13, 1847, provided as follows:

> "May 15, 1847.
>
> At a Circuit Superior Court of Law and Chancery continued and held for Franklin County at the Courthouse on Thursday the 13th day of May 1847 - sitting as a Court of Equity.
>
> Present. The Same Judge as yesterday.
>
> Asa Holland Plff)
against)
Elizabeth Wright, Nelson Abshire and Polly his)
wife Nelson Abshire and John H. Wade)
administrators of John Wright Decd. Mathew)
Wright, John Wright, Pendleton Wright and)
Nancy his wife, William Wright, James Wright,)
Lewis Wright, Otey Wright, Skelton Wright)
Right Wright, Asa Wright, John Nunally and)
Omey his wife and Washington Nunally and)
Rhoda his wife and Stephen Turnbull Defts)
>
> This cause this day came on again to be heard on the papers formerly read and it was argued by Counsel, on consideration whereof, the Court doth adjudge

order and decree that Commissioner Thomas S. Greer do state and settle and adjust the account Current of John H. Wade and Nelson Abshire administrators of John Wright decd. with their Intestates estate, that he specially ascertain the assets of their intestates estate in their hands to be administered on the 11th day of November 1842; that he examine and report the several claims for credits presented by the Plaintiffs Bill, and state whether they were valid claims against the administrators of said Estate at the time they were profered by the said Plaintiff; that he do likewise ascertain whether any payment were made by the Plaintiff to John H. Wade one of the Commissioners appointed to sell the estate of said intestate by the County Court of Franklin, in the part satisfaction of the said plaintiffs bonds refered to by his Bill, and if so, whether the said payments were made with monies or otherwise, and if not made with monies, the nature of said payments, with any other matters specially stated deemed pertinent by himself or required by the said parties to be so stated and report &c the Court doth authorize the said commissioner to enable him to make up said account and report, to examine either of the said parties to this suit on oath, and they are required to attend the said Commissioner for that purpose."

The 1848 Personal Property Tax List for Franklin County, Virginia, listed Elizabeth Wright with the following household:

_____	________	White males above 16 years of age	Slaves above 16 years of age	Slaves above 12 years of age
	Elizabeth Wright	1		

Horses, mules, &c.	4 wheel pleasure carriages and harness & value	Stages and value includ-ing harness	2 Wheel pleasure carriages and Harness, & value	Gold watches
1				

Patent lever or lepine silver watches	Other watches	Metallic clocks	Other clocks	Pianos, and value	Plate over the value of $50

Attorneys paying specific tax, and am't of tax	Physicians and surgeons paying spe-cific tax, and amount of tax	Dentists paying spe-cific tax and amount of tax	Am't of int, or profits on moneys loaned out, or on bonds acquired by purchase, including interest, profits or dividends on state or corporat'n bonds

Am't of monied yearly income over$400, received as salaries or fees of office	Bridges Value	Ferries Value	Newspapers value	
				.10

The 1848 Land Tax List for Franklin County, Virginia, listed John Wright Decd with the following property:

Name of Owner	Residence	Estate whether life or in fee	No of Acres of Land	Residence of Land
John Wright	Decd	In fee	210	Magoty

Distance and bearing from the Court House	Value of Land per acre	Value of improvm	Value of land with improvements	Amt of Tax
12 N	7.00	200.00	1470.00	1.47

Explanation of alterations during the preceding year

The 1848 Land Tax List for Franklin County, Virginia, also listed Elizabeth Wright with the following property:

Name of Owner	Residence	Estate whether life or in fee	No of Acres of Land	Residence of Land
Elizabeth Wright	Franklin	Life	129	Magoty

Distance and bearing from the Court House	Value of Land per acre	Value of improvm	Value of land with improvements	Amt of Tax
12 N	7.00	200.00	903.00	.91

Explanation of alterations
during the preceding year

The 1849 Personal Property Tax List for Franklin County, Virginia, listed Widow E. Wright with the following household on March 13:

	Persons Chargeable With Tax	White males above 16 years of age	Slaves above 16 years of age	Slaves above 12 years of age
Mar 13	Widow E. Wright	1	1	1

Horses, mules, &c.	4 wheel pleasure carriages and harness and value	Stages, and value including harness	Carryalls and harness, and value	2 Wheel pleasure carriages and harness, and value
1				

Gold watches	Patent lever or lepine silver watches	Other watches	Metallic clocks	Other clocks	Pianos, and value

Plate over the value of $50	Attorneys paying specific tax, and am't of tax	Physicians and surgeons paying specific tax amt of tax	Dentists paying specific tax and amount of tax	Am't of int, or profits on moneys loaned out, or on bonds acquired by purchase, including interest, profits or dividends on state or corporat'n bonds

Am't of monied yearly income over $400, received as salaries or fees of office	Bridges - am't of yearly rent or value over $100	Ferries - am't of yearly rent or value over $100	Newspaper printing presses and amount of tax	Total am't of tax. Dollars Cents
				.42

The full text of Court Order Book A/__ dated October 11, 1849, provided as follows:

"October 11, 1849.

At a Circuit Superior Court of Law and Chancery held for Franklin County at the Courthouse on Thursday the 11th day of October 1849 - Sitting as a Court of Equity.

. . . . .

Asa Holland Plff)
against)
Nelson Abshire, Elizabeth Wright)
William Wright Otey Wright, Asa Wright,)
Skelton Wright, John Nunley Washington)
Nunley and John A. Smith. Defts.)

Upon a motion for judgment and award of execution on a forfeited forthcoming bond taken on a writ of Fieri facias sued out of this Court by the Plaintiff against Nelson Abshire and John H. Wade Administrators of John Wright Decd. and the Defendant Elizabeth Wright, the Defendant Nelson Abshire and Polly, his wife & Matthew Wright, John Wright, Pendleton Wright and Nancy his wife, the Defendant William Wright, & James Wright Lewis Wright the Defendant Otey Wright the Defendant Skelton Wright & Right Wright the Defendant Asa Wright the Deft. John Nunly and Omy his wife, & the Defendant Washington Nunley and Rhoda his wife

This day came the Plaintiff by his attorney and it appearing by the oath of a witness that the Defendants have had legal notice of this motion they were solemnly called but came not: Therefore it is considered by the Court that the Plaintiff may have execution against the Defendants for $125.02 cents the penalty of the said forthcoming bond and that he recover against the said Defendats his costs by him in this behalf expended. But this judgment is to be discharged by the payment of $62.57 cents with legal interest thereon from the 19th day of July 1849 till paid and the costs."

The 1850 Personal Property Tax List for Franklin County, Virginia, listed Elizabeth Wright with the following household:

___	Persons Chargeable With Tax	White males above 16 years of age	Male free negroes above sixteen	Slaves above 16 years of age	Slaves above 12 years of age
	Elizabeth Wright	1		1	1

Horses, mules, &c.	4 wheel pleasure carriages and harness and value	Stages, and value including harness	Carryalls and harness, and value	2 Wheel pleasure carriages and harness, and value
1				

Gold watches	Patent lever or lepine silver watches	Other watches	Metallic clocks	Other clocks	Pianos, and value	Harps and value
				1		

Plate over the value of $50	Attorneys paying specific tax, and am't of tax	Physicians and surgeons paying specific tax, and amount of tax	Am't of int, or profits on moneys loaned out, or on bonds acquired by purchase, including interest, profit or dividends on state or corporat'n bonds

Am't of monied yearly income over $400, received as salaries or fees of office	Bridges - am't of yearly rent or value over $100	Ferries - am't of yearly rent or value over $100	Total amount tax. Dollars Cents
			.54½

The 1850 Land Tax List for Franklin County, Virginia, listed Elizabeth Wright with the following property:

Name of Owner	Residence	Taxes whether in fee simple, for life &c	No. of Acres	Description of the land as to water courses, mountains and contiguous tracts
Elizabeth Wright	Franklin	life	129	Magoty

Distance and bearing from the court house	Value of land per acre, including buildings	Sum added to the land on account of buildings	Total Value of the land and buildings	Amount of tax on on the whole tract, at the legal rate
12 NW	7.00	200.00	403.00	.91

Explanation of alterations during the preceding year, especially from whom transferred

On January 10, 1850, at Franklin County, Virginia, D.B. 21/164 Robert A. Scott, as commissioner, conveyed most of the land of John Wright to Robert J. Webb:

> "This Indenture made this 10th day of Janury 1850 between Robert A. Scott a commissioner appointed by a decree of the county court of Franklin by a decree of the said court pronounced in the case of "Skelton Wright & others against Elizabeth Wright & others" of the one part and Robert J. Webb of the other part. Whereas the said Robert A. Scott by the decree of the said court pronounced on the 5th day of June 1849 was appointed a commissioner to convey to the said Webb by proper deed with special warranty the land in the proceedings mentioned which were sold by Stephen Turnbull as commissioner appointed by a decree prounounced in the suit aforesaid on the 6th of January 1845 which land was purchased by said Webb all of which will appear by reference to the record and proceedings of the said suit. Now therefore This Indenture witnesseth that the said Robert A. Scott in compliance with the decree first above mentioned and for and in consideration of the sum of five dollars to him in hand paid at and before the sealing and delivery of these presents, the receipt whereof is hereby acknowledged hath granted bargained and sold and doth by these presents grant bargain sell and convey unto the said Robert J. Webb the tract or parcel of land sold by the said Turnbull commissioner as aforesaid and purchased by the said Webb the same being all the lands of John Wright decd. with the exception of that portion assigned to his widow and a small portion purchased by Asa Wright called the mill tract. The portion hereby intended to be conveyed to the said Webb containing by estimation 200 acres: To have and to hold unto him the said Webb and his heirs &c forever. And the said Robert A. Scott hereby further covenants and agrees to and with the said Webb to warrant and forever defend the right and title to the land herein conveyed or intended to be conveyed free from the claim or claims of him the said Scott and all and every person or persons, claiming by through or under as commissioners as aforesaid, but against no other claim or claims whatever. In testimoney whereof the said Robert A. Scott hath hereto set his hand and affixed his seal the day and year

herein first written.

Ro. A. Scott. Comr

In the Clerk's Office of Franklin County Court the 10" day of January 1850.

This Indenture of bargain and sale between Robert A. Scott, Commissioner, of the one part and Robert J. Webb of the other part, was acknowledged in the said office by the said Scott and admitted to record.

Teste
M. G. Carper C. F. C."

On June 5, 1850, at Court Order Book A/444 the court entered the following order:

"At a Court of Quarter Sessions continued and held for Franklin County at the Courthouse on the 5" day of June 1850.

Present - John Wade, Ira Hurt Joseph Dickinson John S. Hale & Zadack Bernard. Gent'l Justices.
Wright & al. agt. Wright & al. - In Chancery.

The Defendant Otey Wright having attained to the age of 21 years on his motion, It is ordered that this suit be hereafter proceeded in against him in his own name & right without a guardian ad litem and thereupon, This day this cause came on to be heard on the papers formerly read, the deed of assignment from the Defendant Otey Wright to the plaintiff Asa Wright bearing date the _ day of May 1850 the report of advancements made by Commissioner Thomas S. Greer and the report of Commissioner Wm T. Taliafero made in persuance of decretal orders heretofore pronounced in this cause (to which there is no exception) and examination of witnesses and was argued by counsel. Upon consideration whereof the court approving said reports and a statement A filed and made out in this cause to equalize the distribution and apportion the assetts of the estate of the said John Wright Decd. among the distributees of his estate doth confirm them. And it appearing to the court that the slaves in the Bill mentioned were sold as well to pay the debts of the intestate as for the purpose of distribution among the distributees. And that the Defendants John H. Wade and Nelson Abshire who were the Administrators of the intestate as well as the commissioners to sell received at the day of sale one half of the price of the said slaves for the purpose of paying their intestates debts. as well as other sums at an after time without being authorized so to do as the Commissioners of the Court. It is the opinion of the Court that they ought to be regarded as having received the same as so much assetts of their intestate and ought severally to account for the same in this character of administrators. And it appearing also from the said statement A that the bond of the plaintiff Asa Wright given by him for the last payment of the Land in the proceedings mentioned bought by him for the sum of $126:66 dated the 11" day of November 1841 and due and payable on the 11" day of Novem 1844 is paid by a set off of as much against the distributive shares in said Estate due to him in his own right and as assignee of Otey Wright. The court doth adjudge order and decree that the said bond be delivered up to him to be cancelled, and that Robert A. Scott who is hereby appointed a commissioner for the purpose do (at the proper costs of the grantee) convey to the said Asa Wright or his heirs or assigns the said lot of Land in the proceedings mentioned called the "Mill place" by proper deed for that purpose with special warranty. And it also appearing to the court that after allowing to the plaintiff Skelton Wright credit for his distributive share in said intestates estate, and the price for wich the said Land sold at the resale thereof under a decree of this court. That the said Skelton Wright still remains indebted to the other distributees of the said intestate in the sum of $515.70 as of the 31 of January 1847 besides the costs of the two suits in the proceedings mentioned on the two first bonds given for the purchase of said Land. The Court doth therefore adjudge order and decree that Stephen Wood Sheriff of this County who is hereby appointed a receiver for the purpose do proceed to sue out executions on the said judgment and make and collect on the same so much as shall be equal to the said sum of $515.70 with interest from the said 31st day of January 1847 and the costs of said suits, and when collected after deducting his legal commissions divide the same into twelve equal parts, and pay two of those parts to the plaintiff Asa Wright in his own right and as assignee of Otey Wright, pay two other of the said parts to the Defendant William Waid as assignee of John Nunley & wife and William Wright and one of the remaining parts to each of the parties following Viz: Washington Nunley in right of his wife Rhoda, Pendleton Wright in right of his wife Nancy, Right Wright, Matthew Wright, John Wright, James Wright, Lewis Wright and Nelson Abshire in right of his wife Polly. And the Court doth further adjudge order and decree that the Defendant John H. Wade Administrator of John Wright dec'd. do out of the estate of his intestate in his hands to be administered if so much he hath and if not then out of his own proper estate pay to the Plaintiff Asa Wright in his own right and as assignee ot Otey Wright the sum of $189:59 with interest thereon after the rate of six percent per annum from the 1st day of March 1850 till paid, that the same Defendant do in like manner pay to the Defendant William Waid as assignee of John Nunley and wife and William Wright the like sum of $189:58 & with like interest thereon from the 1st day of March 1850. That the same Defendant do in like manner pay to the plaintiffs Washington Nunley & Rhoda his wife the sum of $94.79 & with like interest thereon from the 1st of March 1850. That the same Defendant do in like manner pay to the Defendants Pendleton Wright and Nancy his wife the like sum of $94.79 & with like interest thereon from the 1st day of March 1850. That the same Defendant do in like manner pay to the Defendant Right Wright the like sum of $94:79 & with like interest thereon from the 1st day of March 1850. That the same Defendant do in like manner pay to the Defendant Matthew Wright the like sum of $94:79 & with like interest thereon from the 1st day of March 1850. That the same Defendant do in like manner pay to the Defendant John Wright the like sum of $94:79 with like interest thereon from the 1st day of March 1850. That the same Defendant do in like manner pay to the Defendant James Wright the like sum of $94:79 with like interest thereon from the 1st day of March 1850. That the same Defendant do in like manner pay to the Defendant Lewis Wright the like sum of $94:79 cents with like interest thereon from the 1st day of March 1850. That the same Defendant do in like manner pay to the Defendant Nelson Abshire and Polly his wife the like sum of $94:79 with like interest thereon from the 1st day of March 1850. And that the same Defendant do in like manner pay to the Defendant Nelson Abshire the sum of $591:80 with interest (on $456.54 part) thereof from the 1st day of March 1850. And the Court doth further adjudge order & decree that the Defendant Nelson Abshire administrator of John Wright Decd out of the estate of his intestate in his hands, to be Administered if so much thereof he hath, and if not out of his own proper estate do pay to the Defendant James Wright the sum of $133:81 with like interest thereon from the 1st day of March 1850. That the same Defendant do in like manner pay to the Defendant Lewis Wright the sum of $164:06 with like interest thereon from the 1st day of March 1850. And that he do out of the sum reported in his hands retain to himself in right of his wife Polly the sum of $134:06 with like interest thereon from the 1st of March 1850. And that he do with the sum of $77:14 the residue of the amount in his hands pay the unsatisfied expenses and costs of this suit and after paying the same divide the residue of the said sum of $77:14 into twelve parts and pay the same over to the parties to this suit according to their respective rights as settled by the principles of this decree. And the Court doth further adjudge order and decree that Solomon Pasley, Administrator of Stephen Turnbull Decd (, who was the receiver in this cause) out of the estate of his intestate in his hands to be administered if so much thereof he hath do pay to the Plaintiff Asa Wright transferee of Otey Wright the sum of $121:37 with like interest on $99:20 part thereof from the 1st day of March 1850 that he do in like manner pay to the Defendant William Waid transferee of John Nunley and Naoma his wife and William Wright the sum of $288:12 with like interest on $235.50 part thereof from the 1st day of March 1850. That he do in like manner pay to the plaintiff Washington Nunley and Rhoda his wife the sum of $144:06 with like interest on $119:25 part thereof from the 1st day of March 1850 - That he do in like manner pay to the Defendants Pendleton Wright and Nancy his wife the sum of $134:06 with like interest on $109:85. part thereof from the first of March 1850 till paid - That he do in like manner pay to the Defendant Right Wright the sum of $109:06 with like interest on $89:25 part thereof from the 1st day of March 1850. - That he do in like manner pay to the Defendant Matthew Wright the sum of $119:06 with like interest on $98.50 part thereof from the 1st day of March 1850 - That he do in like manner pay to the Defendant John Wright the sum of $119:06 with like interest on $98:50 part thereof from the 1st day of March 1850 and that he do in like manner pay to the Defendant James Wright the sum of $30:25 with like interest on $24:20 part thereof from the said 1st day of March 1850 until paid. And liberty is reserved to the infant and absent Defendants respectively to show cause against this decree within the time and upon the tenures prescribed by law and liberty is also reserved to the parties respectively to apply hereafter to this Court for such orders or decrees as may become necessary to carry this decree in relation to the said debt due from the said Skelton Wright with full effect and to appoint another receiver from time to time as it may become necessary and to compell the said receivers to account for and pay over the said money as it may be collected, and also to compell the said Abshire to account for and pray over the residue of the said sum of $77:14 if any shall remain after having paid the costs and expences of this suit."

On June 20, 1850, at Franklin County, Virginia, D.B. 21/283 Robert A. Scott, as commissioner, conveyed the Mill Tract to Asa Wright:

"This Indenture made and entered into this 20" day of June 1850 between Robert A. Scott a commissioner acting under a decree of the County Court of Franklin pronounced on the __ day of June 1850 in a suit in Chancery then depending in the said Court in which Skelton Wright and others were plaintiffs and Elizabeth Wright and others were defendants, of the one part and Asa Wright of the other part. Whereas by a decree pronounced in the said suit by the said Court on the 8" day of June 1841, John H. Wade and Nelson Abshire were appointed Commissioners to sell the lands mentioned in the bill and proceedings of the said suit did by virtue of the said decree they sold the said lands and the said Asa Wright being the highest bidder therefor became the purchaser of a tract called "the Mill place" supposed to contain 10 acres at the price of $380.00 which said purchase money it appears has been fully paid. And whereas the said Robert A. Scott was by the decree first herein mentioned appointed a commissioner to convey to the said Asa Wright by deed with special warranty the tract or parcel of land so purchased by him as aforesaid, all of which will more fully appear by reference to the records and proceedings of the suit aforesaid. Now therefore this Indenture Witnesseth that for and in consideration of the premises and for the further consideration of five dollars to him the said Scott in hand paid by the said Asa Wright at and before the sealing and delivery of these presents the receipt whereof is hereby acknowledged hath granted bargained sold and conveyed and by these presents doth give grant bargain sell & convey unto him the said Asa Wright his heirs or assigns the tract or parcel of land herein before described called the Mill place" and supposed to contain 10 acres more or less. To have and to hold to him the said Asa Wright his heirs and assigns, together with all and singular the privileges and appurtenances thereto belonging or in any wise appertaining free from the claim or demand of the said Scott as commissioner as aforesaid and from the claims or demands of all other persons claiming under through or by him the said Ro. A. Scott in his character as commissioner as aforesaid, but against none other. In testimoney whereof the said Robert A. Scott hath hereto set his hand and affixed his seal the day and year herein first written.

Ro. A. Scott

In the Clerk's Office of Franklin County Court the 20' day of June 1850.

This Indenture of bargain and sale between Robert A. Scott, Commissioner, of the one part and Asa Wright of the other part was acknowledged in the said office by the said Scott and admitted to record.

Teste
M. G. Carper C. F. C."

The 1850 Census for Franklin County Virginia, listed an Elizabeth Wright with the following household on October 11, 1850:

Name	Age	Sex	Color	Occupation	Value of Real Estate
Elizabeth Wright	60	F		Farmer	$500
John Wright	25	M			

Place of Birth	Married Within Year	Attended School Within Year	Cannot Read & Write	Deaf Dumb Blind Insane etc.
Virginia				
Virginia				

This record indicates that Elizabeth (Abshire) Wright was born in about 1790.

The 1851 Land Tax List for Franklin County, Virginia, listed Elizabeth Wright with the following property:

Owner	Residence	Estate	# of Acres	Name of Tract
Elizabeth Wright	Franklin	life	129	

Description	Distance	Value	Sum	Total	Amt of Tax
Maggoty Creek	12 NW	7.00		903.00	1.09

Amount of Tax	Explanation

The 1852 Land Tax List for Franklin County, Virginia, listed Elizabeth Wright with the following property:

Owner	Residence	Estate	Acres	Name of Tract
Elizabeth Wright	Franklin	life	129	

Description	Distance	Value	Sum	Total	Amount
Magoty	12 NW	7.00		903.00	1.64

Amount	Explanation

The 1853 Land Tax List for Franklin County, Virginia, listed Elizabeth Wright with the following property:

Owner	Residence	Estate	Acres	Name of Tract
Elizabeth Wright	Franklin	life	129	

Description	Distance	Value	Sum	Total	Amount
Magoty	12 NW	7.00		903.00	1.81

Amount	Explanation

The 1854 Land Tax List for Franklin County, Virginia, listed Elizabeth Wright with the following property:

Owner	Residence	Estate	Acres	Name of Tract
Elizabeth Wright	Franklin	life	129	

Description of the Land	Distance from Court House	Value	Sum Added	Total Value	Amt. of Tax
Magoty	12 NW	7.00		903.00	1.81

Amount of Tax	Explanation of Alterations

The 1855 Land Tax List for Franklin County, Virginia, listed Elizabeth Wright with the following property:

Owner	Residence	Estate	# of Acres	Name of Tract
Elizabeth Wright	Franklin	life	129	

Discription	Distance from CH	Value	Sum	Total	Amount
Magoty	12 NW	7.00		903.00	1.81

Amount for County purposes	Explanation

The 1856 Land Tax List for Franklin County, Virginia, listed Elizabeth Wright with the following property:

Owner	Residence	Estate	# of Acres	Name of Tract
Elizabeth Wright	Franklin	fee	129	

Description	Distance from CH	Value	Sum Added	Total Value	Amt of Tax
Magoty	12 NW	7.00		903.00	3.61

Amount of Tax	Explanation of Alteration

On April 19, 1856, at Franklin County, Virginia, D.B. 24/232 Elizabeth Wright sold her dower land to Otey Wright:

"This Deed made the 19" day of April in the year One thousand eight hundred and fifty six between Elizabeth Wright of the one part & Oatey Wright of the other part all of the County of Franklin and State of Virginia Witnesseth that in consideration of the sum of two hundred Dollars to the said Elizabeth Wright in hand paid by the said Oaty Wright, the receipt whereof is hereby acknowledged, the said Elizabeth Wright does grant unto the said Oaty Wright a certain Tract or parcel of land lying and being in the County of Franklin and State of Virginia on Maggotty Creek it being the same land that was laid off to the said Elizabeth Wright for her dower in the Division of her husband John Wrights lands (and now in her possession) and one Negro man Joshua, to have and to hold the said land with the appertenances and the said Negro Joshua, unto the said Oaty Wright his heirs &c. during her the said Elizabeth Wrights life the said Elizabeth Wright does covenant that she will warrant generally the land and Negro hereby conveyed to the said Oaty Wright and that he shall hold the same free from all incumbrances. Witness the following Signature and seal.

Elizabeth Wright

State of Virginia Franklin County To Wit.

I R. Bush a Justice of the peace for the County and State aforesaid do certify that Elizabeth Wright whose name is signed to the writing on the other side of this Sheet bearing date on the __ day of April in the year of 1856, has acknowledged the same before me in my County aforesaid. Given under my hand this 19" day of April 1856.

R. Bush J. P.

In the Clerks Office of Franklin County Court the 25" day of April 1856.

This Deed from Elizabeth Wright to Otey Wright was Exhibited into the said office and together with the certificates hereon endorsed admitted to Record.

Teste
Ro. A. Scott C. F. C."

The 1857 Land Tax List for Franklin County, Virginia, listed Elizabeth Wright with the following property:

Owner	Residence	Estate	# of Acres	Name of Tract
Elizabeth Wright	Franklin	fee	129	

Description	Distance from CH	Value	Sum Added	Total Value	Amt of Tax
Maggoty Creek	12 NW	6.00	100	774.00	3.10

Amount of Tax	Explanation of Alteration

The 1858 Land Tax List for Franklin County, Virginia, listed Elizabeth Wright with the following property:

Owner	Residence	Estate	# of Acres	Name of Tract
Elizabeth Wright	Franklin	fee	129	

Description	Distance from CH	Value	Sum Added	Total Value	Amt of Tax
Magoty Creek	12 NW	6.00	100	774.00	3.10

Amount of Tax	Explanation of Alteration

The 1859 Land Tax List for Franklin County, Virginia, listed Elizabeth Wright with the following property:

Owner	Residence	Estate	# of Acres	Name of Tract
Elizabeth Wright	Franklin	fee	129	

Description	Distance from CH	Value	Sum Added	Total Value	Amt of Tax
Magoty Creek	12 NW	6.00	100	774.00	3.10

Amount of Tax	Explanation of Alteration

The 1860 Land Tax List for Franklin County, Virginia, listed Elizabeth Wright with the following property:

Owner	Residence	Estate	# of Acres	Name of Tract
Elizabeth Wright	Franklin	Fee	129	

Description	Distance from CH	Value	Sum Added	Total Value	Amt of Tax
Magoty Creek	12 NW	6.00	100	774.00	3.10

Amount of Tax	Explanation of Alteration

On January 18, 1860, at Franklin County, Virginia, D.B. 28/92 Lewis and Louvina Wright appointed Asa Wright their attorney in fact to deal with their interest in the estate of Elizabeth Wright:

> "Know all men by these presents that we Lewis Wright and Louvina his wife of Tippecanoe County and State of Indiana have made constituted and appointed and by these presents do make constitute and appoint Asa Wright of Franklin County in the State of Virginia our true and lawful Attorney for us and in our names place and stead to sell convey assign and set over and transfer to any person or persons on such terms and at such time or place and in whatsoever manner the said Asa Wright may prefer all the right interest title or inheritance which we have or may hereafter have in the real estate and personal estate of Elizabeth Wright who is the mother of the aforesaid Lewis Wright and who now resides in Franklin County in said State of Virginia. Giving and granting to our said Attorney full power and authority to do and perform all and every act and thing whatsoever requisite and necessary to be done in and about the premises as fully to all intents and purposes as we might or could do if personally present with full power of substitution and revocation hereby ratifying and confirming all that our said Attorney or his substitute shall lawfully do or cause to be done by

virtue hereof. In testimony whereof we have hereunto set our hands and seals this 18th day of January A D 1860.

Signed Seal and) Lewis Wright
delivered in the) Louvina Wright
presence of)
Samuel Mustard)
H F Roberts)

The State of Indiana
Tippecanoe County

Personally appeared before me James J. Jones a Notary Public in and for said County Lewis Wright and Lovina Wright his wife the grantors in the foregoing warrant of attorney they being personally known to me and acknowledged the same to be their voluntary act and deed. And the said Lovina Wright wife of the said Lewis Wright being examined by me privately separately and apart from and without the hearing of the said husband and the full contents and purport of said warrant or Power of Attorney being by me made known and explained - declared that she had executed the same of her own free Will and accord and without any coertion or compulsion from her said husband. Witness my hand and Notarial Seal this 18th day of January AD 1860.

James J Jones
Notary Public

In the Clerks Office of Franklin County Court the 1st day of October 1866.

This power of Attorney from Lewis Wright and Lovina Wright his wife to Asa Wright was exhibited into the said Office and together with the certificates hereon endorsed admitted to record. (Revenue Stamps on Power of Attorney as prescribed by law.)

Teste
Ro A. Scott C. F. C"

This record indicates that Elizabeth (Abshire) Wright was still alive and in Franklin County, Virginia, on January 18, 1860.

The 1860 Census for Franklin County, Virginia, listed Elizabeth Wright in the Otey Wright household on August 3, 1860, and her age as 75, indicating a date of birth in about 1785.

The 1860 Census Slave Schedules for Franklin County, Virginia, listed Elizabeth

Wright with the following slave:

Names of Slave Owners	No of Slaves	Age	Sex	Color	Fugitives from the State
Elizabeth Wright	1	35	M	M	

Number manumitted	Deaf & dumb, blind, insane, or idiotic	No. of Slave houses

On December 12, 1864, at Franklin County, Virginia, D.B. 27/399 James C. Smith and Lucy F. Smith sold their interest in the estate of Elizabeth Wright to Otey Wright:

"This Deed made the 12th day of December in the year 1864 between James C. Smith and Lucy F his wife of the first part and Otey Wright of the other part all of the County of Franklin and State of Virginia. Witnesseth that in consideration of the sum of two Hundred and fifty Dollars in hand paid to the said James C. Smith by the said Otey Wright the receipt whereof is hereby acknowledged the said James C Smith and Lucy F his wife do grant unto the said Otey Wright all their interest both real and personal in the Estate of Elizabeth Wright Decd it being the fifth part of four shares of the said Estate. The said estate is now in possession of the said Otey Wright to have and to hold the said Interest unto the said Otey Wright his heirs &c forever and the said James C Smith and Lucy F his wife do covenant that they warrant generally the estate hereby conveyed to the said Otey Wright that he shall hold the same free from them and other persons whatsoever.

Witness the following signatures and seals.

Jas C Smith
Lucy F Smith

State of Virginia)
County of Franklin) to wit

I S Showalter a Justice of the Peace in and for the County and State aforesaid do certify that James C Smith whose name is signed to the writing above bearing date the __ day of December 1864 has acknowledged the same before me in my County aforesaid this 17" day of December in the year of our Lord 1864.

S Showalter JP

State of Virginia)
County of Franklin) to wit

We S Showalter and Daniel Flora two Justices of the Peace in and for the County and State aforesaid do certify that Lucy F Smith the wife of James C Smith whose names are signed to the writing on the other side of this sheet bearing date the __ day of December 1864 pesonally appeared before us in our County aforesaid and being examined by us privily and from her husband and having the writing aforesaid fully explained to her she the said Lucy F Smith acknowledged the said writing to be her act and declared that she had willingly executed the same and does not with to retract it. Given under our hands this 17" day of December 1864.

S Showalter J.P.
Daniel Flora J.P.

In the Clerks Office of Franklin County Court the 2nd day of January 1865

This deed from James C Smith and Lucy F Smith his wife to Otey Wright was exhibited into the said Office and together with the certificates hereon endorsed admitted to record.

Teste - R. A Scott CFC"

This record indicates that Elizabeth (Abshire) Wright had died before December 12, 1864.

On September 3, 1866, at Franklin County, Virginia, D.B. 28/91 Lewis and Lauvina Wright by their attorney in fact Asa Wright sold their interest in the dower estate of Elizabeth Wright to Otey Wright:

"This deed made the 3d day of September in the year 1866 between Asa Wright Attorney for Lewis and Lauvina Wright of the first part and Otey Wright of the Other part both of the County of Franklin and State of Virginia. Witnesseth that in consideration of the sum of Seventy Dollars in hand paid to the said Asa Wright Attorney for Lewis and Lavina Wright by the said Oatey Wright for their entire interest in the estate of Elizabeth Wright Decd both real and personal, the receipt whereof is hereby acknowledged by the said Asa Wright Attorney for Lewis and Lavina Wright do grant unto the said Oatey Wright their entire interest in the estate of of Elizabeth Wright Deceased both real and personal to have and to hold said interest with the appurtenances unto the said Oatey Wright his heirs &c forever. And the said Asa Wright Attorney for Lewis and Lavina Wright do covenant that they will warrant generally the interests hereby conveyed to the said Oatey Wright and that he shall hold the same free from them and all other persons whatsoever. Witness the following signature and Seal.

Asa Wright Attorney in
fact for Lewis and Lavina Wright

State of Virginia)
County of Franklin) SS.

I Thomas J Forbes a Justice of the Peace in and for the County of Franklin and State of Virginia do hereby certify that Asa Wright Attorney for Lewis and Lavina Wright whose name is signed to the writing on the other side bearing date the 3d day of September 1866 has acknowledged the same before me this day in my County aforesaid. Given under my hand this 15th day of September 1866.

Thomas J. Forbes J.P.

In the Clerks Office of Franklin County Court the 1st day of October, 1866.

This deed from Asa Wright attorney for Lewis and Lavina to Otey Wright was exhibited into the said Office and together with the certificates hereon endorsed admitted to record. (Revenue Stamps on Deed as prescribed by law.)

Teste
R A Scott CFC"

On October 12, 1869, at Franklin County, Virginia, D.B. 29/102 Mary Abshire sold all of her interest in the dower estate of Elizabeth Wright to her brother Otey Wright:

"This Indenture made this the twelth day of October in the year of our Lord Eighteen Hundred and sixty nine betwene May Abshire of _ County of Franklin and state of Virginina of the first part, and Otey Wright her brother, of the County of Franklin and state of Virginia of the second part. Witness that the party of the first part for and in consideration of the sum of Eighty Dollars to her in hand paid the receipt whereof is hereby acknowledged dose grant bargin sell convey and confirm unto the said Otey Wright of the second part, and to his heirs all my Wright title claim an intrust in the Estate or dowre of my mother Elizabeth Wright both real and personal lying and being in the County of Franklin and State of Virginia to her and to hold use ocapy possess without any let or hindrance whatever from me and my heirs forever in Witness whereof the said May Abshire of the first part, has hereunto set his hand and seal the day and year above written. Signed sealed and delivered in presence of,

her
Mary X Abshire
mark

State of Virginia) S.S.
County of Franklin)

I, Thomas J. Forbes a Justice of the peace for the County aforesaid and in said State do certify that Mary Abshire whoes name is signed to the writing writing above bearing the 15" day of October 1869" has acknowledge the same before me in my County aforesaid. Given under my hand, this 13" day of October in year 1869".

Thos. J. Forbes JP.

In the Clerks Office of Franklin County Court, the 15" October 1869".

This Deed from Mary Abshire to Otey Wright, was exhibited into the said office and together with the certificates hereon endorsed admitted to record,

(Revenue Stamps placed on deed as prescribed by Law).

Teste
P. Saunders SC"

Mr. Pullen in Virginians and Hoosiers added further about John A. Wright as follows:

"John son of Joseph and Elizabeth Wright, is said to have lived at Republican Hill, presumably Republican in the southern part of Franklin. There were a number of John Anthony Wrights and no doubt John's middle name was Anthony. He recorded himself in his Bible "John A. Wright" and is referred to in the 1839 will of George Wright as "John A. Wright". (WB-5-357)

Marriage bond Franklin - John Wright - Elizabeth Abshire - Lodowick Abshire surety - 8 Feb. 1800. They had ten children and John died 1839, Elizabeth surviving him. His administrators, son-in-law Nelson Abshire and John H. Wade, filed an interim accounting, 6 Mar. 1843 showing that sale of John's personal property took place 15 Nov. 1839 and made partial distribution to Elizabeth, Asa, Nancy, S. (Skelton), Matthew and William Wright. (WB-5-p- 502)

Late in 1800 William H. Wright of Indiana visited in Franklin and returned with

> John Wright's Bible which passed to John's great-g-g-g grand-daughter Imogene (Barker) Pullen, who gave it to the Virginia Historical Society. . . . "

Genealogy Of John J. Wright Of Virginia, Indiana and Kansas by John Calvin Wright stated that:

> "John[7], son of William and Catherine (Doran) Wright, was born about 1780 in Franklin County (the a part of Bedford) Va. He married Elizabeth Kelly of the same county on Septe. 2, 1805. John Vincent, surety. The marriage ceremony was performed by the Rev. Wilson Turner. Little is know of this family."

As set forth above, this identification is incorrect and 1839 John A. Wright, the son of 1830 William Wright, married Elizabeth Abshire.

Genealogy Of John J. Wright Of Virginia, Indiana and Kansas by John Calvin Wright also stated that 1839 John A. Wright was a son of 1845 John Wright of Franklin County and Mary (Abshire) Wright:

> "John[7] son of John[6] and Mary (Abshire) Wright was born about 1774 in Franklin County, Virginia. He married Elizabeth, daughter of William Abshire on Feb. 8, 1800 and died in Franklin County in 1840. Elizabeth was born in Franklin County in 1784-5 and died on Maggottee Creek between 1863-69. After their marriage John and Elizabeth settled on Maggottee Creek and engaged in the business of farming. John and Elizabeth were married by the Rev. Wilson Turner and their marriage Bond was signed by John Vincent. John[7] was the eldest son of John[6] a soldier of the Revolution and who died between Dec. 16, 1844 and Jan. 11, 1845. . . ."

However, as set forth above, 1839 John A. Wright was a son of 1830 William Wright of Franklin County and not the son of 1845 John Wright of Franklin County.

Genealogy Of John J. Wright Of Virginia, Indiana and Kansas by John Calvin Wright stated that the children of 1839 John A. Wright and Elizabeth (Abshire) Wright were the following:

1) Mary "Polly" Wright, born in 1800 or 1801 near Boons Mill, Virginia,
2) Skelton Wright, born in 1804 or 1805 near Boons Mill, Virginia,
3) Anselem Wright, born in 1804 or 1805 near Boons Mill, Virginia,
4) William Wright, born about 1806 or 1807 near Boons Mill, Virginia,
5) John Wright, born about 1809 near Boons Mill, Virginia,
6) Matthew Wright, born about 1811 near Boons Mill, Virginia,

7) Nancy Wright, born about 1813 near Boons Mill, Virginia,

8) Asa Wright, born in 1817 or 1818 near Boons Mill, Virginia,

9) Right Wright, born in 1819 or 1820 near Boons Mill, Virginia,

10) Rhoda Wright, born about 1822 near Boons Mill, Virginia, and

11) Otey Wright, born September 18, 1828, near Boons Mill, Virginia,

The identification of Anselem Wright as a son of 1839 John A. Wright was incorrect. 1883 Anslem Wright of Franklin County was a son of William Wright and Nellie or S. (____) Wright and as set forth in the materials on William Wright (Franklin County) may have been an illigetimate son of 1859 William Wright of Muhlenberg County, Kentucky, and grandson of 1845 John Wright of Franklin County and great grandson of 1809 William Wright of Franklin County.

D.A.R. Application No. 564462 by Grace Bales Howard dated November 2, 1971, stated that John (D) Wright was born in 1747 or 1748 at Fauquier County, Virginia, married Elizabeth Abshire on February 11, 1800, and died on May 25, 1836, at Boonesmille, Franklin County, Virginia, that Elizabeth (Abshire) Wright was born about 1785 and died near Boonesmille, Franklin County, Virginia, after the 1860 Census, and that John (D) Wright and Elizabeth (Abshire) Wright had the following children:

1) Polly (Wright) Abshire, born on March 29, 1801,

2) Nancy (Wright) Wright, born on January 17, 1803,

3) Skelton Wright, born on December 27, 1805,

4) Wright Wright, born on January 30, 1808,

5) Matthew Wright, born on April 11, 1810,

6) John B. Wright, born on March 13, 1812,

7) Omie "Naomi" (Wright) Nunnley, born on March 3, 1814,

8) Asa Wright, born on March 26, 1816,

9) Rhoda (Wright) Meador, born on February 1, 1818,

10) William H. Wright, born on December 11, 1821,

11) James Wright, born on December 13, 1823,

12) Lewis Wright, born on July 7, 1826, and

13) Otey Wright, born on September 18, 1828.

Mrs. Howard incorrectly identified this John A. Wright as the same person as 1845 John Wright of Franklin County, a Revolutionary War pensioner and probably the uncle of 1839 John A. Wright of Franklin County. As set forth above, 1839 John A. Wright of Franklin County was born probably between 1770 and 1780 and could not have served in the Revolutionary War. No source was cited for the date of death of John (D) Wright.

Fifth Generation:

1872 Skelton Wright, His Wife Joanna (Hambrick) Wright, And His Descendants

1872 Skelton Wright was a son of 1839 John A. Wright of Franklin County and Elizabeth (Abshire) Wright. (1809 William[1], 1830 William[2], 1839 John A.[3])

The Family Bible of John A. Wright listed the date of birth of Skelton Wright as December 27, 1805:

> Page 2:
>
> "John A. Wright
>
> John Wright and Elizebeth his Wife was married 11th of february 1800 and there first born Child polley was born 29th of march 1801
> . . . .
>
> Skelton Wright was born 27th of December 1805
> . . . ."

On February 10, 1832, at Franklin County, Virginia, Chancery Court, Virginia State Library Reel 291/699 an execution was issued against Skelton Wright to enforce a judgment for $2 in favor of Elizabeth Pearson:

> "To the Constable of Franklin County Greeting, I command you that of the goods and chattels of Skilly Wright you cause to be made the sum of two dollars, __ cents, with interest from the __ day of __ 183__, till paid, and costs, 30 which Elizebeth pearsone recovered before Bery Booth a Justice of the Peace for the County aforesaid; and that you render to the said Elizebeth Pearson the debt aforesaid, and then make due return thereon, within sixty days. Given under my hand, this 10th day of feb 1832
>
> Benj Booth

To any Sworn Constable of Bedford County to Execute to you are commanded to make the above Execution If found your Bailwick of Franklin County _

Benjamin Booth Jp"

The 1832 Personal Property Tax List for Franklin County, Virginia, listed Skelton Wright with the following household on April 16:

Date	Names of Persons Owning Property	White Tyths	Blacks Over 12 Years	Blacks Over 16 Years
Apl 16	Skelton Wright	1	-	-

Horses Mules		Amount of Tax	
-		-	

The 1833 Personal Property Tax List for Franklin County, Virginia, listed Skelton Wright with the following household on April 12:

Date of List	Owners Names	White Tythes	Blacks over 12 Years	Blacks over 16 Years
Apl 12	Skelton Wright	1	-	-

Horses &c &c		Amt. of tax $	
-		-	

The 1834 Personal Property Tax List for Franklin County, Virginia, listed Skelton Wright with the following household on April 5:

Date of List	Names of Persons	White Tythes	Blacks over 12 Years	Blacks over 16 Years
Apl 5	Skelton Wright	1	-	-

Horses Mules &c		Amount of Tax	
-		-	

The 1840 Personal Property Tax List for Franklin County, Virginia, listed Skelton Wright with the following household:

1840	Names of Owners	Slaves over 12 years of Age	Horses &c		Amount of Taxes
	Skelton Wright	1	1		.08

The 1841 Personal Property Tax List for Franklin County, Virginia, listed Skelton Wright with the following household on May 17:

Date of Receiving Lists from Individuals	Persons Names Chargeable With Tax	No of White Males	Slaves above 12 years old
May 17	Skelton Wright	1	-

Slaves above 16 years old	Horses Mares Mules & Colts	Carriages whether four wheel or two Wheel riding Carriages phea stage wagons with the Vallue thereof	
-	1		.12½

The 1842 Personal Property Tax List for Franklin County, Virginia, listed Skelton Wright with the following household:

Date of Receiving Lists from Individuals	Persons Names Chargeable With Tax	No of White Males Above 16	Slaves above 12 years old
	Skelton Wright	1	-

Slaves above 16 years old	Horses Mares Mules & Colts	Carriages whether 4 wheel or two wheel riding Carriages Carryall and all others with Vallue thereof	Amount of Tax
-	1		.12½

The 1843 Personal Property Tax List for Franklin County, Virginia, listed Skelton Wright with the following household:

______	Names of Persons Taxable	White males over 16 years of age	Slaves over 12 years of age	Slaves over 16 years of age
	Skelton Wright	1		

Horses Colts	Carriages Carryalls and Livery wagons	Pianos(?)	Gold watches	Silver Lever watches	Common silver watches
1					

Wooden clocks	Metal Clocks	Amount of tax
		.14

On February 26, 1844, at Franklin County, Virginia, D.B. 18/313 Skelton Wright conveyed his land to the county sheriff to obtain the protection of the law for insolvent debtors:

> "This Indenture made and entered into this the 26" day of February 1844 between Skelton Wright of the one part, and Saml. Helm Sheriff of Franklin of the other part. Witnesseth that whereas the said Skelton Wright is charged in custody in the jail of Franklin County by virtue of a judgment this day confessed by him at the suit of John H Wade & Nelson Abshire Commissioners, for the sum of $440.00/100 with interest from the 11th day of November 1844 and the costs and the said Skelton Wright having applied to a Justice of the Peace for said County, for the benefit of the Act for the relief of Insolvent debtors in consideration thereof the said Skelton Wright doth hereby bargain sell and grant unto the said Samuel Helm Sheriff as aforesaid one certain tract of Land lying and being in the County of Franklin and Maggotty Creek and containing 200 acres more or less, it being the same land purchased by him under a decree of the County Court of Franklin pronounced in the case of Wright & als vs Wright & als also all the interest of the said Skelton Wright in the estate of his father John Wright Decd. together with his claim for a distributive share of the proceeds of the sales made under and by virtue of the decree pronounced in the aforesaid

case. In witness whereof the said Skelton Wright has hereunto affixed his hand and seal this the 26" day of February 1844.

Test   Skelton Wright
J. A. Early

In the Clerks Office of Franklin County Court the 26" day of February 1844.

This Indenture of bargain and sale between Skelton Wright of the one part, and Samuel Helm Sheriff of Franklin County of the other part was acknowledged in the said Office by the said Wright and admitted to record

Teste
Moses G. Carper. C F C"

The 1845 Personal Property Tax List for Franklin County, Virginia, listed Skelton Wright with the following household:

	Persons Chargeable with tax	White males above 16 years of age	Slaves above 16 years of age	Slaves above 12 years of age
	Skelton Wright	1		

Horses, mules, &c.	4 wheel pleasure carriages and harness and value	Stages, and value including harness	Carryalls and harness, and value	2 Wheel pleasure carriages and harness and value

Gold watches	Patent lever or lepine silver watches	Other watches	Metallic clocks	Other clocks	Pianos, and value

Plate over the value of $50	Attorneys paying specific tax, and am't of tax	Physicians and surgeons paying specific tax, and amount of tax	Dentists paying specific tax and amount of tax	Am't of int, or profits on moneys loaned out, or on bonds acquired by purchase, including interest, pre_ or dividends on state or corporat'n bonds

Am't of monied yearly income over $400, received as salaries or fees of office	Bridges - am't of yearly rent or value over $100	Ferries - am't of yearly rent or value over $100	Newspaper printing presses and amount of tax	Total am't of tax. Dollars Cents

The 1846 Personal Property Tax List for Franklin County, Virginia, listed Skelton Wright with the following household:

____	Persons Chargeable With Tax	White males above 16 years of age	Slaves above 16 years of age	Slaves above 12 years of age
	Skelton Wright	1		

Horses, mules, &c.	4 wheel pleasure carriages and harness and value	Stages, and value including harness	Carryalls and harness, and value	2 Wheel pleasure carriages and harness, and value

Gold watches	Patent lever of lepine silver watches	Other watches	Metallic clocks	Other clocks	Pianos, and value

Plate over the value of $50	Attorneys paying specific tax, and am't of tax	Physicians and surgeons paying specific tax, and amount of tax	Dentists paying specific tax and amount of tax	Am't of int, or profits on moneys loaned out, or on bonds acquired by purchase, including interest, profits or dividends on state or corporat'n bonds

Am't of monied yearly income over $400, received as salaries or fees of office	Bridges - am't of yearly rent or value over $100	Ferries - am't of yearly rent or value over $100	Newspaper printing presses and amount of tax	Total am't of tax. Dollars Cents

The 1847 Personal Property Tax List for Franklin County, Virginia, listed Skelton

Wright with the following household:

	Persons Chargeable With Tax	White males above 16 years of age	Slaves above 16 years of age	Slaves above 12 years of age
	Skelton Wright	1		

Horses, mules, &c.	4 wheel pleasure carriages & harness and value	Stages, and value including harness	Carryalls and harness, and value	2 Wheel pleasure carriages & value

Gold watches	Patent L watches	Other watches	Metallic clocks	Other clocks	Pianos & value

Plate over the value of $50	Attorneys paying specific tax and amount of tax	Physicians &c paying specific tax	Dentists paying specific Tax & amount of tax	Am't of Interest and profits

Am't of monied yearly income over $400	Bridge value -	Ferry - value	Newspaper	Dollars Cents

The 1848 Personal Property Tax List for Franklin County, Virginia, listed Skelton Wright with the following household:

		White males above 16 years of age	Slaves above 16 years of age	Slaves above 12 years of age
	Skelton Wright	1		

Horses, mules, &c.	4 wheel pleasure carriages and harness & value	Stages and value including harness	2 Wheel pleasure carriages and Harness, & value	Gold watches

Patent lever or lepine silver watches	Other watches	Metallic clocks	Other clocks	Pianos, and value	Plate over the value of $50

Attorneys paying specific tax, and am't of tax	Physicians and surgeons paying specific tax, and amount of tax	Dentists paying specific tax and amount of tax	Am't of int, or profits on moneys loaned out, or on bonds acquired by purchase, including interest, profits or dividends on state or corporat'n bonds

Am't of monied yearly income over $400, received as salaries or fees of office	Bridges Value	Ferries Value	Newspapers value	

The 1849 Personal Property Tax List for Franklin County, Virginia, listed Skelton Wright with the following household on February 4:

	Persons Chargeable With Tax	White males above 16 years of age	Slaves above 16 years of age	Slaves above 12 years of age
Feb 4	Skelton Wright	1		

Horses, mules, &c.	4 wheel pleasure carriages and harness and value	Stages, and value including harness	Carryalls and harness, and value	2 Wheel pleasure carriages and harness, and value

Gold watches	Patent lever or lepine silver watches	Other watches	Metallic clocks	Other clocks	Pianos, and value

Plate over the value of $50	Attorneys paying specific tax, and am't of tax	Physicians and surgeons paying specific tax amt of tax	Dentists paying specific tax and amount of tax	Am't of int, or profits on moneys loaned out, or on bonds acquired by purchase, including interest, profits or dividends on state or corporat'n bonds

Am't of monied yearly income over $400, received as salaries or fees of office	Bridges - am't of yearly rent or value over $100	Ferries - am't of yearly rent or value over $100	Newspaper printing presses and amount of tax	Total am't of tax. Dollars Cents

The 1850 Personal Property Tax List for Franklin County, Virginia, listed Skelton Wright with the following household:

___	Persons Chargeable With Tax	White males above 16 years of age	Male free negroes above sixteen	Slaves above 16 years of age	Slaves above 12 years of age
	Skelton Wright	1			

Horses, mules, &c.	4 wheel pleasure carriages and harness and value	Stages, and value including harness	Carryalls and harness, and value	2 Wheel pleasure carriages and harness, and value

Gold watches	Patent lever or lepine silver watches	Other watches	Metallic clocks	Other clocks	Pianos, and value	Harps and value

Plate over the value of $50	Attorneys paying specific tax, and am't of tax	Physicians and surgeons paying speci fic tax, and amount of tax	Am't of int, or profits on moneys loaned out, or on bonds acquired by purchase, including interest, profit or dividends on state or corporat'n bonds

Am't of monied yearly income over $400, received as salaries or fees of office	Bridges - am't of yearly rent or value over $100	Ferries - am't of yearly rent or value over $100	Total amount tax. Dollars Cents

The 1850 Census for Franklin County, Virginia, listed Skelton Wright with the following household on October 9, 1850:

Name	Age	Sex	Color	Occupation	Value of Real Estate
Skelton Wright	45	M		Farmer	$210
Joana Wright	27	F			
Cynthia Wright	11	F			
William Wright	9	M			
John Wright	7	M			
Elizabeth Wright	4	F			
Sarah Wright	1	F			

Place of Birth	Married Within Year	Attended School Within Year	Cannot Read & Write	Deaf Dumb Blind Insane etc.
Virginia				
Virginia				
Virginia				
Virginia				
Virginia				
Virginia				
Virginia				

Neither Hinshaw nor Wingfield listed a marriage bond for Skelton Wright and Joana (_____) Wright.

As will be set forth below, the 1870, 1880, and 1900 Censuses for Madison County, Virginia, listed Giles O. Wright, a son of Skelton Wright and Joanna (Hambrick) Wright, as born in Indiana in about 1857 and these records indicate that the family may have resided in Indiana in about 1857.

The 1860 Census for Madison County, Iowa, listed Skelton Wright with the following household on August 15, 1860, in Grand River Township:

Name	Age	Sex	Color	Occupation
Skelton Wright	54	M		Farmer
Joanna Wright	40	F		
Elizabeth Wright	14	F		
John N. Wright	16	M		
William Wright	18	M		
Sarah Wright	9	F		
Eli Wright	8	M		
Giles O. Wright	5	M		

Real Estate	Personal Property	Born
1200	50	Virginia
		Virginia
		Virginia
		Virginia
		Virginia
		Virginia
		Virginia
		Virginia

This record indicates that Skelton Wright was born in about 1806 and that Joanna (Hambrick) Wright was born in about 1820.

The 1870 Census for Madison County, Iowa, listed Skelton Wright with the following household on August 9, 1870, in Scott Township:

Name	Age	Sex	Color	Occupation
Skelton Wright	65	M	W	Farmer
Joanna Wright	36	F	W	Keeping house
Eli Wright	16	M	W	Farm laborer
Giles Wright	14	M	W	Works on farm
George Wright	6	M	W	At home
Sarah Wright	21	F	W	No Occupation

Real Estate	Personal Property	Born
3180	242	Virginia
		Virginia
		Virginia
		Indiana
		Iowa
		Virginia

This record indicates that Skelton Wright was born in about 1805 and that Joanna (Hambrick) Wright was born in about 1834, but this latter age is clearly a mistaken entry, based on the ages of her children and the other records set forth above.

The 1880 Census for Madison County, Iowa, listed Joanna Wright with the following household on July 28, 1880, in District 113:

Name	Color	Sex	Age	Relationship
Joanna Wright	W	F	55	
Eli A. Wright	W	M	28	Son
Addie Wright	W	F	21	Daughter in law
Sarah D. Wright	W	F	1	Grand Daughter
George W. Wright	W	M	15	Son

Marital Status	Occupation	Born	Father Born	Mother Born
Wd	Keeping house	Virginia	Va	Va
M	Farmer	Virginia	Va	Va
M	Keeping house	Ohio	Mich	Ohio
S		Iowa	Va	Ohio
S	At home	Iowa	Va	Va

This record indicates that Joanna (Hambrick) Wright was born in about 1825. The absence of Skelton Wright from the 1880 Census indicates that he had died between 1870 and 1880.

In her letter dated May 20, 2000, Carlene Martin enclosed a copy of the death certificate of Joanus Wright listing her death on November 27, 1890, at Madison County, Iowa:

"Secretary Of Iowa State Board Of Health:
Return of Deaths in the County of Madison

No.	397
Date of Record:	Dec 27, 1890
1. Name:	Joanus Wright
2. Sex:	Female
3. Color:	White
4. Age:	67
5. Occupation:	Housekeeper
6. Date of Death:	11/27/1890 2:00 a.m.
7. Marital Status:	Widow
8. Nationality:	
9. Where Born:	Virginia
10. Place of Death:	Scott twp, Madison Co Ia
11. Cause of Death:	Congestive Bilious Fever
Complications:	
Duration of Disease:	
Place of Burial:	Winterset
Date of Burial:	2/28/1890
Name and Residence of Physician:	A. C. Baldred, Winterset Ia
Dated:	November 13, 1891

I hereby Certify that the above Return of Deaths is a correct transcript from the Records in this office.

W. C. Newlon, Clerk District Court
E. A. Newlon, Dep Clk"

In her letter dated June 20, 2002, Carlene Martin enclosed a copy of the petition for probate of the estate of Joanna Wright filed on January 10, 1891, at Madison County, Iowa:

"Estate of Joanna Wright
State of Iowa, Madison County, ss:

To the Dist Court of said County:
Your petitioner, Eli A. Wright represents to this Court, that on or about the 27th day of November A.D. 1890, one Joanna Wright died intestate, having at the time of her death personal property in this State, to the amount of about One Hundred Dollars which may be lost or diminished in value, if speedy care not be taken of the same. To the end, therefore, that said property may be collected

and preserved for those who may have a legal interest therein, your petitioner asks that G. W Wright may be appointed Administrator of said estate

Eli A Wright

State of Iowa, Madison County, ss:

I, Eli A Wright the above named petitioner, being duly sworn, say that I have heard read the above petition, and know the contents thereof, and that the same are true as I verily believe, so help me God.

Eli A Wright

Subscribed in my presence, by said Eli A Wright and by him sworn to before me, this 10" day of Jan. A.D. 1891

W. C Newlon Clk
Ed A Newlon Dep.

Administrator's Bond.

Know all men by these presents, That G. W. Wright as principal, and Lem Thornbrugh & J. C. Thornbrugh as sureties, all of the County of Madison, in the State of Iowa, are held and firmly bound unto the County aforesaid, and to all persons herein concerned, in the penal sum of Two Hundred Dollars, for the payment of which, well and truly to be made, we do jointly and severally bind ourselves and our lawful representatives.

Witness our hands and seals, this 10" day of Jan 1891

The condition of the above obligation is such, whereas the above named G. W. Wright on this day appointed by the Dist Court of said County sitting as a Court of Probate, Administrator of the estate of Joanna Wright deceased, late of said County, who died intestate on or about the 27 day of November 1890 to administer all and singular her goods and chattels, moneys, rights, and credits, according to law. Now if the said G. W. Wright shall discharge all the duties which are or may hereafter be required of her by law as such Administrator, then these presents to be void, or otherwise to remain in full force and effect in law.

Witness our hands and seals, the date above written.

G. W. Wright
Lew Thornbrugh
J. C. Thornbrugh

The above bond was approved and filed by me, this 10 day of Jan 1891.

W. C. Newlon
Clerk of the Circuit Court.

State of Iowa, Madison County, ss:

We, Lem Thornbrugh and J. C. Thornbrugh being duly and seveerally sworn, on oath, and each for himself says, that he is a resident of the State of Iowa, that he is one of the above named sureties in the foregoing bond, that he is worth the sum of Two Hundred Dollars over and above all his demands and liabilities, and that he has property liable to execution in the State of Iowa equal to the sum of Two Hundred Dollars

Lem Thornbrugh
J. C. Thornbrugh

Subscribed and sworn to before me by Lem Thornbrugh & J. C. Thornbrugh this 10" day of Jan A.D. 1890

W. C. Newlon Clerk.
Deputy

State of Iowa, Madison County, ss:

I, G. W. Wright do solemnly swear that I will well and truly administer all and singular the goods and chattels, rights, credits, and effects of Joanna Wright deceased, and pay all just claims and charges against her said estate, so far as her assets shall extend, and that I will perform all other acts now or hereafter required by law, to the best of my knowledge and ability.

G. W. Wright

Subscribed and sworn to before me, this 10 day of Janny A.D. 1891

W. C Newlon
Clerk Circuit Court

State of Iowa, To G. W. Wright sends Greeting:

Whereas, The late Joanna Wright departed this life intestate, on the 27 day of November A.D. 1890, being at or immediately previous to his death a resident of the County of Madison, and having property to be administered upon within said County, by means whereof the ordering and granting administration of all and singular the goods, chattels, and credits whereof the said intestate died possessed, in the State of Iowa, and also the auditing, allowing, and final discharging the account thereof, do appertain unto the Circuit Court of Madison County, and the said Court being desirous that the goods, chattels, and credits may be well and faithfully administered, applied, and disposed of doth grant unto you, the said G. W. Wright full power by these presents to administer and faithfully dispose of all and singular the goods, chattels, and credits; to ask, demand, recover, and receive the debts which unto the said intestate, while living, and at the time of his death, did belong, and to pay the debts which the said intestate did owe, after the same shall have been verified, and filed and approved by said Court, as far as such goods, chattels, and credits will thereunto extend and law require; hereby requiring you to make and return to said Court a true and perfect inventory of all and singular the goods, chattels, and credits of the said intestate, within thirty days after the date hereof. And if further personal property, or assets of any kind not mentioned in any inventory that shall have been so made, shall come to your possession or knowledge, to make and return in like manner, a true and perfect inventory thereof forthwith; and also to make a statement showing the condition of said estate within six months from the date hereof and ____ as required by said Court; and the Court aforesaid doth, by these presents, deputise, constitute, and appoint you, the said G. W. Wright Administrator of all and singular the goods, chattels, and credits, which were of the said Joanna Wright

In Testimony Whereof, I W C New1on Clerk of the Dist Court of Madison County in the State aforesaid, have set my hand, and, caused the seal of said Court to be affixed, at Winterset, this 10 day of Jan A.D. 1891

W C Newlon
Clerk Circuit Court."

In her letter dated May 20, 2000, Carlene Martin also enclosed a copy of the affidavit of George W. Wright dated March 28, 1891, regarding the heirs of Joanna Wright:

"To the District Court of Madison County, Iowa:

The undersigned, Administrator of the Estate of Joanne Wright Deceased, would respectfully report as follows, to-wit:

Name of Widow And Heirs	Date of Birth	Residence
Syntha Carrol	" " 1838	unknown
Wm. Wright	9/2/1840	North Yamhill Oregon
Elizabeth Crawford	11/10/1845	Gooe Kansas
Sarah A. Vanscoy	6/10/1849	Omaha Nebraska

Eli A. Wright	7/27/1852	Winterset Iowa
J. O. Wright	4/19/1856	Winterset Iowa
G. W. Wright	11/2/1864	Winterset Iowa
Anna Wright-widow and	4/20/33	Kaw Agency Ind. Ter.
Mary Cain and Esther	- 63	West Duluth Minn.
Lyons heirs at Law of John	- 65	Kaw Agency Ind. Ter.
Wright deceased who was		
son of Joanna Wright decd		

State of Iowa,)
Madison County.)

I, Geo. W. Wright do solemnly swear, that the foregoing is a true and correct list of the names, ages, and residences of the heirs of the estate of Joanna Wright deceased, late of said County so far as I am able to Learn.

Sworn to, before me, and subscribed in my presence, this 28 day of Mar 1891

W C. Newlon Clerk."

In her letter dated June 20, 2002, Carlene Martin enclosed a copy of the petition of Esther Lyons for funds due from the Eastern Cherokees fund appropriated by Congress:

"Commissioner of Indian Affairs
Washington, D.C.

Sir:

I hereby make application for such share as may be due me of the fund appropriated by the Act of Congress approved June 30, 1906, in accordance with the decrees of the Court of Claims of May 18, 1905, and May 28, 1906, in favor of the Eastern Cherokees. The evidence of identity is herewith subjoined.

1. State full name
   English name: Esther Lyon
   Indian name: none
2. Residence: Kaw
3. Town and post office: Kaw
4. County: Kay
5. State: Oklahoma
6. Date and place of birth: Aug 4, 1865 Winterset Iowa
7. By what right do you claim to share? If you claim through more than one relative living in 1851, set forth each claim separately: Esther Wright Lyon

Daughter of John Wright, who is a son of Skeleton Wright and Joe Anna Wright whose maiden name was Joe Anna Hembrick who is known to have Eastern Cherokee blood.

8. Are you married? Yes
9. Name and age of wife or husband: A. L. Lyon age 44 years old
10. Give names of your father and mother, and your mother's name before marriage.
    Father English name: John Wright
    Indian name: same as English
    Mother English name: Anna Wright
    Indian name: same as English
    Maiden name: Anna Evons
11. Where were they born?
    Father: Virginia
    Mother: Indiana
12. Where did they reside in 1851 if living at that time?
    Father In Virginia with parents
    Mother In Iowa with parents
13. Date of death of your father and mother
    Father: about Sept 15 1872
    Mother: Feb 10 1892
14. Where they ever enrolled for annuities, land, or other benefits? If so, state when and where: don't know but I think not
15. Name all your brothers and sisters, giving ages; and if not living, the date of death:
    (1) May Benton July 20 1863
16. State English and Indian names of your grandparents on both father's and mother's side, if possible:
    Father's side Mother's side
    Skelton Wright John Evans
    Joe Ann Wright Anna Evans
17. Where were they born? unknown
18. Where did they reside in 1851, if living at that time?
    on father's side Virginia
19. Give names of all their children, and residence, if living; if not living, give dates of deaths:
    (1) English name: Wm Wright date of death unknown
    English name: Ann Wright date of death unknown
    (2) English name: Joe Wright date of death unknown
    English name: Joe Anna Wright date of death unknown
    (3) English name: John Wright death about Sept 15, 1872
    English name: Eli Wright
    Residence: Winterset, Iowa
    (4) English name: George Wright, Winterset, Iowa
    English name: Elizabeth Wright

Residence: Residence Unknown

(5) English name: Giles _ Wright, Residence Unknown
English: Sarah Wright
Residence: Unknown

20. Have you ever been enrolled for annuities, land, or other benefits? If so state when and where. no

21. To expedite identification, claimants should give the full English and Indian names, if possible, of their paternal, and maternal ancestors back to 1835: Joe Anna Hembreck is a member of the Eastern Cherokee Tribe of Indians and claim is made on the relationship to the Hembrick family

Remarks. (Under this head the applicant may give any additional information that he believes will assist in proving his claims)
I'm not certain the name Hembrick is spelled correctly

I solemnly swear that the foregoing statements made by me are true to the best of my knowledge and belief.

Esther Lyon

Subscribed and sworn to before me this 13 day of February 1905.

My commission expires ____

George M Jacques(?)
Notary Public

Affidavit. (The following affidavit must be sworn to by two or more witnesses who are well acquainted with the applicant.)

Personally appeared before me G. McClary and Susan Pappan(?) who, being duly sworn, on oath depose and say that they are well acquainted with Esther Lyon who makes the foregoing application and statements, and have known her for 35 years and same with years, respectively, and know her to be the identical person she represents herself to be, and that the statements made by her are true, to the best of their knowledge and belief, and they have no interest whatever in her claim.

L. J. McClary
Susan Pappan

Subscribed and sworn to before me this 23 day of February 1907.

George M Jacques
Notary Public"

This record identifies Joanna Wright as Joanna (Hambrick) Wright.

Genealogy Of John J. Wright Of Virginia, Indiana and Kansas by John Calvin Wright stated that:

> "Skelton[8] son of John[7] and Elizabeth (Abshire) Wright was born in 1804-5 in Franklin County, Virginia. He married Joanna ____ about 1838. Skelton began to pay personal property taxes in 1841 and continued to pay each year up to 1852 when he may have followed the general urge to move west. Skelton and his brother Anselem were twins."

It is unclear on what Mr. Wright based the statement that Skelton Wright was a twin brother of Anselem Wright. 1883 Anslem Wright of Franklin County was listed in the marriage license for his second marriage as a son of William and Nelly Wright and in his death certificate as a son of William and S. Wright. There is no record of Anslem Wright being a son of 1839 John A. Wright nor a twin brother of Skelton Wright. Mr. Wright may have assumed such a connection, since they were both born in 1805.

In his email dated May 22, 1999, Paul ____ stated that Skelton Wright died in the 1860's at Madison County, Iowa.

Sixth Generation:

1934 Giles. O. Wright Of Iowa, His Wife Margaret S. Or L. ( ) Wright, And His Descendants

1934 Giles. O. Wright of Iowa was a son of 1872 Skelton Wright and Joanna (Hambrick) Wright. (1809 William[1], 1830 William[2], 1839 John A.[3], Skelton[4])

The 1860 Census for Grand River Township, Madison County, Iowa, listed Giles O. Wright in the Skelton Wright household on August 15, 1860, and his age as 5 and born in Virginia, indicating a date of birth in about 1855.

The 1870 Census for Scott Township, Madison County, Iowa, listed Giles Wright in the Skelton Wright household on August 9, 1860, and his age as 14 and born in Indiana, indicating a date of birth in about 1856, and his occupation as farm worker.

The 1880 Census for Scott Township, Madison County, Iowa, listed Giles O. Wright with the following household on July 28, 1880, in District 113:

Name	Color	Sex	Age	Month Born	Relationship
Giles O. Wright	W	M	23		
Maggie S. Wright	W	F	15		Wife
Fannie M. Wright	W	F	6/12	Nov	Daughter

Marital Status	Occupation	Born	Father Born	Mother Born
M	Laborer	Indiana	Va	Va
M	Keeping house	Iowa	(Mo)	Mo
S		Iowa	Ind	Iowa

This record indicates that Giles O. Wright was born in about 1857 and that Margaret (_____) Wright was born in about 1865.

In her letter dated May 20, 2000, Carlene Martin also enclosed a copy of the affidavit of George W. Wright dated March 28, 1891, regarding the heirs of Joanna Wright:

"To the District Court of Madison County, Iowa:

The undersigned, Administrator of the Estate of Joanne Wright Deceased, would respectfully report as follows, to-wit:

Name of Widow And Heirs	Date of Birth	Residence
. . . .		
J. O. Wright	4/19/1856	Winterset Iowa
. . . .		

State of Iowa,)
Madison County.)

I, Geo. W. Wright do solemnly swear, that the foregoing is a true and correct list of the names, ages, and residences of the heirs of the estate of Joanna Wright deceased, late of said County so far as I am able to Learn.

Sworn to, before me, and subscribed in my presence, this 28 day of Mar 1891

W C. Newlon Clerk."

The 1900 Census for Madison County, Iowa, listed Giles O. Wright with the following household on June 18, 1900, in Scott Township:

Name	Relationship	Color	Sex	Born	Age
Giles O. Wright	Head	W	M	April 1855	45
Margret Wright	Wife	W	F	Aug 1863	36
Leroy Wright	Son	W	M	June 1882	18
Deray (?) Wright	Son	W	M	May 1885	15
William Wright	Son	W	M	Jun 1888	12
Fredie Wright	Son	W	M	Feb 1890	10

Marital Status	Years Married	Children Born	Children Living	Born
M	21			Indiana
M	21	6	4	Iowa
S				Iowa
S				Iowa
S				Iowa
S				Iowa

Father Born	Mother Born	Occupation
Virginia	Virginia	Farmer
Virginia	Virginia	
Indiana	Iowa	
Indiana	Iowa	
Indiana	Iowa	
Indiana	Iowa	

The 1910 Census for Madison County, Iowa, listed Giles O. Wright with the following household on April 15, 1910, in Scott Township:

Name	Relationship	Sex	Color	Age
Jiles O. Wright	Head	M	W	52
Margaret L. Wright	Wife	F	W	46
Fred F. Wright	Son	M	W	20

Marital Status	Years Married	Children Born	Children Living	Born
M	30			Indiana
M	30	6	4	Iowa
S				Iowa

Father Born	Mother Born	Occupation
Indiana	Virginia	Farmer
Virginia	Iowa	
Indiana	Iowa	

This record indicates that Giles Otey Wright was born in about 1858.

The 1920 Census for Madison County, Iowa, listed Giles O. Wright in the William O. Wright household on June 21, 1920, his relationship as father, his age as 67 and born in Indiana, indicating a date of birth in about 1853.

Iowa Cemetery Records available from Ancestry.com listed the gravestone of Giles O. Wright with the following information:

"Name: Giles O. Wright
Death Date: 1934
Page #: 149
Birth Date: 1854
Cemetery: 80
Comment: wif: Margaret C; dau: John H Moore; chi: Leroy; chi: D Ray; chi: Jossup; chi: No name; chi: Ralph C; chi: David"

Seventh Generation:

Leander Leroy Wright, His Wife Daisy E. (   ) Wright, And His Descendants

Leander Leroy Wright was a son of Giles O. Wright and Margaret S. or L. (_____) Wright. (1809 William[1], 1830 William[2], 1839 John A.[3], Skelton[4], Giles O.[5])

The 1900 Census for Madison County, Iowa, listed Leroy Wright in the Giles O. Wright household on June 18, 1900, his relationship as son, and born in June 1882 in Iowa.

The 1910 Census for Madison County, Iowa, listed Roy Wright with the following household on April 23, 1910:

Line Number	Location: Street, Avenue, Road etc.	Location: House number or farm	Location: Dwelling number	Location: Number of family, in order of visitation	Name of each person whose place of abode on April 15, 1910 was in this family. Enter surname first then the given name and middle initial, if any. Include any person living on April 15, 1910. Omit children born since April 15, 1910.
			128	128	Roy Wright
					Daisy Wright
					Mabel M. Wright
					Everet R. Wright
					Ethel M. Wright
					Helen M. Wright

Relationship: Relationship of this person to the head of the family.	Personal Description: Sex	Color or Race	Age at last birthday	Whether single, married, widowed, or divorced	Number of years of present marriage	Mother of how many children: Number born	Mother of how many children: Number now living
Head	M	W	28	M1	8	.	.
Wife	F	W	24	M1	8	5	4
Daughter	F	W	7	S	.	.	.
Son	M	W	4	S	.	.	.
Daughter	F	W	__(?)	S	.	.	.
Daughter	F	W	9/12	S	.	.	.

Nativity (Place of birth of each person and parents of each enumerated. If born in United States, give state or territory. If foreign birth give the country.): Place of birth of this person	Place of birth of Father of this person	Place of birth of Mother of this person	Citizenship: Year of immigration to the U.S.	Whether naturalized or Alien
Iowa	United States	Iowa		

Iowa	Iowa	Iowa
Iowa	Iowa	Iowa
Iowa	Iowa	Iowa
Iowa	Iowa	Iowa
Iowa	Iowa	Iowa

	Occupation		
Whether able to speak English, or, if not, give language spoken.	Trade or profession of, or particular kind of work done by this person.	General nature of industry, business, or establishment in which this person works	Whether an employer, employee, or working on own account.
English	Laborer	Odd jobs	W
English	None		
.	None		
.	None		
.	None		
.	None		

Occupation (cont'd) If an employee.		Education		
Whether out of work on April 15, 1910.	Number of weeks out of work during 1909.	Whether able to read	Whether able to write	Attended school any time since Sept 1, 1900.
no	0	yes	yes	
		yes	yes	

Ownership of Home						
Owned or Rented	Owned free or mortgaged	Farm or house	Number of farm schedule	Whether a survivor of the Union Confederation Army or Navy	Whether blind (both eyes)	Whether deaf and dumb.
R		H	15			

This record indicates that Leander Leroy Wright was born in about 1882.

The 1920 Census for Madison County, Iowa, listed Roy L. Wright with the following household on June 28, 1920:

Line number	Location: Street, avenue, road etc.	Location: House number or farm	Location: Dwelling Number	Location: Number of family, in order of visitation	Name of each person whose place of abode on January 1, 1920 was in this family.
			173	174	Roy L. Wright
					Daisy E Wright
					Everett R Wright
					Helen M Wright
					Grace E Wright
					Lora E Wright
					Nella A Wright

Relation. Relationship of this person to the head of the family.	Tenure. Home owned or rented	Tenure. If owned, free or mortgaged	Personal Description: Sex	Personal Description: Color or Race	Personal Description: Age at last birthday	Personal Description: Single, married, widowed, or divorced
Head	R		M	W	37	M
wife			F	W	34	M
son			M	W	14	S
daughter			F	W	10	S
daughter			F	W	8	S
daughter			F	W	7	S
daughter			F	W	1-6/12	S

Citizenship: Year of immigration to the United States.	Citizenship: Naturalized or alien	Citizenship: If naturalized, year of naturalization.	Education: Attended school any-time since Sept. 1, 1919	Education: Able to read.	Education: Able to write.
				yes	yes
				yes	yes
				yes	yes
			yes	yes	yes
			yes	.	.
			yes	.	.
			.	.	.

Whether able to speak English, or, if not, give language spoken.	Occupation: Trade or profession of, or particular kind of work done by this person.	Occupation: General nature of industry, business, or establishment in which this person works	Occupation: Whether an employer, employee, or working on own account.

Nativity and Mother Tongue

Place of birth of each person and parents of each person enumerated. If born in United States, give state or territory. If foreign birth, give the place of birth, and in addition, the mother tongue.

Person: Place of Birth	Person: Mother Tongue	Father: Place of Birth	Father: Mother Tongue	Mother: Place of Birth	Mother: Mother Tongue
Iowa		Iowa		Iowa	
Iowa		Iowa		Iowa	
Iowa		Iowa		Iowa	
Iowa		Iowa		Iowa	
Iowa		Iowa		Iowa	
Iowa		Iowa		Iowa	
Iowa		Iowa		Iowa	

Able to speak English	Occupation: Trade, profession, or particular kind of work done.	Occupation: Industry, business, or etablishment in which at work.	Occupation: Employer, salary or wage worker, or working on own account.	Number of farm schedule.
yes	Farmer	Gen Farm	OA	171
yes	none			
yes	none			
yes	none			
.	none			
.	none			
.	none			

This record indicates that Leander Leroy Wright was born in about 1883.

The 1930 Census for Madison County, Iowa, listed Leroy Wright with the following household on April 17, 1930:

Place of Abode				
Street, avenue, road etc.	House number (in cities or towns)	Number of dwelling house in order of visitation	Number of family in order of visitation	Name of each person whose place of abode on April 1, 1930 was with this family. Enter surname first, then given name, and middle initial (if any). Omit children born since April 1, 1930
		105	105	Leroy Wright
				Daisy E. Wright
				Everett R. Wright
				Lora L. Wright
				Nellie J. Wright

Relation.	Home Data			
Relationship of this person to the head of the family	Home owned or rented	Value of home if owned, or monthly rental if rented	Radio set	Does this family live on a farm
head	R			yes
wife				
son				
daughter				
daughter				

Personal Description					Education	
Sex	Color or race	Age at last birthday	Marital condition	Age at at first marriage	Attended school or college any time since September 1, 1929	Whether able to read and write
M	W	47	M	19	no	yes
F	W	44	M	16	no	yes
M	W	24	S	.	no	yes
F	W	17	S	.	yes	yes
F	W	12	S	.	yes	yes

Place of birth of each person and parents of each person enumerated and of his or her parents. If born in the U.S., give state or territory. If of foreign birth, give county in which birthplace is now situated.

Place of Birth		
Person	Father	Mother
Iowa	Iowa	Iowa
Iowa	Iowa	Iowa
Iowa	Iowa	Iowa
Iowa	Iowa	Iowa
Iowa	Iowa	Iowa

Mother Tongue or Native Language				Citizenship, etc.		
Lanuage spoken in home before coming to the United States	Code (for office use only) State or M.T.	Country	Nativity	Year of immigration to the U.S.	Natural-ization	Able to speak English
						yes
						yes
						yes
						yes
						yes

Occupation and Industry			Employment	
Occupation Trade, profession, or particular type of work, as spinner, salesman, etc.	Industry Industry or busi-iness, as cotton mill, dry goods store, etc.	Code (for office use only)	Whether actually at work yesterday (or last regular working day) Yes or no	If not, line number on Unemployment
Farmer	Farm		yes	
none	.		.	
Laborer	Farm		yes	
none	.		.	
none	.		.	

Veterans		
Whether a veteran of U.S. military or naval forces		
Yes or no	What war or expedition	Number of farm schedule
no		105
.		
no		
.		
.		

This record indicates that Leander Leroy Wright was born in about 1883.

Iowa Cemetery Records available from Ancestry.com listed the gravestone of Giles O. Wright with the following information:

> "Name: Giles O. Wright
> Death Date: 1934
> Page #: 149
> Birth Date: 1854
> Cemetery: 80
> Comment: wif: Margaret C; dau: John H Moore; chi: Leroy; chi: D Ray; chi: Jossup; chi: No name; chi: Ralph C; chi: David"

This record identifies Leroy Wright as a son of Giles O. Wright.

Eighth Generation:

Everett Ray Wright

Everett Ray Wright was a son of Leander Leroy Wright and Daisy (_____) Wright. (1809 William[1], 1830 William[2], 1839 John A.[3], Skelton[4], Giles Otey[5])

The 1910 Census for Madison County, Iowa, listed Everet R. Wright in the Roy Wright household on April 23, 1910, his relationship as son, age 4 and born in Iowa, indicating a date of birth in about 1916.

The 1920 Census for Madison County, Iowa, listed Everett R. Wright in the Roy L. Wright household on June 28, 1920, his relationship as son, and his age as 14 and born in Iowa, indicating a date of birth in about 1916.

The 1930 Census for Madison County, Iowa, listed Everett R. Wright in the Leroy Wright household on April 17, 1930, his relationship as son, and his age as 24 and born in Iowa, indicating a date of birth in about 1916.

The obituary for David R. Wright dated on January 18, 2006, in The Winterset Madisonian listed his parents as Everett Wright and Mamie (_____) Wright :

> "Wednesday, January 18, 2006
> Obituaries
> David Wright, Missouri
> David R. Wright, 72, of Rockaway Beach, Mo., died Jan. 10, 2006, at St. John's Hospital in Springfield, Mo.
>
> Cremation was handled by Whelchel Funeral Chapels of Forsyth, Mo. No services were held.
>
> David Wright was born Nov. 26, 1933, in Madison County to Everett and Mamie Wright. He resided in Winterset until moving to Rockaway Beach in 1999.
>
> He was preceded in death by a sister, Evelyn.
>
> He is survived by his wife, Norine Wright of Rockaway Beach, Mo.; four sons, Colon Wright of Des Moines, Gary Wright of Garden Grove, and Ralph Wright and Bill Wright, both of Lorimor; two daughters, Shelley Bradford of Garden Grove and Tami Wallace of Murray; a sister, Dorothy Bivins of Winterset; and four grandchildren and three great-grandchildren.
>
> F F F"

Ninth Generation:

2006 David R. Wright Of Taney County, Missouri, His Wife Norine (   ) Wright, And His Descendants

2006 David R. Wright of Taney County, Missouri, was a son of Everett Ray Wright and Mamie (_____) Wright. (1809 William[1], 1830 William[2], 1839 John A.[3], Skelton[4], 1934 Giles O.[5], Everett Ray[5])

David R. Wright was the participant in the Wright DNA Project.

The obituary for David R. Wright was dated on January 18, 2006, in The

Winterset Madisonian and provided as follows:

"Wednesday, January 18, 2006
Obituaries
David Wright, Missouri
David R. Wright, 72, of Rockaway Beach, Mo., died Jan. 10, 2006, at St. John's Hospital in Springfield, Mo.

Cremation was handled by Whelchel Funeral Chapels of Forsyth, Mo. No services were held.

David Wright was born Nov. 26, 1933, in Madison County to Everett and Mamie Wright. He resided in Winterset until moving to Rockaway Beach in 1999.

He was preceded in death by a sister, Evelyn.

He is survived by his wife, Norine Wright of Rockaway Beach, Mo.; four sons, Colon Wright of Des Moines, Gary Wright of Garden Grove, and Ralph Wright and Bill Wright, both of Lorimor; two daughters, Shelley Bradford of Garden Grove and Tami Wallace of Murray; a sister, Dorothy Bivins of Winterset; and four grandchildren and three great-grandchildren.

F F F"

This record identifies David R. Wright as a son of Evertett Wright and Mamie (____) Wright.

Exhibit D

Documentation For Line Of Descent Of Thomas Wright

Kit 38118

Line Of Descent For Thomas Wright, Kit 38118, From 1792 John Wright Of Fauquier County

This exhibit will trace the line of descent of Thomas Wright, Kit 38118, from 1792 John Wright of Fauquier County.

First Generation:

1792 John Wright Of Fauquier County And Elizabeth (Bronaugh) (Darnall) Wright

The line of descent from 1792 John Wright of Fauquier County to 1809 William Wright of Franklin County has been given in my work The Identification Of 1809 William Wright Of Franklin County As The Son Of 1792 John Wright Of Fauquier County and the reader is referred to that work for the documentation relating to that connection.

Second Generation:

1809 William Wright Of Franklin County, Mary (Grant) Wright, And His Descendants

The documentation regarding 1809 William Wright of Franklin County as is the same as that set forth in Exhibit C for David R. Wright.

Third Generation:

1823 James Wright Of Franklin County, His Wife Margaret "Peggy" (Goodman) Wright, And His Descendants

1823 James Wright of Franklin County was a son of 1809 William Wright of Franklin County and Mary (Grant) Wright. (1792 John[1], 1809 William[2])

The 1782 Personal Property Tax List for Bedford County, Virginia, listed one James Wright with the following household:

Name	Free Males above 21 yrs	Slaves	Horses	Cattle	White Ty above 16 yrs	Blk Tithes above 16 yrs
James Wright	1		2		1	

This record indicates that James Wright was born before the summer of 1761.

The 1784 Personal Property Tax List for Bedford County, Virginia, listed James Wright with the following household:

Names	Total Tithes	Tax on Covg. Horses	Whites over 21 Years	Blacks over 16 Years	Blacks under 16
James Wright	1		1		

Total Blacks	No Horses	No Nett Cattle	No Weals Ridg Carriages	Ordinary Licenses
	1			

Franklin County was formed from Bedford County in 1786 and most records relating to James Wright after 1786 are found in that county.

The 1786 Personal Property Tax List for Franklin County, Virginia, listed James Wright with the following household:

By Whom Taken	To Whom Belonging	Total Tithes	Whites Over 21	Whites Under 21
Arthur	James Wright	1	1	0

Slaves Over 16	Slaves Under 16	Horses	Cattle	Studd Horses
0	0	1	0	

The marriage bond of James Wright and Peggy Young was dated October 9, 1786, at Franklin County, Virginia, with David Morgan as surety:

> "Know All Men by these presents that we James Wright And David Morgan are held and firmly bound unto Patrick Henry Esqr Governor or Chief Magistrate of the State of Virginia in the sum of Fifty pounds to the which payment Well and Truly to be made to the said Patrick Henry or to his Successors we Bind Ourselves & each of us Our & each of Our Heirs Exectrs & Admrs Jointly & Severally firmly by these Presents sealed with Our seals & dated this 9th Day of October 1786

The Condition of the Above Obligation is such that Whereas there is a Marriage Shortly Intended to be had & Solemnized Between the Above Bound Jas Wright and Peggy Young - Now if there shall be no Lawful Cause to Obstruct said Marriage then this Obligation to be void else to remain in force

James Wright
David Morgan"

The 1787 Personal Property Tax List for Franklin County, Virginia, listed James Wright with the following household on May 10:

		Whites Over 21	Whites Under 21	Blacks Over 16	Blacks Under 16	Horses	Cattle
May 10	James Wright	1	0	0	0	0	0

The 1789 Personal Property Tax List for Franklin County, Virginia, listed James Wright with the following household on April 22:

		16/ Whites	16 B	12Do	Horses
April 22	James Wright	1	0	0	1

The 1790 Personal Property Tax List for Franklin County, Virginia, listed James Wright with the following household on April 8:

		Whites	Blacks Over 16	Blacks Under 16	Horses	Studs	£ S D
April 8	James Wright	1	0	0	0	2	0 2 0

On February 7, 1791, at Franklin County, Virginia, D.B. 2/173 William Wright, Senr., sold 150 acres of land to James Wright:

"This Indenture made this 7 Day of February 1791 Between William Wright Senr. of Franklin County of the one Part and James Wright of the Said County of the other Part witnesseth that the Said William Wright for the consideration of Thirty five Pounds Current money of Virginia to him in hand paid the Rect. hereof he doth hereby acknowledge hath Given Granted Bargained and Sold and by these Presents do Give Grant Bargain Sell Deliver & Confirm unto the said James Wright his heirs or assigns one Certain Tract or Parcell of Land Containing one hundred & fifty acres be the same more or less and Bounded as followeth to wit Begining at Talbotts Corner white oak Saplin on the Crooked Run thence north seventy five Degrees west fifty four Poles to a Red oak thence north Thirty four Degrees west 20 Poles to a Red oak thence South 82 Degrees West Crossing a Branch seventy Poles to a white oak in the said Line thence new Line by agreement to a Corner white oak on the Bank of Maggottee Creek thence up the Said Creek as it Meanders Crossing the same to the mouth of warfords Branch, thence up the said Branch as it Meanders to a Corner white oak on Charles Vinsons Path thence along the said Path to a Corner red oak in Charles Vinsons Line, thence on his Line to the aforesaid Maggottee Creek thence Down the said Creek as it meanders to Tallbotts & Millers Dividing Line thence on the Said Dividing Line to the Begining Together with the Reversion and Reversions Remainder & Remainders and every Part and Parcell thereof to have and to hold the Above Granted Land and Premises with the Appurtenances Profits and advantages thereunto belonging or any ways appertaining to the said James Wright his heirs and assigns for Ever and the Said William Wright doth for himself his heirs, covenant Grant and agree to and with the said James Wright his heirs and Assigns that he the said William Wright and his heirs the above Granted Land and Premises with the appurtenances unto the said James Wright his heirs and assigns shall and will By these Presents warrant and for Ever Defend in Witness whereof the said William Wright hath hereunto set his hand and seal the Day & Year above written

William Wright

At a Court held for Franklin County on Monday the VII day of February 1791 This Indenture was acknowledged by the within named William Wright to be his Act & Deed and the same was ordered to be Recorded

Teste
Ste Smith ClC"

As set forth in the materials relating to 1809 William Wright, this parcel was a portion of Franklin County Deed 1/324 acquired by William Wright on September 19, 1787. Although Deed 2/173 recited that it was for 150 acres of land, as set forth below, the Land Tax Lists indicate that it was actually for 50 acres of land.

The 1791 Personal Property Tax List for Franklin County, Virginia, listed James Wright with the following household on April 2:

		Whites	Blacks Over 16	Blacks Under 16	Horses	Stud Horses	£ S D
April 2	James Wright	1	0	0	2	0	0 1 0

The 1791 Land Tax List for Franklin County, Virginia, listed James Wright with the following property:

Persons Names	Acres	Average Price	Total Amount	Tax
James Wright	50	0.5.0	12.10.0	

This record reflects the purchase of 50 acres of land by Franklin County Deed 2/173.

The 1792 through 1805 Personal Property Tax Lists and Land Tax Lists continued to list James Wright each year.

On August 24, 1805, at Franklin County, Virginia, D.B. 5/128 James Wright purchased 118 acres of land from Thomas and Ruth McClewain:

> "This Indenture made this 24th day of August 1805, by & between Thomas McClewain, and wife of Franklin County of the one part, and James Wright of the said County of the other part, Witnesseth that the said Thomas McClewain and wife, for and in consideration of 50 pounds to him in hand paid the receipt hereof he doth hereby acknowledge hath given, granted, bargained and sold, and by these Presents doth give, grant, bargain, sell, deliver, and confirm unto the said James Wright, his heirs and assigns forever, a certain Tract or parcel of land, lying and being in Franklin County on the head Branches of white oak bottom Creek, containing 118 acres, be the same more or less, and bounded as followeth, begining at a red oak on the Top of the mountain, thence dividing line by agreement to a Chesnut, thence down the middle ridge to a Gum corner in the Pattant line, N. 12 E. 72 poles to white oak on a high ridge, N. 30 W. 42 poles to a Chesnut tree, N. 15 E. 32 poles to Chesnut tree, N. 39 W. 46 poles to a walnut, N. 28 E. 16 poles to poplar thence new lines N. 26 W. 42 poles to a Hickory on the top of the mountain, S. 43 W. 68 poles to a small Chesnut oak, S. 22 W. 36 poles to a red oak, S. 58 W. 76 poles to a double Chesnut tree, S. 26 W. 70 poles to the Begining, together with the reversion and reversions, remainder and remainders, and every part, and parcel thereof. To have and To hold the above granted Land and premises with appertenances, privileges, profits & advantages thereunto belonging or any ways appertaining, unto the said James Wright, his heirs and assigns for ever and the said Thomas McClewain and wife doth for themselves and their heirs, covenant, grant, and agree to and with the said James Wright, his heirs and assigns, that he the said Thomas McClewain and wife, and their heirs, the above granted Land and premises with the appertenances unto the said James Wright his heirs and assigns, shall warrant and forever defend. In Witness whereof the said Thomas McClewain and wife hath hereunto set their hands, and affixt their seals, the day & year and above written.

Thomas McClewain
Ruth his wife

At a Court held for Franklin County September 2d 1805

This Indenture of bargain and sale between Thomas McClewain & Ruth his wife of the one part and James Wright of the other part was acknowledged by the said Thomas McClewain and Ruth his wife - the said Ruth being first privily examined according to Law - voluntarily relinquished her right of dower in and to the Land & premises conveyed by the said Indenture, which is ordered to be recorded

Teste,
James Callaway C.FC"

On February 3, 1806, at Franklin County, Virginia, D.B. 5/190 James Wright and Peggy Wright sold to Boothe Napper the 118 acres of land purchased in 1805 by Franklin County Deed 5/128:

"This Indenture made this 3d day of February 1806 by & between James Wright and Peggy his wife of Franklin County of the one part & Boothe Napper of the said County of the other part, Witnesseth that the said James Wright and Peggy his wife for and in consideration of forty five pounds current money of Virginia to him in hand paid, the receipt hereof, they doth hereby acknowledge, hath given, granted, bargained & sold, and by these Presents doth give, grant, sell, and deliver and confirm unto Boothe Napper his heirs and assigns for ever, a certain Tract or parcel of Land, lying in Franklin County, on the head branches of White oak bottom Creek, containing 118 acres, be the same more or less, and bounded as follows, Begining at a red oak corner in the Patent line, thence dividing by agreement between Wright and James Abshire to a Chesnut, thence down the ridge to a Gum thence N. 12 E. 72 poles to a white oak on a high ridge, N. 30 W 42 poles to a Chesnut, N. 15 E. 32 poles to a Chesnut, N. 39 W. 46 poles to a Walnut N. 28 E. 16 poles to a Poplar, thence new lines N. 26 W. 42 poles to a Hickory on the Top of the mountain, S. 43 W. 68 poles to a small Chesnut oak S. 22 W. 36 poles to a red oak, S. 58 W 76 poles to a double Chesnut tree, S. 26 W. 70 poles to the Begining, together with the reversion and reversions, remainder and remainders, and every part, and parcel thereof, to have and To hold the above granted Land and premises with the appurtenances, previledges, profits and advantages thereunto belonging or any ways appertaining unto the said Booth Napper his heirs and assigns for ever, and the said James Wright and Peggy his wife, doth for themselves and their heirs covenant, grant, and agree to and with the said Booth Napper his heirs and assigns, that they the said James Wright and Peggy his wife and their heirs, the above granted Land and premises with the appurtenances unto the said Boothe

Napper his heirs and assigns shall and will by these Presents warrant, and forever defend. In Witness whereof the said James Wright & Peggy his wife hath hereunto set their hands and affixt their seals, the day and Year above written.

James Wright
Peggy Wright

At a Court held for Franklin County, February 3d 1806.

This Indenture of bargain and sale between James Wright & Peggy his wife of the one part and Boothe Napper of the other part, was acknowledged by the said James Wright, and Peggy his wife - the said Peggy being first privily examined according to law, voluntarily relinquished her right of dower in and to the Land and Premises conveyed by the said Indenture, was is ordered to be recorded.

Teste,
James Callaway CFC"

On February 14, 1807, at Franklin County, Virginia, D.B. 5/332 James and Peggy Wright sold to John Wright the 50 acres of land purchased from 1809 William Wright by Franklin County Deed 2/173:

"This Indenture made this 14th day of Feby 1807 by and between James Wright of Franklin County of the one part and John Wright of the said County of the other part Witnesseth, that the said James Wright for and in consideration of 120 pounds to him in hand paid the Receipt hereof he doth hereby acknowledge hath given granted Bargained and Sold and by these Presents doth give grant Bargain Sell deliver and confirm unto John Wright his heirs and assigns forever, a certain tract or parcell of land containing 50 acres more or less lying in Franklin County on both sides of Maggottee Creek and bounded as follows begining at a white oak corner in Millers old line thence along said line N 75 degrees West 54 poles to a Red oak thence N 34 West 70 poles to a Red oak then South 82 De West 80 poles to a corner white oak in the sd line made by agreement thence agreement line near a South course to the Creek, thence up the Creek as it meanders to the mouth of a small branch, thence up the same as it meanders to the fork and up the left hand fork to Vinsons old path, and thence along the path to the top of the Ridge to the old cart Road thence along the same as it meanders to the point of the Ridge thence along the agreement line between Wright and Vinson to the Creek, thence down the Creek as it meanders to Bowns old line, thence Along the same line North 20 De East 100 poles to the Begining, together with Reversion and Reversions Remainder and Remainders and every part and parcell thereof to have and to hold the above granted land and premises within appertenances priviledges profit and and advantages thereunto belonging or any wise appertaining unto the said John Wright his heirs and assigns for ever and the said James Wright doth for himself and his heirs covenant grant and agree to and with the said John Wright and his heirs the above granted land and premises with appertenances shall and will by these Presents warrant and forever defend in Witness whereof the said James Wright hath hereunto set his hand and affixt his seal the day and year above written.

Witness		James Wright
Geo. Wright	)	her
Hiram Wright	)	Peggy X Wright
William Brown	)	mark

At a Court held for Franklin County April 6th 1807.

This Indenture of bargain and Sale between James Wright of the one part and John Wright of the other part was acknowledged by the said James Wright & ordered to be recorded

Teste,
James Callaway CFC"

The will of 1809 William Wright dated October 10, 1808, and probated on January 2, 1809, at Franklin County, Virginia, W.B. 1/368 identified James Wright as a son of William:

". . . . I likewise appoint my two sons James Wright and George Wright and Enoch Wright my whole and Sole Executors and trustees. . . ."

On January 11, 1809, at Franklin County, Virginia, D.B. 5/680 James Wright and William Wright sold 200 acres of land to John Vinson:

"This Indenture made this 11" day of January 1809 by and between William Wright Senr. & James Wright both of Franklin County of the one part & John Vinson of the said County of the other part Witnesseth that the sd. William Wright Senr. & James Wright for and in consideration of 100 dollars current money of Virginia to him in hand paid the receipt hereof he doth hereby acknowledge hath given granted bargained & sold, and by these presents doth give grant bargain sell deliver & confirm unto the said John Vinson his heirs & assigns forever, a certain Tract or parcel of Land Containing 200 acres more or less lying & being in the county of Franklin on the south side of Maggottee Creek and bounded as followeth to wit: Begining at a post oak on the top of the ridge near the cart road, thence along Millers old line to a black oak corner in Millers & Browns dividing thence along said line to Maggottee Creek, thence up the Creek as it meanders to a corner Walnut Vinson & Wrights dividing line thence along the same to the Begining Together with the reversion & reversions, remainder and every part & part & parcel thereof To have & to hold the above granted land & premises with appurtenances previledges profits & advantages thereunto belonging or any wise appertaining unto the said John Vinson his heirs & assigns forever, and the said William Wright Senr. & James Wright doth for themselves & their heirs covenant grant & agree to & with the said John Vinson and his heirs & assigns that they the said William Wright Senr. & James Wright and their heirs the above granted Land and premises with appertenances unto the said John Vinson his heirs & assigns shall and will by these presents warrant & forever defend In Witness whereof the sd. William Wright Senr & James Wright hath hereunto set their hands & affixt their seals the day & year above written.

William Wright
James Wright"

The William Wright, Sr., of this record was 1809 William Wright's son 1830 William Wright of Franklin County, who became a "senior" by reason of his father's death.

The 1810 Census for Franklin County, Virginia, listed one James Wright with the following household:

Name of Head of Family	Free White Males	Age	Free White Female	Age	All Other Free Persons	Slaves
James Wright	1	45+	1	26-45		
	2	16-26	2	16-26		
	1	10-16	2	10-16		
	3	0-10	1	0-10		

This record indicates that James Wright was born before 1765 and that Margaret "Peggy" (Young) Wright was born between 1765 and 1794.

The 1810 through 1820 Personal Property Tax Lists for Franklin County, Virginia, continued to list James Wright.

The 1820 Census for Franklin County, Virginia, listed two James Wrights, but one was aged 26 to 45 with a wife aged 16 to 26 and, therefore, could not be 1823 James Wright. The listing for 1823 James Wright gave the following household:

Names of Heads of Families	Free White Males	Age	Free White Females	Age
James Wright	1	45+	1	45+
	1	10-16	1	26-45
	1	0-10	1	16-26
			1	10-16
			2	0-10

Foreigners	Number in Agriculture	Number in Commerce	Number in Manufacture
	1		

Male	Age	Slaves Female	Age	Free Colored Males	Age	Free Colored Females	Age

All Other Persons

The will of James Wright was dated December 12, 1821, probated on May 5, 1823, at Franklin County, Virginia, W.B. 2/629, and provided as follows:

> "In the name of God amen This 12th day of December 1821 I James Wright of Franklin County am sick and weak but of perfect senses mind and memory thanks be to god calling to mind the mortallity of my body knowing that it is appointed for all men once to die I doe hereby appoint this my last will and Testement In manner and form following to wit
>
> Principally and first of all I give and recommend my soul in the hands of Almighty God who give nothing doubting but at the General resurrection I shall receive the same by the mighty power of God
>
> Secondly I recommond my body to the earth to be buried in a Christian like buriel at the discression of my execetors
>
> Thirdly and lastly I recommend my Worldly estate wherewith it has pleased God to bless me in this life I dispose of the same in the manner and form following to wit Item I give and bequeath unto my loving wife Peggy Wright all my Estate both real and personal to her peacably to be enjoyed during her life And after her

death to be equally divided among my children. I also appoint Berry Wright George Wright and James Grant Wright, Three of my children my whole and sole Execetors and trustees of this my last will and Testament in witness whereof I have hereunto set my hand the the day and year above written

Witness	his
Geo Wright	James X Wright
Sucky Smith	mark
Robert Wright	

At a Court held for Franklin County at the Courthouse the 5" day of May 1823

This last will and Testament of James Wright decd. was exhibited into Court and by the oath of George Wright one of the subscribing witnesses hereto

And at a Court held for said County at the Courthouse the 3rd day of January 1825 The said Will was further proved by the oath of Sucky Smith another of the witnesses hereto and ordered to be recorded

And on the motion of James Wright one of the executors in the said Will named who took the oath prescribed by Law and together with George Wright his security entered into and acknowledged his bond in the penalty of two thousand Dollars conditioned according to Law certificate is granted him for obtaining a Probat in due form liberty being reserved to the other executors in the said Will named to join in the probat when they shall think fit

Caleb Tate cfc"

From the will the following family of 1823 James Wright can be identified:

Wife: Peggy Wright

Children: Berry Wright

George Wright

James Grant Wright

The 1829 Personal Property Tax List for Franklin County, Virginia, listed Margaret Wright with the following household on April 4:

Date of Receiving list	Persons Names Charable With Tax	______	Negroes over 12	Horses &c &c &c
April 4	Margaret Wright	-	-	1

	Amount of Tax	
-	.10	

The 1830 Personal Property Tax List for Franklin County, Virginia, listed Margaret Wright with the following household on April 5:

Date	Persons Names Chargeable With Tax	Negroes over 12 years		
April 5	Margaret Wright	-	-	-

Horses &c &c &c		Dollars Cents	Proff
1		.08	

The 1830 Census for Franklin County, Virginia, listed James G. Wright with one female aged 60 to 70 in his household, and this female was almost certainly his mother Margaret "Peggy" (Young) Wright. This record indicates that Margaret "Peggy" (Young) Wright was born between 1760 and 1770.

The 1831 Personal Property Tax List for Franklin County, Virginia, listed Margaret Wright with the following household:

Month Date	Names of Persons chargeable With Tax	Negroes over 12 years		
	Margaret Wright	-	-	-

Horses Mules &c &c		Amount of	
1		.06	

The 1840 Census for Franklin County, Virginia, listed Margaret Wright with the following household:

Names of Heads of Families	Free White Persons Males	Age	Free White Persons Females	Age
Margaret Wright			1	50-60
			1	40-50

Free Colored Persons Male	Age	Free Colored Persons Female	Age	Slaves Males	Age	Slaves Females	Age

	Number of Persons in each Family Employed in					
Total	Mining	Agri-culture	Commerce	Manu-facture and trades	Navigation of the ocean	Navigation of canals lakes and rivers
2						

Learned profes-sions and engineers	Pensioners for Revol-utionary or Military Services included in the foregoing Names	Ages	Deaf and Dumb, Blind and Insane White Persons included in the Foregoing: Deaf and Dumb No.	Ages	Blind

Deaf and Dumb, Blind and Insane White Persons Included in the Foregoing [Continued] Insane and Idiots: Insane and idiots at public charge	Insane and idiots at private charge	Deaf and Dumb, Blind and Insane Colored Persons Included in the Foregoing: Deaf, Dumb, and Blind: Deaf & Dumb	Blind	Insane and Idiots: Insane and idiots at private charge	Insane and idiots at public charge

			Schools, &c.			
Univer-sities or College	Number of Stu-dents	Acade-mies & Grammar Schools	No. of Schol-ars	Primary and Common Schools	No. of Schol-ars	No. of Scholars at public charge
						2

No. of white persons over 90 years of age
<u>in each family who cannot read or write</u>

This record indicates that Margaret "Peggy" (Young) Wright was born between 1780 and 1790, which seems clearly a mistake since she married in 1786. The census data is probably off by 1 or 2 columns and she was probably born closer to 1770 or before.

On January 31, 1844, at Pension File 11901 Peggy (Young) Wright filed her declaration for a pension for the service of 1823 James in the Revolutionary War:

"State of Virginia)
Franklin County) ss. January 31st 1844

On this the thirty first day of January Eighteen hundred and Fortyfour personally appeared before the subscriber a Justice of the peace in and for the County aforesaid Peggy Wright a resident of the State of Virginia in the County of Franklin aged seventyfive years who being first duly sworn according to law doth on her oath make the following declaration in order to obtain the benefit of the provision made by the act of Congress passed July the 7th 1838 entitled An act granting half pay and pensions to certain widows That she is the widow of James Wright who was a revolutionary soldier and to the best of my belief served seven differant tours of three months each three of which tours he served in the Virginia Malitia for himself one tour in the Malitia of Va. as a substitute for James Ray to the best of knowledge and belief it was a three months tour and one three months tour in the virginia malitia as a substitute for George Wright and one other three months tour as a substitute for a man whose name I have forgotten and one other tour of three months as a volunteer. I am unable to state the time my husband entered the service or the period when he left the same ___ were performed previous to our marriage in 1786 the evidence _______ hereto annexed of Moses Greer Jacob Kinsey & Ludwick Kepler as to the services & mariage so far as I now know is the best evidence I can obtain she further declares that she was married to the said James Wright on the 17th day of October one thousand Seven hundred and eighty six that her husband the aforesaid James Wright died on the Eleventh day of March one thousand eight hundred and twenty three that she was not married to him prior to his leaving the service but the marriage took the marriage took place previous to the first day of January Seventeen hundred and ninety four viz. at the time above stated sworn to and subscribed to on the day and year above written.

John Arthur J.P.
Henry Frantz(?)

her
Peggy X Wright
mark

Franklin County to wit

I do hearby certify that according to the appearance of Peggy Wright that she is not able to appear at Court given under my Hand this 31st day of January 1844

John Arthur JP

January 31t 1844

I Moses Greer a clergyman residing in the county of Franklin residing in the same hereby certify that I am well acquainted with Peggy Right who has subscribed and sworn to the above declaration that I believe her to be seventy five years of age that the is reputed and believed in the neighborhood whare she Resides to have been wife of a soldder of the Revolution and that I concur in that opinion Sworn and Subscribed the day and year aforesaid

John Arthur J.P. Moses Greer

State of Virginia)
Franklin County)

personally appeared Ludwick Kepler and made oath that he has been acquainted with the above named James Wright and that he believes him to have been a soldier in the revolutionary war and has heard him say that he served at cabber point and at the dismal swamp and that for upwards of fifty year he has resided in Franklin County and that so far as he knows was raised in the limits of the County aforesaid

John Arthur JP"

This record indicates that Peggy (Young) Wright was born in about 1768 or 1769.

The 1850 Census for Franklin County, Virginia, listed Margaret Wright with the following household on October 21, 1850:

Name	Age	Sex	Color	Occupation	Value of Real Estate
Margaret Wright	84	F			
Mary Wright	50	F			

Place of Birth	Married Within Year	Attended School Within Year	Cannot Read & Write	Deaf Dumb Blind Insane etc.
Virginia				
Virginia				

This record indicates that Margaret "Peggy" (Young) Wright was born in about 1766.

The 1860 Census for Franklin County, Virginia, listed Margaret Wright with the following household on October 4, 1860:

Name	Age	Sex	Color	Occupation	Value of Real Estate
Margt Wright	95	F			
Mary Wright	62	F			

Value of Personal Property	Place of Birth	Married Within Year	Attended School Within Year	Cannot Read & Write	Deaf Dumb Blind Insane etc.
				1	
				1	

This record indicates that Margaret "Peggy" (Young) Wright was born in about 1765.

The death record of John B. Wright was dated on July 15, 1896, at Franklin County, Virginia, and listed the following information for the decedent:

"Place of Death:	Franklin County, Virginia
Line Number:	32
Name of Deceased:	John B. Wright
Race:	White
Sex:	Male
Age:	87
Date of Death:	July 15, 1896
Place:	Franklin County, Virginia
Cause of Death:	Old Age
Name of Parents:	James and Peggy Wright
Birthplace of Deceased:	Franklin County, Virginia
Occupation:	Farmer
Consort of:	Not Stated
Name of Informant:	G. G. Wright

Relation of Informant: Son
Commissioner of the Revenue: F. I. Wray
Date Record Filed: Prior to 1897"

This record confirms the identification of John B. Wright as a son of 1823 James Wright and Margaret "Peggy" (Young) Wright and indicates that he was born in about 1809 at Franklin County, Virginia.

Genealogy Of John J. Wright Of Virginia, Indiana and Kansas by John Calvin Wright stated that James Wright was a son of 1809 William Wright and Mary (Williams) Wright and included the following information regarding this family:

> "On June 27, 1926 the author of these notes went to Franklin County, Virginia and had a conference with Mr. Lewis F. Jamison then living in Boone Mill. Mr. Jamison, together with his son, Curtis Jamison, and his family, lived in the old Jacob Boon house with the old stone chimney which had been erected 140 years before.
>
> Lewis F. Jamison was born in Franklin Co. in 1834 and continued to reside therein to the day of his death. He served four years in the Confederate Army. It was his aunt, Elizabeth Jamison, a daughter of John and Catherine (Boon) Jamison, who married Goodman A. Wright, a son of James Wright.
>
> At the time of my conference with Lewis F. Jamison he was 92 years of age, but his memory was very clear concerining the things that had happened in his early youth. He stated that he was well acquainted with "Peggy" Wright during the period before she died. The United States Census for 1860 for Franklin County, Virginia, page 177, lists her as 95 years of age and living alone with her daughter Mary aged 62.
>
> "Peggy" Wright according to Lewis Jamison lived in a log house, about one mile north of John Jamison's old home (presently owned by Cornelius Jamison a son of Lewis F. Jamison) on the road to Dillon's Mill Post Office and located about two miles from Boone Mill in Franklin Co., Virginia. In 1926 the place was owned by Bessie E. Sink. (According to the early records, the Sink family is spelled Sinck). The Place is more generally known as the J. L. Sink place and was inherited by him from his father, John Sink (1841-1916), Bessie Sink being the wife of J. L. Sink.
>
> Originally, the Sink place on which "Peggy" Wright lived was part of the James Abshire place, and was divided by him among his children. Thomas Abshire fell heir to the place, and he later sold it to Mr. Sink.
>
> James Abshire was a son of Abraham and Phoebe (Wright) Abshire. Phoebe

Wright was the eldest child of James and "Peggy" Wright and hence James Abshire was Peggy's grandson.

Peggy Wright, according to Mr. Jamison was buried in the Abshire burial ground - a public burial ground - located about one-quarter to one-half mile northeast of the Sink place where she formerly lived. He stated that Peggy Wright was a very old lady when she died, that she walked for many years with two canes, and in his opinion must have been from 90 to 95 years of age at her death.

One of the interesting incidents in the life of "Peggy" which came to Mr. Jamison through his father, was the story of a fight that James, husband of Peggy, had with another man who, having succeeded in getting James down on the ground, was suddenly attacked by "Peggy", who took off her shoe and proceeded to knock the man on the head with the heel of it until he became insensible.

Goodman A. Wright, son of James and "Peggy" and a grandfather of the author, was born in 1813. At the age of 22, he married Elizabeth, daughter of John Jamison as shown by the marriage returns on file in the office of the clerk of the county court at Rocky Mount, Va. This marriage occurred on October 27, 1835 with George W. Kelly as the minister. Mr. Lewis F. Jamison stated that he had personally known George W. Kelly, who was a Primitive Baptist minister from Floyd County. A copy of an affadavit made by Lewis F. Jamison is included herewith.

"To Whom It May Concern:

This is to certify that I, Lewis F. Jamison, am a resident of Franklin County, Virginia and have been since the year of my birth in 1834; that I now live in Boone Mill at the home of my son Curtis Jamison; that I am the eldest son of Samuel Jamison, born on March 3rd 1810, and Sarah Webster born in 1812; that Elizabeth Jamison the eldest child of of John Jamison, born October 3rd 1783, and Catherine Boon, born December 3rd, 1785, was a sister of my father and of the same parents; that Elizabeth Jamison married Goodman A. Wright of the same county and neighborhood; that I knew them both from the time of my earliest memory until the year 1856 when they moved to the State of Indiania; that I often visited at their home on Racoon Branch of Little Creek where Goodman A. Wright had a blacksmith Shop where he did general blacksmithing and "ironed new wagons" as a trade; that I now own the three or four acre plat of ground where he then lived; that during my boyhood between the ages from six to twenty two years I often visited and played with their children, Catherine, John, Sarah, Phoebe and baby Samuel; that Goodman A. Wright and Elizabeth his wife were, in the early days of their married live, baptised in the waters of Little Creek and taken into membership in the Church of the Brethern or "Dunkard Church"; and that both were regarded by their neighbors as honored citizens of the community in which they lived being generous and thoughtful of the welfare of others; that their homeland which I now own, is situated about five or six miles southwest of Boone Hill and at that time lay between the plantation of John Jamison on the east, of Andrew Montgomery on the south, and was bounded on the other side by the Boon place.

I further certify that I remember very well Peggy Wright as the mother of Goodman A. Wright; that she was a very old woman at that time; that she frequently came to my father's door where he worked at the shoe makers trade and visited with him; that often when she knocked at his door he would reply, as was his custom, "Come in if you're white" and that she would answer, "I am not very white but I'm coming in anyway"; that she lived in the near neighborhood and had been a widow for many years; that I remember the name of James Wright as being that of her deceased husband and as the father of Goodman A. Wright, and that Goodman A. Wright was a man of great physical strength and was regarded as a leader with the cradle when the wheat harvest was under way.

I further certify that John Jamison, my grandfather and the grandfather of Elizabeth Jamison Wright married Catherine Boon, in Franklin County; that I now live with my son in the old original Boon Home, built about 140 years ago, on the banks of Maggoty Creek, and in the town of Boone Mill.

I further certify that during the war of 1861-65 I enlisted in the 110th Virginia Regiment of Confederate Soldiers; that John A. Wright of the same county was my captain and I believe he became a colonel before the end of the war.

I further certify that I am now in my ninety second year; that I am of sound mind and believe the foregoing statements to be accurate and true.

Signed this 20, day of Jan, in the year of our Lord 1926.

L F Jamison

Notary-

On this the 20 day of Jan 1926 appeared before me Lewis F. Jamison, who is personally known to me as the signer of the foregoing statement, and who being duly sworn attested to the truth of the facts therein.

J. O. Angell
Notary Public.

My commission expires April 26, 1927"

. . . .

Margaret (Young) Wright was the eldest of four children born to James and

Agnes Young."

Fourth Generation:

1896 John B. Wright Of Franklin County, His Wife Jemima (Abshire) Wright, And His Descendants

1896 John B. Wright of Franklin County was the son of 1823 James Wright of Franklin County and Margaret "Peggy" (Young) Wright. (1792 John[1], 1809 William[2], 1823 James[3])

The marriage record of John B. Wright and Jemima Abshire, daughter of Susannah, was dated on December 29, 1831, at Franklin County, Virginia, with Barnabas Arthur as surety and the following affidavit:

"December 27th 1831

Mr caleb Tate Clark of Franklin county court Va can her Arbelle you will please isue licence for John B Wright Jamima Abshire and you will oblige your &c

Test	Abraham Abshire
Tobias Kingray	Susannah X Abshire

Know all Men by these Presents that We John B Wright and Barnabas Arthur are held and firmly bound unto John Floyd Esquire Governor of the Common Wealth of Virginia to which payment well and truly to be made to the said Governor or his successors we bind ourselves and each of us our and each of our heirs Executors and administrators Jointly and Severally firmly by these Presents sealed with our seals and dated this 29 Day of December 1831

The Condition of the above Obligation is such that whereas the above bound John B Wright hath this day Obtained from the Clerks office of the County Court of Franklin a Licence for his Intermarriage with Jemima Abshire of said County now if there shall be no lawful cause to obstruct the said Marriage then the Above Obligation to be Void else to remain in full force and Virtue

Witness		his	
C: Tate	John B	X	Wright
		mark	
		his	
	Barnabas	X	Arthur
		mark	

A list of marrages Celebrated by Mr Moses Greer Jun in the County of Franklin in the year 1831

. . . .

December 29 John Wright To Jummima Abshire"

The 1832 Personal Property Tax List for Franklin County, Virginia, listed John B Wright with the following household on April 17:

Date	Names of Persons Owning Property	White Tyths	Blacks Over 12 Years	Blacks Over 16 Years
Apl 17	John B Wright	1	-	-

Horses Mules		Amount of Tax	
1		.06	

The 1833 Personal Property Tax List for Franklin County, Virginia, listed John Wright (Jas son with the following household on April 12:

Date of List	Owners Names	White Tythes	Blacks over 12 Years	Blacks over 16 Years
Apl 12	John Wright (Jas son	1	-	-

Horses &c &c		Amt. of tax $	
-		-	

The 1834 Personal Property Tax List for Franklin County, Virginia, listed John Wright James son with the following household on April 5:

Date of List	Names of Persons	White Tythes	Blacks over 12 Years	Blacks over 16 Years
Apl 5	John Wright James son	1	-	-

Horses Mules &c		Amount of Tax	
-		-	

In 1834 at Franklin County, Virginia, Chancery Court, Virginia State Library Reel 293/452, John B. Wright was included in "A list of insolvent Tythables in the County Leavy returned by Walter C Callaway Jr. for Henry Carper for the year 1834".

The 1835 Personal Property Tax List for Franklin County, Virginia, listed John Wright (James son with the following household on May 5:

Date of List	Names of Persons	White Tyths	Blacks over 12 Years	Blacks over 16 Years
May 5	John Wright (James son	1	-	-

Horses Mules &c		Amt of Tax	
-		-	

The 1836 Personal Property Tax List for Franklin County, Virginia, listed John Wright Jas son with the following household:

Date of List	Names of Owners	White Tyths	Blacks over 12 Years	Blacks over 16 Years
	John Wright Jas son	1	-	-

Horses Mules &c		Amt of Tax	
1		.06	

The 1837 Personal Property Tax List for Franklin County, Virginia, listed John Wright James son with the following household:

Date of List	Names of Owners	White Tythes	Blacks over 12 Years	Blacks over 16 Years
	John Wright James son	1	-	-

Horses &c	Amt of Tax	
-	-	

The 1840 Census for Franklin County, Virginia, listed John B. Wright with the following household:

Names of Heads of Families	Free White Persons Males	Age	Free White Persons Females	Age
John B Wright	1	20-30	1	15-20
	2	5-10	1	10-15
	1	0-5	1	0-5

Free Colored Persons Male	Age	Free Colored Persons Female	Age	Slaves Males	Age	Slaves Females	Age

Total	Mining	Agri-culture	Commerce	Manu-facture and trades	Navi-gation of the ocean	Naviga-tion of canals lakes and rivers
Number of Persons in each Family Employed In						
7				1		

Learned profes-sions and engineers	Pensioners for Revolu-tionary or Military Services included in the foregoing: Names	Ages	Deaf and Dumb, Blind and Insane White Persons included in the Foregoing: Deaf and Dumb: No.	Ages	Blind

Deaf and Dumb, Blind and Insane White Persons Included in the Foregoing [Continued]: Insane and Idiots: Insane and idiots at public charge	Insane and idiots at private charge	Deaf and Dumb, Blind and Insane Colored Persons Included in the Foregoing: Deaf, Dumb, and Blind: Deaf & Dumb	Blind	Insane and Idiots: Insane and idiots at pri-vate charge	Insane and idiots at public charge

Schools, &c.: Univer-sities or College	Number of Stu-dents	Acade-mies & Grammar Schools	No. of Schol-ars	Primary and Common Schools	No. of Schol-ars	No. of Scholars at public charge

No. of white persons over 90 years of age in each family who cannot read or write

This record indicates that John B. Wright was born between 1810 and 1820, but that is inconsistent with other records for his birth.

The 1841 Personal Property Tax List for Franklin County, Virginia, listed John Wright (Jam son with the following household:

Date of Receiving Lists from Individuals	Persons Names Chargeable With Tax	No of White Males	Slaves above 12 years old
	John Wright (Jam son	1	-

Slaves above 16 years old	Horses Mares Mules & Colts	Carriages whether four wheel or two Wheel riding Carriages phea stage wagons with the Vallue thereof	
-	-		-

The 1842 Personal Property Tax List for Franklin County, Virginia, listed John Wright (Jamson) with the following household:

Date of Receiving Lists from Individuals	Persons Names Chargeable With Tax	No of White Males Above 16	Slaves above 12 years old
	John Wright (Jamson	1	-

Slaves above 16 years old	Horses Mares Mules & Colts	Carriages whether 4 wheel or two wheel riding Carriages Carryall and all others with Vallue thereof	Amount of Tax
-	-		-

The 1843 Personal Property Tax List for Franklin County, Virginia, listed John Wright Jamson with the following household:

	Names of Persons Taxable	White males over 16 years of age	Slaves over 12 years of age	Slaves over 16 years of age
	John Wright Jamson	1		

Horses Colts	Carriages Carryalls and Livery wagons	Pianos(?)	Gold watches	Silver Lever watches	Common silver watches

Wooden clocks	Metal Clocks	Amount of tax
		.14

The 1844 Personal Property Tax List for Franklin County, Virginia, listed Jno. Wright (Jas Son) with the following household:

Dates of Receiving lists	Persons names Chargeable with tax	White Males above 16 years of age	Slaves above 12 years of age	Slaves above 16 years of age
	Jno Wright (Jas Son)	1		

Horses &c	No 4 Wheel Pleasure Carriages and value	No of Carryalls & value	No. Gold Watches	No. Silver Laver or Lapine Watches	No. Other Watches

No. Clocks at 50 Cents	No. Clocks at 25 Cents	No. Pianos and Value	Physicians paying a specific tax	Gold & Silver plate	Interest Received

Deeds Wills& letters of Admns	Total Amount of Tax

The 1845 Personal Property Tax List for Franklin County, Virginia, listed John B Wright with the following household:

	Persons Chargeable with tax	White males above 16 years of age	Slaves above 16 years of age	Slaves above 12 years of age
	John B Wright	1		

Horses, mules, &c.	4 wheel pleasure carriages and harness and value	Stages, and value including harness	Carryalls and harness, and value	2 Wheel pleasure carriages and harness and value

Gold watches	Patent lever or lepine silver watches	Other watches	Metallic clocks	Other clocks	Pianos, and value

Plate over the value of $50	Attorneys paying specific tax, and am't of tax	Physicians and surgeons paying specific tax, and amount of tax	Dentists paying specific tax and amount of tax	Am't of int, or profits on moneys loaned out, or on bonds acquired by purchase, including interest, pre_ or dividends on state or corporat'n bonds

Am't of monied yearly income over $400, received as salaries or fees of office	Bridges - am't of yearly rent or value over $100	Ferries - am't of yearly rent or value over $100	Newspaper printing presses and amount of tax	Total am't of tax. Dollars Cents

The 1846 Personal Property Tax List for Franklin County, Virginia, listed John B Wright with the following household:

	Persons Chargeable With Tax	White males above 16 years of age	Slaves above 16 years of age	Slaves above 12 years of age
	John B Wright	1		

Horses, mules, &c.	4 wheel pleasure carriages and harness and value	Stages, and value including harness	Carryalls and harness, and value	2 Wheel pleasure carriages and harness, and value

Gold watches	Patent lever or lepine silver watches	Other watches	Metallic clocks	Other clocks	Pianos, and value

Plate over the value of $50	Attorneys paying specific tax, and am't of tax	Physicians and surgeons paying specific tax, and amount of tax	Dentists paying specific tax and amount of tax	Am't of int, or profits on moneys loaned out, or on bonds acquired by purchase, including interest, profits or dividends on state or corporat'n bonds

Am't of monied yearly income over $400, received as salaries or fees of office	Bridges - am't of yearly rent or value over $100	Ferries - am't of yearly rent or value over $100	Newspaper printing presses and amount of tax	Total am't of tax. Dollars Cents

The 1847 Personal Property Tax List for Franklin County, Virginia, listed John B Wright with the following household:

	Persons Chargeable With Tax	White males above 16 years of age	Slaves above 16 years of age	Slaves above 12 years of age
	John B Wright	1		

Horses, mules, &c.	4 wheel pleasure carriages & harness and value	Stages, and value including harness	Carryalls and harness, and value	2 Wheel pleasure carriages & value

Gold watches	Patent L watches	Other watches	Metallic clocks	Other clocks	Pianos & value

Plate over the value of $50	Attorneys paying specific tax and amount of tax	Physicians &c paying specific tax	Dentists paying specific Tax & amount of tax	Am't of Interest and profits

Am't of monied yearly income over $400	Bridge value -	Ferry - value	Newspaper	Dollars Cents

The 1848 Personal Property Tax List for Franklin County, Virginia, listed John B Wright with the following household:

_____	________	White males above 16 years of age	Slaves above 16 years of age	Slaves above 12 years of age
	John B Wright	1		

Horses, mules, &c.	4 wheel pleasure carriages and harness & value	Stages and value including harness	2 Wheel pleasure carriages and Harness, & value	Gold watches

Patent lever or lepine silver watches	Other watches	Metallic clocks	Other clocks	Pianos, and value	Plate over the value of $50

Attorneys paying specific tax, and am't of tax	Physicians and surgeons paying specific tax, and amount of tax	Dentists paying specific tax and amount of tax	Am't of int, or profits on moneys loaned out, or on bonds acquired by purchase, including interest, profits or dividends on state or corporat'n bonds

Am't of monied yearly income over $400, received as salaries or fees of office	Bridges Value	Ferries Value	Newspapers value	
				.10

The 1849 Personal Property Tax List for Franklin County, Virginia, listed John B. Wright with the following household on March 5:

	Persons Chargeable With Tax	White males above 16 years of age	Slaves above 16 years of age	Slaves above 12 years of age
Mar 5	John B. Wright	1		

Horses, mules, &c.	4 wheel pleasure carriages and harness and value	Stages, and value including harness	Carryalls and harness, and value	2 Wheel pleasure carriages and harness, and value

Gold watches	Patent lever or lepine silver watches	Other watches	Metallic clocks	Other clocks	Pianos, and value

Plate over the value of $50	Attorneys paying specific tax, and am't of tax	Physicians and surgeons paying specific tax amt of tax	Dentists paying specific tax and amount of tax	Am't of int, or profits on moneys loaned out, or on bonds acquired by purchase, including interest, profits or dividends on state or corporat'n bonds

Am't of monied yearly income over $400, received as salaries or fees of office	Bridges - am't of yearly rent or value over $100	Ferries - am't of yearly rent or value over $100	Newspaper printing presses and amount of tax	Total am't of tax. Dollars Cents

The 1850 Personal Property Tax List for Franklin County, Virginia, listed John B

Wright with the following household:

	Persons Chargeable With Tax	White males above 16 years of age	Male free negroes above sixteen	Slaves above 16 years of age	Slaves above 12 years of age
	John B Wright	2			

Horses, mules, &c.	4 wheel pleasure carriages and harness and value	Stages, and value including harness	Carryalls and harness, and value	2 Wheel pleasure carriages and harness, and value

Gold watches	Patent lever or lepine silver watches	Other watches	Metallic clocks	Other clocks	Pianos, and value	Harps and value

Plate over the value of $50	Attorneys paying specific tax, and am't of tax	Physicians and surgeons paying specific tax, and amount of tax	Am't of int, or profits on moneys loaned out, or on bonds acquired by purchase, including interest, profit or dividends on state or corporat'n bonds

Am't of monied yearly income over $400, received as salaries or fees of office	Bridges - am't of yearly rent or value over $100	Ferries - am't of yearly rent or value over $100	Total amount tax. Dollars Cents

The 1850 Census for Franklin County, Virginia, listed John B. Wright with the following household on October 19, 1850:

Name	Age	Sex	Color	Occupation	Value of Real Estate
John B. Wright	42	M		Farmer	$150
Jemima Wright	46	F			
Nancy Wright	21	F			
James Wright	18	M			
Abraham Wright	16	M			
Robert Wright	14	M			
Margaret Wright	12	F			
William Wright	9	M			
George Wright	2	M			

Place of Birth	Married Within Year	Attended School Within Year	Cannot Read & Write	Deaf Dumb Blind Insane etc.
Virginia				
Virginia				
Virginia				
Virginia				
Virginia				
Virginia				
Virginia				
Virginia				
Virginia				

This record indicates that John B. Wright was born in about 1808 and that Jemima (Abshire) Wright was born in about 1804.

The 1860 Census for Franklin County, Virginia, listed Jno. B. Wright with the following household on October 12, 1860:

Name	Age	Sex	Color	Occupation	Value of Reak Estate
Jno B. Wright	53	M		Farmer	
Jemima Wright	56	F			
Abram Wright	25	M			400
Wm Wright	15	M			
Geo Wright	11	M			
Mahala Mason	35	F			
Nancy Mason	3	F			

Value of Personal Property	Place of Birth	Married Within Year	Attended School Within Year	Cannot Read & Write	Deaf Dumb Blind Insane etc.
				1	
				1	

This record indicates that John B. Wright was born in about 1807 and that Jemima (Abshire) Wright was born in about 1804.

The 1870 Census for Franklin County, Virginia, listed John B. Wright with the following household on October 7, 1870:

Name	Age	Sex	Color	Occupation	Value of Real Estate
John Wright	60	M	W	Farmer	
Jimmima Wright	58	F	W	Keeping house	
George Wright	25	M	W	Farm laborer	
William Wright	23	M	W	Farm laborer	
Joseph Wright	21	M	W	Farm laborer	
Hastie Whitlow	40	F	W	Domestic Servant	

Value of Personal Property	Place of Birth	Married Within Year	Born Within Year	Attended School Within Year	Cannot Read
	Virginia				
	Virginia				
	Virginia				
	Virginia				
	Virginia				
	Virginia				1

Cannot Write	Deaf Dumb Blind Insane or Idiot	Male Citizen Over 21	Male Citizen Over 21 Without Right to Vote
		1	
		1	
1		1	
1		1	
1			

This record indicates that John B. Wright was born in about 1810 and that Jemima (Abshire) Wright was born in about 1820.

The 1880 Census for Franklin County, Virginia, listed John B. Wright in the G. G. Wright household, his relationship as father, and his age as 71, indicating a date of birth in about 1809.

The absence of a listing of Jemima (Abshire) Wright in the 1880 Census indicates that she had probably died before 1880.

The death record of John B. Wright was dated on July 15, 1896, at Franklin County, Virginia, and listed the following information for the decedent:

"Place of Death:	Franklin County, Virginia
Line Number:	32
Name of Deceased:	John B. Wright
Race:	White
Sex:	Male
Age:	87
Date of Death:	July 15, 1896
Place:	Franklin County, Virginia
Cause of Death:	Old Age
Name of Parents:	James and Peggy Wright
Birthplace of Deceased:	Franklin County, Virginia
Occupation:	Farmer
Consort of:	Not Stated
Name of Informant:	G. G. Wright
Relation of Informant:	Son
Commissioner of the Revenue:	F. I. Wray
Date Record Filed:	Prior to 1897"

This record confirms the identification of John B. Wright as a son of 1823 James Wright and Margaret "Peggy" (Young) Wright and indicates that he was born in about 1809 at

Franklin County, Virginia.

DAR Application #388187 for Genevieve (Wright) Smith dated February 24, 1949, stated that John B. Wright was a son of James Wright and Margaret (Young) Wright, was born in 1808, and married Jemima Abshire on December 29, 1831.

From the evidence set forth above and additional evidence set forth below, the children of 1896 John B. Wright of Franklin County and Jemima (Abshire) Wright were the following:

1) Nancy (Wright) Mitchell, born on February 24, 1829, at Virginia,

2) James G. Wright, born on August 11, 1832, at Franklin County, Virginia,

3) Abraham H. Wright, born in about 1832 or in October 1834 or in about 1835 at Franklin County, Virginia,

4) Robert Wright, born in about 1836 or 1838 at Franklin County, Virginia,

5) Margaret Jane (Wright) Mills, born in about 1838 or 1839 or on June 27, 1840, at Franklin County, Virginia,

6) William J. Wright, born in about 1841 or 1845 or 1846 at Franklin County, Virginia,

7) George Greenberry Wright, born in about 1848 or in September 1849 or in about 1850 at Franklin County, Virginia, and

8) Joseph Wright, born in about 1849 at Virginia.

Fifth Generation:

1923 George Greenberry Wright Of Franklin County, His Wife Adness Calla Or Aradnia Caledonia (Hunt) Wright, And His Descendants

1923 George Greenberry Wright of Franklin County was a son of 1896 John B. Wright of Franklin County and Jemima (Abshire) Wright. (1792 John[1], 1809 William[2], 1823 James[3], 1896 John B.[4])

The 1850 Census for Franklin County, Virginia, listed George Wright in the John B. Wright household and his age as 2 and born in Virginia, indicating a date of birth in about 1848.

The 1860 Census for Franklin County, Virginia, listed George Wright in the John B. Wright household and his age as 11, indicating a date of birth in about 1849.

On March 2, 1869, at Franklin County, Virginia, D.B. 29/160 Abram H. Wright, William P. Wright, and George G. Wright purchased a parcel of property from Thomas C. Callaway:

> "This deed maid 2" day March 1869, between Thomas C. Callaway & Susan his wife of the first part and Abram H. Wright, William P. Wright & George G. Wright of the second part. Witness that in consideration of the some of five hundred & 10 dollars to me in hand paid the said Thos. C. Callaway & Susan his wife do grant unto said Abram Wright, William P. Wright & George G. Wright a tract of land lying in the County of Franklin on the headwaters of Blackwater & Maggoty and bounded as follows, beginning at chestnut tree on top of the mountain South 59-1/2, W 76 poles to and old corner hickery S 58 W 49 po to pointers formerly a chestnut oak S 8, W 41 poles to a chestnut Oak, S 50°, 10 East 103 po to a chestnut Oak, S. 15 W 58-1/2 poles to pointers thence with widow Arther's line S 39-1/2, E. 23-1/2 po to a big white Oake head of two branches S 58-1/2 E 48 po to a chestnut oak on top of the mountain thence with top of mountain on the dividing of Blackwater river & Maggoty North 65-1/2 E 28-1/2 po to chestnut tree N 13 E. 18 poles to a hickey tree N 40 E 114 pole to Locust tree N 2 E 31 po to a hickery tree, N 59-1/2 West 58-1/2 po to a chestnut tree, N 43-3/4 N 31.4 poles to a chestnut tree, E 70 to a Gum tree N 49-1/4 W 73 po to a chestnut tree N 73-3/4 West 313 to a chestnut tree S 73-1/2 W 7 poles to a large chestnut Oak, S 39° 20. W 32 poles to a large chestnut, N 11 W 44-1/2 to the beginning, the Beverly tract beginning at a chestnut oake on to of the Ridge thence South 55 E 58 po to a Stump. S 29 W crassing a branch runing East at 14-1/2 po whole lenght of line 20- 1/2 po to a dogwood S 76-1/2, W 65 po a large Rock on to of the Ridge, S 18 E 83-1/2 po to a large chestnut tree plainly marked N 60 W 38 pole to a chestnut Oake on top of the Ridge on the side of a road thence along the said Ridge as it manders N 52 W 20 poles to a chestnut tree on top of Ridge or Knoll N 51-1/2 E 18 po to a small chestnut oak on top of a Knaull N 4° E 12 po N 8° E 10-1/2 poles to a chestnut tree on the point of a spur of the ridge, N 44 E 56 poles to the beginning it being the same that said H. Callaway purchest of John Beverly the said Thomas C. Callaway & Susan his wife do covenant with the said Abram Wright, William P. Wright, & George G. Wright that they will warrant especially the property hereby conveyed. Witness the following signatures date above mentioned.
>
> T C. Callaway
> Susan Callaway

Franklin County to wit,

This is to certify that Thomas C. Callaway and Susan his wife parties to the foregoing deed, personally appeared before us in our said County and acknowledged the same to be their act and deed. Given under our hands & seals. This the 9" day of March 1869.

M T. Greer
D G. Peters

Franklin County to wit,

We M. T. Greer & Daniel G. Peters Justices of the peace for said County do hereby certify that Susan Callaway, wife of Thos C. Callaway, and a party to the foregoing deed bearing date 2" day of March 1869, personally appeared before us in our said County, and being questioned by us seperately and apart from her husband, and having the aforesaid deed fully explained to her, acknowledged the same, and said that she had signed it willingly and did not wish to retract it. Given under our hands & seals. This the 9" of March 1869.

M T. Greer JP
D G. Peter JP.

In the Clerks Office of Franklin County Court the 30" day of March 1870,

This deed from Thomas C. Callaway & Susan his wife to Abram H. Wright, William P. Wright & George G. Wright was exhibited into the said Office and together with the certificates hereon endorsed admitted to Record (Revenue stamps placed on deed"

The 1870 Census for Franklin County, Virginia, listed George Wright in the John B. Wright household and his age as 25 and born in Virginia, indicating a date of birth in about 1845.

The marriage record of George G. Wright and Adness C. Hunt was dated on July 20, 1871, at Franklin County, Virginia, and listed the following information for the parties:

"Marriage License.

Virginia, Franklin County to wit:
To any Person Licensed to Celebrate Marriages:

You are hereby authorized to join together in the Holy State of Matrimony, according to the rites and ceremonies of your Church, or religious denomination, and the laws of the Commonwealth of Virginia George G Wright and Adness C Hunt

Given under my hand, as Clerk of the County Court of Franklin this 19 day of July 1871

Jas J. Carper Clerk

Certificate to Obtain a Marriage License.

Date of Marriage July 20, 1871
Place of Marriage Franklin Co Va
Full Names of Parties Married George G Wright & Adness C Hunt
Age of Husband 21 Years
Age of Wife 18 Years
Condition of Husband (widowed or single) Single
Condition of Wife (widowed or single) Single
Place of Husband's Birth Franklin Co Va
Place of Wife's Birth Pittsylvania Co Va
Place of Husband's Residence Franklin Co Va
Place of Wife's Residence Franklin Co Va
Names of Husband's Parents John B & Jamima Wright
Names of Wife's Parents, Turner J. & Irena V Hunt
(now Irena V Abshire)
Occupation of Husband Farmer

Given under my hand this 19 day of July 1871

Jas J. Carper Clerk.

Minister's Return of Marriage.

I Certify, that on the 20th day of July 1871 at the House of Abraham Haff I united in Marriage the above named and described parties, under authority of the annexed License.

Abraham Haff"

The birth record of George G. Wright, son of George G. Wright and Arriana C. Wright, was dated on April 8, 1872, at Franklin County, Virginia:

"Name of Child: George G. Wright
Date of Birth: April 8, 1872
Father's Name: George G. Wright
Sex: M
Mother's Name: Arriana C Wright
Place: Franklin"

The birth record of Arina E. Wright, daughter of George G. Wright and Amanda C. Wright, was dated on September 2, 1876, at Franklin County, Virginia:

"Name of Child: Arina E. Wright
Date of Birth: September 2, 1876
Father's Name: George G. Wright
Sex: F
Mother's Name: Amanda C Wright
Place: Franklin"

The 1880 Census for Franklin County, Virginia, listed G. G. Wright with the following household on June 4, 1880:

Name	Color	Sex	Age	Month of Birth	Relationship
G. G. Wright	W	M	34		
A. Calla Wright	W	F	26		wife
Cordelia Wright	W	F	8		daughter
Alice Wright	W	F	7		daughter
J. Emma Wright	W	F	3		daughter
John B. Wright	W	M	71		Father

Marital Status	Married During Year	Occupation	Months Unem-ployed	Sickness Blind Deaf & Dumb Idiotic Disabled
M		Farmer		
M		Keeping house		
S		At home		
S		At home		
S		At home		
W		Farmer		

Attended School Within Year	Cannot Read	Cannot Write	Born	Father Born	Mother Born
		1	Virginia	Va	Va
			Virginia	Va	Va
1			Virginia	Va	Va
1			Virginia	Va	Va
			Virginia	Va	Va
	1	1	Virginia	Va	Va

This record indicates that George G. Wright was born in about 1846 and that Adness Calla (Hunt) Wright was born in about 1854.

On July 1, 1884, at Franklin County, Virginia, D.B. 38/52 Abraham H. Wright and George G. Wright purchased 48 acres of land from the estate of Francis M. Arthur:

"This Deed made July 1st 1884, Between Gideon Turner Admx of Francis M Arthur (decd) of the county of Roanoke State of Virginia of the first part and Abraham H Wright and George G. Wright of the County of Franklin and state of Virginia of the second part Witnesseth that for and in consideration of the sum of $200. the receipt of which is hereby acknowledged, the said Gideon Turner Admr. of Francis M. Arthur (decd) does grant to the said Abraham H. Wright and George G. Wright a part of the tract of land known as the "Lousinia" tract and said to contain 48 acres the rest of a tract of 93-1/2 acres to have and to hold. The said Gideon Turner warrants and defends the said property unto the said Abraham H. Wright and George G. Wright against the the claims and demands of all others. Witness the folloing signature and seal. This the 1st day of July A.D. 1884

Gideon Turner

Franklin Co.
State Virginia To wit,

I J W Naff a Justice of the peace for the county of Franklin State of Va do certify that Gideon Turner Admr of Francis M. Arthur (Decd) whose names is signed to the writing above bearing date on the 1st day of July A.D. 1884 personally appeared before me in my county of Franklin and acknowledged the same to be his act. Given under my hand the 1st day of July 1884

J. W. Naff J.P.

In Franklin County Court Clerks Office the 17th day of August 1886

This deed from Gideon Turner administrator of Francis M. Arthur deceased to Abraham H. Wright and George G Wright, Was exhibited in said office and admitted to record.

Teste
Jas J Carper Clk"

On January 23, 1889, at Franklin County, Virginia, D.B. 44/11 George G. Wright and his wife Aradna C. Wright, Abram H. Wright and his wife Nancy A. Wright, and William J. Wright sold 20 acres of land to Lewis M. Moore:

"This Deed made this the 23rd day of January 1889 between Abram H. Wright and Nancy A. Wright his wife William J Wright and Mary J Wright his wife, George G. Wright and Aradna C. Wright his wife of the County of Franklin and State of Virginia of the first part and Lewis M Moore of the same County and State of the second part Witnesseth That the said Abram H. Wright and Nancy A. his wife, William J Wright and Mary J his wife, George G Wright and Aradna C. his wife for and in consideration of the sum of One Hundred Dollars to them in hand paid by the said Lewis M. Moore the receipt whereof is hereby acknowledged have this day bargained and sold to the said Lewis M. Moore and do by these presents grant bargain sell and confirm a certain tract or parcel of land lying in the County of Franklin on the head waters of Maggodee supposed to contain Twenty acres more or less and bounded as follows to wit: by Abram H. Wright and Zackfield Wade and others, together with all and singular the privileges and appurtanances to the aforesaid tract or parcel of land belonging or in any wise appertaining to the only proper use and behoof of him the said Lewis M Moore to have and to hold free from the claim or claims of them the said Abram H. Wright and Nancy A his wife and William J Wright and Mary J. his wife George G. Wright Arandna C. his wife their heirs Executors and administrators and free from the claim or claims of all and every person or persons whomsoever and the said Abram H. Wright and Nancy A his wife and c William J Wright and Mary J his wife George G Wright and Aradna C his wife do for themselves their heirs and warrant and forever defend the title to the aforesaid tract or parcel of land by these presents. In Testimony whereof the said Abram H. Wright and Nancy A his wife William J Wright and Mary J his wife George G Wright and Aradna C. his wife have hereunto set their hands and seals the day and year first writen.

Abram H Wright
her
Nancy A X Wright
mark

	his	
William J.	X	Wright
	mark	
	her	
Mary J	X	Wright
	mark	

George G Wright
Aradnar C Wright

Franklin County To wit:

I C W Mills Justice of the Peace do certify that Abram H Wright and Nancy A. Wright, William J Wright and Mary J Wright, George G. Wright and Aradna C Wright whose names are signed to the writing above bearing date the 23rd day of January 1889 have acknowledged the same to be their act and deed before me in my County. Given under my hand this day and year above written.

C. W. Mills J.P.

Virginia

In the Clerks Office of Franklin County Court the 25 day of October 1893. The foregoing Deed was this day received in said office and upon the Certificate of acknowledgment this day admitted to record

Teste
Jas J. Carper Clerk"

The 1900 Census for Franklin County, Virginia, listed George Wright with the following household:

Location				
In Cities		Number of dwelling houses in the order of visitation	Number of family in the order of visition	Name of each person whose place of abode on June 1, 1900, was in this family.
Street	House Number			
		195	195	George Wright
				Callie Wright
				Laura J. Gutherie
				Isaac S. Wright
				Lauvenia J. Wright
				Kent A. Gutherie
				Robert L. Gutherie

Relation	Personal Description					
Relationship of each person the head the family	Color or race	Sex	Date of Birth Month	Year	Age at last birthday	Whether single, married, widowed, or divorced
Head	W	M	Sept	1849	50	M
Wife	W	F	May	1853	47	M
Daughter	W	F	Aprl	1881	19	M
Son	W	M	May	1892	8	S
G Daughter	W	F	Aug	1889	10	S
G son	W	M	May	1900	1/12	S
Son-in-law	W	M	May	1873	27	M

Personal Description [cont'd]			Nativity: Place of birth of each person and parents of each person enumerated.		
Number of years married	Mother of how many children	Number of these children living	Place of birth of this Person	Place of birth of Father of this person	Place of birth of Mother of this person
28			Virginia	Virginia	Virginia
28	6	5	Virginia	Virginia	Virginia
0	1	1	Virginia	Virginia	Virginia
			Virginia	Virginia	Virginia
			Virginia	Virginia	Virginia
			Virginia	Virginia	Virginia
0			Virginia	Virginia	Virginia

Citizenship			Occupation, Trade, Or Profession of each person Ten Years of age and over.		Education
Year of immigration to the United States	Number of years in the United States	Naturalization	Occupation	Months not employed	Attended school in months
			Farmer	0	
			Housekeeper	0	
			At School		5
			At School		5
			Farm laborer	0	

Education [cont'd]			Ownership Of Home			
Can read	Can write	Can speak English	Owned or rented	Owned free or mortgaged	Farm or house	Number of farm schedule
Yes	Yes	Yes	O	F	F	166
Yes	Yes	Yes				
Yes	Yes	Yes				
Yes	Yes	Yes				
Yes	Yes	Yes				

The 1910 Census for Franklin County, Virginia, listed George G. Wright with the following household on May 4, 1910:

	Location				
Line Number	Street, Avenue, Road etc.	House number or farm	Dwelling number	Number of family, in order of visitation	Name of each person whose place of abode on April 15, 1910 was in this family. Enter surname first then the given name and middle initial, if any. Include any person living on April 15, 1910. Omit children born since April 15, 1910.
			175	175	George G Wright
					Addie C Wright
					Isac Wright

Relationship	Personal Description						
						Mother of how many children	
Relationship of this person to the head of the family.	Sex	Color or Race	Age at last birthday	Whether single, married, widowed, or divorced	Number of years of present marriage	Number born	Number now living
Head	M	W	59	M1	31		
Wife	F	W	53	M1	31	7	6
son	M	W	18	S			

Nativity			Citizenship	
Place of birth of each person and parents of each enumerated. If born in United States, give state or territory. If foreign birth give the country.				
Place of birth of this person	Place of birth of Father of this person	Place of birth of Mother of this person	Year of immigration to the U.S.	Whether naturalized or Alien
Virginia	Virginia	Virginia		
Virginia	Virginia	Virginia		
Virginia	Virginia	Virginia		

	Occupation		
Whether able to speak English, or, if not, give language spoken.	Trade or profession of, or particular kind of work done by this person.	General nature of industry, business, or establishment in which this person works	Whether an employer, employee, or working on own account.
English	Farmer	Home farm	
English	None		
English	Farm labor	Home farm	

Occupation (cont'd) If an employee.		Education		
Whether out of work on April 15, 1910.	Number of weeks out of work during 1909.	Whether able to read	Whether able to write	Attended school any time since Sept 1, 1900.
0		yes	no	
.		yes	yes	
0		yes	yes	yes

Ownership of Home						
Owned or Rented	Owned free or mortgaged	Farm or house	Number of farm schedule	Whether a survivor of the Union Confederation Army or Navy	Whether blind (both eyes)	Whether deaf and dumb.
O	F	F	157			

This record indicates that George G. Wright was born in about 1851 and that Adness

Calla (Hunt) Wright was born in about 1857.

The 1920 Census for Franklin County, Virginia, listed George G. Wright with the following household on February 12, 1920:

	Location				
Line number	Street, avenue, road etc.	House number or farm	Dwelling Number	Number of family, in order of visitation	Name of each person whose place of abode on January 1, 1920 was in this family.
	Mills Mountain Road		114	114	George G Wright
					Callie Wright
					Isaac S Wright
					Sarah L Wright
					Gemima H Wright
					Mildred L Wright

Relation.	Tenure.		Personal Description			
Relationship of this person to the head of the family.	Home owned or rented	If owned, free or mortgaged	Sex	Color or Race	Age at last birthday	Single, married, widowed, or divorced
Head	O	F	M	W	69	M
Wife			F	W	65	M
son			M	W	27	M
daughter in law			F	W	22	M
grand daughter			F	W	4-7/12	S
grand daughter			F	W	2-3/12	S

Citizenship			Education		
Year of immigration to the United States.	Naturalized or alien	If naturalized, year of naturalization.	Attended school any-time since Sept. 1, 1919	Able to read.	Able to write.
				no	no
				no	no
				yes	yes
				yes	yes

Whether able to speak English, or, if not, give language spoken.	Occupation: Trade or profession of, or particular kind of work done by this person.	General nature of industry, business, or establishment in which this person works	Whether an employer, employee, or working on own account.

Nativity and Mother Tongue: Place of birth of each person and parents of each person enumerated. If born in United States, give state or territory. If foreign birth, give the place of birth, and in addition, the mother tongue.					
Person		Father		Mother	
Place of Birth	Mother Tongue	Place of Birth	Mother Tongue	Place of Birth	Mother Tongue
Virginia		Virginia		Virginia	
Virginia		Virginia		Virginia	
Virginia		Virginia		Virginia	
Virginia		Virginia		Virginia	
Virginia		Virginia		Virginia	
Virginia		Virginia		Virginia	

Able to speak English	Occupation: Trade, profession, or particular kind of work done.	Industry, business, or etablishment in which at work.	Employer, salary or wage worker, or working on own account.	Number of farm schedule.
yes	Farmer	General farm	OA	90
yes	none			
yes	Farmer laborer	Home farm	OA	
yes	none			
yes				

This record indicates that George G. Wright was born in about 1851 and that Adness Calla (Hunt) Wright was born in about 1855.

The will of George G. Wright was dated on July 8, 1909, probated on August 2, 1923, at Franklin County, Virginia, W.B. 28/94, and provided as follows:

"In the name of God Amen:

I, George G. Wright of Franklin County, Virginia, do make this my last will and Testament as follows:

1st. I give and devise unto my son Isaac all my real estate consisting of two tracts of land lying in Franklin County, Virginia, on the head waters of Blackwater River, containing, one hundred and two acres, more or less, it being the remainder of my two tracts of land after taking off two small tracts or boundaries of land to be deeded to my two daughters Irene E. & Laura J. upon the following conditions, that is to say he is to pay to Alice Bohon twenty five dollars shortly after decease or before if he wishes to do so as Cordelia Wright has been paid heretofore her part, he is also to take care of and support his mother during her natural life if she survives me.

I appoint R. L. Bohon Executor of this my will and desire that no security be required of him. I hereby revoke all previous wills and codicils heretofore made by me

Witness my hand this 8th day of July 1909.

George G. Wright

Signed and acknowledged by George G. Wright as and for his last will in presence of us who in his presence and in the presence of each other have hereunto subscribed our names as witnesses.

T. J. Wright
W. T. Beckner

Virginia:

In Franklin Circuit Court August 2nd, 1923. The last will and testament of George G. Wright, deceased, was produced in court and proved by the oath of T. J. Wright, one of the subscribing witnesses thereto, who testified that said will was signed, sealed and acknowledged by the Testator in his presence & in the presence of W. T. Beckner, the other subscribing witness thereto, they both being present at the same time, and that said will was attested by him and the said W. T. Beckner at the same time, in the presence of each other and in the presence of and at the request of said Testator, the said will is ordered to be recorded.

Teste,
T. W. Carper, Clerk."

In his email dated March 23, 1999, Stephen David Cabaniss stated that George Greenberrry Wright married Aradnia Caledonia Hunt and that they had the following child:

1) Irene Emma (Wright) Mills.

Sixth Generation:

<u>1957 Isaac Stoner Wright, His Wife Sarah Lutie (Guthrie) Wright, And His Descendants</u>

1957 Isaac Stoner Wright was a son of 1923 George Greenberry Wright of Franklin County and Adness Calla (Hunt) Wright. (1792 John[1], 1809 William[2], 1823 James[3], 1896 John B.[4], 1923 George Greenberry[5])

The 1900 Census for Franklin County, Virginia, listed Isaac S. Wright in the George Wright household, his relationship as son, and his birth in May 1892 at Virginia.

The will of George G. Wright dated on July 8, 1909, and probated on August 2, 1923, at Franklin County, Virginia, W.B. 28/94 listed Isaac Wright as one of his children:

"In the name of God Amen:

I, George G. Wright of Franklin County, Virginia, do make this my last will and Testament as follows:

1st. I give and devise unto my son Isaac all my real estate consisting of two tracts of land lying in Franklin County, Virginia, on the head waters of Blackwater River, containing, one hundred and two acres, more or less, it being the remainder of my two tracts of land after taking off two small tracts or boundaries of land to be deeded to my two daughters Irene E. & Laura J. upon the following conditions, that is to say he is to pay to Alice Bohon twenty five dollars shortly after decease or before if he wishes to do so as Cordelia Wright has been paid heretofore her part, he is also to take care of and support his mother during her natural life if she survives me.

. . . ."

The 1910 Census for Franklin County, Virginia, listed Isaac S. Wright in the George G. Wright household as his son and age 18, indicating a birth in about 1892.

The marriage record of Isaac S. Wright and Sarah Lutie Guthrie was dated on June 10, 1914, at Franklin County, Virginia, and listed the following information for the parties:

"Marriage License

Virginia, Franklin County to-wit:
To any Person Licensed to Celebrate Marriages:

You are hereby authorized to join together in the Holy State of Matrimony according to the rites and ceremonies of your Church, or religious denomination, and the laws of the Commonwealth of Virginia, Isaac Wright and Sarah Lutie Guthrie

Given under my hand, as Clerk of the Circuit Court of Franklin County (or City) this 10 day of June 1914

T W Carper Clerk.

Marriage Certificate
Virginia: In the Clerk's Office of the Circuit Court for the County of Franklin

Date of Marriage, 11 June 1914
Place of Marriage, Franklin Co Va
Full Names of Parties, Isaac Wright and Sarah Lutie Guthrie
Age of Husband 22 years
Condition (single, widowed or divorced) Single
Age of Wife 15 years
Condition (single, widowed or divorced) Single
Race (White or Colored) White
Husband's Place of Birth, Franklin Co Va
Residence, Franklin Co Va
Wife's Place of Birth, Franklin Co Va
Residence, Franklin Co Va
Names of Husband's Parents, Geo. G. Wright and Aradna Wright
Names of Wife's Parents, J H Guthrie and Docia I. Guthrie
Occupation of Husband, Farmer

Given under my hand this 10 day of June 1914

T W Carper Clerk.

Certificate of Time and Place of Marriage

I, D. A. Naff, a Minister of the Church of the Brethren Church, or religious order of that name, do certify that on the 11 day of June 1914, at my house, Virginia, under authority of the above License, I united in Marriage the persons named and described therein. I qualified and gave bond according to law authorizing me to celebrate the rites of marriage in the County (or City) of Franklin, State of Virginia.

Given under my hand this 11 day of June 1914

D. A. Naff M.G."

This record clearly identifies Isaac Wright as a son of George G. Wright and Aradnia Caledonia (Hunt) Wright.

The 1920 Census for Franklin County, Virginia, listed Isaac S. Wright in the George G. Wright with the following household on February 12, 1920:

	Location				
Line number	Street, avenue, road etc.	House number or farm	Dwelling Number	Number of family, in order of visitation	Name of each person whose place of abode on January 1, 1920 was in this family.
	Mills Mountain Road		114	114	George G Wright
					Callie Wright
					Isaac S Wright
					Sarah L Wright
					Gemima H Wright
					Mildred L Wright

Relation.	Tenure.		Personal Description			
Relationship of this person to the head of the family.	Home owned or rented	If owned, free or mortgaged	Sex	Color or Race	Age at last birthday	Single, married, widowed, or divorced
Head	O	F	M	W	69	M
Wife			F	W	65	M
son			M	W	27	M
daughter in law			F	W	22	M
grand daughter			F	W	4-7/12	S
grand daughter			F	W	2-3/12	S

Citizenship			Education		
Year of immigration to the United States.	Naturalized or alien	If naturalized, year of naturalization.	Attended school any-time since Sept. 1, 1919	Able to read.	Able to write.
				no	no
				no	no
				yes	yes
				yes	yes

	Occupation		
Whether able to speak English, or, if not, give language spoken.	Trade or profession of, or particular kind of work done by this person.	General nature of industry, business, or establishment in which this person works	Whether an employer, employee, or working on own account.

Nativity and Mother Tongue

Place of birth of each person and parents of each person enumerated. If born in United States, give state or territory. If foreign birth, give the place of birth, and in addition, the mother tongue.

Person		Father		Mother	
Place of Birth	Mother Tongue	Place of Birth	Mother Tongue	Place of Birth	Mother Tongue
Virginia		Virginia		Virginia	
Virginia		Virginia		Virginia	
Virginia		Virginia		Virginia	
Virginia		Virginia		Virginia	
Virginia		Virginia		Virginia	
Virginia		Virginia		Virginia	

Occupation				
Able to speak English	Trade, profession, or particular kind of work done.	Industry, business, or etablishment in which at work.	Employer, salary or wage worker, or working on own account.	Number of farm schedule.
yes	Farmer	General farm	OA	90
yes	none			
yes	Farmer laborer	Home farm	OA	
yes	none			
yes				

This record indicates that Isaac Stoner Wright was born in about 1893 and that Sarah Lutie (Guthrie) Wright was born in about 1898.

The 1930 Census for Franklin County, Virginia, listed Isaac S. Wright with the following household on April 9, 1930:

Place of Abode				
Street, avenue, road etc.	House number (in cities or towns)	Number of dwelling house in order of visitation	Number of family in order of visitation	Name of each person whose place of abode on April 1, 1930 was with this family. Enter sur-name first, then given name, and middle initial (if any). Omit child-ren born since April 1, 1930
		80	82	Isaac S Wright
				Sarah L Wright
				Hortense Wright
				Mildred Wright
				Cecil Wright
				Clytie Wright
				George Wright
				Blanch Wright
				Callie Wright

Relation. Relationship of this person to the head of the family	Home Data			
	Home owned or rented	Value of home if owned, or monthly rental if rented	Radio set	Does this family live on a farm
Head	O	2000		yes
Wife				
Son				
Daughter				
Son				
Daughter				
Son				
Daughter				
Daughter				

Personal Description					Education	
Sex	Color or race	Age at last birthday	Marital condition	Age at at first marriage	Attended school or college any time since September 1, 1929	Whether able to read and write
M	W	37	M	22	no	yes
F	W	32	M	17	no	yes
M	W	14	S		yes	yes
F	W	11	S		yes	yes
M	W	9	S		yes	yes
F	W	7	S		yes	yes
M	W	5	S		no	
F	W	3	S		no	
F	W	8/12	S		no	

Place of Birth		
Place of birth of each person and parents of each person enumerated and of his or her parents. If born in the U.S., give state or territory. If of foreign birth, give county in which birthplace is now situated.		
Person	Father	Mother
Virginia	Virginia	Virginia
Virginia	Virginia	Virginia
Virginia	Virginia	Virginia
Virginia	Virginia	Virginia
Virginia	Virginia	Virginia
Virginia	Virginia	Virginia
Virginia	Virginia	Virginia
Virginia	Virginia	Virginia
Virginia	Virginia	Virginia

Mother Tongue or Native Language				Citizenship, etc.		
Lanuage spoken in home before coming to the United States	Code (for office use only) State or M.T.	Country	Nativity	Year of immigration to the U.S.	Natural-ization	Able to speak English
						yes
						yes
						yes
						yes
						yes

Occupation and Industry			Employment	
Occupation Trade, profession, or particular type of work, as spinner, salesman, etc.	Industry Industry or busi- iness, as cotton mill, dry goods store, etc.	Code (for office use only)	Whether actually at work yesterday (or last regular working day) Yes or no	If not, line number on Unemployment
Farmer	General farm	VVVV	0	
none				
none				
none				
none				
none				
none				
none				
none				

Veterans: Whether a veteran of U.S. military or naval forces — Yes or no	What war or expedition	Number of farm schedule
non		57

This record indicates that Isaac Stoner Wright was born in about 1893 and that Sarah Lutie (Guthrie) Wright was born in about 1898.

In his emails dated November 17, 2001, Tom Wright stated that Isaac Stoner Wright was a son of George Greenberry Wright and Aranda (Hunt) Wright, was born on May 9, 1892, and married Sarah Guthrie, and died on December 1, 1957, and that Isaac Stoner Wright and Sarah (Guthrie) Wright had the following children:

1) Gemina Hortense Wright, born on May 13, 1915,
2) Mildred Louvina Wright, born on August 7, 1917,
3) Cecil Woodrow Wright, born on November 11, 1919,
4) Clydie Gertrude Wright, born on March 12, 1922,
5) George Stuart Wright, born on November 12, 1924,
6) Blanche Callie Wright, born on August 28, 1927,
7) Beulah Fern Wright, born on August 13, 1929,

8) Beatrice Lottie Wright, born on December 19, 1931,
9) Norman Thomas Wright, born on May 14, 1934,
10) Betty Jane Wright, born on October 7, 1936,
11) Lee Roy Wright, born on October 23, 1938, and
12) Franklin Wilton Wright, born on January 26, 1931.

Seventh Generation:

Norman Thomas Wright, His Wife Joyce (Flora) Wright, And His Descendants

Norman Thomas Wright is the son of 1957 Isaac Stoner Wright and his wife Sarah Lutie (Guthrie) Wright. (1792 John[1], 1809 William[2], 1823 James[3], 1896 John B.[4], 1923 George Greenberry[5], 1957 Isaac Stoner[6])

Norman Thomas Wright is still living and is the father of Thomas Wright, Kit 38118.

Eight Generation:

Thomas Wright

Thomas Wright is the son of Norman Thomas Wright and _____ (____) Wright. (1792 John[1], 1809 William[2], 1823 James[3], 1896 John B.[4], 1923 George Greenberry[5], 1957 Isaac Stoner[6], Norman Thomas[7])

Thomas Wright is still living and is the participant for Kit 38118.

Exhibit E

Documentation For Line Of Descent Of Thomas Carr Wright

Kit 94975

From Justin Glenn:

APPENDIX I (the genealogical record from John Wright III to Thomas Carr Wright).

147. John Wright III (born ca. 1730; married in Price William Co. [Oct. 12, 1753] Ann Williams [born in Prince William Co., 1735/1736; died Oct. 1825, age 89]. By 1771 he was capt. of the Fauquier Co. militia and on April 23 of that same year was commissioned the official surveyor of that county. He sold the last of his property in Fauquier Co., Va., on Sept. 21, 1774, and soon led his family through the Blue Ridge Mountains Gap to the long Indian trail that led southward to the Yadkin River in N.C. He thence headed to the southwestern part of Surry Co. [now Yadkin Co., N.C.], where he settled by Feb. 1775 at the township of Buck Shoals on Deep Creek. Initially laying claim to 1900 acres by "Settlers Rights," he owned five separate tracts of land in the Surry Co. by 1779.

A patriot during the Rev. War, in 1777 he enlisted in Smith's Co., 4th N.C. regt.; he was soon listed as "omitted," however, in a roster dated Sept. 1777. He has been identified [wrongly, no doubt] by A. R. Ritchie [in F. CASSTEVENS, p. 678] with the John Wright listing a claim for 84 months service under Capt. Reese in the *Roster of N.C. Soldiers in the American Rev.* [p. 77, #2060]. This identification is ignored and tacitly contradicted by C. Hoppin's meticulous research on the family. In any event, "our" John Wright was an organizer of "Petty's Meeting House," where he was ordained a deacon June 10, 1783. This church, which subsequently became the Flat Rock Baptist Church, still holds services in Hamptonville, Yadkin Co., N.C. Its old "Minute Book," containing much genealogical information on this large Wright family, has survived and a copy is kept in the Wake Forest U. Library in Winston-Salem.

According to Hoppin's analysis of Surry Co. Order Bk. 2:221, "our" John Wright was one of fifteen men who appeared before the court on Nov. 12, 1787 to be sworn in and empowered to practice as attorney-at-law. Among the fourteen other fledgling lawyers to appear with him that day was 21 year-old Andrew Jackson, future seventh president of the U.S.

John's granddaughter Nancy [Riley] Clark recorded in her 1849 diary that "while serving in the war he took a violent cold that settled on his lungs and eventually caused his death." He died in Surry Co., N.C., Oct. 30, 1789, and Nancy Riley Clark left this account of his passing:

... while on his death bed he suffered much, but bore it all with Christian patience and was perfectly resigned to the will of God. When dying, and gone to all appearance, had ceased to breathe, his wife screamed out of anguish of her heart. She could not give him up. He opened his eyes and said, 'my dear, it is you that keeps me here.' His oldest son then took his mother out of the room and begged her not to make a noise. He then closed his eyes in death ...).

He left an extent will in Surry Co., N.C., dated Oct. 8, 1789:

As it is necessary men should settle their affairs of life before they leave this mortal life, therefore I make this my last Will and Testament. I gave to my daughters Elizabeth Arnold, Nancy Eliott, Agatha Elsbury, Amelia Martin, Lecretia Petty, and Frances Reiley, all of them twenty shillings each.

I give to my son Thomas Wright thirty acres of land which is part of his plantation.

I give to my son Daniel Wright twenty shillings.

I give to my son John Wright two hundred acres of land adjoining Lewis Eliott and Christian Weatherman's land including the field he now has a crop on & feather bed.

I give to my daughter Sally Wright one bay mare and saddle.

I give to my son William Wright & James Wright four hundred acres of land lying on deep Creek adjoining Thomas Jack's land to be equally divided between them.

I give to my son Williams Wright two hundred & seventy acres of land on which I now live but not to possess but one hundred during my wife's life and that to include the field on the south side of the muster ground branch that runs through the plantation bounded on Samuel Arnold's land. It is my will and desire that the three hundred and twenty acres of land I own adjoining John Step'n [i.e., Stephan] and John Elsbery should be sold and the value to be divided between my daughters Rosey and Patsy. I give to my three daughters Sukky, Peggey and Polley Wright ten pounds value each.

My will is that the surveying instruments be sold to buy a horse for use of Estate.

It is my will and desire that my loving wife Anne should have and possess all the rest of my estate together with the plantation I now live on save the hundred acres mentioned and left to son Williams during her lifetime and after to be divided amongst my children whose names are underwritten, namely Nancy [though her name seems to be crossed out, and I agree with J.A.W that her name should be deleted], Sally, Suckey, Peggey, Polley, William, James, Williams, Rosey, and Patsey Wright.

I appoint my beloved wife and son John executors to my last will and testament given under my hand I seal in the year of our Lord One Thousand Seven Hundred and Eighty-Nine and the eighth day of October. [signed by:] John Wright

Test.: Elizabeth Longino

William Elliott

[North Carolina Surry County May Term 1790

The within will was proven by the oath of William Elliott who makes oath that he heard the said Wright publish and declare the same to be his last Will & Testament and he was of sound disposing mind & memory & at the same time he saw Elizabeth Longino sign the same as witness and it was ordered to be recorded. Recorded accordingly, R. L. Williams, C(ounty) C(lerk)]).

Children:

+521. Elizabeth Wright. CA. 1754

522. Nancy Wright (born ca. 1755; married [ca. 1773] Lewis Elliott, and they resided in Surry Co., N.C.).

+523. Agatha Wright. CA. 1756

+524. Thomas Wright. 18 FEB. 1758

+525. Daniel Wright. 27 SEPT. 1759

526. John Wright (born ca. 1761; sheriff of Surry Co., N.C., 1812-1824, he is said to have married and had two sons and one daughter. According to Nancy (Riley)

Clarke Salt's Family Mss., "His wife he left in S.C., his daughter with her. He divided his living and gave his wife one half and took his two sons and moved to Florida. There he died, leaving his sons very much"). According to J.A.W., he m. [Nov. 3, 1790] Ann Mason. It his noteworthy that although he had two older brothers, only he along with his mother were appointed executors. He is apparently the "John Wright" who is listed in the 1820 census Surry Co., N.C., p. 684, with two sons (aged 18 to 26), a wife. In that census only one farm separates his from those of his brother Thomas and his widowed mother Ann. I cannot locate him in the 1830 Florida census).

+527. Amelia Wright. CA. 1763

+528. Sarah Wright. 10 MARCH 1764

+529. Lucretia Wright. 7 JULY 1765

By now we have taken care of the six married daughters and the three grown sons who have left home and established their own households. We have also included the daughter Sarah, who received a special legacy and was unm. and apparently keeping house with her parents when her father wrote his will in 1789. She married soon after her father's death in 1790).

He then made provisions of land for 3 younger sons still at home, and provisions of small legacies for 5 young daughters still at home. Finally, he provided that the older daughter Sally still at home and the 8 younger children still at home should be his residuary legatees and listed them at the end of his will in order of birth.

+530. Frances Wright. 17 FEB. 1767

531. Susan ("Sukky") Wright (born ca. 1769; "may have married Randolph Brown, 1789, Surry Co., N.C." [A. R. RITCHIE, *Sup2*, 107; see also A.R. RITCHIE, 166]). BORN CA. 1769

+532. Margaret "Peggy" Wright. BORN CA. 1771

533. Mary (Polley) Wright (born ca. 1773; said to have married and resided in Surry Co., N.C., but her line is disputed and confused).

+534. William Wright. BORN CA. 1775

+535. James Wright. BORN CA. 1777

+536. Williams Wright. B. 15 APRIL 1779

+537. Rosanna Wright. BORN CA. 1781 [Grave marker 1784; 1850 census says: 1782]

+538. Patsy Wright. 15 OCT. 1784 (In view of her mother's age, perhaps 1782/3 would be more plausible)

Finally, we should note that the above order is very reasonable for the marriages of all the children). [Quotations from C. HOPPIN, "Washington-Wright Connection," *TQ* 4 (1923) 277 (see also 244-280), and NANCY (RILEY) CLARKE SALT, unpubl. Fam. Mss., p. 4, and Surry Co., N.C., Will Bk. 2:160-162; C. HOPPIN, *W.A.*, 1:425-455; A.R. RITCHIE, 49-55, 60, 71, 166; A. R. RITCHIE, *Sup2*, 107, 119; Ritchie in F. CASSTEVENS, *Heritage of Yadkin Co.*, 678; A.L. MARSH, "Marshian Chronicles," unnumbered mss.; J.A.W., *Outline*, 12121]

NEXT GENERATION:

524. Thomas Wright (born in Fauquier Co., Va., Feb. 18, 1758; Rev. War soldier. It was apparently late in 1774 that he began the long trek with his parents from Fauquier Co., Va. to N.C. By Feb. 1775, they had settled in Surry [now Yadkin] Co., N.C., in the township of Buck Shoals on Deep Creek. With the outbreak of the Revolution and the accompanying uprising by the Cherokee Indians, young Thomas served from June to Aug. 1776 in Capt. Jacob Ferree's (or "Ferries") militia company. During this period he helped to build Fort Defiance on the Yadkin River. Shortly after returning home he again volunteered for duty under Capt. Ferree in a N.C. regt. commanded by Col. James Martin. He later served as a militiaman in the spring of 1780 in skirmishes against local Tories.

Meanwhile, in Dec. 1778, he obtained a warrant for 400 acres of land on the south fork of Deep Creek, and soon afterward he married [Jan. 7, 1780] Mary Clanton [born ca. 1759; died June 14, 1844]. A man of some prominence in Surry Co., he represented it in the lower house of the N.C. General Assembly from 1800 to 1803 before being elected to the state senate in 1807 for a one-year term. He was reelected in 1810 to the state senate, where he served continuously until 1817. During the early 1830's he was the senior magistrate of the Surry Co. Court, and was also a prominent member of the Flat Rock Baptist Church until his death on June 22, 1840).

Children:

+1600. John (Philip?) Wright.

1601. Daniel Wright (born Aug. 13, 1784; said to have married Patience ___ and to have had five children. Justus Perkins White, Jr., indicates that this Daniel Wright married [April 27, 1813] Mary Thomas Mitchell [born 1792; died 1824] and that he died in Sedalia, Pettis Co., Mo., March 3, 1874. I note that a Daniel Wright [born in N.C., ca. 1784, appears as a farmer, age 66, in the 1850 census Cooper Co., Mo., married to Margaret D. (born in N.C., ca. 1791) with numerous children, the oldest Samuel born in Ala., ca. 1821).

+1602. Lucy Wright.

+1603. Amelia Wright.

+1604. William Williams Wright.

+1605. Nancy Wright.

+1606. Thomas B. Wright.

+1607. Mary Wright. [W. W. FROST, *FROSTS*, 83-101 (esp. FamBibR, pp. 86-87); Thomas Wright's Rev. War Pension #R.11899 and will (Surry Co. N.C., Will Bk. 4:175), both cited by W. W. FROST, 85, 87; A. R. RITCHIE, 64-67; A. R. RITCHIE, *Sup1*, 36;453-454; F. CASSTEVENS, 679; *DAR P.I.*, 764; 1850 census Cooper Co., Mo., p. 132; FGS by JPW J.A.W., *Outline*, 12121-4]

NEXT GENERATION

1604. William Williams Wright (born in Surry Co., N.C., Feb. 26, 1791; married in Wilkes Co., N.C. [March 28, 1815] his 1st cousin, Sarah Martin [born Sept. 15, 1794; died July 13, 1864]. He acquired property on Hunting Creek in Wilkes Co., N.C., where he held several offices, including justice of the peace and tax collector. He moved with his young family to Madison Co., Ala., ca. 1823, but returned by 1830 to Wilkes Co., where he died Dec. 4, 1870. He was buried in Wright Cem. on Hunting Creek, Wilkes Co., N.C.).

Children:

+4523. Robert Martin Wright.

4524. John Luther Wright (born Sept. 21, 1817; married in Salisbury, Rowan Co., N.C. [June 7, 1846] Mary Shoffe, and he died March 20, 1892).

+4525. Thomas W. Wright.

4526. Williams Martin Wright (born June 3, 1820; married [1850] Adelaide Cauble, and he died April 18, 1899).

4527. David R. Wright (born May 30, 1822; died Aug. 27, 1838).

+4528. Amelia Matilda Wright.

+4529. James William Wright. [A. R. RITCHIE, 65 and *Sup2*, 81; J. HAYES, *Land of Wilkes*, 88; (Anon.), *N.C.: Rebuilding of an Ancient Commonwealth*, 4:515-516; Mrs. W. O. ABSHER, *Heritage of Wilkes Co.*, 471; FamSearch/AF v4.19; *IGI* v4.02, A458609; Anc.com/AWT; J.A.W., *Outline*, 12121-45]

NEXT GENERATION:

4529. James William Wright (born in Ala., Feb. 28, 1826; he moved back to Wilkes Co., N.C. with his family ca. 1836. He taught in local schools and married [July 18, 1861] Frances Almeda Transou [born June 10, 1839; d. May 18, 1907]. At the age of 37 he enlisted as pvt., Co. C, 26th N.C. Inf., CSA, on March 20, 1863. Serving in R. E. Lee's ANV, this famous unit was commanded by "the boy colonel," Col. Henry K. Burgwyn, Jr., who at the age of 21 was killed leading the regt. against the Iron Brigade at Gettysburg on July 1, 1863. Col. Burgwyn was holding the regimental flag when he fell, one of fourteen men who were killed or wounded in succession as they carried their banner in that single assault. Within 30 minutes, 588 out of 803 men in the 26th N.C. Inf. were killed or wounded. James W. Wright survived this slaughter but was wounded two days later in the final phase of the battle. After recuperating at home he rejoined his regt. to participate in the campaigns at the Wilderness, Spotsylvania, and Cold Harbor. He served in the trenches at Petersburg until captured at the Battle of Burgess Mills, Oct. 27, 1864. He was imprisoned at Point Lookout, Md., where he died Jan. 30, 1865).

Child:

+9057. Charles Calvin Wright. [A. M. T. Ball and M. D. W. Gooch in R. T. ABSHER, *Heritage of Wilkes Co.*, 438, 472; (Anon.), *N.C.: Rebuilding an Ancient Commonwealth*, 4:515; A. K. DAVIS, *Boy Colonel*, esp. 292-339; W. FROST, *Frosts*, 88-89; will of J. W. Wright, Wilkes Co., N.C., Will Bk. 5, p. 421-422]

NEXT GENERATION:

9057. Charles Calvin Wright (born on the small family farm in Huntington Creek, Wilkes Co., N.C., Aug. 14, 1862; an only child, he was just two years old when his father died in Confederate service. At the age of seventeen Wright obtained a job teaching school in his native Hunting Creek district of Wilkes Co., N.C., at a salary of $11 per month. He supplemented his income by singing in a popular quartet, "The Big Four," at social functions throughout the region. Elected justice of the peace at the age of 21, he continued his teaching career and served as the county's Superintendent of Schools for 34 years. Throughout this long tenure he achieved vast improvements over what he inherited: "a few log and unpainted frame buildings, as well as an insufficient number of inadequately trained and paid teachers." He was also pres. of both the Wilkes Co. Teachers Assn. and the West Central District Assn. of County Superintendents, and he served on the County Board of Education, State Board of School Examiners, State Text Book Commission, Library Commission, and exec. committee of the State Teachers Assn.

To supplement his inadequate salary as an educator, he also worked as a farmer, living throughout his life on the same small farm at Hunting Creek where he was born. He was instrumental in building the Farmers Alliance "into a powerful force in N.C. politics and economics." Pres. of the Wilkes Co. Farmers Alliance and extremely active in the N.C. Farmers State Alliance, he was an unsuccessful candidate for the state senate in 1890 and 1896. Later he served as a member of the State Board of Agriculture.

A prominent lay leader in the Baptist Church, for 28 years he was a deacon of the Edgewood Baptist Church and superintendent of its Sunday school. He served as moderator of the Brushy Mountain Baptist Assn. for more than twenty years, and from 1917 until his death he served on the board of trustees of the Baptist orphanage at Thomasville, N.C. He married [Sept. 23, 1891] Catharine Land [she also taught in the Wilkes Co. public schools and assisted her husband in the county superintendent's office; she d. Oct. 22, 1943], and he died July 14, 1933).

Children:

13670-h1. Mary Dorris Wright (born June 30, 1892; d. April 10, 1913).

+13670-h2. James Thomas Carr Wright.

+13670-h3. David Ralph Wright.

+13670-h4. Clyde Robert Wright.

+13670-h5. Charles Calvin Wright, Jr. [W. S. POWELL, *Dicty. of N.C. Biog.*, 6:274-275; (Anon.), *N.C.: Rebuilding of an Ancient Commonwealth*, 4:515-516; M. D. W. Gooch in Mrs. W. O. ABSHER, *Heritage of Wilkes Co.*, 471-472; W. W. FROST, *Frosts*, 88-89]

NEXT GENERATION:

13670-h2. James Thomas Carr Wright (born in N.C., May 22, 1894; graduated U. of N.C.-Chapel Hill [A.B., 1917; M.A., 1925]. He taught 34 years at Appalachian State U. in Boone, Watauga Co., N.C., and he married [May 31, 1917] Roxie Sinesca Mastin [born in N.C., ca. 1896]. He died July 14, 1963).

Children:

+16538-b. Charles Olin Wright.

+16538-c. Thomas Carr Wright.

+16538-d. Mary Doris Wright. [R. S. M. Wright and M.D.W. Gooch in ABSHER, 344, 471-472; FROST, *Frosts*, 88-89; (Anon.), *N.C.: Rebuilding of an Ancient Commonwealth*, 4:515-516; 1930 census Watauga Co., N.C., E.D. 6, p. 8B]

NEXT GENERATION:

16538-c. Thomas Carr Wright (born in Watauga Co., N.C., 1921; married [1946] Billie Gordon Smith).

Children:

18252-l. Rebecca Leigh Wright (born 1948).

18252-m. Thomas Carr Wright, Jr. (born 1951).

18252-n. Elizabeth Ann Wright (born 1961). [R. S. M. Wright and M. D.W. Gooch in Mrs. W. O. ABSHER, *Heritage of Wilkes Co.*, 344, 471-472; NCarBI]

Exhibit F

Documentation For Line Of Descent Of James Logan Wright, Jr.

Kit 71409

Line Of Descent From 1713 Francis Wright Of Westmoreland County To James Logan Wright, Jr.

This exhibit will trace the line of descent of James Logan Wright, Jr., from 1713 Francis Wright of Westmoreland County.

First Generation:

1713 Francis Wright Of Westmoreland County, His Wives Anne (Washington) Wright And Martha (Cox) (Wright) Howell, And His Descendants

1713 Francis Wright of Westmoreland County was a son of 1663 Richard Wright of Northumberland County and Ann (Mottram) Wright. (1663 Richard[1])

The will of Richard Wright dated on August 16, 1663, and probated on December 10, 1663, at Northumberland County, Virginia, W.B. 1658-1666/114 listed Francis Wright as one of his children:

> "In the name of God Amen I Richard Wright of Chickacone . . . . doe make this my last will & testement in maner & forme following:
> . . . .
>
> Item I will & bequeath unto my loveing wife Anne Wright the one halfe of my land lying & being upon Machoatick & Patomack River, she takeing that halfe that issues [or ioynes] upon my brother Spencer, & the land to have as long as she lives & after her death to goe to my sonne Francis . . . .
>
> Item I give & bequeath unto my ____ land lying & being upon ____ halfe at present & the other ____ to him & his heirs for ever ____ francis all my money in Engl____ for the dischargeing the ____ education, Likewise I doe ____ Sonne francis Wright my ____ last will & Testament.
> . . . ."

Married Well And Often by Robert K. Headley, Jr., listed the marriage of Francis Wright and Anne Washington as before January 8, 1682/83:

> "Wright, Francis & Washington, Anne; bef. 8 Jan 1682/83; groom was a son of Rich. & Ann (Mottrom) Wright; bride was a dau. of Lt. Col. Jn. Washington; (RapC RB 1682-88:351; RC OB 4:333; WC DW 2:188a; DW 4:1; OB 1675-89:269; Wright 1:130; Wright 2:54)"

On February 25, 1685/6, at Westmoreland County, Virginia, D.B. 4/1 Francis Wright and his wife Ann (Washington) Wright sold Michael Halbrt 100 acres of land which had been granted to Ann (Washington) Wright's father John Washington and descended to her by reason of her father's death:

> "To all christian people to whom these presents shall come, Francis Wright and Ann his wife send greeting in our Lord God everlasting Know Ye that I Francis Wright of the County of Westmoreld in Virga Gentl and I the said Ann daughter of Col John Washington of the County aforesaid decd now wife to the said Francis Wright for good causes and considerations us thereunto moving & more especially for the sum of four thousand pounds of tobacco in cash to us in hand delivered and wherewith we do acknowledge ourselves satisfied and paid, have granted, bargained and sold, aliened, enfeoffed and confirmed and by these presents do grant, bargain, sell, alien enfeoff and confirm unto Michael Halbert one hundred acres of land situate in Westmorld County in Virga. at the head of Madox granted to the said John Washington by patent and now by the death of the said Washington devolving and dissending to Ann his daughter (now wife to the said Wright by hereditary right together with all buildings fences, orchards, woods, rivers, waters, privileges members and appurtinances to the same belonging or in any wise appertaining. To Have and to hold the said messuages or hundred acres of land with its members and appurtenances above recited to him the said Michael Halbert his heirs and assigns forever, And the said Francis Wright and the said Ann his wife do for themselves, their heirs, Executors and Admrs to and for either and every of them covenant, promise grant and agree to and with the said Michael Halbert his heirs and assigns that the said hundred acres of land now is and from time to time and at all times hereafter shall be and remain free and clear and freely and clearly acquitted and discharged of and from all and all manner of former bargains, sails, guifts, grants Feofments, Jointures, Dowers titles of dowers, leases and from all and all manner of other titles, claims, charges and incumbrances of any manner of person or persons whatsoever lawfully claiming the said messuage or hundred acres of land with its members and appurtenances aforesaid. In witness whereof we the said Francis Wright and Ann Wright have hereto put our hands and seals this 25th day of February in the first year of the reign of our Sovereign Lord James the second Annoque Dom: 1685
>
> Signed, Sealed and deli-) Francis Wright
> vered in the presence of us) Ann Wright
> Thomas Baker) John Wright
> Thomas Marshall
> Ann Read
>
> March the 31st 1686. Acknowledged in Court by Francis Wright and then recorded
>
> P. Tho: Marson D.C.C.P.
>
> Westmorld: SS
>
> At a Court held for the said County the 26th day of March 1707.

John Wright Gentl. son and heir apparent of Francis Wright Gent: party to this present conveyance by subscribing his name to the same and by himself in person acknowledged and voluntarily disclaimed any right, title or interest in and to the lands and premises in the said conveyance contained or to any part or parcel thereof for divers and especial considerations at this time him thereunto moving.

Test
Ja: Westcomb Cler Com Pred

Recordatz: primo die April 1707.

Pr. Eund'm Cler'um

Know all men by these presents that I Francis Wright of the County of Westmorld in Virga. do acknowledge and confess myself to be indebted to Michael Halbert his heirs, Exors Admrs in the full and just sum of ten thousand pounds of good tobacco in cash to be paid upon all demands after the date of these presents and to the performance hereof well and truly to be done I do bind myself my heirs and assigns firmly by these presents and in testimony to the truth hereof have hereto put my hand and seal this 25th day of Febry 1685.

Test
Ja: Westcomb Cler. Cler. Com Pred

The condition of this obligation is such that if the above bounded Francis Wright his heirs and assigns do from time to time and at all times hereafter save defend and keep harmless the Michael Halbert his heirs and assigns in the quiet and peacable possession of one hundred acres of land which he holds in right of Ann his wife and now by deed of feofment from the said Wright and Ann his wife granted sold aliened and confirmed to the Michael Halbert his heirs and assigns for a valuable consideration Recd. according to all the parts members and claims and things mentioned in the aforesaid deed of feofment bearing date with these presents And shall and will make such further assurances in law as by the said Michael Halbert and his learned counsel in the law shall be devised, or advised, then this obligation to be void and of none effect, otherwise to stand in full force and virtue.

Signed, Sealed & deli-) Francis Wright
vered in the presents of us) John Wright
Tho: Baker
Tho: Marshall

Westmorld: SS

At a Court held for the said County the 26th day of March 1707.

John Wright, Gentl, son and heir apparent of Francis Wright Gentl. party to the within Bond in open Court acknowledged himself a party to the said bond by subscribing his name thereto and the penalty therein specified to enure and be good and valued to all intents and purposes therein declared against him his heirs, Executors and Admrs to the benefit and advantage of the therein named Michael Halbert according to the true meaning and purport of the said bond.

Test
Ja: Westcomb Cler. Com Ped

Recordatz: primo die Aprilis 1707

Pr Eund'm Cler'um"

This record indicates that Francis Wright had married Ann Washington, daughter of John Washington, prior to February 25, 1685/6, and that they had a son John Wright who was an adult before March 26, 1707.

In his email dated January 31, 2004, Wilburn Dennis Wright stated that the will of Lawrence Washington dated in March 1697/98 and probated at Westmoreland County, Virginia, W.&D.B. 2/133 bequeathed "to my Sister Anne Writts children, One man Servant apiece of our or five years to serve, or Thgree Thousand pounds of Tobacco to purchase the same, to be delivered or paid to them when they arrive to the age of Twenty-years old." This record indicates that Ann (Washington) Wright's children were born after March 1677/78.

On March 25, 1707, at Westmoreland County, Virginia, D.B. 4/4 Francis Wright and his son and heir apparent John Wright sold 200 acres of land to Thomas Goff:

"This Indenture made the 25th day of March 1707 in the fifth year of the reign of our sovereign Lady Ann by the Grace of God of England, Scotland, France and Ireland, Queen Defender of the faith &c and in the year of our Lord one thousand seaven hundred and six Beetween Francis Wright of Westmorld County in the Colony of Virga. Gentl. and John Wright, son and heir apparent of the sd Francis Wright of the one part and Thomas Goff of Richmond County in the Colony aforesaid planter of the other part Witness that they the said Francis Wright and John Wright as well for and in consideration of the sum of five thousand pounds of tobacco and cash to them in hand paid by the said Thomas Goff at and before the ensealing and delivery of these presents the receipt whereof and of every part & parcel thereof the sd Francis Wright and John Wright do hereby confess and acknowledge themselves therewith fully contented satisfied and paid and thereof do acquit, exonerate & forever discharge the said Thomas Goff his heirs, Executors & Admrs and every of them by these presents as also for several other good causes and considerations them the said Francis and John Wright thereunto at this time especially moving, Have given, granted, bargained, sold, aliened enfeoffed and confirmed and by these presents do fully, freely and clearly give grant, bargain sell alien enfeoff and absolutely confirm unto the said Thomas Goff and his heirs forever all that tract or parcel of land which hath been already laid out and surveyed by one Mr. Horton Late of Westmorld County decd by the order of Francis Wright party to these presents unto the said Thomas Goff and Wm Goff late decd adjoining upon the land of Wm Boothe situate in Washington Parish in the County of Westmorld: aforesaid containing by estimation in the whole two hundred acres of land be the same more or less with all houses out houses, tobacco houses, barns, buildings, gardens orchards and edifices whatsoever together with all woods and underwoods, timber trees and trees likely to make timber with and the reversion and reversions, remainder and remainders thereof rents, issues and profits of all and singular the premises aforesaid and all the Estate, right, title, interest, property claim and demand whatsoever of them the said Francis and John Wright of in and to the same and every or any part thereof, but if in case that it shall so happen that the plat and survey of the said two hundred acres of land cannot be found that then and in such case the said Thomas Goff and his heirs at their proper cost and charges shall have the same laid out and surveyed to them by said Francis and John Wright their heirs and assigns upon reasonable request to them or any of them to be made. To Have and to Hold the said two hundred acres of land aforesaid with all their appurtenances unto the said Thomas Goff his heirs and assigns forever to the only sole proper use benefit and behoof of him the said Thomas Goff his heirs and assigns forevermore and to and for none other use intent and purpose whatsoever & the said Francis Wright and John Wright for themselves and their heirs do covenant and grant to and with the said Thomas Goff in manner and form following, (that is to say) that the said Francis Wright and John Wright have or one of them hath at the time of the ensealing and delivery of these presents, a good, true, absolute and indefeasible Estate of Inheritance in pure and absolute fee simple of, in and unto all and singular the premises aforesaid with all its rights, members and appurtenances and being so seized have or one of them hath good right, full power and lawful authority to grant, bargain and sell the same unto Thomas Goff aforesaid his heirs and assigns in manner as aforesaid and the said Francis Wright and John Wright for themselves and their heirs do covenant, promise and grant to and with the said Thomas Goff that he the said Thomas Goff his heirs and assigns shall and may from time to time and at all times forever hereafter have hold, use, occupy, possess and enjoy all and singular the premises aforesaid and every part thereof without the let, suit, trouble, molestation or interruption of them the said Francis Wright and John Wright and their heirs and all and every other person or persons whatsoever and that the premises aforesaid with the appurtenances now are and be and from henceforth forever hereafter shall remain, continue and be unto the said Thomas Goff his heirs and assigns forever free and clear and freely and clearly acquitted, exonerated and discharged of and from all and all manner of former and other gifts, bargains, sales, grants, mortgages, leases, Judgments, Extents, Executions dowers and title of dowers, rents and arrearages of rent and from all other debts charges and incumbrances whatsoever (the chief rent of the Lord of the fee due and to become due from the time of the sale only excepted And the said Francis Wright and John Wright do covenant, promise and grant to and with the said Thomas Goff and his heirs that the said Francis Wright and John Wright and their heirs and all and every other person or persons whatsoever claiming or to claim any right, title or interest of in or to the premises aforesaid & every or any part thereof shall and will upon every reasonable request, costs and charges in the law of him the sd Thomas Goff his heirs make do seal perfect acknowledge suffer and execute or cause to be made done, sealed, perfected, acknowledged suffered and executed all and singular act and acts, thing and things device or devices conveyances and assurances in the law whatsoever for the better and further assurance and suremaking of the premises aforesaid with the appurtenances unto the said Thomas Goff his heirs and assigns forever as by the learned counsel in the law of the said Thomas Goff his heirs and assigns shall reasonably device advice or require. In witness whereof the parties aforesaid have hereunto set their hands and seals the day and year first within written.

Sealed & delivd.) Francis Wright
in the presence of) John Wright
Thomas Sorrell)
Geo. Eskridge)

Westmor'ld: S.S.

At a Court held for the said County the 26th day of March 1707, Francis Wright and John Wright Gentl acknowledged this present conveyance of lands &c to be their proper act and deed and the lands and premises thereby mentioned to be conveyed to the therein named Thomas Goff to be the just right and Inheritance of him the said Thomas Goffe his heirs and assigns forever.

Test
Ja: Westcomb Cler Com Pe'd

Recordatz: primo die April 1707

Pr. Eund'm Cler'um"

On February 21, 1708/9, at Westmoreland D.&W.B. 4/174 Francis Wright and John Wright of Cople Parish, Westmoreland County, sold 200 acres of land to Thomas Robins:

"This Indenture made the twenty first day of February one thousand seven hundred and Eight and in the seventh year of the reign of our Sovereign Lady Ann by the

Grace of God of England Scotland, France and Ireland Queen Defender of the faith &c. Between Francis Wright & John Wright of Cople parish in the County of Westmorld Gentl. of the one part and Thomas Robins of Washington Parish in the said County planter of the other party, Witnesseth that the said Francis Wright and Jno. Wright for and in consideration of five shillings of good and lawful money of England to them in hand paid by the said Thomas Robins at and before the ensealing & delivery of these presents the receipt whereof they do own, Have given, granted, bargained and sold and do by these presents give, grant, bargain and sell unto the said Thomas Robins all their right, title property, benefit claim & demand whatsoever of, in and to two hundred acres of land situate lying and being in the parish of Washington and County aforesaid and beginning at a corner marked hickory of the land of Thomas Marshall and extending East twenty pole to a red oak then North ninety two pole to a marked red oak thence West One hundred and forty pole to a black oak standing in the Westermost line of the Pattent, then South up the said line to a corner marked chesnutt tree Eighty poles, thence East along the Southermost line one hundred and twenty pole to a marked oak of the said Marshalls finally dower the said Marshall's line to the first stacon with all houses, out houses and tobacco houses with all timber and timber trees with all wayes, water and watercourses with all orchards, fences and gardens thereon with all privileges and appurtenances to the same belonging or in any wise appertaining and the reversion and reversions, remainder and remainders, rents issues and profits and all the Estate right, title property, claim and demand whatsoever of them the seaid Francis Wright and John Wright to the same and every part and every part & parcel thereof. To Have and to hold all and singular the tract and parcel of land and premises and every part & parcel thereof hereby bargained and sold or mentioned or intended to be hereby bargained and sold unto the said Thomas Robins his heirs and assigns forever from the day of the date hereof for and during and until the full end and term of one whole year next ensuing - Yielding and paying therefore the rent of one Ear of indian Corn on the feast day of the birth of our blessed Savior if the same shall be lawfully demanded to the end intent and purpose by virtue of these presents and of the Statute for transferring uses into possessions the said Thomas Robins may be in the actual possessions of the premises & thereby enabled to accept a grant of the reversion and Inheritance thereof to him and his heirs forever. In witness whereof the parties abovementioned hath interchangably sett their hands and seals the day and year above mentioned.

Signed, Sealed & deli-) Francis Wright
vered in presence of) John Wright
Nath: Pope)
Jos. Belfield)

Westmorld: S.S.

At a Court held for the said County the 23d day of Febry 1708

Francis and John Wright Gentl personally appeared and acknowledged the within writing or lease of land to Thomas Robins to be their proper act and deed to be and enure to the use therein contained.

Test
Ja: Westcomb Cler. Com Pe'd

Recordatz 28" die Febr'y pre'd

Pr. Eund'm Cler'um"

On August 30, 1711, at Westmoreland County, Virginia, D.&W.B. 7/230 Francis Wright quitclaimed to Francis Spencer 900 acres of land which had been formerly sold by Francis Wright's father Richard Wright to Nicholas Spencer and in which Francis Wright's mother Ann (Mottram) Wright had not properly joined:

"This Indenture made this 30th day of August in the yeare of Our Lord One thousand Seven hundred and Eleven Between Francis Wright of the parish of Cople in the County of Westmorld on the One part and Francis Spencer of the pish and County aforesaid on the Other part Witnesseth that Whereas Richard Wright father of the aforesaid Wright formerly (to Witt) the 18th day of August in the Yeare of Our Lord 1662 sold and Conveyed Over unto Nicholas Spencer esqr father of the aforesaid Francis Spencer a certaine tract of Land lying scituate on Nomony bay Containing Nine hundred acres of land more or less contained in Certaine bounds in the said Deed menconed which said Land was the Just right and inheritance of Ann the daughter of Coll John Mottrom and Wife of the said Richard and Mother of the said Francis Wright and forasmuch as the said Ann did not Joyne in the said sale nor was any party to the said deed nor did not pass her right in the said land as the law requires and that by meanes thereof the same is descended & come to the aforesaid Francis Wright as heir at Law to his mother therefore he the said Francis Wright as well for and in consideracon of the sum of Seven thousand pounds of good sound merchantable Tobacco in Cask to him in hand by the said Francis Spencer already paid and satisfyed the receipt whereof he doth hereby acknowledge and thereof and from every part and parcell thereof he doth acquitt exonerate and forever discharge the said Francis Spencer his heires executors admrs and assignes as alsoe for diverse Other good Causes and Consideracons him the said Francis Wright thereunto especially moveing hath given granted bargained and sold aliened assigned enfeofft remised released and Confirmed and by these presents doth fully Clearly Amply and absolutely give grant bargaine sell Alien Assign enfeoff transferr remise release make Over and Confirm unto the said Francis Spencer the same in his actual possession now being all that his the said Francis Wright his right and tittle of in and to the aforesaid tract of land Containing nine hundred acres be the same more or less being bounded as by the said parties to these prsents is now concluded Confirmed and agreed on (Vizt) Begining at a marked white Oake standing on the maine branch of King Copssco Pond at the head thereof by the road side that that leads from the house of the said Wright to the said Spencers running thence a streight Course to a marked red Oake standing by a swamp or branch that issueth out of Armsbys creek and near the now dwelling house of Samll Chamberlin and thence down the said swamp cove and creek to the head line of the whole dividend of land of the aforesaid Wright or Mattrom thence along the said head line and the water Courses of nominy Bay to the mouth of King Copssco Pond and up the said Pond according to the meanders thereof to the first menconed beginning White Oake together with the revercon and revercons remainder and remainders with the rents issues and profitts of the prmisses and of every part and parcell thereof To Have and to Hold the aforesaid land and premisses with their and every of their appurtenances according to the meets and bounds aforemenconed together with all woods underwoods wayes water Courses orchards fences priviledges and conveniences hereditaments and appurtenances whatsoever to the same the said land and prmisses belonging and in any wayes appertaining unto the said Francis Spencer his heires Executrs admrs and assignes forever free and Clear and freely and Clearly acquitted exonerated and discharged of and from all former and Other gifts grants bargaines sales Joyntures dower titles of dower morgages Judgments extents execucons and encumbrances whatsoever heretofore had made Comitted or done or suffered to be had made Comitted or done by the said Francis Wright or any Other whatsoever Claimeing or pretending to Claime by from or under him the said Francis Wright his heires &c: and the said Francis Wright for himself his heires &c doth Covenant promise grant and agree to and with the said Francis Spencer his heires &c that he the said Francis Wright his heires &c: shall and Will in due form of law acknowledge these prsents in Westmorld County Court (the Justices then sitting within six months from and after the date hereof to the end the same may be enrolled and alsoe that he the said Francis Wright his heires &c shall and Will when thereunto required by the said Francis Spencer his heires &c and at the proper costs and charges in the law of him the said Francis Spencer his heires &c make doe execute signe seale and acknowledge all and every such further & other deed or conveyances and assureances in the law for the better more sure and safe conveying and Confirming the aforesaid bargained and sold land and prmisses unto the aforesaid Francis Spencer his heires &c as by him the said Francis Spencer his heires &c or by his or their Council learned in the law shall be reasonably devised advised or required In Testimony the aforesaid parties to these prsents hath interchangeably hereunto sett their hands and affixed their seales the day and year first above Written, Memorandm (the words the same in his actual possession now being on the eighteenth line was interlined before sealed & signed Frances Wright sealed and delivered in prsence of D McCarty Nath Pope - Westmld SC At a Court held for the said County the 29th day of August 1711 Francis Wright gentl: the above subscriber personally came into Court and acknowledged the above instrument to be his proper act and deed and the lands and prmisses therein menconed to be conveyed to Francis Spencer gentl: to be the Just right and inheritance of him the said Francis Spencer his heires and assignes forever.

Test.
Tho: Sorrell Depty Clu Comp'd

Recordate sixto die Septembris 1711

Pr Eundm Cluum"

This record confirms the identification of Francis Wright as the son of 1663 Richard Wright of Northumberland County as Ann (Mottram) Wright.

Married Well And Often by Robert K. Headley, Jr., listed the marriage of Martha Wright, widow of Francis Wright, and John Howell between August 7, 1713, and April 1, 1714:

> "Howell, John & Wright, Martha (wid.); bet. 7 Aug 1713 - 1 Apr 1714; bride ws the admx. of Maj. Francis Wright; (WC DW 5:200; OB 1705-21:236a, 310, 378a)"

On August 27, 1723, at Westmoreland County, Virginia, D.&W.B 7/292 John Wright exchanged 800 acres of his land in on Machotique River in Cople Parish, Westmoreland County, for 1000 acres of land owned by Henry Lee in Stafford County and in the legal description of the 800 acres John Wright excepted from the exchange 1/2 acre of land where his father Francis Wright was buried:

> "This Indenture made the twenty seventh day of August in the year of Our Lord One thousand seven hundred and twenty three. . . . Between John Wright of the County of Westmorld in Virginia gentleman of the One part and Henry Lee of the County of Westmorld aforesaid gentleman of the Other part Witnesseth that the said John Wright for and in consideracon of the Exchange for One thousand acres of land in Stafford County scituate lying and being on Powells run whereon the said Henry Lee hath now a plantacon or quarter . . . . have granted . . . . unto the said Henry Lee . . . . One . . . . tract . . . . of land . . . . in Cople parish in the aforesaid County of Westmorld and on the mouth of lower Machotique river Containing by estimacon eight hundred acres be the same mor or less being part of a pattent of land formerly granted to Mr John Mottrom by pattent bearing date the thirteenth day of August in the year of Our Lord sixteen hundred and fifty and since by several mean Conveyances or decents become the proper right and inheritance of the said John Wright and is the plantacon and tract of land whereon he now lives (excepting one half acre of the said land being the grave yard on the manour plantacon where Majr Francis Wright father of the said John is buryed as also One other part of the said

> dividend of land Known by the name of time Neck which the said John Wright hath allready given to his brother Richard Wright by deeds bearing date the twenty second day of September in the year of our Lord seventeen hundred and fourteen which said deeds are recorded in the County Court records of Westmorland . . . ."

This record indicates that Francis Wright was buried near the Machotique River in Cople Parish, Westmoreland County, Virginia, and that 1713 Francis Wright of Westmoreland County had a son Richard Wright in addition to his son John Wright.

On August 9, 1744, at Westmoreland County, Virginia, D.&W.B. 10/151 John Kennedy gave his deposition regarding the family of 1713 Francis Wright of Westmoreland County:

> ". . . .
>
> Kennedys Deopons)
> between Wrights)
> Guardian and Lee)
>
> John Kennedy aged forty six years being first sworn saith that fifteen years ago he was overseer for Colo. Henry Lee at the plantation where John Wright formerly did live very near to the land in dispute, that when he first Come to be overseer for Colo. Lee he had occasion for board timber and as he was unacquainted with the lines he applied himself to John Howell (who had intermarried with the mother of Richard Wright and with whom the said Richard Wright then lived being a boy and under the Care of the said Howel) to shew him where to get the said boards that he might not commit a trespass upon any of the neighbours lands and the said Howel directed him to come to a place near the head of Barrs Creeke where he would find a parcel of rich well timbered land close by and adjoining to the place where John Rice a witness in the suit had cut down trees and further told him that he had once forewarned the said John Rice from Clearing the said Ground telling him that he thought it would be of Great Service to Dickie (meaning the said Richard Wright) But that in some short time afterwards going that way the said Howell had desired to see where the line run and after he found out which way the line went he said he was glad he had forewarned the said Rice for that had the said Rice gone on he would have Cleared upon Colo Lees land and this deponant further saith that about a year or two after this happened one Gerrard Davis who had intermarried with a sister of the said Richard Wright Came to the house of this deponant in Company with the said Richard Wright and thier the said Gerrard Davis in the hearing of this deponant pursuaded the said Richard Wright to sue Colo. Lee for more land for that he'd engage the said Wright might recover to Colo. Motrams Back line which this deponant understood to be meant the line runs by the Plff in this survey and in a short time after this the above named John Howell and this deponant were standing for Deer and he this deponant Informed the said Howell of the discourse which he had heard at his house between the said Davis and the said Richard Wright

whereupon the said Howell said to this deponant that Dickie (meaning the said Richard Wright) had better let alone suing the said Lee for if he sued Colo. Lee says he in my life time I shall surely be an evidence against him for as I go along with you home I'll shew you his and Corner (meaning of the said Richard Wright) whereupon they presently after went together to the three triangular trees to which the surveyor in running from the maple for the defendants Survey Came and this deponant and the said Howell standing by the said triangular trees the said Howel pointing to the said Maple and Cove below it told this deponant Wrights lines come from that cove to the maple and from thence to there triangular trees for they are one of Dickies corners (meaning the said Wright and the said Howell farther told this deponant at that time that he had marked these three trees by order of John Wright brother to the said Richard Wright and in his presence and further told this deponant that his other line run from these trees to a point opposite to the mouth of Barrs Creeke and this deponant who lived Eight years in the neighbourhood of the land in Controversy has since several times gone along the said line and has seen old marked line trees all along the said line unless it such parts of the same as have been destroyed by Catterpillars which said line is the same which was run by Colo Henry Lee from a marked white oak upon the bank of the mouth of Barrs Creeke to the said three triangular trees in a reversed course and this deponant was farther told by the said Howell that he the said Howell had formerly lived as a domestick with Major Wright Father of John Wright and that those triangular trees were always in the life time of the said Major Wright and also of his Son John Wright reconed to stand in Colo Motrams Back line till such time as Colo Lee bought the land of the said John Wright and recovered as far as Kurs Tobacco Ground near to the line run by the plff for Motrams Back line which the said Howell told him had ever since been Reckoned Motrams back line and this deponant farther saith that about eleven years ago he became a tennant to the said Richard Wright and lived upon the land now in Controversy between his the said Wrights heir and the said Colo Lee for the space of three Years & in that time the said land was processioned and this deponant saith that he applied to the said Richard Wright to shew him the lines of the said land against the time the processioners should come whereupon the said Wright told this deponant that he would get the above named Howell to shew the lines to the said processioners telling this deponant that the said Howell was best acquanted with the bounds of the said land for that he (meaning the said Howell) was the person who was along with his brother John Wright when he laid of the land for the said Richard and had marked the lines after the said John Wright and this deponant farther saith that the said processioners afterwards in the presence of this deponant did procession the lines and by the defendant in this survey for the bounds of the said Richard Wrights lands and farther saith not - "John Kennedy" The above deposition was sworn to before me - "Edward Ransdill, August 9th 1744

Westmd Sct

At a Court held for the said County the 26th day of June 1745. This deposition of John Kennedy's in an Ejectment in the General Court between Francis Wright an

Infant son of Richard Wright deceased by John Bushrod his Guardian and Thomas McFarlane Plffs and Henry Lee Gent defendant was presented into this Court by the said Lee at whose motion the same is admitted to record

Teste
Geo: Lee CWC

This record indicates that the widow of 1713 Francis Wright of Westmoreland County had remarried after his death to John Howell and that 1713 Francis Wright had the following children:

1) John Wright,
2) Ann (Wright) Davis, wife of Gerrard Davis, and
3) Richard Wright.

The deposition of Thomas Riddle in that same case confirms some of these relationships:

". . . .
Riddells deposi between)
Wrights Guardian and Lee)

Thomas Riddle aged upwards of forty two years being first sworn saith that about nineteen years ago when he had lived as a domestick with John Howell for two years before the said Howell and this deponant were one day standing for deer and amongst other discourse the said Howell then told this deponant that he would shew him the bounds of Dickie Wrights land which his brother John Wright had given him by deed at which time the said Richard Wright was a boy under the Care of the said Howell who was father in law to the said Wright and having first shewn him the water bounds thereof he the said Howell went afterwards with this deponant to the maple Corner of the bounds of the said land noted in the survey or platt from which maple the said deponant was shewn a line of marked trees by the said Howell which run to three triangular oaks shewed as a Corner to the said Richard Wrights land by the deft Colo Lee in the survey and this deponant farther saith that when the said Howel in Company of this deponant Come to the said three trees the said Howell told him that he himself had marked the said three trees as a corner of Richard Wrights land by the order and in the presence of the said John Wright and at the same time the said Howell desired this deponant to take particular notice of the said three trees lest there should hereafter be any dispute about them . . . ."

Second Generation:

1741 Richard Wright Of Westmoreland County, His Wife Elizabeth (Wigginton) (Wright) McFarlane, And His Descendants

1741 Richard Wright of Westmoreland County was a son of 1713 Francis Wright of Westmoreland County and Martha (Cox) Wright. (1663 Richard[1], 1713 Francis[2])

On September 22, 1714, at Westmoreland County, Virginia, D.&W.B. 5/332 John Wright gifted 300 acres of land to his brother Richard Wright, son of John Wright's father Francis Wright:

> "To all Christian people to whom these prsents shall come John Wright of the parish of Cople in the County of Westmorld Gentl: son & heir of Francis Wright late of the parish & County aforesaid Gentl. decd Sendeth Greeting in our Lord God everlasting Now know yee that I the said John Wright for & in consideracon of the natural love & affecion which I have & bear unto my loving brother Richard Wright son of my said father Francis Wright and for divers other causes & consideratons me hereunto more especially moveing Have given & granted and by these prsents doe fully clearly & absolutely give grant & confirm unto the said Richard Wright and the heires of his body lawfully to be begotten for ever all that peice parcell tract tenement & plantacon of land lying scituate & being in the parish & County aforesd in lower Machotique Neck and is bounded as followeth Vizt. Begining at the mouth of a Cove issuing out of a small Creek comonly called the flooding or Oshter Creek runing thence Westerly up the meanders of the said Cove to a small branch at the head thereof lying on the north side of the plantacon where Thomas Appleyard last lived comonly called the old plantacon and up the said branch (crossing the horse path down the said Neck to the said Wrights plantacon) to a marked Maple standing in the said branch thence Southerly up a small discent of swampy ground along a line of marked trees a little to the West of the said ground to three Spanish oakes marked & Standing triangular close to the back line of the land late of Coll: John Mottrom decd but now in the occupacon of the aforesd John Wright thence easterly down the said Mottroms line to a small creek known by the name of Barrs's Creek and issueth into the aforesd. Oshter Creek thence down the same on the West side thereof along the meanders of the said Creek to the mouth of the Cove before menconed to be begun at includeing the old plantacon aforesaid together with the plantacon whereon Wm Haslerigg is now seated containeing three hundred acres of land (be the same more or less) and is part of the same tract of land whereon I now live which formerly was the right & inheritance of the aforesaid John Mottrom together with all & singular the houses outhouses orchards fences gardens way's water water courses woods under woods profitts priviledges conveniences hereditaments emoluments & appurtenances whatsoevr: to the said hereby given & granted land & prmisses belonging or in any way's of right appurtaineing and all the estate right title interest property claime & demand whatsoever of me the said John Wright my heires &c. of in & to the same and every part & parcell thereof with the

revercon & revercons remainder & remainders rents issues & profitts thereof the rents & profitts of the aforesd. granted lands & prmisses with the appurtenances already grown or which hereafter shall grow & become due & oweing for the same or any part thereof by any wayes or meanes whatsoever for & dureing & untill the sd. Richd. Wright shall attaine & be of the full age of eighteen yeares alwayes reserved excepted & foreprized out of this present guift grant & confirmacon to & for the only sole use benefitt & advantage of me the said John Wright my heires &c: To have and to hold the said three hundred acres of land (be the same more or less) with all & singular the prmisses herein before menconed meant or intended to be herein or hereby given granted & confirmed and every part & parcell thereof with their & every of their appurtenances (except before excepted) unto the said Richard Wright and the heires of his body lawfully to be begotten for ever to the only sole proper use benefitt and advantage of him the said Richard Wright and the heires of his body lawfully to be begotten for ever more To be holden of the cheif Lord or Lords of the fee or fees by the rents & services for the same due & of right accustomed to be paid and I the sd. John Wright for my selfe my heires &c. doe hereby covenant promise and grant to & with the sd. Richard Wright and the heires of his body lawfully to be begotten that the aforesd. land and prmisses with their & every of their appurtenances now is & from time to time and at all times for ever hereafter shall be & remaine free & clear and freely & clearly acquitted exonerated & discharged of & from all former & other gifts grants bargaines sales joyntures dowers morgages extents execucons & other incumbrance or incumbrances whatsoever had made comitted done or suffered or which hereafter may be had made done or suffered by me the said John Wright my heires or assignes or by any other person or persons whatsoever by our or any of our consents prvity or procurement and further that I the said John Wright the aforesaid land & prmisses with their & every of their appurtenances as well against me the said John Wright my heires &c: as against all other person or persons whatsoever claimeing or pretending to claime from by or under us any or either of us (any part or parcell of the aforesaid land & prmisses) unto the said Richard Wright and the heires of his body lawfully to be begotten shall & will warrant and by these presents for ever defend and lastly that I the sd. Wright will acknowledge this presen grant in due form of law in Westmorland County Court to the end the same may be recorded and alsoe that my wife Dorothy shall relinquish her right of dower & thirds at the comon law in & to the said lands & prmisses. In Witness & confirmacon whereof I have hereunto sett my hand & affixed my seale this twenty second day of September in the thirteenth yeare of the reign of our Soveraigne Lady Anne of great Britaine &c. and in the yeare of our Lord God one thousand seven hundred & fourteen

Sealed & delivered) J: Wright
in presence of)
Nath Pope)
W: Sturman)

Westmorld SS

At a Court held for the sd. County the 29th day of Sept 1714 John Wright Gentl: personally acknowledged the above Instrument to be his proper act & deed to be & enure to the uses above in the same specified which Youell Watkins accepted in behalfe of Richard Wright and the sd. Watkins alsoe by a power from Dorothy wife of the said John (being duely proved) relinquished the right of dower & thirds of the said Dorothy at the comon law in and to the lands and prmisses above menconed.

Test
Tho: Sorrell DC Cfed

Recordatz 27" die Novoris 1714

Pr. Eundm Cluum"

This record identifies Richard Wright as the son of 1713 Francis Wright of Westmoreland County.

On August 27, 1723, at Westmoreland County, Virginia, D.&W.B 7/292 John Wright exchanged 800 acres of his land in on Machotique River in Cople Parish, Westmoreland County, for 1000 acres of land owned by Henry Lee in Stafford County and in the legal description of the 800 acres John Wright excepted from the exchange 1/2 acre of land where his father Francis Wright was buried and the land which had been gifted to his brother Richard:

"This Indenture made the twenty seventh day of August in the year of Our Lord One thousand seven hundred and twenty three. . . . Between John Wright of the County of Westmorld in Virginia gentleman of the One part and Henry Lee of the County of Westmorld aforesaid gentleman of the Other part Witnesseth that the said John Wright for and in consideracon of the Exchange for One thousand acres of land in Stafford County scituate lying and being on Powells run whereon the said Henry Lee hath now a plantacon or quarter . . . . have granted . . . . unto the said Henry Lee . . . . One . . . . tract . . . . of land . . . . in Cople parish in the aforesaid County of Westmorld and on the mouth of lower Machotique river Containing by estimacon eight hundred acres be the same mor or less being part of a pattent of land formerly granted to Mr John Mottrom by pattent bearing date the thirteenth day of August in the year of Our Lord sixteen hundred and fifty and since by several mean Conveyances or decents become the proper right and inheritance of the said John Wright and is the plantacon and tract of land whereon he now lives (excepting one half acre of the said land being the grave yard on the manour plantacon where Majr Francis Wright father of the said John is buryed as also One other part of the said dividend of land Known by the name of time Neck which the said John Wright hath allready given to his brother Richard Wright by deeds bearing date the twenty second day of September in the year of our Lord seventeen hundred and fourteen which said deeds are recorded in the County Court records of Westmorland . . . ."

This record confirms that 1713 Francis Wright of Westmoreland County had a son Richard Wright in addition to his son John Wright.

Married Well And Often by Robert K. Headley, Jr., listed the marriage of Richard Wright and Elizabeth Wigginton as between November 7, 1721, and December 24, 1732, and the second marriage of Elizabeth (Wigginton) Wright to Thomas McFarlane:

> "Wright, Richard & Wigginton, Elizabeth; bet. 7 Nov 1721 - 24 Dec 1732; bride was a dau. of Wm. (d. WC 1721) & Frances (Johnson) Wigginton (d. WC 1733); she was a wid. by 23 Feb 1741/42 and mar. (2) Thos. McFarlane; (WC DW 5:450; DW 8-2:17; DW 9:209)"

However, as will be set forth below, since Richard Wright was born between about 1710 and 1712, the marriage was probably after about 1726.

On February 27, 1737, at Westmoreland County, Virginia, D.&W.B. 8/333 Richard Wright purchased 100 acres of land from Gerard Davies:

> "This Indenture made the Twentyseventh day of February in the Eleventh Year of the reign of our Sovereign Lord George the Second King of Great Brittain &c and in the Year of our Lord Christ one thousand Seven hundred thirty and Seven Between Gerrard Davies of the parish of Cople and County of Westmorland of the one part And Richard Wright of the Same parish and county of the other part Witnesseth that the Said Gerrard Davies for and in consideration of the Sum of forty five pounds current money of Virginia to him in hand paid by the aforesaid Richard Wright the receipt whereof he doth hereby acknowledge and thereof and Every part thereof and therefrom doth fully clearly and absolutely acquit and Discharge the aforesaid Richard Wright his heirs Executors administrators and assignes and Every of them by these pressents Hath Given Granted bargained Sold aliened released and confirmed and by these presents doth fully clearly and absolutely give grant bargain Sell alien release and confirm unto the said Richard Wright his heirs Executors administrators and assignes forever a certain peice or parchel of Land containing one hundred acres whereon the Said Gerrard Davies now lives Scituate lying and being in Yeocomoco or Nominy Forrest which was formerly Given by James Johnson to his Daughter Elizabeth Johnson mother to the Said Gerrard Davies as may appear by the said Will Together with all houses outhouses Gardens Orchards fences water ways trees woods and underwoods priviledges Liberties profits advantages and hereditaments whatsoever to the said Tract or parchel of Land belonging or any part or parchel thereof in any wise belonging or appertaining and the reversion and reversions remainder and remainders thereof and of Every part thereof And all the Estate rite & title intrest property claim and demand whatsoever

that he the Said Gerrard Davies hath or ought to have of in or to the afd. one hundred acres of Land or any part thereof To have and to hold the aforesaid one hundred acres of Land and all and Singular the premises hereinbefore mentioned and hereby Entended to be granted bargained and Sold unto the Said Richard Wright hereinbefore mentioned his heirs &c forever And he the Said Gerrard Davies for himself his heirs &c. doth hereby covenant and promise to and with the Said Richard Wright his heirs &c. that he the Said Gerrard Davies at the time of the Ensealing and Delivery of these presents is the Sole true and Lawfull owner of the Said Tract or parchel of Land and premises hereby Granted and Sold and of Every part and parcell thereof And further that he the Said Richard Wright his heirs &c. Shall from time to time and at all times forever hereafter peaceably and quietly have hold occupy possess and injoy all and Singular the above Granted Lands and premises with all its rights members and appurtenances thereunto belonging or in any wise appertaining without the Let trouble Hinderance Eviction Expulsion or Interruption _____ appurtances unto the Said Richard Wright his heirs &c Shall and will Warrant and forever Defend by these presents against the claim or claims of him the Said Gerrard Davies his heirs &c. or any other person or persons whatsoever and that the said Gerrard Davies his heirs &c. Shall and will at any time hereafter upon the request and at the proper charges and cost in the Law of the Said Richard Wright his heirs &c. make do Suffer and Execute all and Every Such further and other act and acts thing and things devices and assurances in the Law Whatsoever for the better and more Shure conveying and assureing of all and Singular the Said premises unto the Said Richard Wright his heirs &c according to the true intent and meaning of these presents as by the Said Richard Wright his heirs &c or by his or their Learned Council in the Law Shall be reasonably advised devised or required In Wittness whereof the parties to These presents have Interchangeably Set their hands and Seals the day and Year above Written

Signed Sealed and deli-) Gerrard Davies
vered in presents of)
Peter Cox
Charles Brown
his
Steven Balley
mark

Received of Richard Wright the within consideration of forty five pounds current money of Virginia and acknowledge my Self to be fully satisfied As Witness my hand this Twenty Seven day of February 1737

Peter Cox Gerrard Davies
Charles Brown
his
Steven Balley
mark

Memorandum that on the Twenty Seven day of February one Thousand Seven hundred thirty and Seven Peaceable and quiet possession and Seizin of the Lands and appurtenances within mentioned was made and Delivered by the said Gerrard Davies according to the form and Effect of this deed unto the Said Richard Wright in the present of us whose names are hereunto Subscribed

Peter Cox
Charles Brown
his
Steven Balley
mark

Westmorland SS. At a court held for the Said County the 30th day of May 1738. Gerrard Davies personally acknowledged this deed of Feoffment for Land by him passed to Richard Wright together with the Livery of Seizin and receipt for the consideration money thereon Endorsed to be his proper act and deed; Also Ann the wife of the said Gerrard Davies (being first privately Examined according to Law) personally relinquished her right of Dower and thirds at the common Law of in and to the Lands by the Said deed mentioned to be conveyed all which at the Instance of the Said Wright are admitted to record

Test
G G Turbervile CCW

Recorded the Ninth day of June 1738

Pr. GTCCW"

The will of Richard Wright was dated on March 10, 1740, probated on October 27, 1741, at Westmoreland County, Virginia, W.B. 9/192, and provided as follows:

"In The Name of God Amen I Richard Wright of the parish of Cople and County of Westmoreland being Very Sick weak of body but of Sound and perfect mind and memory praise be given to almighty god for the same, do make and ordain this my Present last will and Testament in manner and form following that is to say, First I commend my soul into the hands of almighty god, who Gave it me hopeing though the merits death and passion of my Saviour Jesus Christ to have full and free pardon and forgiveness of all my Sins, And to Inherit Everlasting life and my Body I commit to the Earth from whence it was Taken to be decently Buryed at the discretion of my Executors hereafter Named And as touching the disposition of all such Temperal Estate as hath pleased Almighty God to bestow upon me I give and Dispose thereof as followeth. First I will that all my my Just debts be truly and Justly paid and discharged Item I give and Bequeath to my God Son William Davis one young Roan mare with a blaise in her forehead one Breeding heifer one young yew, one Breeding Sow, and Suit of Druge Cloughs Vizt, Coat Vest and Breeches to him and his heirs for Ever, Item. I give to my Brother-in-Law Gerrard Davis all my wearing apparel to him and his heirs for Ever, Item I give to my Sister Ann Davis one good Suite of Stuff one pair of Shoes, one pair of Stockings and two Shifts, Item, I give and bequeath unto my Son Francis Wright all that Tract or parcel of Land in Lower mochotick which was given to me by my Brother John Wright. I also give to my Son Francis four Slaves Vizt, Mollattoe Tom, Negroe Tom, Natt and Frank all which land and Negroes I give to him the Said Francis and his heirs forever, and Further my will and desire is that my Son Francis Wright be for himself at the Age of Eighteen years, Item I give and bequeath unto my Daughter Eliza Wright four Slaves Vizt. Negroe Nan Danl Rose and Newman all which Negroes I give to her the said Eliza and her heirs for Ever. Item I give to my Dear and loveing wife Eliza Wright the whole and Sole use of Six Slaves for and during her Natural life as Vizt. Fortune, Charmer, Harry, Old Frank great Frank, and Joe a boy and after her decease I give the Said Negroes with Their Increse to be Equally divided Between my son Francis Wright and My Daughter Eliza Wright and their heirs forever. I also give my Dear and well beloved wife all that Land whereon I now live for and during her Natural life and after her decease I will the Said Land to my Son Francis Wright and his heirs for ever. Item my will and desire is that all the rest and Residue of my Estate Goods and Chattles whatsoever be Equally divided between my wife Eliza my son Francis and daughter Eliza and their heirs for Ever Shair and Shair alike Lastly I do ordain Constitute and appoint my well beloved wife Eliza Wright and my friend John Bushrod Gent, and friend Robt. Middleton Exers of This my Last will and Testament In witness whereof I have Set my Hand and affixed my Seal this 10th day of March 1740

Witness — Richard Wright
Thomas Mcfarlane
Gerrard Davis

Westmoreland SS

At a Court held for the said County the 27th day of October 1741. This Last will and Testament of Richard Wright deceased was Presented in to Court by Elizabeth his Relict and one of his Executors, who made Oath thereto John Bushrod Gent, and Robert Middleton the other Executors in the said will named, not ceareing at present to take the oath of Executors, and Being proved by the oath of Thos Mcfarlane the Surviving witness thereto is admitted to Record and upon the motion of the Said Executrix and her performing what is usual in such cases Certificate is granted her for obtaining a probate hereof In due form - Recorded the 13th day of November 1741

Test
Geo. Turberville __"

The reference to the land in Lower Mochotick given to him by his brother John Wright identifies this Richard Wright as the son of 1713 Francis Wright of Westmoreland County and brother of 1729/30 John Wright of Stafford County. This record identifies the family of 1741 Richard Wright of Westmoreland County as follows:

Wife: Eliza (____) Wright

Children: 1) Francis Wright, and

2) Eliza Wright.

Married Well And Often by Robert K. Headley, Jr., listed the marriage of Elizabeth Wright, widow of Richard Wright, and Thomas McFarlane before July 30, 1745:

> "McFarlane, Thomas & Wright, Elizabeth (wid.); bef. 30 Jul 1745; bride was the rel. of Rich. Wright & a dau. of Wm. (d. WC 1721) & Frances (Johnson) (d. WC 1733) Wigginton; (WC DW 7:348; DW 8-2:17; DW 10:162; DW 12:92; Tucker:146)"

Adventurers of Purse and Person, Virginia 1607-1624/5, 4th edition, by John Frederick Dorman, stated that:

> "28. Mary Ann[4] Cox, (Margaret Fleet[3], Henry[2], Henry[1]) married, as his (1) wife, Francis Wright, son of Richard and Elizabeth (Wigginton) Wright, who left will 5 Dec. 1775-26 March 1793.[105]
>
> . . . .
>
> ---
>
> [105] Westmoreland Co. Deeds & Wills 18, 1787-94, pp. 294-95."

Third Generation:

1776 Francis Wright Of Westmoreland County, His Wives Mary Ann (Cox) Wright And Elizabeth (Middleton) (Wright) Lewis, And His Descendants

1776 Francis Wright of Westmoreland County was a son of 1741 Richard Wright of Westmoreland County and Elizabeth (Wigginton) (Wright) Lewis. (1663 Richard[1], 1713 Francis[2], 1741 Richard[3])

The will of Richard Wright dated on March 10, 1740, and probated on October 27, 1741, at Westmoreland County, Virginia, W.B. 9/192 listed Francis Wright as his son:

> "In The Name of God Amen I Richard Wright of the parish of Cople and County of Westmoreland . . . . do make and ordain this my Present last will and Testament in manner and form following that is to say, ... Item, I give and bequeath unto my

Son Francis Wright all that Tract or parcel of Land in Lower mochotick which was given to me by my Brother John Wright. I also give to my Son Francis four Slaves Vizt, Mollattoe Tom, Negroe Tom, Natt and Frank all which land and Negroes I give to him the Said Francis and his heirs forever, and Further my will and desire is that my Son Francis Wright be for himself at the Age of Eighteen years, ... Item I give to my Dear and loveing wife Eliza Wright the whole and Sole use of Six Slaves for and during her Natural life as Vizt. Fortune, Charmer, Harry, Old Frank great Frank, and Joe a boy and after her decease I give the Said Negroes with Their Increse to be Equally divided Between my son Francis Wright and My Daughter Eliza Wright and their heirs forever. I also give my Dear and well beloved wife all that Land whereon I now live for and during her Natural life and after her decease I will the Said Land to my Son Francis Wright and his heirs for ever. Item my will and desire is that all the rest and Residue of my Estate Goods and Chattles whatsoever be Equally divided between my wife Eliza my son Francis and daughter Eliza and their heirs for Ever Shair and Shair alike . . . ."

On August 9, 1744, at Westmoreland County, Virginia, D.&W.B. 10/151 a surveyor's report was filed in the suit of Wright's Guardian vs. Lee:

"Wrights Guardian &c	)	Westmd County
vs	)	August the 9th 1744
See surveyors report	)	

In obedience to an order of the Honble the General Court the 21st day of April last past

Thomas McFarlane	Plff	)
vs		)
Ferdinande Drednought	deft	)

In Ejectment for two messuages two tenements and three hundred acres of land with the appurtenances in the parish of Cople and County of Westmoreland of the demises of John Bushrod Guardian to Francis Wright, Henry Lee is admitted defendant in the room of the said Drednought. The subscriber on the day appointed in the said order did go upon the lands in Controversy and proceeded to survey and lay out the same as each party did require First the plaintiff directed me to begin at the mouth of a Cove Issuing out of a Creeke Called the Oyster Creeke as at A. in the platt and surveyed in the several meanders of the said Cove going by a plantation where Thomas Appleyard formerly did live and Crossing the horse road and afterwards come within one chain and 13 links to the left of a Corner maple standing in a branch of the said Cove at B the maple is mentioned in the depositions of John Kennady and Thomas Riddle and agreed to by both Plff and deft. to be their Corner thence extending along a marked line mentioned in the depositions of Kennedy and Riddle as laid down in the platt to 3 Triangular oaks marked for a corner Vist two red oaks and one white oak as at C made with red Ink, which oak was shewn by the deft as another Corner of the Plantiffs land and proved by the oaths of John Kennedy and Thomas Riddle and are likewise mentioned in the deposition of Janus Bailey at the request of the Plff I Continued the same Course without any marked trees at 110 po. and 21 links was 8 Chains within an old Corn field at D the said Field formerly tended by Isaac Taylor a tenant on the late Col. Fitshughs land mentioned in the depositions of James Potter & Daniel Jennings, and Nicholas Minor here was shewn by Samuel Attwell as where Mottrams back line Comes through the old Cornfield, thence along Mottrams line S 78° 30m. 117-1/2 poles to a corner marked white oak at E. the line is mentioned in the depositions of the said Attwell, John Barnett and Wm Harding and the white oak is mentioned in the said Attwells deposition to be a corner of Captn McCarty and the now defendant and the deft said it is also a Corner of the Glebe land the plaintiff required me to survey from thence along a line of marked trees N. 40° E at 97 poles Came to a Cove Issuing out of Barres Creeke there angled to the line which was E 6/2 pole to a marked Gum standing on the banks of the Said Cove at Z which line is mentioned in the depons of the said Attwell, Edmund Bulger John Bulger, and John Rice, then the plaintiff required me to survey down the meanders of the said Cove to a marked red oak by Barres Creeke at D made with red Ink this tree the deft said is a line tree in a line which Comes from the aforesaid Triangular oaks to Barres Creeke, again at the request of the defendant I went from thence over Barres Creeke to a marked locust a corner tree at G standing on the bank of Machotique river at the mouth of a small oyster Creeke a corner tree to the land of Captain Daniel McCarty deceased from thence reversed a marked line N. 86° 30' E to the aforesaid Barres Creeke then Crossing Over Barres Creeke to the aforesaid marked red oak at D. made with red ink at the request of the said defendant from E - I continued the line Called mottrams line S. 78° 36 E 179 poles further Came to a Cove at H Issuing out of a Creeke Called by Kennedy and others the parsons Creeke Then the defendant required to lay of the plantiffs land and went to the aforesaid three triangular trees the defendant produced a deed of Gift from John Wright to his brother Richard Wright for three hundred acres of land as termed more or less Contained within certain bounds therein mentioned which deed is dated the 22nd of September Ann Dom 1714 the defendant assertes that the three Triangular trees is the Corner mentioned in the said deed as proved by the oaths of Kennady and Riddle aforesaid and mentioned in the deposition of James Bailey from thence Extending along a line of marked trees proved by the oaths of Kennady and Riddle as mentioned in their depositions and mentioned in the depositions of Kennady as a processioned line I went S. 82° E. 180 pole then Angled to the line the defendant stopt and went the aforesaid marked red oak by the side of Barres Creeke at D made with red Ink from thence I reversed the said marked line the said three triangular trees which reduced to a straight line is from the said three triangular trees to Barres Creeke S. 86° E. 195 poles and laid down in the plat with red Ink in surveying the last mentioned I went near several Elder marked line trees which the deft. asserts to be the line mentioned in the aforesaid deed of Gift therein Called the back line of the land of the late Colo. John Mottram and the deft produced a report of two surveyors (Jointly to the General Court purporting that a line was made by them according to an agreement made between Mr Francis Wright father of the aforesaid John and Richard) who held the land Called Mottrams and Major Thomas Youell to be for the bounds between them which surveyors report is dated the 26th day of September Anno 1687 afterwards at the plffs request I went to the afsd. marked red oak by Barres Creeke at D. made with red Ink from thence surveyed the several meanders Coves & points as laid down In the platt to the first mentioned beginning

Copy
Teste
B Claiborne
p Ben: Walker
C G Court

Surveyed by me
Spence Monroe SWC

Westwd)
Sct)

At a Court Continued and held for the said County the 26th day of June 1745. This platt and survey of land under the hand of Spence Monoe Surveyor of the said County by him made for and between John Bushrod Guardian of Francis Wright an Infant son of Richard Wright deceased and Thomas McFarlane Plaintiffs and Henry Lee Gent defendant in Ejectment in the General Court were presented into this court by the said Lee, at whose motion the same are ordered to be recorded.

Teste
Geo: Lee CWC

Kennedys Deopons between)
Wrights Guardian and Lee)

John Kennedy aged forty six years being first sworn saith that fifteen years ago he was overseer for Colo. Henry Lee at the plantation where John Wright formerly did live very near to the land in dispute, that when he first Come to be overseer for Colo. Lee he had occasion for board timber and as he was unacquainted with the lines he applied himself to John Howell (who had intermarried with the mother of Richard Wright and with whom the said Richard Wright then lived being a boy and under the Care of the said Howel) to shew him where to get the said boards that he might not commit a trespass upon any of the neighbours lands and the said Howel directed him to come to a place near the head of Barrs Creeke where he would find a parcel of rich well timbered land close by and adjoining to the place where John Rice a witness in the suit had cut down trees and further told him that he had once forewarned the said John Rice from Clearing the said Ground telling him that he thought it would be of Great Service to Dickie (meaning the said Richard Wright) But that in some short time afterwards going that way the said Howell had desired to see where the line run and after he found out which way the line went he said he was glad he had forewarned the said Rice for that had the said Rice gone on he would have Cleared upon Colo Lees land and this deponant further saith that about a year or two after this happened one Gerrard Davis who had intermarried with a sister of the said Richard Wright Came to the house of this deponant in Company with the said Richard Wright and thier the said Gerrard Davis in the hearing of this deponant pursuaded the said Richard Wright to sue Colo. Lee for more land for that he'd engage the said Wright might recover to Colo. Motrams Back line which this deponant understood to be meant the line runs by the Plff in this survey and in a short time after this the above named John Howell and this deponant were standing for Deer and he this deponant Informed the said Howell of the discourse which he had heard at his house between the said Davis and the said Richard Wright whereupon the said Howell said to this deponant that Dickie (meaning the said Richard Wright) had better let alone suing the said Lee for if he sued Colo. Lee says he in my life time I shall surely be an evidence against him for as I go along with you home I'll shew you his and Corner (meaning of the said Richard Wright) whereupon they presently after went together to the three triangular trees to which the surveyor in running from the maple for the defendants Survey Came and this deponant and the said Howell standing by the said triangular trees the said Howel pointing to the said Maple and Cove below it told this deponant Wrights lines come from that cove to the maple and from thence to there triangular trees for they are one of Dickies corners (meaning the said Wright and the said Howell farther told this deponant at that time that he had marked these three trees by order of John Wright brother to the said Richard Wright and in his presence and further told this deponant that his other line run from these trees to a point opposite to the mouth of Barrs Creeke and this deponant who lived Eight years in the neighbourhood of the land in Controversy has since several times gone along the said line and has seen old marked line trees all along the said line unless it such parts of the same as have been destroyed by Catterpillars which said line is the same which was run by Colo Henry Lee from a marked white oak upon the bank of the mouth of Barrs Creeke to the said three triangular trees in a reversed course and this deponant was farther told by the said Howell that he the said Howell had formerly lived as a domestick with Major Wright Father of John Wright and that those triangular trees were always in the life time of the said Major Wright and also of his Son John Wright reconed to stand in Colo Motrams Back line till such time as Colo Lee bought the land of the said John Wright and recovered as far as Kurs Tobacco Ground near to the line run by the plff for Motrams Back line which the said Howell told him had ever since been Reckoned Motrams back line and this deponant farther saith that about eleven years ago he became a tennant to the said Richard Wright and lived upon the land now in Controversy between his the said Wrights heir and the said Colo Lee for the space of three Years & in that time the said land was processioned and this deponant saith that he applied to the said Richard Wright to shew him the lines of the said land against the time the processioners should come whereupon the said Wright told this deponant that he would get the above named Howell to shew the lines to the said processioners telling this deponant that the said Howell was best acquanted with the bounds of the said land for that he (meaning the said Howell) was the person who was along with his brother John Wright when he laid of the land for the said Richard and had marked the lines after the said John Wright and this deponant farther saith that the said processioners afterwards in the presence of this deponant did procession the lines and by the defendant in this survey for the bounds of the said Richard Wrights lands and farther saith not - "John Kennedy" The above deposition was sworn to before me - "Edward Ransdill, August 9th 1744

Westmd Sct

At a Court held for the said County the 26th day of June 1745. This deposition of John Kennedy's in an Ejectment in the General Court between Francis Wright an Infant son of Richard Wright deceased by John Bushrod his Guardian and Thomas McFarlane Plffs and Henry Lee Gent defendant was presented into this Court by the said Lee at whose motion the same is admitted to record

Teste
Geo: Lee CWC

Riddells deposi between)
Wrights Guardian and Lee)

Thomas Riddle aged upwards of forty two years being first sworn saith that about nineteen years ago when he had lived as a domestick with John Howell for two years before the said Howell and this deponant were one day standing for deer and amongst other discourse the said Howell then told this deponant that he would shew him the bounds of Dickie Wrights land which his brother John Wright had given him by deed at which time the said Richard Wright was a boy under the Care of the said Howell who was father in law to the said Wright and having first shewn him the water bounds thereof he the said Howell went afterwards with this deponant to the maple Corner of the bounds of the said land noted in the survey or platt from which maple the said deponant was shewn a line of marked trees by the said Howell which run to three triangular oaks shewed as a Corner to the said Richard Wrights land by the deft Colo Lee in the survey and this deponant farther saith that when the said Howel in Company of this deponant Come to the said three trees the said Howell told him that he himself had marked the said three trees as a corner of Richard Wrights land by the order and in the presence of the said John Wright and at the same time the said Howell desired this deponant to take particular notice of the said three trees lest there should hereafter be any dispute about them"

This suit is clearly referencing the land of 1713 Francis Wright of Westmoreland County and 1729/30 John Wright of Stafford County, part of which had been gifted by 1729/30 John Wright to his brother 1741 Richard Wright of Westmoreland County and then passed by 1741 Richard Wright's will to Francis Wright.

The will of Presley Cox dated on February 18, 1766, and probated on September 30, 1766, at Westmoreland County, Virginia, D. & W.B. 14/393 was posted at http://freepages.genealogy.rootsweb.com/~rmbeckman/alhn/doc/presleycoxwill.html and provided as follows:

> "In the Name of God Amen I Presley Cox of Cople parish in Westmoreland County in Virginia being at this time in health both of body and mind but Considering the uncertainty of this life and the impossibility of Knowing how soon the great disposer of all things may please to demand the soul he gave me do think it prudent now to make my last Will and testament which I accordingly do in the following manner and form in the first place I do with great Humility resign my soul to the almighty with stedfast hope that by the meditation (sic! mediation intended?) of my blessed saviour it may Obtain everlasting happiness and my body I would have decently buried by the Discretion of my Executors hereafter mentioned Item I give and bequeath to my son Fleet Cox my great bible and large looking glass which hangs in the Hall and my negro man Dick to him and his heirs forever, Item I give and bequeath to my Grandsons Richard Wright and Presley Wright and my grand Daughter Nancy Wright ten pounds current money of Virginia each to be paid out of my estate by my executors when they arrive to the age of twenty One years or the day of Marriage Item I give to my grandsons Fleet Cox and Presley Cox and my grand daughter Molley Cox ten pounds current money each to e paid Out of my estate by my executors when they arrive to the age of twenty One years or the day of marriage, Item I give to my son William Cox One negro man named Phil One negro man named Tom One negro man named Isae One negro woman named Venney One negro Woman named Nan and her three Children Viz Will, Sett, and nan with all their future increase to him and his heirs forever, Item after my Just debts and the bequests all ready given and bequeathed are fully satisfied and paid then I give the remainder of my estate both real and personal of what nature or kind whatsoever both within doors and without to my son William Cox and his heirs forever lastly I Constitute and appoint my son Fleet Cox and my son William Cox and Frances Wright to be my whole and sole executors of this my last Will and testament hereby revoking and disanuling all Will or Wills by me heretofore made and allowing this only to be my last Will and Testament,
>
> In Witness whereof I have hereunto set my hand and fixt my seal this eighteenth day of February in the year of Our Lord One Thousand seven hundred and sixty six ~

Witness Presly Cox (SL)
George Lamkin)
Peter Lamkin)
John Baley)
her)
Winifred WB Baley)
Mark)

At a Court held for Westmoreland County the 30th day of September 1766, This Will was proved according to law by the oaths of George Lamkin and John Baley Witnesses thereto and Ordered to be recorded V on the motion of William Cox The Executor named in The said Will who made Oath according to law and together with Fleet Cox his security entered into and acknowledged bond with Condition as The law directs certificate is granted him for obtaining a probat Thereof in due form~

Teste,"

This appointment of Frances Wright as an executor and the listing of three grandchildren named Wright in this record identifies the children of Francis Wright as follows:

1) Richard Wright,

2) Presley Wright, and

3) Nancy Wright.

This record also indicates that Presley Cox's daughter who had married Francis Wright had died before February 18, 1766.

Married Well And Often by Robert K. Headley, Jr., listed the marriage of Francis Wright and Elizabeth Middleton well before May 29, 1782, and listed the second marriage of Elizabeth (Middleton) Wright to George Lewis:

"Wright, Francis & Middleton, Elizabeth; well bef. 29 May 1782; bride was a dau. of Benedict & Hannah (Lane) Middleton (d. WC 1785); she mar. (2) Geo. Lewis; (WC DW 16:355; Tidwell:40)"

The will of Francis Wright was dated on December 6, 1775, probated on March 26, 1793, at Westmoreland County, Virginia, W.B. 18/294, and provided as follows:

"In the Name of God Amen I Francis Wright of Westmoreland County do make and ordain this to be my last will and Testament in manner and forme following First I leave my Land I Purchased of Mr. John Rust to be sold to pay my Just debts at Publick oction or Privet Sale as my Executors hereafter named shall think proper and whatever the Land Sells for then will Pay my debts the money to be Eaquely divided between my three sons Benedick Wright Johnson Wiginton Wright & Wright

Wright Secondly I leave to my loving wife Elizabeth the use of my house wherein I now live and the third part of the Land Joining the house during her life I allso leave her the third part of all my Personal Estate for and during her Natrial life and after her death to be Eaquely divided amongst all my Children. Thirdly my will and desire is that all the rest of my Estate not before given shall be Eaquely divided amongst all my Children. I do appoint my loving wife Elizabeth Capt. Bendk. Middleton Junr. & Fleet Cox Executors of this my last will & Testament. As Witness my hand this 6th day of December 1775.

> Fleet Cox Jun. Francis Wright
> Elijah Mood
> Elizabeth Middleton

> At a Court held for Westmoreland County the 26th day of March 1793. On the Motion of Francis Wright it is ordered that this Will be recorded the Heirs at Law consenting thereto.

> Examd. Teste
> J Bland CWC"

This record identifies the family of Francis Wright as follows:

Wife: Elizabeth Wright

Children:
1) Benedick Wright,
2) Johnson Wiginton Wright, and
3) Wright Wright.

However, as will be set forth below, the third son of Francis Wright and Elizabeth (Middleton) Wright was William Wright and the scrivener of the will or the clerk of the court who copied the will apparently miswrote the given name as Wright rather than William.

On November 22, 1776, at Westmoreland County, Virginia, D.B. 19/272 Elizabeth Wright and Fleet Cox, as executors of the will of Francis Wright, sold to Richard Cox 200 acres of land directed to be sold under the will of Francis Wright:

> "This Indenture made the 22nd. day of November in the year of our Lord 1776 Between Elizabeth Wright & Fleet Cox of Cople parish and Westmoreland County Exx, & Exor to the Last will & Testament of Francis Wright deceased of the one part & Richard Cox of the same parish & County aforesaid of the other part Witnesseth that the said Wright did amongst other things in his Will to be sold the Land he purchased of John Rust which was Two hundred Acres be the same more or Less that the aid Elizabeth Wright & Fleet Cox for and in Consideration of the sum of Two hundred acres be the same more or Less that the said Elizabeth Wright & Fleet Cox

for and in Consideration of the sum of Two hundred pounds Current money to them in hand paid at and before the sealing & Delivery of these presents by the said Richd Cox the receipt whereof the said Eliza. Wright & Fleet Cox doth hereby acknowledge themselves therewith fully satisfied and paid & thereof & of every part and parcel thereof doth Clearly Acquit Exonerate and discharge the said Richd Cox his heirs Exors. Admors. by these presents hath given granted bargained sold & Confirmed & by these presents doth fully clearly & absolutely give grant bargain sell & Confirm unto the said Richard Cox his heirs Exors. Admors & assigns forever, Two hundred Acres of Land be the same more or Less which was directed to be sold by the Last will of Francis Wright bearing date the 5th day of December 1775 with all and Singular its rights members Jurisdiction & appurtenances together with all houses Edifices and Appurtenances whatsoever to the said messuage or Tenement & premisses or to any part or Parcel thereof belonging or in any ways appertaining & the reversion & reversions remainder & remainders of all and singular the before mentioned premisses and all rent or rents made of the premisses any part or parcel of of them & also all the estate right title Interest use possession Evidence or claim whatsoever of them the said Eliza. Wright and Fleet Cox in or to the same and all deeds Writings and Evidences whatsoever Toutching or Concerning the premisses or any part or parcel thereof To have and to hold the said two hundred acres of Land be the Same more or Less and all and Singular other the premisses hereby granted and sold Or mentioned to be herein or hereby granted and sold with all and singular of their rights members and appurtenances whatsoever unto the said Richd Cox his heirs Exors Admors and assigns to the only proper use & behoof of him the said Richard Cox his heirs and assigns forever & the said Elizabeth Wright and Fleet Cox for themselves, their heirs &c the said messuage or Tenement with the appurtenances thereunto belonging shall and Will forever Warrant and defend unto the said Richard Cox his heirs and assigns forever by these presents against the Claim or Claims of them the said Elizabeth Wright & Fleet Cox their heirs or assigns and every Other person or persons Whatsoever & the said Eliza. Wright & Fleet Cox for themselves their heirs &c do Covenant promise grant & agree to & with the said Richard Cox his heirs and assigns And every of them by these presents in manner and form following To Wit that the said Elizabeth Wright and Fleet Cox at the time of sealing & delivery of these presents has an Actual pure good & absolute right of the before granted premisses and every part thereof shall be fully vested and executed in and the said Richard Cox his heirs and Assigns According to the true meaning of these _____ and Sold with all and every of their Rights members & Appurtenances of a good pure perfect and Absolute Estate of Inheritance in fee simple without any Condition reversion remainder or Limitation of uses or estates in or to any person whatsoever to Alter change defeat determine or make Void the Same & that the said Richard Cox his heirs & Assigns & every of them shall or may by force and Virtue of these presents from time to time and at all times forever hereafter Lawfully peacably and Quietly have hold Occupy Possess enjoy the said messuage or Tenement and all and Singular the before granted premisses with every of their Appurtenances without any Lawfull let suit Trouble denial Interruption or disturbance of the said Eliza Wright and

Fleet Cox their heirs or assigns or any Other person or persons Whatsoever and that truly and Clearly acquited exonerated & discharged Or Otherwise from time to time well and sufficiently saved & kept harmless the said Eliza Wright & Fleet Cox their heirs Exors. Admors. & assigns of and from all & Singular there Gifts grants bargaining sales Leases Jointers Dowers, Title of Dowers intails rents and arrearages of rents and all Singular other titles Troubles Charges, demands and Incumbrances whatsoever In Witness whereof the Parties to these presents have hereunto set their hands & seals the day & date above Written

Signed Sealed and Deli-) Elizabeth Wright
vered In the presence of) Fleet Cox
William Middleton,
Elijah Moore
Presley Wright
Fleet Cox Junr
Smith King
William King

Received of Richard Cox Two hundred pounds current money of Virginia in full payment for the Consideration within mentioned Witness our hands this 22nd day of November Anno Domini 1776

Teste Elizabeth Wright
Wm Middleton Fleet Cox
Elijah Moore
Presley Wright
Fleet Cox Junr
Smith King
Wm King

Memorandum

That on the 22nd day of Novr. in the year of our Lord good 1776 The within named Eliza. Wright and Fleet Cox made Livery & Seizen of the Lands & appurtenances within mentioned by delivering Turf and Twigg & the ring of the door of the Chief mansion house on the Lands within mentioned unto the within named Richd. Cox in the name of the whole Land & Appurtenances within granted bargained and sold according to the tenor form & effect of the within Deed

Teste
Wm Middleton
Elijah Moore
Presley Wright
Fleet Cox Junr
Smith King
Wm King

Eliza. Wright
Fleet Cox

At a Court held for Westmoreland County Jany 29th 1777 This Indenture together with the rect. & memorandum of Livery & Sezen endorsed were acknd. by the parties thereto & ordered to be recorded

Teste
Presley Thornton Cl. Court

At a Court held for Westmd County the 25th day of Setr 1792 This Indenture &c. being . . . ."

This record indicates that Francis Wright had died between December 6, 1775, the correct date of his will, and November 22, 1776.

A division of the estate of Francis Wright and allotment of the dower interest of Elizabeth Wright was made at the request of Presley Wright and filed on May 27, 1777, at Westmoreland County, Virginia, R.B. 1776-1790/58.

An accounting for the estate of Francis Wright was filed on June 30, 1778, at Westmoreland County, Virginia, R.B. 1776-1790/99.

Married Well And Often by Robert K. Headley, Jr., listed the marriage of Elizabeth Wright, widow of Francis Wright, and George Lewis before August 16, 1786:

> "Lewis, George & Wright, Elizabeth (wid.); bef. 16 Aug 1786; bride was a dau. of Benedict Middleton (d. WC 1785) & the wid. of Francis Wright; (WC DW 16:355; DW 17:217; DW 18:295; RI 7:254)"

Adventurers of Purse and Person, Virginia 1607-1624/5, 3rd edition, by Virginia M. Meyer and John Frederick Dorman, stated that:

> "9. Margaret Fleet[3] (Henry[2], Henry[1]), called Mary in her father's will, married, (bond 17) Oct. 1723[66], Presley Cox of Cople Parish, Westmoreland County, son of Charnock Cox. He left will 18 Feb. 1766 - 30 Sept. 1766.[67]

> Issue: [Cox] 28. Mary Ann[4], married, as his (1) wife, Francis Wright who left will 5 Dec. 1775 - 26 March 1793;[68] . . . . 30. Fleet[4], justice of Westmoreland County, left will 7 Jan. 1791 - 28 June 1791,[70] married Elizabeth Wright; . . . .
>
> ---
>
> [66] Nottingham, *op. cit.*, p. 17.
> [67] Westmoreland Co. Deeds & Wills 14, 1761-68, pp. 393-95.
> [68] Westmoreland Co. Deeds & Wills 18, 1787-94, pp. 294-95.
> . . . .
> [70] Westmoreland Co. Deeds & Wills 18, 1787-94, p. 191."

This record identifies the first wife of Francis Wright as Mary Ann (Cox) Wright.

Adventurers of Purse and Person, Virginia 1607-1624/5, 4th edition, by John Frederick Dorman, stated that:

> "28. Mary Ann[4] Cox, (Margaret Fleet[3], Henry[2], Henry[1]) married, as his (1) wife, Francis Wright, son of Richard and Elizabeth (Wigginton) Wright, who left will 5 Dec. 1775-26 March 1793.[105]
> Issue: [Wright] 89. Richard[5]; 90. Presley[5], married Elizabeth Middleton; 91. Nancy[5], married Matthew Rust.
>
> ---
>
> [105] Westmoreland Co. Deeds & Wills 18, 1787-94, pp. 294-95."

Fourth Generation:

1809 Presley Wright Of Westmoreland County, His Wife Elizabeth (Middleton) Wright, And His Descendants

1809 Presley Wright of Westmoreland County, was a son of 1776 Francis Wright of Westmoreland County and Mary Ann (Cox) Wright. (1663 Richard[1], 1713 Francis[2], 1741 Richard[3], 1776 Francis[4])

The will of Presley Cox dated on February 18, 1766, probated on September 30, 1766, at Westmoreland County, Virginia, D. & W.B. 14/393, and posted at http://freepages.genealogy.rootsweb.com/~rmbeckman/alhn/doc/presleycoxwill.html provided in part as follows:

> "In the Name of God Amen I Presley Cox of Cople parish in Westmoreland County in Virginia . . . . Item I give and bequeath to my Grandsons Richard Wright and Presley Wright and my grand Daughter Nancy Wright ten pounds current money of Virginia each to be paid out of my estate by my executors when they arrive to the

age of twenty One years or the day of Marriage . . . . lastly I Constitute and appoint my son Fleet Cox and my son William Cox and Frances Wright to be my whole and sole executors of this my last Will and testament . . . ."

The appointment of Frances Wright as executor and the listing of a grandchild Presley Wright identifies Presley Wright as a child of Francis Wright.

Adventurers of Purse and Person, Virginia 1607-1624/5, 4th edition, by John Frederick Dorman, stated that:

"28. Mary Ann[4] Cox, (Margaret Fleet[3], Henry[2], Henry[1]) married, as his (1) wife, Francis Wright, son of Richard and Elizabeth (Wigginton) Wright, who left will 5 Dec. 1775-26 March 1793.[105]
Issue: [Wright] 89. Richard[5]; 90. Presley[5], married Elizabeth Middleton; 91. Nancy[5], married Matthew Rust.

[105] Westmoreland Co. Deeds & Wills 18, 1787-94, pp. 294-95."

The inventory and appraisement of the estate of Presley Wright was dated on March 27, 1809, filed on April 24, 1809, at Westmoreland County, Virginia, I.&A.B. 1806-1815/142, and showed an estate of L943, 12s, 8-1/4d.

The Division and Allotment of the estate of Presley Wright was dated July 24, 1812, filed on August 24, 1812, at Westmoreland County, Virginia, I&A.B. 1806-1815/338:

"Anthony	No 1	£100	To	Richard Wright			£76.17.6
Siner	No 2	" 65	"	Sarah Wright	To receive of R.W No. 1	£11:17:6	76.17.6
Nelly	No 3	" 75	"	Eliza Wright	To receive of R.W No. 1	1:17:6	76.17.6
Joe	No 4	" 75	"	Presley Wright	To receive of R.W No. 1	1:17:6	76.17.6
Willis	No 5	" 75	"	George Wright	To receive of M.F.W. No 8	1:17:6	76.17.6
Lucy	No 6	" 70	"	John Wright	To receive of R.W No. 1	6:17:6	76.17.6
Daniel & Ned	No 7	" 75	"	Francis Wright	To receive of M.F.W. No 8	1:17:6	76.17.6
Hanner & Spencer	No 8	" 80	"	Mary F. Wright	To receive of R.W No. 1	:12:6	76.17.6
		£615					£615. - -
		£76:17:6					

Amounts of Account Sale after Debts being Paid £351.11.0½ Divided into eight parts which make each Persons part £43.18.10½. Sarah Wright Received her proportionable part in Bonds George M Wright Recd. his part and John Wright his part, Richard Wright Guardian of Presly Wright Eliza and fanny Wright Received their parts in Bonds

Pursuant to an order of Westmoreland County Court bearing date the 23rd day of March 1812 we the Commissioners have met and Divided the Estate of Presley Wright Deceased Between the legal representatives.

July 24th 1812 William Middleton
William Wright
John Lyell

At a Court held for Westmoreland County the 24th day of August 1812 The Foregoing Acct of the Division of Presley Wright Decd. was Returned and ordered to be Recorded

Teste
Jos. Fox C.W."

This record identifies the eight children and heirs of Presley Wright as follows:

1) Richard Wright,
2) Sarah Wright,
3) Eliza Wright,
4) Presley Wright,
5) George M. Wright,
6) John Wright,
7) Frances Wright, and
8) Mary F. Wright.

On November 2, 1826, in the case of Straughan & Others v. Wright & Others, 4 Rand 493, the court entered the following order:

"This was an appeal from the Chancery Court of Fredericksburg, where William Wright and others filed their bill against Richard Wright and others, praying partition of a tract of land. The facts are set forth at large in the following opinion:

Stanard, for the appellants.
J. Mayo, for the appellees.

November 2. Judge Green delivered his opinion, in which the other Judges concurred.

Richard Wright, by his will dated in 1740, devised to his son Francis, a tract of land in Lower Machodick, which had been given to the testator by his brother John Wright, and also, after the death of is wife, the tract of land on which the testotor lived, to him and his heirs forever. Francis Wright was then, as appears by the will, under the age of eighteen. Francis made his will in December, 1775, and died before the 26th of March, 1776. By this will, he directed that the land he had purchased of John Rust, should be sold for the payment of his debts, and the surplus proceeds of the sale equally divided between his three sons, Benedict Wright, Johnson Wigginton Wright, and Wright Wright. (The testator had no son named Wright Wright, and no attempt is made to shew which of the sons was intended by this name.) He also gave to his wife the dwelling-house and one-third of the land adjoining it, for life; and also, one-third of his personal estate, for life; and after her death, to be equally divided amongst all his children; and directed that all the rest of his estate should be equally divided amongst all his children. On the 26th of March, 1776, the will was proved by three witnesses. The executors qualified; and John Rochester, who was chosen guardian of Presley Wright, the heir at law of Francis Wright, was directed to be summoned to contest the recording of the will. No step was taken on this order, so far as appears. But, on the 26th of March, 1793, the Court in which the will was recorded, made an order in these words: "On the motion of Francis Wright, it is ordered that this will be recorded, the heir at law consenting thereto." On the 13th of November, 1753, Gerard Davis and Thomas M'Farlane and Elizabeth his wife, conveyed 123 acres of land to Francis Wright, which does not appear to have lain adjoining any other land held by Francis Wright. Francis Wright left five children living at the time of his death, Presley, (the eldest son, and heir at law,) Benedict, William, Nancy, and Johnson W. Wright. Such of those children as were alive, and the representatives of one who was dead, filed their bill on the 12th of July, 1820, against the heirs of Presley Wright, who died in 1810, intestate; and afterwards against the purchasers claiming under some of the heirs of Presley Wright, claiming a partition of a tract of land described as containing ___ acres, of which Francis Wright died seised and possessed, and which he was entitled to under the will of Richard Wright. They charge that soon after the death of Francis Wright, Presley Wright entered upon the whole of the said tract of land, and received the rents and profits thereof during his life, and that his heirs, and those claiming under them, have received the rents and profits since his death. . . . ."

This record identifies Francis Wright as the father of Presley Wright.

Fifth Generation:

George M. Wright, His Wife Catherine A. M. P. (   ) Wright, And His Descendants

George M. Wright was a son of 1809 Presley Wright of Westmoreland County and Mary Ann (Cox) Wright. (1663 Richard[1], 1713 Francis[2], 1741 Richard[3], 1776 Francis[4], 1809 Presley[5])

On March 2, 1812, at Westmoreland County, Virginia, D.&W.B. 22/254 George M. Wright sold to Richard Wright all of his interest in the land lately owned by and lived on by Presley Wright:

> "Wright)
> To)
> Wright)
>
> This Indenture made this 2nd day of March Eighteen hundred and twelve. Between Richard Wright of the County of Westmoreland and State of Virginia of the one part and George M. Wright of the County and State aforesaid of the other part. Witnesseth that the said George M. Wright for and in consideration of the sum of 200 dollars to him in hand paid by the said Richard Wright the receipt whereof is hereby acknowledged, Have granted bargain'd and Sold, and by these presents Do grant Sell Alien release and confirm unto him the said Richard Wright and his heirs forever, All the right, title, claim and Interest which he the said George M. Wright has or may have, to that Tract or parcel of Land Situate lying and being in the County of Westmoreland aforesaid whereon Presley Wright lately lived and of which he died Seized, be the same more or less. To have and to Hold the aforemention'd premises or Tract of Land freed and Cleard from all right, title claim or demand either in Law or equity of him the said George M. Wright his heirs Executors or Assigns, or any person or persons claiming under him or through or by him, to the only proper use and behoof of him the said Richard Wright and heirs forever. In Witness whereof the said George M. Wright has hereunto set his hand and affixed his Seal this the day and date first above written.
>
> Sign'd Seal'd & deliver'd) Geo. M. Wright
> in presence of)
> Wm. Wright
> Presly C. Wright
> John Withers
>
> Recd. March 1st 1812 of Richard Wright the within sum of Two hundred dollars in full.
>
> Teste Geo M. Wright

At a Court held for Westmoreland County the 23 day of March 1812. The aforegoing Indenture of bargain and Sale and receipt thereon indors'd from George M. Wright to Richard Wright, were acknowledged in open Court, by the said George M. Wright, and ordered to be recorded

_____ Teste

Jos: Fox Ct. Cur."

This record indicates that George M. Wright was an heir of Presley Wright and, therefore, one of his sons.

The Division and Allotment of the estate of Presley Wright was dated July 24, 1812, filed on August 24, 1812, at Westmoreland County, Virginia, I&A.B. 1806-1815/338 listed George M. Wright as a child and heir of Presley Wright:

"Anthony	No 1	£100	To	Richard Wright			£76.17.6
Siner	No 2	" 65	"	Sarah Wright	To receive of R.W No. 1	£11:17:6	76.17.6
Nelly	No 3	" 75	"	Eliza Wright	To receive of R.W No. 1	1:17:6	76.17.6
Joe	No 4	" 75	"	Presley Wright	To receive of R.W No. 1	1:17:6	76.17.6
Willis	No 5	" 75	"	George Wright	To receive of M.F.W. No 8	1:17:6	76.17.6
Lucy	No 6	" 70	"	John Wright	To receive of R.W No. 1	6:17:6	76.17.6
Daniel & Ned	No 7	" 75	"	Francis Wright	To receive of M.F.W. No 8	1:17:6	76.17.6
Hanner & Spencer	No 8	" 80	"	Mary F. Wright	To receive of R.W No. 1	:12:6	76.17.6
		£615					£615. - -
		£76:17:6					

Amounts of Account Sale after Debts being Paid £351.11.0½ Divided into eight parts which make each Persons part £43.18.10½. Sarah Wright Received her proportionable part in Bonds George M Wright Recd. his part and John Wright his part, Richard Wright Guardian of Presly Wright Eliza and fanny Wright Received their parts in Bonds

Pursuant to an order of Westmoreland County Court bearing date the 23rd day of March 1812 we the Commissioners have met and Divided the Estate of Presley Wright Deceased Between the legal representatives.

July 24th 1812 William Middleton
William Wright
John Lyell

At a Court held for Westmoreland County the 24th day of August 1812 The Foregoing Acct of the Division of Presley Wright Decd. was Returned and ordered to be Recorded

Teste
Jos. Fox C.W."

On April 27, 1815, at Richmond County, Virginia, D.B. 20/23 George M. Wright purchased from Moore F. and Fanny M. Tomlin 180 acres of land:

> "This Indenture made and entered into this 27th day of April in the year of our lord one thousand eight hundred and fifteen in the 39th year of the Commonwealth, between Moore F. Tomlin and Fany M his his wife of the County of Richmond and parish of Lunenburg of the one part, and Geo: M. Wright of the County of Westmoreland & parish of ____ of the other part. Witnesseth that the said Moore F Tomlin and Fanny his wife for and in Consideration of the Sum of One Thousand eight hundred dollars to them in hand paid by the said George M Wright the receipt whereof he the said Moore F Tomlin doth hereby acknowledge and him the said George M. Wright from the same doth acquit exonerate and discharge, Have bargained and Sold and by these presents doth bargain and sell alien and confirm unto the said George M. Wright all and singular the Tract piece or parcel of land lying and being in the County of Richmond and parish of Northfarnham which he the Said Tomlin lately purchased from William Alderson Containing one hundred and eighty acres be the same more or less bounded and described as by the Deed from the said Alderson to the said Tomlin bearing date the 11th day of March last past of Record in the County Court of Richmond will appear referrence thereto being had, together with all and singular the rights, tenements, hereditaments and appurtenances whatsover to the same belonging or in any wise appertaining and the reversion and reversions, remainder and remainders rents issues and profits thereof and every part and parcel thereof unto the said Geo. M. Wright his heirs and assigns forever to have and to hold the said Tract piece or parcel of land, tenements, hereditaments and appurtenances herein before mentioned and intended to be hereby bargained and Sold unto the said Geo. M. Wright his heirs and assigns to his and their only proper use and behoof, and to no other use, whatever forever - and the said Moore T. Tomlin and Fanny M. his wife for themselves, and their heirs do hereby covenant promise & agree to and with the said Geo. M. Wright and his heirs that they the Tomlin & Fanny M. his wife the said Tract piece or parcel of land with the Tenements hereditaments and appurtenancese thereto belonging to him the said Geo: M. Wright his heirs, Exors. admors & assigns shall and will from time to time and at all times forever hereafter, against the claim and demand of them the said Tomlin and Fanny his wife and their heirs and against the Claim of all other

persons whatsoever, warrant and for ever defend by these presents. In Witness whereof the said Moore F. Tomlin & Fanny M. his wife have hereunto set their hands & affixed their Seals the day and year aforesaid.

Signed Sealed & acknowl-) Moore F. Tomlin
edged in the presence of) Fanny M. Tomlin
John Burke
Matilda F Levy
Vin: Bramham
Jere: Garland

Recd. the day of the date of the aforesaid Indenture of the within named George M. Wright the sum of one Thousand eight hundred dollars, the consideration money in full for the land & appurtenances conveyed by the said Deed.

Witnesses Moore F. Tomlin
Matilda F Levy
Vin: Branham
Jere: Garland

Richmond County to wit

We Vincent Bramham and Jeremiah Garland Justices of the peace in the County aforesaid in the State of Virginia do hereby certify that Fanny M. Tomlin the wife of Moore F Tomlin parties to Certain deed for the conveyance of Real Estate to Geo. M. Wright bearing date the 27th day of April 1815 and hereto annexed personally appeared before us in our County aforesaid and being examined by us privately and apart from her husband and having the Deed aforesaid fully explained to her, she the said Fanny M. acknowledged the same to be her act and Deed, and declared that she had willingly signed, sealed & delivered the same, and that she wished not to retract it

Given under our hands and Seals this 27th day of Apl. 1815.

Vin: Bramham
Jere: Garland

At a Court of quarterly Sessions held for the County of Richmond the Sixth day of November 1815.

This Deed of Bargain and Sale from Moore T. Tomlin and Fanny M his wife of the one part, to George M. Wright of the other part with the Receipt thereon Indorsed, was proved in open Court by the Oath of Vincent Bramham, John Burke, and Jeremiah Garland, three of the witnesses to the same subscribed, and admitted to record. The Certificate annexed for the acknowledgment and Privy Examination of the said Fanny M. being returned according to Law, was also admitted to record.

Teste,
Geo. Saunders CRC"

On July 1, 1823, at Richmond County, Virginia, D.B. 21/514 George M. Wright acted as trustee on a deed of trust executed by Edward J. Northen to secure a debt due to Fleet B. Plummer.

On September 10, 1825, at Richmond County, Virginia, D.B. 22/100 George M. Wright conveyed to his wife Catherine M. P. Wright and his children Alexander Wright, Elizabeth M Wright, Mary Ann F Wright, and Emily M Wright and any future children he might have the 180 acres of land purchased by Richmond County Deed 20/123:

"This Indenture this 10th day of September 1825 between George M Wright of Richmond County of the one part and Catharine M P Wright, Alexander Wright, Elizabeth M. Wright, Mary Ann F. Wright & Emily M Wright and the future increase of the bodies of the said George M Wright & the said Catharine M. P. Wright of the othe part Witnesseth that the said George M Wright, as well for and in Consideration of the natural love & affection which he hath & beareth unto the said Catharine M. P. his Wife & Alexander Wright Elizabeth M Wright, Mary Ann F Wright & Emily M Wright his children, and also for the better support maintenance, livelihood & preferment of all, hath Given, Granted, aliened, enfeoffed & confirmed and by these presents do grant, Give, alien, enfeoff and confirm unto the said Catharine M. P. Wright, Alexander Wright their heirs & assigns, all that tract or parcel of land being situate & lying in the County of Richmond near Farnham Church, adjoining the lands of Edwd Saunders, B. M Tomblin, Wm. D McCarty, Jas. Shepherd & Thomas Sydnor & which was heretofore occupied by a certain William Alderson containing One hundred & Eighty acres more or less together with all and singular the Reversion & reversions, Remainder and remainders Yearly and other rents, issues, profits, thereof and every part and parcel thereof: and also my slaves Bill, Lydea, Becky, Hannah, Esther, Maria, Rose, and Nancy, and their future increase; also all my household and Kitchen furniture; plantation Utensils, stocks of horses, cattle & hogs together with their future increase: To have and to hold the said tract or parcel of land, with the tenements, hereditaments and all & singular, other the premises hereby granted & conveyed or mentioned or intended to be hereby to be conveyed, as also the said slaves, goods, chattels & stocks & their future increase, with their & every of the appurtenances of the sd. land unto the said Catharine M. P. Wright, Alexander Wright, Elizabeth M. Wright Mary Ann F Wright & Emily M. Wright and my future children to the only use proper and behoof of the said Conveyers their heirs and assigns forever - and the said George M Wright for himself his heirs &c doth covenant, grant and agree to & with the sd Catharine M P., Alexander,

Elizabeth M. Wright Mary Ann F Wright & Emily M Wright their heirs and assigns, that they their heirs and assigns shall & lawfully may enter from time to time, and at all times hereafter peaceably, and quietly have, hold, use occupy, possess & enjoy the said Real & personal estate hereby granted & confirmed with their & every of their appurtenances, free clear & fully discharged & sufficiently, saved Kept harmless and indemnified of & from & against all former Gifts, grants bargains &c and from the claims of all persons lawfully claiming or to claim under him the said George M Wright. As Witness my hand & seal the Day & year first above Written,

Signed sealed and deli-) C. M. Wright
vered In presence of (3))
Richd. B Plummer)
Ben C. Plummer)
Albert G Plummer)

Richmond County court clerks office the 12th day of September 1825.

This Indenture between George M Wright of the one part, and Catharine M. P. Wright, Alexander Wright Elizabeth M Wright Mary Ann F Wright & Emily M Wright and the future increase of the Bodies of the said George M. Wright and the said Catharine M P. Wright of the other part, was acknowledged by the said George M Wright and admitted to Record

Teste,
Geo. Saunders CRC"

This record identifies the family of George M. Wright as follows:

Wife: Catherine M. P. Wright

Children: Alexander Wright,

Elizabeth M Wright,

Mary Ann F Wright, and

Emily M Wright.

On October 20, 1834, at Westmoreland County, Virginia, D.&W.B. 28/194 George M. Wright and Catherine M. P. Wright conveyed to Robert M. Tomlin certain land pursuant to a decree of the chancery court:

"This Indenture, made and entered into this twentieth day of October, in the year of Our Lord one thousand eight hundred and thirty-four. Between, George M Wright and Catherine M. P. Wright his wife, of the County of Richmond and State of Virginia, of the one part, and Robert M. Tomlin of Nottingham in the County of Prince George and State of Maryland, of the other part. Whereas, by a decree of the Hon'ble the Superior Court of Law and Chancery holden for the county of Richmond aforesaid on the seventeenth day of April in the year before mentioned, it was decreed and ordered, in a chancery suit between the said Robert M. Tomlin, plaintiff, and the said George M. Wright and Catherine M. P. his wife, defendants, that the said defendant should execute a deed of conveyance, according to the directions of the said decree, to the said plaintiff, for the land herein after mentioned and herein and hereby conveyed, or intended so to be; as from the said decree reference thereto being had, more fully and at large will appear: Now therefore, in obedience to the said decree, and in pursuance thereof, This Indenture Witnesseth, that Whereas the said George M Wright and Catherine M P Wright his wife, for a valuable and valid consideration, conveyed, by deed, to Moore F. Tomlin, in his life time a tract or parcel of land, with the appurtenances, called and known by the name of Hagues, lying and being in the County of Westmoreland and State of Virginia; and whereas the said deed to the said Moore F. Tomlin hath been lost or mislaid, and cannot be found, as is alleged by the said Robert M. Tomlin; and whereas the said Moore F. Tomlin hath departed this life since the execution of the deed to him made as aforementioned, and, in the division of the lands which were of him the said Moore F. Tomlin, the said tract called Hagues' hath been allotted to the said Robert M. Tomlin, who is a son of the said Moore F. Tomlin; They the said George M. Wright and Catherine M. P. Wright his wife, for and in consideration of the premises, do, and each of them doth, for themselves and their heirs, remise, release, and altogether from them and their heirs quit claim, and also ratify approve, and confirm, unto the said Robert M. Tomlin, his heirs, and assigns all that tract or parcel of land aforesaid, called and known by the name of Hagues, lying and being in the Said County of Westmoreland, together with all and singular the rights, tenements, hereditaments, and appurtenances whatsoever to the same belonging or in any wise appertaining, and the reverson and reversions, remainder and remainders, rents, issues, and profits thereof, and of every part and parcel thereof. To Have and To Hold the said tract or parcel of land and its appurtenances unto the said Robert M. Tomlin, his heirs, and assigns, to his and their only proper use and behoof, forever. And the said George M. Wright and Catherine M. P. Wright his wife, for themselves and their heirs, do hereby covenant, promise, and agree to and with the said Robert M. Tomlin and his heirs, that they, the said George M. Wright and Catherine M. P. his wife, the said tract or parcel of land, with the tenements, hereditaments, and appurtenances thereto belonging, to him the said Robert M. Tomlin, his heirs, and assigns, from time to time and at all times hereafter, against the claim and demand of them the said George M. Wright and Catherine M. P. his wife and their heirs, and against the claim of all other persons whomsoever, shall and will warrant and forever defend, by these presents. In Witness whereof, the said George M Wright and Catherine M. P. Wright hereunto set their hands and affix their Seals, the day and year above first written.

Signed, sealed, and) G. M. Wright
delivered, in presence of) Catherine M. Wright

Richmond County to wit:

We William D. McCarty and Joseph Palmer Justices of the peace in the County aforesaid in the State of Virginia, do hereby certify that Catherine M. P. Wright, the wife of George M. Wright, parties to the foregoing deed, which bears date the twentieth day of October, in the year One thousand eight hundred and thirty-four, personally appeared before us in Our County aforesaid; and being examined by us privily and apart from her said husband, and having the ded aforesaid fully explained to her, she the said Catherine M. P. Wright acknowledged the same to be her act and deed, and declared that she had willingly signed, sealed and delivered the same, and that she wished not to retract it. Given under our hands and seals, this 20th day of Octr. 1834.

Wm. D. McCarty
Jos: Palmer

Richmond County to wit:

We William D. McCarty and Joseph Palmer justices of the peace for the County aforesaid, do hereby certify that George M. Wright & Catherine M. P. Wright parties to this Deed, hereunto annexed personally appeared before us in our County aforesaid and acknowledged the same to be their act and deed, & desired us to Certify the said acknowledgment to the Clerk of the Court of Westmoreland County in Order that the said deed may be recorded. Given under our hands & Seals this 20th October 1834.

Wm. D. McCarty
Jos. Palmer

At a Circuit Superior Court of Law and Chancery continued and held for Richmond County, at the Court House, on Tuesday the 21st October 1834.

Robert M. Tomlin Plt. vs. George M. Wright and Catherine M. P. his wife defts. In Chancery - This Cause came on again this day to be heard upon the papers formerly read and a deed now here exhibited executed by the defendants to the plaintiff with the privy examination of the feme certified thereon and the certificate of Wm C. McCarty & Joseph Palmer justices of the peace for Richmond County that the same had been acknowledged by the said Geo: M. Wright & Catherine M. P. Wright to be their act and deed and that they, the said George M. & Catherine M. P. had desired the said justices to Certify the said acknowledgement to the Clerk of Westmoreland County Court in Order that the said deed might be recorded, to which deed no objections were made. It is therefore decreed and ordered that the said deed of conveyance be accordingly allowed to be recorded and that the same be delivered after recordation to the plaintiff. And it is further decreed & Ordered that the plaintiff pay to the defendant their costs by them about their Suit in this behalf expended.

A Copy
Teste,
Geo: Saunders C.C.

Clerk's Office of Westmoreland County Court the 27th day of October 1834.

This Deed from George M. Wright and Catherine M. P. his wife to Robert M. Tomlin, was this day presented in my Office, and together with the Certificates of acknowledgment and privy examination thereunder written, and decree thereto appended, admitted to record.

Teste,
William Hutt C.W.C.

Recorded and Examined this 4th day of November 1834.

Teste,
William Hutt C.W.C."

On November 14, 1834, at Westmoreland County, Virginia, D.&W.B. 29/17 George M. Wright and Catherine Wright sold to George Sydnor all of their interest in the land of Frances Wright which was allotted to Frances from the estate of her father Presley Wright:

"This Indenture made and entered into the 14th day of November in the year of Our Lord one thousand eight hundred and thirty four Between George M. Wright and Catherine his wife of the one part of the County of Richmond, and George Sydnor of the County of Westmoreland of the other part Witnesseth that the said George M Wright and Catherine his wife for and in consideration of the sum of Twenty dollars to the said George M. Wright in hand paid by the said Sydnor at and before the ensealing and delivery of these presents the receipt whereof the said George and Catherine his wife do hereby acknowledge, have granted, bargained and sold, and by these presents do grant, bargain and Sell unto the said George Sydnor all the interest right, title or claim whatsoever in that piece or parcel of land which was allotted to Francis Wright, in the division of the Estate of Presley Wright decd. among the distribution of said Presley situate in the County of Westmoreland and adjoining the lot of Eliza Sydnor formerly Eliza Wright and bounded by other Lots belonging to the distributees of Said Presley Wright decd - To have and To hold the said land with the appurtenances unto him the said George Sydnor his heirs & assigns forever. And the said George M. Wright and Catherine his wife, for themselves their and each of their heirs Executors and Admors. do covenant to and with the said George Sydnor his heirs and assigns, that they the said George and

Catherine his wife have a good sure and absolute title in one fourth part of the said lot or parcel of land which was allotted to the said Francis Wright in the division of Her Fathers estate and of which the said Francis died seized and that they the said George M. Wright & Catherine his wife their and each of their Heirs, Exors. &c shall and will from time to time and at all times warrant and defend the title thereof to the said George Sydnor his heirs & assigns against the claim or claims of them the said George & Catherine his wife their or either of their heirs and against the claim or claims of all other persons Whatsoever. In Witness whereof the parties to these have hereto set their hands and affixed their seals.

Witness	G. M. Wright
William Middleton	Catherine M Wright
Bendt. Walker	
Richd. Sydnor	

Westmoreland County to wit:

We William Middleton & Benedict Walker Justices of the peace in the County aforesaid in the State of Virginia, do hereby certify that George M. Wright & Catherine Wright, parties to the foregoing deed bearing date on the 14th day of November, Eighteen hundred and thirty four and hereto annexed personally appeared before us in Our County aforesaid and acknowledged the same to be their act and deed and desired us to certify the said acknowledgment to the Clerk of the County Court of Westmoreland in Order that the said deed may be recorded. Given under our hands & Seals this 14th day of November Eighteen hundred and thirty four

Wm Middleton
Bendt. Walker

Clerk's Office of Westmoreland County Court the 28th day of December 1835.

This deed from George M. Wright and wife to George Sydnor was this day presented in my Office, and with the certificate of acknowledgment thereon endorsed, admitted to record.

Teste,
William Hutt, C.W.C.

Recorded and Examined the 1st day of January, 1836.

Teste,
William Hutt C.C."

This record indicates that George M. Wright was an heir of Frances Wright who was an heir and daughter of Presley Wright and confirms that George M. Wright was a son of Presley Wright.

On April 10, 1839, at Richmond County, Virginia, D.B. 25/58, and pursuant to a decree of the chancery court, George M. Wright and his wife and children sold to Thomas Oldham the 180 cares of land purchased by Richmond Deed 20/123:

> "This Indenture made this 10th day of April 1839 Between George M Wright and Catherine M P his wife, and George N Alderson (Commissioner appointed by Richmond County Court) of the one part, and Thomas Oldham of the other part: Witnesseth: That whereas by a certain cause in the County Court of Richmond in which George M. Wright father and natural Guardian of Alexander Wright, Mary A. F. Wright, Emily M. Wright, John M Wright, George H. Wright, Sarah E Wright, Andrew Wright, the said Alexander Wright and Mary A. F. Wright Emily M. Wright infants over the age of 14 years; and John M Wright, George H Wright, Sarah E Wright and Andrew Wright under the age of 14 years by Richard G Northen Guardian ad litem appointed by Court, and Catherine M. P. Wright plaintiffs & Defendants therein a decree was entered on the 7th January 1839 to the effect following - This cause coming on to be heard by Consent of parties on the Bill, answers of the Defts, exhibits and the examination of witnesses, was argued by counsel, on consideration whereof this Court being of opinion that it is for the benefit of the infant Defendants, and Catherine M. P. Wright the wife of the sd George M Wright, that the tract of land lying near Farnham Church containing about 180 acres now in the possession of the said parties refered to in the said Bill by deed apart of said Bill dated the 10th of September 1825 belonging to the said Infants & their mother aforesaid, Doth order, adjudge & decree, that George N Alderson, who is hereby appointed Commissioner for that purpose, do after advertising the same for four weeks in some paper published in the Town of Fredericksburg or in the City of Richmond, expose to sale the said tract of land: or if he shall Consider that Twelve hundred and fifty dollars offered for said land be a full and fair price, he may close the bargain for the sale thereof. Cash to be paid for the expences of sale and Costs: and for the debts due to Thomas J Meredith, Thomas Oldham and others - The residue to be loaned, taking from the borrower, purchaser or purchasers, Bond with good security, and a deed of Trust upon the premises to secure the payment of the residue of the purchase money - the interest thereof to be annually paid to the said George M Wright Gdn of the said infants or to the said Catherine M. P. Wright the mother, and one of the cestui que trust till the further order of this Court Touching the premises - Right is reserved herein to the parties or any of them from time to time to apply to this Court for any aid in the furtherance of their or either of their rights - The Court doth further order, for the better security of the Perchaser, that the said George M Wright, & Catherine M. P Wright do join the commissioner in the conveyance of the said tract of land, only the said George M Wright to give a general warranty - and the said commissioner is directed to report his proceedings

herein to the Court, and whereas also the said George N Alderson acting as commissioner in pursuance of the decree aforesaid refered to upon due consideration and respection of the premises in said decree mentioned, as well also by the testimony and opinion of others corroborating his judgment & opinion; he did decide & consider, that the said sum of Twelve hundred & fifty dollars was "a full & fair" price for the parcel or tract of land in the said Cause mentioned; and he did close the bargain & sale of the same with Thomas Oldham for that price.

Therefore they the said George M Wright and Catherine M. P. Wright his wife, and George N Alderson for and in consideration of the sum of Twelve hundred and fifty dollars lawful money of the U.S. to the said George N Alderson, commissioner as aforesd. in hand paid by the said Thomas Oldham, the receipt whereof they the said George M Wright, Catherine M. P. Wright and George N Alderson do hereby acknowledge have bargained, sold & conveyed & by these presents do bargain, sell and Convey unto the said Oldham his heirs and assigns, the certain tract or parcel of land in the said cause mentioned, lying & being in the County of Richmond near Farnham Church Coterminous with the lands Christopher Ficklin, Tho: Sydnors estate and Edward S. Saunders & others Containing one hundred & eighty acres be the same more or less, which said tract or parcel of land was duly conveyed by deed bearing date the 10th September 1825 by George M Wright to his wife & children which deed is recorded in Richmond County Court, to which deed & for the proceedings in the suit before referred, reference may be had for further particulars. The said tract or parcel of land To have & to hold with the appurtenances thereto belonging to him the said Thomas Oldham his heirs and assigns, and to the only proper use and behoof of the said Thomas Oldham, his heirs and assigns forever.

And the said George M Wright for himself his heirs, exors & admors, doth hereby covenant to & with the said Thomas Oldham his heirs and assigns, that he the said George M Wright and his heirs the said tract or parcel of land with its appurtenances, unto him the said Thomas Oldham his heirs and assigns, against him the said George M Wright and his heirs and against all persons whomsoever, shall & will by these presents forever defend -

The said George N Alderson conveys the said tract or parcel of land as Commissioner appointed by the Court; and therefore doth not bind himself & his heirs for the title of the same; but that he nor they shall ever set up any claim to the same.

In Witness whereof the parties hereto have signed their names and affixed their seals, the day and year first above written.

Signed sealed & delivered)
in the presence of us)
G. B. Burch
J. H. Shackleford
Benedict Hammock

G. M. Wright
Catherine M. P. Wright
George N Alderson Com

Virginia

At a Court of Monthly session held for Richmond County, at the Court house on monday the 7th day of October 1839.

This Deed of bargain and sale from George M Wright, and Catharine M. P. his wife, and George N Alderson commissioner &c. to Thomas Oldham, was this day presented proved by the oaths of Gibson P Burch and James H Shackleford, two of the subscribing witnesses thereto, and Ordered to lie for further proof - And in the clerks office of the said County on the 19th day of October 1839, the said deed was further proved by the oath of Benedict Hammock another subscribing witness thereto, and admitted to record.

Teste,
Jno F B Jeffries Cl"

This record identifies the expanded family of George M. Wright as follows:

Wife: Catherine M. P. Wright

Children:

1) Alexander Wright, born after April 10, 1818 and before September 10, 1825,
2) Elizabeth M Wright, born after April 10, 1818 and before September 10, 1825,
3) Mary Ann F Wright, born after April 10, 1818 and before September 10, 1825,
4) Emily M Wright, born after September 10, 1825, and before April 10, 1839,
5) John M Wright, born after September 10, 1825, and before April 10, 1839,

6) George H. Wright, born after September 10, 1825, and before April 10, 1839,

7) Sarah E Wright, born after September 10, 1825, and before April 10, 1839, and

8) Andrew Wright, born after September 10, 1825, and before April 10, 1839.

On February 24, 1842, at Richmond County, Virginia, D.B. 25/376 George M. Wright, as trustee, sold to Alexander Bryant land known as the Poplars.

On July 18, 1849, at Richmond County, Virginia, D.B. 27/419 Catharine M. P. Wright and her children purchased from William C. and Virginia Oldham 200 acres of land known as Coxes and Gourds:

> "This Indenture made the 18th day of July 1849 Between William C Oldham and Virginia his wife of the one part and Catharine M P. Wright and her children Mary A. F. Alexander M. Emily M. John M Hamilton G. Sarah E and Andrew Wright of the other part, all of the County of Richmond and State of Virginia: Witnesseth: That the said William C. Oldham and Virginia his wife in Consideration of One Thousand Dollars of lawful money of the Commonwealth of Virginia - secured to be paid to the said William C Oldham his exors admors or assigns by the said Catharine M P. Wright and others, Have bargained and sold and by these presents do and each of them doth bargain and sell unto the said Catharine M P Wright, and her children aforesaid their heirs and assigns a certain piece or parcel of land and premises being a part of the tract of land Known by the name of Coxes and Gourds lying & being in the County of Richmond & State of Virginia, supposed to contain Two Hundred Acres be the same more or less adjoining the land of Robert B Neasome, Wm Webb, Sally Critcher & others Begining at a Corner red Oak on the S.E. side of the road leading from Farnham Church to Oldhams Mill, with the land of Robert B Neasome, thence with said Neasoms land to the swamp to the line of Wm Webb thence up said swamp with the land of said Webb to a corner Ash tree in the line of said Webb where the line is to commence which divides this land from the other portion of said Oldhams land (near an old bridge) in the branch which makes dower from Sally Critchers spring thence a North easterly Course up said branch by sundry Marked trees to the land of Farnham Church property (called Sallys) thence a south westerly course up a valley & Hill with said land last mentioned by sundry marked trees to the line of Sally Critcher, thence with her line to a corner stone on the Northwest side of said main road before mentioned, at the corner of Robert C Wooddys land thence along said main road to the Beginning, with all and singular the appurtenances to the same belonging or in any wise appertaining To Have And To Hold the said land & premises herein before mentioned unto the said Catharine M. P. Wright, and here children hereinbefore mentioned, their heirs and assigns

forever. And the said William C Oldham and Virginia his wife for themselves and their heirs, the said land before mentioned or intended to be sold unto the said Catharine M P. Wright and her children herein before mentioned their heirs and assigns free from the claim or claims of them the said William C Oldham & Virginia his wife And of all and every person or persons whatsoever shall will and do warrant and forever defend by these presents. In Witness whereof the said William C Oldham and Virginia his wife have hereunto set their hands and seals the day & year first above written.

Wm C Oldham
Virginia Oldham

Richmond County Sc

We Chas W Smith and Richd A Payne Justices of the peace in the County aforesaid in the state of Virginia do hereby Certify that Virginia the wife of Wm C Oldham parties to a certain Deed bearing date on the 18th day of July 1849 and hereto annexed personally appeared before us in our County aforesaid, and being examined by us privily and apart from her husband and having the Deed aforesaid fully explained to her she the said Virginia acknowledged the same to be her act and deed and declared that she had willingly signed sealed and delivered the same and that she wished not to retract it Given under our hands and seals this 18th day of July 1849

Chas W Smith
Richd A Payne

Clerks Office of Richmond County Court the 6' day of August 1849

This Deed of bargain and sale from Wm C Oldham and Virginia his wife to Catharine M P Wright and her children, was this day presented, acknowledged before me in my office aforesaid by the said Wm C Oldham, and with the certificate annexed admitted to record.

Teste,
J. S. Jeffries CC"

The 1850 Census for Richmond County, Virginia, listed George M. Wright with the following household on August 10, 1850:

Name	Age	Sex	Color	Occupation	Value of Real Estate
George M. Wright	63	M		Farmer	$1000
Catharine A. M Wright	56	F			
Hamilton Wright	20	M			
Sarah E. Wright	17	F			
Andrew Wright	15	M			

Place of Birth	Married Within Year	Attended School Within Year	Cannot Read & Write	Deaf Dumb Blind Insane etc.
Westmoreland County				
Westmoreland County				
Richmond County				
Richmond County				
Richmond County				

This record indicates that George M. Wright was born in about 1787 in Westmoreland County and that Catharine A. M. P. (_____) Wright was born in about 1794 in Westmoreland County.

Sixth Generation:

1869 John M. Wright Of Richmond County, His Wive Elizabeth F. (Mothershead) (Dudley) Wright And Virginia S. (Parry) Wright, And His Descendants

1869 John M. Wright of Richmond County was a son of George M. Wright and Catherine A. M. P. (_____) Wright. (1663 Richard[1], 1713 Francis[2], 1741 Richard[3], 1776 Francis[4], 1809 Presley[5], George M.[6])

On April 10, 1839, at Richmond County, Virginia, D.B. 25/58, and pursuant to a decree of the chancery court, George M. Wright and his wife and children sold to Thomas Oldham the 180 cares of land purchased by Richmond Deed 20/123:

> "This Indenture made this 10th day of April 1839 Between George M Wright and Catherine M P his wife, and George N Alderson (Commissioner appointed by Richmond County Court) of the one part, and Thomas Oldham of the other part: Witnesseth: That whereas by a certain cause in the County Court of Richmond in

which George M. Wright father and natural Guardian of Alexander Wright, Mary A. F. Wright, Emily M. Wright, John M Wright, George H. Wright, Sarah E Wright, Andrew Wright, the said Alexander Wright and Mary A. F. Wright Emily M. Wright infants over the age of 14 years; and John M Wright, George H Wright, Sarah E Wright and Andrew Wright under the age of 14 years by Richard G Northen Guardian ad litem appointed by Court, and Catherine M. P. Wright plaintiffs & Defendants therein a decree was entered on the 7th January 1839 to the effect following - This cause coming on to be heard by Consent of parties on the Bill, answers of the Defts, exhibits and the examination of witnesses, was argued by counsel, on consideration whereof this Court being of opinion that it is for the benefit of the infant Defendants, and Catherine M. P. Wright the wife of the sd George M Wright, that the tract of land lying near Farnham Church containing about 180 acres now in the possession of the said parties refered to in the said Bill by deed apart of said Bill dated the 10th of September 1825 belonging to the said Infants & their mother aforesaid, Doth order, adjudge & decree, that George N Alderson, who is hereby appointed Commissioner for that purpose, do after advertising the same for four weeks in some paper published in the Town of Fredericksburg or in the City of Richmond, expose to sale the said tract of land: or if he shall Consider that Twelve hundred and fifty dollars offered for said land be a full and fair price, he may close the bargain for the sale thereof. Cash to be paid for the expences of sale and Costs: and for the debts due to Thomas J Meredith, Thomas Oldham and others - The residue to be loaned, taking from the borrower, purchaser or purchasers, Bond with good security, and a deed of Trust upon the premises to secure the payment of the residue of the purchase money - the interest thereof to be annually paid to the said George M Wright Gdn of the said infants or to the said Catherine M. P. Wright the mother, and one of the cestui que trust till the further order of this Court Touching the premises - Right is reserved herein to the parties or any of them from time to time to apply to this Court for any aid in the furtherance of their or either of their rights - The Court doth further order, for the better security of the Perchaser, that the said George M Wright, & Catherine M. P Wright do join the commissioner in the conveyance of the said tract of land, only the said George M Wright to give a general warranty - and the said commissioner is directed to report his proceedings herein to the Court, and whereas also the said George N Alderson acting as commissioner in pursuance of the decree aforesaid refered to upon due consideration and respection of the premises in said decree mentioned, as well also by the testimony and opinion of others corroborating his judgment & opinion; he did decide & consider, that the said sum of Twelve hundred & fifty dollars was "a full & fair" price for the parcel or tract of land in the said Cause mentioned; and he did close the bargain & sale of the same with Thomas Oldham for that price.

Therefore they the said George M Wright and Catherine M. P. Wright his wife, and George N Alderson for and in consideration of the sum of Twelve hundred and fifty dollars lawful money of the U.S. to the said George N Alderson, commissioner as aforesd. in hand paid by the said Thomas Oldham, the receipt whereof they the said George M Wright, Catherine M. P. Wright and George N Alderson do hereby acknowledge have bargained, sold & conveyed & by these presents do bargain, sell and Convey unto the said Oldham his heirs and assigns, the certain tract or parcel of land in the said cause mentioned, lying & being in the County of Richmond near Farnham Church Coterminous with the lands Christopher Ficklin, Tho: Sydnors estate and Edward S. Saunders & others Containing one hundred & eighty acres be the same more or less, which said tract or parcel of land was duly conveyed by deed bearing date the 10th September 1825 by George M Wright to his wife & children which deed is recorded in Richmond County Court, to which deed & for the proceedings in the suit before referred, reference may be had for further particulars. The said tract or parcel of land To have & to hold with the appurtenances thereto belonging to him the said Thomas Oldham his heirs and assigns, and to the only proper use and behoof of the said Thomas Oldham, his heirs and assigns forever.

And the said George M Wright for himself his heirs, exors & admors, doth hereby covenant to & with the said Thomas Oldham his heirs and assigns, that he the said George M Wright and his heirs the said tract or parcel of land with its appurtenances, unto him the said Thomas Oldham his heirs and assigns, against him the said George M Wright and his heirs and against all persons whomsoever, shall & will by these presents forever defend -

The said George N Alderson conveys the said tract or parcel of land as Commissioner appointed by the Court; and therefore doth not bind himself & his heirs for the title of the same; but that he nor they shall ever set up any claim to the same.

In Witness whereof the parties hereto have signed their names and affixed their seals, the day and year first above written.

Signed sealed & delivered)
in the presence of us)
G. B. Burch
J. H. Shackleford
Benedict Hammock

G. M. Wright
Catherine M. P. Wright
George N Alderson Com

Virginia

At a Court of Monthly session held for Richmond County, at the Court house on monday the 7th day of October 1839.

This Deed of bargain and sale from George M Wright, and Catharine M. P. his wife, and George N Alderson commissioner &c. to Thomas Oldham, was this day presented proved by the oaths of Gibson P Burch and James H Shackleford, two of the subscribing witnesses thereto, and Ordered to lie for further proof - And in the clerks office of the said County on the 19th day of October 1839, the said deed was further proved by the oath of Benedict Hammock another subscribing witness thereto, and admitted to record.

Teste,
Jno F B Jeffries Cl"

This record identifies John M. Wright as a son of George M. Wright and Catherine M. P. Wright.

The marriage consent of for the marriage of John M. Wright and Elizabeth T. Dudley was dated on December 28, 1849, at Richmond County, Virginia:

"The Clerk of Richmond County is hereby granted permision to ishue a licence to Mr. Jno. M. Wright for the union of himself in marriage to the undersigned

Elizabeth T. Dudly

John M Wright)
with) certificate
Elizabeth T Dudley)

proven 28th Decr 1849 by the oath of Saml D Mothershead. License issued"

Marriages Of Richmond County, Virginia 1668-1853 compiled by George H. S. King listed the marriage of John M. Wright and Elizabeth T. Dudley on December 28, 1849, in Richmond County, Virginia:

"Wright, John M. and Elizabeth T. Dudley*, bond 28 December 1849. Samuel D. Mothershead (b). MBB., p. 330"

The 1850 Census for Richmond County, Virginia, listed John M. Wright with the following household on August 10, 1850:

Name	Age	Sex	Color	Occupation	Value of Real Estate
John M. Wright	22	M		Inn Keeper	$1000
Elizabeth F. Wright	22	F			
Hamilton Dudley	8	M			
Henry B. Scott	35	M		Doctor	
Lydia Ann Pitman	40	F			

Place of Birth	Married Within Year	Attended School Within Year	Cannot Read & Write	Deaf Dumb Blind Insane etc.
Richmond County	1			
Richmond County	1			
Richmond County				
Richmond County				
Northumberland County				

This record indicates that John M. Wright and Elizabeth F. (Mothershead) (Dudley) Wright were born in about 1828 in Richmond County. The Hamilton Dudley in the household was Elizabeth F. (Mothershead) (Dudley) Wright's son by her first marriage.

The death record of Elizabeth T. Wright was dated on May 26, 1859, at Richmond County, Virginia:

"Name	Elizabeth T. Wright
White	1
Colored	
Free	
Slave	
Name of Owner of slave	
Sex	Female
Date of Death	May 26, 1859
Place of Death	Richmond County
Cause of Death	Typhoid fever
Age	37 years
Name of parents	Samuel Mothershead
Place of Birth	Richmond County
Occupation	
Marital Status	Married
Informant	John M. Wright
Relationship	Husband"

The 1860 Census for Richmond County, Virginia, listed John M. Wright two doors from George M. Wright with the following household on August 1, 1860:

Name	Age	Sex	Color	Occupation	Value of Real Estate
John M. Wright	33	M		Merchant	3500
James S. Wright	9	M			
Affia E. Wright	4	F			
Hamilton M. Dudley	16	M			
Joseph Douglas	21	M		Clerk	

Value of Personal Property	Place of Birth	Married Within Year	Attended School Within Year	Cannot Read & Write	Deaf Dumb Blind Insane etc.
2000	Virginia				
	Virginia				
	Virginia				
	Virginia				
	Virginia				

This record indicates that John M. Wright was born in about 1827. The absence of Elizabeth F. (Mothershead) (Dudley) Wright from the household reflects her death on May 26, 1859.

The marriage record of John M. Wright and Virginia S. Parry was dated on April 3, 1865, at Richmond County, Virginia:

"Marriage License.
Virginia - County of Richmond to wit:
To any Person Licensed to Celebrate Marriages:

You are hereby authorized to join together in the Holy State of Matrimony, according to the rites and ceremonies of your Church, or religious denomination, and the laws of the Commonwealth of Virginia, John M. Wright and Virginia S. Parry

Given under my hand, as Clerk of the County Court of said County, this 3d day of April 1865

Geo. W. Sydnor Clerk Pro Tem.

Certificate to Obtain a Marriage License,

Time of Marriage, April 3d 1865
Place of Marriage, Richmond County Va

Full Names of Parties married, John M Wright Virginia S Parry
Age of Husband, Thirty Eight years
Age of Wife, Twenty two
Condition of Husband, (widowed or single,) widowed
Condition of Wife, (widowed or single,) Single
Place of Husband's Birth, Richmond County Va
Place of Wife's Birth, Essex County Va
Place of Husband's Residence, Richmond County Va
Place of Wife's Residence, Richmond County Va
Names of Husband's Parents, George M & Catharine M. P. Wright
Names of Wife's Parents, John H & Virginia Parry
Occupation of Husband, Farmer

Given under my hand this 3d day of April 1865.

Geo. W. Sydnor Clerk Pro tem.

Minister's Return Of Marriage.

I Certify, that on the 3rd day of April 1865, at Farham Richmond County Va, I united in marriage the above named and described parties, under authority of the annexed License.

Ro. Wmson Minister Gospel"

The 1870 Mortality Schedule for Richmond County, Virginia, listed the death of John M Wright in December 1849 in Richmond County, Virginia:

Name of Decedent	Age	Sex	Color	Born	Married or Widowed
John M Wright	42	M	W	Virginia	M

Month of Death	Occupation	Cause of Death
Decr	Merchant	Dropsy

This record indicates that John M. Wright was born in about 1828.

The 1870 Census for Richmond County, Virginia, listed John M. Wright with the following household on July 12, 1870:

Name	Age	Sex	Color	Occupation	Value of Real Estate
John M Wright	47	M	W	Merchant	$2000
Virginia S Wright	26	F	W	Keeping House	
William A Wright	4	M	W		
Emma V Wright	2	F	W		
Fannie B Wright	3/12	F	W		

Value of Personal Property	Place of Birth	Married Within Year	Born Within Year	Attended School Within Year	Cannot Read
$200	Virginia				
	Virginia				
	Virginia				
	Virginia				
	Virginia				

Cannot Write	Deaf Dumb Blind Insane or Idiot	Male Citizen Over 21	Male Citizen Over 21 Without Right to Vote

1

This record indicates that John M. Wright was born in about 1823 and that Virginia (____) Wright was born in about 1844. The continued listing of John M. Wright after his death was probably because his death occurred within one year of the census. His age was probably given by his wife Virginia who may not have known his year of birth of about 1827 or 1828.

Seventh Generation:

1928 James Seaborn Wright Of Teller County, Colorado, His Wives Eugenia Belle (Renshaw) Wright And Grace (Kelley) Wright, And His Descendants

1928 James Seaborn Wright of Teller County, Colorado, was a son of 1869 John M. Wright of Richmond County, Virginia, and Elizabeth F. (Mothershead) (Dudley) Wright. (1663 Richard[1], 1713 Francis[2], 1741 Richard[3], 1776 Francis[4], 1809 Presley[5], George M.[6], 1869 John M.[7])

The 1860 Census for Richmond County, Virginia, listed James S. Wright in the John M. Wright household on August 1, 1860, and his age as 9 and born in Virginia, indicating a date of birth in about 1851.

The 1880 Census for Wise County, Texas, listed J. S. Wright with the following household in June 1880:

Name	Color	Sex	Age	Month of Birth	Relationship
J S Wright	W	M	26		
Egenie Wright	W	F	18		Wife
Minnie Wright	W	F	2		D
James Wright	W	M	1		Son

Marital Status	Married During Year	Occupation	Months Unem-ployed	Sickness Blind Deaf & Dumb Idiotic Disabled
		Drummer		
		Keeps house		

Attended School Within Year	Cannot Read	Cannot Write	Born	Father Born	Mother Born
			Va	Va	Va
			Tx	Ky	Tenn
			Tx	Va	Tx
			Tx	Va	Tx

This record indicates that James Seaborn Wright was born in about 1854 and that Eugenia Belle (Renshaw) Wright was born in about 1862.

In his letter dated September 19, 2006, Thad Tatum enclosed a transcription of a series letters from James Seaborn Wright to his son James Logan Wright which indirectly identify his family relationships:

First Letter:

"Cripple Creek, Colo.
Oct 29, 1913

James Logan Wright
Decatur, Texas

My Dear Son,

As I have not heard from you in a long time, thought I would drop a line. Of course I heard of all of your troubles through Minnie and would and should have written you then, but the fact is I did not know what to say. Such things are very delicate to deal with and most people don't want you to say anything to them about such troubles. I know I was that way. I simply did not want to hear of them, but my belief is that if married people can't get along, the best way is to separate and the quicker the better and the sooner it is forgotten the better for all concerned.

Now for instance the woman that I married here that would not allow my children to come to see me. Why she done that knowing that I would not stand it. She wanted a separation, and she knew that would be sure to bring it about. Then you can see I would be better off without her. Now Logan, my son, I want to ask a great favor of you. I am down and out financially speaking, and I want you to help me some if you possibly can.

. . . . Then there is something I want to talk to you about when I can see you. You know you have never been much of a hand to write is one reason I have never said anything to you. I have comming to me a good big bunch of money left by a cousin of mine that my Mother raised from the time he was 3 months old, and I called him Brother. He was my mother's nephew from the Mothershead side of the family. We parted in 1866. He went to Bolivia, S. America and me to Texas. We parted in Baltimore City. Well, he made as it appears lots of wealth, never married, lived and died a batchelor and left the estate to my sister and myself. which is in the hands of trustees and of course nothing can be done untill final settlements with the courts. . . . You see my half sister, Julia, that died in Texas and my half brother Billie who lives in Baltimore City are not heirs in this atall, my cousin being of no relation to them whatever, and sister and myself are the only remaining of the Mothershead's side of the family. Only for us the family is extinct.

. . . . Hoping to hear from you at your earliest, I am as ever your affectionate father,
Jas. S. Wright 117 West Warren

Logan, when you read this, burn at once. I have found out in life it is always best to keep your own _____. Now you see one reason this woman that bears my name could come in and it is best for you children that she know nothing. That is the reason she has never gotten a divorce. She thinks I might get something. So Keep all to yourself."

The Minnie referred to would be James Seaborn Wright's daughter Minnie Elizabeth (Wright) Allen. The woman he married and from whom he was separated would be his second wife Grace (Kelley) Wright. His mother would be Elizabeth F. (Mothershead) (Dudley) Wright. His father was John M. Wright who remarried after the death of Elizabeth to Virginia Parry. The half- brother Billie would be his half-brother William A. Wright.

Second Letter:

"Cripple Creek, Colo.
Monday night, March 23, 1914

James L. Wright
Decatur, Texas (Forwarded to Waxahachie)

My Dear Son,

Yours to hand a few days ago. Was glad to hear from you but sorry to hear of your circumstances. . . . . Today I would have been in Texas selling goods only for family troubles. . . . .

Now Logan, my son, I know nothing at all of your trouble. Minnie has never written anything in regard to it. When Walter was here in September, 1912, I thought he acted strange but told me nothing, only that he did not think that you and your wife would live together very long. . . . . Now in both of my separations there was nothing criminal in either of the ladies concerned. The first was your mother, poor woman. . . . .

When your poor mother died in California, your Aunt Rhoda Renshaw was with her, ...

. . . . Let me know in your next where you think you will go and for present, believe me as ever your affectionate father, James S. Wright

117 West Warren Ave.
CC Colo.

. . . ."

James Seaborn Wright's first wife was Eugenia Belle Renshaw and Aunt Rhoda Renshaw would be her sister. The family troubles of James Logan Wright, Sr., would be his divorce from his first wife Alice Lucille (Clements) Wright.

Third Letter:

Cripple Creek, Colo.
April 19th, 1918

Mrs. Jas. Logan Wright
Waxahachie, Texas

My Dear Daughter,

Some time has gone by since I heard from you, Logan and my little grand daughter, Margaret Eugenia. . . . . By the way, I had an aunt named Margaret. My mother's sister, Miss Margaret Mothershead, died when she was about 20 years of age, before I was born. . . .

Now don't think for a moment that I object to any one marrying, oh no, but it is simply this. Dad is out of the game, and as it is now 12:30 AM, I will bring this random letter to a close, remaining as ever your affectionate father,

Jas. S. Wright
117 W. Warren Ave.

Tell Logan howdy, kiss little Margaret for me.

Write soon. Dad"

The reference to Margaret Mothershead confirms the identity of James Seaborn Wright's mother as Elizabeth F. (Mothershead) (Dudley) Wright. The will of Samuel Mothershead dated September 9, 1829, and probated on March 2, 1840, at Richmond County, Virginia, W.B. 9/332 listed among others his daughters Elizabeth Mothershead and Margaret Mothershead. The granddaughter referred to would be Margaret Eugenia (Wright) Tatum, born on November 26, 1917, in Waxahachie, Texas.

Fourth Letter:

"Cripple Creek, Colo.
May 6th, 1925

James Logan Wright

Waxahachie, Tex.

My Dear Son,

Yours just to hand. Contents duly noted. . . . .

Now in regard to your age. You were born in the month of August, 1879. Minnie was born in April, 1878. The dates of the month, that is the day I can't say. There was about 14 months difference in yours and Minnie's ages. Say you were born the last of August, 1879, it then would only be 4 months until 1880. . .
Your father,

Jas. S. Wright

. . . .
You say Oscar Allen (Minnie's husband) died . . . . Your father,

Jas. S. Wright"

The dates of birth of his children Minnie Wright and James Logan Wright are consistent with the 1880 Census set forth above. The identification of Minnie Wright's husband as Oscar Allen is consistent with the Renshaw family materials set forth below.

Our Renshaw Cousins compiled by Bernice Everitt, 1984, stated that:

"Eugenia Bell Renshaw, the family beauty, married James Seaborn Wright at age 15. Her parents reluctantly approved this marriage. They felt that Jennie was too young but they also recognized that James Wright, coming from a good southern family, would make an excellent husband for their headstrong, pretty daughter. He was an educated man from Richmond and Boston.

The marriage was not a happy one. Eugenia contracted tuberculosis and her father sent her to California hoping that a change in climate would improve her health. Her brother, Dr. John Renshaw, said later that the climate near San Francisco where she went was not a good climate for her health. She died at age 25, leaving three young children to be reared by her parents:

1. Minnie Elizabeth Wright who married O. G. Allen,
2. James Logan Wright who married:
    (1) Alice Lucille Clements
    (2) Lola May Curlin
    (3) Mayme Scarborough (Wosnig)
3. Walter Mothershead Wright - who never married

H. Eugenia Belle Renshaw Wright
b. 12 Aug 1861, Decatur, Texas
d. 13 Mar 1887, Lakeport, California
m. 1876
James Seaborn Wright
b. 1844 in Virginia
d. 31 Oct 1928, Cripple Creek, Colorado
children: Minnie Elizabeth Wright Allen, James Logan Wright, Walter Mothershead Wright

. . . .

H1 James Logan Wright
b. 16 Aug 1879, Decatur, Texas
d. 9 Dec 1938, Legion, Texas
bur. Waxahachie, Texas
He served in Spanish American War. Attended Decatur Baptist College and old Fort Worth University
m. (1) Alice Lucille Clements
b. 1890, Decatur, Texas
d. 28 Dec 1966, Kerrville, Texas
children: Jennee Warren Wright Lawhorn

. . . .

H2 James Logan Wright
m. (2) 2 Jun 1915
Lola May Curlin, daughter of Jackson Valentine Curlin and Margaret Emma Calvert
b. 10 Jan 1877, Union City, Tennessee
d. 23 Dec 1922
children: Margaret Eugenia Wright Tatum, James Logan Wright, Jr. These children were reared by their grandmother Curlin after the death of Lola May Curlin Wright

. . . .

H23 3. James Logan Wright, Jr.
b. 12 Apr 1920, Waxahachie, Texas
m. 30 Aug 1946
Stella White (Haslam), daughter of Sinclair White and Vannie Morrison
b. 19 May 1919, Ennis, Texas
occ. Assistant Manager of Sears in Amarillo and Lubbock, Texas before establishing a Ben Franklin store in Wilburton, Oklahoma
children: James Logan Wright III, Elizabeth Wright Tyrrell

. . . .

H2 James Logan Wright
m. (3) Mayme Scarborough (Wosnig)

. . . ."

Renshaw Reflections by Grace Parke Renshaw, Gateway Press, Inc., Baltimore, 1983, stated that:

> "g. Eugenia Belle Renshaw b 12 Aug 1861 Decatur TX d 1886 Lakeport, CA m 1876 James Seaborn Wright
> Ch: Logan, Walter and Minnie Wright"

In his letter dated September 5, 2006, Thaddeus A. Tatum enclosed a family report which stated that:

> "James Seaborn Wright first married Eugenia Belle (Jennie) Renshaw in Decatur, Wise Co, Texas in 1878. Her parents were Dr William Renshaw and Sarah Worthington Renshaw. They moved to Texas from Sparta, Tennessee about 1859. . . .
>
> Eugenia Belle Renshaw Wright divorced James Seaborn Wright in the mid 1880's. She later developed tuberculosis, and her family sent her to Lakeport, California in the mistaken belief that her health would improve in that climate. She died in Lakeport. Their children, who were raised by the Renshaw grandparents in Decatur, were:
>
> 1. Minnie Wright, born June, 1878 in Decatur, Texas, who married but had no children and died in Fort Worth, Texas I believe in 1929.
>
> 2. James Logan Wright (Sr), born August, 1879 in Decatur, Texas; died at the Veterans hospital in Legion, Texas in December, 1938.
>
> 3. Walter Mothershead Wright, born January 22, 1882 in Decatur, Texas; never married and had no children; died in Osdick, San Bernardino Co, California on July 28, 1928 of tuberculosis.
>
> James Seaborn Wright moved to Cripple Creek, Colorado after the divorce in the mid-1880's. He married secondly Grace Kelley in 1893 in Cripple Creek. They had two children, one of whom died in infancy. The surviving daughter, Gertrude Wright, was born in 1896. Grace Kelley Wright had either left or divorced James Seaborn Wright by 1900 because she was living in her father's household with their daughter in the 1900 census. We know nothing more about Gertrude Wright. James S Wright died in Cripple Creek October 31, 1928 and was buried there. . . ."

Eighth Generation:

1938 James Logan Wright Of Kerr County, Texas, His Wives Alice Lucille (Clements) Wright, Lola May (Curlin) Wright, And Mayme (Scarborough) (Wosnig) Wright, And His Descendants

1938 James Logan Wright of Kerr County, Texas, was a son of 1928 James Seaborn Wright of Teller County, Colorado, and Eugenia Belle (Renshaw) Wright. (1663 Richard[1], 1713 Francis[2], 1741 Richard[3], 1776 Francis[4], 1809 Presley[5], George M.[6], 1869 John M.[7], 1928 James Seaborn[8])

The 1900 Census for Wise County, Texas, listed James L. Wright in the John W. Hogg(?) household on June 9, 1900:

Location				
In Cities				
Street	House Number	Number of dwelling houses in the order of visitation	Number of family in the order of visition	Name of each person whose place of abode on June 1, 1900, was in this family.
		215	218	John W Hogg(?)
				Eva D. Hogg
				Maud J. Hogg
				Eugenia Hogg
				Chas. B Simmons
				Velma Simmons
				James L. Wright
				Lucy Edmonds

Relation	Personal Description					
Relationship of each person the head the family	Color or race	Sex	Date of Birth Month	Year	Age at last birthday	Whether single, married, widowed, or or divorced
Head	W	M	Mar.	1848	52	M
Wife	W	F	Feb	1855	45	M
Daughter	W	F	Nov.	1881	18	S
Daughter	W	F	Jan.	1884	16	S
S in law	W	M	Nov.	1869	30	M
Daughter	W	F	Mar.	1877	23	M
nephew	W	M	Aug.	1879	20	S
guardian(?)	W	F	May	1875	25	S

Personal Description [cont'd]			Nativity		
			Place of birth of each person and parents of each person enumerated.		
Number of years married	Mother of how many children	Number of these children living	Place of birth of this Person	Place of birth of Father of this person	Place of birth of Mother of this person
28	.	.	Texas	Georgia	Alabama
28	2	2	Tennessee	Illinois	Tennessee
.	.	.	Texas	Texas	Tennessee
.	.	.	Texas	Texas	Tennessee
0	.	.	Mississippi	Alabama	Mississippi
0	0	0	Texas	Texas	Tennessee
.	.	.	Texas	Maryland	Texas
.	.	.	Texas	Alabama	Texas

Citizenship			Occupation, Trade, Or Profession of each person Ten Years of age and over.		Education
Year of immi-gration to the United States	Number of years in the United States	Natural-ization	Occupation	Months not employed	Attended school in months)
			Stockman & farmer	0	.
			.	.	.
			At School	.	9
			At School	.	8
			Physician	.	.
			.	.	.
			Farm laborer	4	.
			.	.	.

Education [cont'd]			Ownership Of Home			
Can read	Can write	Can speak English	Owned or rented	Owned free or mortgaged	Farm or house	Number of fam schedule
yes	yes	yes	O	O	F	
yes	yes	yes				
yes	yes	yes				
yes	yes	yes				
yes	yes	yes				
yes	yes	yes				
yes	yes	yes				
yes	yes	yes				

The 1920 Census for Ellis County, Texas, listed James L. Wright with the following household on January 14, 1920:

	Location				
Line number	Street, avenue, road etc.	House number or farm	Dwelling Number	Number of family, in order of visitation	Name of each person whose place of abode on January 1, 1920 was in this family.
	Marvin Avenue	104	314	396	James L. Wright
					Lola M Wright
					Margaret E Wright

Relation.	Tenure.		Personal Description			
Relationship of this person to the head of the family.	Home owned or rented	If owned, free or mortgaged	Sex	Color or Race	Age at last birthday	Single, married, widowed, or divorced
Head	R		M	W	40	M
Wife			F	W	42	M
Daughter			F	W	2-2/12	S

Citizenship			Education		
Year of immigration to the United States.	Naturalized or alien	If naturalized, year of naturalization.	Attended school any-time since Sept. 1, 1919	Able to read.	Able to write.
				yes	yes
				yes	yes
				.	.

Nativity and Mother Tongue

Place of birth of each person and parents of each person enumerated. If born in United States, give state or territory. If foreign birth, give the place of birth, and in addition, the mother tongue.

Person		Father		Mother	
Place of Birth	Mother Tongue	Place of Birth	Mother Tongue	Place of Birth	Mother Tongue
Texas		Virginia		Texas	
Tennessee		Tennessee		Kentucky	
Texas		Texas		Tennessee	

Occupation				
Able to speak English	Trade, profession, or particular kind of work done.	Industry, business, or etablishment in which at work.	Employer, salary or wage worker, or working on own account.	Number of farm schedule.
yes	Tanner	Own shop	O.A.	
yes	None	.	.	
.	None	.	.	

The 1930 Census for Wood County, Texas, listed James L. Wright with the following household on April 18, 1930:

Place of Abode				
Street, avenue, road etc.	House number (in cities or towns)	Number of dwelling house in order of visitation	Number of family in order of visitation	Name of each person whose place of abode on April 1, 1930 was with this family. Enter surname first, then given name, and middle initial (if any). Omit children born since April 1, 1930
		195	212	James L Wright
				Mollie L Wright
				Clydes R Wright
				James D Wright

Relation.	Home Data			
Relationship of this person to the head of the family	Home owned or rented	Value of home if owned, or monthly rental if rented	Radio set	Does this family live on a farm
Head	O		R	yes
wife				
Daughter				
son				

Personal Description					Education	
Sex	Color or race	Age at last birthday	Marital condition	Age at at first marriage	Attended school or college any time since September 1, 1929	Whether able to read and write
M	W	53	M	30	No	Yes
F	W	42	M	19	No	Yes
F	W	21	S		yes	Yes
M	W	13	S		yes	Yes

Place of Birth		
Place of birth of each person and parents of each person enumerated and of his or her parents. If born in the U.S., give state or territory. If of foreign birth, give county in which birthplace is now situated.		
Person	Father	Mother
Texas	Texas	Texas
Texas	Texas	Texas
Texas	Texas	Texas
Texas	Texas	Texas

Mother Tongue or Native Language				Citizenship, etc.		
Lanuage spoken in home before coming to the United States	Code (for office use only) State or M.T.	Country	Nativity	Year of immigration to the U.S.	Natural-ization	Able to speak English
						yes
						yes

Occupation and Industry			Employment	
Occupation Trade, profession, or particular type of work, as spinner, salesman, etc.	Industry Industry or busi-iness, as cotton mill, dry goods store, etc.	Code (for office use only)	Whether actually at work yesterday (or last regular working day) Yes or no	If not, line number on Unemployment
Dr	MD	9294		
None	.			
Teacher	Public school	9494		
None	.			

Veterans: Whether a veteran of U.S. military or naval forces — Yes or no	What war or expedition	Number of farm schedule
No		196
.		
No		
.		

Our Renshaw Cousins compiled by Bernice Everitt, 1984, stated that:

"Eugenia Bell Renshaw, the family beauty, married James Seaborn Wright at age 15. . . . . She died at age 25, leaving three young children to be reared by her parents:

. . . .

2. James Logan Wright who married:

   (1) Alice Lucille Clements
   (2) Lola May Curlin
   (3) Mayme Scarborough (Wosnig)

. . . .

H1 James Logan Wright
b. 16 Aug 1879, Decatur, Texas
d. 9 Dec 1938, Legion, Texas
bur. Waxahachie, Texas
He served in Spanish American War. Attended Decatur Baptist College and old Fort Worth University
m. (1) Alice Lucille Clements
b. 1890, Decatur, Texas
d. 28 Dec 1966, Kerrville, Texas
children: Jennee Warren Wright Lawhorn

. . . .

H2 James Logan Wright
m. (2) 2 Jun 1915
Lola May Curlin, daughter of Jackson Valentine Curlin and Margaret Emma Calvert
b. 10 Jan 1877, Union City, Tennessee
d. 23 Dec 1922
children: Margaret Eugenia Wright Tatum, James Logan Wright, Jr. These children were reared by their grandmother Curlin after the death of Lola May Curlin Wright

. . . .

H2 James Logan Wright
m. (3) Mayme Scarborough (Wosnig)

. . . ."

In his letter dated September 5, 2006, Thaddeus A. Tatum enclosed a family report which stated that:

"James Seaborn Wright first married Eugenia Belle (Jennie) Renshaw in Decatur, Wise Co, Texas in 1878. . . . . Their children, who were raised by the Renshaw grandparents in Decatur, were:

. . . .
2. James Logan Wright (Sr), born August, 1879 in Decatur, Texas; died at the Veterans hospital in Legion, Texas in December, 1938.
. . . .
James Logan Wright (Sr) was the only child who had children. He was born August 16, 1879 in Decatur, Texas. He died December 9, 1838 at the Veterans hospital in Legion, Texas. He married first Alice Lucille Clenents in Decatur, Tx about 1908. They had one daughter named Jennee Warren Wright, born January 10, 1910 in Decatur, Texas. Alice developed mental problems (schizophrenia) while the daughter was a young girl and was sent to the mental institution in Rusk, Texas. James Logan Wright then divorced her. She was in and out of several mental institutions during her life, died in 1966, and is buried in the same Denton, Texas cemetery as her daughter Jennee. Jennee was raised by her Clements grandparents from about age 3. . . .

James Logan Wright (Sr) migrated to Dallas about 1913 and worked as a tinner in the Dallas area. He met in Waxahchie and married there secondly Lola May Curlin on June 2, 1915. She was working as a legal assistant when he met her. Lola May Curlin was born January 10, 1877 in Union City , Tennessee. She died in Waxahchie on December 23, 1922. . . .

The children of James Logan Wright Sr and Lola May Curlin Wright were:

1. Margaret Eugenia Wright, born in Waxahachie on November 26, 1917. She married Thaddeus Alto Tatum Jr., . . .

2. James Logan Wright Jr., born April 12, 1920 in Waxahachie, Texas. He married Stella White, ..."

Ninth Generation:

James Logan Wright, Jr., His Wife Stella (White) (Haslam) Wright, And His Descendants

James Logan Wright, Jr., was a son of 1938 James Logan Wright of Kerr County, Texas, and Lola May (Curlin) Wright. (1663 Richard[1], 1713 Francis[2], 1741 Richard[3], 1776 Francis[4], 1809 Presley[5], George M.[6], 1869 John M.[7], 1928 James Seaborn[8], 1938 James Logan[9])

Our Renshaw Cousins compiled by Bernice Everitt, 1984, stated that:

"
. . . .
H23 3. James Logan Wright, Jr.
b. 12 Apr 1920, Waxahachie, Texas

m. 30 Aug 1946
Stella White (Haslam), daughter of Sinclair White and Vannie Morrison
b. 19 May 1919, Ennis, Texas
occ. Assistant Manager of Sears in Amarillo and Lubbock, Texas before establishing a Ben Franklin store in Wilburton, Oklahoma
children: James Logan Wright III, Elizabeth Wright Tyrrell

. . . ."

In his letter dated September 5, 2006, Thaddeus A. Tatum enclosed a family report which stated that:

". . . .
James Logan Wright (Sr) migrated to Dallas about 1913 and worked as a tinner in the Dallas area. He met in Waxahchie and married there secondly Lola May Curlin on June 2, 1915. . . . .

The children of James Logan Wright Sr and Lola May Curlin Wright were:

. . . .
2. James Logan Wright Jr., born April 12, 1920 in Waxahachie, Texas. He married Stella White, born May 19, 1919 in Ennis, Texas, on Aug 30, 1946 in Dallas or Ennis, Texas. He was her second husband. They met as college students at Trinity University in Waxahachie. . . ."

Exhibit G

Documentation For Line Of Descent Of Werter Gregory Wright III

Kit 123670

Line Of Descent From 1713 Francis Wright Of Westmoreland County To Werter Gregory Wright III

This exhibit will trace the line of descent of Werter Gregory Wright III from 1713 Francis Wright of Westmoreland County.

First Generation:

1713 Francis Wright Of Westmoreland County, His Wives Anne (Washington) Wright And Martha (Cox) (Wright) Howell, And His Descendants

The documentation for this generation is the same as the documentation for James Logan Wright set forth in Exhibit F.

Second Generation:

1741 Richard Wright Of Westmoreland County, His Wife Elizabeth (Wigginton) (Wright) McFarlane, And His Descendants

The documentation for this generation is the same as the documentation for James Logan Wright set forth in Exhibit F.

Third Generation:

1776 Francis Wright Of Westmoreland County, His Wives Mary Ann (Cox) Wright And Elizabeth (Middleton) (Wright) Lewis, And His Descendants

The documentation for this generation is the same as the documentation for James Logan Wright set forth in Exhibit F.

Fourth Generation:

<u>1836 Benedict Wright Of Westmoreland County, His Wife Mary "Molly" (Rust) Wright, And His Descendants</u>

1836 Benedict Wright of Westmoreland County was a son of 1776 Francis Wright of Westmoreland County and Elizabeth (Middleton) (Wright) Lewis. (1663 Richard[1], 1713 Francis[2], 1741 Richard[3], 1776 Francis[4])

The will of Francis Wright Dated on December 6, 1775, and probated on March 26, 1793, at Westmoreland County, Virginia, W.B. 18/294, and listed Benedick Wright as one of his sons:

> "In the Name of God Amen I Francis Wright of Westmoreland County do make and ordain this to be my last will and Testament in manner and forme following First I leave my Land I Purchased of Mr. John Rust to be sold to pay my Just debts at Publick oction or Privet Sale as my Executors hereafter named shall think proper and whatever the Land Sells for then will Pay my debts the money to be Eaquely divided between my three sons Benedick Wright Johnson Wiginton Wright & Wright Wright Secondly I leave to my loving wife Elizabeth the use of my house wherein I now live and the third part of the Land Joining the house during her life I allso leave her the third part of all my Personal Estate for and during her Natrial life and after her death to be Eaquely divided amongst all my Children. Thirdly my will and desire is that all the rest of my Estate not before given shall be Eaquely divided amongst all my Children. I do appoint my loving wife Elizabeth Capt. Bendk. Middleton Junr. & Fleet Cox Executors of this my last will & Testament. As Witness my hand this 6th day of December 1775.
>
> Fleet Cox Jun. Francis Wright
> Elijah Mood
> Elizabeth Middleton
>
> At a Court held for Westmoreland County the 26th day of March 1793. On the Motion of Francis Wright it is ordered that this Will be recorded the Heirs at Law consenting thereto.
>
> Examd. Teste
> J Bland CWC"

<u>Married Well And Often</u> by Robert K. Headley, Jr., listed the marriage of Benedict Wright first to Mary "Molly" Rust on January 20, 1792, at Westmoreland County, Virginia, and second to Hannah Claughton in 1807 at Westmoreland County, Virginia:

"Wright, Benedict & Rust, Mary "Molly"; b. 20 Jan 1792; Jn. Rust (sec.); bride was a dau. of Vincent Rust (d. WC 1794) who gave his cons. & Ann Bailey; Benedict Wright mar. (2) Hannah Claughton, WC, 1807; (WC DW 19:95; RI 7:461; MLB WC; MLB WC2; JFL annotations to MLB WEC)"

On June 22, 1793, at Westmoreland County, Virginia, R.B. 7/254 an accounting for the estate of Francis Wright was filed:

"Wright Francis)
Executors Account) The Estate of Francis Wright deceased

In Account with George Lewis who intermarried with Elizabeth Wright Ex.

Cr

		Tobacco	
To Board and Sundry Charges against	Benedict Wright	106 23.6.0	
To Ditto	Johnson W Wright	106 24.1.0	
To Ditto	William Wright		23.2.3
		212 10.9.3	

	lb Tobo			
To Vincent Marmaduke Sheriff for	6909.7/2			
To Thomas Sanford Sheriff for	258	8.6. 1	£5.13.11	Certificate Tax
To Benjn Branham Sheriff Richd for	51	5.6.10½	1.15. 6	ditto
	1205	15.2. 7	7. 9. 5	

By Hire of Negroe Fay from 1783 to 1792 both inclusive	51.10.0
By Cash of Presly Wright	12. 5.9
By the proportions of the three Children Benedict Johnson and William of the Stock furniture &c	56.19.3
	£120.15.0

In obedience to an order of the worshipfull Court of Westmoreland County bearing Date the 25 day of June 1793 we have Examined the account of George Lewis who intermarried with Elizabeth Wright Executrix of Francis Wright Deceased, with the Estate of the said deceased and report that he Exhibited an account according to the above Debits and that those respecting Taxes &c were without vouchers and that it appears that the said Estate should have Credits agreeable to those stated above. Given under our hands the 22d day of June 1793

Samuel Rust
Chrisr. Collins
John Yeatman

At a Court held for Westmoreland County the 22d day of June 1793. This Account of the Settlement of the Executorship on the Estate of Francis Wright Deceased, returned pursuant to a former order of this court and ordered to be Recorded

Examd   Teste
                         J Bland CWC"

This record identifies Benedict Wright as a child of Francis Wright and Elizabeth (Middleton) (Wright) Lewis.

The 1810 Census for Westmoreland County, Virginia, listed Benedict Wright with the following household:

Name of Head of Family	Free White Males	Age	Free White Female	Age	All Other Free Persons	Slaves
Benedict Wright	1	26-45	1	16-26		
	1	0-10	1	0-10		

This record indicates that Benedict Wright was born between 1765 and 1784.

The 1820 Census for Westmoreland County, Virginia, listed Benedict Wright with the following household:

Names of Heads of Families	Free White Males	Age	Free White Females	Age	Foreigners
Benedict Wright	1	45+	1	45+	
	1	16-26	1	26-45	
	1	0-10	1	16-26	
			2	0-10	

Number in Agriculture	Number in Commerce	Number in Manufacture	Slaves Male	Age
8			1	45+
			2	26-45
			2	14-26
			4	0-14

Slaves Female	Age	Free Colored Males	Age	Free Colored Females	Age	All other Persons
2	45+					
1	14-26					
1	0-14					

This record indicates that Benedict Wright was born before 1775.

On November 2, 1826, in the case of Straughan & Others v. Wright & Others, 4 Rand 493, the court entered the following order:

> "This was an appeal from the Chancery Court of Fredericksburg, where William Wright and others filed their bill against Richard Wright and others, praying partition of a tract of land. The facts are set forth at large in the following opinion:
>
> Stanard, for the appellants.
> J. Mayo, for the appellees.
>
> November 2. Judge Green delivered his opinion, in which the other Judges concurred.
>
> Richard Wright, by his will dated in 1740, devised to his son Francis, a tract of land in Lower Machodick, which had been given to the testator by his brother John Wright, and also, after the death of is wife, the tract of land on which the testotor lived, to him and his heirs forever. Francis Wright was then, as appears by the will, under the age of eighteen. Francis made his will in December, 1775, and died before the 26th of March, 1776. By this will, he directed that the land he had purchased of John Rust, should be sold for the payment of his debts, and the surplus proceeds of the sale equally divided between his three sons, Benedict Wright, Johnson Wigginton Wright, and Wright Wright. (The testator had no son named Wright Wright, and no attempt is made to shew which of the sons was intended by this name.) He also gave to his wife the dwelling-house and one-third of the land adjoining it, for life; and also, one-third of his personal estate, for life; and after her death, to be equally divided amongst all his children; and directed that all the rest of his estate should be equally divided amongst all his children. On the 26th of March, 1776, the will was proved by three witnesses. The executors qualified; and John Rochester, who was chosen guardian of Presley Wright, the heir at law of Francis Wright, was directed to be summoned to contest the recording of the will. No step was taken on this order, so far as appears. But, on the 26th of March, 1793, the Court in which the will was recorded, made an order in these words: "On the motion of Francis Wright, it is ordered that this will be recorded, the heir at law consenting thereto." On the 13th of November, 1753, Gerard Davis and Thomas M'Farlane and Elizabeth his wife, conveyed 123 acres of land to Francis Wright,

which does not appear to have lain adjoining any other land held by Francis Wright. Francis Wright left five children living at the time of his death, Presley, (the eldest son, and heir at law,) Benedict, William, Nancy, and Johnson W. Wright. Such of those children as were alive, and the representatives of one who was dead, filed their bill on the 12th of July, 1820, against the heirs of Presley Wright, who died in 1810, intestate; and afterwards against the purchasers claiming under some of the heirs of Presley Wright, claiming a partition of a tract of land described as containing ___ acres, of which Francis Wright died seised and possessed, and which he was entitled to under the will of Richard Wright. They charge that soon after the death of Francis Wright, Presley Wright entered upon the whole of the said tract of land, and received the rents and profits thereof during his life, and that his heirs, and those claiming under them, have received the rents and profits since his death. . . . ."

This record identifies Francis Wright as the father of Benedict Wright.

The 1830 Census for Westmoreland County, Virginia, listed Benedict Wright with the following household:

Names Heads of Families	Free White Males	Age	Free White Females	Age
Benedict Wright	1	50-60	1	40-50
	1	10-15	1	20-30
	1	0-5	2	15-20
			1	5-10

Slaves Male	Age	Slaves Female	Age	Free Colored Males	Age	Free Colored Females	Age
1	36-55	1	55-100				
2	10-24	1	36-55				
2	0-10	2	24-36				
		1	10-24				
		3	0-10				

	White Persons included in the foregoing				
Total	Deaf & Dumb Under 14	Deaf & Dumb 14 to 25	Deaf & Dumb 25+	Blind	Aliens - Foreigners & Naturalized
21					

Slaves and Colored Persons, included in the foregoing			
Deaf & Dumb under 14	Deaf & Dumb 14 to 25	Deaf & Dumb 25+	Blind
			1

This record indicates that Benedict Wright was born between 1770 and 1780 and in conjunction with the 1820 Census between 1770 and 1775.

In April 1837 in the case of Wrights v. Oldham and Others, 8 Leigh 304, the court entered the following order:

> "Benedict Middleton, by his last will and testament, made in May 1782, and admitted to record in September 1785, after directing that all his just debts be duly paid by his executors, devised and bequeathed as follows:
>
> 'Item, I lend unto my dear wife, Hannah Middleton, during her natural life, the use of all my lands and one half of my negroes and personal estate.
>
> Item, I give and bequeath the other half of my negroes and personal estate to be equally divided among my grandson Benedict Lamkin, and five daughters, Elizabeth Lewis, Jane Wroe, Hannah Middleton, Martha Middleton and Ann Middleton, to them and each of their heirs forever.
> . . . .
> and it is my will and desire, that my daughter Elizabeth Lewis may only have her life in what I have given her as above, that is, one sixth part of my whole estate, real and personal, and after her decease I give and bequeath the same to be equally divided among my grandchildren that she had by her first husband Francis Wright deceased, and the child she now has or may have by George Lewis her present husband, to them and their heirs forever,
> . . . .'
>
> Elizabeth Lewis died in 1793, in the life time of Hannah Middleton the widow, leaving issue three sons, Benedict Wright, William Wright and Johnson W. Wright, children of her first husband Francis Wright, and one daughter, Hannah Lewis, the child of her second husband George Lewis. Johnson W. Wright died in 1803, leaving issue a son, Benedict D. Wright, and a daughter Polly R. Wright, who afterwards intermarried with Samuel J. Boothe. Hannah Lewis the daughter of Elizabeth Lewis intermarried with Samuel Clark, and died in 1815, leaving issue two daughters, Judith and Betsy, the last named of whom afterwards intermarried with Marcellus Windsor.
> . . . ."

This record identifies Benedict Wright as a son of Francis Wright and Elizabeth (Middleton) (Wright) Lewis.

On March 1, 1838, at Westmoreland County, Virginia, D.&W.B. 29/404 Enoch G. Jeffreys, Elizabeth Jeffreys, and Francis W. Wright sold to W. J. Courtney 1-1/2 acres of land formerly owned by the late Benedict Wright:

> "This Indenture made and entered into this 1st day of March 1838 between Enock G Jeffreys Elizabeth Jeffreys his wife & Francis W Wright of the County of Westmoreland and State of Virginia of the one part and William J Courtney of the County and State aforesaid of the other part Witnesseth that the said E G Jeffreys & Elizabeth his Wife and F W Wright for and in consideration of the sum of Nine dollars to them in hand paid By the said W J Courtney the receipt whereof is Hereby Acknowledged by the said Jeffreys wife & Wright for themselves and their Heirs have this day Bargained sold and delivered and by these presents do fairly and firmly bargain sell and deliver unto the said William J Courtney and his Heirs forever a certain messuage or peace of land lying on the main road leading to Kinsale near the sign bord Leading to Smithers Mill and Being in the County aforesaid Adjoining the land of W P Courtney & Jeremiah Thrift up to a hicorey tree Containing an area of One & a half acres more or less and being the land formerly Held by George V C Hudson & then by Benedict Wright Late of the said County to have and to hold the said Messuage pease of Land unto him the said W J Courtney his Heirs and assigns forever to Gether with all & singular the privileges the appurtinances Houses out houses ways & Water Courses thereto belonging or in any wise Appertaining in fee simple and said E G Jeffreys & wife and F W Wright doth hereby warrant and defend the right of said land free from the claim or claims of themselves their heirs and all other persons whatsoever in testimony whereof we and each of us have hereunto set our hands and seals this day And year as above written signed sealed and Ackd
>
> In the presents of Jeremiah Jeffreys
>
> Francis W Wright
> Enoch G Jeffreys
>
> Virginia
>
> Clerk's Office of Westmoreland County Court the 25th day of June 1838
>
> This deed from Enoch G Jeffreys and Elizabeth his wife and Francis W Wright to William J Courtney was this day presented in my office acknowledged by the said Jeffries and Wright and admitted to record
>
> Teste
> William Hutt CC

Recorded and examined 26" June 1838

Teste
William Hutt CC"

This record indicates that Benedict Wright had died before March 1, 1838.

On February 26, 1844, at Westmoreland County, Virginia, R.B. 31/460 a report and division of the estate of Benedict Wright among his heirs dated December 4, 1843, was filed:

"We the undersigned Commissioners appointed under an an Order of the County Court of Westmoreland held on the 22nd day of February 1841, to divide the land whereof Benedict Wright died possessed among the heirs & to assign to Hannah Wright widow of Benedict Wright her dower - make the following report to wit: To Hannah Wright 54 acres 2 Rods, marked on the plat herewith annexed, by the word "Dower" Lot No 1, valued at $332, to Francis W. Wright, subject to the payment of $87.50¢ Lot No 2, valued at $229.50 to receive of Francis W Wright $15, to Mortrom M Wright Lot No 3, valued at $229.50; to receive of Francis W Wright $15, to Lewis H Dix who intermarried with Mary A Tapocot grandaughter of Benedict Wright, Lot No 4 valued at $216, to receive of Francis W Wright $28.50 cts, To James M Wright Lot No 5 valued at $216. to receive of Francis W Wright $28.50, to Enoch G Jeffries who intermarried with Elizabeth C Wright & Lot No 6 valued at $244, to receive of Francis W Wright 50 Cents, to Wm B Robinson who intermarried with Ann W Wright

Given under our hands & seals this 4" day of December 1843.

Robert Bailey
James English
Jos. Wheelwright

[Map Not Included]

Westmoreland County, May 10" 1841,

Surveyed platted calculated and divided the above figure of land lying in the County aforesaid belonging to the heirs of Benedict Wright decd, Bounded as follows, Beginning at A the corner of Wm J Courtneys fence near the sign board directing to Kensale & Smithers mill and running thence with Courtneys line N 43° & 23 poles to B. a stob opposite a pine & Cedar Corner to the premises and John Bailey thence with John & Robert Baileys line S 46° E 46 poles Thence S 48° E 46 po. thence S 46° E 37 po. to the main road leading to Kinsale thence S 45° 38' E 153.8 po. to C.

a red oak corner to the premises C. B. Hudson & side line to E G. Jeffries, thence with Hudsons line S 41-1/2° W 8 po. thence S 48-1/2° W 8 po. to a swamp (Mr Wrights spring run) thence across the swamp up a flat & run S 63° W 10.9 po. thence S 37° W 16 po. thence S 60° W 7 po. thence S 52-1/2° W 9 po. thence S 68-1/2° W 8 po. thence S 32 W 13.5 po. to D, the middle of the road leading to Hamilton Hall, Corner to the premises C B Hudson & Side line to Smithers heirs, thence up the road N 18-1/2° W 70 po. to E in the main road Corner to Smithers heirs thence S 49 W 35 po. thence S 33° W 127.3 po. to F. a marked white oak Corner to this in Smithers line thence N 72-1/2° W 36 po. to G. the center of the swamp corner to this in Smithers line thence up the swamp N 31° W 22.4 po. thence N 5-1/2° W 14 po. thence N 36° E 13 po. thence N 16-1/2° E 16 po. thence N 18-1/2° E 22 po. thence N 38° E 12 po. thence N 7-1/2° E 20 po. thence N 12-1/2° W 40 po. thence N 23-1/2° W 24 po. thence N 30-1/2° W 14 po, thence N 36-1/2° W 60 po. to H, the main road leading to Smithers mill thence S 56-1/2° W 6 po. thence S 48° W 10 po. thence S. 50 W 12 po. thence S 27-1/2° W 28 po thence S 13-1/2 W 34 po. thence S 3° W 26 po. thence S 27° W 25 po thence S 47° W 34.7 po, to I. at Gilberts swamp, corner to this & Presley Cox's heirs thence up the swamp N 33° W 32 po. thence N 15° W 7 po. thence N 36° W 12 po. thence N 59-1/2 W 10 po. thence N 26° W 5.2 po to J, corner to this & John Hazard, thence with Hazzards line N 30-1/2 E 32 po thence N 24° E 26 po. thence N 17-1/2° E 18 po. thence N 26° E 12 po thence N 29-1/2° E 72.4 po. to K, Corner to this in Wm J Courtneys line thence with Courtneys line S 46-1/2° E 12 po. thence S 31-1/2° E 24 po. thence S 56-1/2° E 25.4 po to the Beginning, containing an area of Three hundred and forty two acres 4-1/2 poles.

James W. English Sr

The red lines and letters show the division lines and Corners.

L M is the line between the widows dower and Francis W Wright, L poplr M is at E, G Jeffries's 2 line

N.O. is the line between Francis W Wright & E G Jeffries, The road to Kinsale

P.Q. is the line between E G Jeffriess & L Dix P. is a stob, 2 is a marked Cedar P is 50 po from Kinsale road

R.S. is the line between E G. Jeffriess & James W. Wright R a stob 10 poles from gate S. Holly at the swamp.

J. W. English

Virginia,
At a court held for Westmoreland County the 26th day of February 1844.

This report and Division of the estate of Benedict Wright decd, was returned and Ordered to be recorded.

Teste,
William Hutt CC

Recorded and Examining

Teste,
William R Lisson DC"

This record identifies the family of Benedict Wright as follows:

Wife: Hannah Wright

Children: 1) Francis W. Wright,
2) Mottrom M. Wright,
3) James M. Wright,
4) Elizabeth C. (Wright) Jeffries, and
5) Ann W. (Wright) Robinson,

Grandchild: 1) Mary A. (Tapocot) Dix.

Fifth Generation:

<u>1891 Francis W. Wright Of Westmoreland County, His Wife Jane (Jeffries) Wright, And His Descendants</u>

1891 Francis W. Wright of Westmoreland County was a son of 1836 Benedict Wright of Westmoreland County and Mary (Rust) Wright. (1663 Richard[1], 1713 Francis[2], 1741 Richard[3], 1776 Francis[4], 1836 Benedict[5])

On March 1, 1838, at Westmoreland County, Virginia, D.&W.B. 29/404 Enoch G. Jeffreys, Elizabeth Jeffreys, and Francis W. Wright sold to W. J. Courtney 1-1/2 acres of land formerly owned by the late Benedict Wright:

"This Indenture made and entered into this 1st day of March 1838 between Enock G Jeffreys Elizabeth Jeffreys his wife & Francis W Wright of the County of Westmoreland and State of Virginia of the one part and William J Courtney of the County and State aforesaid of the other part Witnesseth that the said E G Jeffreys & Elizabeth his Wife and F W Wright for and in consideration of the sum of Nine dollars to them in hand paid By the said W J Courtney the receipt whereof is Hereby Acknowledged by the said Jeffreys wife & Wright for themselves and their Heirs have this day Bargained sold and delivered and by these presents do fairly and firmly bargain sell and deliver unto the said William J Courtney and his Heirs forever a certain messuage or peace of land lying on the main road leading to Kinsale near the sign bord Leading to Smithers Mill and Being in the County aforesaid Adjoining the land of W P Courtney & Jeremiah Thrift up to a hicorey tree Containing an area of One & a half acres more or less and being the land formerly Held by George V C Hudson & then by Benedict Wright Late of the said County to have and to hold the said Messuage pease of Land unto him the said W J Courtney his Heirs and assigns forever to Gether with all & singular the privileges the appurtinances Houses out houses ways & Water Courses thereto belonging or in any wise Appertaining in fee simple and said E G Jeffreys & wife and F W Wright doth hereby warrant and defend the right of said land free from the claim or claims of themselves their heirs and all other persons whatsoever in testimony whereof we and each of us have hereunto set our hands and seals this day And year as above written signed sealed and Ackd

In the presents of Francis W Wright
Jeremiah Jeffreys Enoch G Jeffreys

Virginia

Clerk's Office of Westmoreland County Court the 25th day of June 1838

This deed from Enoch G Jeffreys and Elizabeth his wife and Francis W Wright to William J Courtney was this day presented in my office acknowledged by the said Jeffries and Wright and admitted to record

Teste
William Hutt CC

Recorded and examined 26" June 1838

Teste
William Hutt CC"

On February 26, 1844, at Westmoreland County, Virginia, R.B. 31/460 a report and division of the estate of Benedict Wright among his heirs dated December 4, 1843, was filed:

"We the undersigned Commissioners appointed under an an Order of the County Court of Westmoreland held on the 22nd day of February 1841, to divide the land whereof Benedict Wright died possessed among the heirs & to assign to Hannah Wright widow of Benedict Wright her dower - make the following report to wit: To

Hannah Wright 54 acres 2 Rods, marked on the plat herewith annexed, by the word "Dower" Lot No 1, valued at $332, to Francis W. Wright, subject to the payment of $87.50¢ Lot No 2, valued at $229.50 to receive of Francis W Wright $15, to Mortrom M Wright Lot No 3, valued at $229.50; to receive of Francis W Wright $15, to Lewis H Dix who intermarried with Mary A Tapocot grandaughter of Benedict Wright, Lot No 4 valued at $216, to receive of Francis W Wright $28.50 cts, To James M Wright Lot No 5 valued at $216. to receive of Francis W Wright $28.50, to Enoch G Jeffries who intermarried with Elizabeth C Wright & Lot No 6 valued at $244, to receive of Francis W Wright 50 Cents, to Wm B Robinson who intermarried with Ann W Wright

Given under our hands & seals this 4" day of December 1843.

Robert Bailey
James English
Jos. Wheelwright

[Map Not Included]

. . . ."

This record identifies Francis W. Wright as a son of Benedict Wright.

The 1850 Census for Westmoreland County, Virginia, listed Francis W. Wright with the following household on August 9, 1850:

Name	Age	Sex	Color	Occupation	Value of Real Estate
Francis W. Wright	36	M		Farmer	1000
Jane J. Wright	30	F			
Sarah A Wright	9	F			
Henry B Wright	7	M			
William Wright	4	M			
Mary F Wright	1	F			

Place of Birth	Married Within Year	Attended School Within Year	Cannot Read & Write	Deaf Dumb Blind Insane etc.
Va				
Va				
Va				
Va				
Va				
Va				

This record indicates that Francis W. Wright was born in about 1814 and that Jane (Jeffries) Wright was born in about 1820.

The 1860 Census for Westmoreland County, Virginia, listed F. W. Wright with the following household on August 14, 1860:

Name	Age	Sex	Color	Occupation	Value of Real Estate
F. W. Wright	46	M		Farmer	900
J. Wright	40	F			
S. Wright	18	F			
H. Wright	16	M			
W. Wright	14	M			
B. Wright	6	M			

Value of Personal Property	Place of Birth	Married Within Year	Attended School Within Year	Cannot Read & Write	Deaf Dumb Blind Insane etc.
176	Va				
	Va				
	Va				
	Va				
	Va				
	Va				

This record indicates that Francis W. Wright was born in about 1814 and that Jane (Jeffries) Wright was born in about 1820.

The 1870 Census for Westmoreland County, Virginia, listed Francis Wright with the following household on July 5, 1870:

Name	Age	Sex	Color	Occupation	Value of Real Estate
Francis Wright	55	M	W	Farmer	800
Jane Wright	49	F	W	Keeping house	
James W Wright	23	M	W	Labourer	
Robt B Wright	17	M	W	Labourer	
Sarah Ann Wright	28	F	W	at home	
Lucy Graham	10	F	B	Domestic servt	

Value of Personal Property	Place of Birth	Married Within Year	Born Within Year	Attended School Within Year	Cannot Read
150	Virginia				1
	Virginia				1
	Virginia				.
	Virginia				.
	Virginia				.
	Virginia				1

Cannot Write	Deaf Dumb Blind Insane or Idiot	Male Citizen Over 21	Male Citizen Over 21 Without Right to Vote
1		1	
.		.	
.		1	
.		.	
.		.	
1		.	

This record indicates that Francis W. Wright was born in about 1815 and that Jane (Jeffries) Wright was born in about 1821.

The 1880 Census for Westmoreland County, Virginia, listed Frank and Jane Wright in the Ben Wright household in June 1880:

Name	Color	Sex	Age	Month of Birth	Relationship
Ben Wright	W	M	27		.
Frank Wright	W	M	67		Father
Jane Wright	W	F	60		Mother
Sarah King	W	F	30		Sister

Marital Status	Married During Year	Occupation	Months Unem-ployed	Sickness Blind Deaf & Dumb Idiotic Disabled
M		Farmer		.
M		At home		Insane
S		Keeping house		.
S		at home		.

Attended School Within Year	Cannot Read	Cannot Write	Born	Father Born	Mother Born
			Va	Va	Va
			Va	Va	Va
			Va	Va	Va
			Va	Va	Va

This record indicates that Francis W. Wright was born in about 1813 and that Jane (Jeffries) Wright was born in about 1820 and that Francis W. Wright had become insane.

The 1900 Census for Westmoreland County, Virginia, listed Jane Wright in the R. B. Wright household on June 14, 1900, her relationship as mother, her birth in April 1820 in Virginia, her marital status as widow, and that she had had five children of who two were living.

In his email dated June 3, 2008, Werter Gregory Wright III enclosed a photograph of the tombstones of Francis W. Wright and Jane J. Wright located in the Wright Family Cemetery on his farm in Westmoreland County, Virginia:

"Francis W. Wright
Born 1815
Died
April 9, 1891

Jane J. Wright
Born
Nov. 22, 1820
Died
Jan. 17, 1902"

In his telephone conference dated June 7, 2008, Werter Gregory Wright III stated that Francis W. Wright married Jane Jeffries, daughter of Jeremiah and Jane Jeffries.

Sixth Generation:

<u>1921 Robert Benjamin Wright Of Westmoreland County, His Wife Ella Victoria (Lewis) Wright, And His Descendants</u>

1921 Robert Benjamin Wright of Westmoreland County was a son of 1891 Francis W. Wright of Westmoreland County and Jane (Jeffries) Wright. (1663 Richard[1], 1713 Francis[2], 1741 Richard[3], 1776 Francis[4], 1836 Benedict[5], 1891 Francis W.[6])

The 1860 Census for Westmoreland County, Virginia, listed B. Wright in the Francis W. Wright household on August 14, 1860, and his age as 6 and born in Virginia, indicating a date of birth in about 1854.

The 1870 Census for Westmoreland County, Virginia, listed Robert B. Wright in the Francis Wright household on July 5, 1870, and his age as 17 and born in Virginia, indicating a date of birth in about 1853.

The 1880 Census for Westmoreland County, Virginia, listed Ben Wright with the following household in June 1880:

Name	Color	Sex	Age	Month of Birth	Relationship
Ben Wright	W	M	27		.
Frank Wright	W	M	67		Father
Jane Wright	W	F	60		Mother
Sarah King	W	F	30		Sister

Marital Status	Married During Year	Occupation	Months Unemployed	Sickness Blind Deaf & Dumb Idiotic Disabled
M		Farmer		.
M		At home		Insane
S		Keeping house		.
S		at home		.

Attended School Within Year	Cannot Read	Cannot Write	Born	Father Born	Mother Born
			Va	Va	Va
			Va	Va	Va
			Va	Va	Va
			Va	Va	Va

This record indicates that Robert Benjamin Wright was born in about 1853.

The 1900 Census for Westmoreland County, Virginia, listed R. B. Wright with the following household on June 14, 1900:

Location				
In Cities				
Street	House Number	Number of dwelling houses in the order of visitation	Number of family in the order of visition	Name of each person whose place of abode on June 1, 1900, was in this family.
	240	240	241	R B Wright
				Ella Wright
				Werter Wright
				Jane Wright
				Sarah A King

Relation: Relationship of each person the head the family	Personal Description: Color or race	Sex	Date of Birth: Month	Date of Birth: Year	Age at last birthday	Whether single, married, widowed, or or divorced
Head	W	M	May	1852	48	M
Wife	W	F	Apr	1859	41	M
Son	W	M	May	1886	14	S
mother	W	F	Apr	1820	80	Wd
Sister	W	F	May	1856	55	Wd

Personal Description [cont'd]: Number of years married	Mother of how many children	Number of these children living	Nativity: Place of birth of each person and parents of each person enumerated. Place of birth of this Person	Place of birth of Father of this person	Place of birth of Mother of this person
15	.	.	Virginia	Virginia	Virginia
15	1	1	Virginia	Virginia	Virginia
.	.	.	Virginia	Virginia	Virginia
.	5	2	Virginia	Virginia	Virginia
.	0	0	Virginia	Virginia	Virginia

Citizenship: Year of immigration to the United States	Number of years in the United States	Naturalization	Occupation, Trade, Or Profession of each person Ten Years of age and over. Occupation	Months not employed	Education: Attended school in months)
			Farmer		
			.		
			Clerk		
			.		
			Dressmaker		

Education [cont'd]			Ownership Of Home			
Can read	Can write	Can speak English	Owned or rented	Owned free or mortgaged	Farm or house	Number of fam schedule
yes	yes	yes	O	F	F	171
yes	yes	yes				
yes	yes	yes				
yes	yes	yes				
yes	yes	yes				

This record indicates that Robert Benjamin Wright was born in May 1852 and that Ella Victoria (Lewis) Wright was born in April 1859.

The 1910 Census for Westmoreland County, Virginia, listed Benjamin Wright with the following household on May 7, 1910:

	Location				
Line Number	Street, Avenue, Road etc.	House number or farm	Dwelling number	Number of family, in order of visitation	Name of each person whose place of abode on April 15, 1910 was in this family. Enter surname first then the given name and middle initial, if any. Include any person living on April 15, 1910. Omit children born since April 15, 1910.
			197	197	Benjamin Wright
					Victoria Wright
					Werter Wright
					Sarah King
					George Clarke

Relationship	Personal Description						
						Mother of how many children	
Relationship of this person to the head of the family.	Sex	Color or Race	Age at last birthday	Whether single, married, widowed, or divorced	Number of years of present marriage	Number born	Number now living
Head	M	W	57	M1	25	.	.
Wife	F	W	49	M1	25	2	1
son	M	W	24	S	.	.	.
sister	F	W	68	Wd	.	.	.
servant	M	B	20	S	.	.	.

Nativity			Citizenship	
Place of birth of each person and parents of each enumerated. If born in United States, give state or territory. If foreign birth give the country.				
Place of birth of this person	Place of birth of Father of this person	Place of birth of Mother of this person	Year of immigration to the U.S.	Whether naturalized or Alien
Virginia	Virginia	Virginia		
Virginia	Virginia	Virginia		
Virginia	Virginia	Virginia		
Virginia	Virginia	Virginia		
Virginia	Virginia	Virginia		

	Occupation		
Whether able to speak English, or, if not, give language spoken.	Trade or profession of, or particular kind of work done by this person.	General nature of industry, business, or establishment in which this person works	Whether an employer, employee, or working on own account.
English	Farmer	General farm	W
English	none	.	.
English	Laborer	Home farm	W
English	none	.	.
English	Laborer	General farm	W

Occupation (cont'd) If an employee.		Education		
Whether out of work on April 15, 1910.	Number of weeks out of work during 1909.	Whether able to read	Whether able to write	Attended school any time since Sept 1, 1900.
no	0	yes	yes	.
.	.	yes	yes	.
no	0	yes	yes	.
.	.	yes	yes	no
no	0	yes	yes	.

Ownership of Home				Whether a survivor of the Union Confederation Army or Navy	Whether blind (both eyes)	Whether deaf and dumb.
Owned or Rented	Owned free or mortgaged	Farm or house	Number of farm schedule			
O	F	F	139			

This record indicates that Robert Benjamin Wright was born in about 1853 and that Ella Victoria (Lewis) Wright was born in about 1861.

The 1920 Census for Westmoreland County, Virginia, listed Robert B. Wright with the following household on February 7, 1920:

	Location				
Line number	Street, avenue, road etc.	House number or farm	Dwelling Number	Number of family, in order of visitation	Name of each person whose place of abode on January 1, 1920 was in this family.
On road from Acorn to Kings mill			54	56	Robert B. Wright
					Ella V. Wright
					Werter G. Wright
					Margret B. Wright
[Separated in listing by two households]					
					Mary V. Wright
					Werter G. Wright Jr.

Relation.	Tenure.		Personal Description			
Relationship of this person to the head of the family.	Home owned or rented	If owned, free or mortgaged	Sex	Color or Race	Age at last birthday	Single, married, widowed, or divorced
Head	O	F	M	W	67	M
Wife			F	W	61	M
Son			M	W	33	M
Daughter in law			F	W	32	M
Daughter			F	W	5	S
Grandson			M	W	1	S

Citizenship			Education		
Year of immigration to the United States.	Naturalized or alien	If naturalized, year of naturalization.	Attended school any-time since Sept. 1, 1919	Able to read.	Able to write.
			.	yes	yes
			.	yes	yes
			.	yes	yes
			.	yes	yes
			no	no	no
			no	.	.

Nativity and Mother Tongue

Place of birth of each person and parents of each person enumerated. If born in United States, give state or territory. If foreign birth, give the place of birth, and in addition, the mother tongue.

Person		Father		Mother	
Place of Birth	Mother Tongue	Place of Birth	Mother Tongue	Place of Birth	Mother Tongue
Virginia		Virginia		Virginia	
Virginia		Virginia		Virginia	
Virginia		Virginia		Virginia	
Virginia		Virginia		Virginia	
Virginia		Virginia		Virginia	
Virginia		Virginia		Virginia	

Occupation				
Able to speak English	Trade, profession, or particular kind of work done.	Industry, business, or etablishment in which at work.	Employer, salary or wage worker, or working on own account.	Number of farm schedule.
yes	Farmer	General farm	Em	46
yes	None	.	.	.
yes	Farm laborer	Home farm	.	.
yes	None	.	.	.
.	None	.	.	.
.	None	.	.	.

This record indicates that Robert Benjamin Wright was born in about 1853 and that Ella Victoria (Lewis) Wright was born in about 1859.

In his email dated June 3, 2008, Werter Gregory Wright III enclosed a photograph of the tombstones of Robert Benjamin Wright and Victoria Lewis Wright located in the Wright Family Cemetery on his farm in Westmoreland County, Virginia:

"In Memory Of
R. B. Wright
May 31, 1852
Jan. 26, 1921
I have fought a good fight
I have finished my course
I have kept the faith

Victoria L. Wright
Oct. 24, 1858
Aug. 30, 1951"

In his telephone conference dated June 7, 2008, Werter Gregory Wright III stated that Robert Benjamin Wright was a son of Francis W. Wright and Jane (Jeffries) Wright and married Ella Victoria Lewis.

Seventh Generation:

1954 Werter Gregory Wright Of Westmoreland County, His Wife Margaret Lee (Brown) Wright, And His Descendants

1954 Werter Gregory Wright, Sr., of Westmoreland County was a son of 1921 Robert Benjamin right of Westmoreland County and Ella Victoria (Lewis) Wright. (1663 Richard[1], 1713 Francis[2], 1741 Richard[3], 1776 Francis[4], 1836 Benedict[5], 1921 Robert Benjamin[6])

The 1900 Census for Westmoreland County, Virginia, listed Werter Wright in the R. B. Wright household on June 14, 1900, his relationship as son, his birth in May 1886, in Virginia, and his occupation as clerk.

The 1910 Census for Westmoreland County, Virginia, listed Werter Wright in the Benjamin Wright household on May 7, 1910, his relationship as son, his age as 24 and born in Virginia, indicating a date of birth in about 1886, and his occupation as laborer.

The 1920 Census for Westmoreland County, Virginia, listed Werter G. Wright in the Robert B. Wright household on February 7, 1920:

Line number	Location: Street, avenue, road etc.	Location: House number or farm	Location: Dwelling Number	Location: Number of family, in order of visitation	Name of each person whose place of abode on January 1, 1920 was in this family.
On road from Acorn to Kings mill			54	56	Robert B. Wright
					Ella V. Wright
					Werter G. Wright
					Margret B. Wright
[Separated in listing by two households]					
					Mary V. Wright
					Werter G. Wright Jr.

Relation. Relationship of this person to the head of the family.	Tenure. Home owned or rented	Tenure. If owned, free or mortgaged	Personal Description: Sex	Personal Description: Color or Race	Personal Description: Age at last birthday	Personal Description: Single, married, widowed, or divorced
Head	O	F	M	W	67	M
Wife			F	W	61	M
Son			M	W	33	M
Daughter in law			F	W	32	M
Daughter			F	W	5	S
Grandson			M	W	1	S

Citizenship			Education		
Year of immigration to the United States.	Naturalized or alien	If naturalized, year of naturalization.	Attended school any-time since Sept. 1, 1919	Able to read.	Able to write.
			.	yes	yes
			.	yes	yes
			.	yes	yes
			.	yes	yes
			no	no	no
			no	.	.

Nativity and Mother Tongue

Place of birth of each person and parents of each person enumerated. If born in United States, give state or territory. If foreign birth, give the place of birth, and in addition, the mother tongue.

Person		Father		Mother	
Place of Birth	Mother Tongue	Place of Birth	Mother Tongue	Place of Birth	Mother Tongue
Virginia		Virginia		Virginia	
Virginia		Virginia		Virginia	
Virginia		Virginia		Virginia	
Virginia		Virginia		Virginia	
Virginia		Virginia		Virginia	
Virginia		Virginia		Virginia	

Occupation				
Able to speak English	Trade, profession, or particular kind of work done.	Industry, business, or etablishment in which at work.	Employer, salary or wage worker, or working on own account.	Number of farm schedule.
yes	Farmer	General farm	Em	46
yes	None	.	.	.
yes	Farm laborer	Home farm	.	.
yes	None	.	.	.
.	None	.	.	.
.	None	.	.	.

This record indicates that Werter Gregory Wright, Sr., was born in about 1887 and that Margaret Lee (Brown) Wright was born in about 1888.

The 1930 Census for Westmoreland County, Virginia, listed Werter Wright with the following household on May 19, 1930:

Place of Abode				
Street, avenue, road etc.	House number (in cities or towns)	Number of dwelling house in order of visitation	Number of family in order of visitation	Name of each person whose place of abode on April 1, 1930 was with this family. Enter surname first, then given name, and middle initial (if any). Omit children born since April 1, 1930
		157	160	Werter Wright
				Margaret Wright
				Mary V Wright
				Gregory Wright
				Victoria Wright
				John Pase(?)

Relation.	Home Data			
Relationship of this person to the head of the family	Home owned or rented	Value of home if owned, or monthly rental if rented	Radio set	Does this family live on a farm
Head	O			yes
Wife				
Daughter				
Son				
Mother				
boarder				

Personal Description					Education	
Sex	Color or race	Age at last birthday	Marital condition	Age at at first marriage	Attended school or college any time since September 1, 1929	Whether able to read and write
M	W	44	M	27	no	yes
F	W	43	M	26	no	yes
F	W	16	S	.	yes	yes
M	W	10	S	.	yes	yes
F	W	69	Wd	.	no	yes
M	neg	20	S	.	no	yes

Place of Birth

Place of birth of each person and parents of each person enumerated and of his or her parents. If born in the U.S., give state or territory. If of foreign birth, give county in which birthplace is now situated.

Person	Father	Mother
Virginia	Virginia	Virginia
Virginia	Virginia	Virginia
Virginia	Virginia	Virginia
Virginia	Virginia	Virginia
Virginia	Virginia	Virginia
Virginia	Virginia	Virginia

Mother Tongue or Native Language				Citizenship, etc.		
Lanuage spoken in home before coming to the United States	Code (for office use only) State or M.T.	Country	Nativity	Year of immigration to the U.S.	Natural-ization	Able to speak English
	74					
	74					
	74					
	74					
	74					
	74					

Occupation and Industry			Employment	
Occupation Trade, profession, or particular type of work, as spinner, salesman, etc.	Industry Industry or busi-iness, as cotton mill, dry goods store, etc.	Code (for office use only)	Whether actually at work yesterday (or last regular working day) Yes or no	If not, line number on Unemployment
Farmer	General farm	VVVV	yes	
none	.	.	.	
none	.	.	.	
none	.	.	.	
none	.	.	.	
Farm laborer	General farm	VIVV	yes	

Veterans Whether a veteran of U.S. military or naval forces		
Yes or no	What war or expedition	Number of farm schedule
no		7

This record indicates that Werter Gregory Wright, Sr., was born in about 1886 and that Margaret Lee (Brown) Wright was born in about 1887.

In his email dated June 8, 2008, Werter Gregory Wright III enclosed a photograph of the tombstones of Werter Gregory Wright and Margaret Brown Wright located in the Ebenezer Church Cemetery, Westmoreland County, Virginia:

"Werter Gregory Wright
1885 - 1954

Margaret Brown Wright
1887 - 1972"

Eighth Generation:

2000 Werter Gregory Wright Of Westmoreland County, His Wife Frances Christine (Packett) Wright, And His Descendants

2000 Werter Gregory Wright, Jr., of Westmoreland County was a son of 1954 Werter Gregory Wright, Sr., of Westmoreland County and Margaret Lee (Brown) Wright. (1663 Richard[1], 1713 Francis[2], 1741 Richard[3], 1776 Francis[4], 1836 Benedict[5], 1921 Robert Benjamin[6], 1954 Werter Gregory[7])

The 1920 Census for Westmoreland County, Virginia, listed Werter Gregory Wright, Jr., in the Robert B. Wright household on February 7, 1920, his relationship as grandson, his age as 1 and born in Virginia, indicating a date of birth in about 1919.

The 1930 Census for Westmoreland County, Virginia, listed Gregory Wright in the Werter Wright household, his relationship as son, his age as 10 and born in Virginia, indicating a date of birth in about 1920.

In his email dated June 8, 2008, Werter Gregory Wright III enclosed a photograph of the tombstone of Werter Gregory Wright, Jr., located in the Ebenezer Church Cemetery, Westmoreland County, Virginia:

"Werter Gregory Wright, Jr.
U. S. Army W. W. II
June 17, 1919 - May 20, 2000"

Ninth Generation:

Werter Gregory Wright III

Werter Gregory Wright III is the son of 2000 Werter Gregory Wright, Jr., of Westmoreland County and Frances Christine (Packett) Wright and is the living participant in the Wright DNA Project.

Exhibit H

Documentation For Line Of Descent Of Peter Wright

Kit 108246

From Burke's Commoners

WRIGHT, OF BOLTON-ON-SWALE.

WRIGHT, JOHN-EDWARD, esq. of Bolton-on-Swale, in the county of York, born in 1765, *m.* first, 4th September, 1786, Anne. daughter of George Allan, esq. of Blackwell Grange, in the palatinate of Durham (see vol. i. p. 42), and by her, who died 21st March, 1797, has had issue,

JAMES-ALLAN, born 8th June, 1789, captain in the Durham Militia, who died unmarried 4th, and was buried in the family vault of the Allans of Blackwell Grange, at Darlington Church, 8th January, 1834.
JOHN-ALLAN, *b.* 17th December, 1793, lieutenant in the Royal Navy.
Anne, died unmarried in 1829.
Elizabeth, died young in 1798.
Catharine, died unmarried in 1831.

He wedded, secondly, in 1798, Agnes, daughter of John M'Kerrell, esq. of Hill House, in the county of Ayr, and has three other daughters, viz.

Charlotte.
Eleanor, *m.* in 1825, to F. G. Spilsbury, esq. and died in 1833.
Margaret, m. to William Hussey, esq. of Glasgow.

Mr. Wright succeeded his father 20th April, 1806.

Lineage.

This family, one of remote antiquity in the North of England, has been settled for centuries in the county of York.

JOHN WRIGHT, of Plowland, in Holderness, wedded at the close of the fourteenth, or in the beginning of the fifteenth century, Alice, daughter and co-heir of John Ryther, son and heir of Gilbert Ryther, who died seized of Alford Well and Sutton, and grandson of Sir William Ryther, knt. By this lady he had a son and successor,

ROBERT WRIGHT, of Plowland, who espoused, first, Anne, daughter of Thomas Grimston, esq. and grand-aunt of Sir Marmaduke Grimston, high sheriff for Yorkshire in 1598, by whom he had a son, WILLIAM, his heir. He married, secondly, Ursula, daughter of Nicholas Pudston, esq. of Haybon, and had two other sons and three daughters, viz. John, Christopher; Ursula, the wife of John Constable, of Hatfield, Alice, and Martha. The eldest son,

WILLIAM WRIGHT, of Plowland, wedded the daughter of — Thornton, and had (with another son, Robert, of Foston, born in 1572, who married, and had issue)

FRANCIS WRIGHT, of Sowerby, in the county of York, who *m.* the sister of Henry Markham,* and was father of

FRANCIS WRIGHT, of Bolton-on-Swale in the county of York, who died about the year 1651, leaving, by Grace, his wife, daughter of — Beckwith, esq. of Aldborough, in the same shire, one son and three daughters, viz.

FRANCIS, his heir.
Elizabeth, *m.* to Frinian, alias Ninian, Anderson, of Gales, in Yorkshire.
Jane, *m.* to John Palliser, of Kirby Wiske, also in Yorkshire.
Grace, *m.* to Thomas Meryton, esq. of Castle Levington, in the same county, son of George Meryton, D.D. Dean

* This gentleman's son and heir, Henry Markham, esq. died *s. p.* and divided his property, at Bolton, between his cousins, Francis Wright, of Sowerby, and another Francis Wright, also his own cousin.

of Peterborough, and subsequently of York.

His only son,

THE REV. FRANCIS WRIGHT, D.D. of Bolton-on-Swale, espoused Anne, daughter of the Very Rev. George Meryton, Dean of York, and, by her, who died 29th March, 1670, had six sons and two daughters, namely,

I. Francis, who died *s. p.*
II. GEORGE, heir to his father.
III. Thomas.
IV. Richard.
V. Christopher.
VI. William.
I. Anne, *m.* to Thomas Hewardine of Maltby, and died 5th October, 1671, leaving issue.
II. Grace, *m.* to — Blakiston, of Old Malton, in Yorkshire.

Dr. Wright died in 1655, and was succeeded by his eldest surviving son,

GEORGE WRIGHT, esq. of Bolton-on-Swale, born in 1629, who *m.* first, Beatrice, daughter of James Mauleverer,† esq. of Arncliffe, in Yorkshire, by Beatrice, daughter of Sir Timothy Hutton, of Marske, (by his wife, Elizabeth, daughter of Sir George Bowes, of Streatlam, in the county palatine of Durham, the knight marshall, who suppressed the great northern rebellion, headed by the potent earls of Westmoreland and Northumberland, *temp. Queen* ELIZABETH,) and had issue,

I. Francis, aged 7, in 1665, died 22nd September, 1684.
II. George, of Bolton, born 10th August, 1662.
III. Richard, *b.* 5th July, 1664.
I. Anne, aged nine years, in 1665.
II. Beatrice, aged six years, in 1665.

Mr. Wright wedded, secondly, a lady named Margaret, but of what family is not recorded, and left at his decease, 6th June, 1674, another son,

JOHN WRIGHT, esq. of Bolton-on-Swale, proprietor of estates at Bolton-on-Swale, Greenbury, Ellerton, Scorton, and in the parish of Catterick, in the county of York, and of property at Newcastle-on-Tyne. He *m.* Margaret Greathead, and, by her, who died 4th August, 1748, had issue to survive infancy,

I. JOHN, his heir.
II. Thomas, *b.* 20th December, 1737.
III. Francis, *b.* 5th August, 1739.
IV. Baines, *b.* 26th April, 1743.
V. Richard, *b.* 29th July, 1748.
I. Elizabeth, *m.* to William Pennyman Consett, esq. of Normanby, in Yorkshire.
II. Martha, *b.* 30th June, 1744.

Mr. Wright died 11th June, 1748, and was succeeded by his eldest son,

JOHN WRIGHT, esq. of Bolton-on-Swale, who *m.* Miss Eleanor Page, by whom, who died in 1822, aged ninety-five, had two sons and four daughters, viz.

I. JOHN-EDWARD, his heir.
II. George, *b.* 11th May, 1771, who *m.* a daughter of — Griffith, esq. of St. Asaphs, in Wales, and dying about the year 1807, left two sons,
    Edward-Baines, *b.* 20th March, 1805, died in March, 1825.
    George-Nathan, *b.* 21st March, 1806.
I. Eleanor, *m.* 27th March, 1793, to John Nicholson, esq.
II. Barbara-Crowe.
III. Margaret, *m.* 13th November, 1788, to the Rev. John Dehane.
IV. Sarah-Harriett, died an infant, 27th March, 1775.

Mr. Wright died at Leeds, 20th April, 1806, and was *s.* by his son, the present JOHN-EDWARD WRIGHT, esq. of Bolton-on-Swale.

Arms—Quarterly, 1st and 4th, or, a fesse chequy arg. and az. between three eagles' heads, erased of the third, for WRIGHT: 2nd and 3rd az. three crescents, or, for RYTHER.

Crest—A unicorn passant regardant, quartered, arg. and az. armed or.

Estates—In the counties of York and Durham.

Seat—Leatherhead.

† He was great-great-grandson of Sir William Mauleverer, knt. of Arncliffe, by Jane, daughter of Sir John Conyers, of Sockburne, in Durham. This ancient family, which but recently became extinct, was descended, in a direct male line, from Sir Richard Mauleverer, knt. who came into England with William the Conquerer, by whom he was appointed master of the forests, chases, and parks north of Trent.

Exhibit I

Documentation For Line Of Descent Of Peter Wright

Kit 108246

From Dudgale's Visitation

LANGBARGH WAPENTAKE. *Stokesley*, 25° *Aug.* 1665.

WRIGHT OF BOLTON UPON SWALE.

ARMS.—Quarterly:
1 and 4. Or, a fess componée argent and azure between three eagle's heads erased of the last, a canton gules.
2. Azure, three crescents or.
3. .... a lion rampant .... charged with an annulet.

CREST.—A unicorn passant regardant argent, armed or, unguled azure.

Will'm Wright of Plowland in co. Ebor. = ..., daughter of ...... Thorneton.

Robert Wright of Foston. =

Francis Wright of Sowerby in com. Ebor. = ...

Francis Wright of Bolton super Swale in co. Ebor. died in a° 1651, or thereabouts. = Grace, daughter of ...... Beckwith of Aldbrough in com. Ebor.

Christopher Wright of Sowerby in co. Ebor. =

Francis Wright of Bolton, died a° 1665. = Anne, daugh. of George Meryton, Deane of Yorke.

1. Elizabeth, wife of Trinian alias Ninian Anderson of Gales in com. Ebor.

2. Jane, wife of John Palleser of Kirby Wiske in com. Ebor.

3. Grace, wife of Thomas Meryton of Castle Levinton in com. Eborum.

1. Francis Wright, obijt sine prole.

2. George Wright of Bolton in co. Ebor. æt. 36 an. 25° Aug. a° 1665. = Beatrice, da. of James Maleverer of Arncliffe in co. Ebor. Esqr.

3. Thomas.
4. Richard.
5. Christoph^r.
6. Will'm.

1. Anne, wife of Thomas Hewardin of Maltby in co. Ebor.

2. Grace, wife of John Blakeston of Old-Malton in co. Ebor.

3. Richard, æt. 1 ann.

2. George, æt. 3 ann.

1. Francis, æt. 7 ann. 25 Aug. 1665.

1. Anne, æt. 9 ann.

2. Beatrice, æt. 6 an. 1665.

Exhibit J

Documentation For Line Of Descent Of Peter Wright

Kit 108246

From Diane Hayter Family Report

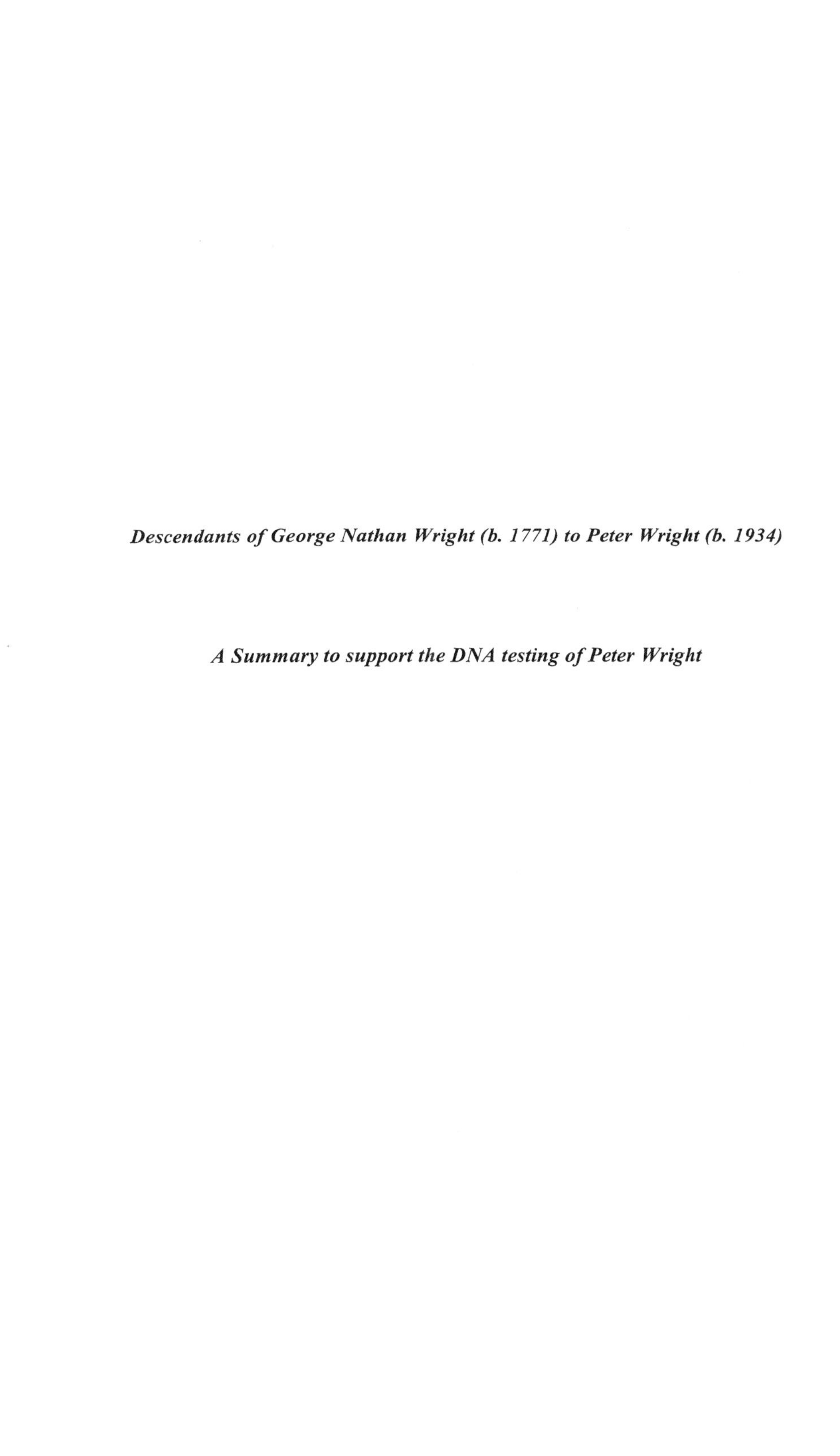

Descendants of George Nathan Wright (b. 1771) to Peter Wright (b. 1934)

A Summary to support the DNA testing of Peter Wright

Index

Index to Figures

Compiled by Robert Hale and Diane Hayter
www.ourgenealogy.co.uk
July 2008

Summary

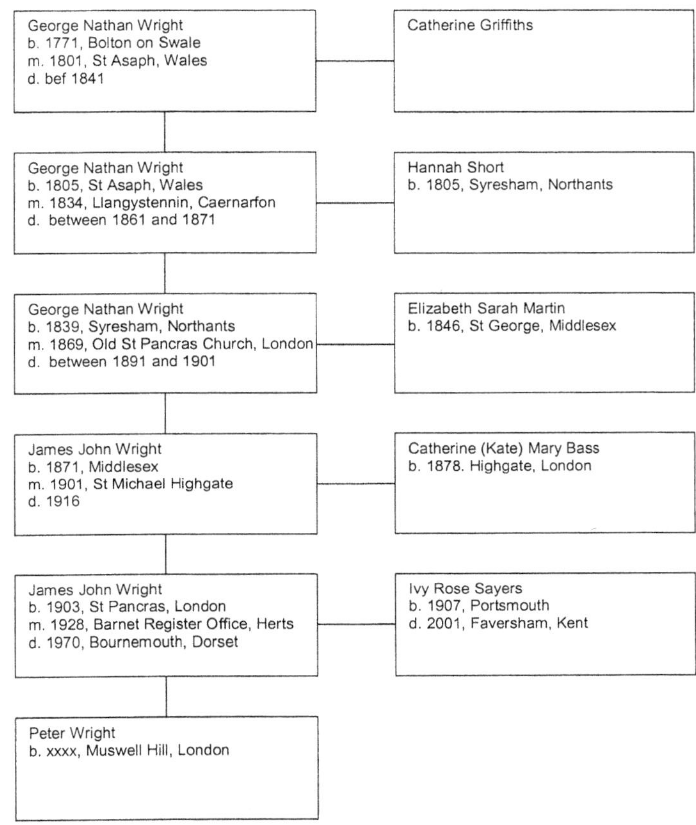
George Nathan Wright
b. 1771, Bolton on Swale
m. 1801, St Asaph, Wales
d. bef 1841
Catherine Griffiths
George Nathan Wright
b. 1805, St Asaph, Wales
m. 1834, Llangystennin, Caernarfon
d. between 1861 and 1871
Hannah Short
b. 1805, Syresham, Northants
George Nathan Wright
b. 1839, Syresham, Northants
m. 1869, Old St Pancras Church, London
d. between 1891 and 1901
Elizabeth Sarah Martin
b. 1846, St George, Middlesex
James John Wright
b. 1871, Middlesex
m. 1901, St Michael Highgate
d. 1916
Catherine (Kate) Mary Bass
b. 1878. Highgate, London
James John Wright
b. 1903, St Pancras, London
m. 1928, Barnet Register Office, Herts
d. 1970, Bournemouth, Dorset
Ivy Rose Sayers
b. 1907, Portsmouth
d. 2001, Faversham, Kent
Peter Wright
b. xxxx, Muswell Hill, London

BMD Registers and Census Returns

		BMD			Census Returns						
#	Name	B	M	D	1841	1851	1861	1871	1881	1891	1901
1	George N Wright		B 14								
2	George N Wright				1 (35) School master Syresham	2 (46) Penman St. Pancras	4 (56) Auction Porter Pancras				
3	George N Wright		C 16		1 (1) - Syresham	3 (11) Errand Boy St. Pancras	5 (21) General Labourer Pancras	6 (31) Painter house Pancras	7 (41) Painter Islington	9 (51) Painter St Pancras	*2
4	James J Wright		C 17						7 James (10) Scholar	9 John (20) General Labourer	11 James (30) ? Founder
5	James J Wright										
6	Peter Wright										

Format for each census box

x (y) x = figure for census return. (y = age given in return)
name name is given for James John Wright, as it changes between census returns.
occupation
location

B - Marriage Bond (Fig. 14)
C - Certificate
*2 - George's widow Elizabeth

Detail

The direct line from George Nathan Wright (b. c1771 in Bolton on Swale) to Peter Wright (b. 1934, Muswell Hill, London) is given below. Peter Wright provided the DNA sample used in the analysis.

Generation No. 1

1. **George Nathan[2] Wright** (son of John Wright[1]) was born c. 1771 in Bolton on Swale, Yorkshire. He married **Catherine Griffiths**

George Nathan Wright:
Christening: 11 May 1771, Bolton on Swale, Yorkshire (from IGI)

Catherine Griffiths:
Possible death 24 May 1805 – Diserth, St Asaph (from burial records at Hawarden, Flintshire records office):

Marriage: 20 Jun 1801, St Asaph, Wales (from Marriage Bond & Parish Register)

Marriage Bond
The marriage bond index is searchable at http://www.llgc.org.uk/index.php?id=485 The relevant entries read:
GRIFFITH, Catharine, sp., St. Asaph, FLN. 1801, Jun 20. At St. Asaph. George Wright. A,B. 140/15
WRIGHT, George, bach., Bolton, YKS. 1801, Jun 20. At St. Asaph, FLN. Catharine Griffith. A,B. 140/15..

The parish register for their marriage (at Figure 14) is interesting as the date given for the wedding is 22 June 1780, almost 21 years earlier than the date given in the marriage bond index. Figure 14 states that the marriage was by licence and the only George Wright and Catherine Griffiths bond (licence) found for St. Asaph is the 1801 bond..

Also the entry in the marriage register immediately before George and Catherine, on the same page, is dated 1st June 1801.

It also appears that John Griffith the first child of George and Catherine was base born, according to St. Asaph burial register, which states 'John Griffith (Wright) base born son of George Wright and Catherine Griffith.'. John was buried on 6th May 1801, and as he had his mothers maiden name, we can assume George and Catherine were not married at this time.

Therefore the view is that the marriage bond date for the wedding is correct, and the marriage register entry needs further investigation.

Children of George Wright and Catherine Griffiths are:

2 i. John Griffith[3] (Wright), base born c. 1800 in St Asaph, Wales; died 1801 in St Asaph.
Burial: 06 May 1801, St Asaph
From St. Asaph burial records - 'John Griffith (Wright) base born son of George Wright and Catherine Griffith.'

3 ii. John Wright, born c. 1802; died 1802 in St Asaph. (from parish register)
Burial: 17 Oct 1802, St Asaph (from parish register)

4 iii. Edward Baynes Wright, born 29 Mar 1803 in Gwernglefryd, St Asaph, Wales.
Christening: 18 Jan 1804, St Asaph, Wales (from parish register)

\+ 5 iv. George Nathan Wright, born c. 1805 in St Asaph, Wales; died Aft. 1861.

Generation No. 2

5. George Nathan[3] **Wright** was born c. 1805 in St Asaph, Wales, and died Aft. 1861. He married **Hannah Short** 19 Nov 1834 in Llangystennin, Caernarfon. She was born c. 1805 in Syresham, Northamptonshire, and died Aft. 1861.

Checked the St Asaph parish records but couldn't find a baptism record. There were no other entries for Wrights or Rights around that time in St Asaph.

1841 Census – living with/next door to his wife's brother and mother?
1861 Census – maybe near St Pancras workhouse.
http://www.workhouses.org.uk/index.html?StPancras/StPancras.shtml

Based on births of children, George moved from North Wales to Syresham, Northamptonshire (his wife's home) between Sept 1837 and Sept 1838, and then to St. Pancras area of London between 1846 and 1849.

Children of George Wright and Hannah Short are:

6 i. Charlotte Maria[4] Wright, born c. Aug 1835 in Llangystennin, Caernarvon, Wales.
Christening: 30 Aug 1835, Llangystennin, Caernarvon, Wales

7 ii. Catharine Wright, born 19 Aug 1836 in Llangystennin, Caernarvon, Wales.
Christening: 09 Sep 1838, Llangystennin, Caernarvon, Wales

8 iii. Barbara Wright, born 18 Sep 1837 in Llangystennin, Caernarvon, Wales. She married Charles James Bartlett c. Mar 1877 in St Giles, London, Middlesex; born 08 Feb 1846 in Marylebone, Middlesex; died Bet. 1881 - 1891.

Barbara was a witness at her brother George's wedding still named Wright so she was unmarried.
Christening: 09 Sep 1838, Llangystennin, Caernarvon, Wales

\+ 9 iv. **George Nathan Wright**, born c. Sep 1839 in Syresham, Northamptonshire; died Bef. 1901.

10 v. John Wright, born c. 1841 in Syresham, Northamptonshire.
Christening: 07 Feb 1841, Syrensham, Northamptonshire

\+ 11 vi. Edward Wright, born c. 1843 in Syresham, Northamptonshire.
12 vii. James Wright, born c. 1846 in Syresham, Northamptonshire.
13 viii. Mary Wright, born c. 1849 in St Pancras, London.
14 ix. Amy Wright, born c. 1851 in St Pancras, London.

Generation No. 3

9. George Nathan[4] **Wright** was born c. Sep 1839 and was christened on 29 Sep 1839, Syresham, Northamptonshire, and died Bef. 1901. He married **Elizabeth Sarah Martin** 26 Sep 1869 in Old St Pancras Church, daughter of John Martin and Martha. She was born c. Jun 1846 in St George, Middlesex.

Children of George Wright and Elizabeth Martin are:

15 i. George[5] Wright, born 1870 in Middlesex.
\+ 16 ii. **James John Wright**, born 1871 in Middlesex; died c. 1916.
17 iii. Edith Wright, born 1872 in Middlesex.
18 iv. Edwin/Edward Wright, born 1875 in Middlesex.
19 v. Alice Wright, born 1876 in Middlesex.
20 vi. Henry Wright, born 1880 in Middlesex.

21 vii. Margaret Wright, born 1892 in St Pancras, London.

11. Edward[4] Wright was born c. 1843 and christened on 30 Apr 1843 in Syresham, Northamptonshire. He married **Mary Ann Coldwell** in c. Sept 1863. She was born c. 1847 in Gravesend, Kent.

1871 - 8 Johnson Street St Pancras - Carpenter.

1863 3rd Quarter Marriage Register
Coldwell Mary Ann Pancras 1b 242
Wright Edward Pancras 1b 242

Children of Edward Wright and Mary are:
22 i. Sarah[5] Wright, born 1865 in St Pancras, London.
23 ii. Edward Wright, born 1870 in St Pancras, London.

Generation No. 4

16. James John[5] Wright was born 1871 in Middlesex, and died c. 1916. He married **Catherine (Kate) Mary Bass** 07 Sep 1901 in St Michael Highgate, daughter of Thomas Bass and Mary Smith. She was born 09 Mar 1878 in Dorothy Cottages, Highgate, Middlesex, and died 25 Jan 1964 in Totteridge, Barnet.

Notes for James John Wright: Occupation Type Dresser. Died when son James was 12.
Wife Kate was a midwife

Children of James Wright and Catherine Bass are:
\+ 24 i. James John[6] Wright, born 11 Aug 1903 in St Pancras, London; died 01 Jan 1970 in Bournemouth.
25 ii. Katherine Elsie Wright, born c. Dec 1904 in St Pancras, London.
\+ 26 iii. Edith May Wright, born 1909 in Finchley; died 2006 in Bournemouth.
27 iv. Tim Wright, born 1910.
28 v. Isabel Wright, born c. Mar 1912 in Barnet.
29 vi. Reginald A Wright, born 1913.
\+ 30 vii. Dorothy A Wright, born c. Dec 1917 in Finchley; died 2006 in Bournemouth.

Generation No. 5

24. James (Jim) John[6] Wright was born 11 Aug 1903 in St Pancras, London, and died 01 Jan 1970 in Bournemouth. He married **Ivy Rose Sayers** 20 Oct 1928 in Barnet Register Office, daughter of William Sayers and Eliza Wilkinson. She was born 06 Apr 1907 in Portsmouth, and died c. Apr 2001 in Faversham, Kent.

Wedding notes: In 1828 When James got married he was living at 2 The Vale, Halliwick Road, Friern Barnet. Ivy was living at 5 Ivy Villas, Oakleigh Road, Friern Barnet. Her parents did not attend the wedding.

Personal memories.
Nan spent most of the war working as a bus conductress in London and bringing up 3 children on her own as Grandad, Jim had gone off to France in the army. They spent a few years in Wales while the worst of the bombs hit London. I have been told stories of Hodges farm where they lived for a while (near Amroth).

Uncle Alan was born at the end of the war, Nan was very ill after his birth and money was very tight. I remember a tale of only having mashed potatoes and spring onions to eat.

What a character! She used to call me a young tart, I don't think tart meant the same thing to her! After Jim died, Ivy came to live with us for I think 6 months of the year and to my Uncles for the other 6 months. I loved having her there! During that time she got to know my other Grandad, Ernie quite well, he was a widower and used to come every Sunday for lunch. One day he "popped the question"!

Ivy (my Mum's Mum) married Ernie (My Dad's Dad) in 1972? It was all in the local paper at the time, my Mum and Dad became step brother and sister.

Children of James Wright and Ivy Sayers are:
+ 31 i. Norman[7] Wright, born 1929; died 2006 in Spain.
+ 32 ii. June Wright, born xxxx in Muswell Hill.
+ 33 iii. Peter Wright, born xxxx.
+ 34 iv. Alan Wright, born xxxx.

26. Edith May[6] Wright was born 1909 in Finchley, and died 2006 in Bournemouth. She married **(1) ? Neil**. She married **(2) Bill Martin**.

Child of Edith Wright and ? Neil is:
35 i. Pam[7] Neil.

30. Dorothy A[6] Wright was born c. Dec 1917 in Finchley, and died 2006 in Bournemouth. She married **(1) Edward Dolby**. She married **(2) Vincent Simpson**.

Notes for Dorothy A Wright:
Dolly was a toddler when James and Ivy were courting. Say she was 3 or 4 when James was 19/20.

Married age c. 18

Births 4th Quarter 1917
Wright Dorothy A Bass Barnet 3a 556

Children of Dorothy Wright and Edward Dolby are:
36 i. Jean[7] Dolby.
37 ii. Ronnie Dolby.

Generation No. 6

31. Norman[7] Wright was born 1929, and died 2006 in Spain. He married **Maisie Etheridge**. She died 2003.

Child of Norman Wright and Maisie Etheridge is:
38 i. Melvyn[8] Wright, born c. xxxx.

32. June[7] Wright was born xxxx in Muswell Hill. She married **George Douglas Hayter** xxxx, son of Ernest Hayter and Florence Litten. He was born xxxx in Tottenham.

Children of June Wright and George Hayter are:
39 i. David John[8] Hayter, born xxxx. He married (1) Susan Margaret Twynham xxxx. He married (2) Susan Margaret Norris xxxx in Broadstairs, Kent.

David Hayter and Susan Twynham: - Marriage: xxxx - Divorce: xxxx

40 ii. Antony James Hayter, born xxxx. He married Linda Alison Jones xxxx; born xxxx.

41 iii. Diane Jane Hayter, born xxxx in Epping, Essex. She married (2) Neil Collinson xxxx in Llanteg, Pembrokeshire; born xxxx in Manchester. - Divorce: xxxx

33. Peter[7] Wright was born xxxx. He married **Audrey Ship**.

Child of Peter Wright and Audrey Ship is:

42 i. Deborah[8] Wright, born xxxx. She married Mark Hill xxxx.

34. Alan[7] Wright was born xxxx. He married **Phyllis**. She was born xxxx.

Children of Alan Wright and Phyllis are:

43 i. Dean[8] Wright, born xxxx. He married Linda.
44 ii. Vanessa, born xxxx.
45 iii. Darren, born xxxx.

Figure 1 - 1841 Census – George Nathan Wright

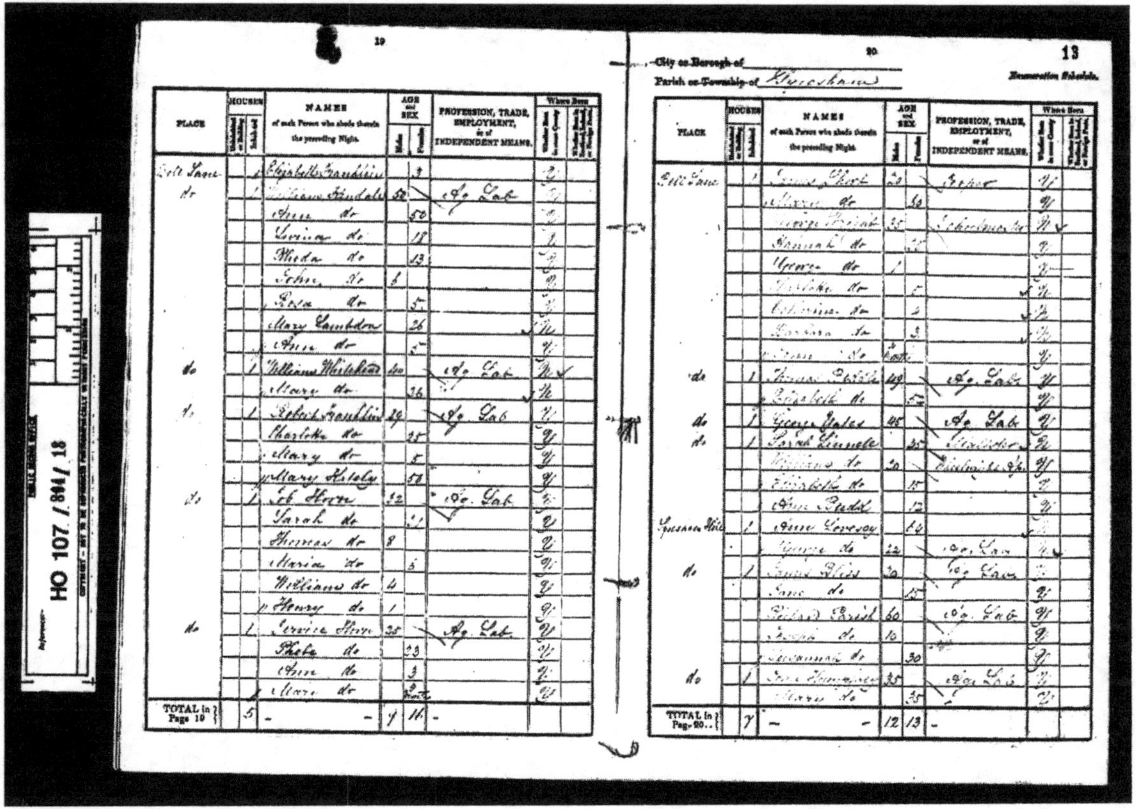

HO 107 / 844 / 18

19

20

13

Figure 2 - 1851 (page 1) George Wright

No.	Parish of St Pancras — Name of Street, Place, or Road, and Name or No. of House	Name and Surname of each Person who abode in the house, on the Night of the 30th March, 1851	Relation to Head of Family	Condition	Age of Males	Age of Females	Rank, Profession, or Occupation	Where Born
20	1 Ashby St	Ann [illegible]	Daur			14		Midx St Pancras
21		William [illegible]	Head	Mar	30		Rail Labr	Do Do
		Sarah Do	Wife	Mar		30		Do Do
22	7 Ashby St	William Skinner	Head	Mar	[illegible]		Journeyman Painter	Do Do
		Anne Do	Wife	Mar		46		Do Do
		Charles Do	Son		14		Errand Boy	Do Do
		James Do	Son		10		Scholar	Do Do
23		Edward Rowland	Head	Mar	[illegible]		Stoker Gas Works	Midx Westminster
		Anne Do	Wife	Mar		41		Essex Frank[illegible]
		Richard Do	Son		[illegible]		Rail Labr	Midx Westminster
24		Sophia Wood		Widow		40	Charwoman	Yorkshire Leeds
25		John Selly	Head	Mar	[illegible]		Costermonger Greengrocer	Midx St Pancras
		Lucy Do	Wife	Mar		[illegible]		Gloucestershire [illegible]
26		Robert Bull	Head	Mar	[illegible]		Hawker Cooper	Midx St Pancras
		Mary Do	Wife	Mar		46		Do Do
27		George Wright	Head	Mar	[illegible]		Penman	North Wales St Asaph
		Hannah Do	Wife	Mar		[illegible]		Northamptonshire [illegible]
		Charlotte Do	Daur	U		[illegible]	[illegible]	N Wales Carnarvon
		Catherine Do	Daur			[illegible]	Do	Do Do
		Barbara Do	Daur			13	Do	Do Do

Figure 3 - 1851 (page 2)

21

Parish or Township of	Ecclesiastical District of	City or Borough of	Town of	Village of
St Pancras		Marylebone		

No. of Householder's Schedule	Name of Street, Place, or Road, and Name or No. of House	Name and Surname of each Person who abode in the house, on the Night of the 30th March, 1851	Relation to Head of Family	Condition	Age of Males	Age of Females	Rank, Profession, or Occupation	Where Born	Whether Blind, or Deaf-and-Dumb
87	[illegible] St	George Wright	Son		11		Errand Boy	N Wales Caernarvon	
		John Do	Son		9		Do Do	Northampton [illegible]	
		Edward Do	Son		7		Scholar	Do Do	
		James Do	Son		5		Do	Do Do	
		Mary Do	Daur			2		Midx St Pancras	
		Ann Do	Daur			[illegible]		Do Do	
88	8 Ashby St	[illegible] Lindsey	Head	Mar	53		Shoemaker	Devon Plymouth	
		Phillippa Do	Wife	Mar		49		Cornwall Bodmin	
		Elizabeth Do	Daur	U		23		Midx St Pancras	
		Maria Do	Daur	U		18		Do Do	
		Henry Do	Son		15		Errand Boy	Do Do	
89		Joseph Duncan	Head	Mar	48		Journeyman Painter	Midx St Pancras	
		Sarah Do	Wife	Mar		50		Do Clerkenwell	
90		James Hunn	Head	Mar	25		[illegible]	Do Soho	
		Jane Do	Wife	Mar		26		Do St Pancras	
		Hannah Do	Daur			5		Do Do	
91		Benjamin Watts	Head	Mar	28		Lab Gas Works	Do Do	
		Isabella Do	Wife	Mar		26		Do Do	
		Isabella Do	Daur			2		Do Do	
Total of Houses	1			Total of Persons	9	10			

Figure 4 - 1861 (page 1)

PUBLIC RECORD OFFICE	Reference — R.G. 9 117	COPYRIGHT PHOTOGRAPH—NOT TO BE REPRODUCED PHOTOGRAPHICALLY WITHOUT PERMISSION OF THE PUBLIC RECORD OFFICE, LONDON

The undermentioned Houses are situate within the Boundaries of the

Page 11								
Parish [or Township] of Pancras	City or Municipal Borough of	Municipal Ward of Parochial No 6	Parliamentary Borough of Marylebone	Town of	Hamlet or Tything, &c., of	Ecclesiastical District of Old St Pancras Part of		

No. of Schedule	Road, Street, &c., and No. or Name of House	Houses Inhabited	Uninhabited (U), or Building (B)	Name and Surname of each Person	Relation to Head of Family	Condition	Age of Males	Age of Females	Rank, Profession, or Occupation	Where Born	Whether Blind, or Deaf-and-Dumb
				Arthur Stephens	Son	—	1			Middx Pancras	
	Eve Terrace			Jane "	Daur	—		13	Scholar	" "	
	Old St Pancras Church						—	—	Omitted in first line of Page 6		
	Church Terrace			Pancras Workhouse							
60	10	1		William Hutchinson	Head	Widr	47		Marine Store Dealer	Surrey Walworth? / Middx Pancras	
				Hannah "	Sister	Unmar		30		" Edgware	
61	9	1		Joseph Harding	Head	Mar	59		Farmer	Bucks [illegible]	
				Emma "	Wife	Mar		48		Middx Pancras	
				John "	Son	Unmar	20		Farmer Son	Hertford St Albans	
				Thomas Nash	Nephew	—	16		Blacksmith & Farmer	Essex Harlow	
62	8	1		William Abraham?	Head	Married	26			Middlesex Pancras	
				Susan "	Wife	Mar		26		" "	
				William "	Son		5			" "	
				Alfred "	Son		3			" "	
				Edwin "	Son		1			" Marylebone	
63				Mary Greer	Head	Widow		68	Dairywoman	Bucks Amersham	
64	7	1		Thomas Allen	Head	Unmar	64		Bronze manufacturer Master	Middlx Pancras	
				Mary Starck	Servant	Unmar		72	Domestic Servant	Middx London	
65	6	1		Bartley Wilson	Head	Widr	45		Brush Maker Jour	" "	
				Walter "	Son	Unmar	17		Cabinet Maker Jour	" "	
				Ellen "	Daur	do		15		" "	
				Rebecca Smith	Aunt	do		25		Kent Greenwich	
				Phebe Washington	Visitor	do		21	Laundress	N Wales St Asaph	
66				George Wright	Head	Mar	56		Auctioneer Broker	Northampton [illegible]	
				Hannah "	Wife	Mar		56			
7	Total of Houses	5			Total of Males and Females		13	10			

Eng.—Sheet D.

Figure 5 - 1861 (page 2)

PUBLIC RECORD OFFICE	Reference — R.G. 9 117	COPYRIGHT PHOTOGRAPH—NOT TO BE REPRODUCED PHOTOGRAPHICALLY WITHOUT PERMISSION OF THE PUBLIC RECORD OFFICE, LONDON

9 [Page 11

The undermentioned Houses are situate within the Boundaries of the

Parish [or Township] of	City or ~~Municipal~~ Borough of	~~Municipal~~ Ward of	Parliamentary Borough of	Town of	~~Hamlet or Tything, &c., of~~	Ecclesiastical District of
Pancras		Parochial No. 6	Marylebone			St Pancras (East ?)

No. of Schedule	Road, Street, &c., and No. or Name of House	Houses Inhabited	Houses Uninhabited (U.) or Building (B.)	Name and Surname of each Person	Relation to Head of Family	Condition	Age of Males	Age of Females	Rank, Profession, or Occupation	Where Born	Whether Blind, or Deaf-and-Dumb
	Church Terrace			Catherine Wright	Daur	Unmar		24	Laundress	N Wales Llangue[illegible]	
				Barbara "	do	do		23	Dressmaker	do do	
				George "	Son	do	21		General Labourer	Northampton Syresham	
				Edward "	Son	do	18		do do	" "	
				Mary "	Daur	do		12	Scholar	Middlx Pancras	
				Anne "	Daur	do		10	Scholar	Dunster Somerset	
67				William Moody	Head	Mar	57		Private Watchman	Middlx Holborn	
				Jane "	Wife	Mar		47		" Pancras	
				Jane "	Daur	Unmar		23		" "	
				Charlotte "	Do	"		20	Laundress	" "	
				William "	Son	"	12		Scholar	" "	
				Elizabeth "	Daur	"		10	do	" "	
68	5	1		William Bellamy	Lodger	Unmar	36		Cattle Dealer &	Huntingdonsh Sawtry	
69				Ann ? Pierce	Head	Widow		36	House proprietor	Middlx Marylebone	
				Annie "	Daur			6		" Islington	
70				Thomas Milner	Head	Mar	32		Iron ? Traveller	" Covent Garden St Pauls	
				Eliza "	Wife	Mar		27		" Pancras	
				Anne "	Daur			6		" "	
				James "	Daur	—		4			
				Alfred Ward	Boarder	Unmar	23		Bankers Clerk	Essex Colchester	
71				Stephen Skinner	Head	Mar	47		Shoemaker Jour	Kent Tonbridge	
				Eliza "	Wife	Mar		48	Tailoress	Worcester Crowle	
75	3	1		Thomas Hewitt	Head	Mar	65		Chairmaker Jour	Surrey Lambeth	
				Mary "	Wife	Mar		68		N.K.	
6	Total of Houses...	2			Total of Males and Females...		9	15			

Eng.—Sheet D.

Figure 6 – 1871 – George N Wright

The undermentioned Houses are situate within the Boundaries of the

*Civil Parish [or Township] of	City or Municipal Borough of	Municipal Ward of—	Parliamentary Borough of	Town of	Village or Hamlet, &c., of	Local Board, or [Improvement Commissioners District] of	Ecclesiastical District of
St Pancras	London	[illegible]	Marylebone				[illegible]

No. of Schedule	ROAD, STREET, &c., and No. or NAME of HOUSE	HOUSES In-habited	HOUSES Uninhabited (U.), or Building (B.)	NAME and Surname of each Person	RELATION to Head of Family	CONDITION	AGE of Males	AGE of Females	Rank, Profession, or OCCUPATION	WHERE BORN	Whether 1. Deaf-and-Dumb 2. Blind 3. Imbecile or Idiot 4. Lunatic
1	[illegible]	1		John [illegible]	Head	Mar	[illegible]		[illegible]	[illegible]	
				Eliza do	Wife	Mar		[illegible]		[illegible]	
2				[illegible] do	Head	[illegible]	[illegible]		[illegible]	Middlesex London	
				[illegible]	[illegible]	[illegible]		16	General Servant	[illegible]	
3				William [illegible]	Head	Mar	[illegible]		[illegible]	[illegible]	
				[illegible] do	Wife	Mar		[illegible]		[illegible]	
				Emma [illegible] do	[illegible]			[illegible]		do do	
4	[illegible]	1		Charles [illegible]	Head	Mar	[illegible]		[illegible]	do do	
				Martha do	Wife	Mar		[illegible]		do do	
				Charles do	Son	[illegible]	[illegible]		[illegible]	do do	
				Thomas do	Son	[illegible]	[illegible]		[illegible]	do do	
				[illegible] do	Son	[illegible]	6			do do	
				Martha do	[illegible]	[illegible]		[illegible]		do do	
				[illegible]	[illegible]	[illegible]	[illegible]	[illegible]	[illegible]	do [illegible]	
				Charles do	[illegible]		1			do do	
				[illegible]	[illegible]		[illegible]			[illegible]	
5	2			George N Wright	Head	Mar	[illegible]		[illegible]	[illegible]	
				Elizabeth do	Wife	Mar		[illegible]		[illegible]	
				[illegible] do	[illegible]	[illegible]	1			do [illegible]	
				[illegible] do	Son	[illegible]	[illegible]			do do	
6	[illegible]			[illegible]	Head	Mar	[illegible]		[illegible]	do [illegible]	
				[illegible] do	Wife	Mar		[illegible]		do do	
7	3 [illegible]	1		[illegible]	Head	Mar	[illegible]		[illegible]	do [illegible]	
				[illegible] do	Wife	Mar		[illegible]	[illegible]	[illegible]	
7	Total of Houses..	3			Total of Males and Females..		[illegible]	[illegible]			

* Draw the pen through such of the words as are inappropriate.

Eng.—Sheet N.

Figure 7 - 1881 – George Nathan Wright

Page 38]

The undermentioned Houses are situate within the Boundaries of the

Civil Parish [or Township] of	City or Municipal Borough of	Municipal Ward of	Parliamentary Borough of	Town or Village or Hamlet of	Urban Sanitary District of	Rural Sanitary District of	Ecclesiastical Parish or District of
Islington		Thornhill	Finsbury				St Michael's

No. of Schedule	ROAD, STREET, &c., and No. or NAME of HOUSE	HOUSES Inhabited	HOUSES Uninhabited (U.), or Building (B.)	NAME and Surname of each Person	RELATION to Head of Family	CONDITION as to Marriage	AGE last Birthday of Males	AGE last Birthday of Females	Rank, Profession, or OCCUPATION	WHERE BORN	(1) Deaf-and-Dumb (2) Blind (3) Imbecile or Idiot (4) Lunatic
	B. Beaconsfield										
413	14 P	1		George N. Wright	Head	Mar	[illegible]		Printer	Northampton	
				Elizabeth "	Wife	"		34		Middlesex	
				George "	Son	Un	11		Scholar	"	
				James "	Son	"	10		"	"	
				Edith "	Dau	"		9	"	"	
				Edwin "	Son	"	6		"	"	
				Alice "	Dau			3	—	"	
				Henry	Son		1		—	"	
414	15 P		U								
415	16 P	1		Henry Ballam[illegible]	Head	Mar	33		Mattress Maker	St Pancras	
				Elizabeth "	Wife	"		33		Bristol	
				Percy "	Son	Un	13		Scholar	S. "	
				Lillah "	Dau	"		11	"	"	
				Francis "	Son	"	8		"	Reading	
				Florence "	[illegible]	"		6	"	"	
				Charles "	Son		3		—	Bristol	
				William "	"		1		—		
				Edward	"		5 Mo			Middx	
416	17 P		U 1								
417	18 P	1		Francis [illegible]	Head	Mar	35		Stableman	Gloucestershire	
				Harriett "	Wife			30		Hampshire	
				Edith "	Dau	Un		4	Sch	Bloomsbury	
				Florence "	"			3	—	Fulham	
				John "	Son		1		—	Islington	
	Total of Houses...	3	2	— Total of Males and Females...			12	10			

NOTE.—Draw the pen through such of the words of the headings as are inappropriate.

Figure 8 - 1881 – Possible James Wright

PUBLIC RECORD OFFICE

Reference:- R.G. 11/151

The undermentioned Houses are situate within the Boundaries of the [Page 47

Civil Parish [or Township] of	City or Municipal Borough of	Municipal Ward of	Parliamentary Borough of	Town or Village or Hamlet of	Urban Sanitary District of	Rural Sanitary District of	Ecclesiastical Parish or District of
Marylebone	—	New Church St	Marylebone	—	—	28	St Barnabas

No. of Schedule	ROAD, STREET, &c., and No. or NAME of HOUSE	HOUSES Inhabited	HOUSES Uninhabited (U.), or Building (B.)	NAME and Surname of each Person	RELATION to Head of Family	CONDITION as to Marriage	AGE last Birthday of Males	AGE last Birthday of Females	Rank, Profession, or OCCUPATION	WHERE BORN	(1) Deaf-and-Dumb (2) Blind (3) Imbecile or Idiot (4) Lunatic
6	Total of Houses...	1		Total of Males and Females...			9	16			

NOTE.—Draw the pen through such of the words of the headings as are inappropriate.

Eng.- Sheet E.

Figure 9 - 1891 – George N Wright

Administrative County of London — The undermentioned Houses are situate within the Boundaries of the — Page 54

Civil Parish of St Pancras | Municipal Ward of Gt Portland [illegible] | Parliamentary Borough or Division of East St Pancras | Ecclesiastical Parish or District of Old St Pancras

No. of Schedule	Road, Street, &c., and No. or Name of House	Houses Inhabited	Uninhabited	No. of rooms occupied if less than five	Name and Surname of each Person	Relation to Head of Family	Condition as to Marriage	Age Males	Age Females	Profession or Occupation	Employer	Employed	Neither	Where Born	(1) Deaf-and-Dumb (2) Blind (3) Lunatic, Imbecile or Idiot
1439	19 Aldenham St			2	Catherine Maloney	Head	Wid		58	Sewing Machinist		X		London St Lukes	
					James "	Son	S	26		Railway Porter		X		" Chelsea	
					Arthur "	"	Married	27		" [illegible]		X		" St Pancras	
					[illegible] "	"	"		18	Chairwoman		X		" "	
					Arthur L "	G Son		1						" Islington	
1440	21 do	1			John J Coppock	Head	"	58		Moulding [illegible]		X		Surrey Lambeth	
					[illegible] "	Wife	"		51					London City	
					John J "	"	S	30		Drapers Warehouseman		X		" St Pancras	
					Elizabeth E "	Daur	"		27					" St "	
					George "	Son	"	23		" Clerk		X		" "	
					Alfred "	"	"	19		" " [illegible]		X		" "	
					Henry "	"	"	18		Chemical Porter		X		" "	
					James Fitzgerald	[illegible]	"	29		Fishmongers Clerk		X		" "	
1441				1	Maria Hayward	Head	Wid		36	Laundress		X		" "	
					Elizabeth "	Daur			9	Scholar				" "	
					Rose "	"			6	"				" "	
					James "	Son		3						" "	
1442	23 do	1		2	Thomas Bailey	Head	Head	38		Farrier Smith		X		" Highgate	
					Maud "	Wife	M		40					" Cork	
1443				2	George N Wright	Head	"	51		Painter		X		Northampton	
					Elizabeth "	Wife			43					London St Pancras	
					George "	Son	S	21		Typefounder		X		" "	
					John "	"	"	20		General Labourer		X		" "	
					Edward "	"	"	16		Scholar				" "	
					Alice "	Daur			13	"				" "	
					Henry "	Son		12						" "	
1444				1	William Wilson	Head	M	40		General Labourer				" —	
					Elizabeth "	Wife	"		36					" —	
1445				2	George Powell	Head	"	58		Cabinet maker		X		Bridgnorth Salop	
					Elizabeth "	Wife	"		48					Norwich city	
	Total of Houses and of Tenements with less than Five Rooms	2		6	Total of Males and Females			18	12						

NOTE.—Draw the pen through such of the words of the headings as are inappropriate.

Reference:- RG12/126 — PUBLIC RECORD OFFICE

Figure 10 - 1891 - Edward & Mary Ann Wright

Administrative County of London — The undermentioned Houses are situate within the Boundaries of the — Page 16

Civil Parish: Islington | Municipal Borough: Finsbury | Municipal Ward: | Urban Sanitary District: | Town or Village or Hamlet: St Mary Islington | Rural Sanitary District: | Parliamentary Borough or Division: West Islington | Ecclesiastical Parish or District: St [illegible]

No. of Schedule	Road, Street, &c., and No. or Name of House	Houses Inhabited	Rooms (if less than five)	Name and Surname of each Person	Relation to Head of Family	Condition as to Marriage	Age (Males)	Age (Females)	Profession or Occupation	Employer	Employed	Neither	Where Born
	222 York Rd			Mary Mutton	Daur	S		[illegible]	Violin String Seeker [illegible]		X		London Islington
				Millie do	Daur	S		[illegible]	Scholar				do do
				Alice do	Daur	S		[illegible]	do				do Islington
				Thomas do	Son	S	[illegible]		do				do St Pancras
88			1	William Summers	Head	M	[illegible]		Carman		X		Essex Chelmsford
				Betsy do	Wife	M		[illegible]	Violin String Maker [illegible]		X		London St Pancras
				Ernest do	Son	S	2						do Islington
89			2	Michael Adams	Head	M	[illegible]		Violin String Maker	do	X		London Whitechapel
				Louisa do	Wife	M		60					do Clerkenwell
				Henry do	Son	S	30		Drover		X		do Smithfield
90	223 do	1	2	James Reeves	Head	M	47		Boot & Shoe Maker	X			Kent Deptford
				[illegible] M do	Wife	M		47	Boot Machinist		X		Surrey Farnham
91	224 do	1	2	Edward Wright	Head	M	46		B. Machine Hand		X		Northamptonshire
				Mary A. do	Wife	M		46					Kent Gravesend
				Edward do	Son	S	22		Glass Beveller [illegible]		X		London Islington
				John do	Son	S	18		G. Labourer		X		do do
				George do	Son	S	10		Scholar				do do
				Emmie do	Daur	S		2					do do
92			2	John Gunning	Head	M	34		G. Labourer		X		London St Pancras
				Lydia do	Wife	M		33					Surrey Peckham
				Mary F. do	Daur	S		2					London Islington
				John do	Son	S	6						do do
				Frederick do	Son	S	[illegible]						do do
93			1	Emma George	Head	S		34	Living on own Means				Surrey Peckham
94			1	Mary Stevens	Head	Wid		69	Living on own Means				Kent Bromley
				Frederick Harvey	Grandson	S	16		Van Guard [illegible]		X		London Islington
95			1	William Newton	Head	M	55		Farrier [illegible]		X		Surrey [illegible]
				Elizabeth do	Wife	M		55					London Holborn
96	226 do	1	2	Charles Branch	Head	M	[illegible]		Fireman		X		West Drayton
				Elizabeth do	Wife	M		29					London
				Ann do	Daur	S		[illegible]					do
9	Total of Houses and of Tenements with less than Five Rooms	3	9	Total of Males and Females			16	15					

Note.—Draw the pen through such of the words of the headings as are inappropriate.

RG12/159

Figure 11 - 1901 Elizabeth Wright (widow)

Administrative County London — The undermentioned Houses are situate within the boundaries of the — Page 17 — 87

Civil Parish of St Pancras (part) | Ecclesiastical Parish of St Anne Brookfield (part 1) | County Borough, Municipal Borough, or Urban District of St Pancras | Ward of Municipal Borough or of Urban District of Ward one (part) | Rural District of | Parliamentary Borough or Division of North St Pancras | Town or Village or Hamlet of

No. of Schedule	Road, Street, &c., and No. or Name of House	Inhabited	Name and Surname of each Person	Relation to Head of Family	Condition as to Marriage	Age Males	Age Females	Profession or Occupation	Employer, Worker, or Own account	If Working at Home	Where Born	Deaf and Dumb, Blind, Lunatic, Imbecile
			Gordon J Rogers	Son	S	3					London Islington	
			Ellen L Rose	Visitor	S		79	Laundress	Worker		London Pancras	
104	16 Lulot St	1	Barbara Bartlett	Head	Wid		62	Laundress Ironer	Worker		Carnarvon [illegible]	
105			Elizabeth Wright	Head	Wid		56				London Paddington	
			George do	Son	S	31		Telephone [illegible]	Worker		London Pancras	
			James do	Son	S	30		[illegible]	Worker		do do	
			Harry do	Son	S	25		Telephone [illegible]	Worker		London Islington	
			Margaret do	Daur	S		9				London Pancras	
106	17 do	1	Thomas Drew	Head	M	49		House Painter	Worker		Devon Plymouth	
			Charlotte do	Wife	M		45				London Pancras	
			Thomas do	Son	S	18		London Railway	Worker		London Pancras	
			Mary A do	Daur	S		16				do do	
			Charlotte do	Daur	S		14				do do	
			Charles F do	Son	S	11					do do	
			George H do	Son	S	9					do do	
			Arthur E do	Son	S	6					do do	
107	18 Lulot St	1	Isaac Butler	Head	M	49		Hard [illegible] Turner	Worker		Worcs Birmingham	
			Emma do	Wife	M		46				do	
			Emily do	Daur	S		22	[illegible] Maid	Worker		do	
			Minnie do	Daur	S		20	Servant [illegible]	Worker		do	
			John do	Son	S	16		[illegible] Washer	Worker		London Pancras	
			Dorah do	Daur	S		3				London Pancras	
108			William Rolfe	Head	M	29		General Labourer	Worker		Middlesex Enfield	
			Mary do	Wife	M		26				Beds Shillington	
			Amy do	Daur	S		7				London Islington	
			Charlie do	Son	S	4					London Pancras	
			Nellie do	Daur	S		3				do do	
			Percy do	Son	S	1					do do	
109	20 do	1	John West	Head	M	36		General Labourer	Worker		Beds Luton	
			Eliza do	Wife	M		33				London Islington	
110			William Grant	Head	M	34		[illegible] Labourer	Worker		Devon Exeter	
Total of Schedules of Houses and of Tenements with less than Five Rooms: 7		4	Total of Males and of Females			16	15					

Note.—Draw your pen through such words of the headings as are inapplicable.

Eng.—Sheet F.

PUBLIC RECORD OFFICE REFERENCE :- RG 13/156

Figure 12 - 1901 – Mary Ann Wright (Widow)

Administrative County: London — The undermentioned Houses are situate within the boundaries of the — Page 7 — 85

Civil Parish of Islington East — Ecclesiastical Parish of St Matthew [illegible] — County Borough, Municipal Borough, or Urban District of Islington — Ward of Municipal Borough or of Urban District of [illegible] Holloway — Rural District of — Parliamentary Borough or Division of [illegible] — Town or Village or Hamlet of —

No. of Schedule	Road, Street, &c., and No. or Name of House	Houses Inhabited	Name and Surname of each Person	Relation to Head of Family	Condition as to Marriage	Age last Birthday: Males	Age last Birthday: Females	Profession or Occupation	Employer, Worker, or Own account	If Working at Home	Where Born	Infirmity
40	220 York Rd	X	Thomas Perman	Head	M	50		[illegible] Labourer	Worker		Maida Vale London	
			Eliza Perman	Wife	M		45				Maida Vale do	
41	222 York Rd	1	George Golddew	Head	M	23		Barber Hairdresser	Own account		[illegible] naturalised	
			Milly Golddew	Wife	M		22				[illegible] naturalised	
			Alby Golddew	Son	S	1					Islington London	
			Fanny Golddew	Daug	S		[illegible]				Islington London	
42	222 York Rd		Sarah E. Avenell	Wife	M		40	[illegible]	Worker		[illegible] India	
			Caroline E. Avenell	Daug	S		19	[illegible]	do		Islington London	
			Arthur J. Avenell	Son	S	14		[illegible]	do		Islington do	
			Ellen Avenell	Daug	S		10	Scholar			Islington do	
43	222 " "		Louis Boulden	Head	M	35		[illegible] Driver	Worker		Smithfield do	
			Mary Boulden	Wife	M		36				Holborn do	
			Louis Boulden	Son	S	15		[illegible] Boy	Worker		Blackfriars do	
			Emily Boulden	Daug	S		13				" do	
			Mary Boulden	Daur	S		8				Clerkenwell do	
			[illegible] Boulden	Daug	S		5				Clerkenwell do	
			Fred Boulden	Son	S	4					Clerkenwell do	
			[illegible] Boulden	Daug	S		1				Holloway do	
44	222 " "		J. S. [illegible]	Head	Wid		40	Housekeeper [illegible] Family	Worker	At Home	Holloway do	
			Henry Perman	Son	S	21		[illegible]	do		Chatham Kent	
			[illegible]	Son	S	18		[illegible]			Holloway London	
			[illegible]	Son	S	16		[illegible] Guard			Holloway do	
			John [illegible]	Son		14		[illegible] Guard			" do	
			Susan [illegible]	Daugt			13				" do	
			Eliza [illegible]	Niece			10				" do	
			Francis Palmer	Boarder	S		19	[illegible] Maker	Worker		" do	
45	224 York Road	1	Mary Ann Wright	Head	Wid		65				North[illegible] Kent	Blind
			John Wright	Son	S	25		[illegible] Constable [illegible]		[illegible]	Islington London	
			Emmy Wright	Daught	S		12				Islington do	
Total of Schedules of Houses and of Tenements with less than Five Rooms		6	Total of Males and of Females			12	17					

Note.—Draw your pen through such words of the headings as are inapplicable.

Figure 13 - 1901 – George Wright

Administrative County: London
The undermentioned Houses are situate within the boundaries of the
Civil Parish of St Pancras (part) — Ecclesiastical Parish of Holy Trinity (part) — County Borough, Municipal Borough, or Urban District of St Pancras (part) — Ward of Municipal Borough or of Urban District of North (part) — Parliamentary Borough or Division of West St Pancras (part)
Page 68 31

No. of Schedule	Road, Street, &c., and No. or Name of House	Houses Inhabited	Uninhabited	Name and Surname of each Person	Relation to Head of Family	Condition as to Marriage	Age (Males)	Age (Females)	Profession or Occupation	Employer, Worker, or Own account	Where Born
369				John Archer	Head	M	33		General Labourer	Worker	Cheshunt
				Rebecca do	Wife	M		29			London St Pancras
				Samuel do	Son		10				do do
				John do	Son		5				do do
				Charlie do	Son		2				do do
370				Samuel French	Head	M	61		Night Watchman	Worker	Lincs Swinstead
				Jane do	Wife	M		56			do do
				Jessie do	Son		26		Marine Store Dealer	Own account	London Islington
				Florrie do	Daur			8			do do
371	10 Harmood Pl	1		George Wright	Head	M	30		General Carman	Worker	do St Pancras
				Isabella do	Wife	M		28			do do
				Alice do	Daur			10			do do
				Maud do	Daur			6			do do
				George do	Son		[illegible]				do do
372				Annie Taylor	Head	Wid		59			do Lambeth
				George do	Son	S	21		Railway Carter	Worker	do St Pancras
				George Lacey	Boarder	S	23		[illegible]	do	do do
				Tom [illegible]	Boarder	S	22		Painter	do	do do
				Isabella Taylor	Granddaur			10 months			do Whitechapel
373	11 do	1		William Pym	Head	M	35		Labourer Midland Rly	Worker	Leicestershire
				Caroline do	Wife	M		34			London St Pancras
	Pianofactory		1								
374	Augusta Cottage do	1		John Cowton	Head	M	58		Horsekeeper Groom	Worker	Herts Berkhamstead
				Hannah Cowton	Wife	M		56			Northants Northampton
				John do	Son	S	34		Horsekeeper Groom	Worker	London St Pancras
				William do	Son	S	24		Railway [illegible]	do	do do
				George do	Son		17		[illegible]	do	do do
				Hannah do	Daur			16	[illegible] maker	do	do do
				Frederick do	Son		13				do do
6	Total of Schedules of Houses and of Tenements with less than Five Rooms: 5	3	1	Total of Males and of Females			17	11			

Note—Draw your pen through such words of the headings as are inapplicable.

PUBLIC RECORD OFFICE REFERENCE :- RG 13/135 CROWN COPYRIGHT - NOT TO BE REPRODUCED WITHOUT PERMISSION

Figure 14 - Parish Register – George Wright and Catherine Griffith

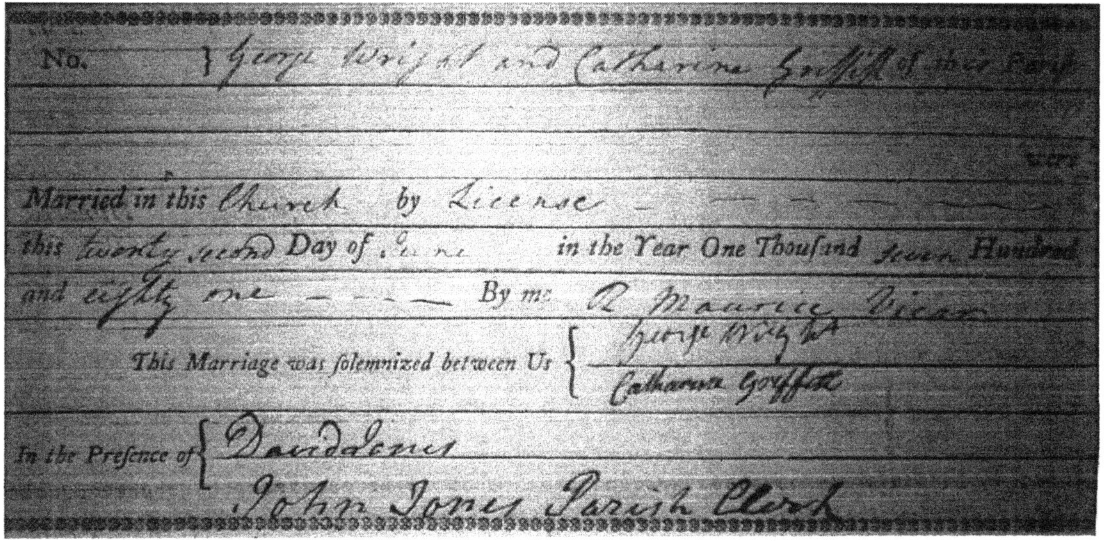

No. George Wright and Catherine Griffith of this Parish

were

Married in this Church by License

this twenty second Day of June in the Year One Thousand seven Hundred

and eighty one By me R Maurice Vicar

This Marriage was solemnized between Us { George Wright / Catherine Griffith

In the Presence of { David Jones / John Jones Parish Clerk

Figure 15 - Parish Register – Christening of Edward Baynes Wright

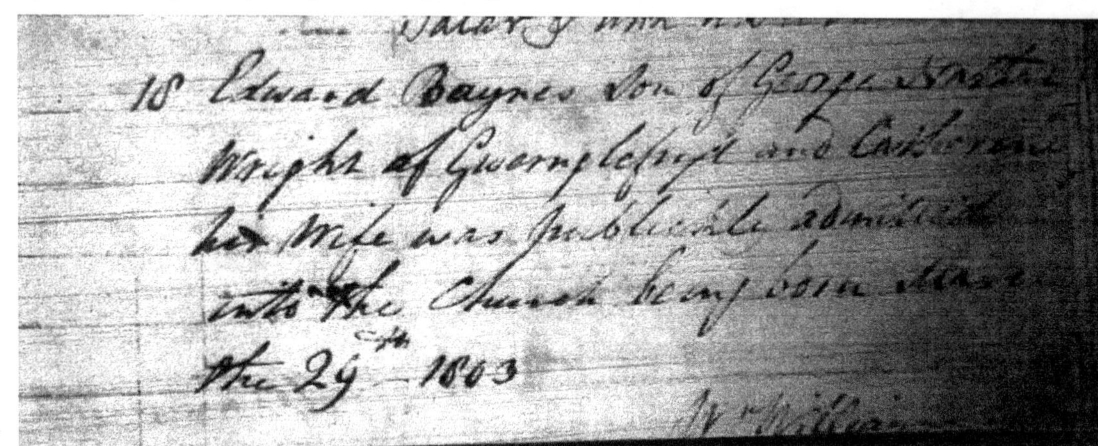

18 Edward Baynes Son of George [illegible]
Wright of [illegible] and Catherine
his Wife was publickly admitted
into the Church being born [illegible]
the 29th 1803

Figure 16 - Marriage Certificate - George Wright and Elizabeth Martin

CERTIFIED COPY OF AN ENTRY OF MARRIAGE

GIVEN AT THE GENERAL REGISTER OFFICE

Application Number COL153656

1869. Marriage solemnized at Old St Pancras in the Parish of Old St Pancras in the County of Middlesex

No.	When Married.	Name and Surname.	Age.	Condition.	Rank or Profession.	Residence at the time of Marriage.	Father's Name and Surname.	Rank or Profession of Father.
91	Sept 26 1869	George Nathan Wright	full	Bachelor	Painter	St Pancras	George Nathan Wright	Labourer
		Elizabeth Sarah Martin	full	Spinster		St Pancras	John Martin	Coachman

Married in the Parish Church according to the Rites and Ceremonies of the Established Church, by or after Banns by me, W R Arrowsmith

This Marriage was solemnized between us, George Wright, Elizabeth Sarah Martin; in the Presence of us, F W Slingsby, Barbara Wright

CERTIFIED to be a true copy of an entry in the certified copy of a register of Marriages in the Registration District of St Pancras

Given at the GENERAL REGISTER OFFICE, under the Seal of the said Office, the 12th day of May 2007

MXD 217219

CAUTION: THERE ARE OFFENCES RELATING TO FALSIFYING OR ALTERING A CERTIFICATE AND USING OR POSSESSING A FALSE CERTIFICATE. © CROWN COPYRIGHT

WARNING: A CERTIFICATE IS NOT EVIDENCE OF IDENTITY.

NJR

Figure 17 – 1901 Marriage Certificate – James Wright & Kate Bass

CERTIFIED COPY OF AN ENTRY OF MARRIAGE

GIVEN AT THE GENERAL REGISTER OFFICE

COL178979

1901. Marriage solemnized at Highgate in the Church of St. Michael in the County of Middlesex

No.	When Married.	Name and Surname.	Age.	Condition.	Rank or Profession.	Residence at the time of Marriage.	Father's Name and Surname.	Rank or Profession of Father.
92	September 7 1901	James John Wright	30	Bachelor	Printing Material Manufacturer	31 North Road Cottages Highgate	George Nathan Wright	Decorator
		Kate Mary Bass	23	Spinster	-	31 North Road Cottages Highgate	Thomas Henry Bass	Bricklayer

Married in the Church of St. Michael according to the Rites and Ceremonies of the Church of England by or after Banns by me, Philip B. [illegible]

This Marriage was solemnized between us, James John Wright, Kate Mary Bass

in the Presence of us, Beatrice Maud Best, Charles Abraham Allen

CERTIFIED to be a true copy of an entry in the certified copy of a Register of Marriages in the Registration District of Edmonton

Given at the General Register Office, under the Seal of the said Office, the 8th day of March 2006

MXC 482040

WARNING: A CERTIFICATE IS NOT EVIDENCE OF IDENTITY.

GIM

Exhibit K

Documentation For Descendants Of George Meryton Or Meriton

BIRDFORTH WAPENTAKE. *Threske*, 23° *Aug.* 1665.

LOCKWOOD OF SOWERBY.

ARMS.—........ a chevron .... between three cinquefoils ....
No proofe made of these armes.

Clare, daughter to Anthony Byerley of Pickhall in com. Ebor. first wife. = Richard Lockwood of Sowerby in com. Ebor. died a° 1645, or thereabouts. = Dorothy, daughter of Anthony Atkinson of Wensley in com. Ebor. second wife.

2. Elizabeth, wife of Raphe Atkinson of Wensley in com. Ebor.
1. Clare, wife of .... Best of ...... in com. Ebor.
2. John Lockwood.
1. Mathew Lockwood of Sowerby, æt. 35 ann. 23° Aug. a° 1665. = Barbara, daugh. and coheire of Thomas Beckwith of Aketon in com. Ebor. Esqr.
Dorothy, wife of John Hamerton of Purston in co. Ebor.

2. Thomas, æt. 11 an. 1665.
1. Richard, æt. 12 an. 23° Aug. 1665.
Barbara, æt. 9 an. 1665.

LANGBARGH WAPENTAKE. *Stokesley*, 25° *Aug.* 1665.

MERYTON OF CASTLE LEVENTON.

ARMS.—Sable, on a chevron or three roses gules, a canton ermine.
No proofe made of these armes.

George Meryton, D[r] in Divinity, Chaplain to Qu. Anne (wife to K. James), Deane of Peterborough, and after of Yorke, died in a° 1624. = Mary, daughter of ...... Rande of ...... in com. Lincoln, son to ...... Rande, Bisshop of Lincolne.

4. John Meryton of Moulton in com. Ebor. = ⊥
3. Robert, obijt sine prole.
2. Thomas Meryton of Castle Leventon in co. Ebor. died in a° 1652. = Grace, daugh. of Francis Wright of Bolton upon Swale in com. Ebor.
1. George Meryton, died without issue.
1. Mary, wife of Thomas Moyser of Nun-Appleton in com. Ebor.
2. Anne, wife unto Franc. Wright, son of Franc. Wright of Bolton upon Swale in co. Ebor.

4. Richard.
5. John.
2. Thomas.
3. Paul Meryton, marr. Meriam, daugh. of .... Lyster of .....
1. George Meryton of Castle Leventon, æt. 30 an. et 11 mensium 25 Aug. 1665. = Mary, daughter of John Palleser of Kirkby super Wiske in co. Ebor.
1. Grace, wife of Francis Palleser of Dublyn in Ireland.
2. Anne, wife of Thomas Palleser of the citty of Westminst[r], grocer.

3. John.
2. George.
1. Thomas, æt. 8 annorum et 10 mens. 25 Aug. 1665.

Other Heritage Books by Robert N. Grant

Identifying the Wrights in the Goochland County, Virginia Tithe Lists, 1732-84

The Identification of 1792 John Wright of Fauquier County, Virginia; As Not the Son of 1729/30 John Wright of Stafford County, Virginia

The Identification of 1809 William Wright of Franklin County, Virginia, as the Son of 1792 John Wright of Fauquier County, Virginia, and Elizabeth (Bronaugh) (Darnall) Wright

Wright Family Birth Records (1853-1896) and Marriage Records (1788-1915): Franklin County, Virginia, 1853-1896

Wright Family Birth Records, 1853-1896; Marriage Records, 1761-1900; Census Records, 1810-1900, in Amherst County, Virginia

Wright Family Birth Records, 1853-1896; Marriage Records, 1808-1910; Census Records, 1810-1900; Patent Deeds and Land Grants; Deed Records, 1808-1910; Death Records, 1853-1896; Probate Records, 1808-1900, in Nelson County, Virginia

Wright Family Birth Records (1853-1896) and Marriage Records (1782-1900): Campbell County, Virginia

Wright Family Birth Records, Marriage Records, and Personal Property Tax Lists: Appomattox County, Virginia

Wright Family Census Records, Deed Records, Land Tax Lists, Death Records and Probate Records: Appomattox County, Virginia

Wright Family Census Records: Bedford County, Virginia, 1810-1900

Wright Family Census Records: Campbell County, Virginia, 1810-1900

Wright Family Census Records: Franklin County, Virginia, 1810-1900

Wright Family Death Records (1853-1920), Cemetery Records by Cemetery, and Probate Records (1782-1900): Campbell County, Virginia

Wright Family Death Records (1854-1920), Cemetery Records by Cemetery, and Probate Records (1785-1928): Franklin County, Virginia

Wright Family Death, Cemetery and Probate Records: Bedford County, Virginia

Wright Family Deed Records (1782-1900) and Land Tax List (1782-1850): Campbell County, Virginia

Wright Family Land Grants (1785-1900) and Deed Records (1785-1897): Franklin County, Virginia

Wright Family Land Grants, Deed Records, Land Tax List, Death Records, Probate Records: Prince Edward County, Virginia

Wright Family Land Records: Bedford County, Virginia

Wright Family Land Tax Lists: Franklin County, Virginia, 1786-1860

Wright Family Land Tax Records: Amherst County, Virginia, 1782-1850

Wright Family Land Tax Records: Nelson County, Virginia, 1809-1850

Wright Family Patent Deeds and Land Grants, 1761-1900, Deed Records, 1761-1903; Chancery Court Files, 1804-1900; Death Records, 1853-1920; Cemetery Records by Cemetery; and Probate Records, 1761-1900, in Amherst County, Virginia

Wright Family Personal Property Tax Lists: Amherst County, Virginia, 1782-1850

Wright Family Personal Property Tax Lists: Campbell County, Virginia, 1785-1850

Wright Family Personal Property Tax Lists: Franklin County, Virginia, 1786-1850

Wright Family Personal Property Tax Lists: Nelson County, Virginia, 1809-1850

Wright Family Personal Property Tax Records for Bedford County, Virginia, 1782 to 1850

Wright Family Records: Births in Bedford County, Virginia

Wright Family Records: Land Tax List, Bedford County, Virginia, 1782-1850

Wright Family Records: Lynchburg, Virginia Birth Records (1853-1896), Marriage Records (1805-1900), Marriage Notices (1794-1880), Census Records (1900), Deed Records (1805-1900), Death Records (1853-1896), Probate Records (1805-1900)

Wright Family Records: Marriages in Bedford County, Virginia

Wright Family Records: Prince Edward County, Virginia Birth Records, Marriage Records, Election Polls, and Tithe List, Personal Property Tax List, Census

www.ingramcontent.com/pod-product-compliance
Lightning Source LLC
Chambersburg PA
CBHW071712300426
44115CB00010B/1394

9780788449352